AI Adoption and Diffusion in Education

Gamze Sart
Istanbul University-Cerrahpaşa, Turkey

Funda Hatice Sezgin
Istanbul University-Cerrahpaşa, Turkey

IGI Global
Scientific Publishing
Publishing Tomorrow's Research Today

Vice President of Editorial	Melissa Wagner
Managing Editor of Acquisitions	Mikaela Felty
Managing Editor of Book Development	Jocelynn Hessler
Production Manager	Mike Brehm
Cover Design	Phillip Shickler

Published in the United States of America by
IGI Global Scientific Publishing
701 East Chocolate Avenue
Hershey, PA, 17033, USA
Tel: 717-533-8845
Fax: 717-533-8661
Website: https://www.igi-global.com E-mail: cust@igi-global.com

Library of Congress Cataloging-in-Publication Data

Names: Sart, Gamze, 1967- editor. | Sezgin, Funda H., editor.
Title: AI adoption and diffusion in education and public administration / Edited by Gamze Sart, Funda Sezgin.
Other titles: Artificial intelligence adoption and diffusion in education and public administration
Description: Hershey, PA : Information Science Reference (an imprint of IGI Global), [2025] | Includes bibliographical references and index. | Summary: "The publication will research the AI adoption and diffusion in education and public administration. Use and importance of AI in education and daily life has been increasing day by day. Thefore, this edited book will be a guide for the countries to see the employment of AI in both education and public administration"-- Provided by publisher.

Identifiers: LCCN 2024042576 (print) | LCCN 2024042577 (ebook) | ISBN 9798369379493 (hardcover) | ISBN 9798369379509 (paperback) | ISBN 9798369379516 (ebook)
Subjects: LCSH: Artificial intelligence--Educational applications--Cross-cultural studies. | Public administration--Technological innovations--Cross-cultural studies.
Classification: LCC LB1028.43 .A372 2024 (print) | LCC LB1028.43 (ebook) | DDC 418.0071/1--dc23/eng/20241018
LC record available at https://lccn.loc.gov/2024042576
LC ebook record available at https://lccn.loc.gov/2024042577

British Cataloguing in Publication Data
A Cataloguing in Publication record for this book is available from the British Library.

Table of Contents

Detailed Table of Contents

The utilisation of artificial intelligence (AI) in the field of education has witnessed a notable surge in recent years, with growth of technology. This increase has given rise to a number of ethical issues. This study will provide a comprehensive examination of the ethical implications of AI in education. A bibliometric analysis of studies conducted in this field will be conducted through the analysis of existing studies in the literature. The bibliometric analysis allows for the numerical analysis of the relationships between the keywords identified in the study and studies conducted on the intersection of AI and ethics in education. It also accesses and evaluates data such as the number of publications in this field, countries, authors, publication years, citation counts, and keywords. The data obtained provide insight into the evolution of the discourse on the ethical implications of AI in education within academic literature. The findings of this study indicate that a crucial step in the development of AI applications in education is to establish a clear ethical framework.

The incorporation of Artificial Intelligence (AI) into higher education is altering both curriculum design and administrative operations. This chapter investigates how AI is being exploited to tailor learning experiences, expedite administrative chores, and enhance decision-making in educational institutions. AI-driven curriculum design encourages adaptive learning environments, allowing students individualized learning routes based on their unique requirements and preferences. Meanwhile, AI boosts administrative efficiency by automating routine activities, optimizing resource allocation, and boosting student support services. Despite the transformational potential, AI adoption also creates obstacles linked to ethical considerations, data protection, and the need for faculty training. By reviewing case studies of effective

Currently, artificial intelligence is used in many different ways in many different sectors - for example, in the diagnosis of diseases in the field of health by processing data, for inventory management in logistics management, and for customer service in tourism. Artificial intelligence is also used in higher education institutions in different fields such as intelligent learning systems and data management. There are different studies in the literature on the use of artificial intelligence in higher education. Considering its importance, analyzing the studies in the literature comprehensively is important for understanding the applications and making it easier for educational institutions to experience an artificial intelligence adaptation process. This study aims to analyze the existing studies in the literature through bibliometric analysis. Initially, in the bibliometric method, the existing literature is obtained by searching a database in line with the search words. After that, the existing literature is analyzed in different dimensions such as time and quantity.

The concept of Artificial Intelligence (AI), which was first used in the 1950s, can perform tasks that require human intelligence by using various algorithms and computer programs. This chapter aims to evaluate AI tools that can be used in universities. Firstly, the AI tools used in universities were researched from the literature, then Fuzzy Multi-Criteria Decision Making was applied to determine which of these tools should be prioritized. Five criteria (perceived ease of use, perceived usefulness, personalization, interaction, trust) obtained from expert opinions and the literature were weighted and the AI tools that were determined as alternatives were prioritized. Fuzzy numbers, first presented to the literature by Zadeh in 1965, aid in decision-making because it is frequently impossible to utilize precise formulations during evaluations. Since 1965, extensions of fuzzy numbers have been developed and integrated into multi criteria decision making methods. The decision making method to be used in this study is also integrated with the use of intuitionistic fuzzy numbers.

This study examines the role of artificial intelligence (AI) technologies in the education of students with disabilities and provides a comprehensive assessment of how these technologies can transform educational processes. Also, the study explores the impact of AI-based technologies such as speech recognition, text-to-speech, and automated captioning systems in increasing accessibility for students with disabilities. In evaluating AI-based technologies tailored to the educational needs of students with disabilities, multi-criteria decision-making methods such as fuzzy logic and the Fuzzy CoCoSo method were utilized. The analysis results demonstrate that these technologies contribute substantially to enhancing students' learning motivation, supporting academic success, and developing independent mobility skills. This study addresses the contributions of AI to educational accessibility from a perspective of social justice and equity and offers recommendations for the effective use of AI-supported accessibility technologies in this field.

To enhance the calibre of decisions, artificial intelligence technologies have been included in educational administration. The use of artificial intelligence in school administration is covered in this chapter. Out of the 130 journal articles that were downloaded from peer-reviewed journals, 50 articles were chosen for review. According to the review's findings, artificial intelligence has been applied to educational administration in several areas, including performance and assessment, faculty management, student management, course management, and student recruiting and admission. Lack of expertise and skills, ethical issues, financial difficulties, and infrastructure issues were the main obstacles to the use of AI in school administration.

This chapter highlights the transformative impact of Artificial Intelligence on the education sector in Bangladesh, reshaping the learning experience for students. It emphasizes how AI fosters personalized learning, increases access to resources, and enhances skill development, while also addressing challenges like infrastructural limitations, teacher readiness, and societal resistance. The discussion includes important ethical considerations, such as data privacy and algorithmic fairness, underscoring the need for responsible integration. By synthesizing existing literature, the paper clarifies the complex relationship between AI and education and suggests avenues for further research. Collaboration among policymakers, administrators, students, and technology developers is crucial to ensure that AI benefits all learners in Bangladesh. The research highlights some key issues that are of the essence to inform the discussion on AI in education and as guidelines for developing a more inclusive and operational structure for education in Bangladesh.

This part analyzes the integration of Artificial Intelligence (AI) in German Higher Education Institutions (HEIs), highlighting its transformative potential and associated challenges. AI technologies are increasingly employed to enhance teaching, streamline administration, and accelerate research. Despite their benefits, concerns regarding transparency, equity, data privacy, and accountability are raised. Anticipated European regulations, such as the proposed Artificial Intelligence Act, are expected to further shape AI application in academia. Using empirical case studies from German universities, this manuscript illustrates successful AI integration while addressing the challenges of balancing innovation with ethical and legal considerations. The manuscript concludes with strategic recommendations for policymakers, educators, and technology developers to promote responsible AI adoption, emphasizing the importance of ethical frameworks, human oversight, and interdisciplinary collaboration. This study provides valuable insights into the current and future landscape of AI in HEIs.

Preface

Artificial Intelligence (AI) has emerged as a transformative force across numerous domains, reshaping how we approach challenges and innovate solutions. Among the many fields impacted by this technology, education stands out as pivotal areas where AI has both profound and evolving implications. Recognizing this, we present *AI Adoption and Diffusion in Education*, a comprehensive exploration of AI's integration into Education.

As editors of this volume, we have curated a collection of contributions from leading researchers, practitioners, and thought leaders, each offering a unique perspective on the adoption and diffusion of AI. This book examines the increasing importance of AI in education, serving as a valuable resource for countries seeking to understand and implement AI strategies effectively.

The book addresses a broad spectrum of readers—professional researchers, educators, managers, government officials, and policymakers. By doing so, it underscores the ubiquity of AI and its potential to drive efficiency, enhance decision-making, and foster innovation in education. The chapters within this book delve into key topics such as the impact of AI on education, its role in enhancing learning experiences, and its employment in higher education.

We hope this volume will not only serve as a guide for understanding AI's transformative potential but also inspire actionable strategies to maximize its benefits. As AI continues to evolve, its role in shaping the future of education becomes ever more critical.

We extend our gratitude to the contributing authors for their insightful work and to the readers who will engage with this volume. It is our belief that this book will provide valuable insights, fostering informed dialogue and action in the dynamic intersection of AI and education.

ORGANIZATION OF THE BOOK

Chapter 1: Examining Artificial Intelligence and Ethics in Education with Bibliometric Analysis

In this chapter, the editors explore the burgeoning intersection of artificial intelligence (AI) and ethics within the education sector. Employing bibliometric analysis, the study provides a comprehensive overview of existing literature, highlighting trends, key contributors, and thematic developments. By analyzing publication data, including citation metrics, geographic origins, and keyword associations, the chapter maps the evolution of discourse surrounding the ethical dimensions of AI in education. The findings underscore the critical need for an ethical framework to guide the integration of AI technologies into educational practices. This chapter offers valuable insights for researchers, educators, and policymakers navigating this evolving landscape.

Chapter 2: AI in Higher Education: Revolutionizing Curriculum and Administration

This chapter examines the transformative impact of AI on higher education, focusing on curriculum design and administrative functions. By leveraging AI-driven adaptive learning systems, institutions are now able to personalize learning experiences to meet diverse student needs. Concurrently, AI has streamlined administrative operations by automating routine tasks, enhancing decision-making processes, and optimizing resource management. While the benefits are substantial, the integration of AI presents challenges, including ethical considerations, data security, and the necessity of faculty training. Through case studies of successful AI applications, this chapter provides a forward-thinking perspective on how institutions can harness AI to revolutionize education and administration.

Chapter 3: Employment of AI in Higher Education

The deployment of AI technologies in higher education is reshaping institutional dynamics and pedagogical methods. This chapter highlights the applications of AI in areas such as admissions, scheduling, and assessments, emphasizing the potential for creating equitable and personalized learning environments. It also addresses the challenges associated with AI adoption, including ethical dilemmas and risk management. By advocating for increased awareness among educational leaders and policymakers, the chapter underscores the importance of strategic implementation to sustain and expand the capabilities of higher education institutions through AI-driven innovation.

Chapter 4: Artificial Intelligence in Education and Its Importance

This chapter investigates the impact of generative AI technologies, like ChatGPT, on higher education. Drawing on a large-scale survey of university students in Pakistan, it evaluates their knowledge, willingness, skills, and technological support related to ChatGPT usage. The findings reveal high levels of awareness and interest but identify gaps in technical proficiency and institutional support. Public universities demonstrated greater adoption rates, while gender differences were negligible. The chapter concludes with actionable recommendations for fostering awareness and integration of generative AI in higher education, emphasizing its potential to enhance teaching and learning experiences.

Chapter 5: An In-Depth Bibliometric Analysis to Understand the Impact and Future of Artificial Intelligence in Higher Education

This chapter conducts an exhaustive bibliometric analysis to assess the applications and impact of AI in higher education. By reviewing the existing literature, the authors identify trends and gaps in research, shedding light on how AI has been used for intelligent learning systems and data management. The analysis spans various dimensions, including publication frequency and thematic shifts, providing educational institutions with a roadmap for adapting AI technologies effectively. This chapter serves as a resource for educators and administrators aiming to understand the evolving role of AI in academia.

Chapter 6: Evaluation of Artificial Intelligence Tools for Universities with Fuzzy Multi-Criteria Decision-Making Methods

This chapter evaluates AI tools utilized in universities using the Fuzzy Multi-Criteria Decision Making (MCDM) method. By analyzing factors such as usability, personalization, and trust, the study ranks AI tools to identify those most suited for higher education environments. Drawing on expert opinions and literature, the chapter integrates fuzzy logic to address uncertainties in decision-making. This rigorous evaluation offers practical insights for university administrators seeking to prioritize and implement effective AI solutions.

Chapter 7: Evaluation of AI-based Accessibility Technologies for Disabled Higher Education Students Using Fuzzy CoCoSo Method

Focusing on AI's role in enhancing accessibility for students with disabilities, this chapter employs the Fuzzy CoCoSo method to evaluate technologies such as speech recognition and automated captioning. The findings highlight the transformative potential of AI in fostering equity and independence in educational settings. By addressing challenges and providing actionable recommendations, the chapter emphasizes AI's contributions to social justice and inclusivity in higher education.

Chapter 8: The Application of Artificial Intelligence in Educational Administration

This chapter reviews the integration of AI technologies in educational administration, analyzing 50 peer-reviewed studies. Applications range from faculty and student management to performance assessments and recruitment. Despite the clear advantages, challenges such as ethical concerns, financial constraints, and infrastructural gaps persist. This comprehensive review provides insights into leveraging AI for improved decision-making and administrative efficiency in educational settings.

Chapter 9: The Role of Teachers in an AI-Enhanced Educational Landscape

This chapter explores the evolving role of educators in an AI-driven educational ecosystem. While AI tools automate administrative tasks and personalize learning, human-centric skills such as empathy, creativity, and critical thinking remain indispensable. Advocating for professional development and policy reforms, the chapter underscores the need for a balanced approach where educators and AI tools collaborate to create supportive and engaging learning environments.

Chapter 10: Edufusion: Integrating Artificial Intelligence with Teaching Practices to Enhance Learning Experiences

Investigating the integration of AI into traditional teaching practices, this chapter examines its potential to transform pedagogical methods and improve learning outcomes. Through literature reviews and empirical research, the chapter highlights the dynamic interplay between AI and education, offering a detailed analysis of its implications for teaching strategies and institutional practices.

Chapter 11: Artificial Intelligence and the Future of Education in Bangladesh: Impact, Challenges, and Ethical Implications of AI on Student Learning

This chapter explores the transformative impact of AI on education in Bangladesh, addressing its benefits, challenges, and ethical considerations. By synthesizing existing research, the study highlights how AI enhances access, personalization, and skill development, while also tackling infrastructural and societal barriers. It advocates for collaborative efforts among stakeholders to ensure equitable and responsible AI integration.

Chapter 12: The Utilization of Artificial Intelligence in Higher Education Institutions in Germany: Opportunities and Challenges of AI in HEIs

Focusing on German Higher Education Institutions (HEIs), this chapter examines AI's integration into teaching, administration, and research. Empirical case studies illustrate both opportunities and challenges, including ethical concerns and regulatory implications. The chapter concludes with strategic recommendations for promoting responsible AI adoption while balancing innovation with transparency and accountability.

Chapter 13: Exploring Knowledge, Will, Skills, Technological Support, and Use of ChatGPT in Higher Education: A Cross-sectional Survey

This chapter presents findings from a survey of university students in Pakistan, exploring their engagement with ChatGPT. High levels of knowledge and willingness contrast with moderate skills and technological support, revealing a need for institutional initiatives to facilitate AI adoption. The chapter offers insights for policymakers and educators aiming to harness generative AI for enhanced learning experiences.

CONCLUSION

In an era characterized by rapid technological advancements and unprecedented global challenges, the chapters in this edited volume offer a comprehensive examination of the transformative potential of artificial intelligence, machine learning, and advanced computational methods across diverse domains. The insights presented in this book highlight both the opportunities and the challenges posed by these innovative technologies. The authors have masterfully explored critical areas such as the integration of AI in educational enrollment systems and teaching.Together, these studies underscore a shared vision: leveraging technology responsibly and strategically to create sustainable, inclusive, and adaptable systems that respond to the evolving needs of our societies.

As editors, we believe that this collection provides a valuable contribution to the growing body of knowledge on the interplay between technology and human-centered systems. It is our hope that readers—whether scholars, practitioners, or policymakers—will find inspiration and practical guidance within these pages, fostering further exploration and innovation in their respective fields.

This book serves not only as a reflection of current advancements but also as a call to action for interdisciplinary collaboration, ethical considerations, and a balanced approach to technological adoption. By embracing the principles of transparency, inclusivity, and sustainability, we can collectively navigate the complexities of this digital age to achieve a better, more equitable future.

Chapter 1
Examining Artificial Intelligence and Ethics in Education With Bibliometric Analysis

Ecenur Alioğulları
Istanbul University-Cerrahpaşa, Turkey

Duygu Tüylü
Gelisim University, Turkey

Aslıhan Sağıroğlu
Istanbul Arel University, Turkey

ABSTRACT

The utilisation of artificial intelligence (AI) in the field of education has witnessed a notable surge in recent years, with growth of technology. This increase has given rise to a number of ethical issues. This study will provide a comprehensive examination of the ethical implications of AI in education. A bibliometric analysis of studies conducted in this field will be conducted through the analysis of existing studies in the literature. The bibliometric analysis allows for the numerical analysis of the relationships between the keywords identified in the study and studies conducted on the intersection of AI and ethics in education. It also accesses and evaluates data such as the number of publications in this field, countries, authors, publication years, citation counts, and keywords. The data obtained provide insight into the evolution of the discourse on the ethical implications of AI in education within academic literature. The findings of this study indicate that a crucial step in the development of AI applications in education is to establish a clear ethical framework.

DOI: 10.4018/979-8-3693-7949-3.ch001

INTRODUCTION

The use of AI in education has increased in recent years thanks to the development and rapid advancement of technology. With the use of AI in education, learning processes become faster and more effective. In this way, students' success is also positively affected. Many benefits can be achieved by optimizing learning by incorporating digital systems into educational processes. Examples of these are automatic evaluation systems and smart educational assistants, digital guidance applications. Thanks to all these systems, student performance can be monitored. Student and teacher interactions are also facilitated with AI in education. In addition to these positive situations brought by the use of AI in education, some ethical problems also arise. These ethical problems cause a number of concerns. Among the ethical problems of AI applications in the field of education, privacy problems related to students' personal data may arise. At the same time, these ethical problems lead to some concerns such as equality and justice (Turan et al. 2022). Considering the deep impact of AI on individual learning processes, it is inevitable to consider these technologies within an ethical framework. The impact of AI applications on society is not limited to education alone; It also has significant effects on individuals' lives and the social structures they are in (Keskin and Sevli, 2024). Therefore, the number of studies investigating the relationship between AI and ethics in education is increasing, but a more comprehensive understanding is still needed in this area.

As a result of the literature study, it has been revealed that AI applications in education have an important research area in terms of ethical concerns. AI is a field of study that can create intelligent computer programs such as problem solving, revealing the meaning of complex systems, processing information, and producing new algorithms (Nilsson, 1991). One of the most repeated words in the literature in the field of AI and ethics is transparency. Yu and Yu argued that transparency is very important in AI applications and is essential for users to ensure trust (Yu and Yu, 2023). Holmes and his colleagues argue that AI applications are important in the field of education but emphasize that ethical situations are difficult to implement (Holmes et al. 2022). Seo and his colleagues conducted an analysis with certain participants to measure the impact of AI applications in education and to determine the situations of various security and privacy risks of AI systems (Seo et al. 2021). Despite the positive aspects of AI in the learning process of students, this study analyzed these processes due to the ethical elements brought by these systems (Akgun and Greenhow, 2022). Another study has discussed the advantages and disadvantages of using generative AI in educational environments in detail (AlAli, 2024). In Valerio's study, a survey was conducted by examining the perceptions of AI and the ethical situations of AI in an educational institution in Zamboanga. According to the findings obtained from the survey study, it was argued that more importance should be given to the ethical situations in AI applications used in education and that these areas should be focused on. Similarly, they argued that more research should be done to reduce ethical concerns in the education sector (Valerio, 2024). In another study, they addressed the applications of artificial intelligence in education in a multidimensional manner, emphasizing the importance of important ethical issues such as privacy and access to people's information (Eden et al. 2024). Considering all this literature review, it was observed that AI applications in education are important and ethical situations create concerns. Taking the necessary precautions to reduce concerns in ethical situations is another element in the literature.

Due to the high number of recent topics in these areas, a bibliometric analysis is conducted in this study after determining the concepts of AI and ethics in education with appropriate keywords. The present study provides a comprehensive analysis of the existing literature on this topic. In this study, the studies in the web of science database with the keywords determined in the field of artificial intelligence and ethics in education is analyzed with bibliometrics. As a result of this analysis, important information such as the publication years of the studies, the countries where they were published, author networks, word clouds, the citations received by the authors, and the sources in which the studies were published the most were provided. In the first stage of this study, an introduction to the concepts of AI and ethics in education is given, and then the relevant studies and literature review in this field are included in the second part. The third part includes the methodology, and the stages of how bibliometric analysis is performed. The fourth part of the study includes findings, performance analysis and scientific mapping. The fifth and last part of the study includes the results and discussion.

RELATED STUDIES

AI is a field that can be used in different disciplines. In AI ethics, which is formed with the use of AI, ethical problems are addressed. It consists of a wide and important area where ethical principles, ethical rules, ethical regulations, ethical norms, theories and guidelines are discussed in AI ethics. The concept of AI is also called machine ethics in some studies (Siau and Wang, 2020). With AI ethics, AI that aims to eliminate unethical problems and behaves ethically can be achieved (Stupp, 2019). Ethics is a concept that investigates the basis of any concept or concepts morally and reveals what is right and wrong for societies. Ethics also includes concepts such as justice and equality. It is also a guide to how things should be by investigating the logical phenomenon of the work or situation under consideration (Liao, 2020). According to the study of Cointe and his colleagues, the concept of ethics is divided into three dimensions. The concept of ethics is a philosophical discipline that describes how a person should behave towards others. We can explain the three dimensions discussed in this study as follows: Firstly, in consequentialist ethics, a person is considered ethical only if he/she evaluates the consequences of each choice and chooses the option that leads to the highest moral outcome. It is also referred to as utilitarian ethics as the decisions made are usually aimed at providing the best overall outcomes. The second ethical concept from the dimensions is duty ethics. Accordingly, in duty ethics, a person is considered ethical only if he/she respects the obligations, duties and rights related to certain situations. The holder of duty ethics (also known as duty ethics or obligation ethics) behaves in accordance with the norms determined by society. The last dimension is virtue ethics. In virtue ethics, a person is considered ethical only if he/she acts and thinks in line with certain moral values (e.g. courage, justice, etc.). The individual with virtue ethics should show an intrinsic motivation to be evaluated favourably by others (Cointe, 2016). Ethical conflicts describe the situation that arises when every available option violates an established ethical principle and a decision must be made (Kirkpatrick, 2015). AI researchers recognise that machine ethics is an important element in the extent to which autonomous systems can interact with humans. Therefore, research has emerged focussing on technical methods for these systems to respect human rights and only perform actions that follow acceptable ethical principles. However, this topic still remains unclear for many AI practitioners and requires an in-depth examination. Moreover, existing survey studies on AI governance have generally focussed on the psychological, social and legal dimensions of the challenges (Etzioni and Etzioni, 2017).

The ethical issues arising from the nature of AI fall into different categories. We can list them as follows: In the first category, there are ethical problems arising from AI. We can divide them into 3 as follows: 1. Transparency, 2. Data security and confidentiality, 3. Independence, goal setting and accountability, In the second category, there are ethical problems arising from the human element. These are 1. accountability, 2. ethical standards, 3. human rights laws. In the third category, there are ethical problems arising from the social impact of ethical AI problems. These are 1. automation and job replacement, 2. accessibility, 3. democracy and civil rights. We can explain all these subcategories as follows. Firstly, explanations of ethical problems arising from the nature of AI will be given.

Transparency: Machine learning, especially with deep neural networks, is one of the main technologies of AI today. However, it is quite difficult to explain and understand the inference processes of machine learning, which is often referred to as a 'black box'. The uncertainty of these systems causes algorithms or models to become complex for users and developers. This essentially leads to transparency issues. Lack of transparency not only leads to problems of explanation, but also creates difficulties in human monitoring and guidance of machine learning or AI.

Therefore, transparency and explainability is one of the most discussed weaknesses of AI (Larsson and Heintz, 2020).

Data security and privacy: The success of AI is largely associated with training data. Often, large volumes of data, including personal and private data, are required to train an AI system, especially with a deep learning model. Leaking personal information or misuse of data are serious ethical issues that concern every individual, institution, organisation and even the state. Data security and privacy are important issues faced during the development and implementation of AI technology (Dilmaghani et al.2019).

Independence, goal setting and accountability: Here, the independence of AI refers to the ability of the system to control itself without direct human intervention. Thanks to this autonomy, social rules and some responsibilities are also successfully realised. With the advancement of the field of AI, the autonomy and responsibility of existing AI robots has been possible to a certain extent. Independence, goal setting and autonomy are important elements in AI in order to purify the system from morally harmful factors. However, the realisation of all these elements is a challenging question and issue (Sullins, 2011; Huang et al. 2022). We can explain the ethical problems arising from the human element in the second category as follows.

Accountability: When AI fails to successfully execute an external command, it is desirable to find the answer to the question of who should take responsibility. The unintended outcome can be caused by many factors, such as software codes, data input, incorrect operations or other elements. Therefore, accountability is an ethical issue that concerns the human elements involved in the design, implementation, deployment and use of AI (Timmermans et al. 2010).

Ethical Standards: The ultimate goal of AI in relation to ethics is to create a system that can act in accordance with ethical principles and exhibit ethical behaviour. Therefore, in order for AI to be considered ethical, it is important to set comprehensive and unbiased ethical standards in the field of education or regulation. Researchers and practitioners who want to develop ethical guidelines for AI should have a good grasp of existing ethical theories and principles (Brendel et al. 2021).

Human Rights Laws: Both designers and engineers who are practitioners of AI should be trained on how AI systems should be for human rights. Some important problems may occur in AI processes without knowing human rights laws. Basic human rights trainings are important to eliminate all these problems. We can give examples of some published human rights laws: Universal Declaration of Human Rights, International Human Rights Law, Charter of the United Nations, International Covenant on Economic, Social and Cultural Rights, International Covenant on Civil and Political Rights (Aizenberg and Hoven 2020). The explanations of ethical problems arising from the social impact of ethical AI problems in the third category are as follows:

Automation and Workplace Displacement: When robots are used instead of human labor in institutions, AI ethical situations will be directly affected by this situation. Therefore, automation and workplace displacement situations can also be counted among the ethical situations that cause concern (Wang and Siau, 2019).

Accessibility: It is desired for everyone to have equal and easy access to the AI field. When these situations are not present, ethical problems arise in AI (Houwen et al. 2023).

Democracy and Civil Rights: In order for trust in the AI field to be established, ethical elements must be provided within the scope of democracy and civil rights (Leslie et al. 2021).

In addition to artificial intelligence, various decision support models are also used in the education sector to test students' success and professional development. In one study, tests and evaluations used in the field of guidance applied to follow the personal and professional development of students in educational institutions were discussed in a web-based decision support system (Çil et al. 2014). The application of artificial intelligence in the field of education is becoming increasingly prevalent. With the use of AI in the education sector, the aforementioned ethical problems are increasing. In addition to these negative aspects of using AI in education, there are also positive aspects. Thanks to AI in education, student and teacher interaction increases and students' learning levels can increase successfully. AI also provides ease of access to information. In this sense, it facilitates the lifelong learning process by helping students' learning support (Pedro et al. 2019). Some studies on AI and ethics in education are as follows. Another study looked at the opportunities and potential ethical issues presented by artificial intelligence in education. Subsequently, a thematic analysis was conducted with the objective of defining and developing a framework of ethical principles. This was achieved by undertaking a review of the pertinent ethical policies and guidelines for AI in education. Each principle was examined from the perspective of basic education stakeholders (Nguyen et al., 2023). The article classifies individuals into three categories based on their distinct responsibilities in AI education: programmers, teachers, and students. Furthermore, it provides guidance and recommendations tailored to these three roles. The challenges in AI training fall into three primary categories: Algorithmic irrationality, data incompleteness, and content inaccuracies. Consequently, the article once more categorises individuals as programmers, teachers, and students in accordance with their respective responsibilities in AI education (Sijing et al. 2018). A top-down approach was employed for the development of artificial moral agents, with the objective of implementing an ethics-by-design solution for teaching and learning processes. This approach was aligned with the principles of values congruence in AI (Córdova et al., 2022). In another study, the authors investigated the interconnections between contemporary research on AI in education, including its impact on reducing teachers' workloads, enhancing student learning, influencing assessments, and advancing smart tutoring systems (Chaudhry & Kazim, 2022).

In order to analyse the studies on AI and ethics in education in more detail, bibliometric analysis is effective. Although bibliometrics is a quantitative analysis method, it describes the characteristics of the literature in the relevant field with numerical data (Haddow, 2013). Some bibliometric analysis studies in the fields of AI in education or ethics in AI can be given as follows.

Prahani et al. (2022) conducted bibliometric analysis to focus on the trends of AI in education. The results show that AI trends in education have increased in the last five years. At the same time, it has been observed that the research focus in this field in the last decade has mostly addressed students. Other areas of interest are as follows: Engineering education issues, teaching techniques, e-learning based education, educational structure, curriculum. Song and Wang (2020) included in their study a bibliometric analysis of the development of educational AI research worldwide in the last two decades. Maphosa and Maphosa (2023), in their study, addressed bibliometric analysis and topic modelling approach for 304 articles published in the scopus database on AI in higher education between 2012-2021. Sharma et al. (2024) evaluated 251 academic articles published between 2014 and 2023 to examine the intersection of AI and education. This review shows a growing interest in the potential of AI to improve educational outcomes and address inequalities. The research emphasises the importance of addressing ethical issues in AI-integrated education, targeting the rapid increase in annual publication numbers from 2019 onwards. Rodrigues et al. (2024) conducted a systematic literature review examining the relationship between academic ethics and AI (AI) using bibliometrics in order to eliminate the literature confusion on this topic, given the challenges and opportunities facing the education and academic field. Ivanova et al. (2024) aimed to examine and outline the impact of AI (AI) on educational applications, which is an important issue considering its increasing use and prevalence on a global scale. A bibliometric method is applied to create the 'overall picture' using bibliographic data obtained from scientific databases such as Scopus and Web of Science (WoS). Data on publications related to the keyword 'AI and education' in the last 5 years were analysed and processed with the Biblioshiny tool in the R environment in order to create a descriptive structure of scientific production, measure the impact of scientific publications, monitor collaboration models, and identify key research areas and new trends. In his study, Talan (2021) analysed the studies in the literature on the use of AI in the field of education with bibliometric aspects. Delen et al. (2024) analysed the research trends in educational AI studies published in the WoS database. This study carried out a bibliometric analysis of 4673 articles published between 1975 and 2023. Zheltukhina et al. (2024) aimed to conduct a bibliometric analysis and comprehensive evaluation of publications related to ChatGPT in educational research. This study also aims to present bibliometric findings to interpret research patterns and themes of ChatGPT application in educational research. Metli (2023) conducted a bibliometric analysis of 6498 articles from 1980-2022 in the field of AI in education. Durak et al. (2024) conducted a bibliometric analysis study on AI and learning roles in the field of education in the WoS database between 2013-2023. Polat et al. (2024) discussed the bibliometric analysis of the use of chatgbt in education for 212 studies with the scopus database. Bahroun et al. (2023) addressed the transformative effect of the education sector in AI with bibliometric analysis by including medical education and engineering field. Li (2023) discussed a bibliometric study evaluating the use of big data and AI in education between 2010-2023. Radu et al. (2024) In the context of transition to competence-based approach in education, this study deals with bibliometric analysis to identify emerging trends, challenges and opportunities at the intersection of AI and Competence-based Education (CEE). Guechair (2024) conducted a bibliometric analysis in the field of AI in education between 2010 and 2024 with the help of scopus database. Ilham et al. (2024) conducted a bibliometric analysis on AI in education and identified AI in general learning, medical education and higher education as research foci. Abuhassna et al. (2024) used bibliometric method to analyse the long-term outcomes of AI and its impact on students' learning processes. Pua et al. (2021) aimed to identify and analyse the main topics using key terms on AI in education. The study method is to perform bibliometric analysis of 8,660 articles published between 2000 and 2020 using CiteSpace software and to perform key terms and clustering analysis. The studies summarised above are given in Table 1.

Table 1. Recent bibliometric analyses in the field of artificial intelligence and ethics in education

Authors	Year	Title	Journal
Zheltukhina et al.	2024	A bibliometric analysis of publications on ChatGPT in education: Research patterns and topics	Online J. Commun. Media Technol
Abuhassna et al.	2024	The Information Age for Education via Artificial Intelligence and Machine Learning: A Bibliometric and Systematic Literature Analysis	International Journal of Information and Education Technology
Ilham et al.	2024	Artificial Intelligence Research in Education: A Bibliometric Analysis.	Journal on Education
Guechair	2024	Artificial Intelligence in Education: A Comprehensive Bibliometric Study on Scopus	ATRAS journal
Radu et al.	2024	Artificial intelligence and competency-based education: A bibliometric analysis	Amfiteatru Economic
Polat et al.	2024	A Bibliometric Analysis of Research on ChatGPT in Education	International Journal of Technology in Education

continued on following page

Table 1. Continued

Authors	Year	Title	Journal
Durak et al.	2024	Artificial Intelligence in Education: A Bibliometric Study on Its Role in Transforming Teaching and Learning	International Review of Research in Open and Distributed Learning
Delen et al.	2024	Understanding the Growth of Artificial Intelligence in Educational Research through Bibliometric Analysis	Sustainability
Ivanova et al.	2024	A Bibliometric Analysis of Artificial Intelligence in Teaching.	Informatics
Rodrigues et al.	2024	Artificial intelligence: threat or asset to academic integrity? A bibliometric analysis	Kybernetes.
Sharma et al.	2024	The Intersection of AI, Ethics, and Education: A Bibliometric Analysis.	In 2024 International Conference on Computing and Data Science
Bahroun et al.	2023	Transforming education: A comprehensive review of generative artificial intelligence in educational settings through bibliometric and content analysis	Sustainability
Li	2023	Big data and artificial intelligence in education: A bibliometrics study from 2010 to 2023	IEEE World Conference on Applied Intelligence and Computing (AIC)
Metli	2023	Articles on education and artificial intelligence: A bibliometric analysis.	Journal of Social Sciences and Education, 6(Education Special Issue)
Maphosa and Maphosa	2023	Artificial intelligence in higher education: a bibliometric analysis and topic modeling approach	Applied Artificial Intelligence,
Prahani et al.	2022	Artificial intelligence in education research during the last ten years: A review and bibliometric study.	International Journal of Emerging Technologies in Learning
Talan	2021	Artificial intelligence in education: A bibliometric study	International Journal of Research in Education and Science
Pua et al.	2021	Identification and Analysis of Core Topics in Educational Artificial Intelligence Research: A Bibliometric Analysis.	Cypriot Journal of Educational Sciences
Song and Wang	2020	A bibliometric analysis of worldwide educational artificial intelligence research development in recent twenty years	Asia Pacific Education Review

METHODS

Bibliometric Analysis is the numerical analysis of publications and the relationships between these publications in a specific field over a specific period. This analysis method is used to determine scientific developments, trends, and key contributions in a specific research area. Such analyses, which are conducted through metrics such as publication numbers, citation networks, author collaborations, and distribution of subject headings, allow researchers to evaluate the current state of the field and predict future research trends. The foundations of bibliometric analysis were laid in the 1950s and over time it has become an important method used especially in the evaluation of scientific publications and research outputs. With bibliometric analysis, the literature is systematically scanned and combined, thus helping to provide researchers with special methodologies. In addition, bibliometric analysis guides researchers in developing original methodologies by revealing gaps in the literature and the most popular topics. In this context, it becomes possible to understand the fundamental dynamics of the field and to discover new research opportunities. The findings obtained as a result of bibliometric studies allow for the determination of how the relevant discipline has developed, the identification of problems or deficiencies, and the discussion of corrections or suggestions that need to be made in this context. (Yilmaz, 2017).These findings contribute to understanding the evolution of the field and current research trends, while also supporting strategic decisions in research methods and topic selection. These data provided by bibliometric analyses make it possible to develop insights into the future directions of the discipline and to offer suggestions that will increase the quality of research.

Figure 1. Research process stages

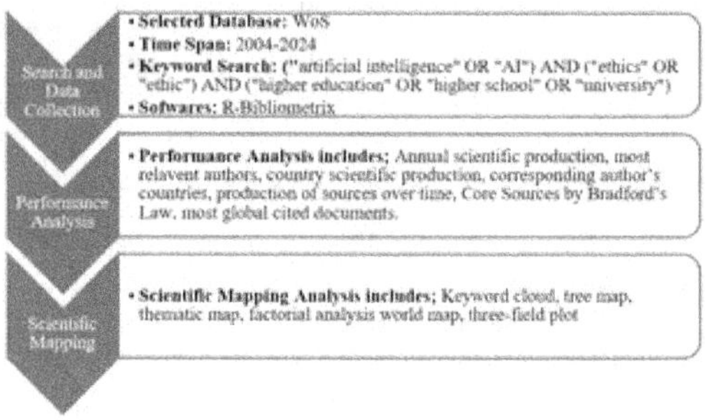

In the study, firstly, keywords are determined and data are obtained from the WoS database. The research theme is AI and ethics in higher education education, and the keywords "artificial intelligence", "AI", "ethics", "ethic", "higher education", "higher school", "university" are used as search criteria. The aim of the study is to analyze the subject from an interdisciplinary perspective rather than evaluating the ethical aspects of the use of AI in higher education. Then, two analyses are performed, namely performance analysis and scientific mapping. In the performance analysis, the number of published studies per year, the most influential authors, the number of publications by country, the countries of the responsible authors, the number of publications by journals, Basic Sources according to Bradford Law, and the most cited publications are examined. In the Science Mapping section; keyword cloud, tree map, thematic map, factor analysis, and three-file plot study are included. The methodology of the study is explained in detail in Figure 1.

RESULTS

The purpose of a literature review is to evaluate existing literature and identify potential areas for future research and the limits of current knowledge. When conducting a literature review, the process is usually sequential and follows defined search terms and criteria. The aim of this process is to identify gaps and potential research areas in the research field by systematically analyzing relevant studies.

WoS is one of the databases with very high data quality that is frequently used for bibliometric analysis (Mingers and Leydesdorff, 2015). This database evaluates the quality of publications according to certain academic standards and provides the opportunity to use it as a platform where indexed journals are included (Ulu and Türkan, 2024).

In this study, WoS database, which is a comprehensive repository of academic literature covering various disciplines, is used. On 15 October 2024, 297 articles from 209 sources were identified and incorporated into the study following a search of the WoS database using the pertinent keywords. The fundamental statistical data pertaining to the articles gathered in this context are presented in Figure 2.

Figure 2. General data information

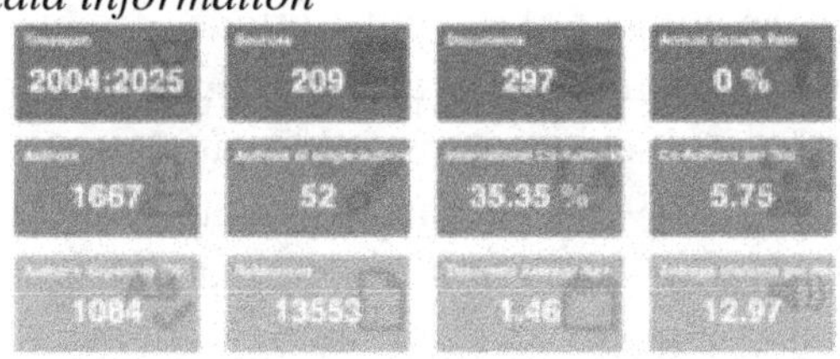

Within the scope of the study, 297 articles from 209 journals in the WoS database are analysed. The first article on the subject was published in 2004 and all articles from 2004-2024 are included in the analysis. The annual growth rate of the studies on this topic is 0% and the average age of the articles is 1.46 years. While 52 of 297 articles were published by a single author, the remaining 245 were published by multiple authors and the number of co-authors per article was found to be 5.75.

209 articles had 1084 keywords, 13553 references and an average of 12.97 citations per article.

Results of Performance Analysis

The objective of performance analysis is to identify groups of scientific actors (countries, universities, researchers) and evaluate the impact of their work based on bibliographic data. Furthermore, the extraction of information on the intellectual, social or conceptual structure of a research field can be conducted using science mapping analysis based on bibliographic networks (Gutiérrez-Salcedo, M., 2018). The following analyses are conducted according to these headings: Annual Scientific Production, Most Relevant Authors, Country Scientific Production, Corresponding Author's Countries, Production of Sources over Time, Core Sources by Bradford's Law, and Most Global Cited Documents.

Figure 3. Annual scientific production

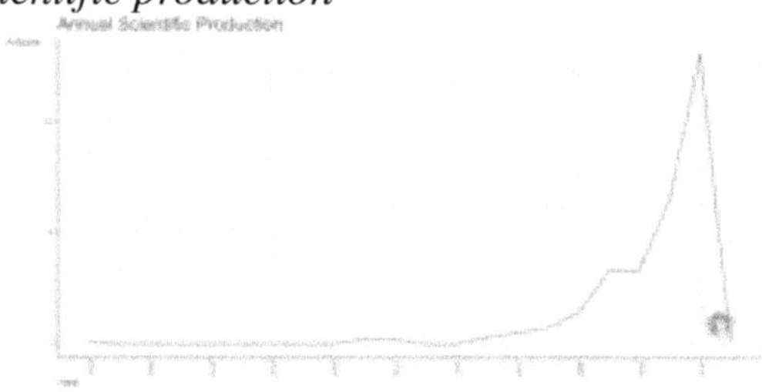

Figure 3 illustrates the number of scientific articles produced per year between 2004 and 2024. While the number of articles produced remained low and static between 2004 and 2016, an increase is observed in 2016. The upward trajectory reached a notable level in 2019 and reached its zenith in 2023. In 2024, a decline is observed due to incomplete data, but it is anticipated that the upward trend will resume once the data is complete. This upward trend in the number of articles indicates that this field is a nascent area of research.

Figure 4. Most relevant authors

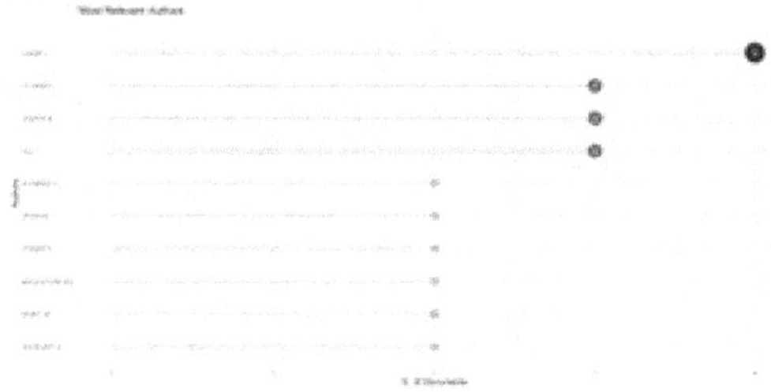

Figure 4 illustrates the ten most influential authors in the field. It is evident that Qadir has a dominant presence, with four articles, while Flordi, Gupta and Liu, the most prolific authors, follow with three articles each. Collectively, the top ten authors have contributed 25 articles over the span of 21 years.

Figure 5. Country scientific production

Figure 5 presents a global map indicating the countries with the highest levels of scientific productivity. A total of 72 countries have conducted studies on this subject, 41 of which have conducted nine or fewer studies. The USA is in the leading position with 267 papers, followed by the UK with 185 and China with 157. The top 10 countries are the USA, the UK, China, Canada, Australia, Germany, Spain, Italy, the Netherlands and Japan. It can be seen that countries with a higher level of economic development contribute more to the field.

Figure 6. Corresponding author's countries

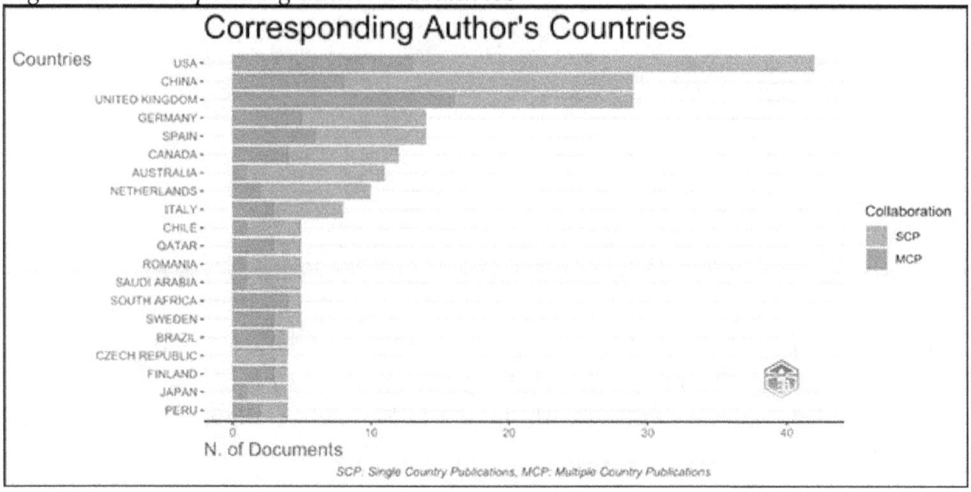

Figure 6 illustrates the scientific output of the corresponding authors from a range of countries. The data is presented in two formats: the number of single-country publications (SCP) and the number of multi-country publications (MCP). The United States of America is the country with the highest scientific production, with 13 (31%) of the total 42 articles being multinational (joint) and 29 being single-national. The United Kingdom follows the United States in terms of the number of articles, but in contrast to the United States, 16 (55.2%) of the 29 articles are multinational (joint). This illustrates that some countries are inclined to reinforce international collaboration. This graph underscores the significance of cooperation in scientific studies and the role of certain countries within these networks.

Figure 7. Production of sources over time

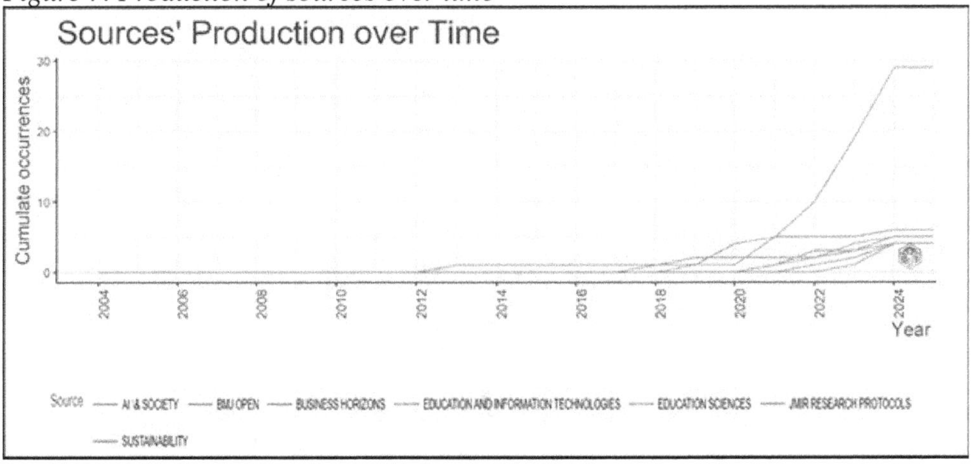

Figure 7 illustrates the quantity of scientific output from various sources over time. The journal BMJ Open is notable for having published the greatest number of articles on this subject after 2020. The journal has reached its peak in 2023 and is by far the most prolific source. The number of articles published by Business Horizons and AI Society has increased since 2020, although it has not reached the same level as that of BMJ Open. These journals continue to make a significant scientific contribution and demonstrate a balanced increase. In the top ten journals with the highest number of publications in this field, a total of 66 articles have been identified over the 20-year period analyzed, with more than half of them being published in the top three journals.

Figure 8. Core sources by Bradford's law

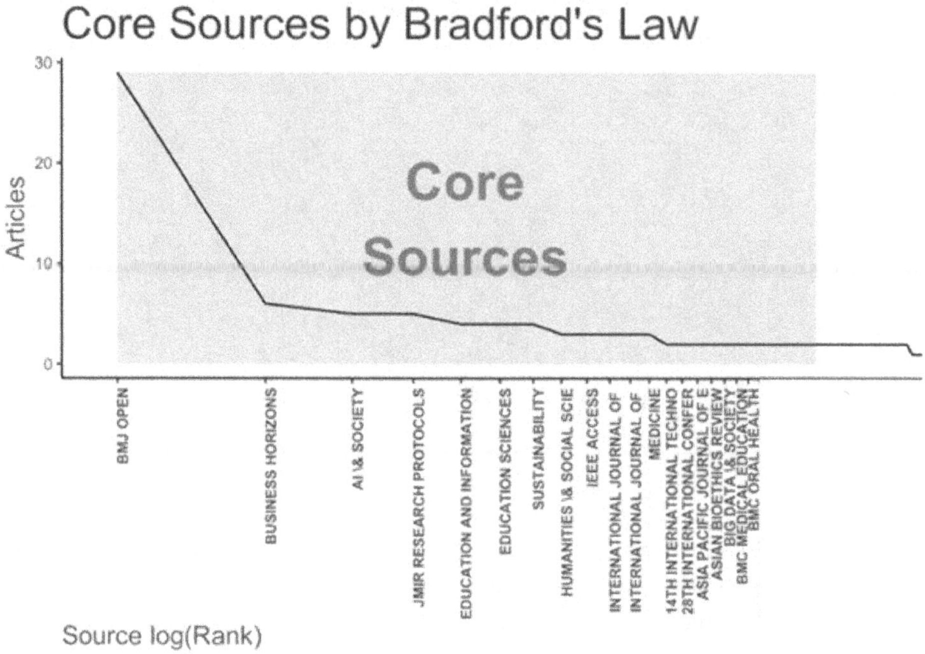

The law formulated by Bradford in 1934 elucidates the manner in which literature pertaining to a specific topic is distributed across journals (Bradford, 1934; Garfield, 1980). In his 1980 paper, Garfield offers the following explanation of Bradford's Law: "In order to construct a bibliography on a specific topic, it is necessary to identify a small number of core journals that will contain approximately one-third of the articles within that field. The remaining third of articles are distributed across a second group of journals, which contains a larger number of titles. The largest group, comprising a substantial number of journals, provides the remaining third. This law states that accumulation of knowledge in a particular field are concentrated in certain journals, with the remainder distributed across a wider range of sources. Figure 8 illustrates the main sources according to Bradford's law. The initial determination of the first 26 journals of 209 publication places is designated as Region 1, the subsequent 59 journals between 27 and 85 are classified as Region 2, and the remaining 124 journals between 86 and 209 are assigned to Region 3. It is established that between two and 29 articles were published in Region 1. In Regions 2 and 3, it is observed that there was only one article on the subject.

Figure 9. Most global cited documents

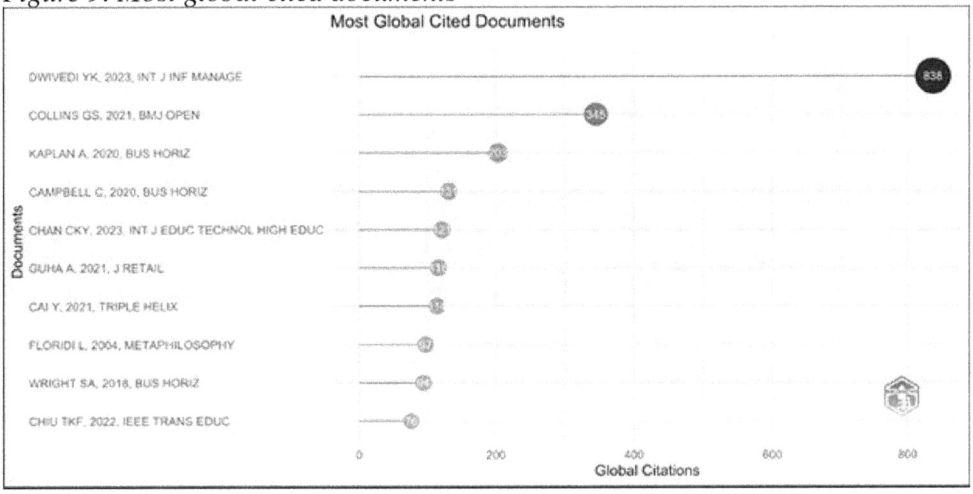

Figure 9 illustrates the most frequently cited papers published between 2004 and 2024. Dwivedi (2023) is the most highly cited paper with 838 citations and has notably increased its citation average in 2023. Collins (2021), who ranks second, has 345 citations. The ten most frequently cited authors account for 55.44% of the total number of citations.

Results of Science Mapping

Science mapping is a technique that is commonly employed to ascertain the significance of the interconnections between variables (Chen, 2017). In this context, a range of analytical tools, including keyword clouds, tree maps, thematic maps, factorial analysis world maps and three-field plot analyses are subjected to scrutiny.

Figure 10. Keyword cloud

In the context of academic studies, it is common practice to include more than one keyword. The objective of this analysis is to examine the relationship between the utilization of AI in universities and ethical considerations, with a view to identifying potential research areas that may be of interest.

A word cloud is a visualization tool that demonstrates the frequency of use of keywords in scanned articles, associating this frequency in a proportional manner according to the dimensions of the words. As illustrated in Figure 10, the most frequently used keywords in the articles are 'artificial intelligence', 'ethics', 'technology', 'students' and 'AI' respectively. The ten most frequent keywords constitute 28.26% of the total number of keywords.

Figure 11. Tree map

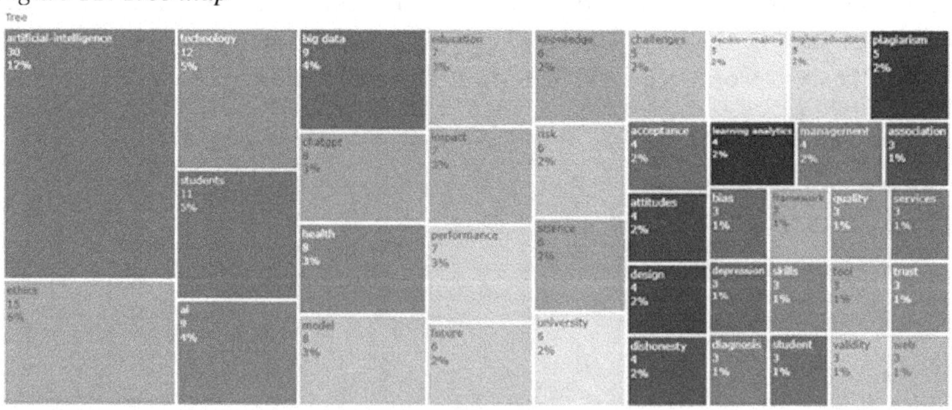

Figure 11 illustrates the prevalence of keywords in a keyword tree map as means of comparison. This analysis is more detailed than that provided by the word cloud graph and offers insight into the ratio of each keyword to the total number of keywords employed. While the usage rate of the keyword 'artificial-intelligence' is 11%, the usage rate of the keyword 'web' is 1%.

Figure 12. Thematic map

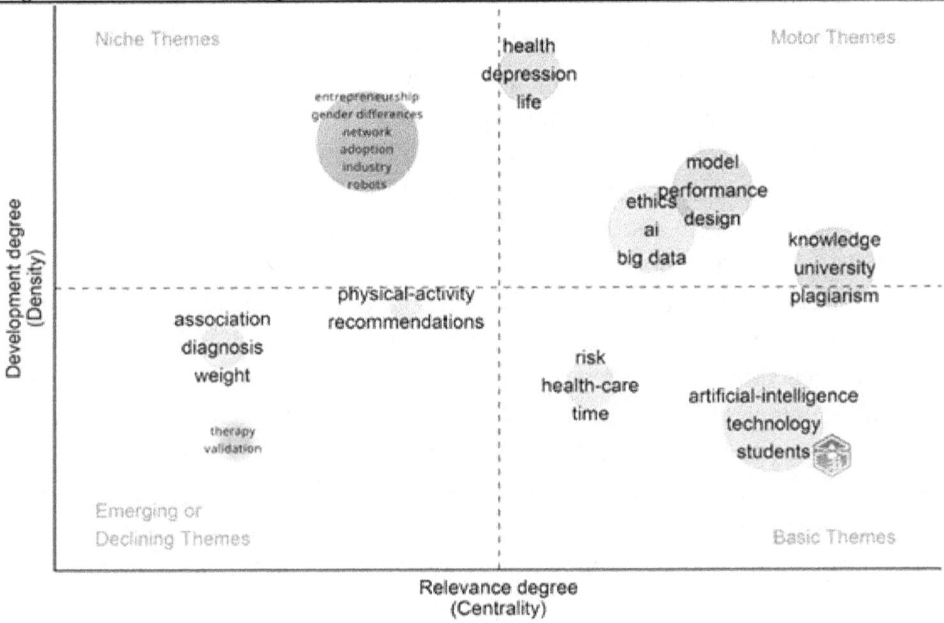

The analysis of keyword networks represents a significant methodology for the identification of relationships and connections between concepts, based on the co-occurrence of keywords. The principal objective of keyword (synonym) analysis is to elucidate the conceptual structure of publications. This analysis is conducted through the co-occurrence map and keyword clusters of words that indicate common concepts or a specific ideology. Figure 12 presents a thematic map for the keywords employed in the analyzed articles.

Thematic mapping is a technique that presents a visual representation of the interconnections between topics. Thematic maps are often framed on the axes of centrality (x-axis) and intensity (y-axis). Intensity refers to the level of development of a particular theme, while centrality measures the importance of the theme in the overall context. Thematic maps are divided into four sections, allowing readers to examine the themes under four quadrants.

The themes situated in the lower left quadrant of the thematic map encompass subjects that have diminished significance or are exhibiting potential for an upward trajectory. It is possible to cease researching these themes or to continue developing them. Themes situated in the lower right quadrant are referred to as basic schemes and have typically been subjected to extensive research. The upper left quadrant contains developed but isolated niche themes. These are typically specific to a particular field and are not widely used. The upper right quadrant contains well-developed themes that are often the focus of research. These are considered important areas of study for researchers. The evaluation of themes according to their quadrants and how researchers will address these themes helps them to determine their research strategies.

The concepts of 'association', 'diagnosis', 'weight', 'therapy', 'physical activity' and 'recommendations' in the left sub-quadrant, 'Emerging or Declining Themes', may have lost importance or attracted less attention. Consequently, these concepts can be removed from the research or redeveloped. The concepts of "risk," "health care," "time," "AI," "technology," and "students" in the lower right quadrant, Basic Themes, are concepts that are frequently encountered and intensively studied in research. In the upper left quadrant, Niche Themes, the concepts of 'entrepreneurship', 'gender differences', and 'networks' represent more specific topics that are not widely used, although they are quite developed. In the upper right quadrant, designated as Motor Themes, the concepts of "health," "depression," "life," "ethics," "AI," "big data," "model," "performance," "design," "knowledge," "university," and "plagiarism" represent advanced and high-intensity topics. These concepts, which have high centrality, have become the focus of researchers and have gained an important place in the literature.

Figure 13. Factorial analysis world map

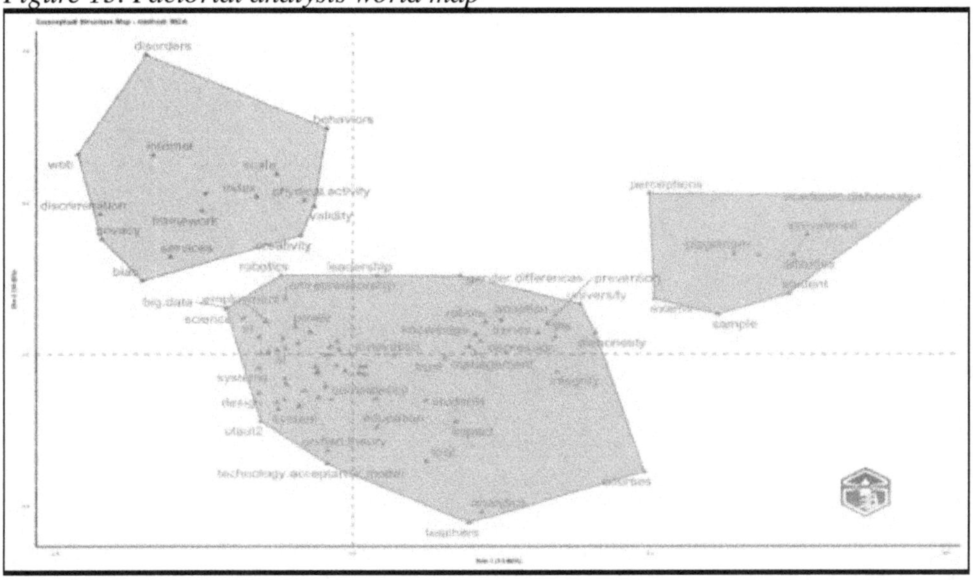

The conceptual structure map in Figure 13 is created using multiple correspondence analysis (MCA). This method is a widely recognized technique for reducing the number of dimensions in order to examine the relationships between a collection of categorical variables. The keywords generated from the WoS database are visually organized and three clusters are created from a total of 1084 keywords. Cluster 1 (green) predominantly encompasses concepts related to behavior and communication tools, whereas Cluster 2 (blue) brings together concepts related to education and those related to AI. Cluster 3 (red) is characterized by ethical concepts and includes words related to behavioral patterns. The triangular shapes represent the individual factors related to the clusters.

Figure 14. Three-field plot

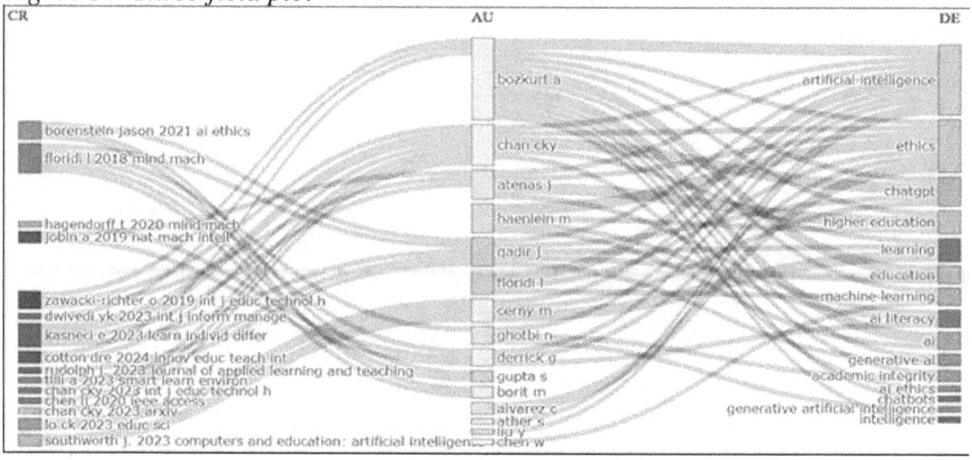

Figure 14 presents a three-field graph, which serves as a visual tool for elucidating the relationships between 15 sources, 15 authors, and 15 keywords obtained from the search. The size of box, the more connections they have with other fields. The width of the relationship between two fields is also a measure of the strength of the relationship between them. For example, it can be seen that the author named Aras Bozkurt, who is ranked first, uses 12 keywords in his work that he uses in three different sources.

CONCLUSION AND DISCUSSION

This chapter encompasses an examination of the number of articles on the ethical examination of the use of AI in universities, the most influential authors, the most productive countries, and the sources with the most publications. The increasing use of AI in the field of education brings with it important ethical issues, which makes it necessary to establish ethical frameworks to ensure the responsible use of AI in education. The findings of the study facilitated the delineation of the scope and of this field by elucidating the position and evolution of AI and ethics in the academic literature. A more conscious and systematic approach to the ethical dimensions of the use of AI in education will provide great benefits in terms of the adoption of sustainable AI applications.

The ethical examination of the use of AI in universities was first studied in the literature in 2000 and progressed with small increases until 2016. This upward trend became evident in 2019 and reached its peak in 2023. Based on this situation, it can be commented that the use of AI is increasing and ethical problems are increasing with it. The utilisation of AI also gives rise to ethical concerns, including those pertaining to data privacy, student privacy, the potential for biased algorithms, and the question of responsibility. However, the adoption of AI in academia, as well as in daily life, is increasing interest in this process by both students and academic staff. In addition, the evaluation of AI tools highlights the importance of transparency and ethical auditing for academic institutions. With the inclusion of AI in the field of education, there has been a need for investigation to determine and regulate the ethical responsibilities brought about by this development for universities. In this context, investigation on the ethical use of AI in universities is a promising development and it is desired that this increase continues to increase. A number of reasons, such as the advanced research institutions, large technology companies, significant financial resources and competitive environment within universities in the USA, have made the USA a leading country in the studies conducted in this field. Countries with a large number of multi-country publications stand out in terms of their capacity to produce scientific output, solid research resources and various financial supports. This also shows that these countries have an important role in international research. Such collaborations are very important in addressing global issues and providing a broad perspective on interdisciplinary issues. In this analysis, it is seen that the most frequently mentioned keywords are 'AI,' 'ethics,' 'technology,' 'students' and 'AI'. This situation reveals that the use of AI in education is frequently addressed with its ethical dimensions and evaluated in terms of the effects it may have on students. The frequency of use of keywords shows that the topic has high potential for various research areas at the intersection of education, AI and ethics. This result can be a guide for future research. While themes such as 'association' and 'therapy' can be considered as topics that have lost their importance or received less attention, the main themes such as 'AI' and 'students' represent the main topics that form the main structure of the research. In addition, niche themes such as 'entrepreneurship' and 'gender differences' reflect studies focusing on more specific areas, while themes with high centrality and intensity such as 'ethics' and 'big data' have gained an important place in the literature by forming the focus of research.

This study aims to increase awareness of the ethical use of AI applications in education and examines key issues in the literature within a conceptual framework. At the same time, the analyses conducted shed light on strategic areas that researchers can focus on, and can be applied to primary and high school levels in the future, allowing for the creation of an important data source for wider age groups. Such an extended analysis can be useful in understanding the perceptions and reactions of different age groups regarding the ethical use of AI; thus, it can play an important role in obtaining comprehensive data that guides the development of educational policies and future research.

REFERENCES

Abuhassna, H., Awae, F., Adnan, M. A., Daud, M., & Almheiri, A. S. (2024). The information age for education via artificial intelligence and machine learning: A bibliometric and systematic literature analysis. *International Journal of Information and Education Technology (IJIET)*, 14(5).

Aizenberg, E., & Van Den Hoven, J. (2020). Designing for human rights in AI. *Big Data & Society*, 7(2), 2053951720949566.

Akgun, S., & Greenhow, C. (2022). Artificial intelligence in education: Addressing ethical challenges in K-12 settings. *AI and Ethics*, 2(3), 431–440. PMID: 34790956

AlAli, R., & Wardat, Y. (2024). Opportunities and Challenges of Integrating Generative Artificial Intelligence in Education. *International Journal of Religion*, 5(7), 784–793.

Bahroun, Z., Anane, C., Ahmed, V., & Zacca, A. (2023). Transforming education: A comprehensive review of generative artificial intelligence in educational settings through bibliometric and content analysis. *Sustainability*, 15(17), 12983.

Bradford, S. C. (1934). Sources of information on specific subjects. *Engineering (London)*, 137, 85–86.

Brendel, A. B., Mirbabaie, M., Lembcke, T. B., & Hofeditz, L. (2021). Ethical management of artificial intelligence. *Sustainability*, 13(4), 1974.

Chaudhry, M. A., & Kazim, E. (2022). Artificial Intelligence in Education (AIEd): A high-level academic and industry note 2021. *AI and Ethics*, 2(1), 157–165. PMID: 34790953

Chen, C. (2017). Science mapping: A systematic review of the literature. *Journal of Data and Information Science*, 2(2), 1–40.

Çil, İ., Tokat, M. A., Türkan, Y. S., & Doğan, N. (2014). "E-guidance and counseling decision support system in elementary and high schools", H. U. Journal of Education, 29, (29-2),34-56.

Cointe, N., Bonnet, G., & Boissier, O. (2016, May). Ethical Judgment of Agents' Behaviors in Multi-Agent Systems. In AAMAS,1106-1114.

Collins, G. S., Dhiman, P., Navarro, C. L. A., Ma, J., Hooft, L., Reitsma, J. B., & Moons, K. G. (2021). Protocol for development of a reporting guideline (TRIPOD-AI) and risk of bias tool (PROBAST-AI) for diagnostic and prognostic prediction model studies based on artificial intelligence. *BMJ Open*, 11(7), e048008. PMID: 34244270

Córdova, P. R., & Vicari, R. M. (2022, August). Practical ethical issues for artificial intelligence in education. In International Conference on Technology and Innovation in Learning, Teaching and Education (pp. 437-445). Cham: Springer Nature Switzerland.

Delen, I., Sen, N., Ozudogru, F., & Biasutti, M. (2024). Understanding the growth of artificial intelligence in educational research through bibliometric analysis. *Sustainability*, 16(16), 6724.

Dilmaghani, S., Brust, M. R., Danoy, G., Cassagnes, N., Pecero, J., & Bouvry, P. (2019). Privacy and security of big data in AI systems: A research and standards perspective, in *Proc. IEEE Int. Conf. Big Data*, 5737–5743.

Durak, G., Çankaya, S., Özdemir, D., & Can, S. (2024). Artificial intelligence in education: A bibliometric study on its role in transforming teaching and learning. *International Review of Research in Open and Distributed Learning*, 25(3), 219–244.

Dwivedi, Y. K., Kshetri, N., Hughes, L., Slade, E. L., Jeyaraj, A., Kar, A. K., & Wright, R. (2023). Opinion Paper:"So what if ChatGPT wrote it?" Multidisciplinary perspectives on opportunities, challenges and implications of generative conversational AI for research, practice and policy. *International Journal of Information Management*, 71, 102642.

Eden, C. A., Chisom, O. N., & Adeniyi, I. S. (2024). Integrating AI in education: Opportunities, challenges, and ethical considerations. Magna Scientia Advanced Research and Reviews, 10(2), 006-013.

Etzioni, A., & Etzioni, O. (2017). Incorporating ethics into artificial intelligence. *The Journal of Ethics*, 21, 403–418.

Garfield, E. (1980). Citation indexing. *Journal of Information Science*, 2(1), 47–47.

Guechair, S. (2024). Artificial intelligence in education: A comprehensive bibliometric study on scopus (2010-2024). *Atras Journal*, 5(3), 445–463.

Gutiérrez-Salcedo, M., Martínez, M. Á., Moral-Munoz, J. A., Herrera-Viedma, E., & Cobo, M. J. (2018). Some bibliometric procedures for analyzing and evaluating research fields. *Applied Intelligence*, 48, 1275–1287. DOI: 10.1007/s10489-017-1105-y

Haddow, G. (2013). Bibliometric research. In *Research methods: Information, systems and contexts* (pp. 219–244). Tilde University Press.

Holmes, W., Porayska-Pomsta, K., Holstein, K., Sutherland, E., Baker, T., Shum, S. B., & Koedinger, K. R. (2022). Ethics of AI in education: Towards a community-wide framework. *International Journal of Artificial Intelligence in Education*, •••, 1–23.

Houwen, B. B., Nass, K. J., Vleugels, J. L., Fockens, P., Hazewinkel, Y., & Dekker, E. (2023). Comprehensive review of publicly available colonoscopic imaging databases for artificial intelligence research: Availability, accessibility, and usability. *Gastrointestinal Endoscopy*, 97(2), 184–199. PMID: 36084720

Huang, C., Zhang, Z., Mao, B., & Yao, X. (2022). An overview of artificial intelligence ethics. *IEEE Transactions on Artificial Intelligence*, 4(4), 799–819.

Ilham, R., Giatman, M., & Maksun, H. (2024). artificial intelligence research in education: A bibliometric analysis. *Journal of Education*, 6(2), 13467–13479.

Ivanova, M., Grosseck, G., & Holotescu, C. (2024, February). Unveiling insights: a bibliometric analysis of artificial intelligence in teaching. In Informatics (Vol. 11, No. 1, p. 10). MDPI.

Keskin, D., & Sevli, O. 2024, Eğitimde Yapay Zekâ Ve Etik. International Topkapı Congress III.

Kirkpatrick, K. (2015). The moral challenges of driverless cars. *Communications of the ACM*, 58(8), 19–20.

Larsson, S., & Heintz, F. (2020). Transparency in artificial intelligence. *Internet Policy Review*, 9(2).

Leslie, D., Burr, C., Aitken, M., Cowls, J., Katell, M., & Briggs, M. (2021). Artificial intelligence, human rights, democracy, and the rule of law: a primer. arXiv preprint arXiv:2104.04147.

Li, J. (2023, July). Big data and artificial intelligence in education: A bibliometrics study from 2010 to 2023. In *2023 IEEE World Conference on Applied Intelligence and Computing (AIC)* (pp. 400-406). IEEE.

Liao, S. M. (Ed.). (2020). *Ethics of artificial intelligence*. Oxford University Press.

Maphosa, V., & Maphosa, M. (2023). Artificial intelligence in higher education: A bibliometric analysis and topic modeling approach. *Applied Artificial Intelligence*, 37(1), 2261730.

Metli, A. (2023). Articles on education and artificial intelligence: A bibliometric analysis. Journal of Social Sciences and Education, 6(Education Special Issue), 279-312.

Mingers, J., & Leydesdorff, L. (2015). A review of theory and practice in scientometrics. *European Journal of Operational Research*, 246(1), 1–19.

Nguyen, A., Ngo, H. N., Hong, Y., Dang, B., & Nguyen, B. P. T. (2023). Ethical principles for artificial intelligence in education. *Education and Information Technologies*, 28(4), 4221–4241. PMID: 36254344

Nilsson, N. J. (1991). Logic and artificial intelligence. *Artificial Intelligence*, 47(1-3), 31–56.

Pedro, F., Subosa, M., Rivas, A., & Valverde, P. (2019). Artificial intelligence in education: Challenges and opportunities for sustainable development.

Polat, H., Topuz, A. C., Yildiz, M., Taslibeyaz, E., & Kursun, E. (2024). A bibliometric analysis of research on chatgpt in education. *International Journal of Technology in Education*, 7(1), 59–85.

Prahani, B., Rizki, I., Jatmiko, B., Suprapto, N., & Tan, A. (2022). Artificial intelligence in education research during the last ten years: A review and bibliometric study. [iJET]. *International Journal of Emerging Technologies in Learning*, 17(8), 169–188.

Pua, S., Ahmad, N. A., & Khambari, M. N. M. (2021). Identification and analysis of core topics in educational artificial intelligence research: A bibliometric analysis. *Cypriot Journal of Educational Sciences*, 16(3), 995–1009.

Radu, C., Ciocoiu, C. N., Veith, C., & Cătălin, R. (2024). Artificial intelligence and competency-based education: A bibliometric analysis. *Amfiteatru Economic*, 26(65), 220–240.

Rodrigues, M., Silva, R., Borges, A. P., Franco, M., & Oliveira, C. (2024). Artificial intelligence: Threat or asset to academic integrity? A bibliometric analysis. *Kybernetes*.

Seo, K., Tang, J., Roll, I., Fels, S., & Yoon, D. (2021). The impact of artificial intelligence on learner–instructor interaction in online learning. *International Journal of Educational Technology in Higher Education*, 18, 1–23. PMID: 34778540

Sharma, R., Kumar, P., Singh, D. K., Suri, D., Rajput, P., & Kumar, S. (2024, April). The intersection of ai, ethics, and education: a bibliometric analysis. In *2024 International Conference on Computing and Data Science (ICCDS)* (pp. 1-6). IEEE.

Siau, K., & Wang, W. (2020). Artificial intelligence (AI) ethics. *Journal of Database Management*, 31(2), 74–87.

Sijing, L., & Lan, W. (2018, August). Artificial intelligence education ethical problems and solutions. In 2018 13th International Conference on Computer Science & Education (ICCSE) (pp. 1-5). IEEE.

Song, P., & Wang, X. (2020). A bibliometric analysis of worldwide educational artificial intelligence research development in recent twenty years. *Asia Pacific Education Review*, 21(3), 473–486.

Stupp, C. (2019). Fraudsters used AI to mimic CEO's voice in unusual cybercrime case: Scams using artificial intelligence are a new challenge for companies, Accessed: Feb. 10, 2022. [Online]. Available: https://www.wsj.com/articles/fraudsters-use-ai-tomimic-ceos-voice-in-unusual-cybercrime-case-11567157402

Sullins, J. P. (2011). When is a robot a moral agent? In Anderson, M., & Anderson, S. L. (Eds.), *Machine Ethics* (pp. 151–161). Cambridge Univ. Press.

Talan, T. (2021). Artificial intelligence in education: A bibliometric study. *International Journal of Research in Education and Science*, 7(3), 822–837.

Timmermans, J., Stahl, B. C., Ikonen, V., & Bozdag, E. (2010). The ethics of cloud computing: A conceptual review, in Proc. IEEE 2nd Int. Conf. Cloud Comput. Technol. Sci., 614–620.

Turan, T., Turan, G., & Küçüksille, E. (2022). Yapay zekâ etiği: Toplum üzerine etkisi. *Mehmet Akif Ersoy Üniversitesi Fen Bilimleri Enstitüsü Dergisi*, 13(2), 292–299.

Ulu, M., & Türkan, Y. S. (2024). *Bibliometric Analysis of Traffic Accident Prediction Studies from 2003 to 2023: Trends, Patterns, and Future Directions*. Traffic Transportation.

Valerio, A. (2024). Anticipating the impact of artificial intelligence in higher education: Student awareness and ethical concerns in Zamboanga City, Philippines. *Cognizance Journal of Multidisciplinary Studies*, 4(6), 10–47760.

Wang, W., & Siau, K. (2019). Artificial intelligence, machine learning, automation, robotics, future of work and future of humanity: A review and research agenda. *Journal of Database Management*, 30(1), 61–79.

Yilmaz, G. (2017). Restoranlarda Bahşiş İle İlgili Yayınlanan Makalelerin Bibliyometrik Analizi. Seyahat ve Otel İşletmeciliği Dergisi, 65–79. https://doi.org/DOI: 10.24010/soid.335082

Yu, L., & Yu, Z. (2023). Qualitative and quantitative analyses of artificial intelligence ethics in education using VOSviewer and CitNetExplorer. *Frontiers in Psychology*, 14, 1061778. PMID: 36968737

Zheltukhina, M. R., Sergeeva, O. V., Masalimova, A. R., Budkevich, R. L., Kosarenko, N. N., & Nesterov, G. V. (2024). A bibliometric analysis of publications on ChatGPT in education: Research patterns and topics. *Online Journal of Communication and Media Technologies*, 14, e202405.

KEY TERMS AND DEFINITIONS

Artificial Intelligence: "It is a field of computer science that aims to solve problems that generate meaning from data and are based on learning and creativity, often associated with business intelligence."

Higher Education: "These are educational and training institutions where the highest level of education is provided through an educational program and where research and development are carried out."

Ethics: "It is the branch of philosophy that examines and explains moral concepts, judgments and standards of behavior."

Bibliometric Analysis: "Bibliometric Analysis is the numerical analysis of publications and the relationships between these publications in a specific field over a specific period"

Chapter 2
AI in Higher Education: Revolutionizing Curriculum and Administration

Mustafa Kayyali
https://orcid.org/0000-0003-3300-262X
HE Higher Education Ranking, Syria

ABSTRACT

The incorporation of Artificial Intelligence (AI) into higher education is altering both curriculum design and administrative operations. This chapter investigates how AI is being exploited to tailor learning experiences, expedite administrative chores, and enhance decision-making in educational institutions. AI-driven curriculum design encourages adaptive learning environments, allowing students individualized learning routes based on their unique requirements and preferences. Meanwhile, AI boosts administrative efficiency by automating routine activities, optimizing resource allocation, and boosting student support services. Despite the transformational potential, AI adoption also creates obstacles linked to ethical considerations, data protection, and the need for faculty training. By reviewing case studies of effective AI integration in universities, this chapter gives a forward-looking picture of the future of higher education and administration in the era of AI.

INTRODUCTION

The rapid growth of technology has brought about extraordinary transformations in different areas, and higher education is no exception (Marshall, 2018). In recent years, Artificial Intelligence (AI) has emerged as one of the most disruptive forces in academia, changing not only the way students learn but also how institutions run (Yadav, 2019). The potential of AI resides in its ability to change curriculum

DOI: 10.4018/979-8-3693-7949-3.ch002

design, customize educational experiences, and expedite administrative operations, therefore boosting the overall efficiency of academic institutions. As we approach an era marked by data-driven decision-making and automated solutions, the role of AI in higher education has extended beyond a basic tool to aid with traditional chores; it has become an intrinsic component of educational innovation and institutional strategy. AI's influence in higher education encompasses a wide spectrum of applications. In the field of teaching and learning, AI-powered platforms are being used to develop tailored learning environments that adapt to specific student needs. These systems assess data such as students' progress, behavior, and preferences to deliver customized recommendations and interventions, enabling learners to improve at their own speed. This method signals a substantial shift from traditional, one-size-fits-all educational models, allowing for more adaptable and responsive learning experiences. In addition, AI is facilitating new types of pedagogy, such as intelligent tutoring systems, virtual learning assistants, and AI-based content development, which are enhancing both in-person and online educational delivery.

On the administrative side, AI has the ability to address some of the most significant difficulties faced by educational institutions today (Pedro et al, 2019). Universities and colleges often battle with managing huge volumes of data, whether it includes student records, financial information, or operational operations (Attaran et al, 2018). AI can automate many of these regular administrative duties, including admissions processing, resource allocation, and academic advising, so freeing up staff to focus on more strategic efforts. For example, AI-powered chatbots can handle student requests and deliver rapid responses, boosting the quality and efficiency of student services. Moreover, AI's predictive analytics capabilities help institutions to anticipate future demands and trends, increasing decision-making processes linked to enrollment management, student retention, and course offers.

However, the integration of AI into higher education is not without its hurdles. While AI provides great potential, it also brings important ethical, legal, and social challenges that need to be properly explored. Issues including as data privacy, algorithmic bias, and the potential for job displacement among professors and administrative personnel are some of the primary dilemmas that institutions must confront. The collecting and analysis of huge volumes of personal data to power AI systems raise worries about the security and confidentiality of student information. Furthermore, the reliance on algorithms to make key decisions about student development and institutional operations risks perpetuating existing biases if not properly monitored and supervised. Ensuring transparency, accountability, and fairness in AI applications will be vital to attaining their full potential without aggravating social disparities.

The emergence of AI also needs a considerable cultural and organizational adjustment within educational institutions (Benbya et al, 2020). Faculty members, administrators, and students must gain new abilities to effectively engage with AI technologies. This includes understanding how AI systems work, acknowledging their limitations, and incorporating them into current educational and administrative frameworks. To achieve this, colleges must invest in faculty development programs that provide educators with the essential tools and knowledge to harness AI in their teaching and research. Similarly, administrators must be trained to use AI-driven systems for decision-making and resource management, ensuring that new technologies are implemented in a way that corresponds with institutional aims and values. The potential for AI to drive transformation in higher education is great, but its impact will depend partly on how well institutions negotiate the intricacies of AI adoption. Early adopters of AI in higher education have already proved its capacity to improve learning outcomes, streamline processes, and cut costs (Hannan & Liu, 2023). For example, colleges that have integrated AI into their admissions processes have observed improvements in enrollment rates and student satisfaction. Similarly, universities adopting AI-driven analytics for academic advising and retention initiatives have been able to provide more tailored help to at-risk students, leading to increased graduation rates. These accomplishments imply that AI has the potential to address some of the most persistent difficulties confronting higher education, including access, cost, and student success.

This chapter digs into the transformational impact that AI is playing in transforming both curriculum design and administrative operations within higher education. Through an evaluation of the current level of AI adoption in academia, we investigate the ways in which AI is changing established educational models and offering new avenues for institutional efficiency. We will also emphasize the ethical considerations and problems that accompany the widespread use of AI in higher education, bringing insights into how institutions might avoid risks while reaping the benefits of AI-driven innovation. Finally, by offering real-world case studies of AI integration in universities, we give a path for educational institutions wanting to leverage AI's full potential to better both teaching and administration. As we stand on the brink of a new era in higher education, AI presents great prospects to rethink the future of learning and institutional management, but its success will ultimately rest on intelligent and inclusive implementation strategies.

AI-Driven Curriculum Design and Personalization

Artificial Intelligence (AI) has changed several sectors of higher education, but arguably nowhere is its impact more evident than in curriculum design and customization (Kayyali, 2024). The old style of curriculum development—characterized by static, one-size-fits-all courses—has increasingly given way to dynamic, data-driven approaches that adapt to individual learning needs. AI technologies now enable instructors to develop courses that are not only more flexible but also more responsive to the different requirements and learning styles of students. This shift constitutes a considerable divergence from established educational paradigms, presenting the promise for a more individualized and effective learning experience. One of the most fundamental benefits of AI-driven curriculum design is its capacity to personalize learning experiences to individual individuals. Historically, educators had the issue of establishing curricula that suited the demands of vast, diverse student groups (Sleeter & Carmona, 2017). This sometimes led to generalist teaching strategies that could fail to captivate specific students or leave others under-challenged. AI modifies this equation by providing for a more granular understanding of each student's unique learning preferences, skills, and shortcomings. Through complex algorithms and data analytics, AI can track student performance in real time, providing insights into their progress, comprehension, and engagement (Xu, 2024). Based on this data, AI can offer individualized learning routes, modifying the curriculum to better meet the needs of each learner (Kayyali, 2021). For example, an AI-driven system might propose extra exercises or reading materials to a student who is struggling with a certain idea, while presenting more advanced content to a student who has already mastered it. This level of customisation guarantees that students receive tailored support when needed, while those who excel are not held back by a set pace. The ability to differentiate learning in real-time is a tremendous leap forward in the pursuit of inclusive education, enabling educators to handle individual differences more effectively than ever before.

Moreover, AI-driven curriculum design encourages the establishment of adaptive learning environments (Yekollu et al, 2024). Unlike static course materials, AI-powered platforms can be modified in real-time based on student input and performance. This adaptive learning technique promotes student engagement by giving more relevant, timely, and tailored content. A student who excels in a certain subject can be urged to investigate more complex themes or participate in project-based learning, while a student who struggles can receive additional scaffolding or even immediate tutoring from AI-powered assistants. This versatility makes learning more dynamic and responsive, creating an atmosphere in which each student's educational path is unique and continually growing. Another area where AI is pushing innovation in curriculum design is through the use of intelligent tutoring systems (ITS) (Dermeval et al, 2018). These AI-based systems are designed to deliver tailored instruction and feedback, typically simulating the interactions between a student and a human tutor. Intelligent tutoring systems harness enormous amounts of data to predict student needs, direct learning courses and offer individualized interventions. They can assess student replies, find patterns of misunderstanding, and give targeted remediation. Over time, ITS systems grow more polished in their ability to enable tailored learning, offering an experience that is analogous to one-on-one tutoring but at scale. This not only improves learning results but also serves to level the playing field for children who may not have access to personalized tutoring outside the classroom.

The integration of AI into curriculum design is not restricted to boosting the learning experience for individual students (Chen et al, 2020). It also holds significant promise for revolutionizing how courses and entire programs are designed. AI may examine trends in student performance, course comments, and even employment results to provide insights into the effectiveness of the curriculum. Based on this data, colleges can make more informed judgments regarding which courses to offer, how to sequence them, and what learning objectives should be prioritized. For example, an AI system might determine that students who study a particular sequence of courses tend to struggle in succeeding modules. With this understanding, educators and administrators may tailor the curriculum to better prepare students for the difficulties ahead, guaranteeing easier transitions between subjects and more cohesive learning experiences. Beyond increasing the design of individual courses, AI is also being utilized to construct transdisciplinary curricula that match the evolving demands of the modern workforce. As the global economy becomes increasingly digital, multidisciplinary knowledge and skills are becoming more crucial. AI can examine job market data, industry trends, and academic research to discover developing fields and skill sets that are in demand (Alekseeva et al, 2021). Based on this analysis, educational institutions can build new programs that integrate areas like data science, artificial intelligence, and digital marketing with traditional disciplines such as business, humanities, or the social sciences. The capacity to build a curriculum that responds to real-world demands in real-time means that students are better equipped for their jobs, and armed with the skills necessary to succeed in a fast-changing world. Another intriguing aspect of AI-driven curriculum design is its capacity to support lifelong learning (Markauskaite et al, 2022). As the pace of technological development accelerates, ongoing learning and upskilling have become vital. AI-powered learning platforms can offer individualized suggestions to learners throughout their careers, proposing new courses, certificates, or learning materials based on their developing requirements and professional goals. By monitoring trends in their work performance, hobbies, and areas for improvement, AI may create personalized learning experiences that correspond with each individual's career trajectory. This strategy encourages learners to take charge of their educational experiences, always adjusting and expanding in response to the demands of the labor market.

As intriguing as AI-driven curriculum design and personalization may be, it also comes with hurdles that educators and institutions must negotiate. One important concern is the risk of over-reliance on AI systems, which might potentially limit the function of human instructors in the learning process (Kayyali, 2024). While AI can deliver tailored learning routes and adaptive content, it cannot duplicate the humanity, creativity, and mentorship that human professors contribute to education. Therefore, educators need to keep a major role in directing and creating the curriculum, ensuring that AI is used to supplement, rather than replace, human contact (Pedro et al, 2019). Ethical considerations also play a key role in AI-driven curriculum design. The use of AI systems to collect and analyze student data raises problems regarding privacy and permission. Institutions must be clear about how they use data and ensure that student's personal information is secured. Additionally, the algorithms that underpin AI-based customization must be carefully constructed to prevent reinforcing biases or perpetuating disparities. A truly inclusive approach to AI-driven education demands continual attention to guarantee that these systems are fair, transparent, and accountable. AI-driven curriculum design and personalization reflect a transformational shift in the landscape of higher education. By using the potential of AI, universities can build more flexible, dynamic, and personalized learning experiences that respond to the different needs of students. While problems exist, notably in terms of ethical considerations and the need to maintain human control, the potential benefits of AI in curriculum design are obvious. As AI technologies continue to improve, their ability to enhance education will only rise, creating exciting prospects for the future of learning.

AI in Administrative Functions: Efficiency and Innovation

The importance of Artificial Intelligence (AI) in higher education extends far beyond the classroom, where it plays a crucial role in enhancing administrative activities (Ahmad et al, 2021). Traditionally, university administration has been burdened by labor-intensive operations that take a large amount of time, manpower, and resources. From admissions to student services, financial administration, and resource allocation, these processes generally follow inflexible, manual workflows that can contribute to inefficiencies and delays. AI offers a disruptive solution by streamlining these activities, allowing universities to become more efficient, responsive, and innovative. This transition not only lessens the administrative burden on staff but also increases the entire student experience, allowing institutions to focus more on their main mission: instruction and research.

One of the most immediate applications of AI in higher education management is in admissions (Zawacki-Richter et al, 2019). For years, the admissions process has been a laborious, paper-based procedure where personnel pore through hundreds of applications, transcripts, and recommendation letters. This is not only time-consuming but also prone to human error and bias. AI can substantially speed up this process through the use of machine learning algorithms that can examine applications, assess qualifications, and even forecast which applicants are most likely to succeed. By automating this initial screening phase, institutions can decrease administrative expenses, shorten response times, and ensure a more objective evaluation of prospects (Spring et al, 2022). AI systems can go beyond only assessing academic qualifications. They may examine a wide range of applicant data, including extracurricular activities, social media accounts, and even personal writings, to develop a holistic image of each individual. This kind of analysis helps universities better match students with programs that meet their interests and skills. In doing so, AI can lead to improved retention rates and more successful academic journeys, as students are put in environments that are more aligned with their abilities and objectives. This kind of customization in the admissions process would have been inconceivable a decade ago, but AI makes it possible at scale. AI's potential to streamline administrative activities is also obvious in the field of course scheduling and enrollment management. Scheduling has long been a logistical burden for universities, with administrators needing to negotiate classroom availability, faculty schedules, and student preferences, all while assuring compliance with degree requirements and accrediting criteria. AI-driven solutions can optimize these complicated variables, creating timetables that suit the needs of all stakeholders while increasing resource efficiency. By examining patterns in course enrollment data, AI can also forecast which classes are likely to be over- or under-subscribed, enabling institutions to make better-informed decisions about course offerings and personnel requirements. This not only enhances student satisfaction by ensuring that popular courses are available but also helps colleges manage resources more effectively.

Similarly, AI-powered systems can assist with student advice and degree preparation (Majjate, 2023). Traditional advising focuses on manual processes where advisers work individually with students to guide them through course selections and graduation requirements. While personal interaction is vital in this process, it can be time-consuming and vulnerable to discrepancies. AI can improve advising by assessing student data, identifying gaps in their progress, and offering the best courses for fulfilling degree requirements (Khare et al, 2018). AI-driven platforms can develop individualized degree plans for students based on their academic performance, job objectives, and course availability, allowing for more efficient planning and minimizing the possibility of delays in graduation. Advisors can then use this information to have more effective, focused conversations with students, boosting the quality of assistance provided. Beyond student-facing functions, AI is also making a substantial impact on internal administrative procedures, particularly in financial management and human resources. Managing budgets, grants, and funding allocations in higher education is a very complex undertaking that demands careful preparation and execution. AI systems can assess historical financial data, estimate future demands, and offer solutions for optimal resource allocation. By delivering data-driven insights, AI allows institutions to make better-educated decisions about how to deploy finances, whether for faculty recruiting, research programs, or facility enhancements (Bates et al, 2020). This kind of financial knowledge enables colleges to function more efficiently and make strategic investments that support their long-term objectives.

In human resources, AI is transforming recruitment, onboarding, and staff management (Mer, 2023). Traditionally, hiring processes in higher education are lengthy and can be riddled with issues, including attracting diverse talent and ensuring fairness in hiring practices. AI-powered recruitment tools can help find individuals who are the best fit for faculty and staff roles by assessing their skills, experiences, and even personal qualities (Rathnayake, C., & Gunawardana, 2023). These platforms can also assure equal employment by eliminating unconscious bias in the selection process. By automating portions of the hiring process, such as candidate screening and interview scheduling, AI frees up human resources workers to focus on more strategic objectives, such as faculty development and staff retention. One of the most prominent applications of AI in university administration is the usage of AI-powered chatbots and virtual assistants. These systems are increasingly being implemented to address a wide range of student requests, from answering questions about financial aid to providing information on course registration and campus events. Unlike human personnel, chatbots are available 24/7, ensuring that students receive prompt solutions to their inquiries regardless of when they ask them (Kooli, 2023). This not only increases the student experience but also decreases the effort for administrative staff, who are sometimes overwhelmed with routine requests that could be handled by an automated system. Moreover, these AI-driven tools can continue to learn from their interactions with students, boosting their ability to give accurate and relevant information over time (Saaida, 2023). In student services, AI is proven to be a game-changer in managing everything from housing assignments to mental health care. AI-driven solutions may monitor student preferences and behaviors to optimize housing placements, ensuring that students are assigned to dormitories that best suit their needs (Chiu et al, 2023). In the field of student well-being, AI is being utilized to identify at-risk students and provide early treatments. By monitoring behavioral patterns, academic achievement, and engagement levels, AI can flag students who may be suffering and connect them with the necessary support resources, such as counseling or academic advising. This proactive approach to student support is a key innovation, as it enables colleges to address concerns before they worsen, thereby enhancing retention and student achievement.

Despite the obvious advantages of AI in administrative activities, its application is not without hurdles. One of the key problems is the ethical consequences of depending on AI for decision-making (Rodgers et al, 2023). While AI systems can handle massive amounts of data and deliver meaningful insights, they can also bring new forms of bias if not adequately regulated. For example, if an AI system is educated on biased data, it may perpetuate inequities in areas such as admissions, hiring, or resource allocation. Therefore, it is crucial that universities create transparent AI systems, frequently audit their algorithms, and ensure that human oversight remains an integral part of decision-making processes. Data privacy is another key worry (Yanamala et al, 2024). As AI systems collect and analyze increasingly huge datasets, colleges must ensure that student and staff information is protected (Teng et al, 2023). This involves sophisticated data governance procedures and compliance with standards such as the General Data Protection Regulation (GDPR) in Europe or the Family Educational Rights and Privacy Act (FERPA) in the United States (Fiero & Beier, 2022). Institutions must be upfront about how data is gathered, utilized, and stored, and establish clear principles for data security and privacy. Looking to the future, AI will continue to drive innovation in university administration, enabling institutions to become more nimble, responsive, and student-centered. As AI systems become more advanced, they will not only increase operational efficiency but also provide deeper insights into how colleges may better serve their students and communities. The incorporation of AI into administrative activities signifies a significant transformation in how universities work, offering a future where decision-making is faster, more informed, and more egalitarian. AI's position in administrative activities is altering higher education in dramatic ways (Alexander, 2020). From streamlining admissions and course scheduling to boosting financial management and student services, AI is enabling universities to function with greater efficiency and innovation. However, the successful application of AI demands careful consideration of ethical considerations and data privacy issues, as well as a commitment to preserving human oversight in decision-making processes (Nassar & Kamal, 2021). As universities continue to embrace AI-driven solutions, they will be better positioned to manage the complexity of modern education and deliver a more personalized, efficient, and meaningful experience for their students and staff.

Challenges and Ethical Considerations in AI Adoption

As artificial intelligence (AI) continues to find its way into the fabric of higher education, it carries with it a plethora of problems and ethical dilemmas. While AI offers better efficiency, tailored learning, and enhanced decision-making capabilities, its implementation is not without risk. The introduction of any new technology—especially one as powerful and disruptive as AI—inevitably generates issues about its long-term influence on institutions, educators, students, and society at large. To ensure that the use of AI in higher education is both responsible and sustainable, universities must address a range of problems and ethical considerations, each requiring significant study and careful planning.

1. Bias in AI Algorithms

One of the most important problems regarding AI adoption is the issue of bias incorporated into AI algorithms (Schwartz, 2022). AI systems are built on large volumes of data, and the outputs they generate are only as good as the data they learn from (Belenguer, 2022). If the data used to train AI models is biased, the system may unwittingly exacerbate existing inequities. In the context of higher education, this could mean that AI-powered systems for admissions, grading, or even individualized learning paths might disproportionately favor certain groups of students over others. For instance, students from underrepresented backgrounds could face systematic disadvantages if the data used to create these AI systems fails to portray the diversity of human experience. Bias can also occur in more subtle ways (Akter et al, 2021). Even if an AI system seems neutral on the surface, it might still perpetuate injustices depending on criteria such as socioeconomic position, color, or gender. For example, if AI is used to predict student achievement, it may reward students who come from more affluent educational backgrounds while dismissing the potential of students from less-resourced situations. This kind of bias can undermine the primary objective of higher education: to offer equitable chances for learning and growth. Addressing bias in AI systems requires institutions to establish rigorous protocols for data collecting, model training, and system evaluation (Ferrara, 2023). It's not enough to believe that AI is naturally objective—institutions must actively endeavor to ensure that the algorithms they deploy are transparent, fair, and accountable. This may require conducting regular audits of AI systems to uncover bias, as well as incorporating diverse teams in the design and deployment of AI technologies to prevent unconscious bias from influencing outcomes.

2. Data Privacy and Security Concerns

AI's power to study and interpret huge volumes of data is both its greatest strength and a significant ethical challenge. In higher education, AI systems rely on the collection of student data to create individualized learning experiences, optimize administrative tasks, and enhance decision-making (Ahmad et al, 2022). However, the increased dependence on AI also raises worries about data privacy and security. Students, faculty, and staff entrust educational institutions with sensitive personal information—ranging from academic records and financial data to behavioral patterns and biometric data. The question of how this data is stored, processed, and safeguarded becomes essential when AI is involved. Data breaches, illegal access, and misuse of personal information are genuine hazards that come with AI adoption (Olabanji et al, 2024). If educational institutions do not have comprehensive data protection rules in place, they risk mistakenly divulging sensitive information, leading to a loss of trust among students and other stakeholders. Furthermore, the expanding usage of AI-powered surveillance tools, such as facial recognition systems on campuses, raises worries about student privacy and the possibility of invasive monitoring (Choung et al, 2024). To prevent these dangers, colleges must create explicit norms on data privacy and security when deploying AI technologies. This includes implementing tight rules for data encryption, access control, and compliance with privacy legislation such as the General Data Protection Regulation (GDPR) in Europe or the Family Educational Rights and Privacy Act (FERPA) in the United States. Additionally, colleges should create an open discourse with students and staff regarding the ethical use of AI and data, ensuring that individuals have a clear awareness of how their data is being used and the right to opt out of specific forms of data gathering.

3. The Impact on Employment and Academic Roles

The rise of AI in higher education throws into doubt the future function of human professors, administrators, and support workers (Mellul, 2018). As AI systems become more capable of handling jobs previously carried out by humans—such as grading coursework, providing student feedback, and managing administrative processes—there is a rising concern that AI could lead to job displacement. While AI might clearly make certain activities more efficient, it is vital to analyze how its adoption may affect the workforce within educational institutions. For instance, if AI systems take over mundane duties such as admissions processing or course scheduling, what will happen to the human staff members who once handled these responsibilities? Similarly, if AI technologies are utilized to aid in teaching, will educators find themselves displaced by computers, or will their responsibilities develop to focus on areas where human abilities are irreplaceable, such as mentorship, critical thinking facilitation, and emotional support?

The ethical problem here is to ensure that AI is used to complement rather than replace human responsibilities in education (Schiff, 2022). Rather than perceiving AI as a danger to employment, institutions should research methods to integrate AI into the workforce in a way that empowers educators and staff. This can encompass retraining and reskilling campaigns to assist staff adapt to new AI-driven workflows, as well as increasing collaboration between humans and AI systems. The goal should be to develop a balance where AI tackles repetitive, time-consuming jobs, allowing humans to focus on higher-order cognitive and emotional tasks that need creativity, empathy, and interpersonal connection.

4. Student Autonomy and Agency

AI's potential to provide individualized learning experiences offers numerous benefits, but it also raises questions about student autonomy and agency (van der Vorst & Jelicic, 2019). In a future where AI systems can analyze student behavior, anticipate learning outcomes, and prescribe specific educational courses, there is a concern that students would become unduly dependent on these technologies, losing the ability to make independent decisions about their own learning journeys. Moreover, there is a delicate line between personalization and manipulation. If AI systems are designed to urge students in particular directions based on algorithmic predictions, students could feel pressured to take a course they did not completely choose for themselves. The ethical problem here is to achieve a balance between the benefits of AI-powered customization and the protection of student autonomy. Universities must ensure that students have control over their educational decisions, even while AI technologies give guidance and support. This involves building AI systems that make recommendations rather than dictating decisions, allowing students to opt in or out of certain features, and fostering a culture of critical thinking where students are encouraged to challenge the proposals made by AI.

5. Accountability and Transparency

A very important ethical consideration in AI adoption is the problem of accountability (Ahmad, 2024). When choices are made by AI systems—whether it's picking students for admission, grading assignments, or predicting future academic success—it can be tough to discern who is accountable for those decisions. If an AI system makes an error or creates an unjust outcome, who is held accountable? Is it the developers of the AI, the educational institution that deployed it, or the individuals that rely on the system?

To solve this dilemma, institutions must promote transparency in their use of AI (Saaida, 2023). This requires making AI systems and their decision-making processes understandable to all stakeholders, including students, professors, and administrators. Institutions should explicitly describe how AI technologies are being utilized, what data is being collected, and how choices are being made. Furthermore, colleges must develop clear processes for accountability, ensuring that there are systems in place to address grievances and remedy errors when they occur.

6. The Digital Divide and Accessibility

While AI has the potential to democratize education by making individualized learning accessible to all, it could also worsen existing disparities if not deployed appropriately (Bulathwela et al, 2024). Access to AI-powered products frequently depends on stable internet connectivity, advanced technological infrastructure, and digital literacy abilities. Students from low-income households or rural locations may encounter hurdles to adopting these technologies, thereby expanding the divide between wealthy and underprivileged people. To ensure that AI use in higher education is inclusive, colleges must overcome the digital gap. This may involve investing in infrastructure to support students in remote or underserved places, delivering digital literacy programs to help students utilize AI tools, and ensuring that AI systems are developed with accessibility in mind. Only by addressing these discrepancies can AI truly realize its promise of making education more egalitarian.

As AI begins to dominate higher education, colleges must navigate a complicated ethical terrain. While the benefits of AI—such as better efficiency, individualized learning, and improved decision-making—are evident, the obstacles and hazards cannot be overlooked. Bias, data privacy, employment displacement, student autonomy, accountability, and the digital divide are all crucial concerns that deserve deliberate attention (Du, 2024). Ultimately, the effective use of AI in higher education will depend on a commitment to ethical norms, openness, and diversity. Universities must engage in continuing talks with students, professors, and staff to ensure that AI is employed in ways that accord with their core values and mission. By addressing these concerns head-on, educational institutions can leverage the power of AI while ensuring the rights, privacy, and well-being of all stakeholders.

Case Studies: Successful Integration of AI in Universities

The successful integration of Artificial Intelligence (AI) in universities is a developing trend globally, as institutions aim to enhance educational experiences, expedite administrative procedures, and encourage a culture of innovation. By reviewing individual case studies of colleges that have effectively incorporated AI, we can better grasp the tangible benefits, the techniques taken to overcome hurdles, and how AI is altering higher education. These case studies highlight how institutions have personalized AI solutions to their unique needs, establishing models that can serve as inspiration for others wishing to go on a similar road.

1. Carnegie Mellon University: Pioneering Personalized Learning

Carnegie Mellon University (CMU) has been at the forefront of integrating AI into educational practice, particularly through its work on personalized learning (Chine et al, 2022). One of CMU's most famous endeavors is the founding of the Open Learning Initiative (OLI), which employs AI to personalize educational content to the requirements of individual students. OLI plans to give a more tailored learning experience by employing AI algorithms to monitor student performance in real time and adapt the content accordingly. For example, in a mathematics course employing OLI, if a student has difficulties with a certain idea, the AI system will give additional exercises and resources suited to that exact area of difficulty. Conversely, if the student exhibits mastery, the system may eliminate repetition, allowing them to progress more swiftly through the course. This method not only boosts learning results but also helps students remain interested by presenting content that is relevant to their ability level (Dönmez, 2024). By recording and analyzing data on student performance, OLI gives educators deep insights into how students are performing. professors can utilize this data to detect patterns, such as which concepts students often struggle with or where further guidance may be needed. This information helps educators to make data-driven decisions about course design and teaching tactics, boosting the overall educational experience. Carnegie Mellon's approach to AI-driven individualized learning serves as an example of how institutions might employ technology to adapt to the various requirements of students. By ensuring that learning experiences are flexible and responsive, CMU has shown how AI may be implemented into the curriculum to benefit both students and educators.

2. University of Helsinki: AI for Administrative Efficiency

The University of Helsinki has effectively integrated AI to improve its administrative procedures, decreasing bureaucracy and boosting the efficiency of student services (Kallio et al, 2020). One of the most popular instances is the usage of AI-powered chatbots to handle routine requests from students and staff. These chatbots, named "Emma" and "Valtteri," were created to answer issues about admissions, course registration, and general university procedures. Before the introduction of AI chatbots, the university's administrative personnel were overwhelmed by the volume of requests they received every day, many of which were repeated and time-consuming (Deacon & Plumbley, 2024). By applying AI, the university was able to automate these regular processes, allowing personnel to focus on more complicated and value-added work. The chatbots are available 24/7, offering rapid solutions to typical questions, which has dramatically boosted student satisfaction. Emma and Valtteri are not only capable of answering simple concerns, but they also learn from each contact, growing more successful over time. Through machine learning algorithms, the chatbots continuously improve their responses based on the data they collect. If a query falls outside the chatbot's capabilities, it is escalated to a human staff member, ensuring that students always receive the support they need. The University of Helsinki's deployment of AI for administrative duties has lowered response times, saved operational costs, and allowed staff to concentrate on tasks that require human judgment and knowledge. The success of this effort illustrates how AI can alter the efficiency of administrative operations, decreasing bottlenecks and improving the overall experience for students and staff alike.

3. Arizona State University: AI in Student Support and Retention

Arizona State University (ASU) is highly renowned for its creative use of AI in aiding student achievement and retention (Azcona, 2019). One of ASU's signature AI initiatives is its "Success Coach" program, which leverages AI to monitor student progress and deliver real-time interventions when students exhibit signs of academic struggle. The method combines data from numerous sources, including grades, attendance records, and participation in extracurricular activities, to identify children who may be in danger of falling behind. Once the AI system recognizes a possible issue, it triggers a reaction from a "Success Coach," who reaches out to the student with individualized advice and resources. This proactive strategy helps students address difficulties before they become insurmountable, enhancing retention rates and ensuring that students receive the support they need to succeed. ASU has also implemented AI into its student advising system. The university's AI-powered advisor, "EOSS," gives tailored help to students as they navigate course selections, degree requirements, and career preparation. The advisor employs predictive analytics to offer courses that fit with students' academic strengths and career ambitions, helping them stay on pace for graduation (Tybroski, 2023). The results of ASU's AI-driven student support efforts have been spectacular. Since implementing these programs, the university has witnessed a considerable boost in retention rates, particularly among first-year students. The AI technologies have not only improved academic performance but have also boosted the whole student experience by offering individualized, data-driven help at every stage of the educational journey.

4. University College London: AI in Research and Knowledge Creation

University College London (UCL) has successfully integrated AI into its research ecosystem, utilizing the capabilities of AI to accelerate knowledge generation and discovery (Westgarth, 2022). UCL's AI-driven research platform, "UCLP," employs machine learning algorithms to evaluate enormous amounts of academic literature, uncover new patterns, and offer potential research collaborations based on common interests among faculty members. For example, UCLP can examine hundreds of academic papers in a matter of minutes, revealing patterns and links that could take human researchers weeks or months to uncover. The method has been particularly useful in multidisciplinary research, as it identifies common themes across diverse fields and recommends innovative research topics that academics might not have considered otherwise. In addition to funding research, UCL has employed AI to streamline the process of grant applications. The AI system supports researchers in identifying potential funding opportunities that correspond with their skills and research objectives (Dwivedi et al, 2021). By examining historical grant successes and failures, the AI can make recommendations on how to improve bids, boosting the odds of winning money. UCL's use of AI in research has expedited the speed of innovation, enabling faculty members to focus on high-level thinking and problem-solving while automating time-consuming administrative activities. This incorporation of AI into the research process emphasizes the potential for AI to change knowledge generation in higher education.

5. Tsinghua University: AI in Campus Management

Tsinghua University, one of China's leading colleges, has adopted AI in campus administration, employing smart technology to boost the efficiency and sustainability of its operations (Nong et al, 2023). The institution has deployed an AI-powered smart campus system that monitors energy use, building usage, and environmental conditions across its wide campus. The AI system optimizes the university's energy usage by evaluating data from sensors put throughout the campus. It automatically changes heating, cooling, and lighting depending on real-time occupancy data, ensuring that energy is used efficiently. This has led to significant financial savings and a reduction in the university's carbon impact, coinciding with Tsinghua's environmental objectives. In addition to energy management, Tsinghua's AI system monitors campus safety by evaluating data from security cameras, access control systems, and emergency response systems (Zou et al, 2024). The AI may recognize anomalous patterns of behavior or unauthorized access to restricted locations, alerting campus security to potential threats. This proactive approach to campus safety has increased security while decreasing the need for ongoing human surveillance. Tsinghua's smart campus effort highlights how AI may be integrated into the physical management of university campuses, generating more sustainable and secure environments for students and staff. The university's success with AI-powered campus administration has prompted other institutions to seek similar solutions.

6. Deakin University: AI-Powered Learning Analytics

Deakin University in Australia has made tremendous gains in employing AI to enhance learning through data analytics (Ifenthaler & Gibson, 2020). The university's AI-driven learning analytics platform, "CLOUD," collects data on student engagement, performance, and learning behaviors from multiple digital sources, including learning management systems and online examinations. CLOUD leverages this data to present professors with meaningful insights into how students are interacting with course materials, which resources they find most useful, and where they are suffering. Based on this information, professors can change their teaching approaches, provide targeted feedback, and offer additional support to students who may be in danger of underperforming. Students also benefit directly from the AI system. CLOUD gives individualized recommendations for study resources and activities, helping students stay interested and on track with their studies. The system can identify kids who are slipping behind and provide them with targeted tools to address their individual issues. Deakin's use of AI-powered learning analytics has led to greater student engagement and academic success, as well as more effective teaching tactics. The university's experience with AI integration in learning analytics illustrates the potential for AI to alter the way institutions understand and support student learning.

These case studies highlight how AI, when intelligently and strategically incorporated, may greatly improve the academic, administrative, and operational operations of universities. By addressing the individual demands of their institutions, these colleges have successfully harnessed AI to increase educational outcomes, streamline operations, and build more sustainable, secure, and supportive learning environments. As AI technology continues to grow, these case studies offer examples of how other institutions might harness its potential to change the future of higher education.

Future Trends: AI's Potential to Transform Education and Administration

The rapid growth of Artificial Intelligence (AI) is poised to deliver dramatic improvements to education and university management in the coming years (Kayyali, 2024). As AI technologies become more powerful and accessible, their potential to disrupt higher education extends beyond present uses, paving the way for creative methods in teaching, learning, management, and policy-making. The future promises tremendous possibilities, with AI positioned to play a vital role in generating more personalized, efficient, and scalable educational experiences, as well as altering the character of administrative activities. In this part, we discuss some significant future developments that show AI's potential to transform the landscape of higher education and its administration.

1. Hyper-Personalized Learning Paths

One of the most promising future developments in education is the evolution of hyper-personalized learning paths powered by AI (Singh & Kaunert, 2024). While current AI-driven personalization modifies content and tempo to match individual student needs, future AI systems will carry this concept much further, enabling individualized educational experiences that are not merely responsive but also anticipatory. AI algorithms will have the ability to forecast a student's learning needs and preferences in real time, offering ideal learning materials, methodology, and support mechanisms based on each student's individual learning style, cognitive development, and emotional state (Alam, 2023). Imagine a world where students no longer follow standardized curriculums but instead proceed through custom-designed learning journeys. AI will be able to curate information from a worldwide reservoir of educational resources, picking the most appropriate materials based on the student's strengths, interests, and future career objectives. These technologies will also integrate powerful data analytics to continually update learning tactics, enabling students to negotiate complex educational courses while guaranteeing that no one falls behind. This level of customization will enhance student engagement, raise motivation, and considerably improve learning outcomes, particularly for kids who have difficulty with traditional educational methods.

2. AI-Powered Lifelong Learning

The concept of lifelong learning is becoming increasingly relevant as the globe experiences fast technological and economic developments (Rieckmann, 2018). The future of education will be marked by a shift away from the traditional idea of education as a finite phase and toward a dynamic, lifelong process. AI will play a significant role in supporting this shift by offering continuous learning opportunities that are flexible, tailored, and accessible to learners of all ages. AI-powered platforms will allow users to smoothly migrate between formal education, career development, and personal growth activities (Khamis, 2024). These platforms will employ AI to monitor changes in the job market, emerging technologies, and individual learning goals, ensuring that learners are equipped with the skills and knowledge necessary to adapt to altering workforce demands. This ongoing engagement between the student and AI will provide a fluid educational experience, where individuals may upgrade their skill sets in real time as new demands arise, making education more relevant and responsive than ever before. AI-driven lifelong learning will encourage a more inclusive and accessible education system. By reducing obstacles to entry and enabling scalable, on-demand learning experiences, AI can democratize education, ensuring that learners from all backgrounds have the opportunity to achieve in an increasingly competitive global landscape.

3. The Rise of AI-Generated Educational Content

As AI continues to advance, one of the most exciting possibilities is the creation of AI-generated educational content (Alasadi & Baiz, 2023). Future AI systems will have the power to develop educational resources such as textbooks, lesson plans, evaluations, and even interactive simulations. AI-generated content will be regularly updated and enhanced based on the latest research and educational trends, ensuring that students and instructors always have access to the most relevant and cutting-edge information. In addition to traditional educational content, AI could provide immersive learning experiences that mix virtual and augmented reality (VR/AR) technology . Imagine AI-driven simulations that allow students to study historical events, conduct intricate scientific experiments, or connect with virtual mentors—all from the comfort of their own homes. These experiences will not only make learning more engaging and participatory but will also broaden access to high-quality education, particularly for children in underserved or rural places. As AI-generated material grows more sophisticated, educators will move from content creators to content curators and facilitators. Professors will employ AI technologies to select and adjust the most relevant resources for their students, freeing them to focus on higher-level duties such as mentorship, critical thinking development, and nurturing creativity.

4. Smart Campus Management and Sustainability

AI's influence on higher education will not be confined to the classroom; it will also revolutionize the way colleges run their physical campuses and operations (George & Wooden, 2023). In the future, colleges will progressively embrace AI-powered "smart campus" systems that optimize resource management, promote sustainability, and improve the overall student experience. Smart campus systems will leverage AI to monitor and control many aspects of campus infrastructure, such as energy usage, building occupancy, and environmental conditions. AI algorithms will assess real-time data from sensors put across the campus to ensure optimal energy efficiency, cutting waste and lowering costs. For example, AI might automatically change heating, cooling, and lighting systems based on occupancy patterns, delivering a more comfortable environment while decreasing the university's carbon footprint. AI will be utilized to increase campus safety by integrating surveillance systems, access controls, and emergency response mechanisms (Mayeke et al, 2024). AI-powered security systems will be able to detect possible threats, such as unauthorized entry or suspicious conduct, in real time, alerting campus authorities before incidents occur. This proactive approach to campus safety will give students and staff a more secure learning environment. AI-driven campus management solutions will also boost operational efficiency by automating regular administrative duties. Whether it's managing facilities, scheduling classes, or planning events, AI will expedite administrative operations, allowing university staff to focus on more strategic and mission-critical activities.

5. Ethical AI and Responsible Innovation

As AI becomes increasingly ingrained in higher education, the importance of ethical AI and responsible innovation will take center stage (Bentley, 2023). Universities will play a vital role in defining the development and deployment of AI technologies, ensuring that they are utilized in ways that are equitable, transparent, and aligned with human values. In the future, institutions will need to build complete frameworks for ethical AI governance. This will require setting standards for the appropriate use of AI, ensuring that data privacy is respected, and eliminating biases in AI systems that could perpetuate inequality. Universities will also need to incorporate AI ethics into their courses, enabling students with the skills and knowledge to manage the ethical problems posed by AI in their future jobs. Universities will be tasked with establishing a culture of responsible innovation, where AI technologies are produced and applied in ways that promote societal well-being. This will require coordination between educators, technologists, policymakers, and industry leaders to guarantee that AI is utilized for the greater good.

6. AI-Augmented Decision Making in University Administration

University administration is set to benefit greatly from the inclusion of AI-augmented decision-making tools (Mullangi et al, 2023). As AI grows more capable of evaluating huge volumes of data, university officials will increasingly rely on AI tools to support choices relating to strategic planning, budgeting, enrollment management, and faculty recruitment. In the future, AI will provide administrators with predictive analytics that can estimate student enrollment trends, identify at-risk students, and recommend interventions to increase retention and graduation rates. AI-powered decision-support systems will also help colleges optimize resource allocation by assessing data on student demographics, course demand, and program performance. These insights will enable colleges to make better-educated, data-driven decisions that line with their long-term objectives. AI-augmented decision-making will also extend to faculty and staff recruiting (Shmueli & Ray, 2024). AI algorithms will scan job applications, rate candidates' skills, and even anticipate their prospective fit within the university's culture. By automating the recruitment process, AI will help colleges attract top talent and ensure that they hire individuals who are aligned with their academic and institutional missions.

7. Collaborative AI and Human-Centered Learning Environments

While AI will probably play a larger role in education, the future will likely see a balance between AI-driven technology and human-centered learning settings (Shneiderman, 2020). Rather than replacing educators, AI will act as a tool that enhances their talents, allowing them to focus on promoting creativity, critical thinking, and emotional intelligence—skills that AI cannot imitate. In this future vision, professors will interact with AI technologies to create dynamic, student-centered learning environments. AI will handle the more technical aspects of teaching, such as grading, data analysis, and content delivery, while professors focus on offering individualized mentorship, stimulating debates, and developing a feeling of community among students. The future of education will prioritize the creation of hybrid learning environments that mix the finest of AI-driven technology with the irreplaceable value of human connection. In this setting, educators will play a fundamental role as facilitators of learning, guiding students through a world where AI is a constant presence, but human interactions and critical thinking remain at the core of the educational experience.

The potential for AI to change education and university administration is large and diverse (Bates et al, 2020). From hyper-personalized learning experiences to AI-powered campus administration, the future of higher education will be defined by the seamless integration of AI technologies that boost both academic and operational outcomes. As colleges continue to use AI, they must do so ethically, ensuring that these technologies are employed in ways that promote diversity, transparency, and ethical innovation. The trends discussed in this part provide a view into the future of AI in education, presenting a vision of a more efficient, personalized, and forward-thinking higher education system.

CONCLUSION

The advent of Artificial Intelligence (AI) in higher education constitutes one of the most significant revolutions in the academic landscape in recent decades. The tremendous impact AI has on curriculum design, personalized learning, and administrative processes heralds a future where higher education institutions are more adaptable, data-driven, and efficient. As AI technologies continue to advance and mature, their potential to alter education at both individual and institutional levels becomes even more obvious. However, with this great promise comes a complex set of problems that must be carefully addressed to ensure that the benefits of AI are realized while reducing any downsides. The revolutionary impact of AI in curriculum design is one of the most promising advances in modern education. By using AI's ability to analyze large volumes of data, educational institutions can build personalized learning experiences that respond to individual student needs and learning styles. This departure from the old, standardized educational model offers a more dynamic, flexible, and inclusive approach to learning, where students can proceed at their own pace and receive individualized help. The use of AI in adaptive learning systems, intelligent tutoring platforms, and AI-generated content is already showing promise in both online and face-to-face learning contexts. As AI technologies evolve, we are likely to observe a more dramatic trend toward a fully tailored curriculum, allowing for more effective teaching tactics, more engagement, and enhanced learning results.

Equally significant is AI's role in transforming administrative operations within higher education organizations. Administrative efficiency is typically an ignored part of the academic ecosystem, yet it plays a critical role in molding the student experience and institutional performance. AI-driven solutions can expedite different operational processes, from admissions and course scheduling to financial management and student support services. By automating mundane processes and applying predictive analytics to better decision-making, AI enables institutions to allocate resources more effectively, cut operational costs, and improve service delivery. For instance, AI-powered chatbots are already offering 24/7 help to students, answering concerns regarding enrollment, financial aid, and course registration, thereby decreasing the administrative strain on personnel. Moreover, AI's ability to evaluate student data in real time can assist administrators in recognizing patterns and trends, enabling institutions to make educated decisions about student retention, academic performance, and resource allocation.

Despite these advantages, the integration of AI into higher education also raises a series of problems that institutions must solve to ensure responsible and ethical usage of these technologies. One of the most serious problems is the issue of data privacy and security. AI systems rely significantly on data to function efficiently, and the gathering, storage, and analysis of personal information raise issues about confidentiality and the potential misuse of data. Educational institutions must establish robust data protection measures and adhere to strict privacy standards to respect the rights of students and professors. Failure to do so could diminish faith in AI systems and jeopardize their effectiveness.

Another challenge comes in the ethical implications of AI decision-making, particularly concerning algorithmic prejudice. AI systems are only as unbiased as the data they are trained on, and if the data reflects existing inequities or prejudices, there is a risk that AI could perpetuate these biases in its decision-making processes. This is especially concerning when AI is used for high-stakes choices, such as university admissions, grading, or financial assistance distribution. To reduce these dangers, institutions must guarantee that AI systems are transparent, routinely reviewed, and subject to human control. This will help to maintain justice and accountability, ensuring that AI helps, rather than hinders, the goal of educational equity. The incorporation of AI into higher education needs a cultural shift within academic organizations. Faculty, administrators, and students alike must be equipped with the skills and knowledge to effectively engage with AI technologies. Faculty development programs will be vital in helping educators understand how to incorporate AI into their teaching practices and research efforts. Meanwhile, administrators will need to adopt a more data-driven approach to management, employing AI insights to optimize institutional operations. Equally crucial is developing a culture of continual learning among students, who must be prepared to work alongside AI systems in their academic and professional lives. Institutions that invest in establishing AI literacy and fostering a collaborative, innovation-driven atmosphere will be better positioned to negotiate the hurdles of AI integration and maximize its possibilities. The successful deployment of AI in higher education will require a careful, planned strategy. Institutions must reconcile the demand for technical innovation with a commitment to ethical standards and human-centric values. This includes not only addressing the technical aspects of AI, such as data management and algorithmic transparency but also considering the larger social, cultural, and ethical ramifications of AI use. As AI becomes increasingly interwoven in the fabric of higher education, institutions must be diligent in ensuring that these technologies are employed in ways that enhance, rather than reduce, the quality of education.

Looking ahead, the future of AI in higher education has great promise. AI can alter the way we teach, learn, and administer academic institutions, delivering more personalized, efficient, and accessible educational experiences. By harnessing AI to its best potential, higher education may become more inclusive, delivering chances for lifelong learning to a broader and more diverse community of students. However, fulfilling this promise will require continual investment in research, infrastructure, and human resources. Institutions must remain committed to investigating creative AI applications while retaining a focus on ethical considerations, equality, and student-centered learning.

In conclusion, AI is not simply a technology tool but a catalyst for rethinking the entire educational ecosystem. Its significance in transforming both curriculum and administration suggests a paradigm shift that will determine the future of higher education. By integrating AI ethically and strategically, institutions can not only improve their operations and educational offerings but also play a leading role in influencing the future of learning in an increasingly digital world. The road ahead is loaded with opportunity, but it is also riddled with challenges that require careful consideration. Only by addressing these difficulties head-on can higher education institutions fully leverage the revolutionary power of AI to build more dynamic, inclusive, and future-ready educational environments.

REFERENCES

Ahmad, A. Y. A. B. (2024). Ethical implications of artificial intelligence in accounting: A framework for responsible ai adoption in multinational corporations in Jordan. *International Journal of Data and Network Science*, 8(1), 401–414.

Ahmad, S. F., Alam, M. M., Rahmat, M. K., Mubarik, M. S., & Hyder, S. I. (2022). Academic and administrative role of artificial intelligence in education. *Sustainability*, 14(3), 1101.

Ahmad, S. F., Rahmat, M. K., Mubarik, M. S., Alam, M. M., & Hyder, S. I. (2021). Artificial intelligence and its role in education. *Sustainability*, 13(22), 12902.

Akter, S., McCarthy, G., Sajib, S., Michael, K., Dwivedi, Y. K., D'Ambra, J., & Shen, K. N. (2021). Algorithmic bias in data-driven innovation in the age of AI. *International Journal of Information Management*, 60, 102387.

Alam, A. (2023). Harnessing the Power of AI to Create Intelligent Tutoring Systems for Enhanced Classroom Experience and Improved Learning Outcomes. In *Intelligent Communication Technologies and Virtual Mobile Networks* (pp. 571–591). Springer Nature Singapore.

Alasadi, E. A., & Baiz, C. R. (2023). Generative AI in education and research: Opportunities, concerns, and solutions. *Journal of Chemical Education*, 100(8), 2965–2971.

Alekseeva, L., Azar, J., Giné, M., Samila, S., & Taska, B. (2021). The demand for AI skills in the labor market. *Labour Economics*, 71, 102002.

Alexander, B. (2020). *Academia next: The futures of higher education*. Johns Hopkins University Press.

Attaran, M., Stark, J., & Stotler, D. (2018). Opportunities and challenges for big data analytics in US higher education: A conceptual model for implementation. *Industry and Higher Education*, 32(3), 169–182.

Azcona, D. (2019). Artificial Intelligence in computer science and mathematics education (Doctoral dissertation, Dublin City University).

Bates, T., Cobo, C., Mariño, O., & Wheeler, S. (2020). Can artificial intelligence transform higher education? *International Journal of Educational Technology in Higher Education*, 17, 1–12.

Belenguer, L. (2022). AI bias: Exploring discriminatory algorithmic decision-making models and the application of possible machine-centric solutions adapted from the pharmaceutical industry. *AI and Ethics*, 2(4), 771–787. PMID: 35194591

Benbya, H., Davenport, T. H., & Pachidi, S. (2020). Artificial intelligence in organizations: Current state and future opportunities. *MIS Quarterly Executive*, 19(4).

Bentley, C., Aicardi, C., Poveda, S., Magela Cunha, L., Kohan Marzagao, D., Glover, R., & Acar, O. A. (2023). A framework for responsible AI education. Available at *SSRN* 4544010.

Bulathwela, S., Pérez-Ortiz, M., Holloway, C., Cukurova, M., & Shawe-Taylor, J. (2024). Artificial intelligence alone will not democratise education: On educational inequality, techno-solutionism and inclusive tools. *Sustainability*, 16(2), 781.

Chen, L., Chen, P., & Lin, Z. (2020). Artificial intelligence in education: A review. *IEEE Access : Practical Innovations, Open Solutions*, 8, 75264–75278.

Chine, D. R., Brentley, C., Thomas-Browne, C., Richey, J. E., Gul, A., Carvalho, P. F., & Koedinger, K. R. (2022, July). Educational equity through combined human-AI personalization: A propensity matching evaluation. In *International Conference on Artificial Intelligence in Education* (pp. 366-377). Cham: Springer International Publishing.

Chiu, T. K., Moorhouse, B. L., Chai, C. S., & Ismailov, M. (2023). Teacher support and student motivation to learn with Artificial Intelligence (AI) based chatbot. *Interactive Learning Environments*, •••, 1–17.

Choung, H., David, P., & Ling, T. W. (2024). Acceptance of AI-Powered Facial Recognition Technology in Surveillance Scenarios: Role of Trust, Security, and Privacy Perceptions. *Technology in Society*, •••, 102721.

Deacon, T., & Plumbley, M. D. (2024, June). Working with AI Sound: Exploring the Future of Workplace AI Sound Technologies. In *Proceedings of the 3rd Annual Meeting of the Symposium on Human-Computer Interaction for Work* (pp. 1-21).

Dermeval, D., Paiva, R., Bittencourt, I. I., Vassileva, J., & Borges, D. (2018). Authoring tools for designing intelligent tutoring systems: A systematic review of the literature. *International Journal of Artificial Intelligence in Education*, 28, 336–384.

Dönmez, E. (2024). The Future of Education: AI-Supported Reforms in the USA and China. In *Global Agendas and Education Reforms: A Comparative Study* (pp. 135–150). Springer Nature Singapore.

Du, Y. (2024). The Digital Divide: Mapping the Ethics of Artificial Intelligence. *Journal of Student Research*, 13(2).

Dwivedi, Y. K., Hughes, L., Ismagilova, E., Aarts, G., Coombs, C., Crick, T., & Williams, M. D. (2021). Artificial Intelligence (AI): Multidisciplinary perspectives on emerging challenges, opportunities, and agenda for research, practice and policy. *International Journal of Information Management*, 57, 101994.

Ferrara, E. (2023). Fairness and bias in artificial intelligence: A brief survey of sources, impacts, and mitigation strategies. *Sci*, 6(1), 3.

Fiero, A. W., & Beier, E. (2022). New global developments in data protection and privacy regulations: Comparative analysis of European Union, United States, and Russian legislation. *Stan. J. Int'l L.*, 58, 151.

George, B., & Wooden, O. (2023). Managing the strategic transformation of higher education through artificial intelligence. *Administrative Sciences*, 13(9), 196.

Hannan, E., & Liu, S. (2023). AI: New source of competitiveness in higher education. *Competitiveness Review*, 33(2), 265–279.

Ifenthaler, D., & Gibson, D. (Eds.). (2020). *Adoption of data analytics in higher education learning and teaching*. Springer.

Kallio, T. J., Kallio, K. M., & Blomberg, A. (2020). From professional bureaucracy to competitive bureaucracy–redefining universities' organization principles, performance measurement criteria, and reason for being. *Qualitative Research in Accounting & Management*, 17(1), 82–108.

Kayyali, M. (2021). Positive Impact of High Technology on Higher Education.

Kayyali, M. (2024a). Future possibilities and challenges of AI in education. In *Transforming education with generative AI: Prompt engineering and synthetic content creation* (pp. 118–137). IGI Global.

Kayyali, M. (2024b). Immersive Technologies: Virtual and Augmented Reality in Higher Education. In Reshaping Learning with Next Generation Educational Technologies (pp. 99-114). IGI Global.

Kayyali, M. (2024c). The Future of Higher Education in an Uncertain World. In *Building Resilient Education Models Post Crisis* (pp. 42–55). IGI Global.

. Khamis, R. (2024). AI-Powered Learning Experience Platforms: Investigating Personalized Learning in the Workplace.

Khare, K., Stewart, B., & Khare, A. (2018). Artificial intelligence and the student experience: An institutional perspective. The International Academic Forum (IAFOR).

Kooli, C. (2023). Chatbots in education and research: A critical examination of ethical implications and solutions. *Sustainability*, 15(7), 5614.

Majjate, H., Bellarhmouch, Y., Jeghal, A., Yahyaouy, A., Tairi, H., & Zidani, K. A. (2023). AI-powered academic guidance and counseling system based on student profile and interests. *Applied System Innovation*, 7(1), 6.

Markauskaite, L., Marrone, R., Poquet, O., Knight, S., Martinez-Maldonado, R., Howard, S., & Siemens, G. (2022). Rethinking the entwinement between artificial intelligence and human learning: What capabilities do learners need for a world with AI? *Computers and Education: Artificial Intelligence*, 3, 100056.

Marshall, S. J. (2018). Shaping the University of the Future. Springer, 10, 978-981.

Mayeke, N. R., Arigbabu, A. T., Olaniyi, O. O., Okunleye, O. J., & Adigwe, C. S. (2024). Evolving Access Control Paradigms: A Comprehensive Multi-Dimensional Analysis of Security Risks and System Assurance in Cyber Engineering. *Asian Journal of Research in Computer Science*, 17(5), 108–124.

Mellul, C. (2018). Emerging technologies in higher education and the workplace: An assessment. *Future*, •••, 223.

Mer, A. (2023). Artificial intelligence in human resource management: Recent trends and research agenda. Digital Transformation, Strategic Resilience. *Cyber Security and Risk Management*, 111, 31–56.

Mullangi, K., Dhameliya, N., Anumandla, S. K. R., Yarlagadda, V. K., Sachani, D. K., Vennapusa, S. C. R., & Patel, B. (2023). AI-Augmented Decision-Making in Management Using Quantum Networks. *Asian Business Review*, 13(2), 73–86.

Nassar, A., & Kamal, M. (2021). Ethical dilemmas in AI-powered decision-making: A deep dive into big data-driven ethical considerations. *International Journal of Responsible Artificial Intelligence*, 11(8), 1–11.

Nong, L., Liu, G., Tang, C., & Chen, Y. (2023). The Design and Implementation of Campus informatization in Chinese Universities: A Conceptual Framework. *Sustainability*, 15(6), 4732.

Olabanji, S. O., Oladoyinbo, O. B., Asonze, C. U., Oladoyinbo, T. O., Ajayi, S. A., & Olaniyi, O. O. (2024). Effect of adopting AI to explore big data on personally identifiable information (PII) for financial and economic data transformation. Available at *SSRN* 4739227.

Pedro, F., Subosa, M., Rivas, A., & Valverde, P. (2019). Artificial intelligence in education: Challenges and opportunities for sustainable development.

Rathnayake, C., & Gunawardana, A. (2023). The role of generative ai in enhancing human resource management recruitment, training, and performance evaluation perspectives. *International Journal of Stochastic Analysis*, 8(11), 13–22.

Rieckmann, M. (2018). Learning to transform the world: Key competencies in Education for Sustainable Development. Issues and trends in education for sustainable development, 39(1), 39-59.

Rodgers, W., Murray, J. M., Stefanidis, A., Degbey, W. Y., & Tarba, S. Y. (2023). An artificial intelligence algorithmic approach to ethical decision-making in human resource management processes. *Human Resource Management Review*, 33(1), 100925.

Saaida, M. B. (2023). AI-Driven transformations in higher education: Opportunities and challenges. *International Journal of Educational Research and Studies*, 5(1), 29–36.

Schiff, D. (2022). Education for AI, not AI for education: The role of education and ethics in national AI policy strategies. *International Journal of Artificial Intelligence in Education*, 32(3), 527–563.

Schwartz, R., Schwartz, R., Vassilev, A., Greene, K., Perine, L., Burt, A., & Hall, P. (2022). Towards a standard for identifying and managing bias in artificial intelligence (Vol. 3, p. 00). US Department of Commerce, National Institute of Standards and Technology.

Shmueli, G., & Ray, S. (2024). Reimagining the Journal Editorial Process: An AI-Augmented Versus an AI-Driven Future. *Journal of the Association for Information Systems*, 25(1), 10.

Shneiderman, B. (2020). Human-centered artificial intelligence: Three fresh ideas. *AIS Transactions on Human-Computer Interaction*, 12(3), 109–124.

Singh, B., & Kaunert, C. (2024). Future of Digital Marketing: Hyper-Personalized Customer Dynamic Experience with AI-Based Predictive Models. In Revolutionizing the AI-Digital Landscape (pp. 189-203). Productivity Press.

Sleeter, C., & Carmona, J. F. (2017). *Un-standardizing curriculum: Multicultural teaching in the standards-based classroom*. Teachers College Press.

Spring, M., Faulconbridge, J., & Sarwar, A. (2022). How information technology automates and augments processes: Insights from Artificial-Intelligence-based systems in professional service operations. *Journal of Operations Management*, 68(6-7), 592–618.

Teng, Y., Zhang, J., & Sun, T. (2023). Data-driven decision-making model based on artificial intelligence in higher education system of colleges and universities. *Expert Systems: International Journal of Knowledge Engineering and Neural Networks*, 40(4), e12820.

Tybroski, M. (2023). Developing Career Readiness Among Collegiate Student Staff Members (Doctoral dissertation, Arizona State University).

. van der Vorst, T., & Jelicic, N. (2019). Artificial Intelligence in Education: Can AI bring the full potential of personalized learning to education?.

Westgarth, T., Chen, W., Hay, G., & Heath, R. (2022). Understanding UK Artificial Intelligence R&D commercialisation and the role of standards. Tech. rep. For the Department of Digital, Culture, Media and Sport, and the Office for Artificial Intelligence. Oxford Insights. URL: https://assets. publishing. service. gov. uk/government/uploads/system/uploads/attachment_data.

Xu, Z. (2024). AI in education: Enhancing learning experiences and student outcomes. *Appl. Comput. Eng*, 51, 104–111.

Yadav, K. (2019). Disruptive innovative technologies in higher education. *International Journal of Advanced Education and Research*, 4(1), 49–54.

Yanamala, A. K. Y., Suryadevara, S., & Kalli, V. D. R. (2024). Balancing Innovation and Privacy: The Intersection of Data Protection and Artificial Intelligence. *International Journal of Machine Learning Research in Cybersecurity and Artificial Intelligence*, 15(1), 1–43.

Yekollu, R. K., Bhimraj Ghuge, T., Sunil Biradar, S., Haldikar, S. V., & Farook Mohideen Abdul Kader, O. (2024, February). AI-Driven Personalized Learning Paths: Enhancing Education Through Adaptive Systems. In International Conference on Smart Data Intelligence (pp. 507-517). Singapore: Springer Nature Singapore.

Zawacki-Richter, O., Marín, V. I., Bond, M., & Gouverneur, F. (2019). Systematic review of research on artificial intelligence applications in higher education–where are the educators? *International Journal of Educational Technology in Higher Education*, 16(1), 1–27.

Zou, Y., Zhong, N., Chen, Z., & Zhao, W. (2024). Bridging digitalization and sustainability in universities: A Chinese green university initiative in the digital era. *Journal of Cleaner Production*, 469, 143181.

Chapter 3
Employment of AI in Higher Education

Rituraj Jain
https://orcid.org/0000-0002-5532-1245
Marwadi University, India

Kumar J. Parmar
https://orcid.org/0000-0002-2502-5680
Marwadi University, India

Damodharan Palaniappan
https://orcid.org/0009-0003-0721-3068
Marwadi University, India

T. Premavathi
https://orcid.org/0009-0003-0172-2021
Marwadi University, India

ABSTRACT

AI deployment in higher learning is consequently changing the dynamics in the functioning mode of institutions and modes of delivery of knowledge. This chapter covers the prospects, issues and strategies associated with adoption of AI in an environment of higher learning and teaching: its use, deployment, and promotion. Technologies powered by AI have been adopted in higher learning institutions to improve the management functions interference such as admission, timetabling and assessment. University education however should create AI setups where all students are accorded the necessary consideration. It has intended to effectively raise awareness to the educational leaders and policymakers on how to use AI for enhancing school development and on the same note how to minimize on the risks that may arise because of the technology. The general aim therefore is to improve,

DOI: 10.4018/979-8-3693-7949-3.ch003

equitable and personalized teaching and learning conditions that will help extend the capacity of institutions sustainably through the advancement of technology.

1. INTRODUCTION

It is worth to note that the entire tertiary education system is in a process of dramatic transformation which is associated with rapid developments and application of artificial intelligence. Some time ago, AI remained the province of movies and books, but it is now becoming a reality that is changing education as we know it. This chapter covers the current and future capabilities of Artificial Intelligence in higher institutions, the advantages and benefits AI can bring to the academia, establishing the ethical concerns and dilemmas that come with integrating AI into universities and colleges. The modern learner is the primary beneficiary of the performance enhancement hence the importance of ensuring that quality learning is delivered effectively and efficiently especially bearing in mind the present environment that Universities and colleges are operating In.

1.1 Purpose and Scope

This chapter seeks to cover the topic of what AI is, how it is being used in higher learning institutions, the advantages of applying this technology and the disadvantages and the /or ethical questions arising from application of this technology in the higher learning institutions. We will also look at how AI is adopted across different segments of the higher education value chain including learning management systems, knowledge Trucks intelligent tutoring systems, automated administrative processes, and predictions. In addition, the paper will also examine the ethical issues underpinning AI and learning such as data privacy, algorithmic bias and the issue of fairness to all stakeholders. We used a literature review method to gather sufficient information on the use of AI in educational scenarios and from relevant literature and research papers from academic and industrial sources.

1.2 AI: Introduction to its Use in Colleges and Universities

AI is permeating higher education on multiple fronts, transforming both teaching and administrative tasks. (Kamalov et al., 2023) In the realm of teaching and learning, AI is being leveraged to - Personalize Learning: Another area is that artificial intelligence can address each student's learning gaps, pace of learning, and preferred learning style to enhance the student learning. Enhance Student Support: An ITS gives assistance to students, grading, and encouragement and takes up the role of a tutor and teacher alongside other teachers and is always available, online. Automate Assessment and Feedback: AI solutions can involve the process of marking the assignments and give the student instant feedback at the same time saving the instructors time for more constructive activities. Beyond the classroom, AI is streamlining administrative tasks and providing valuable insights through data analysis - Improve Admissions Processes: This can also help in recruiting students where by the applicant details are help analyzed to determine potential and chance of success. Enhance Institutional Effectiveness: Automated tools in analytics can help detect patterns, forecast student performance, and guide institutional decisions that will enhance students' achievement. Automate Administrative Tasks: AI also helps to manage the administrative work related to scheduling, record keeping and financial aid processing so that the staff spent more time with pertinent activities.

1.3 The Growth of AI in the Higher Learning Institution

The use of artificial intelligence in education is not newly experienced, but it is the result of the findings from the earlier 1960s and recent advancements. In the beginning, AI studies addressed the application of the concept in education with the creation of intelligent tutoring systems. However, the constraints in compute and the nature of learning of human beings gave huge challenges (Balta, 2023). As years advanced AI's possibilities developed too, so correct learning analytics, adaptive learning environments and prediction models became more detailed. 87 Currently big data, cloud, and machine learning advances have taken AI into higher levels of application in higher learning institutions to achieve maximum results. Parallel demand in tough and updated computing systems and improvement in techniques of learning and data mining spearheaded the revival of interest in applying AI in education. Key milestones include:

1970s-1980s: Introduction of the first intelligent tutoring systems – SCHOLAR and BUGGY and showed how AI could be used to achieve customized learning. 1990s-2000s: Introduction of learning management systems and the relatively increased provision of educational data creating basis on which the concept popularized as data Based Education. 2010s-Present: New breakthroughs in machine learning, deep learning, and natural language processing have created highly specialized technologies tested for their ability to assistant in the learning process, to perform tasks autonomously, and to analyze data and derive meaningful information. Since the emergence of the AI technologies, which is progressing at an enormous rate, the integrated opportunities to transform teaching-learning and educational management processes are becoming more and more apparent. The subsequent sections will discuss the particular use of AI, advantages and disadvantages, problems, and ethical issues of AI implementation in higher learning institutions (Onesi-Ozigagun et al., 2024).

1.4 Impact of AI Integration

The integration of AI is no longer a futuristic vision for higher education but rather a strategic imperative for institutions seeking to remain relevant and competitive in the 21st century (Ahmad et al., 2023). Here's why AI is increasingly seen as essential for modernizing higher education - Meeting Evolving Student Needs: Modern learners, or as some people call them Generation C, have been exposed to technology and as learners demand that education be individualized and fun. Here's how AI can assist institutions in meeting these emerging new expectations: TIMER Content, Learning Maps, and Instant Assistance. Enhancing Educational Effectiveness: Artificial Intelligence can contribute greatly to the improvement of education competence of teachers and learners. Using AI to look at student data can help find out which students are at risk early on and help pin point specific students that need help for their classes as well as give the instructors tools to know how to approach the specific students with a better learning plan.

Addressing Affordability and Accessibility: AI also proves have capability with respect to the current concerns of the affordability and accessibility in higher education. Tasks that usually take a lot of time manually can become less expensive to accomplish when decided by computers while Artificial Intelligence can bring education closer to students who cannot easily access them due to geographical factors. Preparing Students for the Future Workforce: With AI setting its pace to revolutionize industries all over the world, then higher learning institutions should be able to prepare the learners for this new world. Some of the ways of achieving this aim is by including the AI into the curriculum as well as offering student's experiences in how they could acquire AI literacy. Driving Innovation and Research: Many AI technologies are being developed today in universities around the world as research is central to the learning institutions. The necessity for AI integration in higher education goes beyond the question of how to remain future-oriented and adjust to the rapidly growing quantity of technologies. That makes it quite a revolutionary change in the overall educational system focusing on personal data and individual learner's needs. However, if integrated AI is applied responsibility, society can amaze by its learning opportunity for all students since it can create a new and very efficient learning environment (Kamalov et al., 2023).

2. AI IN ADMINISTRATIVE PROCESSES

As with the tendency to revolutionize the teaching and learning processes, AI also enjoys great attention concerning its ability to revolutionize the organizational processes in higher learning institutions. With these features, AI is significantly changing how universities operate, allocate their resources, and most importantly, how they engage with the students: AI helps to automate certain processes, offer analytics/data insights, and improve the work organization flow.

2.1 Enhancing Efficiency in Administrative Tasks

This section demonstrates that administrative duties take up a good proportion of the staff and institutional time. AI provides a strong improvement of these processes by enabling automation, thus saving the efforts of staff members on more significant and important tasks (Onesi-Ozigagun et al., 2024). Here are some key areas where AI is making a difference - Admissions and Enrollment: Through data inputs, including quantitative results like GPA, test scores or students' writings, AI systems can perform group analysis of applicants to determine who has great potential to succeed in a particular capacity. This can help in cutting the time spent on admissions, in enhancing the admissions decision-making and in elimination of bias (Onesi-Ozigagun et al., 2024). Course Scheduling and Timetabling - Developing effective course sections and schedules necessary to address the student needs and preferences, faculty teaching availability and constraints and classroom requirements is a rather daunting task. Then schedules can be planned effectively without sharp conflicting hours by using the historical data, the students' preferences, and faculties' constraints available to AI algorithms.

Grading and Assessment: AI can mechanize the process of grading knowing that which type of tests for example multiple choice questions or assignments are typically set. This also reduces the amount of time needed for instructors to assign feedback while at the same time improving the speed at which students learn and correct themselves (Sil et al., 2024). Financial Aid and Billing: AI can be best applied in financial aid where the application of eligibility and processing of student applications and disbursement of funds can be done through an automated system. It can also enhance the accuracy of bills and manage payments effectively while also assisting students to access financial advice tailored for their needs (Kamalov et al., 2023). Student Services and Support: Chatbots and virtual assistants can save the staff's time replying to frequently asked questions, responding to students at any time, and explaining how to register for classes or apply for a financial aid Innocent.

2.2 Case Studies

Many universities in all corners of the globe are already on the receiving end of AI in administrative solutions. Here are a few notable examples - Georgia Institute of Technology: The professors at Georgia Institute of Technology used an AI avatar called 'Jill Watson' for posing answers to questions from students in an online bulletin board. Jill was able to handle thousands of student concerns happily which proves the potential of AI for improving student engagement. Arizona State University: ASU employs and integrates AI solutions in student services, including course search and matchmaking, proactively advising students based on their academic strengths, and weakness and career aspirations. Balta notes that the university has registered positive changes in output measures such as retention and graduation statistics for students. University of Melbourne: AI is used at the University of Melbourne to schedule classes appropriately thus smart utilization of classroom facilities and better students' satisfaction with course offering.

2.3 Chat bots and Virtual assistances

Many universities and colleges are now using chatbots and virtual assistants to help students 24/7 while minimizing the workload of administrative employees (Chamorro-Atalaya et al., 2023). These AI-powered tools can - Answer Frequently Asked Questions: Current tasks that several times engage students include inquiries about admissions, course offerings, campus services and accommodation, among others, and with a chatbot, students receive immediate responses, thus limiting correspondences to the relevant offices (N.Thombre, 2023). This means that some of the student queries that include admissions details, course to be taken, services, and facilities available in a campus can be answered by chatbots and this will allow offices to reduce the number of emails and phone calls that are received. By adopting these virtual assistants, students can also be assisted to complete complex business activities including course registration, financial aid or enrollment verifications having the right information and support to effectively complete these tasks. Additionally, chatbots are employed on a hourly, day and night method availability to support the students and that is very important to the students living in different time zones or perhaps the ones with lots of other things to attend to. (Chamorro-Atalaya et al., 2023) These include the student's academic records, interest, and career development aspirations, to offer student-specific guidance and recommendations that will help them in their academic

Guide Students Through Processes: This provides an opportunity to attend to the need of multiplicity of students and helping students through complex administrative procedures of, for instance, course registration, financial aid application or enrollment verification among others by providing them with an assistant that has all the information that they might need to complete those processes successfully. These AI-powered virtual assistants can show students how they should complete each task, answer questions that students may have throughout the process, and in some cases, complete the form on the student's behalf when asked – these sorts of essential administrative tasks may become more doable and less intimidating with the help of virtual assistants. These functions liberate staff time to work on value-added student services and other relevant strategic chores (Annuš, 2023). Provide 24/7 Support: It also means that they can be accessible to the students in contrast to the human staff for they are functional round the clock. This is especially important for learners across various time zones or those having numerous other commitments (Annuš, 2023).

2.4 Data Analysis and Decision Making

Personalized Learning and Support: AI can also utilize data captured through adaptive and analytic learning to identify the pattern of learning, student's inclination towards kind of learning and their performance which in turn can be used to offer unique learning experience. This can result to better learning sessions for the side of the students. AI does this by delivering content that meets the needs of the learner, offering feedback and support whenever required and affording learners' autonomy by taking on clerical work and rendering routine tutorials. For instance, with the use of adaptive learning which encompasses an integration of an artificial intelligent framework which could track the progress of each learner and in the process provide a mechanism to ensure appropriate challenge levels are presented for students to guarantee motivation. Third, there are some characteristics of the intelligent tutoring systems, such as real-time feedback and support which can allow students practice what they are weak at or having the right information when they need it. Such an approach not only optimizes learning achievement but also enhances a positive climate of feelings that inculcate better quality learning among all forms of student acceptability by incorporating requirements to suit them personally and academically (Ober et al., 2023).

3. AI IN TEACHING AND LEARNING

In general, AI's ability to revolutionize higher learning is predicated on its ability to improve and individualize the process of teaching and learning. From the use of autonomy in delivering educational content, student-friendly support, and assistance in performance of redundant tasks, AI enables both the learner as well as the teacher to accomplish more (Vrabie, 2024).

3.1 Personalized Learning

The conventional model of learning delivery where the same content, methodology, and pace is applied across a class destabilizes the class and ignores unique learners. Today's AI is introducing new approaches such that the learning experiences are designed based on different factors such as personal abilities of the learners, their disabilities, their learning abilities as well as their rate of learning. Adaptive Learning Platforms: Such platforms have incorporated AI algorithms that make them choose the difficulty levels and the rate of passing content based on a learner's performance. Proactively, the system continues to assign difficult work as the student advances or returns to already completed tasks where the student seems to be poor in. This makes the learning process to be more effective since the students are more and more engaged by the kind of teaching methods being adopted by the tutor. For example, such platforms as Khan Academy and Duolingo already adapt and recommend the model and the tasks required by using AI technologies (Baillifard et al., 2023). Personalized Learning Paths: For instance, AI can use data of a student's academic records, expressed preferences, career aspirations and even learning habits to proscribe learning routes. These paths may necessarily comprise one or several courses, an online resource, or activities that would fit the student to a tee and his or her learning goals. This sense of connection might prove quite useful for learners who remain uncertain about majors or future occupations (Tlili et al., 2023).

Customized Content Delivery: With the help of cognitive technologies, AI can even suggest what text, video, or simulation-based learning interfaces would be best for a particular student for building effective instruction. This makes it possible to present to the students what they would easily understand and grasp to get the most out of the information being passed. Picture a system that understands whether a student is a visual, an auditory, or a kinesthetic learner, and knowing this, serves up the information to the student in a preferred mode (Abdamia et al., 2023).

Algorithm for AI-Powered Personalized Learning:

1. Input: Enter data with the student, course content and learning objectives.
2. Initialize: It is necessary to determine the first level of the content and the feedback mechanism.
3. Analyze Student Data: Request for a pull of the performance history and the way in which the learning takes place.
4. Select the appropriate content: Based on the learning model chosen that is best suited his skill with regards to the learning style of the student.
5. Engagement: How much time is spent, number of quiz attempts and the level of accuracy to the response.

6. Adaptation of Difficulty: It has been established to increase the difficulty level if the reflected correct scores or to decrease it or provide content remedial if wrong scores.
7. Provide Feedback: Provide the student feedback as soon as each activity in the lesson is completed
8. Monitor Progress: Find out the performance in terms of accuracy and time taken to complete a certain test.
9. Adapt Learning Path: Propose: basic content or complex content according to the student progress and if needed, report to instructors.
10. Adaptive Content Generation: Develop different tests or practices for learners
11. Auto-Gracin: Provide feedback to the grade student submissions through the use of machine learning models
12. Report Generation: Inform the student and the educator concerning the performance of the student.

Transitioning into the ALP-description, The AI-Powered Personalized Learning Algorithm is intended for designing learning scenarios in accordance with the need, preference and academic accomplishment of the learner. It can also directly retrieve pertinent data regarding a student including learning profile –visual, audial- and academic history. By putting the course content and learning objectives into this system, it starts at an appropriate difficulty level for this student and introduces a real-time feedback process. The tool looks at the past performance of the student combined with the way that the student learns then makes the best content decision. The presented difficulty level then gets dynamically adjusted according to how fast the student progresses through the material presented to him/her. In different words and simple example, when the student does well to answer a question, I raise the level of difficulty, but when the student does poorly or fails to answer that specific question, it offers more content the student needs for him/her to comprehend the material properly. From the time the student begins to interact with the content, the algorithm tracks engagement metrics: time on-task, the results of the quiz and the accuracy of the answer given. The algorithm can give feedback as soon as the activity is over so that the students can understand where they made the mistake in the learning process. This is to ensure that performance is being monitored and that such aspects as the accuracy rate and time taken to complete a specific kind of learning content gap is determined. It takes the learning level up or down or to a different area, to a simpler or more complex level depending on the circumstances. However, adaptive content is then created algorithmically. It can be a sort of quiz or an exercise which the student can take as a practice in those fields where the student has to practice more. Evaluation will be provided according to the advice given by an online grading system, derived from the result of machine learning algorithms. Using it instead for something like this will enable teachers to save much more time to do something much bigger and much more important. Finally, there is an important level of detailed reports on performance that are prepared to assist the students and other people, who supervise their results as well as their choice of further effective strategies. This is the way in which the algorithm personalizes and creates an active learning approach, leading to better results.

3.2 Intelligent Tutoring Systems

ITS powered by AI are Intelligent Tutoring Systems that respond to students' need for an easily approachable personal tutor whom they can rely on at any time of day and any day of the week for advice, for answers to questions that may flood their inset thoughts, and for encouragement. Real-Time Feedback and Support: With ITS, students will be able to receive comments on their work in real time, with instructions on what should be improved. Another advantage of students receiving instant answers is to assist students in avoiding formation of wrong ideas. For instance, an ITS for writing could give grammar and style suggestions during their typing as they complete a paper, instead of when the paper is ready for submission. Personalized Problem Sets and Exercises: AI can be used in devising personalized classes and more specifically in devising of problem sets and exercise that the student has to do with most difficulty. This makes sure that all students are engaged adequately as well as bent sup to do more practice on contents in which they seem to struggle most.

3.3 Improving the Learning Resources

AI is not just revolutionizing the education process for students; it is also revolutionizing the generation and presentation of learning materials. Through natural language processing and generative AI models, educators now have the potential of automating the process of developing quality learning materials including notes, lecture slides, and probably even text books. Challenges: (Kadaruddin, 2023) Some of the possibilities of AI integration that can effectively facilitate classroom learning include the following; Summarize research articles for students, create quizzes from the content of the lecture, create overdoses to make students understand complex lessons, and use of simulation that may depict what students are learning. Further, through AI, training can be provided in the perspective of the student as the language used, the examples and multimedia used can be adjusted to the needs of a student as well as his or her background. This leaves the educators more time to work on nurturing the discourse and directing the students' learning and to come up with innovative, reconstruction learning resources. Automated Content Creation: The innovative application of AL can help the instructors in developing quality content for teaching, including notes, power point presentations, and text books. For instance, machines can come up with an overview of a long research paper that a student might be forced to read in class, produce questions based on a teacher's lecture content or even design simulation tests. This leaves educators available to devote more time to other more creative and more engaging ways of teaching (Ruiz-Rojas et al., 2023).

Multimedia Content Generation: AI can create multimedia content namely attractive videos, animations as well as graphics that can increase student interest and improve learning. For instance, AI can be employed in rendering additional dimensions for better understanding of concepts in science or developing timeliness for historical occurrences (Vrabie, 2024). Content Personalization and Adaptation: AI can also individualize the contents of what is learned, the language, and examples given that fit the learner's personal experience and prior knowledge.

3.4 Assessment and Evaluation

AI can also positively impact the assessment and evaluation process outlining opportunities for both educators and students. In the proposed AI solutions for automated grading, plagiarism detection, and feedback in ways that are more efficient, academic integrity, and informative to the student for learning purposes (Onesi-Ozigagun et al., 2024). The utilization of program grading for mechanical checks frees instructors to spend more time on meaningful communication; in turn, the use of plagiarism identification aids promotes academic integrity. Of course, AI may also review student work to make recommendations and give suggestions for correcting mistakes towards achieving mastery. Such levels of individual analysis can do a lot, providing students with the sense of control over the learning process and the ability to advance step by step consciously and with purpose. Automated Grading: AI can help to facilitate grading of all the multiple-choice questions, saving instructors' time to focus on more engaging with the students. It also enables feedback to be given as soon as they are written which is also good for students.

Plagiarism Detection: There is also use of artificial intelligence in teaching i.e in the case of detecting plagiarism in students' work by use of plagiarism detection software. It also helps instructors in preventing plagiarism and make students aware of cheating in their academic years. Personalized Feedback and Recommendations: AI can analyze student work and afford reaction and suggestion of the improvement on individual basis, if possible. For instance, an intelligent writing tutor that automatically analysis a student's writing performance may be able to diagnose the student's weakness whether in grammar, organization or argumentation, and recommend on the improvement strategies that are likely to enhance their writing ability. Such type of feedback can be much more individualized than general remarks, which may enhance students' awareness of their learner profile (Kim, 2023).

3.5 Challenges and Ethical Considerations

There are vast opportunities of utilizing AI in education, so it is high time to be aware of the prospects and problems as well as considering the major ethical concerns of implementing such an effective tool into educational process. One of them is the question of data protection and, moreover, data security. The technology driven education system based on artificial intelligence can also track and compile student's information such as personal information, performance records and even behaviors (Ayala-Pazmiño, 2023). Data Privacy and Security: Advanced I'I' structures need humongous data inputs for AI systems to work at optimal levels. Students' data should be collected, kept, used and shared responsibly and in an ethical manner, and students' privacy should also be protected. Bias and Fairness: Meaning; an AI algorithm is the reflection of the data on which the algorithm maker fed the algorithms. This means that if in the training data set there were biases, the AI system might also reinforce them or even intensify them. There is a growing need to create and apply fair, unbiased, and essentially equitable AI systems for students.

The Role of Educators: As AI continues to grow, it is therefore noteworthy to wonder about the place of the pedagogical agent in machine learning. As we see, there are many opportunities for automation when using AI, but the human factor is still important in education. Teachers will also have to shift their competencies to the practices that cannot be replicated using ALs, including reasoning, inventiveness, and socio-emotional growing. Applying AI in teaching and learning can go far to transform education by enhancing the teaching – learning process for all learners. By automating tasks, personalizing learning pathways, and providing data-driven insights, AI can free up educators to focus on what they do best: support their learning endeavors while facing students in the acts of knowing and learning directly (Kamalov et al., 2023). Nevertheless, the AI integration in education provoked many discussions regarding privacy, values, and the educator role. In this way, the use of the presented AI-based approach will not replace the teacher, but will become an integral part of the educational process, which, in turn, will become more efficient, open, and trustworthy for all the members of the learning process (Bulut, 2024).

4. AI IN RESEARCH AND KNOWLEDGE CREATION

Outside the classroom, AI is already revolutionizing the world of research and production of knowledge at quite a fast pace. Boy and girls, accelerate the analysis of data; enabling researchers to solve multifaceted problem and enhancing research collaboration across disciplinary boundaries. It has become apparent that by using artificial intelligence features, researchers are able to find solutions to new questions, to optimize their cooperation with other scientists, and accelerate the processes of identifying scientific discoveries that could possibly improve people's lives. Through outsourcing time-consuming tasks, improving the integration of knowledge, and promoting interfiled collaboration, AI is transforming the research environment and improving the speed of knowledge advancement (Balta, 2023).

4.1 AI-Powered Research Tools

In many areas of research today, it is not just the amount of information produced that is mind boggling, but also the type of information produced. AI brings high effective ways of handling, analyzing, and utilizing such big amounts of the information flood. Scholars have no other option than leveraging AI technologies to help them manage the huge flows of information available. Such complex analytics features help extend the range of findings and suggest new hypotheses which might be useful for further experimenting with the instances quicker than with simple statistics measures (Wang et al., 2023). AI thus allows people to do research and extend knowledge by providing a means of analyzing large quantities of data with far less effort than without its aid; it thus provides researchers the opportunity to shift from mechanical and tedious tasks to more challenging and abstract activities that release their breakthroughs across various fields of study; This is according to Hasselgren & Oprea 2024.

Data Analysis and Pattern Recognition: One way in which AI can be particularly useful to the forensic researcher is its ability to make predictions from the data that may not be obvious when analysed by a human analyst. This capability proves most useful in vertically oriented disciplines such as genomics, astrophysics, and climatology, where scientists handle large data sets. For example, AI is being used to analyze genomic data to identify potential drug targets for diseases like cancer (Artificial intelligence for science: The easy problems and the hard problems, 2024).

Literature Review and Knowledge Synthesis: Scouring large databases to determine which studies are relevant and which best compile the current body of knowledge can prove to be a very tedious endeavour. As such an AI-powered tools can speed up and even bring to a whole new level this process by analyzing thousands of articles and finding important conclusions or, even, a connection between results of different studies. Now, semantic assistants like Semantic Scholar are already helping researchers to make sense of a massive and disparate field of scientific documents.ls to manage, analyze, and extract meaningful insights from this data deluge. Researchers are increasingly turning to AI-powered tools to navigate the vast troves of information at their fingertips. These advanced analytics capabilities enable researchers to uncover hidden patterns, identify promising avenues for further exploration, and expedite the discovery process (Wang et al., 2023).

By automating the analysis of large datasets, AI frees up researchers to focus on the more creative and conceptual aspects of their work, leading to groundbreaking advancements across diverse fields of study (Hasselgren & Oprea, 2024). Data Analysis and Pattern Recognition: AI algorithms excel at identifying patterns and trends in large datasets that might not be apparent to human researchers. This capability is particularly valuable in fields like genomics, astronomy, and climate science, where researchers grapple with massive datasets. For example, AI is being used to analyze genomic data to identify potential drug targets for diseases like cancer (Artificial intelligence for science: The easy and hard problems, 2024). Literature Review and Knowledge Synthesis: Sifting through mountains of research articles to identify relevant studies and synthesize existing knowledge is a time-consuming but essential part of the research process. AI-powered tools can automate and accelerate this process by scanning thousands of articles, identifying key findings, and even highlighting connections between different studies that might not be immediately obvious. Tools like Semantic Scholar are already being used by researchers to navigate and understand the vast landscape of scientific literature (Lo et al., 2023). Experiment Design and Optimization: The design of an experiment is very of paramount importance in science. AI can also help researchers to conduct experiments more efficiently giving measurements that are more likely to be significant. For example, AI algorithms may help to learn experimental parameters, as well as estimate possible results and recommend other possible experimental configurations (Carobene et al., 2023).

4.2 Enhancing Collaboration

Team work is necessary in scientific development, but is often negatively affected by the distance between people, specialty, and the overload of data. AI can also reduce such barriers to increase collaboration within research activities as outlined by Lin et al., 2022. Facilitating Interdisciplinary Research: AI can help to establish the interaction between researchers from different fields which do not necessarily interact with each other by finding key subjects and possible points of intersection. For instance, AI could introduce a computer scientist working on new machine learning approaches to a biologist discovering the structure of intricate biological systems and so on (Gao & Wang, 2023). Cross-Institutional Collaboration: AI can also help concert researchers working in different institutions since belongings to the same platform aid in sharing information resources, coordinating and communicating on the various projects. This can be especially useful for many-layered research involving multiple groups of specialists located in various parts of the world (Yager, 2024). Breaking Down Language Barriers: The other area that researchers can benefit from AI is through translation, this makes them have access to research work done in their area of study across the world. This has the potential to lead to a diversification as well as a globalization of the research community.

4.3 AI-Driven Discovery

However, there is a growing involvement of AI not only in supporting existing research activities, but also in advancing scientific research (Alowais et al., 2023). Generating Hypotheses and Identifying New Research Questions: Based on the data, AI can draw out many features that can be indicative of anomalous behavior, or new hypotheses for research questions. This can also unveil totally different sorts of new scientific exploration. For instance, AI has used machine learning to predict novel drug candidates by learning from the chemical fingerprints of different compounds and their biological activities (Hasselgren & Oprea, 2024) (Mullowney et al., 2023).

Accelerating Drug Discovery and Development: AI is making a significant impact in the pharmaceutical studies and particularly improving the speed of drug discovery and development. Current AI techniques can search extensive databases of chemical substances and determine the efficacy and potential pharmacology of drug targets as well as design new drugs with given characteristics (Hasselgren & Oprea, 2024). Personalized Medicine and Healthcare: Consequently, AI is opening for a new era of individualized medicine; that is medicine delivered based on the patient. Machine learning algorithms can estimate the development of previously stated diseases based on patients' personal records, genetic predisposition, and lifestyle, and then prescribe preventive measures or therapy (Varnosfaderani & Forouzanfar, 2024). AI integration is Already changing the face and process of how scientific research is conducted in the research space. AI assists in improving the speed of research processes and its organization, supports cooperation, and assists in making breakthroughs to be made in various branches. With the increasing development of AI technologies, it can be assumed that its role as an innovative potential in the context of research will only increase in the future (Duede et al., 2024).

4.4 Effects on Academic Publishing

The traditional model of academic production is also changing under the influence of AI solutions. In the following areas, artificial intelligence solutions are applied to support the manuscript preparation and publishing: production, peer review, and distribution. Another area that AI has had a huge-effect on academic publishing is in the preparation of manuscripts. AI offers tools to enhance the quality of research papers by offering research writers a grammar and spell check as well as writing style recommendations in real-time. They can also help with citation and formatting and other related matters to ensure that researchers can devote more time in substantive issues. The issues outlined in this section are some of the most important ones that would carry the spectator's attention. Automated Manuscript Screening and Peer Review: The field of AI can help in the peer review procedure by prescreening manuscripts according to its relevance, uniqueness as well as ethic policies. This may be useful to speed up a publication, bypass the editors and reviewers, and thus lighten the workload on their part (Bengio et al., 2024).

5. CHALLENGES IN IMPLEMENTING AI IN HIGHER EDUCATION

On one hand these are the potential benefits of integrating AI in higher education but achieving all these benefits involve challenges. University must uncloak a system of challenges that include technological, ethical, and cultural to innovate AI in the learning-teaching-facilitation, research and education processes and functions.

5.1 Technological Barriers

Utility and effectiveness of AI necessitate strong technologic commitment and sophisticated, which presents problems for extensive institutions (Vrabie, 2024). Infrastructure Requirements: The AI systems especially the ones that take on the learning machines feature a very large computing power and storage space. Businesses might require plumbing, or investment into the infrastructure to support the demands of these AI applications. This can of course be a massive challenge financially particularly for those institutions that are relatively small and hence might not be financially buoyant to do so. Cost of AI Solutions: Educational technologies and AI tools, applications, and platforms that can be integrated into education may not be cheap. Subscription and licensing fees, implementation cost, maintenance cost put pressure on institutional budget. Further, the fast and continuous advancement of AI functionalities implies that institutions may incur frequent costs on updates and malfunctions (Onesi-Ozigagun et al., 2024).

Integration with Existing Systems: AI tools may perfectly dovetail with conventional learning management systems, other institutional solutions, and student information systems to an extent that it can be technically challenging. That is why data must be compatible and interoperable with other systems that an AI application will work on them, since their openness is stipulated (Kamalov et al., 2023). Lack of Technical Expertise: AI system development, including designing, implementing, as well as sustaining, necessitates professional technical skills. Hiring qualified personnel to serve institutions in AI may be difficult, and this becomes worse because of the shortage resulting from its application in different fields today (Starting Up AI, 2024).

5.2 Moral and Ethical Implication

Process involving AI has several ethical concerns which many institutions need to consider when implementing AI. Data Privacy and Security: Student data is a key aspect of most of the AI systems by which institutions collect and analyze large amounts of data from students, thus there is a violation of student's privacy. Down at the institutional level, therefore, there are needed protocols to follow regarding data collection, storage, utilization, and privacy, guided by FERPA and other regulatory laws. It is therefore necessary that instructors, teachers and professors do be transparent to the students, and this is to make the students understand how their data is being used. Bias in AI Algorithms: AI algorithm reflects the data set used to train it. However, if the training data included some bias, for examples ethnic, gender or other, the AI system in turn will also likely reproduce and often deepen the prejudice, which means that students with certain characteristics will be treated unfairly. For institutions, it means that they cannot relax and watch the AI systems possibly becoming or initially being opaque with bias in applying their power and prescience (Chen, 2023).

5.3 Resistance to Change

The adoption of new technologies such as integration of artificial intelligence in organizations always undergo social resistance from personnel who are rigid with norms. Faculty and Staff Concerns: It is possible that initiative may be lacking in the introduction of AI on campuses due to concerns about negative impact on employment, unfamiliarity with AI and doubts about its efficacy. It is therefore recommended that institutions must set aside funds to train the faculty and staff for them to appreciate and feel competent on their ability to apply AI in their work.

6. STRATEGIES FOR SUCCESSFUL AI DEPLOYMENT IN HIGHER EDUCATION

These research findings thus propose that it is possible to meaningfully adopt AI in higher learning institutions if the process involves a systems approach. Here's a breakdown of key strategies.

6.1 Formal Structure and Action Plan

Specifically, as institutions explore AI adoption, they need to evaluate their institutional capabilities and create a plan. This requires performing a broad need analysis to determine where AI can solve a particular problem or contribute to improvement of an existing situation, as student support services being relieved by AI chatbots. Also, it is high time that institutions assessed their technological structure, control and handling of data, and possible vulnerabilities that may come with absorption of the AI (Onesi-Ozigagun et al., 2024). Lastly, for the developmental of these initiatives, various institutions should also ensure the right resource management through financial, staffing and professional development support.

6.2 Cultivating an AI–Ready Environment

Clearly, the introduction of AI is not just a technical process; it is organizational as well. This has a very critical implication to institutions, where they must create cultures that allow for experimentation, promote the innovation as well as ensure that the various stakeholders are active participants in the entire AI drive. Organizing and soliciting the participation of the people in the faculty and staff is vital in creating awareness and acceptances of new changes. Promote AI Literacy: Develop faculty staff and student awareness and sensitivity to AI in terms of knowledge, utility, potential risks and opportunities. Address Concerns and Resistance: To date, Luddite worries about job loss, the invasion of privacy, and algorithmic unfairness must be front and addressed explicitly. Transparency is key. Encourage Experimentation and Innovation: Allow the faculty to try out AI tools for teaching and learning, in a risk-free environment. Recognize and Reward Early Adopters: Exhibit extended pilot case studies of artificial intelligence that has been adopted in the organization and appreciate the efforts of the faculty and staff in implementing the system.

7. ENGAGING STUDENTS AND FACULTY TO THE CONCEPT OF ARTIFICIAL INTELLIGENCE

In the world dominated by artificial intelligence, it becomes essential for universities to develop AI competent student and faculty population. This means preparing them to live, work and practice in an AI world by offering them knowledge and ethical standards they require.

7.1 Developing AI Competencies: Why AI Literacy Matters

Dubious as the concept of AI literacy might be, it is not simply an optional asset; it is a fundamental competence for the world of work and the world at large. The disposition of AI across different sectors calls for the student to have a basic appreciation of how to interact with AI and how best to utilize this technology to be employable and make a positive impact in their respective fields in future. Likewise, faculty should have a good understanding of AI to incorporate it into various teaching and research functions to promote the achievement of enhanced learning outcomes of students (Ge & Hu, 2020). AI literacy encompasses a broad range of knowledge and skills, including: Foundational Understanding: Understanding general knowledge about AI, its subdivisions (machine learning, natural language processing, etc.) and industries they are used in.

Critical Thinking: AI's strengths and weaknesses, identifying real and fake claims about the technology, and understanding if and how the programs are prejudiced. Ethical Awareness: Describe the use of AI, its potential harm, privacy concerns, bias, and efficient work disruption, and appropriate AI development. Practical Skills: In terms of application, for students it may mean applying AI services to their study or art projects. For faculty, it could include the ways of using AI in teaching or putting AI to use in data analysis in research. Benefits of AI Literacy - Students: AI literacy educates society for an economy and job market in which artificial intelligence plays a huge role. It enables them to be prepare for the different job markets around the world that seem to change with time and be productive members of society with the spread of Artificial Intelligence.

7.2 Use of Artificial Intelligence in Curriculum

It is important now to integrate AI education into different fields. Here are some examples: Introductory AI Courses: Teach introductory classes that can be taken by students with any prior background, which explore concepts, uses, and effects of AI. AI-Specific Majors and Minors: Enact unique courses which will target student intending to be developers in artificial intelligence, data scientists, or other similar professions. AI Integration Across Disciplines: Introduce AI modules or case studies into rather specialized courses in various departments of the university, demonstrate how different fields including health, finance, arts etc, are applying AI. Project-Based Learning: The conclusion is that involve students in course activities where they must work on developing or on using an AI application.

7.3 Faculty Development Programs

Supporting the preparedness and readiness of the faculty into taking charge of the changing facet in education, AI is a must. AI Literacy Workshops: Provide awareness sessions for basic concepts of AI and inclusion of AI in teaching, handling the ethical issues. Hands-on Training: Offer AI proof of concept alongside professional development workshops that teach the selected AI tools useful to the disciplines of the intended faculty. Faculty Learning Communities: Support formation of communities of practice where faculty members can discuss, compare their experiences, successes, and obstacles in the implementation of AI. Incentives for Innovation: Support adoption of AI through recognition, grants or course buyouts for faculties to try Innovative applications in teaching and learning as well as research. As a result of investing in student and faculty AI literacy programs, higher learning institutions prepare the next generation of citizens for both the AI opportunities and the AI risks and dilemmas.

8. FUTURE TRENDS AND OPPORTUNITIES IN AI FOR HIGHER EDUCATION

Though the integration of AI in higher education is not fully realized, the idea of change it can bring is huge. This section aims at giving a sneak view of what future holds in store about the trends.

8.1 Emerging AI Technologies

Several emerging AI technologies are poised to significantly impact higher education: Part of these are enhanced learning analytics for increased understanding of students learning, adaptive learning delivery technologies that adapts instruction in real-time as well as virtual and augmented reality learning environments. Evaluation and feedback will also be partially integrated into AI integrated solutions, applied to grading and students will be also given timely feedback. Moreover, the progress of XAI is concerned with the reasoning behind AI choices to enhance confidence and let educators understand how AI is used in instruction. Advanced Learning Analytics: AI will become less limited to learning analytics but will furnish more enriched information on student learning patterns, and more accurate performance estimations, to provide intensive interaction.

Adaptive Learning Platforms: True AI will lead to dynamic, real-time learning paths in which content, difficulty level, as well as instructional approaches, are customized to the student's need and or learning achievements. Virtual and Augmented

Reality (VR/AR) Enhanced Learning: AI will be involved in design and development of engaging and interactive learning utilizing VR/AR, simulation and practice using virtual labs, and individual virtual classrooms. AI-Powered Assessment and Feedback: With regards to assignments where rubrics are applicable, AI will carry the task of grading and providing feedback personal to the students.

8.2 Future Learning Environments

As the AI technologies progress further, the conventional model of instruction is going to change and this may result in new context for learning using AI. The adoption of some of these AI technologies in higher learning will help transform the way learners acquire their knowledge and how some professors disseminate that knowledge. As a result, integrating AI into learning and educational process can help to: …er education has the potential to revolutionize how students learn and how educators teach. By providing personalized learning experiences, automating administrative tasks, and delivering real-time feedback, AI can create a more inclusive and effective learning environment (Mello et al., 2023).

8.3 New Roles and Responsibilities

This paper also identifies how AI will change the nature of work in higher education for students and faculty as AI becomes more embedded across colleges and universities. Students will increasingly take on more active and engaged roles in their learning, leveraging AI-powered tools to personalize their educational journeys, monitor their progress, and collaborate with peers and instructors in new ways (Ahmad et al., 2023). The rise of AI in education will lead to the emergence of new roles and responsibilities: Learning Experience Designers: Such professionals will focus on creating exciting and meaningful learning experiences that use artificial intelligence technologies. AI Ethics Officers: Since the deployment of AI is bound to become more and more commonplace in educational environments, there will of course be the need for professionals who will oversee ethical flaws and possible AI misuses or with potential bias.

CONCLUSION

AI integration in higher learning is one of the transformative processes in future learning methods for students and innovative practices for faculties. When applied to this sector, AI can greatly increase productivity, adapt instruction methods to students' abilities, and consequently – achieve better learning results. However, it must be done cautiously. To enhance the benefits of AI, it must address ethical issues and risks, with proper intentions that minimize biased results. Of even greater importance is the notion that these tools should be available to learners from all backgrounds since AI advancement is already here for students. AI is one of the most promising zones in the development of technologies that, therefore, lies at the same potential of the future of HE. Through propelling sustained advancements in the field, promoting increased institutional and interdisciplinary 'connectivity', and maintaining a strong and steadfast values-oriented approach to vocational AI, we can unlock the full potential of AI and bring about a transformation in learning which will benefit all.

REFERENCES

Abbas, N., Imran, A., Manzoor, R., Hussain, T., & Hussain, M H A I. (2023, August 16). Role of Artificial Intelligence Tools in Enhancing Students' Educational Performance at Higher Levels., 36-49. https://doi.org/DOI: 10.55529/jaimlnn.35.36.49

Abdamia, N., Puteh, F., & Jah, N J A. (2023, April 10). Investigating Learning Modalities among Diploma Students., 12(2). https://doi.org/DOI: 10.6007/ijarped/v12-i2/16552

Ahmad, S., Umirzakova, S., Mujtaba, G., Amin, M., & Whangbo, T. K. (2023, January 1). Education 5.0: Requirements, Enabling Technologies, and Future Directions. Cornell University. https://doi.org//arxiv.2307.15846DOI: 10.48550

Ahmad, S. F., Han, H., Alam, M. M., Rehmat, M. K., Irshad, M., Arraño-Muñoz, M., & Ariza-Montes, A. (2023, June 9). Impact of artificial intelligence on human loss in decision making, laziness and safety in education. *Palgrave Macmillan*, 10(1). Advance online publication. DOI: 10.1057/s41599-023-01787-8 PMID: 37325188

AlGhamdi, R., Buhari, S M., & Alassafi, M O. (2020, November 1). FROM TEACHING TO COACHING: A CASE STUDY OF A TECHNICAL COMMUNICATION COURSE. International Academy of Technology, Education and Development. https://doi.org/DOI: 10.21125/iceri.2020.0285

Alowais, S. A., Alghamdi, S. S., Alsuhebany, N., Alqahtani, T., Alshaya, A., Almohareb, S. N., Aldairem, A., Alrashed, M., Saleh, K. B., Badreldin, H. A., Yami, M. S. A., Harbi, S. A., & Albekairy, A. (2023, September 22). Revolutionizing healthcare: The role of artificial intelligence in clinical practice. *BioMed Central*, 23(1). Advance online publication. DOI: 10.1186/s12909-023-04698-z PMID: 37740191

Annuš, N. (2023, May 25). Chatbots in Education: The impact of Artificial Intelligence based ChatGPT on Teachers and Students., 7(4), 366-370. https://doi.org/DOI: 10.59287/ijanser.739

Artificial intelligence for science: The easy and hard problems. (2024, September 3). https://www.aimodels.fyi/papers/arxiv/artificial-intelligence-science-easy-hard-problems

Ayala-Pazmiño, M. (2023, May 2). Artificial Intelligence in Education. *Exploring the Potential Benefits and Risks.*, 8(3), 892–899. DOI: 10.33386/593dp.2023.3.1827

Baillifard, A., Gabella, M., Lavenex, P. B., & Martarelli, C. S. (2023, January 1). Implementing Learning Principles with a Personal AI Tutor: A Case Study. Cornell University. https://doi.org/DOI: 10.48550/arXiv.2309

Balta, N. (2023, June 15).. . *Embracing the Future: AI's Transformative Potential in Educational Research*, 6(2), 1–2. DOI: 10.31757/euer.624

Bengio, Y., Hinton, G. E., Yao, A. C., Song, D., Abbeel, P., Darrell, T., Harari, Y. N., Zhang, Y., Lan, X., Shalev-Shwartz, S., Hadfield, G. K., Mouret, J., Maharaj, T., Hutter, F., Baydin, A. G., McIlraith, S. A., Gao, Q., Acharya, A., Krueger, D., & Mindermann, S. (2024, May 24). Managing extreme AI risks amid rapid progress. *American Association for the Advancement of Science*, 384(6698), 842–845. DOI: 10.1126/science.adn0117 PMID: 38768279

Bulut, O., Beiting-Parrish, M., Casabianca, J. M., Slater, S., Jiao, H., Song, D., Ormerod, C. M., Fabiyi, D. G., Ivan, R., Walsh, C., Rios, O., Wilson, J. M., Yildirim-Erbasli, S. N., Wongvorachan, T., Liu, J. X., Tan, B., & Morilova, P. (2024, June 27). The Rise of Artificial Intelligence in Educational Measurement: Opportunities and Ethical Challenges. Cornell University. https://doi.org/DOI: 10.48550/arXiv.2406

Bulut, O., Beiting-Parrish, M., Casabianca, J. M., Slater, S., Jiao, H., Song, D., Ormerod, C. M., Fabiyi, D. G., Ivan, R., Walsh, C., Rios, O., Wilson, J. M., Yildirim-Erbasli, S. N., Wongvorachan, T., Liu, J. X., Tan, B., & Morilova, P. (2024, June 27). The Rise of Artificial Intelligence in Educational Measurement: Opportunities and Ethical Challenges. Cornell University. https://doi.org//arxiv.2406.18900DOI: 10.48550

Bureau, U. C. (2024, April 19). Starting Up AI. https://www.census.gov/library/working-papers/2024/adrm/CES-WP-24-09.html

Carobene, A., Padoan, A., Cabitza, F., Banfi, G., & Plebani, M. (2023, November 30). Rising adoption of artificial intelligence in scientific publishing: Evaluating the role, risks, and ethical implications in paper drafting and review process. *De Gruyter*, 62(5), 835–843. DOI: 10.1515/cclm-2023-1136 PMID: 38019961

Chamorro-Atalaya, O., Huarcaya-Godoy, M., Durán-Herrera, V., Nieves-Barreto, C., Suarez-Bazalar, R., Cruz-Telada, Y., Alarcón-Anco, R., Huayhua-Mamani, H., Vargas-Díaz, A., & Balarezo-Mares, D. (2023, September 30). Application of the Chatbot in University Education: A Systematic Review on the Acceptance and Impact on Learning. *Tresorix Ltd*, 22(9), 156–178. DOI: 10.26803/ijlter.22.9.9

Chen, Z. (2023, September 13). Ethics and discrimination in artificial intelligence-enabled recruitment practices. *Palgrave Macmillan*, 10(1). Advance online publication. DOI: 10.1057/s41599-023-02079-x

Dave, M., & Patel, N. (2023, May 26). Artificial intelligence in healthcare and education. *Springer Nature*, 234(10), 761–764. DOI: 10.1038/s41415-023-5845-2 PMID: 37237212

Davenport, T H., & Glaser, J. (2022, October 31). Factors governing the adoption of artificial intelligence in healthcare providers. Springer Science+Business Media, 1(1). https://doi.org/DOI: 10.1007/s44250-022-00004-8

Duede, E., Dolan, W. W., Bauer, A., Foster, I., & Lakhani, K. R. (2024, May 23). Oil & Water? Diffusion of AI Within and Across Scientific Fields. Cornell University. https://doi.org//arxiv.2405.15828DOI: 10.48550

Fontenelle-Tereshchuk, D. (2024, January 10). Academic writing and ChatGPT: Students transitioning into college in the shadow of the COVID-19 pandemic. Springer Science+Business Media, 3(1). https://doi.org/DOI: 10.1007/s44217-023-00076-5

Gao, J., & Wang, D. (2023, January 1). Quantifying the Benefit of Artificial Intelligence for Scientific Research. Cornell University. https://doi.org//arxiv.2304.10578DOI: 10.48550

Ge, Z., & Hu, Y. (2020, April 1). Innovative Application of Artificial Intelligence (AI) in the Management of Higher Education and Teaching. *IOP Publishing*, 1533(3), 032089–032089. DOI: 10.1088/1742-6596/1533/3/032089

Hasselgren, C., & Oprea, T. I. (2024, January 23). Artificial Intelligence for Drug Discovery: Are We There Yet? *Annual Reviews*, 64(1), 527–550. DOI: 10.1146/annurev-pharmtox-040323-040828 PMID: 37738505

Kadaruddin, K. (2023, August 2). Empowering Education through Generative AI. *Innovative Instructional Strategies for Tomorrow's Learners.*, 4(2), 618–625. DOI: 10.56442/ijble.v4i2.215

Kamalov, F., Calonge, D. S., & Gurrib, I. (2023, August 16). New Era of Artificial Intelligence in Education: Towards a Sustainable Multifaceted Revolution. *Multidisciplinary Digital Publishing Institute*, 15(16), 12451–12451. DOI: 10.3390/su151612451

Kamalov, F., & Gurrib, I. (2023, January 1). New Era of Artificial Intelligence in Education: Towards a Sustainable Multifaceted Revolution. Cornell University. https://doi.org/DOI: 10.48550/arXiv.2305

Khosravi, H., Shum, S B., Chen, G., Conati, C., Tsai, Y., Kay, J., Knight, S., Martínez-Maldonado, R., Sadiq, S., & Gašević, D. (2022, January 1). Explainable Artificial Intelligence in education. Elsevier BV, 3, 100074-100074. https://doi.org/DOI: 10.1016/j.caeai.2022.100074

Kim, N. (2023, February 28)... *Strengthening the Self-feedback on College Writing Classes.*, 17(1), 47–62. DOI: 10.46392/kjge.2023.17.1.47

Lin, Y., Frey, C. B., & Wu, L. (2022, January 1). Remote Collaboration Fuses Fewer Breakthrough Ideas. Cornell University. https://doi.org//arxiv.2206.01878DOI: 10.48550

Lo, K., Chang, J. C., Head, A., Bragg, J., Zhang, A. X., Trier, C., Anastasiades, C., August, T., Authur, R., Bragg, D., Bransom, E., Cachola, I., Candra, S., Chandrasekhar, Y., Chen, Y., Cheng, E. Y., Chou, Y., Downey, D., Evans, R. L., . . . Weld, D. S. (2023, January 1). The Semantic Reader Project: Augmenting Scholarly Documents through AI-Powered Interactive Reading Interfaces. Cornell University. https://doi.org//arxiv.2303.14334DOI: 10.48550

M U D., & Thombre, D. (2023, June 24). Admission BOT: Unleashing the Potential of Neural Networks in Streamlining the Admission Process., 5(3). https://doi.org/DOI: 10.36948/ijfmr.2023.v05i03.3989

Muhie, Y. A., & Woldie, A. B. (2020, January 1). Integration of Artificial Intelligence Technologies in Teaching and Learning in Higher Education., 10(1), 1-7. http://www.sapub.org/global/showpaperpdf.aspx?doi=10.5923/j.scit.20201001.01

Mullowney, M. W., Duncan, K., Elsayed, S. S., Garg, N., Hooft, J. J. J. V. D., Martin, N. I., Meijer, D., Terlouw, B. R., Biermann, F., Blin, K., Durairaj, J., González, M. G., Helfrich, E. J. N., Huber, F., Leopold-Messer, S., Rajan, K., Rond, T. D., Santen, J. V., Sorokina, M., & Medema, M. H. (2023, September 11). Artificial intelligence for natural product drug discovery. *Nature Portfolio*, 22(11), 895–916. DOI: 10.1038/s41573-023-00774-7 PMID: 37697042

Núñez, J L M., Harris, P., Fernández, R P., Abbas, A., & Radovanović, D. (2023, January 1). Does intrinsic motivation mediate perceived artificial intelligence (AI) learning and computational thinking of students during the COVID-19 pandemic? Elsevier BV, 4, 100128-100128. https://doi.org/DOI: 10.1016/j.caeai.2023.100128

Ober, T M., Lehman, B., Gooch, R., Oluwalana, O., Solyst, J., Phelps, G., & Hamilton, L S. (2023, August 7). Culturally Responsive Personalized Learning: Recommendations for a Working Definition and Framework. Wiley, 2023(1), 1-14. https://doi.org/DOI: 10.1002/ets2.12372

Onesi-Ozigagun, O., Ololade, Y. J., Eyo-Udo, N. L., & Ogundipe, D. O. (2024, April 10). REVOLUTIONIZING EDUCATION THROUGH AI: A COMPREHENSIVE REVIEW OF ENHANCING LEARNING EXPERIENCES. *Fair East Publishers*, 6(4), 589–607. DOI: 10.51594/ijarss.v6i4.1011

Perkins, M. (2023, February 22). Academic integrity considerations of AI Large Language Models in the post-pandemic era: ChatGPT and beyond. *University of Wollongong*, 20(2). Advance online publication. DOI: 10.53761/1.20.02.07

Rane, M V., Apte, V M., Nerkar, V N., Roja, M M., & Rajput, K. (2021, March 5). Automated Timetabling System for University Course. https://doi.org/DOI: 10.1109/esci50559.2021.9396906

Rani, M., Bala, J., & Varjani, S. (2023, June 19).. . *Scope and Challenges of Multimedia in Education Sector.*, 5(3). Advance online publication. DOI: 10.36948/ijfmr.2023.v05i03.3868

Resnick, M. (2024, March 27). Generative AI and Creative Learning: Concerns, Opportunities, and Choices. https://doi.org/DOI: 10.21428/e4baedd9.cf3e35e5

Rodway, P., & Schepman, A. (2023, January 1). The impact of adopting AI educational technologies on projected course satisfaction in university students. Elsevier BV, 5, 100150-100150. https://doi.org/DOI: 10.1016/j.caeai.2023.100150

Ruiz-Rojas, L. I., Acosta-Vargas, P., De-Moreta-Llovet, J., & González, M. (2023, July 25). Empowering Education with Generative Artificial Intelligence Tools: Approach with an Instructional Design Matrix. *Multidisciplinary Digital Publishing Institute*, 15(15), 11524–11524. DOI: 10.3390/su151511524

Sil, P., Chaudhuri, P., & Raman, B. (2024, January 1). Can AI Assistance Aid in the Grading of Handwritten Answer Sheets? Springer Science+Business Media, 291-298. https://doi.org/DOI: 10.1007/978-3-031-64312-5_35

Southgate, E. (2020, July 27). Artificial intelligence, ethics, equity and higher education: a 'beginning-of-the-discussion' paper. https://apo.org.au/node/307359

Taneja, K., Maiti, P., Kakar, S., Guruprasad, P., Rao, S., & Goel, A K. (2024, January 1). Jill Watson: A Virtual Teaching Assistant Powered by ChatGPT. Springer Science+Business Media, 324-337. https://doi.org/DOI: 10.1007/978-3-031-64302-6_23

Tlili, A., Sun, T., Denden, M., Kinshuk, K., Graf, S., Fei, C., & Wang, H. (2023, May 23). Impact of personality traits on learners' navigational behavior patterns in an online course: A lag sequential analysis approach. *Frontiers of Medicine*, 14. Advance online publication. DOI: 10.3389/fpsyg.2023.1071985 PMID: 37292512

Vacalares, S. T., Clarin, E., Lapid, R., Malaki, M., Plaza, V., & Barcena, M. (2023, May 30). Factors affecting the writing skills of the education students: A descriptive study. *GSC Online Press*, 18(2), 1192–1201. DOI: 10.30574/wjarr.2023.18.2.0931

Varnosfaderani, S. M., & Forouzanfar, M. (2024, March 29). The Role of AI in Hospitals and Clinics: Transforming Healthcare in the 21st Century. *Multidisciplinary Digital Publishing Institute*, 11(4), 337–337. DOI: 10.3390/bioengineering11040337 PMID: 38671759

Vrabie, C. (2024, July 14). Artificial Intelligence from Idea to Implementation. How Can AI Reshape the Education Landscape? Cornell University. https://doi.org//arxiv.2407.20236DOI: 10.48550

Wang, L., Fu, T., Du, Y., Gao, W., Huang, K., Liu, Z., Chandak, P., Liu, S., Katwyk, P. V., Deac, A., Anandkumar, A., Bergen, K. J., Gomes, C. P., Ho, S., Kohli, P., Lasenby, J., Leskovec, J., Liu, T., Manrai, A. K., & Žitnik, M. (2023, August 2). Scientific discovery in the age of artificial intelligence. *Nature Portfolio*, 620(7972), 47–60. DOI: 10.1038/s41586-023-06221-2 PMID: 37532811

Wang, T., Lund, B., Marengo, A., Pagano, A., Mannuru, N. R., Teel, Z. A., & Pange, J. (2023, May 31). Exploring the Potential Impact of Artificial Intelligence (AI) on International Students in Higher Education: Generative AI, Chatbots, Analytics, and International Student Success. *Multidisciplinary Digital Publishing Institute*, 13(11), 6716–6716. DOI: 10.3390/app13116716

Yager, K. G. (2024, June 24). Towards a Science Exocortex. Cornell University. https://doi.org//arxiv.2406.17809DOI: 10.48550

Zimmerle, J C. (2021, January 2). Safe, Sound, and Private: Promoting Data Protection for Students. Taylor & Francis, 38(1), 1-18. https://doi.org/DOI: 10.1080/07380569.2021.1882203

Chapter 4
Artificial Intelligence in Education and Its Importance

Şule Darıcan
https://orcid.org/0000-0002-0688-6020
Istanbul Aydın University, Turkey

ABSTRACT

Artificial intelligence technologies have pioneered significant transformations in numerous industries and are increasingly being adopted in the field of education. AI offers meaningful contributions to the management of information and teaching processes in education with its capability to learn, make intelligent predictions, solve complex problems, and adapt to different languages. With personalized learning experiences, AI has the potential to play an important role in determining areas of improvement by analyzing student performance, while also making teaching methods more effective for teachers. AI applications such as automatic assessment, language recognition, and content analysis provide convenience in fields such as foreign language teaching. The use of learning analytics to monitor student progress increases the efficiency of education systems and supports academic success by providing customized feedback. The aim of this study is to examine the importance of AI in education with its innovative solutions, potential applications, and strategies to improve education systems.

DOI: 10.4018/979-8-3693-7949-3.ch004

INTRODUCTION

Since the beginning of the twenty-first century, artificial intelligence systems have begun to play an important role in many areas of society. The rapid advancement of technology has facilitated the integration of these systems into daily life and made artificial intelligence one of the most important elements of our age. This situation has led to significant changes in numerous fields such as education, health, economy, and industry.

Artificial intelligence is a field that focuses on developing computers, machines, and other systems with human-like intelligence characterized by cognitive abilities, learning, adaptation, and decision-making skills. AI first emerged alongside computers and computer-based technologies. Over time, web-based and online intelligent education systems have become prevalent in the field of education. Eventually, with the integration of embedded computer systems, humanoid robots and web-based chatbots have begun to be used to perform the tasks of instructors independently or in collaboration with them. The use of these technologies has allowed instructors to perform administrative functions such as reviewing and grading student assignments more efficiently, increasing the quality of teaching activities. Since these systems utilize machine learning and adaptability elements, they are also used to customize the curricula and course content to individual student needs. This has encouraged the adoption and long-term use of AI, which has positively improved the overall experience and learning quality of students (Chen et.al., 2020).

Integrated computers, sensors, and similar technologies have facilitated the integration of artificial intelligence into machines and other elements such as buildings and robots. Chassignol et al. (2018) define AI as an area of computer science aimed at developing cognitive abilities similar to human intelligence, whereas Sharma (2019) defines AI as machines that have the capacity to imitate the human mind. Pokrivcakova (2019) emphasizes that AI applications in the field of education are systems created through the collaboration of experts from different disciplines with the aim of helping teachers and developing the knowledge and skills of learners. Wartman et al. (2018) state that this technology has the ability to imitate human cognition and actions. In general, AI stands out as a field that focuses on development of machines that can perform human-like functions including complex capabilities such as speech, recognition, visual perception, and decision-making.

AI has gained significant momentum with the global development of science and technology, as is evidenced by its wide usage in numerous fields (Pannu, 2015). As it is increasingly integrated into educational environments and teaching processes, AI is gaining more importance in this field and attracts attention with its apparent advantages over traditional teaching methods (Chassignol et al., 2018; Roll and Wylie, 2016). While optimizing the learning environment, AI facilitates student excitement, initiative and creativity, and makes classroom management more efficient for teachers (Colchester et al., 2017; Yang and Bai, 2020; Tuomi, 2018; Wang, 2020). In this context, AI applications in education offer opportunities for reform in this field through the integration of teaching and learning (Huang, 2021).

Applications of AI in education clearly demonstrate the significant advantages offered by intelligence-based systems. The effects of AI are manifested through various benefits such as improved learning outcomes, efficiency in time and cost, and global access to high quality education. Personalized learning and intelligent tutoring systems play an important role in increasing academic success, especially for disadvantaged groups. The global reach of AI and its potential for expansion offer richer and more effective learning experiences for students in both developed and developing countries. In addition, automated grading systems provide significant cost and time savings since teachers spend a large portion of their time on grading papers and related tasks (Kamalov, et al., 2023). AI emerges as a technology that creates revolutionary changes in education; it reshapes educational processes and enriches learning experiences with the development of human-like systems with cognitive abilities. The AI tools used in educational processes have the potential to increase academic success by improving learning outcomes, providing cost and time efficiency, as well as personalized learning opportunities for disadvantaged groups. The positive effects of AI in education have the potential to reform the field and shape the future of educational systems.

CONCEPTUAL FRAMEWORK

What is Artificial Intelligence?

Artificial intelligence can be defined as an interdisciplinary field that aims to imitate the cognitive functions of human intelligence. This discipline aims to develop machines with human-like thinking abilities that can solve complex problems by drawing from various disciplines such as computer science, mathematics, psychology, neuroscience, and engineering. Artificial intelligence aims to facilitate learning, understanding, and decision-making processes by modeling human intelligence from both theoretical and applied aspects; in this context, it creates interactive systems using methods such as algorithms, data analysis, and machine learning. Today, artificial intelligence has a wide range of applications from automated processes to intelligent assistants, playing an important role in many sectors such as technology, health, finance, and education. In the field of education, AI transforms teaching methods, enriches learning experiences, and provides support to teachers.

Artificial intelligence has made significant progress in the 21st century and has found its place in institutions. In fact, in the 1940s and 1950s, scientists from the disciplines of mathematics, engineering, and computer science conducted research to explore the potential of artificial brains and define machine intelligence. In 1950, Alan Turing introduced the famous "Turing Test" that determined the concept of "Machine Intelligence." In this context, the origins of AI date back to the workshop held at Dartmouth College in 1965, where John McCarthy convinced the participants to adopt the term "Artificial Intelligence." This event is also considered the beginning of the first "Golden Age" of AI (Lui, 2018). Initially, studies in the field of artificial intelligence focused on developing programs that can solve certain problems. For example, Alan Turing's "Turing Test" questioned the ability of artificial intelligence to think like humans. In the 1960s and 1970s, basic knowledge-based systems and the first machine learning algorithms emerged (Nilsson, 1998).

In the 1990s, the increase in basic computational power and the expansion of access to larger data sets were among the main factors of the revival in the field of artificial intelligence. During this period, innovative techniques such as artificial neural networks and powerful machine learning algorithms such as support vector machines were developed. Artificial neural networks have significantly increased the capacity of data processing and machine learning through layered architectures and backpropagation algorithms, significantly increasing effectiveness in solving complex problems. This rebirth of artificial intelligence has arisen the interest of researchers and engineers in the academic and industrial fields on this subject and paved the way for the discovery of new application areas. For example, AI applications in sectors such as finance, healthcare, and automation facilitate the efficiency of systems and strengthen decision support mechanisms. This situation has led to increased research and development in the field of AI and encouraged interdisciplinary collaborations. Ultimately, the 1990s was as a period in which the basic theoretical frameworks and application areas of artificial intelligence took shape and matured.

Since the mid-2000s, applications of artificial intelligence based on machine learning and deep learning have achieved significant success in areas such as image recognition, language processing, and data analysis (LeCun, et al., 2008). Deep learning uses multilayered artificial neural networks to automatically extract meaningful features, especially from large and complex data sets. This process allows the model to perform with high accuracy on new data.

Today, AI has a crucial role in many sectors including education, healthcare, finance, automotive, and retail. In the education sector, AI-based systems aim to increase student success by providing personalized learning experiences. Additionally, analytical tools have been developed to help teachers manage course content and learning materials more effectively. The impact of AI is expected to increase in the future (Chui et al., 2016), which has the potential to provide greater automation and efficiency in both business processes and individuals' daily lives.

Artificial Intelligence in Education and Application Areas

Artificial intelligence in education (AIEd) is an innovative field with the potential to transform educational processes at the intersection of technology and learning sciences. This field aims to create flexible and inclusive learning environments by personalizing learning experiences through artificial intelligence technologies to improve student-teacher interactions and curriculum design. The development of AIEd offers significant opportunities to increase effectiveness in education and optimize teaching methods.

Applications of AI in education have been the focus of academic research for over 30 years. The discipline aims to support both formal education and lifelong learning in different learning environments, such as traditional classrooms and workplaces. By integrating AI and learning sciences (education, linguistics, sociology, psychology, anthropology, and neuroscience), AIEd contributes to the development of flexible, inclusive, and effective learning environments, as well as other AIEd tools. The main scientific goal of AIEd is to open the 'black box' of learning by making often implicit computational forms of educational, psychological, and social knowledge explicit. In this context, AIEd provides deep and detailed insights into how learning occurs, facilitating the study of the effects of learners' socio-economic and physical contexts and technology. These insights provide a foundation for the development of future AIEd software and inform approaches to non-technological learning strategies. For example, AIEd offers crucial support to instructors in understanding the micro steps of the students in learning physics and identifying common misconceptions (Luckin et al. 2016).

In general, the education system consists of four main components: student, teacher, curriculum, and learning environment. The quality of the interactions between these components is directly related to the quality of the educational process. The use of artificial intelligence in education has the potential to deeply affect the learning experiences of teachers and students. Artificial intelligence solutions, which can be applied in a wide range from traditional classroom environments to digital platforms, offer significant opportunities for personalizing learning processes and optimizing teaching methods, as well as increasing student success. In this context, applications enhanced by artificial intelligence are considered a strategic tool to increase the effectiveness in education.

At present, artificial intelligence is widely used in education and its applications are not limited to knowledge-based approaches. Data and logic-based artificial intelligence methods offer various opportunities in different aspects of educational process. These applications include personalized learning systems, dialogue systems, exploratory learning supports, data mining in education, student performance analysis, intelligent teacher assistants, chatbots, support systems for students with special needs, robot interactions with children, artificial intelligence-supported assessment tools, and automatic test creation systems. The main purpose of these technologies is to enrich the learning experience of students and provide administrative support to educational institutions. For instance, areas such as course programs and personnel management, exam organization, and cybersecurity measures directly contribute to school management while indirectly affecting teaching processes (Holmes et al., 2019). Artificial intelligence is an interdisciplinary research field that covers various areas such as machine learning, algorithm development, and natural language processing. This technology plays an important role in reshaping educational materials and methods. Among the innovative solutions offered by AI in education are supporting students' learning processes through individualized learning platforms, providing teachers with the opportunity to conduct performance evaluations with automatic evaluation systems, and performing analysis on learners' behaviors with facial recognition technologies. In this context, the use of AI in the field of education provides significant opportunities for improving the learning experience and the effectiveness of teaching practices.

Personalized Learning

Personalized learning has emerged in recent years as a promising teaching method to meet different learner needs. Personalized learning is defined as "teaching that is accelerated in accordance with learning needs, adapted to learning preferences, and shaped according to the special interests of individuals" (Bernacki, 2021).

Personalized learning dates back to the long-term work of John Dewey, who advocated the idea of placing learners at the center of education in the early 20th century. Dewey encouraged a student-centered approach to education by emphasizing the importance of the learning experience and the needs of individuals in education. He argues that learning is not just about the transfer of information, but also requires the student to actively participate, explore, and learn in their own unique ways. In this context, personalized learning represents an effort to provide education that is appropriate for each student's individual needs and learning styles. Dewey's work paved the way for the development of more customized and interactive approaches in education systems. It became clear that educators should utilize diverse teaching methods in accordance with the different abilities and interests of their learners.

Dewey's ideas inspired the development of personalized learning approaches in today's education. The concept began to take shape when educational reformers criticized the standard approach to the industrialized education system and began to seek different solutions to address diversity (Redding, 2016). For example, the Personalized System of Instruction (PSI), introduced by Fred Keller in 1968, emphasizes self-paced learning, mastery learning, and small group instruction, which is considered an early effort to implement personalized instruction approaches and a precursor to personalized learning (Keller, 1968). The foundations of personalized learning are based on John Dewey's philosophy of student-centered education. Dewey emphasized the role of individual experiences in education and argued that effective learning occurs with the active participation of students. Educational reforms so far tended to develop new pedagogical approaches that take student diversity into account, and in this context, the Personalized System of Instruction, introduced by Fred Keller in 1968, is considered an early example of personalized learning practices.

In recent years, education systems in countries such as the United Kingdom, the United States, Finland, and Canada have been shifted towards personalized learning practices to meet the increasing diversity among students and provide quality education to all students. These efforts aim to achieve equality and inclusiveness in the field of education with approaches that focus on personal learning needs and different learning styles. Personalized learning aims to increase educational success and improve the overall effectiveness of the education system by providing learning experiences that are appropriate for the individual needs of students. In this context, educational reforms and policies focus on the development of innovative strategies for diversifying teaching methods and improving learning environments.

Personalized learning systems, i.e. adaptive learning platforms, are among the most important AI applications in education. These systems provide varying learning materials based on individual needs. For instance, instead of reading a textbook or solving problems on a question sheet, students learn the course content through interactive media. Comparisons of test scores show that using personalized learning systems to learn a subject lead to higher scores compared to traditional instruction methods. A recent study by Microsoft in 2018 on over 2,000 students and teachers from Singapore, United States, United Kingdom, and Canada revealed that AI contributes to the learning progress of students. These platforms identify the gaps in students' knowledge and adapt the relevant tools to support progress. While these systems create learning models based on students' knowledge level, current platforms do not yet involve learners' emotional and social states. Accelerated by the widely adopted distant education practices throughout the COVID-19 pandemic, personalized learning systems present an improved experience of distant education that has the potential to reshape K-12 education in the future (Akgun and Greenhow; 2022).

Artificial intelligence assesses not only the information provided, but also the learning processes and emotional states of students, offering a more personalized, flexible, and engaging learning experience for students (Luckin, et al, 2016). Consequently, learning environments (e.g. schools) can be improved in various ways by teachers and students using artificial intelligence. In other words, artificial intelligence offers important advantages to everyone involved in the educational process, improving the tasks in the process in various ways.

Intelligent Tutoring Systems

Intelligent Tutoring Systems (ITS) are computerized learning environments that provide feedback based on learning processes through computational models. These systems aim to provide adaptable and effective learning experiences in accordance with the individual needs of students. Within educational technologies, subgroups that provide feedback specifically for students seeking help are determined as Dialogue Systems and Pedagogical Conversational Agents, which offer interactions similar to raising hands in the classroom environment. These technologies can simulate natural language use by interacting with users and thus support learning processes by providing specific feedback to students (Wollny et al., 2021).

Most ITSs are implemented with expert system technology and computer models that support this technology. Intelligent Tutoring Systems were first introduced in the 1970s and have acquired an important place among innovative approaches in the field of education. These systems cover the subcategories of educational technologies that integrate object-oriented systems, databases, communication infrastructures, and artificial intelligence methods. Students can use Intelligent Tutoring Systems to learn without human intervention through interactive learning experiences that can be adapted to individual needs (Zafari et al., 2022). This process demonstrates the potential of Intelligent Tutoring Systems to create student-centered learning environments. In particular, the automation of the teaching process allows teachers to use their time more efficiently, while allowing students to make progress at their own pace. In this context, Intelligent Tutoring Systems have an important role in providing personalized learning experiences in education and enable future educational technology research.

Intelligent Tutoring Systems optimize the learning experience by offering step-by-step, well-defined, and structured instructions for students in subjects such as mathematics or physics. ITS creates a structured learning roadmap with learning materials and activities, responding to individual misconceptions and success rates, based on subject knowledge and pedagogical principles. Along with the students' progress, ITS modifies the difficulty level and offers instructions when necessary. All these processes are designed to help students learn a particular subject effectively. In this respect, ITS offers an innovative approach to education by responding to individual learning needs. Intelligent tutoring systems can take many forms, but they typically include several AI models; AI models are highly simplified computational representations of certain knowledge about the real world (such as the semantic networks, ontologies, or knowledge graphs used by SCHOLAR). The models of ITS represent information specific to learning. Generally, information related to the subject matter is represented in a domain model, information related to effective teaching is represented in a pedagogical model, and information related to the student is represented in a learner model. The ITS algorithm utilizes these three models to create a series of activities for each student. Intelligent Tutoring Systems (ITS) are systems that provide customized educational experiences to individual students using a set of artificial intelligence models. These systems adapt students' learning activities using three main models: Domain Model, Pedagogical Model, and Learner Model (Holmes et al., 2019). Figure 1 below demonstrates how domain, pedagogical, and learner models can be linked in an ITS.

Figure 1. ITS architecture with pedagogy, domain, learner, and open learner models (Holmes et al., 2019)

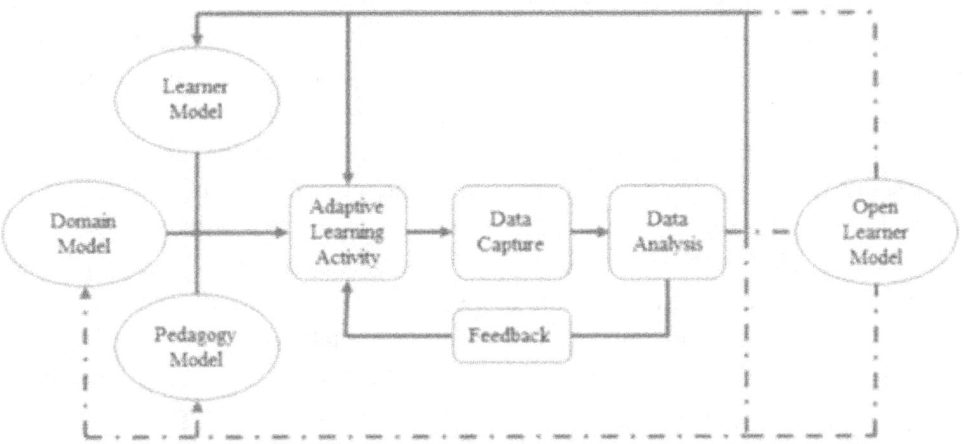

Domain Model: This model represents information related to the subject matter that ITS aims to teach students. For example, it includes information such as mathematical operations or the causes of historical events. The domain model usually focuses on well-structured and defined subjects; fields such as mathematics and physics are frequently used subjects for Streamed Learning Systems.

Pedagogy Model: This model involves information on effective learning and teaching methods obtained from research in educational sciences and teaching experts. For example, concepts such as appropriate educational approaches, individualized feedback, and Vygotsky's zone of convergent development are included in this model. The pedagogy model balances the difficulty level of the activities presented to students and provides appropriate feedback according to their learning needs.

Learner Model: This model provides information about the student's learning status and includes information such as the student's previous interactions, materials they struggle with, and misunderstandings. The system may also include information about other students who have learned similar topics in the past. This model is used to design personalized learning paths based on students' individual needs and experiences.

When they are combined, these three models form the basis of the ITS algorithm and decide which activities are to be presented to students and how they are adapted. For instance, in a mathematics ITS, the domain model might include information on binary equations, the pedagogical model might reflect effective teaching strategies, and the student model might reflect the student's achievements and difficulties in this subject. These constructions come together to support the learning process and create a personalized educational experience.

Automatic Essay Scoring Systems

Automated essay scoring systems stand out as an important application of artificial intelligence in education. By automating assessment processes, AI provides acceleration and has the potential to provide personalized feedback to students.

One of the primary motivations for the development of automated essay scoring systems (AES) has been the need to score student writing, such as large-scale, course-intensive university courses and the entrance exams. Recently, massive open online course (MOOC) providers such as EdX, Coursera, and Udacity have included automated scoring engines to grade the written work of thousands of students. While early systems typically provided an overall writing quality score, some now offer students guidance, sample writing materials, and detailed feedback to help them improve their writing. These systems include the Educational Testing Service's Criterion Online Writing Evaluation Service, Turnitin's Revision Assistant, Pearson's Write to Learn, Grammarly, and Chegg's WriteLab (Murphy, 2019).

Using machine learning and natural language processing (NLP) techniques, AI can analyze student responses in detail, from multiple-choice questions to essays and oral answers. AI-based scoring tools are particularly useful in assessing complex assignments such as essay writing and problem solving. In this way, educators' workload is reduced, while the grading is more consistent and accurate. Providing instant feedback provides a more unbiased assessment process by minimizing human biases and assessment errors. These features allow educators to spend more time on other tasks, such as syllabus development and student engagement. In addition, AI has less limitations than teachers, allowing them to offer more detailed feedback. Since examining mistakes is a crucial component of learning, providing detailed feedback has a critical role in understanding the subject. Automatic AI-enabled evaluation tools are able to analyze performance and determine the points in which students may need further support (Vittorini et al., 2021).

Feedback is associated with cybernetics, control and systems theory, and is at the foundation of artificial intelligence because it is the most straightforward element of human-machine interaction. Mirchi et al. have developed a system called Virtual Operative Assistant, which provides feedback based on performance analysis, using AI for simulation in the medical field. Similarly, Janpla and Piriyasurawong examined the use of AI in test generation for e-learning and developed intelligent software for online exams (González-Calatayud et al,2021).

Automated essay scoring and the integration of artificial intelligence in education play a critical role in the evolution of today's education systems. Artificial intelligence increases teaching effectiveness by accelerating assessment processes and providing feedback customized to students' needs; this encourages students to be more actively involved in their learning process. Furthermore, the adoption of this innovative technology by MOOC (Massive Open Online Course) platforms has the potential to reach a wide audience and democratize learning opportunities. However, effective use of these systems requires a learning environment in which educators can provide guidance and support without eliminating the human factor.

Dialogue-Based Tutorial Systems

Within the framework of intelligent tutorial systems (ITS), SCHOLAR has, in a sense, enabled the development of dialogue-based instructional systems. Dialog-Based Instructional Systems (DBTS) are discussed in conjunction with Jaime Carbonell's SCHOLAR. SCHOLAR differs from other Intelligent Instructional Systems (ITS) in at least one respect. While traditional ITSs aim to present individualized educational materials and learning activities, SCHOLAR encourages students to interact through dialogues on the subject. This dialogue-centered approach has led to the development of a version of ITS known as DBTS. Traditionally, these systems involved individualized instructional materials and learning activities (this is the main feature of ITSs), while SCHOLAR guides students on the subjects utilizing a dialogue-centered approach (Carbonell, 1970). Unlike ITSs, dialogue-based tutoring systems (DBTSs) use techniques such as fuzzy logic developed for this specific purpose. Dialogue-based tutoring systems help learners understand subjects more deeply by encouraging active participation. This interactive approach not only helps students acquire knowledge, but also improves critical thinking. One of the important systems that can be an example of DBTS is CIRCSIM designed by Rovick and Michael (1986).

One of the first examples of DBTS, CIRCSIM-Tutor, teaches through problem solving. For instance, the system offers a definition of a physiological change and asks the student to make a prediction about the effect of this change on several physiological variables. It then starts a dialogue to fix the mistakes of the student in their predictions. It consists of seven modules: the teaching planner, the student model, input comprehension, text generator, screen manager, problem solving, and knowledge base. The teaching planner consists of two levels: a lesson planner and a discourse planner. The lesson planner creates lesson objectives and divides them into discourse tasks. The discourse planner manages the exchange between the teacher and student. Most tasks are carried out in the form of questions. When the student gives an unexpected answer to a question, the planner adds new tasks to the learning plan to achieve the learning outcome (Zhou et al 1999).

Among the dialogue-based tutoring systems are AutoTutor and WatsonTutor. AutoTutor has been developed by researchers at the Institute for Intelligent Systems at the University of Memphis, which is a computer tutor that mimics a human tutor, to recreate the dialogue patterns of human tutors (Graesser et al., 1999). As a tutoring system that works based on the use of natural language, AutoTutor has yielded significant learning outcomes in a variety of areas, including computer literacy, physics, and critical thinking.

Careful decisions had to be made about when teachers should be imitated and when idealized teaching strategies that humans could not easily implement should be employed (Graesser 2011; Graesser et al., 2009). AutoTutor integrates patterns identified in regular teaching protocols (Graesser et al., 2009, 1995) and idealized strategies derived from basic learning research (e.g., modeling-reinforcement-extinction, learning progressions). The primary research goal was to determine which features promote learning and student motivation (Graesser 2011; Graesser et al., 2012a, b). Overall, AutoTutor has been highly effective as a learning technology. AutoTutor yielded learning outcomes of 0.8σ (standard deviation units) on average over control groups that read static teaching materials (e.g., textbooks) and was implemented for the same amount of time (Graesser 2011; Graesser et al., 2012b). Inspired by human teachers and implementing well-defined teaching methods, AutoTutor offers students significant gains by enriching the learning experience. The significant learning gains over static resources demonstrate the potential of such interactive systems in education.

AUTOTUTOR is a complex system that mimics a human teacher by engaging in a natural language dialogue with learners. AutoTutor creates challenging questions that require about a paragraph of knowledge to answer correctly. An example question in the field of conceptual physics is: "When a headless car is rear-ended, occupants typically sustain neck injuries. Explain why the occupants in this situation sustain neck injuries." A perfect answer to this question is three to seven sentences long, but the initial answers given by real human learners typically range from one word to two sentences. AutoTutor helps the learner construct an improved answer that demonstrate their knowledge level and adaptively corrects any problems in their answer. The dialogue between AutoTutor and the learner typically lasts 50 to 200 speaking rounds for a single challenging question (Graesser, et al., 2005). AutoTutor is a sophisticated system that simulates the teaching process by engaging in a natural language dialogue with learners. The challenging questions test the depth of students' knowledge, while providing opportunities to develop their typically short answers. They provide a guiding platform for students to expand their thinking. The system provides adaptive feedback to uncover students' knowledge and improve their answers. This process increases the intensity of interaction, enriching the learning experience.

An AutoTutor instructional dialogue typically proceeds through a five-step instructional framework: (1) The instructor presents a problem, (2) The student attempts to respond, (3) The instructor provides a short feedback, (4) Collaborative interaction occurs to develop the answer, and (5) The instructor checks the student's understanding (Graesser et al., 1995). The AutoTutor instructional dialogue is a structured learning process that actively engages students. The instructor's questions stimulate thinking, while the feedback provided develops the student's responses. Collaborative interactions reinforce learning, and checking the student's understanding increases the effectiveness of the process. These stages create a dynamic interaction that supports learning.

Another dialogue-based tutoring system, Watson Tutor, is designed to provide the opportunity to interact with content and self-assess by expressing their thoughts in their own words. The aim of these activities is to improve learning outcomes. It reaches these goals by coordinating a series of learning activities following a well-defined dialogue strategy. Activities used include (Afzal, 2019):

- Starting with broad questions and then delving deeper into the topic; providing clues and identifying misconceptions along the way.
- Suggesting related questions that students frequently ask instructors and encourage discovery.
- Incorporating relevant multimedia content to facilitate further learning.
- Conducting compare and contrast activities to test basic understanding of concepts.

Watson Tutor and AutoTutor are both interactive tutoring systems that support student learning. However, there are some important differences between them.

While Watson Tutor guides students through natural language dialogues, AutoTutor offers interaction in a question-answer format. Watson Tutor focuses on improving students' understanding with an approach aimed at deepening their cognitive processes. AutoTutor, on the other hand, aims to help students understand the subject by introducing new information during the learning process. While Watson Tutor aims to provide in-depth understanding by focusing on existing knowledge, AutoTutor prioritizes enriching the learning experience by transferring new information. These differences play an important role in determining which system will be more effective according to the needs of the users. Watson Tutor is an interactive tutoring system that guides students' review sessions using natural language dialogues. Like AutoTutor and CIRCSIM, it aims to go beyond introducing new information and provide students with a deeper understanding of their previously acquired knowledge.

Advantages of Using Artificial Intelligence in Education

Following UNESCO's 2030 Agenda for Sustainable Development, the role of teachers has changed significantly in order to ensure quality and equal access worldwide, which is one of the main goals of this agenda (ODS4). Technological evolution creates a technological ecosystem, defined as "a metaphor that expresses a necessary evolution in traditional education systems formed by the combination of different software components and services that share a certain semantic data flow." Part of this evolution is shaped by the impact of algorithms and computerization in education. For this reason, many people fear that "AI-supported robots will soon completely replace human teachers." Although this may seem like a threat, it also presents an opportunity (Vivar and Penalvo, 2023).

The advantages of using AI in education are diverse and all-encompassing. Based on current research, the contributions of AI-based methods to learning and teaching processes can be systematically summarized with the following list (Owoc, 2019).

- The first advantage is the existence of a system that provides automatic evaluation of answer sheets submitted by students by modeling teacher behavior. This system analyzes knowledge levels and utilizes advanced algorithms to process them. In addition, it contributes to the learning process by providing detailed feedback to students. The system also facilitates development of personalized teaching plans, thus suggesting compatible and effective learning paths for each student's individual needs. This approach aims to increase efficiency in education and improve the quality of learning outcomes.
- Secondly, spaced repetition method provides reviews when the student is close to forgetting it. The SuperMemo app, introduced by Polish inventor Peter Wozniak, is based on the spaced repetition method. This app tracks

what the user has learned and when. Using artificial intelligence techniques, the app can detect when the user is closest to forgetting something and make suggestions for reviewing information.

- The third advantage is that feedback provided by machine learning and language processing improve the quality of evaluations. For example, a chatbot can collect feedback through a conversation like a human interviewer, with minimal effort from the user. Furthermore, each conversation can be adjusted to the personality of the student. A chatbot can also determine reasons for certain ideas.
- Fourth, the use of virtual facilitators can support teachers in classroom work. For example, a teaching assistant named Jill Watson (JW) was introduced in the Knowledge-Based Artificial Intelligence (KBAI) course held at the Georgia Institute of Technology. Since the spring semester of 2016, JW has been independently responding to student interactions in various online discussion forums within the scope of the KBAI course, answering frequently asked routine questions, and sharing weekly announcements. This practice supports the learning process by providing immediate answers to students' questions while reducing the burden on teachers.
- Fifth, Watts has developed a chat campus based on IBM Watson cognitive computing technologies. Students at Deakin University ask IBM Watson 1600 questions per week to learn details about campus life and education on the cloud. In the 12 months since Watson was implemented, this innovative solution has answered more than 55,000 student questions. In addition, the school is improving the use of Watson, training the system to understand new information.
- Personalized learning can be considered the sixth artificial intelligence application in education. In general, this concept refers to various educational programs in which the learning pace and teaching strategies are customized to suit the specific needs of each individual. In particular, educational content is adapted to the learning preferences and individual interests of each student, making learning experience more effective. This approach offers the potential to improve educational outcomes by allowing students to learn at their own pace while increasing their motivation.
- Cheating is a significant concern of all teachers. In this context, AI-supported anti-cheating systems stand out as another AI application offered in the field of education. Proctoring is a software designed to secure the identity of the student during the exam and to restrain cheating attempts. Thanks to this system, a supervisory tool is available at all times, increasing exam security and ensuring integrity. Artificial intelligence is integrated into this supervision

process, providing instant monitoring and analysis capabilities, thus contributing to the prevention of fraudulent actions in educational processes.

- The final solution proposed by Watts is data accumulation and personalization. For example, learning grammar rules can be supported by examples from the subject that is of interest to the individual. This approach can make learning processes more effective, especially by increasing motivation.

Researchers summarize the scenarios regarding the use of artificial intelligence in educational processes for various stakeholders as follows: Individuals participating in educational processes can benefit from customized and individual learning opportunities provided by artificial intelligence. Professionals operating in pedagogical and scientific-pedagogical fields apply artificial intelligence technologies to increase education quality and improve pedagogical competences. Managers of educational institutions can gain the ability to manage and direct changes within the institution more effectively with the opportunities offered by artificial intelligence technologies. In addition, e-learning resources reduce costs and produce more effective learning materials by using artificial intelligence technologies (Yuskovych-Zhukovska, 2022). Artificial intelligence has a crucial role in the restructuring of the education system and deeply affects management, teaching and learning processes. The function of artificial intelligence, which was initially limited to simple computer-aided teaching applications, has undergone a significant evolution over time. Today's modern artificial intelligence systems make the educational experience richer by using artificial intelligence-supported chatbots along with web-based platforms, robot technologies and systems integrated into devices.

Disadvantages of Using Artificial Intelligence in Education

Although artificial intelligence has the potential to revolutionize the education system, it also causes some concerns.

Factors that are often overlooked in AI applications include adequate assessment of cost and financing, teacher training and continuous professional development, complementary curriculum support and implementation of pedagogical strategies, and parents being a stakeholder in the learning process (Nye, 2015). An integrated assessment of these factors is a critical requirement for the most efficient use of the potential of AI in education. The interaction of these factors with each other is a factor that directly affects the success of AI applications. If these factors are not considered, the impact of AI projects may be limited, and the expected results may not be achieved. Therefore, adopting a comprehensive and multidimensional approach to AI integration in education is indispensable to increase success and ensure sustainable impact.

In modern society, artificial intelligence requires constant innovation and information support for development. Both the development and sustainability of artificial intelligence require significant financial investments. The design and continuous functionality of intelligent educational tools require a qualified technical team and high research and development costs. The evolution of artificial intelligence systems necessitates constant updating and renewal of these systems to adapt to dynamic educational needs. Changes in educational processes increase the need for continuous training for personnel, which can create significant cost elements. Therefore, investments in terms of time, resources, and educational expenses become inevitable. The constantly changing educational environment and demands require teachers and other educational personnel to receive continuous training and updates to keep their professional knowledge and skills up to date. The establishment of a systematic training mechanism for effective artificial intelligence integration is of great importance (Guan, 2023).

Data privacy and security concerns are another significant issue in all technological advances. Personal data, contact information, and location details can be exposed to various threats, such as cyberattacks and government surveillance. These issues are also present in AI applications in the field of education. With the integration of AI tools in educational institutions, sensitive data such as students' personal information, academic records, and behavioral patterns are collected and processed. This poses significant risks to stakeholders due to the possibility of unauthorized access or misuse of such data. Violation of individuals' privacy rights and the possibility of discriminatory practices are among the main related threats. In addition, inadequate data security measures can lead to data breaches or leaks, which can increase concerns in this regard and weaken trust in AI-based education systems. Data privacy and security issues brought about by AI applications in education are a result of analysis and personalization processes based on large amounts of student data. In this context, there is a challenge of striking a delicate balance between leveraging the potential to transform education while at the same time protecting data privacy and security (Kamalov, et al., 2023)

Ensuring fairness is of critical importance in using AI applications in education. As AI is being improved, developing countries are at risk of further deepening educational divides through new technologies. Just as the digital divide separates those who have internet access from those who do not, the widening algorithmic divide also poses the danger of missing out on many educational opportunities offered by AI. Since most AI algorithms come from developed countries, they cannot fully consider the specific conditions of developing countries and cannot be directly applied (Yu, 2020). The education sector must overcome significant obstacles, such as the basic infrastructure and technological deficiencies required for AI to enhance learning.

According to Chassignol et al. (2018), while artificial intelligence has a transformative potential in education, the social and emotional dimensions of learning should also be considered. Effective learning is facilitated with the personalization and increased efficiency provided by artificial intelligence-supported technologies, as well as the social interaction and individual guidance provided by the human teacher. Therefore, artificial intelligence should be considered as a complementary tool in the role of teachers, and the importance of social interaction should never be ignored. Although the use of artificial intelligence-based systems provides many advantages in terms of the quality of education, a system in which teachers are completely disabled will not be functional. Because artificial intelligence systems are based on big data analysis, even if they undertake the task of personal teaching, they can sometimes give wrong results in special cases (Chassignol et al., 2018)

O'Neil (2016) discusses the effects of biases in AI algorithms on discriminatory practices in education, indicating that this situation can lead to ethical issues. Studies examining how teachers adopt AI applications are also important. In addition, a study by Huang et al. (2021) draws attention to research results indicating that AI applications may negatively affect students' commitment to learning. Finally, AI systems ignoring the human factor in education can weaken teacher-student interaction. This can negatively affect students' social and emotional development and weaken their educational experiences.

CONCLUSION

According to Edward Fredkin, director of the Massachusetts Institute of Technology (MIT) Artificial Intelligence Laboratory and a faculty member at Carnegie Mellon University, there are three important events that have occurred throughout history. The first of these is the creation of the universe, and the second is the beginning of life. The third event, which Fredkin finds as important as the beginning of life, is the emergence of artificial intelligence (Copeland, 1998).

Artificial intelligence technologies, with the wide range of opportunities and innovative solutions they offer in the field of education, have the potential to radically transform the learning process. This study examines the critical importance of AI applications in education, the innovative solutions they provide in classrooms and education systems, application areas and future strategies in detail, and examines the ways they contribute to the development of education. AI plays a major role in increasing student success, optimizing teaching processes and developing pedagogical competencies of teachers by supporting individualized learning experiences.

AI applications in education not only address the individual learning needs of students, but also offer opportunities to modernize teaching methods. In this respect, the use of AI in education is of critical importance in terms of creating an educational environment that is suitable for the requirements of the technological age. However, ethical issues such as data privacy, algorithmic biases, teacher training and continuous professional development must be considered for the effective integration of AI in education. Education systems should develop more comprehensive and multidimensional approaches by taking these elements into account.

In conclusion, while the use of AI in education provides various advantages, it also poses some issues in practice. Ethical, social, and emotional dimensions should be addressed without ignoring the human factor, and these elements should be considered in the development of AI applications. Educational institutions should continuously adapt to changes to make the education systems of the future more effective, accessible, and inclusive by utilizing the innovative opportunities offered by artificial intelligence.

Providing equal opportunities in education, ensuring data security, and supporting teachers' professional development through methods that allow them to benefit from artificial intelligence technologies are of crucial importance for sustainable education systems. Strategic steps to be taken to maximize the potential of AI in education, to provide students with richer, more engaging, and more effective learning experiences, and ultimately to increase the quality of education will form the basis of future success in education.

In summary, the integration of artificial intelligence in education is not only a technology investment, but also part of a reform that will structurally transform education systems and support individual and social development. In this process, effective cooperation between all stakeholders is a critical requirement for the sustainability of the transformation in education. Innovative solutions provided by artificial intelligence in education will be an important tool in creating a more effective and fair learning environment in the future.

Suggestions for the sustainability of education systems are as follows;

Innovative Educational Practices: Educational institutions should adopt innovative teaching methods by encouraging the integration of new technologies, which will increase student engagement and motivation.

Continuous Professional Development: Educational programs should be regularly offered to teachers to provide information about AI and other new technologies. Teachers should be armed with the necessary skills to use new technologies effectively.

Data Security and Privacy: With the use of AI in education, the security and privacy of data is of utmost importance. Education systems must comply with data protection laws and be transparent about protecting student data.

Providing Equal Opportunities: AI applications in education should provide equal access to all students. Educational resources should target disadvantaged groups and promote social equality.

REFERENCES

Afzal, S., Dempsey, B., D'Helon, C., Mukhi, N., Pribic, M., Sickler, A., & Wilde, L. (2019). The personality of AI systems in education: Experiences with the Watson tutor, a one-on-one virtual tutoring system. *Childhood Education*, 95(1), 44–52. DOI: 10.1080/00094056.2019.1565809

Akgun, S., & Greenhow, C. (2022). Artificial intelligence in education: Addressing ethical challenges in K-12 settings. *AI and Ethics*, 2(3), 431–440. DOI: 10.1007/s43681-021-00096-7 PMID: 34790956

Bernacki, M. L., Greene, M. J., & Lobczowski, N. G. (2021). A systematic review of research on personalized learning: Personalized by whom, to what, how, and for what purpose(s*)?Educational Psychology Review*, 33(4), 1675–1715. DOI: 10.1007/s10648-021-09615-8

Carbonell, J. R. (1970). AI in CAI: An artificial-intelligence approach to computer-assisted instruction. *IEEE Transactions on Man-Machine Systems*, 11(4), 190–202. DOI: 10.1109/TMMS.1970.299942

Chassignol, M., Khoroshavin, A., Klimova, A., & Bilyatdinova, A. (2018). Artificial Intelligence trends in education: A narrative overview. *Procedia Computer Science*, 136, 16–24. DOI: 10.1016/j.procs.2018.08.233

Chen, L., Chen, P., & Lin, Z. (2020). Artificial intelligence in education: A review. *IEEE Access : Practical Innovations, Open Solutions*, 8, 75264–75278. DOI: 10.1109/ACCESS.2020.2988510

Chui, M., Manyika, J., & Miremadi, M. (2016). Where machines could replace humans-and where they can't (yet). *The McKinsey Quarterly*, •••, 1–12.

Colchester, K., Hagras, H., Alghazzawi, D., & Aldabbagh, G. (2017). A survey of artificial intelligence techniques employed for adaptive educational systems within e-learning platforms. *Journal of Artificial Intelligence and Soft Computing Research*, 7(1), 47–64. DOI: 10.1515/jaiscr-2017-0004

Copeland, J. (1993). *Artificial intelligence: A philosophical introduction*. John Wiley & Sons.

González-Calatayud, V., Prendes-Espinosa, P., & Roig-Vila, R. (2021). Artificial intelligence for student assessment: A Systematic Review. *Applied Sciences (Basel, Switzerland)*, 11(12), 5467. DOI: 10.3390/app11125467

Graesser, A. C. (2009). Inaugural editorial for Journal of Educational Psychology. *Journal of Educational Psychology*, 101(2), 259–261. DOI: 10.1037/a0014883

Graesser, A. C., Chipman, P., Haynes, B. C., & Olney, A. (2005). AutoTutor: An intelligent tutoring system with mixed-initiative dialogue. *IEEE Transactions on Education*, 48(4), 612–618. DOI: 10.1109/TE.2005.856149

Graesser, A. C., Conley, M. W., & Olney, A. M. (2012a). Intelligent tutoring systems. In Graham, S., & Harris, K. (Eds.), APA Educational Psychology Handbook: Vol. 3. *Applications to Learning and Teaching* (pp. 451–473). American Psychological Association.

Graesser, A. C., D'Mello, S. K., Hu, X., Cai, Z., Olney, A., & Morgan, B. (2012b). AutoTutor. In McCarthy, P., & Boonthum-Denecke, C. (Eds.), *Applied natural language processing: Identification, investigation, and resolution (ss* (pp. 169–187). IGI Global. DOI: 10.4018/978-1-60960-741-8.ch010

Graesser, A. C., Person, N. K., & Magliano, J. P. (1995). Collaborative dialogue patterns in naturalistic one-toone tutoring. *Applied Cognitive Psychology*, 9(6), 1–28. DOI: 10.1002/acp.2350090604

Graesser, A. C., Wiemer-Hastings, K., Wiemer-Hastings, P., & Kreuz, R.Tutoring Research Group. (1999). AutoTutor:A simulation of a human tutor. *Cognitive Systems Research*, 1(1), 35–51. DOI: 10.1016/S1389-0417(99)00005-4

Guan, H. (2023). Advantages and Challenges of Using Artificial Intelligence in Primary and Secondary School Education. *Journal of Education. Humanities and Social Sciences*, 22, 377–383.

Holmes, W., Bialik, M., & Fadel, C. (2019). *Artificial intelligence in education:promises and implications for teaching and learning*. Center for Curriculum Redesign.

Huang, J., Saleh, S., & Liu, Y. (2021). A review on artificial intelligence in education. *Academic Journal of Interdisciplinary Studies*, 10(3), 206–217. DOI: 10.36941/ajis-2021-0077

Kamalov, F., Santandreu Calonge, D., & Gurrib, I. (2023). New era of artificial intelligence in education: Towards a sustainable multifaceted revolution. *Sustainability (Basel)*, 15(16), 12451. DOI: 10.3390/su151612451

Keller, F. S. (1968). Good-bye, teacher.... *Journal of Applied Behavior Analysis*, 1(1), 79–89. DOI: 10.1901/jaba.1968.1-79 PMID: 16795164

LeCun, Y., Bottou, L., Bengio, Y., & Haffner, P. (1998). Gradient-based learning applied to document recognition. *Proceedings of the IEEE*, 86(11), 2278–2324. DOI: 10.1109/5.726791

Liu, J., Kong, X., Xia, F., Bai, X., Wang, L., Qing, Q., & Lee, I. (2018). Artificial intelligence in the 21st century. *IEEE Access : Practical Innovations, Open Solutions*, 6, 34403–34421. DOI: 10.1109/ACCESS.2018.2819688

Luckin, R., Holmes, W., Griffiths, M., & Forcier, L. B. (2016). *Intelligence unleashed: An argument for AI in Education*. Pearson.

Murphy, R. F. (2019). Artificial intelligence applications to support k-12 teachers and teaching: A review of promising applications, opportunities, and challenges. Perspective. *RAND Corporation* (1-20).

Nilsson, N. J. (1998). *Artificial intelligence: a new synthesis*. Morgan Kaufmann.

Nye, B. D. (2015). Intelligent tutoring systems by and for the developing world: A review of trends and approaches for educational technology in a global context. *International Journal of Artificial Intelligence in Education*, 25(2), 177–203. DOI: 10.1007/s40593-014-0028-6

O'Neil, C. (2016). *Weapons of Math Destruction: How Big Data Increases Inequality and Threatens Democracy*. Crown Publishing Group.

Owoc, M. L., Sawicka, A., & Weichbroth, P. (2019, August). Artificial intelligence technologies in education: benefits, challenges and strategies of implementation. In *IFIP International Workshop on Artificial Intelligence for Knowledge Management* (pp. 37-58). Cham: Springer International Publishing.

Pannu, A. (2015). Artificial intelligence and its application in different areas. *Artificial Intelligence*, 4(10), 79–84.

Pokrivcakova, S. (2019). Preparing teachers for the application of AI-powered technologies in foreign language education. *Journal of Language and Cultural Education*, 7(3), 135–153. DOI: 10.2478/jolace-2019-0025

Preston, J., & Bishop, M. (2006). Essays on Searle and Artificial Intelligence, Oxford: Clarendon Press, 2002, pp. xvi+ 410.

Redding, S. (2016). Competencies and personalized learning. *Handbook On Personalized Learning For States, Districts, And Schools*, 3-18.

Roll, I., & Wylie, R. (2016). Evolution and revolution in artificial intelligence in education. *International Journal of Artificial Intelligence in Education*, 26(2), 582–599. DOI: 10.1007/s40593-016-0110-3

Sharma, R. C., Kawachi, P., & Bozkurt, A. (2019). The landscape of artificial intelligence in open, online and distance education: Promises and concerns. *Asian Journal of Distance Education*, 14(2), 1–2.

Vittorini, P., Menini, S., & Tonelli, S. (2021). An AI-based system for formative and summative assessment in data science courses. *International Journal of Artificial Intelligence in Education*, 31(2), 159–185. DOI: 10.1007/s40593-020-00230-2

Vivar, J. M. F., & Peñalvo, F. J. G. (2023). Reflexiones sobre la ética, potencialidades y retos de la Inteligencia Artificial en el marco de la Educación de Calidad (ODS4). *Comunicar: Revista Cientifica De Comunicacion y Educacion*, (74), 37–47.

Wartman, S. A., & Combs, C. D. (2018). Medical education must move from the information age to the age of artificial intelligence. *Academic Medicine*, 93(8), 1107–1109. DOI: 10.1097/ACM.0000000000002044 PMID: 29095704

Wollny, S., Schneider, J., Di Mitri, D., Weidlich, J., Rittberger, M., & Drachsler, H. (2021). Are we there yet?-a systematic literature review on chatbots in education. *Frontiers in Artificial Intelligence*, 4, 654924. DOI: 10.3389/frai.2021.654924 PMID: 34337392

Yang, S., & Bai, H. (2020). The integration design of artificial intelligence and normal students' education. [). IOP Publishing.]. *Journal of Physics: Conference Series*, 1453(1), 012090. DOI: 10.1088/1742-6596/1453/1/012090

Yu, P. K. (2020). Legal Studies Research Paper Series The Algorithmic Divide and Equality in the Age of Artificial Intelligence. *Florida Law Review*, 72(19), 331–389.

Yuskovych-Zhukovska, V., Poplavska, T., Diachenko, O., Mishenina, T., Topolnyk, Y., & Gurevych, R. (2022). Application of artificial intelligence in education. Problems and opportunities for sustainable development. *BRAIN. Broad Research in Artificial Intelligence and Neuroscience*, 13(1Sup1), 339-356.

Zafari, M., Bazargani, J. S., Sadeghi-Niaraki, A., & Choi, S. M. (2022). Artificial intelligence applications in K-12 education: A systematic literature review. *IEEE Access : Practical Innovations, Open Solutions*, 10, 61905–61921. DOI: 10.1109/ACCESS.2022.3179356

Zhou, Y., Freedman, R., Glass, M., Michael, J. A., Rovick, A. A., & Evens, M. W. (1999, July). Delivering hints in a dialogue-based intelligent tutoring system. In *AAAI/IAAI* (pp. 128-134).

ADDITIONAL READING

Ahmad, S. F., Alam, M. M., Rahmat, M. K., Mubarik, M. S., & Hyder, S. I. (2022). Academic and administrative role of artificial intelligence in education. *Sustainability (Basel)*, 14(3), 1101. DOI: 10.3390/su14031101

Alhumaid, K., Naqbi, S., Elsori, D., & Mansoori, M. (2023). The adoption of artificial intelligence applications in education. *International Journal of Data and Network Science*, 7(1), 457–466. DOI: 10.5267/j.ijdns.2022.8.013

Nalbant, K. G. (2021). The importance of artificial intelligence in education: A short review. *Journal Of Review in Science and Engineering*, 2021, 1–15.

KEY TERMS AND DEFINITIONS

Artificial Intelligence: A technology in which features of human intelligence are exhibited by computers.

Artificial Intelligence in Education: The use of information processing systems based on artificial intelligence in the field of education, which can participate in human-performed processes such as learning, adapting, synthesizing, self-regulating, and using information.

Expert Systems: A computer software that uses data and inference to solve complex problems that often require significant human expertise. A typical expert system consists of several components, such as a knowledge base, an inference engine, and a user interface.

Chapter 5
An In-Depth Bibliometric Analysis to Understand the Impact and Future of Artificial Intelligence in Higher Education

Hacer Yumurtaci Aydogmus
https://orcid.org/0000-0002-2307-0840
Alanya Alaaddin Keykubat University, Turkey

Ufuk Aydogmus
Alanya Alaaddin Keykubat University, Turkey

Yusuf Sait Turkan
https://orcid.org/0000-0001-7240-183X
Istanbul University-Cerrahpasa, Turkey

ABSTRACT

Currently, artificial intelligence is used in many different ways in many different sectors - for example, in the diagnosis of diseases in the field of health by processing data, for inventory management in logistics management, and for customer service in tourism. Artificial intelligence is also used in higher education institutions in different fields such as intelligent learning systems and data management. There are different studies in the literature on the use of artificial intelligence in higher education. Considering its importance, analyzing the studies in the literature comprehensively is important for understanding the applications and making it easier for educational institutions to experience an artificial intelligence adaptation process.

DOI: 10.4018/979-8-3693-7949-3.ch005

This study aims to analyze the existing studies in the literature through bibliometric analysis. Initially, in the bibliometric method, the existing literature is obtained by searching a database in line with the search words. After that, the existing literature is analyzed in different dimensions such as time and quantity.

INTRODUCTION

In 1950, Alan Turing (1950) put forth a conceptual framework for the potential of machines to think in his article "Computing Machinery and Intelligence". In the subsequent five-plus decades, artificial intelligence (AI) has demonstrated remarkable advancements and pervasive integration into numerous domains of human endeavor. Since the 1980s, the field of AI has been subdivided into distinct research domains, including machine learning, knowledge-based systems, and pattern recognition. In the contemporary era, artificial intelligence (AI) has become an indispensable component of both business operations and daily life. Currently, deep learning and machine learning, the two most prominent sub-branches of AI, are capable of making sophisticated predictions and analyses due to the use of multi-layered neural networks and big data analytics. Ünlü (2019) stated that with the development of computational power in recent years, deep ANN architectures have begun to be used to reveal hidden patterns from an extremely complex data set. The development has resulted in the implementation of innovative applications in a number of fields, including technology, finance, health, manufacturing, and the education sector. The advancement and evolution of AI applications in numerous domains of education is accompanied by a notable increase in the adoption of AI in these same domains (Roll and Wylie, 2016). The rapid expansion of AI in the field of higher education, particularly at the university level, has given rise to a surge in discourse and prompted researchers to investigate the impact of AI on higher education.

Machine learning, deep learning, and reinforcement learning are critical to AI's success in the education sector. These fields have reached a point where they are indispensable to AI's capabilities. At the beginning of AI, the goal was clear: to create machines that could perform as well as humans on specific tasks. Machine learning was the first step in this process. The emergence of machine learning was based on the idea of identifying and recognizing hidden patterns in accordance with human learning style and the perspective that computers learn without coding for certain tasks (Hurley, 2019; Rield, 2019). Later, deep learning, developed to understand complex structures in higher-dimensional data (Hinton, 2007), provided better prediction results in big data (Lecun et. al, 2015). Deep learning applications have found much larger application areas, especially in the field of e-learning, which has spread rapidly with the advances in internet technology (Muniasamy and Alasiry, 2020). Deep learning has achieved significant success in areas such as image and voice recognition and has been used in many studies that have brought about groundbreaking developments in the education sector (Hernández-Blanco et al., 2019). Reinforcement learning (RL) is a computational paradigm for sequential decision making and goal-oriented learning (Wiering and Otterlo, 2012; Sutton and Barto, 2018). RL differs from supervised and unsupervised learning in that it focuses on the agent learning through direct contact with its environment. It has found application in many areas of the education sector, including techniques for the teacher-student framework, examination systems, educational content, personalized content, and applications in e-learning (Mon et al., 2023).

The advent of AI has precipitated substantial transformations in the realm of higher education, among other sectors. The application of AI in educational contexts presents a range of potential benefits, including the ability to tailor learning experiences, monitor student progress, and assess the effectiveness of educational materials. In the field of education, AI can be utilized to determine the factors affecting student performance (Baradwaj and Pal, 2011), predict student success (Koçoğlu et al., 2017), develop learning tools and learning techniques (Kavitha et al., 2018). In addition, AI has been utilized to develop novel learning methodologies (Khare and Stewart, 2018; Taneri, 2020), identify at-risk students at an earlier stage (Minaei-Bidgoli et al., 2003; Baneres, 2019), and monitor and enhance curriculum and resource management (Muniasamy & Alasiry, 2020). In educational institutions, it is essential to evaluate a range of factors and leverage new technologies to enhance guidance and psychological counseling services (Cil et al. 2014). Furthermore, AI technologies have the potential to facilitate personalized and adaptable learning processes that diverge from conventional learning and teaching approaches (Florea & Radu, 2019). Students may benefit from personalized support throughout the learning process, facilitated by AI-supported learning platforms and digital assistants, which could enhance their engagement in the learning process. For faculty members, automation in evaluation processes and facilities such as the analysis of student performance can reduce the workload and create an opportunity to focus more on teaching processes. Moreover, university administrators may benefit from more efficient analyses in strategic decision-making processes through the use of big data analytics, which could lead to improvements in education policies. For parents, AI facilitates more precise monitoring of their children's academic progress. In the context of higher education, the application of AI in these and related domains can have both positive and negative implications. On the one hand, AI can enhance learning outcomes, the quality of education, and the ease with which knowledge is acquired. On the other hand, it can also have adverse effects on various aspects of the educational process, including performance management. There is a common concern that AI may impede students' ability to think independently and express themselves effectively, potentially disrupting their cognitive and linguistic development (Shrivastava, 2022; Dwivedi et al., 2023). Another significant concern is the potential for academic fraud with AI-supported chatbots (Meckler and Verma, 2022). Furthermore, the potential for bias and privacy concerns in the use of AI for identifying at-risk students raises ethical considerations (Baneres et al., 2019).

While the number of studies in the literature examining the role of AI in education is increasing over time, it is essential to conduct a comprehensive analysis of these studies in the existing literature. In this context, bibliometric analysis represents an effective tool for examining the impact of AI on higher education. A bibliometric analysis is a method used to reveal the structure of the literature, research trends, and important sources of studies conducted on a specific subject in the field of education, as in many other fields (Aydogmus et al., 2023). A bibliometric analysis of studies conducted on AI in higher education can inform future research, identifying trends and potential gaps in the existing body of knowledge in this field. Accordingly, this study will present a bibliometric analysis of studies conducted in the field of AI in higher education and a detailed analysis of the frequency of use of the word "effect" by the most influential authors & publications in the data source. The second part of the study presents the methodology employed, namely bibliometric analysis. Furthermore, it delineates the analytical steps undertaken. In the third section, the results of the bibliometric analysis are presented and subsequently interpreted. The conclusion section includes analysis of the publications included in the data file with suggestions for future research and comments on the impact of artificial intelligence on higher education using the existing data file.

METHOD

Bibliometric analysis is a fundamental methodological tool for assessing the impact and trends of scientific research. Originally conceived in the 1950s, bibliometrics was developed to quantitatively assess the impact of scholarly publications; this approach has proven invaluable in mapping the growth and dissemination of knowledge within and across disciplines. Derek J. de Solla Price and Eugene Garfield are credited with laying the foundation for modern bibliometric methods, which form the basis for much of today's research assessment (Godin, 2006). Over time, bibliometric analysis studies have evolved into a more comprehensive analytical review method used to track scientific progress, evaluate publication performance, and identify influential researchers and emerging areas of research.

Bibliometrics is essentially the statistical study of publication data. Through the application of quantitative measures such as citation counts, co-authorship analysis, and journal impact factors, bibliometric methods provide a lens for evaluating the dissemination and reception of scientific knowledge. This method can reveal research trends, assess the scholarly impact of individual studies, and measure the reach of particular research fields or journals (Gutiérrez-Salcedo et al., 2017). In addition, bibliometrics can help institutions and researchers identify highly cited works, prominent authors, and prolific areas of study. Such insights are particularly valuable in fields with high publication volumes, where bibliometric analysis can guide the allocation of research funding, identify productive research collaborations, and inform the development of academic policies. Central to many bibliometric analyses is the Web of Science (WoS) database, a comprehensive indexing platform managed by Clarivate Analytics. WoS is widely used because of its extensive catalog of high-quality publications across multiple disciplines and its historical depth, with records dating back to the early 20th century. The platform includes major citation indexes such as the Science Citation Index Expanded (SCIE), the Social Sciences Citation Index (SSCI), and the Arts & Humanities Citation Index (AHCI). These indices allow researchers to track citations, visualize the impact of publications over time, and analyze interdisciplinary connections within research outputs (Shukla et al., 2019). WoS's robust infrastructure makes it particularly well-suited for bibliometric analyses, providing reliable data on citation counts, journal impact metrics, and other key publication attributes.

Figure 1. Steps of the bibliometric analysis procedure

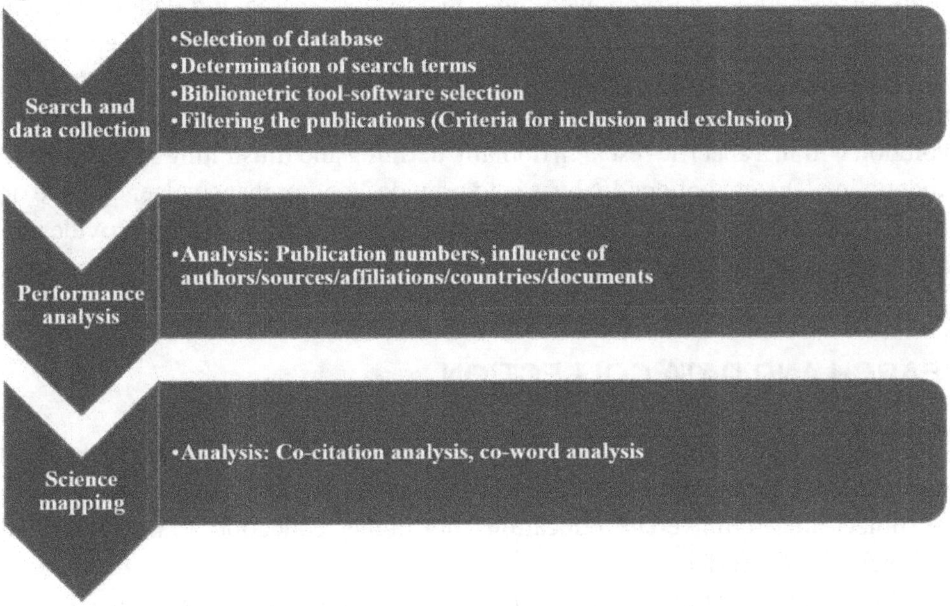

In practice, bibliometric analysis can serve several purposes within the scientific community. First, it facilitates trend analysis, allowing researchers to observe shifts in research priorities and the emergence of new areas of inquiry. For example, by evaluating keyword frequencies and citation networks within a field, scholars can identify growing topics and anticipate future research directions. Second, bibliometrics supports performance evaluation at both the individual and institutional levels. Metrics derived from bibliometric analysis, such as the h-index and journal impact factor, are widely used to measure the influence and reach of researchers and academic institutions. These metrics are often considered in academic promotions, funding decisions, and institutional rankings, although it is worth noting that the use of bibliometric indicators in such evaluative contexts has been the subject of ongoing debate, particularly regarding issues of fairness and accuracy in representing research quality. Bibliometric studies also provide insight into patterns of collaboration within academia. Co-authorship networks, for example, can reveal influential partnerships and research clusters, highlighting scholars who serve as bridges between different disciplines or research groups. This aspect of bibliometric research has been instrumental in promoting interdisciplinary studies and supporting strategic research partnerships, thereby fostering the growth of collaborative networks across scientific fields. In summary, bibliometrics is a powerful, data-driven approach to understanding the scope and impact of scholarly communication.

As shown in Figure 1, the analysis of scientific literature was conducted using bibliometric methods and followed three main steps: search and data collection, performance analysis, and science mapping. Performance analysis and science mapping are critical components in bibliometric analysis, providing essential tools for examining a research field. By combining these methods, we explore the thematic evolution within a specific research domain, defining and illustrating its conceptual subdomains. The goal of our analysis is to provide a comprehensive perspective on university education and artificial intelligence. In addition, this study provides insights from the literature on the impact of artificial intelligence on higher education.

SEARCH AND DATA COLLECTION

In this study, Bibliometrix (v.4.0.0) programs were used to analyze the data and create some tables and pictures. A search was carried out using a search query in the subject area ((“university education” or “higher education”) and (“artificial intelligence”) and (effect)).

Table 1 shows that of the 178 documents in the dataset, 134 were articles, 26 were papers, and the rest editorial materials and reviews. The publications were published in 126 different sources, the average number of citations per publication was 8.966 and a total of 9590 references were used in 178 publications. All the publications are the work of a total of 647 different authors.

Table 1. Main information of data

Description	Results
Main Information About Data	
Timespan	1997:2024
Sources (Journals, Books, Etc)	126
Documents	178
Annual Growth Rate %	17,73
Document Average Age	1,46
Average Citations Per Doc	8,966
References	9590
Document Contents	
Keywords Plus (ID)	342
Author's Keywords (DE)	730
Authors	
Authors	647
Authors Of Single-Authored Docs	23
Authors Collaboration	
Single-Authored Docs	23
Co-Authors Per Doc	3,84
International Co-Authorships %	28,65
Document Types	
Article	110
Article; Early Access	24
Article; Proceedings Paper	2
Editorial Material	2
Proceedings Paper	24
Review	16

RESULTS OF PERFORMANCE ANALYSIS

The number of publications, citation-based impact indicators and journal impact indicators can be used in the performance analysis phase (Gutiérrez-Salcedo et al., 2018). In this study, the number of publications, the most productive authors, the most cited publications, the journals and affiliations with the most publications, and the prominent countries were used as performance indicators.

Number of Publications

The annual number of publications between 1997 and 2024 is presented in Figure 2 Between 1997 and 2019, a total of 11 publications were realized and it can be said that studies on the subject were sporadic for this time period. As of 2020, it is understood that publications started to increase. Accordingly, it is understood that the subject is quite up to date. It is also seen that the number of publications for the year 2024 is almost equal to the total of previous years. During the high-yield active period of 2020–2024, publication numbers reached a maximum of 82 in 2024. The number of publications by years is given in Figure 2.

Figure 2. Document numbers published from 1997 to 2024

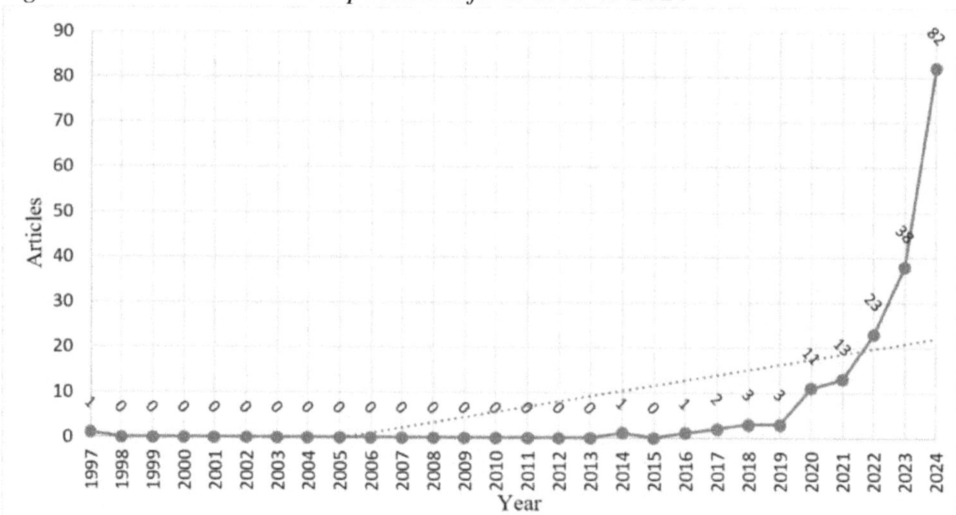

According to the Figure 2, it can be stated that the concept of "artificial intelligence" has gained more attention in the field of higher education over time and is still up to date. It is understood that the 2020 pandemic also had an impact on this.

Figure 3 shows that the average citations per article peaked in 2020 and 2023, with a general decline in 2022. From this figure, the average annual number of citations was between 0.2 and 0 until 2016, but started to increase after 2016. Between 2017 and 2019, the value between 0.3 and 0.6 increased as of 2020. The fact that 2020 is the year in which the number of publications also increased shows us the connection between the two figures (2 and 3).

Figure 3. The number of annual cited paper

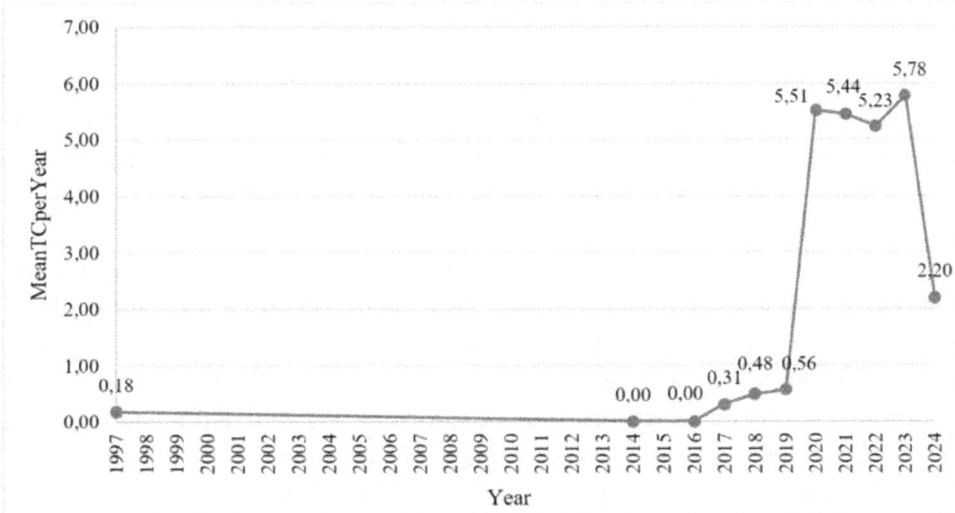

Author Influence

In this study, there were 647 authors in entirety.

Table 2. Most relevant authors

Authors	Articles		Authors	Articles
Chiu TKF	4		Luo X	2
Carballido BV	2		Moorhouse BL	2
Chai CS	2		Ouya S	2
Chen SY	2		Ouyang F	2
Degboe BM	2		Rodríguez ME	2
Essel HB	2		Segbenya M	2

continued on following page

Table 2. Continued

Authors	Articles		Authors	Articles
Gaglo K	2		Sharma S	2
Gao ZY	2		Slimi Z	2
Guerrero-roldán AE	2		Vlachopoulos D	2
Jiao PC	2		Wu M	2
Kossingou GM	2		Yu ZG	2
Li X	2		Zhong LY	2

Table 2 shows the top 24 most influential authors with two or more publications in the dataset. Thomas K.F. Chiu from The Chinese University of Hong Kong dominates the research field with 4 publications since 2022, followed by 23 authors with 2 publications each in the database analysis. The remaining 623 authors contributed one publication each.

The four publications of Chiu, who has the highest number of publications, are analyzed and the effects they examine for AI are explained here. First, the study by Sing et al. (Chiu is the 4th author) in 2022 was reviewed and used a structural equation model to identify the relationships between students' perceived usefulness, attitude towards using AI, subjective norms towards learning about AI, basic literacy about AI, and behavioral intentions towards learning about AI. In addition, the moderating effects of preparedness, social good, and optimism on the research model were also examined and various moderating effects were found between students' perceptions of preparedness, social good, and optimism towards AI. In his study in 2023, Chiu aimed to investigate how generative AI changes school education from the perspective of teachers and leaders. With questionnaires completed by 88 school teachers and leaders from diverse backgrounds, the focus was on the overall impact of Chatgpt and Midjounery on school education. Chiu et al. (2023) noted that as AI evolves technologically, it will inevitably bring numerous changes to classroom practice, however, research on AI in education reflects a weak connection to pedagogical perspectives or teaching approaches. In their study, they used self-determination theory as the underlying framework to investigate how teacher support moderates the effects of student expertise on need satisfaction and intrinsic motivation to learn with AI technologies. Xia, Chiu, Chai (2023) examined the moderating effects of need satisfaction and gender in predicting self-regulated learning (SRL) among Grade 9 students. The results showed that girls perceived more need support than boys. In predicting SRL, autonomy and competence need satisfaction were moderated by both gender and AI knowledge, whereas relatedness need satisfaction was moderated only by gender. Especially among girls, autonomy and competence effects predict SRL more strongly when AI knowledge is low.

Figure 4. Authors with the highest local citations

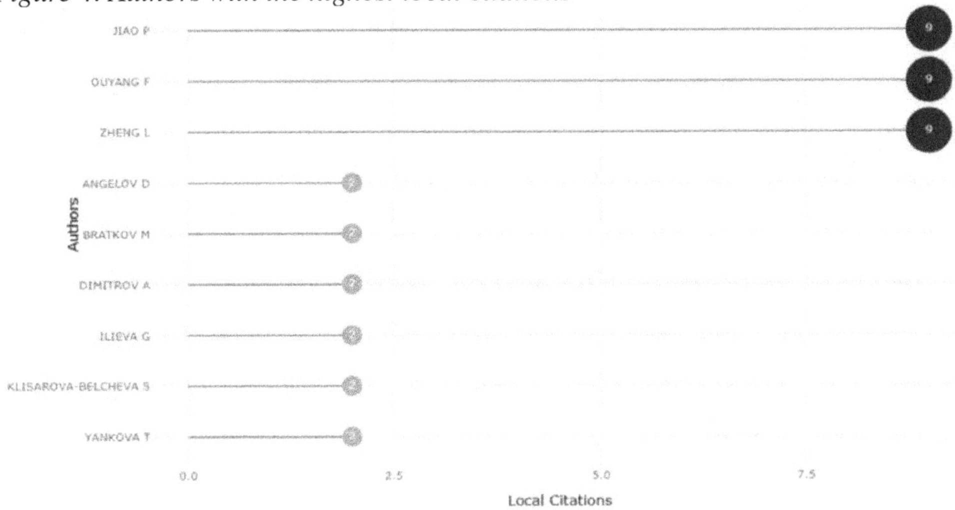

This study also examined authors based on local citation counts. Figure 4 showcases authors with two or more local citations, with Pengcheng Jiao, Fan Ouyang and Luyi Zheng leading the list, each receiving nine local citations. This shows that their work has a significant impact in academic environments and is frequently referenced. They are followed by Delian Angelov, Marin Bratkov, Angel Dimitrov, Galina Ilieva, Stanislava Klisarova-Belcheva, and Tania Yankova, each with two local citations. Furthermore, among the 647 authors analyzed, 32 authors received a single local citation, while 606 authors received no local citations. This distribution reflects that a small group of selected authors have a significant impact on the local academic environment, while others have a more limited impact. These findings provide a deeper understanding of academic impact measurement by helping to identify frequently cited works and authors in the literature.

Influential Sources

In this study, an analysis was conducted on the number of articles published in selected academic journals.

Figure 5. Most relevant sources

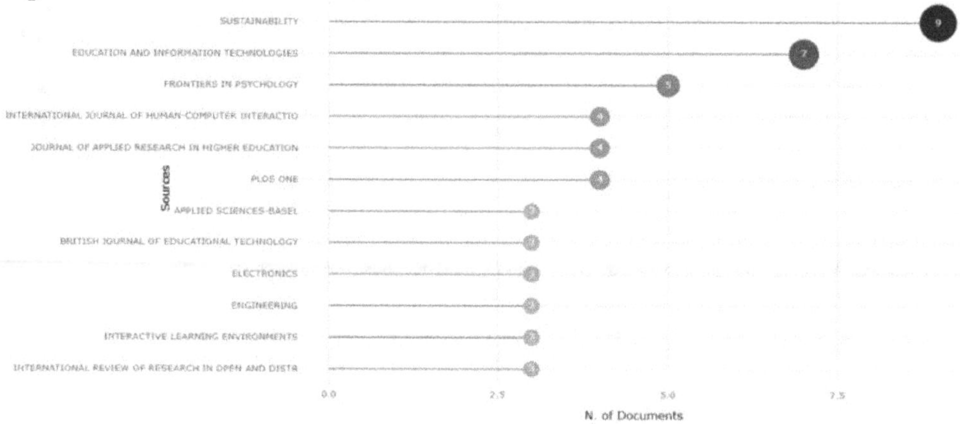

Figure 5 presents the journals with the greatest impact within the research topics and the number of articles published in each. The journals with the highest number of articles include *Sustainability* (9 articles), *Education and Information Technologies* (7 articles), *Frontiers in Psychology* (5 articles), *International Journal of Human-Computer Interaction* (4 articles), *Journal of Applied Research in Higher Education* (4 articles), and *PLOS ONE* (4 articles). These journals cover interdisciplinary topics, appealing to a broad academic audience with a focus on sustainability, educational technologies, psychology, human-computer interaction, and higher education. Additionally, journals such as *Applied Sciences-Basel*, *British Journal of Educational Technology*, *Electronics*, *Engineering*, *Interactive Learning Environments*, and *International Review of Research in Open and Distributed Learning* each feature 3 articles. These journals exert a significant influence, particularly in fields such as educational technologies, engineering, electronics, and interactive learning environments. This analysis highlights the journals most frequently preferred by academic communities and indicates where specific topics are more extensively covered, thereby guiding researchers in source selection. The figure includes a total of 12 journals, each with at least three publications. Within the dataset, consisting of 126 sources, the remaining 114 sources feature two publications in 13 journals and a single publication in 101 journals.

Figure 6. Most local cited sources

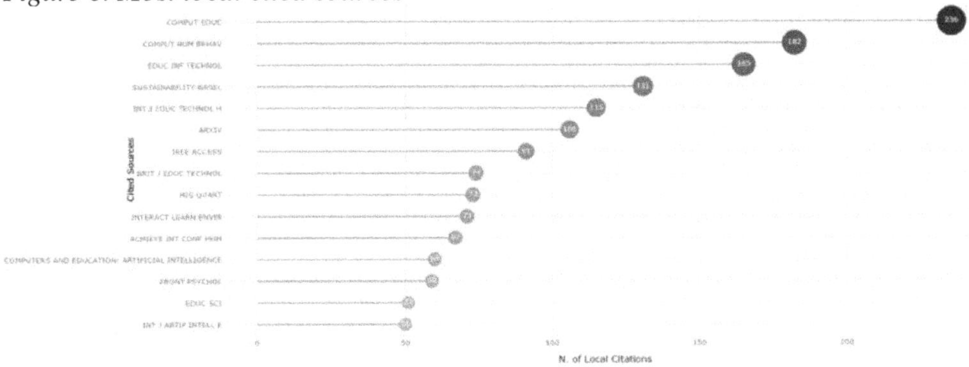

In the realm of academic research, the impact of scientific journals is often measured by their citation counts, which reflect their significance and influence within respective fields. In this bibliometric analysis, the sources with the highest local citations were identified, and Figure 6 displays sources with a total of 50 or more local citations. Computers & Education leads the list with 236 local citations. It is followed by Computers in Human Behavior with 182 local citations and Education and Information Technologies with 165 local citations. Sustainability (Basel) has 131 local citations, and all these journals reflect the growing interest in sustainable practices in education and their intersection with technology.

Other notable sources include the International Journal of Educational Technology in Higher Education with 115 local citations, arXiv with 106 local citations, and IEEE Access with 91 local citations, representing both formal and informal publication channels that facilitate the rapid dissemination of technological advancements and educational practices. British Journal of Educational Technology and MIS Quarterly, with 74 and 73 local citations respectively, highlight the integration of educational technology and management information systems. Interactive Learning Environments, which publishes articles on all aspects of the design and use of interactive learning environments in a very broad sense, and Frontiers in Psychology, a multidisciplinary journal that publishes advances in psychological research, are also on the list and can highlight the psychological and interactive components necessary for effective educational technology.

Furthermore, the presence of conferences such as the ACM/IEEE International Conference on Human-Robot Interaction, with 67 local citations, underscores the importance of conferences where innovative research is often presented for the first time. Finally, sources such as Computers and Education: Artificial Intelligence, Education Sciences, and the International Journal of Artificial Intelligence in

Education, with 50-60 local citations, reflect the growing interest in AI as a transformative tool in education.

Figure 7. Temporal distribution of sources with the highest number of publications

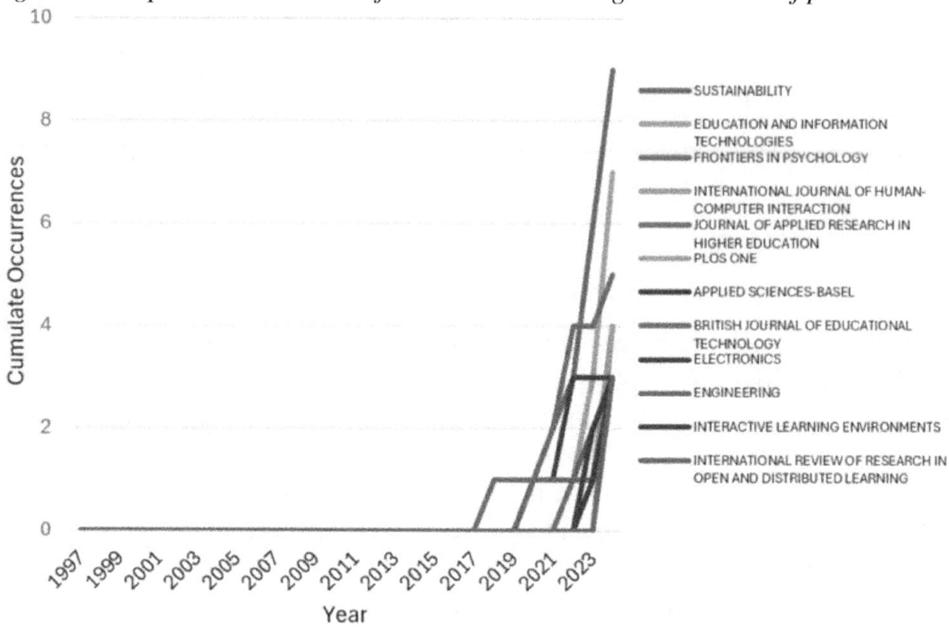

Figure 7 illustrates the yearly distribution of articles published in the various interdisciplinary sources listed in Figure 5, highlighting an upward trend in academic interest. The sources examined in this study include Sustainability, Education and Information Technologies, Frontiers in Psychology, International Journal of Human-Computer Interaction, Journal of Applied Research in Higher Education, PLOS ONE, Applied Sciences - Basel, British Journal of Educational Technology, Electronics, Engineering, Interactive Learning Environments, and the International Review of Research in Open and Distributed Learning. A marked increase in publication volume since 2020 appears directly linked to the acceleration of digitalization in education and the widespread adoption of technological solutions. This trend reflects a growing interest in technological innovations within teaching and learning, as well as a heightened focus on these subjects by researchers. Additionally, the impact of the COVID-19 pandemic likely contributed to the increased number of publications starting in 2020.

In particularly, Sustainability and Education and Information Technology have emerged as increasingly preferred outlets, reflecting the growing academic interest in educational technology and sustainability. Similarly, the journals Frontiers in Psychology and International Journal of Human-Computer Interaction have garnered significant interest in response to the growing focus on human factors and interactive learning experiences. The significant increase in publications in 2023 and 2024 across all sources underlines the diversity and academic appeal of research in interdisciplinary fields such as education, psychology, engineering and human-computer interaction. These findings suggest that innovative educational approaches and interdisciplinary research are increasingly being embraced by the academic community and researchers showing more interest in these areas. The fact that current issues such as digital transformation and sustainability in education are on the research agenda contributes to the enrichment of the academic literature in these fields.

Table 3. Sources' local impact by h index

Source	h_ index	g_ index	m_ index	TC	NP	PY_ start
Education and Information Technologies	5	7	1,667	201	7	2022
Sustainability	4	9	0,571	96	9	2018
Frontiers in Psychology	3	5	0,6	85	5	2020
Applied Sciences-Basel	2	3	0,4	12	3	2020
British Journal of Educational Technology	2	3	1	59	3	2023
Computer Applications in Engineering Education	2	2	0,071	12	2	1997
Education Sciences	2	2	0,5	16	2	2021
Educational Technology \& Society	2	2	0,5	65	2	2021
Engineering	2	3	0,4	73	3	2020
Interactive Learning Environments	2	3	1	126	3	2023
International Journal of Educational Technology in Higher Education	2	2	0,667	90	2	2022
International Journal of Human-Computer Interaction	2	3	2	10	4	2024
Journal of Applied Research in Higher Education	2	4	0,667	27	4	2022
Plos One	2	3	1	9	4	2023

Table 3 presents an analysis of the impact values and local influence of academic sources based on metrics such as the h-index. According to the data, the journal Education and Information Technologies stands out with the highest impact value, possessing an h-index of 5 and accumulating a total of 201 citations since 2022. Similarly, Sustainability has an h-index of 4, reflecting a notable impact in environmental and sustainability issues, with nine of its publications receiving 96 citations since 2018.

The journal Frontiers in Psychology maintains an h-index of 3, underscoring its contributions to the psychology domain, with 85 citations since 2020, reaching a broad readership. Journals such as the British Journal of Educational Technology and Interactive Learning Environments have also generated substantial impact through recent publications, accruing 59 and 126 citations from articles published in 2023, respectively.

Additionally, journals like the International Journal of Educational Technology in Higher Education and the Journal of Applied Research in Higher Education contribute valuable insights into technological applications in education, with articles published in 2022 and 2024 earning 90 and 27 citations, respectively. Overall, this analysis demonstrates the significant impact of these journals within specific fields and their enduring influence in academic literature. Through metrics such as the h-index and other bibliometric indicators, understanding the local and global impacts of these sources holds substantial importance for guiding academic work and accumulating knowledge.

Influential Affiliations

The study analyzed the most impactful affiliation, focusing on the academic publication performance of universities with five or more publications, as presented in Table 4. According to the data, the Bucharest University of Economic Studies (Romania) ranks the highest with 11 publications. This is followed by the Chinese University of Hong Kong (Hong Kong) and Zhejiang University (China), each with 10 publications. Anadolu University (Turkey) also stands out with 9 publications, a count it shares with Erasmus University (Netherlands). Another prominent affiliation from China, Peking University, appears with 8 publications, matched by University of Cape Coast (Ghana) and Universidad Privada Boliviana (Bolivia). Universitat Oberta de Catalunya (Spain) and King Abdulaziz University (Saudi Arabia) contribute with 7 and 6 publications, respectively. National Yunlin University of Science and Technology (Taiwan) and Beijing Language and Culture University (China) are included in the list with 6 and 5 publications, respectively. These data indicate that these universities play an active role in the global academic landscape, demonstrating high research productivity.

Table 4. Most relevant affiliations

Affiliation	Articles
Bucharest University of Economic Studies, Romania	11
Chinese University of Hong Kong, Hong Kong	10
Zhejiang University, China	10
Anadolu University, Turkey	9
Erasmus University, Netherlands	9

continued on following page

Table 4. Continued

Affiliation	Articles
Peking University, China	8
University of Cape Coast, Ghana	8
Universidad Privada Boliviana, Bolivia	8
Universitat Oberta de Catalunya, Spain	7
King Abdulaziz University, Saudi Arabia	6
National Yunlin University of Science and Technology, Taiwan	6
Beijing Language and Culture University, China	5

Figure 8. Temporal distribution of affiliations with the highest number of publications

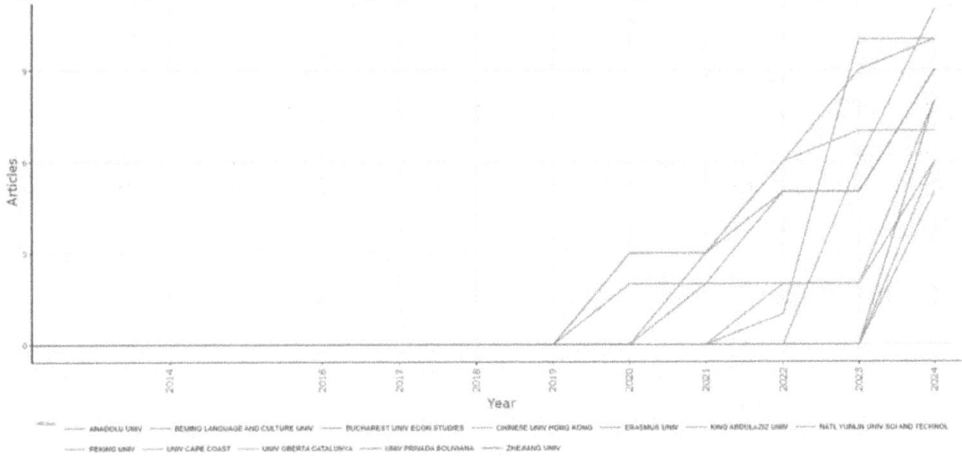

Figure 8 provides a detailed examination of changes over time in the academic publication output of the 12 universities with the highest publication counts. The data reveal that while certain affiliations have recorded significant increases in publication productivity, others have shown relatively stable or declining trends.

According to the analysis, since 2020, the Bucharest University of Economic Studies (Romania) has emerged as one of the affiliations with the most substantial growth, marking a notable surge in publications during 2023-2024. This suggests that investments in research activities and strategies aimed at enhancing international visibility have been successful for this Romanian university. A similar trend is observed for the Chinese University of Hong Kong, which has maintained a consistent rise in publication output since 2022, further solidifying its presence in academia. Similarly, Zhejiang University (China) has attracted attention with its publication growth in the 2022-2024 period. Anadolu University (Turkey) also displayed a rising publication performance starting in 2021, enhancing its contributions to the international academic literature.

On the other hand, Erasmus University (Netherlands) and Universidad Privada Boliviana (Bolivia) increased their publication counts in 2023, gaining visibility on both regional and global levels. Peking University (China) and University of Cape Coast (Ghana) also demonstrated notable increases in 2023, assuming more prominent roles on the academic stage.

In contrast, universities like Universitat Oberta de Catalunya (Spain) and King Abdulaziz University (Saudi Arabia) exhibited periodic increases in publication output; however, these increases were less pronounced and sustainable compared to other affiliations. For instance, while National Yunlin University of Science and Technology (Taiwan) recorded a significant rise in 2024, it appears to reflect a more periodic surge rather than sustained long-term growth. Similarly, Beijing Language and Culture University (China) displayed a similar pattern, though without the robust increase seen in other universities. The differences in publication performance among affiliations may be linked to factors such as research funding, international collaborations, and academic strategies. In this context, bibliometric analyses provide valuable insights into the publication strategies and research presence of academic affiliations.

Influential Countries

Within the scope of the study, the productivity of the countries was discussed from different perspectives.

Table 5. Most relevant countries

Country	Freq		Country	Freq		Country	Freq
China	185		Ghana	14		Bolivia	8
USA	47		Peru	14		Iran	8
Spain	34		South Korea	14		Oman	8
India	32		Mexico	13		Portugal	8
Malaysia	25		UK	13		South Africa	8
Germany	19		Pakistan	12		Turkey	8
Netherlands	19		Australia	11		Thailand	7
Saudi Arabia	19		Russia	9		Tunisia	7
Romania	17						

Table 5 examines the ranking and academic productivity of the countries with the highest number of publications. According to the data, China leads by a wide margin with 185 publications, reflecting its substantial investments in scientific research and its influence on the international academic stage. The USA ranked second with 47 publications, Spain and India ranked third and fourth with 34 and 32 publications respectively, and Malaysia ranked fifth with 25 publications. These five countries have significant global impact, aided by their national research capacities and extensive academic collaboration networks. The first 5 countries in the table account for about half of the total productivity of countries with 47.5%. Other countries, such as Germany, the Netherlands, Saudi Arabia, and Romania, also stand out with 17 or more publications.

Countries such as Ghana, Peru, South Korea, Mexico, and the United Kingdom also good positions, each with 13-14 publications, showcasing their national academic capacities at the international level. They are followed by Pakistan, Australia, Russia, Bolivia, Iran, Iran, Oman, Portugal, South Africa and Turkey, each with between 8 and 12 publications. Thailand and Tunisia, with 7 publications each, complete the top 25 countries list. Outside of these top 25, the remaining 37 countries each contributed between 1 and 6 publications, maintaining a more limited scope of global academic contributions.

This analysis highlights the contribution levels of specific countries to the international scientific literature. Leading countries like China and the USA play a decisive role in academic productivity, while other countries make significant regional and global contributions to knowledge production.

Figure 9. Corresponding author's countries

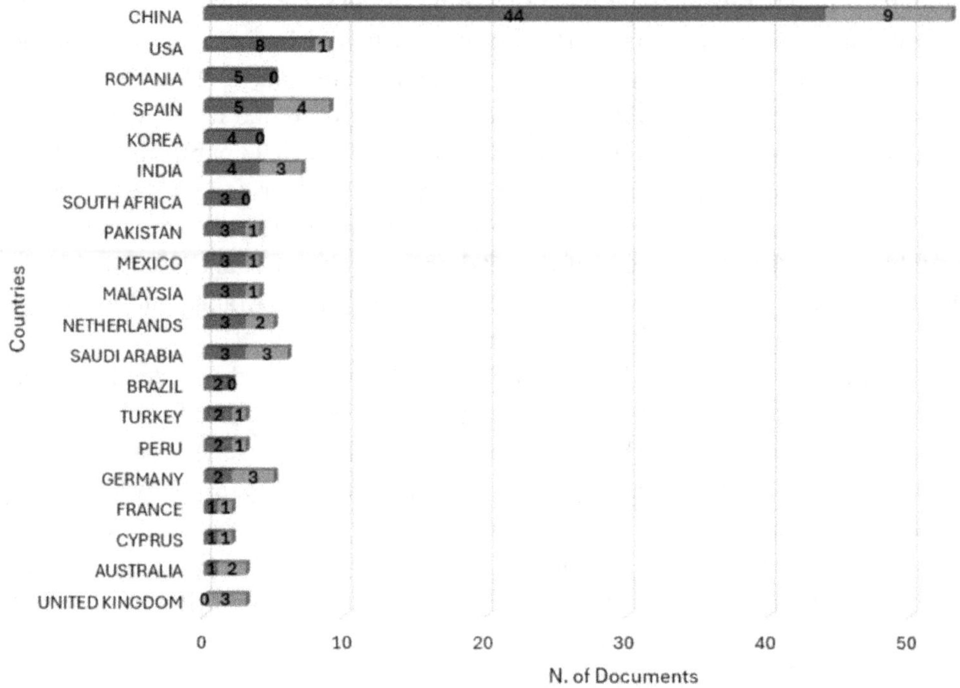

Figure 9 shows the 20 most productive countries in terms of corresponding authors. SCP (single country paper) shows the number of publications produced by authors from that country only, while MCP (multiple country paper) shows the number of publications that include co-authors from other countries as well as the relevant country.

This differentiation allows for an evaluation of both local academic productivity and the extent of international research collaboration. China stands out as the leading country, with a total of 53 publications. Of these, 44 are SCPs, highlighting a high level of independent local research output. However, the presence of 9 MCPs indicates that China engages in international collaborations to a limited extent. The United States ranks second, with a total of 9 publications. Of these, 8 are SCPs, suggesting a strong preference for single-country research initiatives. With only 1 MCP, the United States demonstrates limited international collaboration relative to its overall output. Spain and India also feature prominently, with 9 and 7 publications, respectively. Spain shows a balanced distribution between SCP (5) and MCP (4) publications, indicating a relatively high inclination toward international collaboration. India displays a similar pattern, with 4 SCPs and 3 MCPs, reflecting a balanced approach between independent and collaborative research efforts. Romania and Germany, each with 5 publications, show different structures in their research outputs. Romania's publications consist entirely of SCPs, underlining a focus on local research independence. In contrast, Germany's mix of 2 SCPs and 3 MCPs shows a moderate but significant involvement in international collaboration. Countries such as Saudi Arabia, South Africa, and Korea provide valuable but comparatively smaller contributions, each showing varying levels of international collaboration. For instance, Saudi Arabia's equal split between SCP (3) and MCP (3) publications highlights a balanced approach to collaborative research. South Africa, with solely SCP (3) publications, indicates a limited engagement in international partnerships. Other countries, including Turkey, Australia, and the United Kingdom, show lower publication counts but participate in international collaborations to some extent, as evidenced by their MCP contributions. This bibliometric analysis reveals geographical differences in research collaboration patterns. These findings provide a foundation for deeper exploration into the factors promoting international collaborations and the influence of local research policies on publication trends.

Table 6. Most cited contries

Country	TC	Average Article Citations	Country	TC	Average Article Citations
China	737	13,90	U Arab Emirates	40	20,00
Netherlands	121	24,20	Pakistan	39	9,80
Spain	81	9,00	Thailand	39	19,50
Turkey	78	26,00	United Kingdom	35	11,70
Germany	77	15,40	Saudi Arabia	31	5,20

Figure 10. Most cited contries

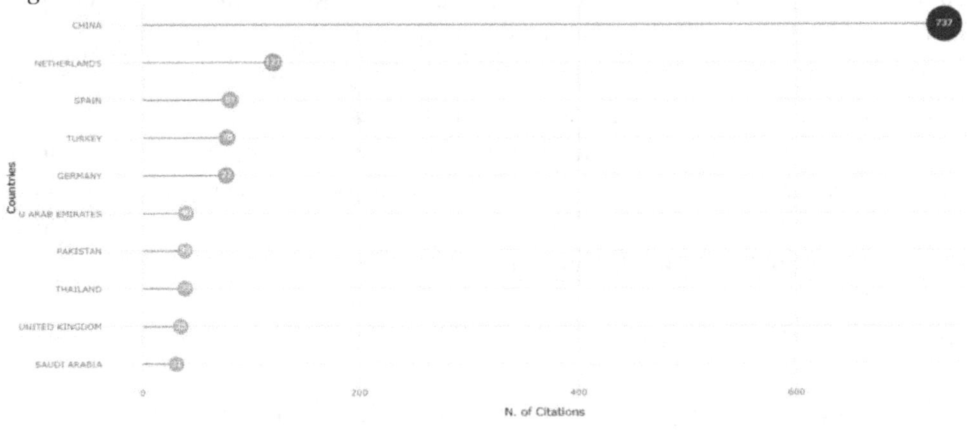

Table 6 and Figure 10 illustrate countries with a total citation count exceeding 30, along with their respective average citation counts. The data encompass countries such as China, the Netherlands, Spain, Turkey, Germany, the United Arab Emirates, Pakistan, Thailand, the United Kingdom, and Saudi Arabia. Notable differences in citation counts among these countries are clearly observable. As indicated by the chart, China stands out with 737 citations, significantly surpassing other countries and holding the highest citation count in this domain. This reflects China's influence in the research field and underscores the magnitude of its contributions to academic literature. However, when examining average citation counts, China has an average of 13.90, which is lower than that of some other countries. This suggests that while China has a large volume of publications, the average impact per publication is comparatively lower. The Netherlands ranks second with a total citation count of 121 and an average citation count of 24.20, positioning it above China in terms of citation impact. This indicates that, although the Netherlands produces fewer publications, its research outputs tend to receive more citations, thus reflecting a higher impact. Turkey, with a total of 78 citations, is also among the prominent countries and stands out with an average citation count of 26.00. This data indicates that studies originating from Turkey are particularly impactful and occupy a significant place in the international academic literature. Germany demonstrates a similar pattern with a total citation count of 77 and an average of 15.40. Countries such as the United Arab Emirates, Pakistan, and Thailand have comparable total citation counts, ranging from 39 to 40 citations, placing them within this table. Their average citation counts are recorded at 20.00, 9.80, and 19.50, respectively. These figures highlight that research from the United Arab Emirates and Thailand, in particular, commands notable impact, emphasizing the influence of research output from these countries. The United Kingdom and Saudi Arabia, with total citation counts of 35 and 31, respectively, are positioned at the lower end of the table. The United Kingdom's average citation count of 11.70 indicates a relatively modest impact of its publications. Meanwhile, Saudi Arabia, with an average citation count of 5.20, has the lowest average among the countries listed. In summary, the relationship between total citation counts and average citation values for each country reveals distinct differences between academic productivity and the impact of these publications. These data illuminate how scientific output and influence vary by country, with some countries generating a larger quantity of studies, while others produce relatively fewer but more impactful works.

Influential Documents

In this study, publications with the highest citation value were examined.

Table 7. Most local cited documents

Document (Author, Year, Source)	Year	Local Citations
Ouyang F, 2022, Educ Inf Technol	2022	9
Ilieva G, 2023, Information	2023	2
Vinichenko MV, 2020, Entrep Sustain Iss	2020	1
Prinsloo P, 2020, Big Data Soc	2020	1
Leoste J, 2021, Computers	2021	1
Yang ACM, 2021, Educ Technol Soc	2021	1
Raffaghelli JE, 2022, Comput Educ	2022	1
Raza SA, 2022, J Appl Res High Educ	2022	1
Martins RM, 2023, Inform Educ	2023	1
Pisica AI, 2023, Societies	2023	1
Jafari F, 2024, J Appl Res High Educ	2024	1
Maheshwari G, 2024, Educ Inf Technol	2024	1

Table 7 includes documents with a local citation count of 1 or more. Such an analysis demonstrates the extent to which research topics and articles garner attention in local scholarly communities and identifies which studies receive higher citation rates. The distribution of local citations in the table reveals a concentration of interest in studies published as of 2022, indicating that these works have particularly resonated within the local context. The document with the highest local citation count is a study by Ouyang (2022), published in Education and Information Technologies, which stands out with 9 local citations. This suggests that Ouyang's 2022 study has garnered significant, displaying a strong impact in this area. Although the other studies listed have lower local citation counts, each has evidently made a distinct impact within its respective field. For example, Ilieva's 2023 study, published in Information, has received 2 local citations. Despite being relatively recent, this study has already resonated within the local academic environment and has been noted by other researchers in its field. All remaining studies have received 1 local citation, suggesting that these documents, while creating modest impact, are still utilized as references by local researchers. These studies were published between 2020 and 2024, with most released in the past four years. Notably, the studies by Jafari and Maheshwari, published in 2024, have already received local citations despite their recent release, hinting at their potential to gain further citations in the future. Moreover, the presence of studies published in various journals, such as Big Data and Society and Entrepreneurship and Sustainability Issues, underscores the breadth of interest within local academic circles across different fields. Analyses like these are instrumental in identifying academic trends and areas of interest, providing bibliometric data that can highlight scholarly engagement with particular studies and guide the direction of future research by identifying topics of growing importance within the academic community.

Table 8. Most global cited documents

Paper (Author, Year, Source)	Total Citations	TC per Year
Ouyang F, 2022, Educ Inf Technol	122	40,67
Bozkurt A, 2021, Sustainability	68	17,00
Chiu TKF, 2023, Interact Learn Environ-A	65	32,50
Kuang K, 2020, Engineering	65	13,00
Chiu TKF, 2023, Interact Learn Environ	61	30,50
Wang Y, 2021, Educ Technol Soc	58	14,50
Marcinkowski F, 2020, Fat20: Proceedings Of The 2020 Conference On Fairness, Accountability, And Transparency	58	11,60
Wu R, 2024, Br J Educ Technol	57	57,00
Dekker I, 2020, Front Psychol	57	11,40
Essel HB, 2022, Int J Educ Technol High Educ	56	18,67
Kong F, 2020, Int J Emerg Technol Learn	55	11,00
Raffaghelli JE, 2022, Comput Educ	51	17,00

Papers with a global citation count of 50 or more are presented in the Table 8. This table shows valuable insights into the international academic impact of specific studies. For each article, both the total citation count and the annual average citation rate are provided. At the top of the table is an article by Ouyang (2022), published in *Education and Information Technologies*, which stands as the most highly cited work with a total of 122 global citations and an impressive annual average of 40.67 citations. This high citation count indicates that Ouyang's work has generated considerable interest in the field of educational technology, suggesting a substantial international impact. Another notable study in the table is by Bozkurt (2021), published in *Sustainability*, with a total of 68 citations and an annual average of 17.00 citations, reflecting significant academic interest and broad acceptance by an international audience. Two distinct studies published by Chiu (2023) in *Interactive Learning Environments* each received a global citation count of 65 and 61, with annual citation rates of 32.50 and 30.50, respectively. These figures reflect the rapid expansion and influence of research focused on interactive learning environments within the educational technology sector. Despite being recently published in 2023, these studies have gained considerable traction, indicating a high demand for innovative approaches within education technology. Another impactful work in the table is by Wang (2021), published in *Educational Technology & Society*, with

58 total citations and an annual average of 14.50 citations. Marcinkowski's (2020) study, presented at the *Conference on Fairness, Accountability, and Transparency*, also stands out with 58 citations and an annual average of 11.60. Additionally, Wu's (2024) article in the *British Journal of Educational Technology*, with 57 citations and an extraordinary annual average of 57.00, highlights rapid interest despite its recent publication. This very high citation rate underlines how quickly the study has become a key focus in the field. The high citation counts not only advance knowledge within these areas but also shape academic discourse within these disciplines. In conclusion, bibliometric analyses such as this are invaluable for identifying the studies that receive the most attention within academic communities and understanding the topics that hold greater importance on a global scale. This table, through the lens of global citation counts, provides direction for future research in areas such as educational technology and sustainability, highlighting emerging trends that are likely to influence research trajectories in the years to come.

When Table 7 and Table 8 are considered together, authors such as Ouyang F and Raffaghelli JE stand out in both tables with their locally and globally cited studies. The studies of these authors have resonated within both local academic circles and the international scholarly community, highlighting the broader perspective through which their academic impact can be assessed. Ouyang F, with a 2022 publication in Education and Information Technologies, emerges as the most cited author in both tables. This work has garnered 9 local citations and an impressive 122 global citations, with an annual average citation rate of 40.67, indicating a significant international impact. In contrast, while Raffaghelli JE's 2022 study, published in Computers and Education, has received a single citation at the local level, it has attracted 51 citations globally, with an annual average of 17.00 citations, signifying a notable international impact. This pattern suggests that while Raffaghelli's work has generated significant interest globally, it has seen more limited recognition locally. These comparisons illustrate how local and global citation metrics can reveal differing levels of academic engagement with specific works, offering insights into the varying impact of research within both narrower and broader scholarly contexts. As such, these bibliometric analyses highlight the increasing importance of educational technology within academic discourse and underscore the capacity of research in this field to engage a diverse readership globally.

Ouyang, the author of the publication with the highest number of citations in Table 7, is also the author in Figure 4. There are also three authors in this publication and these three authors are the top three authors with 9 citations in Figure 4. Ouyang et al. (2022), which has the highest number of citations (both local and global), is a systematic review of empirical research on the application of AI in online higher education. Specifically, this literature review examines the functions of empirical research, the algorithms used in empirical research, and the impact and implications of empirical research. They stated that there are limited literature reviews examining the purposes and effects of applying AI techniques in the context of online higher education, and that gaining a deep understanding of the empirical impact of AI applications in online higher education is a major challenge, so they collected, reviewed and summarized the empirical research of AI in online higher education. In their study, they focused on the questions of "what are the functions of AI applications", "which AI algorithms are used to realize these functions" and "what are the effects and implications of AI applications on teaching and learning processes" in online higher education. In the section examining the answer to the third question, four positive impacts are emphasized. These four impacts are listed as a high quality of AI-enabled prediction with multiple input variables, a high quality of AI-enabled recommendations based on student characteristics, an improvement of students' academic performances and an improvement of online engagement and participation. Furthermore, Ouyang et al. (2022), based on a literature review of various articles, reported that innovative applications of AI in online higher education help to reform instructional design and development methods and advance the structures of an intelligent, networked, personalized and lifelong education system.

RESULTS OF SCIENCE MAPPING

Co-citation Analysis

Co-citation analysis is a method used to better understand the evolution of important topics in a particular field of study. It entails assessing the references mentioned by the scientific publications that are part of the chosen dataset and examining the connections between the cited publications.

As seen in Table 1, a total of 9590 references were used in the documents included in the dataset. In this study, papers and sources were analyzed for co-citation analysis.

Figure 11. The co-citation network of cited papers

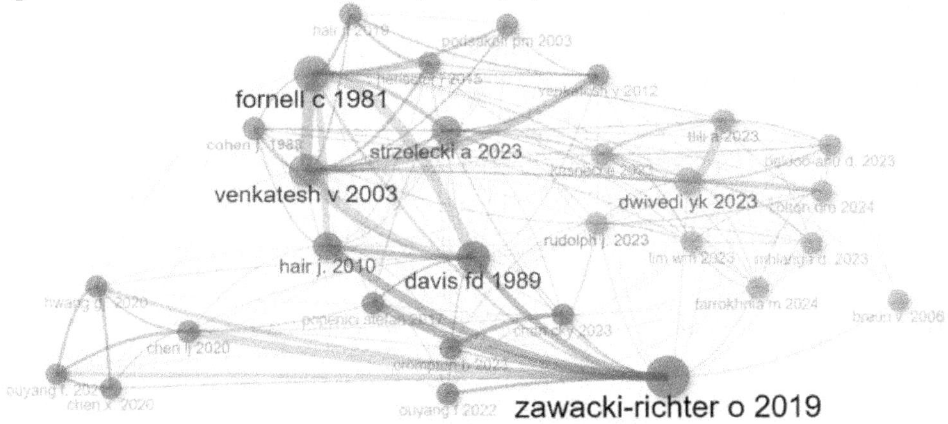

As seen in Figure 11, the most cited papers are Zawacki-Richter (2019), Davis (1989) and Hair (2010) in the red cluster, while Venkatesh (2003), Strzelecki (2023) and Fornell (1981) in the blue cluster, Rudolph (2023) and Dwivedi (2023) in the blue cluster, chen (2020) is in the fourth cluster. Each of these clusters represents the research interest, referred to as the theme of the study (Rao and Shukla, 2023). 30 nodes were included in the analysis, and it is seen that the red cluster has a higher density among the four clusters obtained.

Figure 12. The co-citation network of sources

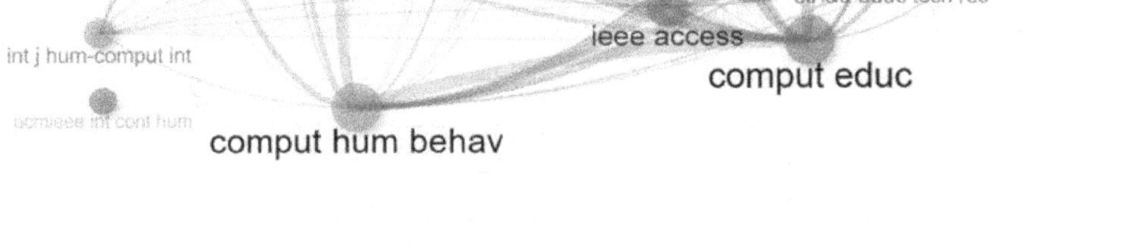

When the co-citation analysis is performed for the sources in the dataset, five different clusters are obtained for 25 nodes as shown in Figure 12. When the sources are analyzed by subject, the blue group focuses more on educational technology, while the red group includes journals in technology and applied sciences. The green and purple groups focus on more specific areas such as human-computer interaction and learning environments.

Co-word Analysis

Identifying the frequency distributions of keywords could uncover promising opportunities for future research (Kevork and Vrechopoulos 2009, from Khaldi and Prado-Gascó, 2021).

Figure 13. The co-occurrence of author's keywords density diagram

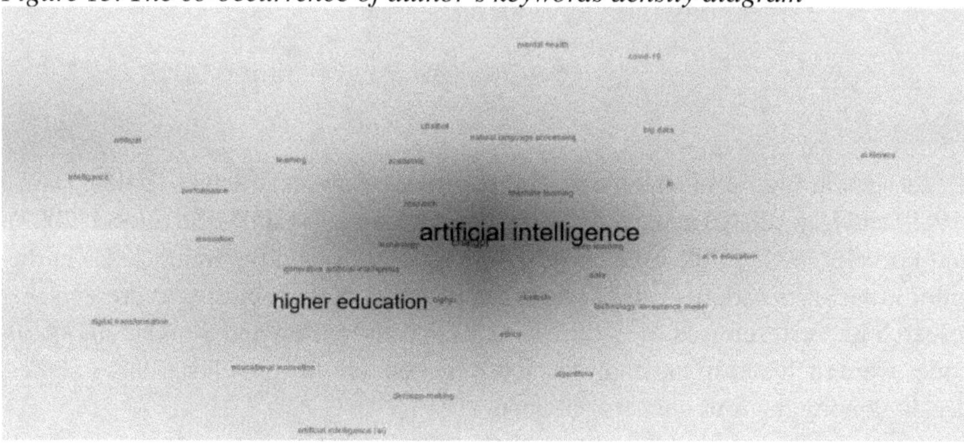

Out of a total of 730 author's keywords, the two most frequently occurring keywords were artificial intelligence and higher education. The "effect" author's keyword has a total of 12 occurrences different types as shown at Table 10.

Table 9. The co-occurrence of author's keywords

Author's Keywords	Frequency		Author's Keywords	Frequency
artificial intelligence	68		technology	10
higher education	51		chatbot	9
education	24		learning	9
chatgpt	22		higher	8
AI	10		machine learning	7

The results of the co-word analysis shown in Table 9 indicate a marked research interest in the intersection of "artificial intelligence" (68 occurrences) and "higher education" (51 occurrences), underlining the growing relevance of AI applications in educational contexts. In particular, terms such as "education" (24 occurrences), "ChatGPT" (22 occurrences) and "technology" (10 occurrences) reveal an emphasis on the integration of generative AI technologies, especially conversational agents, into learning environments. Furthermore, "AI", "chatbot" and "learning" (9-10 occurrences each), "machine learning" (7 occurrences) and "deep learning" (6 occurrences) emerged as key terms. "The presence of the phrases "technology acceptance model" (5 occurrences) and "performance" (5 occurrences) emphasizes the importance of assessing the effectiveness and user acceptance of AI applications in education, especially understanding how these technologies affect student engagement and learning effectiveness.

Table 10. Forms where "effect" appears as a author's keyword.

Author's Keywords	Frequency		Author's Keywords	Frequency
effect size	1		learning effect	1
effective teaching	1		model of learning effects	1
effectiveness	1		moderation effects	1
effects of ai on libraries	1		overall effect	1
intervention effects	1		testing effect	1
judicial effectiveness	1		treatment effect estimation	1

Figure 14. The co-occurrence of keyword plus density diagram

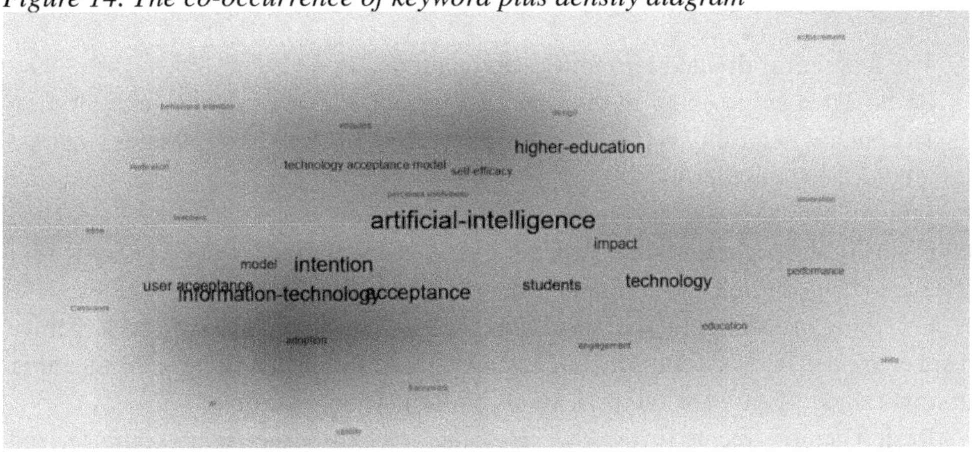

Out of a total of 342 keyword plus, the two most frequently occurring keywords were acceptance (29 occurrences), artificial-intelligence (24 occurrences), higher education (18 occurrences), intention (17 occurrences), information-technology (13 occurrences). The impact keyword plus has a total of 10 occurrences, while the effect keyword has never been used.

Thematic Map

The thematic map diagram presents an analysis of themes across two dimensions: centrality and density. The horizontal axis represents the degree of centrality, while the vertical axis indicates the degree of development density.

Figure 15. Thematic map

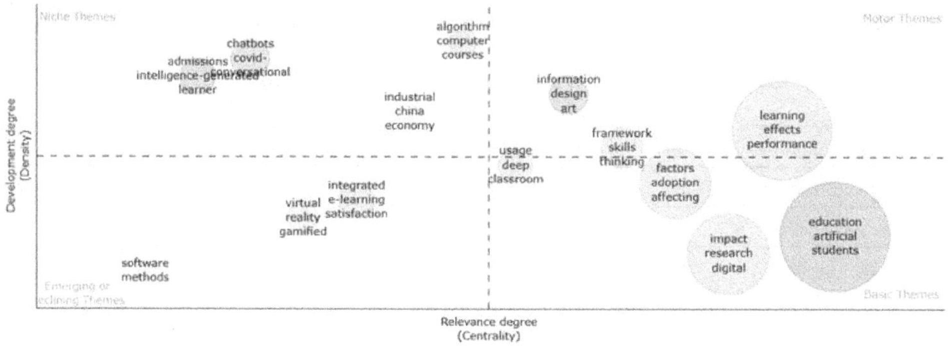

The diagram is divided into four main quadrants:

Niche Themes: Located in the upper left quadrant, these themes exhibit high density but low centrality, representing specific areas of expertise. Examples include "chatbots" and "covid."

Motor Themes: Positioned in the upper right quadrant, these themes show both high density and high centrality, indicating critical and well-developed topics within the field. "Algorithm" and "computer courses" are examples of such themes.

Emerging or Declining Themes: Found in the lower left quadrant, these themes display low density and centrality, suggesting they are either emerging or diminishing in importance. "Software" and "methods" fall into this category.

Basic Themes: Located in the lower right quadrant, these themes are characterized by high centrality but low density, indicating fundamental yet underdeveloped topics within the field. Examples include "education" and "artificial students."

CONCLUSION

The rapid integration of AI into current technologies has sparked the fourth industrial and learning revolution, making the development of curricula for AI education a key strategic initiative for global education authorities (Sing et al., 2022).

In this study, a bibliometric analysis was conducted on the use of artificial intelligence in higher education and its effects. The fact that there has been an increase in publications in this field in recent years shows that the field is up-to-date. In addition, the high number of publications in the last four years may be due to the impact of the covid-19 pandemic and the importance given to distance education systems in higher education.

Bibliometric analysis is an important guide in perceiving the trends in a particular field of study. Bibliometric analysis can reveal research trends, assess the scholarly impact of individual studies, and measure the reach of particular research fields or journals (Gutiérrez-Salcedo et al., 2017). According to the findings of this study, the most influential author is Chiu, who has 4 publications. The three most locally cited authors (Ouyang, Jiao and Zheng) are co-authors on the same publication, which has the highest number of citations locally and globally. This publication presented a systematic literature review, mainly focused on finding answers to three questions from the literature. In our study, we focus on the last of these three questions, "the effects of artificial intelligence", and explain this publication.

In other parts of the bibliometric analysis, the most productive source is Sustainability magazine, the most productive institution is Bucharest University of Economic Studies and the most productive country is China. According to the co-citation analysis conducted within the scope of the study, the most highly cited reference is Zawacki-Richter (2019). In this study, it is stated that although Artificial Intelligence in Education (AIEd) has been around for about 35 years, it is still unclear to educators how to utilize it pedagogically on a broader scale and how it can have a truly meaningful impact on teaching and learning in higher education. Through a systematic review, this article examines research on AI applications in higher education covering the period 2007-2018. According to Zawacki-Richter et al. (2019), it reflects the lack of critical reflection on the challenges and risks of AIEd, the weak connection to theoretical pedagogical perspectives, and the need for further exploration of ethical and educational approaches to the implementation of AIEd in higher education. It is also stated that the scarcity of authors affiliated with education departments identified as a result of the systematic review is evidence of the need for educational perspectives on technological developments.

In this study, a thematic map was prepared for future studies. According to this map shown in Figure 15, studies on chatbots, artificial intelligence and learning, and the acceptance of these systems are suggested. At the same time, mixed reality and education systems, personalized learning platforms, artificial intelligence-supported assessment systems, multidisciplinary studies in the field of technology and education are recommended.

REFERENCES

Aydogmus, H. Y., Turkan, Y. S., & Aydogmus, U. (2023). A Bibliometric Analysis of Higher Education and the Sustainable Development Goals. In Advances in educational marketing, administration, and leadership book series (pp. 1–25). https://doi.org/DOI: 10.4018/978-1-6684-8356-5.ch001

Baneres, D., Rodríguez-Gonzalez, M. E., & Serra, M. (2019). An early feedback prediction system for learners at-risk within a first-year higher education course. *IEEE Transactions on Learning Technologies*, 12, 249–263.

Baneres, D., Rodríguez-Gonzalez, M. E., & Serra, M. (2019). An early feedback prediction system for learners at-risk within a first-year higher education course. *IEEE Transactions on Learning Technologies*, 12, 249–263.

Baradwaj, B. K., & Pal, S. (2011). Mining educational data to analyze students' performance. *International Journal of Advanced Computer Science and Applications*, 2, 63–69.

Bota-Avram, C. (2023). Bibliometric analysis of sustainable business performance: Where are we going? A science map of the field. *Economic research-. Ekonomska Istrazivanja*, 36(1), 2137–2176.

Chiu, T. K. (2023). The impact of Generative AI (GenAI) on practices, policies and research direction in education: A case of ChatGPT and Midjourney. *Interactive Learning Environments*, •••, 1–17.

Chiu, T. K., Moorhouse, B. L., Chai, C. S., & Ismailov, M. (2023). Teacher support and student motivation to learn with Artificial Intelligence (AI) based chatbot. *Interactive Learning Environments*, •••, 1–17.

Çil, İ., Tokat, M. A., Türkan, Y. S., & Doğan, N. (2014). E-guidance and counseling decision support system in elementary and high schools. *H. U. Journal of Education*, 29, (29-2),34-56.

Dwivedi, Y. K., Kshetri, N., Hughes, L., Slade, E. L., Jeyaraj, A., & Kar, A. K.. (2023). "So what if ChatGPT wrote it?" multidisciplinary perspectives on opportunities, challenges, and implications of generative conversational AI for research, practice, and policy. *International Journal of Information Management*, 71, 102642. DOI: 10.1016/j.ijinfomgt.2023.102642

Florea, A. M., & Radu, S. (2019, May). Artificial intelligence and education. In 2019 22nd International Conference on Control Systems and Computer Science (CSCS) (pp. 381-382). IEEE.

Godin, B. (2006). On the origins of bibliometrics. *Scientometrics*, 68(1), 109–133. DOI: 10.1007/s11192-006-0086-0

Gutiérrez-Salcedo, M.. (2017). Some bibliometric procedures for analyzing and evaluating research fields. [Preprint]. *Applied Intelligence*. Advance online publication. DOI: 10.1007/s10489-017-1105-y

Hernández-Blanco, A., Herrera-Flores, B., Tomás, D., & Navarro-Colorado, B. (2019). A systematic review of deep learning approaches to educational data mining. *Complexity*, 2019(2019), 1306039.

Hinton, G. E. (2007). Learning multiple layers of representation. *Trends in Cognitive Sciences*, 11, 428–434. PMID: 17921042

Hurley, R. (2019). *Data Science: A Comprehensive Guide to Data Science, Data Analytics, Data Mining, Artificial Intelligence, Machine Learning, and Big Data*. Independently Published.

Kavitha, P., Moorthy, B. K., Sudharshan, P. S., & Aarthi, T. (2018). Mapping artificial intelligence and education. In 2018 International Conference on Communication, Computing and Internet of Things (IC3IoT); IEEE: Piscataway, NJ, USA, pp. 165–168.

Khaldi, H., & Prado-Gascó, V. (2021). Bibliometric maps and co-word analysis of the literature on international cooperation on migration. *Quality & Quantity*, 55, 1845–1869. DOI: 10.1007/s11135-020-01085-4

Khare, K., & Stewart, B. (2018). Artificial Intelligence and the Student Experience: An Institutional Perspective. *IAFOR Journal of Education*, 6(3), 63–78.

Koçoğlu, F. Ö., Emre, ˙. I. E., & Erol, Ç. S. (2017). Observation of Success Status of Employees in E-Learning Courses in Organizations with Data Mining. *International Journal of E-Adoption*, 9, 38–49.

LeCun, Y., Bengio, Y., & Hinton, G. (2015). Deep learning. *Nature*, 521(7553), 436–444. PMID: 26017442

Meckler, L., & Verma, P. (2022) Teachers are on alert for inevitable cheating after the release of ChatGPT. The Washington Post. Available at: https://www.washingtonpost.com/education/2022/12/28/chatbot-cheating-ai-chatbotgpt-teachers/ (Accessed August 15, 2024).

Minaei-Bidgoli, B., Kashy, D. A., Kortemeyer, G., & Punch, W. F. (2003, November). Predicting student performance: an application of data mining methods with an educational web-based system. In 33rd Annual Frontiers in Education, 2003. FIE 2003. (Vol. 1, pp. T2A-13). IEEE.

Mon, B. F., Wasfi, A., Hayajneh, M., Slim, A., & Ali, N. A. (2023). Reinforcement Learning in Education: A Literature Review. *Informatics (MDPI)*, 10(3), 74. DOI: 10.3390/informatics10030074

Muniasamy, A., & Alasiry, A. (2020). Deep Learning: The Impact on Future eLearning. *International Journal of Emerging Technologies in Learning*, 15(1), 188–199. DOI: 10.3991/ijet.v15i01.11435

Muniasamy, A., & Alasiry, A. (2020). Deep Learning: The Impact on Future eLearning. *International Journal of Emerging Technologies in Learning*, 15(1), 188–199. DOI: 10.3991/ijet.v15i01.11435

Ouyang, F., Zheng, L., & Jiao, P. (2022). Artificial intelligence in online higher education: A systematic review of empirical research from 2011 to 2020. *Education and Information Technologies*, 27(6), 7893–7925.

Rao, P. K., & Shukla, A. (2023). Sustainable strategic management: A bibliometric analysis. *Business Strategy and the Environment*, 32(6), 3902–3914.

Riedl, M. O. (2019). Human-centered artificial intelligence and machine learning. *Human Behavior and Emerging Technologies*, 1, 33–36.

Roll, I., & Wylie, R. (2016). Evolution and revolution in artificial intelligence in education. *International Journal of Artificial Intelligence in Education*, 26, 582–599.

Shrivastava, R. (2022). Teachers fear ChatGPT will make cheating easier than ever. Forbes. Available at: https://www.forbes.com/sites/rashishrivastava/2022/12/12/teachers-fear-chatgpt-will-make-cheating-easier-than-ever/?sh=5b0ab2ac1eef (Accessed on July 5, 2024).

Shukla, A. K., Janmaijaya, M., Abraham, A., & Muhuri, P. K. (2019). Engineering applications of artificial intelligence: A bibliometric analysis of 30 years (1988–2018). *Engineering Applications of Artificial Intelligence*, 85, 517–532. DOI: 10.1016/j.engappai.2019.06.010

Sing, C. C., Teo, T., Huang, F., Chiu, T. K., & Xing Wei, W. (2022). Secondary school students' intentions to learn AI: Testing moderation effects of readiness, social good and optimism. *Educational Technology Research and Development*, 70(3), 765–782.

Sutton, R. S., & Barto, A. G. (2018). *Reinforcement Learning: An Introduction*. MIT Press.

Taneri, G. U. (2020). Artificial Intelligence & Higher Education: Towards Customized Teaching and Learning, and Skills for an AI World of Work. Research & Occasional Paper Series: CSHE. 6.2020. Center for Studies in Higher Education.

Turing, A. M. (1950). Computing machinery and intelligence-AM Turing. *Mind*, 59(236), 433–450.

Ünlü, R. (2019). An assessment of imbalanced control chart pattern recognition by artificial neural networks. In *Artificial Intelligence and Machine Learning Applications in Civil* (pp. 240–258). Mechanical, and Industrial Engineering., DOI: 10.4018/978-1-7998-0301-0.ch013

Wiering, M. A., & Van Otterlo, M. (2012). Reinforcement learning. *Adaptation, Learning, And Optimization*, 12(3), 729.

Xia, Q., Chiu, T. K., & Chai, C. S. (2023). The moderating effects of gender and need satisfaction on self-regulated learning through Artificial Intelligence (AI). *Education and Information Technologies*, 28(7), 8691–8713.

Zawacki-Richter, O., Marín, V. I., Bond, M., & Gouverneur, F. (2019). Systematic review of research on artificial intelligence applications in higher education–where are the educators? *International Journal of Educational Technology in Higher Education*, 16(1), 1–27.

Chapter 6
Evaluation of Artificial Intelligence Tools for Universities With Fuzzy Multi-Criteria Decision-Making Methods

Hacer Yumurtaci Aydogmus
https://orcid.org/0000-0002-2307-0840
Alanya Alaaddin Keykubat University, Turkey

Ufuk Aydogmus
Alanya Alaaddin Keykubat University, Turkey

ABSTRACT

The concept of Artificial Intelligence (AI), which was first used in the 1950s, can perform tasks that require human intelligence by using various algorithms and computer programs. This chapter aims to evaluate AI tools that can be used in universities. Firstly, the AI tools used in universities were researched from the literature, then Fuzzy Multi-Criteria Decision Making was applied to determine which of these tools should be prioritized. Five criteria (perceived ease of use, perceived usefulness, personalization, interaction, trust) obtained from expert opinions and the literature were weighted and the AI tools that were determined as alternatives were prioritized. Fuzzy numbers, first presented to the literature by Zadeh in 1965, aid in decision-making because it is frequently impossible to utilize precise formulations during evaluations. Since 1965, extensions of fuzzy numbers have been developed and integrated into multi criteria decision making methods. The decision making method to be used in this study is also integrated with the use of intuitionistic fuzzy

DOI: 10.4018/979-8-3693-7949-3.ch006

numbers.

INTRODUCTION

Artificial intelligence, also referred to as AI and defined as machines that imitate human intelligence, is a significant technical advancement that has caused a global debate. It includes creating artificial intelligence with the ability to observe, learn, and analyze data. Given that AI collects data, identifies patterns and automates decision-making processes, it can be described as "automation based on relationships" (Okulich-Kazarin et al., 2024).

In higher education, the capability approach emphasizes what students can achieve with technology, rather than documenting these measures of access to technology. This is significant since the same resources might yield varying results for different persons. The approach also acknowledges that each person has unique abilities and needs. It can be applied to the evaluation of digital educational resources and their usage, such as assessing the capabilities of AI in the classroom to enhance educational outcomes. Moreover, it stresses the meaningful integration of AI, considering how this technology can support the diverse needs of learners (Markauskaite et al., 2022; Carvalho et al., 2022).

Artificial intelligence (AI) has recently garnered significant attention from educational researchers (Hmoud et al., 2024) and has begun to be employed by universities to enhance the quality of higher education services. AI tools are expected to assist university instructors in the teaching process. Additionally, students are utilizing AI to help them complete their assignments (Okulich-Kazarin et al., 2024).

Generative artificial intelligence can influence various aspects of student learning, such as the contextual and motivational dimensions (Hmoud et al., 2024). The integration of generative artificial intelligence (AI) tools with instructional design matrices represents a novel and promising approach to addressing the evolving demands of modern education. By leveraging AI's capabilities, educators can provide personalized learning experiences, adaptive content generation, and real-time support for students. The use of an instructional design matrix brings structure and coherence to the educational process, ensuring alignment with learning objectives and enhancing the effectiveness of teaching strategies. This combined approach enhances student engagement and motivation, offering educators new opportunities to create dynamic and inclusive virtual classrooms (Ruiz-Rojas et al., 2023).

A challenge, however, is the lack of knowledge among teachers regarding generative AI tools and systematic processes for designing micro-curricular activities that facilitate the development and management of large-scale virtual learning environments. Addressing this would enable teachers to effectively design and manage

AI-supported digital resources with innovative educational strategies, promoting the creation of massive virtual classrooms (García-Peñalvo & Corell, 2020).

In this book chapter, firstly, studies on the use of artificial intelligence in higher education from the literature are presented. Then, the IFTOPSIS method used in this study was explained with its steps under the title of material and method, and important concepts related to fuzziness were given beforehand. Under the title of application, the criteria definitions determined based on literature and expert opinions, alternatives to be evaluated were presented, and then the results obtained with the application of the method were given. Finally, the study was evaluated and concluded.

LITERATURE REVIEW

The inevitable role of artificial intelligence (AI) tools in every aspect of contemporary life, including the field of foreign language teaching and learning, cannot and should not be overlooked. Although the exact trajectory of AI's development cannot be immediately and definitively predicted, it is evident that AI is already shaping trends in foreign language learning. Given the current generation's heavy reliance on technology, integrating ChatGPT into the English language curriculum in tertiary education could significantly boost student motivation (Marjanovikj-Apostolovski, 2024).

As technology continues to advance, the integration of generative AI tools into various sectors, including education, has gained momentum (Shahzad et al., 2024). Numerous studies have been conducted on the use of AI tools in higher education, and when examining these studies on a yearly basis, it is clear that the past two years have seen a particularly significant acceleration. The number of publications in 2023-2024 has surpassed those of previous years. This section presents examples from studies, especially from the past two years.

In a study conducted in 2023, responses generated by ChatGPT to existing assessment prompts from ten courses across seven Australian universities were analyzed to explore how ChatGPT could impact assessment in engineering education. The strengths and weaknesses of current assessment practices were addressed, and opportunities for leveraging ChatGPT to facilitate learning were discussed. Since artificial intelligence is rapidly evolving, this analysis established a benchmark for ChatGPT's performance in responding to engineering education assessment prompts as of early 2023. The findings indicated a need for changes in existing practices, as ChatGPT was able to generate valid responses to many assessments with only minor adjustments to the input prompts, and future versions trained on larger datasets are expected to perform even better (Nikolic et al., 2023).

McGrath et al. (2023) focused on the adoption of artificial intelligence in higher education practices by examining university instructors' relationships with emerging technologies. Their study employed an experimental philosophy approach with three objectives: i) to identify university instructors' intuitions regarding their responsibility to adopt new AI technologies, ii) to understand the conditions under which university instructors find AI defensible and are thus willing to integrate such tools and services into their daily practices, and iii) to determine instructors' self-reported knowledge about AI.

An empirical study involving 534 university students adapted the UTAUT2 model, indicating that attitudes toward ChatGPT are shaped by performance expectancy, effort expectancy, social influence, facilitating conditions, hedonic motivation, and habit (Strzelecki, 2023). Among English-as-a-foreign-language learners, perceived ease of use, perceived usefulness, and general attitudes toward ChatGPT closely align with their overall perceptions of the tool (Liu & Ma, 2024). Most studies have explored learners' attitudes toward ChatGPT through the lens of technology acceptance (Liu & Ma, 2024; Strzelecki, 2023).

This study employed a person-centered approach (latent profile analysis) and thematic analysis to uncover students' attitudes and behavioral intentions toward ChatGPT. Utilizing a rigorous stratified random sampling approach, the study conducted a mixed-methods investigation based on representative data collected from 850 Chinese university students (Zhang et al., 2024).

The study (Liu & Ma, 2024) aims to provide empirical insights into how English-as-a-foreign-language learners perceive and utilize ChatGPT, a highly capable AI chatbot from OpenAI's GPT family, beyond the classroom setting. Structural equation modeling analyses revealed that while Perceived Ease of Use does not directly predict learners' Attitude, it can influence Attitude through the full mediation of Perceived Usefulness. The findings also suggest that learners who hold positive attitudes toward the usefulness of ChatGPT are more likely to exhibit a higher level of Behavioral Intention, which in turn strongly predicts their Actual Use of ChatGPT for English learning outside the classroom.

Hmoud et al. (2024) aimed to investigate the characteristics of students' task motivation within the context of artificial intelligence, particularly in relation to ChatGPT. The researchers conducted interviews with 15 students about their experiences with ChatGPT to collect data. They used both inductive and deductive content analysis to explore students' motivation while learning with ChatGPT. To identify categories and subcategories of motivation, the researchers utilized MAXQDA 2022. Five main categories emerged: task enjoyment, reported effort, outcome evaluation, perceived relevance, and interaction.

In a study by Strzalkowski et al. (2024) in the field of patient health education, the readability and accuracy of ChatGPT-4 and Google Gemini in answering questions about an eye disease were evaluated in comparison with two human experts. The study concluded that, despite requiring higher levels of training, both AI tools handled questions effectively, delivering mostly accurate answers with few critical errors.

Smerdon (2024) conducted a study on the use of AI tools by undergraduate students in their assignments. The study sought to statistically compare the grade point averages (GPAs) and performances of students who used AI tools versus those who did not, based on surveys. While students using AI tools had higher GPAs, there was no statistically significant effect on overall student performance.

Kohnke (2024) examined how students enrolled in an English for Academic Purposes course at a Hong Kong university perceived generative AI tools and traditional grammar-checking tools. The findings showed that students viewed generative AI tools as more comprehensive and authoritative, due to their ability to provide detailed explanations and contextual insights that enhance language proficiency. However, the study also highlighted concerns over overreliance, data privacy, and fair access to premium features. It examined the ethical and pedagogical implications of integrating such tools into higher education and emphasized the need for institutional guidance.

Another study conducted in 2024 explored the awareness, acceptance, and adoption of ChatGPT in higher education institutions across China using the Technology Acceptance Model. Survey data collected from university students revealed that awareness of ChatGPT significantly influenced the intention to adopt it (Shahzad et al., 2024).

Okulich-Kazarin et al. (2024) evaluated student responses via electronic surveys from eight Eastern European universities, aiming to comprehensively explore the use of artificial intelligence in higher education in relation to Sustainable Development Goal 4.3's focus on "non-violent" learning environments. The study emphasized the integration of smart education and AI in creating such environments. Given the challenge of directly measuring "non-violent" learning environments, the researchers focused on students' views regarding the impact of AI tools on the educational process as a unified and indivisible entity.

In addition to the artificial intelligence studies in the field of education obtained from the above-mentioned literature, an additional search was made in the WoS database for the book chapter. ("artificial intelligence" AND ""multi-criteria decision" AND ("higher education" OR "university" OR "universities")) were selected as topic for the search. The search revealed four publications that were not directly relevant to the subject of this chapter. For the first article obtained from the literature, the aim was to diagnose patients at high risk of prostate cancer. A dataset of 78 patients from Necmettin Erbakan University Meram Medical Faculty was used, and an artificial neural network was established regarding the consistency of the convergence coefficients calculated using the Fuzzy TOPSIS method. In the second study, a methodology for predicting antibiotic resistance has been proposed, and a multi-objective evolutionary search strategy has been addressed. To select the best prediction model, a multi-criteria decision-making process has been suggested. With the results obtained, this study contributes to the literature by using fuzzy MCDM methods in the selection of AI tools for higher education.

MATERIALS AND METHOD

Decision-making is very challenging when there is risk and ambiguity. Many qualitative or quantitative decision-making techniques that have been researched in the literature can be applied to get around these challenges. The most popular quantitative decision-making technique is Multi-Criteria Decision-Making Methods (MCDM), which allows the selection of the best option from the list of available options as well as the ranking of those options.

To select the best alternative from a range of alternatives, experts today employ a variety of empirical and scientific techniques. Experiences can be useful in decision-making in a limited number of relevant fields; they cannot be used universally. Regardless of the environment under study, selecting the optimal option in any given situation can be done effectively and efficiently by applying a scientific technique. Many professionals employ the MCDM, which is considered one of the most significant scientific methodologies. The concept of MCDM is put out when a decision maker takes into account many attributes. This approach assigns a significant portion of routine decisions made in human communities and organizations to itself (Alinezhad and Khalili, 2019). Fuzzy numbers is a helpful tool for handling decisions involving ambiguous and imprecise phenomena. It allows for the qualification of imprecise information as well as the reasoning and decision-making of incomplete and ambiguous data. This makes it possible to include qualitative elements in decision-making issues (Zadeh, 1965 and Zadeh 1975; from Nieto-Morote and Ruz-Vila, 2012).

Preliminaries: Basic Definitions of Intuitionistic Fuzzy Sets

Accordingly, the general definitions of IFS by Atanassov (1986) are explained in following items:

Definition 1: X is assumed as a non-empty set. Also, let the IFS in the X set be defined by α. m_α and n_α are defined as membership and non-membership degrees of IFS:

$$\alpha = \{x, a_\alpha(x), b_\alpha(x); x \in X\} \quad (1)$$

where a_α: X → [0,1] and b_α: X → [0,1] and their sum must not exceed 1.

$$0 \leq a_\alpha(x) + b_\alpha(x) \leq 1 \quad (2)$$

Hesitancy degree (Π) is found for α as in Eq. (3):

$$\Pi_\alpha(x) = 1 - a_\alpha(x) - b_\alpha(x) \quad (3)$$

Definition 2: X= (a_X, b_X) and Y= (a_Y, b_Y) are defined as an IFS. Addition and multiplication operations for X and Y are performed as shown below:

$$X \oplus Y = \left(a_X + a_Y - a_X a_Y, b_X b_Y\right) \quad (4)$$

$$X \otimes Y = \left(a_X a_Y, b_X + b_Y - b_X b_Y\right) \quad (5)$$

Definition 3: X=(a_X, b_X) is described as an IFS. For set A, the score function S(X) and the accuracy function H(X) are calculated in the following Eqs. (6) and (7):

$$S(X) = a_X - b_X \quad (6)$$

$$H(X) = a_X + b_X \quad (7)$$

Definition 4: Let it be defined as two IFS, X= (a_X, b_X) and Y= (a_Y, b_Y). The normalized Euclidean and normalized Taxicab distances between IFS are calculated by the following formulas:

$$d_E(X, Y) = \sqrt{\frac{1}{2n}\sum_{i=1}^{n}(a_X - a_Y)^2 + (b_X - b_Y)^2 + (\Pi_X - \Pi_Y)^2} \quad (8)$$

$$d_T\left(X, Y\right) = \frac{1}{n}\sum_{i=1}^{n}\left(|a_X - a_Y| + |b_X - b_Y| + |\Pi_X - \Pi_Y|\right) \quad (9)$$

Definition 5: Let the decision matrix for each decision makers be shown by $W = \left[X_{lr}\right]_{k*s}$, where l =1, 2, . . ., k is a set of *k* criteria and r=1, 2, . . ., s. X_{lr} represents idea of DM *r* with resprct to the criterion *l*. By this way, intuitionistic fuzzy numbers can be shown as $X_{lr} = \left(a_{X_{lr}}, b_{X_{lr}}, \Pi_{X_{lr}}\right)$. Intuitionistic fuzzy weighted averaging (IFWA) operator is formulated by Xu (2007) as shown in Eq. (10):

$$Z = \text{IFWA}=\left(1 - \prod_{r=1}^{s}\left(1 - a_{X_{lr}}\right)^{\varnothing_r}, \prod_{r=1}^{s} b_{X_{lr}}{}^{\varnothing_r}, \prod_{r=1}^{s}\left(1 - a_{X_{lr}}\right)^{\varnothing_r} - \prod_{r=1}^{s} b_{X_{lr}}{}^{\varnothing_r} \quad (10)$$

where Z= (a_Z, b_Z, Π_Z), l =1, 2, . . ., k; and $\varnothing_r$ is represented in Eq. (11):

$$\varnothing_r = \frac{a_r + \Pi_r\left(\frac{a_r}{a_r + b_r}\right)}{\sum_{r'=1}^{s} a_{r'} + \Pi_{r'}\left(\frac{a_{r'}}{a_{r'} + b_{r'}}\right)} \tag{11}$$

Description of Intuitionistic Fuzzy TOPSIS Method

Steps of the Intuitionistic Fuzzy TOPSIS method which was improved by Boran et al. (2009) are shown as follows. In addition, intuitionistic fuzzy weighted averaging (IFWA) operator will be used for creating decision matrix.

Step 1: Decision matrix is prepared for each decision maker with intuitionistic fuzzy numbers. To evaluate the alternatives, the scale developed for intuitionistic fuzzy numbers by Alkan and Kahraman (2021) will be implemented as shown in Table 1.

Step 2: After preparing decision matrices for each decision maker, aggregated intuitionistic decision matrix is occured. Evaluations of decision makers are integrated in aggregated intuitionistic decision matrix by using Equations 10 and 11 with IFWA operator. By this way, the decision makers may have different weights in the working model according to their experience and knowledge on the relevant subject will be provided by equation 11.

Table 1. Intuitionistic fuzzy linguistic terms used for alternative selection

Linguistic Terms	IFS	
	m	n
Certainly High Value (CHIV)	.9	.1
Very High Value (VHIV)	.8	.15
High Value (HIV)	.7	.25
Above Average Value (AAVV)	.6	.35
Average Value (AVV)	.5	.45
Under Average Value (UAVV)	.4	.55
Low Value (LOV)	.3	.65
Very Low Value (VLOV)	.2	.75
Certainly Low Value (CLOV)	.1	.9

Step 3: Aggregated intuitionistic fuzzy criterion weight matrix are prepared in this phase. Firstly, weights consisting of intuitionistic fuzzy criterion pairs were established by the decision makers. Intuitionistic fuzzy number linguistic scales

found by Alkan and Kahraman (2021) are used to state the weights of the criteria are shown in Table 2.

Table 2. Intuitionistic fuzzy linguistic terms used for criterion weights

Linguistic Terms	IFS	
	m	n
Absolutely High Importance (AHI)	0.90	0.10
Very High Importance (VHI)	0.80	0.15
High Importance (HI)	0.70	0.25
Above Average Value (AAV)	0.60	0.35
Average Value (AV)	0.50	0.45
Under Average Value (UAV)	0.40	0.55
Low Importance (LI)	0.30	0.65
Very Low Importance (VLI)	0.20	0.75
Absolutely Low Importance (ALI)	0.10	0.90

After, individual evaluations of decision makers were transformed into aggregated intuitionistic fuzzy criterion weight matrix with Equation 12. Let be a set of intuitionistic fuzzy pairs ($<m_{i,1},n_{i,1}>,<m_{i,2},n_{i,2}>$). The value of k_i in the formula is the number of decision makers (Atanassov, 2020).

$$< \mu(C_i), \nu(C_i) > = <\frac{\sum_{j=1}^{ki} m_{i,j}}{k_i}, \frac{\sum_{j=1}^{ki} n_{i,j}}{k_i}> \tag{12}$$

Step 4: Weighted intuitionistic fuzzy decision matrix is occured by multiplying intuitionistic fuzzy decision matrix with aggregated intuitionistic fuzzy criterion weight matrix as explained in Equation 4.

Step 5: Positive ideal solutions ($A^* = (m_{A^*}, n_{A^*})$) and negative ideal solutions ($A^- = (m_B^-, n_B^-)$) are prepared for weighted intuitionistic fuzzy decision matrix by the help of Equations 13, 14, 15 and 16 respectively. J_1 represents criterion is benefit-oriented, and J_2 represents the cases of the criterion being cost-oriented in these equations.

$$m_{A^*} = \{(maks\, m_A | j \in J_1), (min\, m_A | j \in J_2) \tag{13}$$

$$n_{A^*} = \{(min\, n_A | j \in J_1), (maks\, n_A | j \in J_2) \tag{14}$$

$$m_{A-} = \{(min\, m_A | j \in J_1), (maks\, m_A | j \in J_2) \tag{15}$$

$$n_{A-} = \{(maks\, n_A | j \in J_1), (min\, n_A | j \in J_2) \tag{16}$$

Step 6: After determining positive and negative ideal solutions, positive separation measures (S^*) and negative separation measures (S^-) are calculated by using normalized Euclidean distance (Szmidt ve Kacprzyk, 2004) in Equation (17) and Equation (18).

$$S^* = \sqrt{\frac{1}{2n}\sum_{i=1}^{n}(m_A - \mathrm{m}_{A*})^2 + (n_A - \mathrm{n}_{A*})^2 + (\Pi_A - \Pi_{A*})^2} \quad (17)$$

$$S^- = \sqrt{\frac{1}{2n}\sum_{i=1}^{n}(m_A - \mathrm{m}_{A-})^2 + (n_A - \mathrm{n}_{A-})^2 + (\Pi_A - \Pi_{A-})^2} \quad (18)$$

Step 7: Relative closeness coefficients (C_i) are calculated by using Equation 19.

$$C_i = \frac{S^-}{S^* + S^-} \quad (19)$$

Step 8: Lastly, alternatives are ranked with relative closeness coefficients. The higher alternative with relative closeness coefficient is determined as best alternative in IFS-TOPSIS method.

APPLICATION

Determination of Criteria And Alternatives

We established five criteria for evaluating the alternatives after talking with the three experts and reviewing the literature on the AI tools in higher education. These criteria encompass perceived ease of use (PEOU), perceived benefit (PB), personalization (Per), interaction (Int) and trust (Tr). Detailed explanations of the criteria are given below in sub-items:

Perceived Ease of Use (PEOU) plays a crucial role in students' preference for AI-based tools. This concept refers to the perception of how effortless and easy it is to use a technology by its users. Students place great importance on the clarity and usability of the tools they use, especially in educational processes. If a technological tool is perceived as complex and challenging to use, students' inclination to adopt that tool can be negatively impacted. With the increasing prevalence of AI tools, evaluations based on perceived ease of use have become more significant. The effective use of AI technologies in education is not only related to the innovations offered by the technology itself but also to how users perceive and comfortably adapt to it (Al Darayseh, 2023; Gayan Nayanajith, 2020).

Studies on the acceptance of AI in education have revealed that perceived ease of use is one of the most critical factors in technology acceptance models. A systematic review by Kelly et al. (2023) indicated that perceived ease of use strongly influences users' behavioral intentions in the process of adopting AI technologies (Kelly et al., 2023). This implies that students' ability to learn and adapt to AI-based systems easily enhances their willingness to use these technologies. In today's educational landscape, where technology is widely used, students' ability to use these tools effortlessly encourages more active participation in technology.

Perceived ease of use is not considered a standalone factor in the adoption of AI-based systems. The experiences users have during the learning and application processes of these technologies are closely related to their perceptions of how useful the systems are. In a study by Gayan Nayanajith (2020), it was found that both e-security and perceived ease of use played a significant role in the adoption of AI technologies in banking systems. This research demonstrated that the perception of ease of use is not only linked to the learning phase of the technology but also to users' trust in its security. Similarly, a study by Lopes et al. (2024) examined the impact of AI-supported systems in the context of e-commerce. The study found that perceived ease of use strengthened users' shopping intentions, with personalized shopping experiences offered by AI-supported systems facilitating decision-making processes and encouraging greater adoption of the technology (Lopes et al., 2024). In another study by Park and Kim (2023) on AI-supported digital health content, it was shown that perceived ease of use increased users' interest and intention to use such technologies. In a study particularly focused on students, AI-based chatbots were found to provide support in critical areas such as depression management, and the perception of ease of use enhanced this support (Park & Kim, 2023).

Perceived ease of use plays a critical role in technology acceptance models related to AI-based educational technologies. Sohn and Kwon (2020) compared various technology acceptance models and investigated the impact of perceived ease of use on the adoption of AI-based smart products. The results showed that the perception of ease of use was an important factor in users' adoption of these products (Sohn & Kwon, 2020). In a study by Sudaryanto et al. (2023), it was also noted that perceived ease of use was a decisive factor in accounting students' adoption of AI technologies. This study revealed that students' digital competencies and perceptions of how effortlessly they could use AI tools played a significant role in their adoption of the technology (Sudaryanto et al., 2023).

In conclusion, one of the most important factors students consider when choosing AI tools is their perception of how easy these tools are to use. Perceived ease of use is critically important in reducing the complexity of technology and enabling users to interact comfortably with it. For AI tools to be effectively adopted in education, perceptions of the ease of use of these technologies need to be positively shaped.

Therefore, PEOU has been identified as one of the criteria discussed in this book chapter.

Perceived Benefit (PU): One of the most important factors that students consider when using AI tools is how these tools will contribute to their academic performance. This concept, known as "Perceived Usefulness," refers to students' evaluation of how beneficial they find AI tools. The more useful a particular AI tool is perceived to be, the more likely students are to prefer using that technology. Specifically, when students believe that AI tools will make a tangible contribution to their educational process, their inclination to use these tools increases (Gerlich, 2023).

Perceived usefulness is not limited solely to contributing to academic success. It also encompasses the ability of students to access information more quickly, expedite decision-making processes, and receive personalized recommendations. These advantages offered by AI-based systems make students' educational experiences more effective and efficient (Kim, 2020). For instance, Kim's (2020) study highlights that AI-driven interactive recommendation systems save students time in information retrieval and help them adopt more complex decision-making strategies. This indicates that AI tools not only facilitate access to information but also enable students to make higher-quality choices in their education (Kim, 2020).

Personalization (Per): The personalization capabilities of AI tools are one of the primary reasons students increasingly prefer these technologies today. Personalization enhances the educational experience by providing content tailored to students' learning styles, individual needs, and performance. In this context, AI offers a customized approach that optimizes students' learning processes and accounts for their individual differences, rather than a one-size-fits-all educational model. Bhutoria (2022) describes the role of AI in education as a system tailored to meet students' specific needs. By utilizing big data and machine learning techniques, AI can analyze each student's learning habits and skills, delivering the most suitable content for each individual (Bhutoria, 2022). Similarly, Hashim et al. (2022) note that AI-assisted learning systems track student performance, offering personalized solutions that make the learning process more efficient (Hashim et al., 2022).

Maghsudi et al. (2021) emphasize that AI-based personalized education systems can identify students' individual strengths and weaknesses, providing them with the most appropriate learning paths. AI analyzes previous learning experiences to offer personalized learning pathways and long-term strategies. In this process, students' areas of weakness are identified, enabling more effective learning (Maghsudi et al., 2021). Mehendale (2023) asserts that such AI-supported systems increase student motivation, promote academic success, and ensure that education becomes accessible to everyone.

Rasheed et al. (2023) highlight that the use of AI in education personalizes learning processes, increasing students' interest in learning and positively impacting their academic performance. Tapalova and Zhiyenbayeva (2022) emphasize AI's transformative power in education, stating that personalized learning pathways provide students with 24/7 access and adapt educational processes to their individual needs. Van der Vorst and Jelicic (2019) argue that AI-supported educational tools can reduce teachers' workloads while providing students with one-on-one educational support, thereby enhancing the efficiency of education.

The positive impact of AI-supported personalized education systems on students' academic success, motivation, and overall educational experience underscores the increasing importance of these technologies in education. As these systems become more widely used in the future, they will enable a more personalized learning experience for each student, further improving the efficiency of educational processes.

Interaction (Int): With the increasing use of AI tools in education, their contribution to the student experience has become increasingly important. One of the key factors that students consider when choosing AI tools is how these technologies interact with them. Tools with a high level of interaction are perceived by students as more effective, user-friendly, and motivating. The interaction provided by AI stands out through its ability to respond to individual student needs, offering a personalized experience in educational processes.

Davis et al. (2024) examined AI's capacity to identify students' learning needs and deliver content accordingly. AI can monitor student performance, provide real-time feedback, and offer the most suitable learning methods for each student. This type of interaction allows students to experience more efficient learning processes. The research emphasized that interaction enables students to recognize their deficiencies and address them immediately through timely interventions.

In particular, in the education of healthcare professionals, the research by Mohammad and Fahad Mohammad (2024) highlights that AI improves the efficiency of educational processes by offering interactive tools. This interaction with students accelerates their professional development and underscores the growing importance of digital tools in education. In disciplines like healthcare education, AI tools play a critical role in creating interactive learning environments that are responsive to students' individual needs.

Okulich-Kazarin (2024) explored the impact of AI on student interaction within sustainable learning environments. The study linked AI tools' contribution to learning processes with the interaction they facilitate, which has the potential to enhance the quality of learning. This interactive structure provided by AI increases student engagement, leading to a deeper understanding and greater success in education.

Santos et al. (2024) examined how AI can be used in special education. AI personalizes instruction interactively according to students' needs and adapts learning materials during the process. Such interaction helps create inclusive and accessible learning environments, ensuring that students with different abilities receive equal education.

Interaction has become one of the main reasons why students prefer AI-supported educational tools. These tools respond sensitively to students' individual learning processes, offering them the most suitable learning experience, and significantly contributing to students' ability to achieve their educational goals.

Trust (Tr): As AI technologies are increasingly used in the field of education, trust has become one of the critical factors students consider when choosing these tools. The data security and privacy policies of AI tools directly impact students' trust in and preference for these technologies. Therefore, reliability is crucial for the widespread use of AI technologies in sensitive areas such as education. The trustworthiness of AI tools has been extensively addressed in various academic studies. Ryan (2020) stated that trusting AI, much like in human relationships, involves expectations of responsibility and assurance. However, it was noted that considering AI systems as fully trustworthy could raise ethical concerns. Particularly in cases where AI cannot align with human moral norms, it was argued that rather than trust, a certain level of "dependence" on AI should be developed. In this sense, trust in AI is grounded more in rational considerations than in the interpersonal trust seen in human relationships.

Omrani et al. (2022) highlighted the European Commission's efforts to develop highly reliable AI and emphasized the importance of trust for user groups like students. This study suggested that trust in AI is directly linked to concerns about the ethical use of AI and data security. In this context, it was emphasized that trust can only be enhanced through not just technological improvements but also by ensuring the ethical use of AI.

A study by Schmidt et al. (2020) stressed the importance of transparency and traceability in increasing trust in AI systems. Understanding how AI systems work and the data on which decisions are based can enhance users' trust, including that of students. However, the research also found that transparency does not always increase trust and, in some cases, can create distrust among users (Schmidt et al., 2020). This finding highlights that strategies to build trust through transparency must be carefully considered.

In conclusion, it is clear that students place great importance on the trust factor when choosing AI tools. The data security, transparency, ethical use, and appropriateness of AI tools for educational contexts significantly influence trust and, consequently, the rate at which these technologies are adopted. Building trust is not only about technological capabilities but also about designing these systems in a way that meets user needs and expectations. Ensuring these trust elements is essential for the successful use of AI tools in educational environments.

Four AI tools, namely virtual reality and augmented reality tools, chatbots for education, learning management systems and collaborative AI tools, were identified to be used in the study. Virtual reality and augmented reality has the potential to provide students with hands-on experiences, enhance the acquisition of complex concepts, develop critical thinking skills and prepare them for real-world challenges. Despite the great importance of digitalization, the use and effective inclusion of tools such as VR/AR in higher education courses is currently limited to isolated actions by university institutions (Kosmas et al., 2024). Chatbots with artificial intelligence were developed for a number of uses. After reviewing relevant technological developments, Caldarini et al. proposed that rule-based information retrieval and generative chatbots could be examples of chatbots (Lin & Yu, 2024). Learning management systems, which is considered as one of the important web-based innovations in the educational environment, according to McGill and Klobas (2009), is known as an information system that facilitates e-learning through the processing, storage and dissemination of educational materials. It is also used to support the management and related communication of learning contexts (Ashrafi et al., 2022). Collaborative AI tools; can help students work together and communicate, monitor contributions and progress, and get insights into both individual and group dynamics (Abu-Ghuwaleh & Saffaf, 2023).

RESULTS OF ANALYSIS

Within the scope of the study, a fuzzy multi-criteria decision-making model is created in order to use artificial intelligence effectively in higher education activities. For evaluating and prioritizing the artificial intelligence tools for higher education, VR and AR tools, chatbots for education, learning management systems and collaborative AI tools are determined as alternatives represented by A1, A2, A3 and A4 respectively in application model. In addition, 5 criteria will be handled to evaluate alternatives named as perceived ease of use (PEOU), perceived benefit (PB), personalization (PER), interaction (INT) and trust (TR) respectively.

To choose the the most appropiate alternative for artificial intelligence tool in higher education, intiutinistic fuzzy TOPSIS (IFS-TOPSIS) will be handled. Solution of the defined problem with IFS-TOPSIS method will be shown with application steps as follows.

Step 1: Decision matrix is perpared including evaluations of decision makers (DM) with four alternatives (VR and AR tools, chatbots for education, learning management systems and collaborative AI tools) and five criteria (Perceived ease of use, perceived benefit, personalization, interaction and trust) with intuitionistic fuzzy numbers. For determining the alternatives by the decision makers, the scale in Table 1 which developed for intuitionistic fuzzy sets by Alkan and Kahraman (2021) will be used. According to intuitionistic fuzzy linguistic scale, evaluations of each decision makers are given with linguistic scale and intuitionistic fuzzy numbers Table 3 and Table 4 respectively.

Table 3. Linguistic evaluations of decision makers for artificial intelligence tools selection problem

Alternatives/ Criteria	Decision Makers	A1	A2	A3	A4
PEOU	DM1	AAV	VHV	CHV	HV
	DM2	AV	HV	CHV	AAV
	DM3	HV	VHV	VHV	HV
PB	DM1	CHV	HV	VHV	CHV
	DM2	HV	VHV	VHV	VHV
	DM3	VHV	HV	CHV	CHV
PER	DM1	HV	AAV	VHV	VHV
	DM2	AAV	HV	VHV	VHV
	DM3	HV	HV	VHV	CHV
INT	DM1	CHV	VHV	HV	CHV
	DM2	VHV	HV	HV	HV
	DM3	CHV	VHV	HV	VHV
TR	DM1	HV	VHV	CHV	VHV
	DM2	AAV	HV	VHV	VHV
	DM3	HV	VHV	CHV	VHV

Table 4. Evaluations of decision makers for artificial intelligence tools selection problem with intuitinositic fuzzy numbers

Alternatives/ Criteria	Decision Makers	A1	A2	A3	A4
PEOU	DM1	0.6, 0.35	0.8, 0.15	0.9, 0.1	0.7, 0.25
	DM2	0.5, 0.45	0.7, 0.25	0.9, 0.1	0.6, 0.35
	DM3	0.7, 0.25	0.8, 0.15	0.8, 0.15	0.7, 0.25

continued on following page

Table 3. Continued

Alternatives/ Criteria	Decision Makers	A1	A2	A3	A4
PB	DM1	0.9, 0.1	0.7, 0.25	0.8, 0.15	0.9, 0.1
	DM2	0.7, 0.25	0.8, 0.15	0.8, 0.15	0.8, 0.15
	DM3	0.8, 0.15	0.7, 0.25	0.9, 0.1	0.9, 0.1
PER	DM1	0.7, 0.25	0.6, 0.35	0.8, 0.15	0.8, 0.15
	DM2	0.6, 0.35	0.7, 0.25	0.8, 0.15	0.8, 0.15
	DM3	0.7, 0.25	0.7, 0.25	0.8, 0.15	0.9, 0.1
INT	DM1	0.9, 0.1	0.8, 0.15	0.7, 0.25	0.9, 0.1
	DM2	0.8, 0.15	0.7, 0.25	0.7, 0.25	0.7, 0.25
	DM3	0.9, 0.1	0.8, 0.15	0.7, 0.25	0.8, 0.15
TR	DM1	0.7, 0.25	0.8, 0.15	0.9, 0.1	0.8, 0.15
	DM2	0.6, 0.35	0.7, 0.25	0.8, 0.15	0.8, 0.15
	DM3	0.7, 0.25	0.8, 0.15	0.9, 0.1	0.8, 0.15

Step 2: Aggregated IF decision matrix is constructed by using Eqs. (10) and (11) considering with weights of three decision makers are equal (0,33) and shown in Table 5.

Table 5. Aggregated intuitionistic fuzzy decision matrix

	A1	A2	A3	A4
PEOU	0.604, 0.343	0.767, 0.180	0.871, 0.116	0.666, 0.283
PB	0.815, 0.158	0.734, 0.214	0.838, 0.133	0.871, 0.116
PER	0.666, 0.283	0.666, 0.283	0.796, 0.152	0.838, 0.133
INT	0.871, 0.116	0.767, 0.180	0.696, 0.253	0.815, 0.158
TR	0.666, 0.283	0.767, 0.180	0.871, 0.116	0.796, 0.152

Step 3: Weights of criteria are found by decision makers' opinions with intuitionistic fuzzy number linguistic scales found by Alkan and Kahraman (2021) as shown in Table 2. Finally, clustered intuitionistic fuzzy criterion weight matrix are pepared in Table 6 and Table 7 by using Equation 12 respectively.

Table 6. Linguistic expressions of decision makers for criteria

DMs/Criteria	DM1	DM2	DM3	Criterion Type
PEOU	A	VH	H	Benefit
PB	H	AH	AH	Benefit
PER	AH	H	VH	Benefit
INT	VH	VH	AA	Benefit
TR	AA	H	A	Benefit

Table 7. Clustered intuitionistic fuzzy criterion weight matrix

Criteria	IFSs Weight
PEOU	0.666, 0.283
PB	0.833, 0.15
PER	0.8, 0.166
INT	0.733, 0.216
TR	0.6, 0.35

Step 4: Weighted intuitionistic fuzzy decision matrix is perepared by multiplying intuitionistic fuzzy decision matrix with clustered intuitionistic fuzzy criterion weight matrix by using Equation 5. Weighted intuitionistic fuzzy decision matrix is calculated and shown in Table 8.

Table 8. Weighted intuitionistic fuzzy decision matrix

	A1	A2	A3	A4
PEOU	0.403, 0.529	0.511, 0.413	0.580, 0.367	0.444, 0.486
PB	0.679, 0.284	0.611, 0.332	0.698, 0.263	0.726, 0.249
PER	0.532, 0.402	0.532, 0.402	0.637, 0.294	0.670, 0.278
INT	0.639, 0.308	0.562, 0.358	0.510, 0.415	0.597, 0.340
TR	0.399, 0.534	0.460, 0.467	0.522, 0.426	0.478, 0.449

Step 5: Positive ideal solutions and negative ideal solutions are prepared by using Equations 13, 14, 15 and 16 respectively and listed in Table 9.

Table 9. Positive and negative ideal solutions

	Positive Ideal Solutions	Negative Ideal Solutions	Criterion Type
PEOU	0.580, 0.367	0.403, 0.529	Benefit
PB	0.726, 0.249	0.611, 0.332	Benefit
PER	0.670, 0.278	0.532, 0.402	Benefit
INT	0.639, 0.308	0.510, 0.415	Benefit
TR	0.522, 0.426	0.399, 0.534	Benefit

Step 6: Positive separation measures (S*) and negative separation measures (S-) are determined by using positive ideal solutions, negative ideal solutions and normalized Euclidean distance with Equation 17 and Equation 18 as shown in Table 10.

Step 7: Relative closeness coefficients (Ci) are also determined by using Equation 19 and listed in Table 10.

Table 10. Separation measures and the relative closeness coefficients

Alternatives	S^*	S^-	C_i
A1	0.059	0.111	0.349
A2	0.062	0.088	0.416
A3	0.109	0.055	0.662
A4	0.092	0.062	0.597

Step 8: Finally, alternatives are ranked according to relative closeness coefficients. The higher alternative with relative closeness coefficient is determined as best alternative. As a result, A3 (learning management systems) is determined as best alternative. Alternatives which are selected for Artificial Intelligence Tools Selection Problem are ranked as A3, A4, A2 and A1 respectively according to IFS-TOPSIS method approach.

CONCLUSION

In this study, a multi-criteria decision-making (MCDM) model has been applied to effectively evaluate artificial intelligence (AI) tools in higher education, using the Intuitionistic Fuzzy TOPSIS method. The findings on the application of multi-criteria decision making method as well as literature reviews on the use of artificial intelligence in higher education are presented. The increasing role of AI in education and the benefits it provides show that AI is an important tool for addressing the challenges faced by instructors in teaching processes. It has been found that AI enhances the effectiveness of education by personalizing student learning processes and enabling adaptive instructional materials. Moreover, the findings of the study emphasize the need to increase the awareness of instructors regarding AI-based tools. The support provided by AI in managing complex tasks, such as large-scale virtual classrooms, contributes to a better understanding of technological developments in education. In this context, it is clear that systematic training programs for instructors and strategies for the use of digital tools should be developed.

Intuitionistic Fuzzy TOPSIS method, as applied in the study, provided a comprehensive framework for the multidimensional evaluation of AI tools, allowing decision-makers to compare the performance of each tool based on various criteria. The five key criteria employed in the study—perceived ease of use, perceived usefulness, personalization, interactivity, and trust—were identified as critical factors influencing the selection of technological tools in education. These criteria not only pertain to the functionality of the tools but also to how they shape the user experience.

The analysis revealed that perceived usefulness (PB) and personalization (PER) were the most heavily weighted criteria. This finding suggests that, for AI tools to be successfully implemented in education, it is not enough for them to be merely functional; they must also address individual student needs and provide tangible benefits. In this context, learning management systems emerged with the highest proximity coefficient, performing exceptionally well in both perceived usefulness and personalization criteria. This result aligns with the flexible structure of learning management systems, which enables student-centered solutions and adapts to individual learning processes.

Collaborative AI tools, ranked second, demonstrated significant performance, particularly in the criteria of interactivity and personalization. The potential of these tools to enhance collaboration and interaction among students highlights the growing importance of collaborative learning in educational technologies. The preference for these tools is driven by their ability to encourage individual contributions and provide collaborative environments. This finding indicates that the acceptance of collaborative learning tools, increasingly employed in the field of educational technology, is likely to rise in the future.

On the other hand, VR/AR tools and educational chatbots ranked third and fourth, respectively. Although these tools offer innovative and advanced technologies in education, they underperformed in comparison to other tools, especially in the criteria of ease of use and interactivity. This indicates that there are still technical and pedagogical challenges in integrating VR/AR tools and chatbots into educational environments. To ensure wider adoption, these tools need to be optimized with user-friendly interfaces and enhanced to provide more effective interaction with students.

The method employed in the study provided a robust analytical framework for understanding the performance of AI tools based on different criteria. By considering the weightings assigned by decision-makers, the strengths and weaknesses of each AI tool were identified. Notably, the relatively lower scores for some tools in the trust (TR) criterion suggest that the perception of trust in the use of technology in educational settings needs to be improved. Trust is a critical factor for the acceptability of AI technologies in education, underscoring the need to enhance the reliability of these tools for broader adoption.

In conclusion, this study offers a multidimensional evaluation framework for selecting AI tools in higher education and clearly highlights the criteria on which these tools stand out. Learning management systems have demonstrated superior performance compared to other tools by offering student-centered flexibility and personalization. These findings provide valuable insights for the effective integration of technological tools in higher education and serve as essential guidance for shaping digitalization strategies in education. The development of policies to promote the effective use of AI tools in higher education and their broader adoption will contribute to the improvement of educational processes. Further research is needed to understand the future potential of AI-supported educational technologies and to use these technologies more effectively. In particular, more studies are required on how multi-criteria decision-making methods can be used in the selection and evaluation of such technologies. This can make significant contributions to the processes of selecting and implementing the most appropriate AI solutions for educational institutions.

REFERENCES

Abu-Ghuwaleh, M., & Saffaf, R. (2023). Integrating AI and NLP with project-based learning in STREAM education.

Al Darayseh, A. (2023). Acceptance of artificial intelligence in teaching science: Science teachers' perspective. *Computers and Education: Artificial Intelligence*, 4, 100132.

Alinezhad, A., & Khalili, J. (2019). *New methods and applications in multiple attribute decision making (MADM)* (Vol. 277). Springer.

Alkan, N., & Kahraman, C. (2021). Circular intuitionistic fuzzy TOPSIS method: Pandemic hospital location selection. *Journal of Intelligent & Fuzzy Systems*, 42(1), 1–22.

Almansour, M., & Alfhaid, F. M. (2024). Generative artificial intelligence and the personalization of health professional education: A narrative review. *Medicine*, 103(31), e38955. PMID: 39093806

Ashrafi, A., Zareravasan, A., Rabiee Savoji, S., & Amani, M. (2022). Exploring factors influencing students' continuance intention to use the learning management system (LMS): A multi-perspective framework. *Interactive Learning Environments*, 30(8), 1475–1497.

Atanassov, K. (1986). Intuitionistic fuzzy sets. *Fuzzy Sets and Systems*, 20(1), 87–96.

Atanassov, K. (2020). Circular intuitionistic fuzzy sets. *Journal of Intelligent & Fuzzy Systems*, 39(5), 5981–5986.

Bhutoria, A. (2022). Personalized education and artificial intelligence in the United States, China, and India: A systematic review using a human-in-the-loop model. *Computers and Education: Artificial Intelligence*, 3, 100068.

Boran, F. E., Genç, S., Kurt, M., & Akay, D. (2009). A multi-criteria intuitionistic fuzzy group decision making for supplier selection with TOPSIS method. *Expert Systems with Applications*, 36(8), 11363–11368.

Carvalho, L., Martinez-Maldonado, R., Tsai, Y. S., Markauskaite, L., & De Laat, M. (2022). How can we design for learning in an AI world? *Computers and Education: Artificial Intelligence*, 3, 100053.

Davis, C. (2024). Artificial Intelligence in Education: Enhancing Learning Experiences through Personalized Adaptation. *International Journal of Cyber and IT Service Management*, 4(1), 26–32.

García-Peñalvo, F. J., & Corell, A. (2020). The COVID-19: The enzyme of the digital transformation of teaching or the reflection of a methodological and competence crisis in higher education. *Campus Virtuales*, 9(2), 83–98.

Gayan Nayanajith, D.A. (2020). Customers' Perceptions of E-Security and Ease of Use on Artificial Intelligence Enabled E-Banking Adoption.

Gerlich, M. (2023). Perceptions and acceptance of artificial intelligence: A multidimensional study. *Social Sciences*, 12(9), 502.

González, R. A. G., & Bonilla, M. H. S. (2022). Education and artificial intelligence: Immersive theme nodes. *Electronic Journal of Educational Technology*, 82, 59–77. DOI: 10.21556/edutec.2022.82.2633

Hashim, S., Omar, M. K., Ab Jalil, H., & Sharef, N. M. (2022). Trends on technologies and artificial intelligence in education for personalized learning: Systematic literature. *Journal of Academic Research in Progressive Education and Development*, 12(1), 884–903.

Hmoud, M., Swaity, H., Hamad, N., Karram, O., & Daher, W. (2024). Higher education students' task motivation in the generative artificial intelligence context: The case of chatgpt. *Information (Basel)*, 15(1), 33.

Kelly, S., Kaye, S. A., & Oviedo-Trespalacios, O. (2023). What factors contribute to the acceptance of artificial intelligence? A systematic review. *Telematics and Informatics*, 77, 101925.

Kim, J. (2020). The influence of perceived costs and perceived benefits on AI-driven interactive recommendation agent value. *Journal of Global Scholars of Marketing Science*, 30(3), 319–333.

Kohnke, L. (2024). Exploring EAP students' perceptions of GenAI and traditional grammar-checking tools for language learning. *Computers and Education: Artificial Intelligence*, 7, 100279.

Kosmas, P., Nisiforou, E., & Vrasidas, C. (2024). Transforming higher education teaching through the integration of virtual and augmented reality. In *INTED2024 Proceedings* (pp. 2604-2612). IATED.

Lin, Y., & Yu, Z. (2024). A bibliometric analysis of artificial intelligence chatbots in educational contexts. *Interactive Technology and Smart Education*, 21(2), 189–213.

Liu, G., & Ma, C. (2024). Measuring EFL learners' use of ChatGPT in informal digital learning of English based on the technology acceptance model. *Innovation in Language Learning and Teaching*, 18(2), 125–138.

Lopes, J. M., Silva, L. F., & Massano-Cardoso, I. (2024). AI Meets the Shopper: Psychosocial Factors in Ease of Use and Their Effect on E-Commerce Purchase Intention. *Behavioral Sciences (Basel, Switzerland)*, 14(7), 616. PMID: 39062439

Maghsudi, S., Lan, A., Xu, J., & van Der Schaar, M. (2021). Personalized education in the artificial intelligence era: What to expect next. *IEEE Signal Processing Magazine*, 38(3), 37–50.

Marjanovikj-Apostolovski, M. (2024). ChatGPT as a learning tool in an undergraduate advanced academic english course at south east european university. Journal of Teaching English for Specific and Academic Purposes, 243-254.

Markauskaite, L., Marrone, R., Poquet, O., Knight, S., Martinez-Maldonado, R., Howard, S., & Siemens, G. (2022). Rethinking the entwinement between artificial intelligence and human learning: What capabilities do learners need for a world with AI? *Computers and Education: Artificial Intelligence*, 3, 100056.

McGrath, C., Pargman, T. C., Juth, N., & Palmgren, P. J. (2023). University teachers' perceptions of responsibility and artificial intelligence in higher education-An experimental philosophical study. *Computers and Education: Artificial Intelligence*, 4, 100139.

Mehendale, P. (2023). Personalization in Education through AI. *European Journal of Advances in Engineering and Technology*, 10(3), 60–65.

Mohd Rahim, N. I., & Iahad, A., N., Yusof, A. F., & A. Al-Sharafi, M. (2022). AI-based chatbots adoption model for higher-education institutions: A hybrid PLS-SEM-neural network modelling approach. *Sustainability*, 14(19), 12726.

Nieto-Morote, A., & Ruz-Vila, F. (2012). A fuzzy multi-criteria decision-making model for construction contractor prequalification. *Automation in Construction*, 25, 8–19.

Nikolic, S., Daniel, S., Haque, R., Belkina, M., Hassan, G. M., Grundy, S., & Sandison, C. (2023). ChatGPT versus engineering education assessment: A multidisciplinary and multi-institutional benchmarking and analysis of this generative artificial intelligence tool to investigate assessment integrity. *European Journal of Engineering Education*, 48(4), 559–614.

Okulich-Kazarin, V., Artyukhov, A., Skowron, Ł., Artyukhova, N., & Wołowiec, T. (2024). When Artificial Intelligence Tools Meet" Non-Violent" Learning Environments (SDG 4.3): Crossroads with Smart Education. Sustainability (2071-1050), 16(17).

Okulich-Kazarin, V., Artyukhov, A., Skowron, Ł., Artyukhova, N., & Wołowiec, T. (2024). When Artificial Intelligence Tools Meet" Non-Violent" Learning Environments (SDG 4.3): Crossroads with Smart Education. *Sustainability (2071-1050), 16*(17).

Omrani, N., Rivieccio, G., Fiore, U., Schiavone, F., & Agreda, S. G. (2022). To trust or not to trust? An assessment of trust in AI-based systems: Concerns, ethics and contexts. *Technological Forecasting and Social Change*, 181, 121763.

Orozco, M. P., Pytel, P., & Pollo-Cattaneo, M. F. (2020). Implementation methodology of a chatbot as a virtual tutor in the educational field for universities in Latin America. In Serna, E.M. (Ed.), Formative Research in Engineering(pp. 218–226). Antioquia Research Institute (IAI).

Park, D. Y., & Kim, H. (2023). Determinants of intentions to use digital mental healthcare content among university students, faculty, and staff: Motivation, perceived usefulness, perceived ease of use, and parasocial interaction with AI Chatbot. *Sustainability*, 15(1), 872.

Rasheed, Z., Ghwanmeh, S., & Abualkishik, A. Z. (2023). Harnessing Artificial Intelligence for Personalized Learning: A Systematic Review. *Data and Metadata*, 2, 146–146.

Ruiz-Rojas, L. I., Acosta-Vargas, P., De-Moreta-Llovet, J., & Gonzalez-Rodriguez, M. (2023). Empowering education with generative artificial intelligence tools: Approach with an instructional design matrix. *Sustainability*, 15(15), 11524.

Ryan, M. (2020). In AI we trust: Ethics, artificial intelligence, and reliability. *Science and Engineering Ethics*, 26(5), 2749–2767. PMID: 32524425

Santos, S. M. A. V., da Silva, C. G., de Carvalho, I. E., & de Castilho, L. P., das Neves Meroto, M. B., Tavares, P. R., dos Reis Pires, R., de Oliveira Rodrogues Moniz, S. S. (2024). The art of personalization of education: Artificial Intelligence on the stages of special education. *Contribuciones. Ciencia y Sociedad*, 17(2), e4971–e4971.

Schmidt, P., Biessmann, F., & Teubner, T. (2020). Transparency and trust in artificial intelligence systems. *Journal of Decision Systems*, 29(4), 260–278.

Shahzad, M. F., Xu, S., & Javed, I. (2024). ChatGPT awareness, acceptance, and adoption in higher education: The role of trust as a cornerstone. *International Journal of Educational Technology in Higher Education*, 21(1), 46.

Smerdon, D. (2024). AI in essay-based assessment: Student adoption, usage, and performance. *Computers and Education: Artificial Intelligence*, 7, 100288.

Sohn, K., & Kwon, O. (2020). Technology acceptance theories and factors influencing artificial Intelligence-based intelligent products. *Telematics and Informatics*, 47, 101324.

Strzalkowski, P., Strzalkowska, A., Chhablani, J., Pfau, K., Errera, M. H., Roth, M., & Guthoff, R. (2024). Evaluation of the accuracy and readability of ChatGPT-4 and Google Gemini in providing information on retinal detachment: A multicenter expert comparative study. *International Journal of Retina and Vitreous*, 10(1), 61. PMID: 39223678

Strzelecki, A. (2023). To use or not to use ChatGPT in higher education? A study of students' acceptance and use of technology. *Interactive Learning Environments*, •••, 1–14. DOI: 10.1080/ 10494820.2023.2209881

Sudaryanto, M. R., Hendrawan, M. A., & Andrian, T. (2023). The Effect of Technology Readiness, Digital Competence, Perceived Usefulness, and Ease of Use on Accounting Students Artificial Intelligence Technology Adoption. In *E3S Web of Conferences* (Vol. 388, p. 04055). EDP Sciences.

Szmidt, E., & Kacprzyk, J. (2004). A similarity measure for intuitionistic fuzzy sets and its application in supporting medical diagnostic reasoning, In International conference on artificial intelligence and soft computing (pp. 388-393). Berlin, Heidelberg: Springer Berlin Heidelberg.

Tapalova, O., & Zhiyenbayeva, N. (2022). Artificial intelligence in education: AIEd for personalised learning pathways. *Electronic Journal of e-Learning*, 20(5), 639–653.

Torres, M. T. M., Álvarez, L. M. S., & Osorio, A. S. O. (2022). Initialstudy of a chatbot for virtual modality students from the inter-American school of librarianship. *Library Research*, 36(90), 13–30. DOI: 10.22201/iibi.24488321xe.2022.90.58452

U.S. Department of Education. Artificial Intelligence and Future of Teaching and Learning: Insights and Recommendations., Washington, DC, (2023)

Van der Vorst, T., & Jelicic, N. (2019). Artificial Intelligence in Education: Can AI bring the full potential of personalized learning to education? 30th European Conference of the International Telecommunications Society (ITS): "Towards a Connected and Automated Society", Helsinki, Finland, 16th-19th June, 2019, International Telecommunications Society (ITS), Calgary

Xu, Z. (2007). Intuitionistic fuzzy aggregation operators. *IEEE Transactions on Fuzzy Systems*, 15(6), 1179–1187.

Zhang, Y., Yang, X., & Tong, W. (2024). University students' attitudes toward ChatGPT profiles and their relation to ChatGPT intentions. *International Journal of Human-Computer Interaction*, •••, 1–14.

Chapter 7

Evaluation of AI-Based Accessibility Technologies for Disabled Higher Education Students Using Fuzzy Cocoso Method

Eren Kamber
Alanya Alaaddin Keykubat University, Turkey

ABSTRACT

This study examines the role of artificial intelligence (AI) technologies in the education of students with disabilities and provides a comprehensive assessment of how these technologies can transform educational processes. Also, the study explores the impact of AI-based technologies such as speech recognition, text-to-speech, and automated captioning systems in increasing accessibility for students with disabilities. In evaluating AI-based technologies tailored to the educational needs of students with disabilities, multi-criteria decision-making methods such as fuzzy logic and the Fuzzy CoCoSo method were utilized. The analysis results demonstrate that these technologies contribute substantially to enhancing students' learning motivation, supporting academic success, and developing independent mobility skills. This study addresses the contributions of AI to educational accessibility from a perspective of social justice and equity and offers recommendations for the effective use of AI-supported accessibility technologies in this field.

DOI: 10.4018/979-8-3693-7949-3.ch007

INTRODUCTION

The rapid development of both hardware and software technologies has transformed instructional methods, enabling educators to create more engaging and technology-enhanced learning experiences. As these advancements continue, technology's role in enhancing academic skills becomes even more crucial. The flexibility offered by digital tools allows students to engage with learning content anywhere and anytime, reinforcing the need to integrate technology within educational settings (Geist, 2011).

Inclusive education has also become a central issue in global education systems, particularly regarding students with disabilities. Since the early 18th century, educational policymakers have increasingly recognized the value of creating inclusive school environments that accommodate diverse student needs. This "full inclusion" approach, as adopted by various countries, seeks to ensure equal access to education regardless of student differences (Onaga & Martoccio, 2008).

With the emergence of artificial intelligence (AI) in the mid-20th century, AI applications have expanded significantly within our fast-evolving digital landscape. Heightened expectations—driven by media, industry experts, and scientific advancements—have fueled AI's applications across various fields, including education, healthcare, and finance (Chan & Zary, 2019). Although there is no universally agreed definition of AI, it is broadly understood as an interdisciplinary field combining elements from computer science, psychology, linguistics, neuroscience, and philosophy, among other disciplines (Chen et al., 2020).

AI is fundamentally structured around three main paradigms: symbolic (logic- and knowledge-based), statistical (probabilistic and machine learning models), and subsymbolic (embodied intelligence and heuristic search). These paradigms allow AI to address diverse challenges across domains such as perception, reasoning, knowledge management, and communication. Today, AI is used in fields ranging from automotive and finance to medicine and education (Russell & Norvig, 2016).

The influence of AI-powered technologies is now embedded in everyday life, reshaping how people think, act, and communicate. As AI has advanced—especially with the rise of Artificial Neural Networks (ANN) and Deep Learning (DL)—its applications have grown substantially, offering new potential across many sectors (Chan & Zary, 2019).

Specifically, the use of AI in education, known as Artificial Intelligence in Education (AIEd), focuses on developing technologies that can perform cognitive tasks similar to human learning and problem-solving processes (Baker et al., 2019). Through advanced techniques like Natural Language Processing (NLP) and interactive chatbots, AI enhances educational environments, making learning more personalized and engaging (Alhawiti, 2014; Karsenti, 2019). In addition, AI-based tools in education have led to innovations like educational data mining and learning analytics, supporting data-driven decision-making in instructional design (Romero & Ventura, 2020).

These AI systems enable students to learn at their own pace while offering teachers data-driven insights to better support individual learning needs. Moreover, AI can deliver personalized practice exercises and assignments, adapted to the unique skill levels and challenges of each student, further fostering a tailored learning experience (Vincent-Lancrin & Van der Vlies, 2020; Karsenti, 2019).

In this study, the transformative impact of technology in education is examined, with a specific focus on artificial intelligence (AI) applications that support the educational processes of individuals with disabilities. Initially, the study evaluates the effects of using technological tools in education on enhancing individuals' academic skills and making the educational process more accessible. Following this, it discusses how AI-supported systems personalize students' learning experiences and assist teachers in making data-driven decisions. The challenges faced by individuals with disabilities in education, along with inclusive educational practices aimed at these individuals, are also key focuses of this research. Within this context, the role of AI-supported learning tools in improving accessibility for students with disabilities is analyzed. Additionally, the study examines various support systems offered by AI technologies in education and the potential of these systems to strengthen students' independent learning abilities.

In addition, the study summarizes the results of a literature review conducted to assess the feasibility of AI-based assistive tools for individuals with disabilities. The findings of this study make significant contributions by presenting innovative technological solutions that support the participation of individuals with disabilities in educational processes, thereby shedding light on steps that can be taken to achieve equity in education.

The Fuzzy CoCoSo (Combined Compromise Solution) method is employed to prioritize AI-supported accessibility technologies for students with disabilities in this study. The method is distinguished as an effective tool for evaluating alternatives in multi-criteria decision-making problems characterized by uncertainty and fuzzy data. Through the use of Fuzzy CoCoSo, evaluations were conducted across different alternatives and criteria to measure the potential contributions of AI-based technologies in education.

LITERATURE REVIEW

Disability in Education

Students with intellectual disabilities often face significant challenges in developing a positive self-concept, maintaining a proactive attitude towards career exploration, and making autonomous career decisions—challenges that can stem from learned helplessness (Kang & Cho, 2021). Limited access to career information and structured decision-making tools further compounds these issues, leaving these students with insufficient opportunities to explore potential career paths effectively (Hitchings et al., 2001).

Debate continues over the full inclusion of students with disabilities in mainstream education systems, yet successful integration requires educational institutions to foster an environment that embraces diversity and innovation. This involves supporting educational staff and ensuring flexible, constructive approaches to outcomes, assessments, and overall learning processes (Alqaryouti, 2010).

Historical milestones have greatly influenced the development of education for students with disabilities, including the early 20th-century mandate for universal education, the global recognition of human rights from the 1950s onward, and the adoption of inclusive, humanistic educational philosophies. Despite the ratification of the United Nations Convention on the Rights of Persons with Disabilities (UNCRPD) in 2006 by numerous countries, many still struggle to align with international standards, facing challenges in both policy conceptualization and practical implementation for inclusive education (Karellou, 2019).

Globally, there has been a notable increase in both the number and variety of support requests made by university students with disabilities. These requests vary widely, from visible physical disabilities to invisible mental health or psychological conditions, many of which require flexible, adaptive support strategies as students progress through their studies (Rose, 2010).

A review of global literature reveals persistent obstacles for students with disabilities in higher education, highlighting the complexities of achieving equal opportunity in this setting. While all students face transitional challenges entering postsecondary education, those with disabilities experience additional barriers due to reduced support networks, lack of role models, limited self-advocacy skills, insufficient or ineffective accommodations, low expectations from others, and restricted access to both mainstream and assistive technologies (Burgstahler, 2012).

Research has also explored the willingness of college faculty to provide accommodations for students with learning disabilities. These accommodations include aids such as tape recorders, note-takers, laptops, and early access to syllabi. However, faculty were less inclined to offer extra credit or alternative assignments, showing neutral attitudes towards other adjustments like extended deadlines and instructor notes (Skinner et al., 2007).

Within the European Union, support for students with disabilities varies considerably by country, as education policies are shaped primarily by individual member states rather than EU-wide mandates. Some countries, like Portugal, Germany, and Greece, offer preferential enrollment procedures, and support systems range from technical aids (e.g., Braille materials, recorded lectures) to special examination accommodations (Karellou, 2019).

Many higher education institutions still treat disability as a distinct area managed by student support services, rather than integrating it into institutional policies and practices. A shift toward the 'social model' of disability, which considers environmental and cultural factors, could enhance the retention and success of students with disabilities. By embedding inclusive practices in university policies and training personnel in inclusive pedagogy, institutions not only support students with disabilities but also create a more inclusive learning environment for all (Karellou, 2019).

AI Functions in Disability Education

The integration of artificial intelligence (AI) in educational environments has grown significantly in recent years. Scholars in the field of AI in education (AIEd) emphasize that AI technologies can enable personalized learning, improve learning efficacy, support teachers and students in structured activities, and create more interactive classroom experiences (Hopcan et al., 2022).

Luckin et al. (2016) highlight that AIEd equips students with essential skills for the modern world, such as creativity and critical thinking, by allowing for the monitoring and assessment of complex skillsets. This technology also provides insights into effective instructional methods and the types of learning contexts that best foster these skills.

As an interdisciplinary field, AIEd has garnered academic interest for over three decades, bringing together diverse disciplines to design adaptive and personalized AI-driven learning tools. These tools encourage learning across varied contexts, supporting students regardless of location or traditional educational limitations (Luckin et al., 2016).

AI technologies such as intelligent robots and adaptive learning platforms have been increasingly adopted in K-12 and higher education. They allow for personalized learning tailored to individual needs, providing an alternative to conventional educational approaches that may not suit all learning styles, abilities, or preferences. Through AI, educators can address each student's unique needs more effectively, thereby supporting a truly individualized learning experience (Della Ventura, 2019).

For students with disabilities transitioning to adulthood, career education is essential to ensure effective career planning and development. Implementing advanced technologies that offer innovative learning experiences is key to making career education accessible and impactful for these students (Hong & Kim, 2024).

Structured and customized career education plays a vital role for students with intellectual disabilities in promoting independence and facilitating societal integration (Lombardi et al., 2018; Soresi et al., 2008).

AI-enhanced tools are increasingly recognized for their advantages over conventional educational technologies in supporting students' learning processes. AI technologies enable instructors to deliver adaptive, personalized learning experiences that align with individual learners' unique needs, while also offering essential support for those with learning disabilities (Chen et al., 2020; Kharbat et al., 2021). AI-based tutoring systems, text-to-speech software, and speech recognition applications assist students with disabilities in their learning, making knowledge acquisition more accessible and customized to individual capabilities (Hopcan et al., 2022; Barua et al., 2022).

Placing students at the core of their learning journey, AI technologies empower learners to take a more active role. For students with intellectual disabilities, this targeted approach can address underlying barriers to learning, rather than focusing solely on behavior. Integrating AI into educational programs has shown to increase engagement, motivation, and focus among these students, thus enhancing their educational experience (Martínez et al., 2023; Hong & Kim, 2024).

In the last 25 years, AI in education has evolved with tools such as "teacher bots" that function as teaching assistants, delivering content, providing feedback, and tracking student progress (Bayne, 2015). The continued development of these applications demonstrates AI's potential to offer targeted support, identify learning gaps, and streamline routine tasks, allowing teachers to focus on adaptive, student-centered instruction (Chan & Zary, 2019).

Studies on AI Functions in Disability Education

In recent years, the application of artificial intelligence (AI) in education has broadened significantly, especially in programs tailored for students with intellectual disabilities. The integration of AI into these educational contexts is anticipated to achieve specific learning and developmental outcomes (Hopcan et al., 2022; Marino et al., 2023). This study, therefore, aims to assess the effectiveness of an AI-driven career education program for students with intellectual disabilities, with a particular focus on its impact on students' career self-efficacy and learning flow. Specifically, this research addresses the following questions: 1) How does participation in an AI-based career education program affect the career self-efficacy of students with intellectual disabilities? 2) How does it influence their learning flow? (Hong & Kim, 2024).

In the context of medical education, AI has primarily been utilized for individualized learning support, offering personalized feedback while avoiding potential issues related to curriculum assessment and the digitalization of sensitive exams. The need for accurate data handling and methodological improvements is critical to advancing AI integration in the medical field. Additionally, incorporating AI into the medical curriculum could equip future professionals with the necessary skills to leverage AI algorithms effectively (Chan & Zary, 2019).

One of AI's key roles in educational settings is the facilitation of personalized learning, which involves tailoring educational content to the unique needs of each student (Karsenti, 2019). Given the growing significance of Artificial Intelligence in Education (AIEd), this field warrants a comprehensive review. In a recent systematic analysis of 45 influential AIEd studies, key trends emerged: 1) AIEd research interest and influence have steadily grown; 2) deep learning technologies are not yet widely implemented in educational settings; 3) traditional AI tools, such as natural language processing, are commonly used in education, whereas more advanced techniques remain less explored; 4) many studies utilizing AI technology lack an in-depth engagement with established educational theories (Chen et al., 2020).

AI is also gaining traction in non-academic university services. For instance, institutions like Griffith, Northwestern, and Oklahoma have implemented chatbots to assist students by answering queries and providing support outside of regular hours. Such systems, also applied in libraries, student services, and academic advising, offer personalized assistance, support students with special needs, streamline administrative tasks, and facilitate assessments (Brown et al., 2020).

Special education, particularly through Universal Design for Learning (UDL), has also benefited from AI tools. UDL is a framework that promotes accessibility for all students by focusing on three key principles: engagement, representation, and expression. AI-based digital tools support these principles, enhancing the learning experience for both mainstream and special education students (Banes & Behnke, 2019).

In alignment with the United Nations Sustainable Development Goal (SDG) 4, which seeks to provide inclusive and equitable quality education for all, AI technology shows promise in supporting students with disabilities and those in vulnerable situations. For instance, AI is seen as a potential tool to ensure equal access to vocational training and educational opportunities for marginalized groups, including students with disabilities (UN, 2020).

This study provides insights into the trends in AI-related research within special education by conducting a systematic review of 29 studies published between 2008 and 2020. Most of these studies, originating primarily from the United States, focus on skill development through a quantitative research approach, examining both cognitive and affective learning factors within diverse school settings. Software-based AI applications are the most common, with many studies focusing on supporting learners with autism spectrum disorders (Hopcan et al., 2022).

Barriers to AI Integration in Disability Education

While technological advancements and disability support services have expanded educational opportunities, these innovations risk reinforcing stigma if not grounded in a comprehensive understanding of the complex, socio-political dimensions of disability. Beyond approaches that focus on mere integration or compensation, an intersectional perspective is essential to truly address the diverse and layered experiences of individuals with disabilities. By framing accessibility in higher education as a matter of social justice and human rights, this approach calls for structural and ideological shifts aimed at meaningful inclusion. An intersectional intervention model moves beyond reductionist solutions, targeting systemic inequities that contribute to the underrepresentation and high dropout rates among disabled students in higher education (Liasidou, 2014).

Barriers to inclusion are often rooted in multiple domains, including the physical environment, where students encounter challenges in accessing campus facilities, classrooms, accommodations, libraries, and support services (Holloway, 2001). Attitudinal obstacles further complicate inclusion, manifesting as negative perceptions from peers without disabilities (Liasidou, 2014) and exclusionary practices from university staff (Madriaga, 2007). Redpath et al. (2013) note that a significant barrier stems from limited awareness among faculty regarding the varied needs of disabled students. This lack of awareness frequently forces students to repeatedly request the same accommodations, which are essential for their learning. Examples of such accommodations include providing lecture notes or slides in advance (Hopkins, 2011) and permitting lecture recordings (Mortimore, 2013). These unaccommodating practices hinder full inclusion, placing students with disabilities at a disadvantage relative to their non-disabled peers.

Application Areas of AI in Higher Education

Artificial intelligence (AI) can be used in many areas to increase access and participation in education for students with disabilities. These technologies can improve students' academic performance, support independent learning skills, and reduce barriers in education (Chen et al., 2020). Here are some important areas of use and contributions in this area:

Personalized Learning and Support (Ayeni et al., 2024)

Personalized Learning Experience: AI can provide customized content according to students' learning pace and needs. This can help students with learning disabilities understand lessons better.

Language and Voice Support: AI-based voice assistants and translation applications allow students with hearing or visual impairments to access course materials more easily (Chen et al., 2021).

Accessibility Technologies (Anderson, 2024)

Voice Recognition and Text-to-Speech Applications: AI-based voice recognition systems allow students with physical disabilities to take notes or use computers. Text-to-speech software can also help visually impaired students listen to materials.

Automatic Subtitle and Translation Systems: Automatic subtitle creation in live lectures or video content for hearing-impaired students increases accessibility.

Supportive and Assistive Applications

Mental Health and Counseling Support: AI can monitor students' mental health and recommend counseling support if needed. This can be useful for stress and anxiety management (Liu et al., 2024).

Task and Time Management: AI-powered agendas, reminders, and task managers for students can help develop regular study habits, especially for students with disabilities who have difficulties such as attention deficit or hyperactivity disorder (Subashini and Krishnaveni 2021).

Interaction and Social Participation Support (Sibalija et al., 2020)

Development of Social Skills: AI can provide virtual interactions or simulations to students to develop social skills. This can help students with spectrum disorders such as autism to be more successful in social environments.

Interactive Chatbots and Support Systems: Chatbots that can quickly answer students' questions can increase the independence of students with disabilities by meeting simple needs.

Adaptation of Educational Materials (Dei, 2025)

Automatic Summarization and Simplification: AI can summarize or simplify texts, allowing students with learning disabilities to understand content more easily.

Visual and Auditory Supports: Provides alternative formats for course materials for students with visual or hearing impairments (Mills et al., 2023).

Accessibility and Guidance Technologies (Jansen and Colombo, 2024).

On-Campus Navigation and Assistive Robots: AI-supported navigation applications and assistive robots can be developed for students with visual or physical disabilities to easily navigate the campus.

Augmented Reality (AR) and Virtual Reality (VR): VR and AR technologies integrated with AI allow students with physical disabilities to participate in laboratory experiments or other applied courses in a virtual environment (Arranz-Paraíso and Arranz-Paraíso, 2024).

Fuzzy Logic

Decisions can be made under certainty or uncertainty. Making decisions under certainty is easier because there are many methods developed. Making decisions under uncertainty, on the contrary, is quite difficult. Environments where decisions are made under uncertainty and at the same time the goals and constraints are not clear are called fuzzy environments (Bellman and Zadeh, 1970).

Classical logic progresses by taking the value of "1" if the judgment is true and "0" if it is false. Fuzzy logic, which was introduced by Lotfi A. Zadeh in 1965 and is the principle of uncertain knowledge, deals with partial truth expressions instead of true or false expressions in classical logic. Thus, it is understood that the degree of truth of a proposition in fuzzy logic can be any real number between 0 and 1. As a result, unlike classical logic, which is based on definite judgments, fuzzy logic can easily work with uncertain judgments. For this, it uses membership functions.

One of the most suitable areas for the use of fuzzy set theory is decision analysis. Multi-criteria decision problems are generally very suitable for modeling using fuzzy set theory because of the complexity they contain and the criteria whose values can be verbal but cannot be defined very well (Kamber et al., 2024).

In different situations and environments, decision making to select different alternatives is one of the most important and difficult tasks of those in the management level. Today's rapidly changing and most competitive environment requires a business to have a detailed decision-making process in order to be successful. Decision making should be carried out not only by using information but also with the help of advanced decision-making techniques. Therefore, making the right decisions is necessary to gain advantage in a competitive environment. In addition, more than one purpose and criteria are included in this decision-making process. Therefore, it will be beneficial for businesses to use MCDM methods that take all criteria into consideration when making important decisions (Soner and Önüt, 2006: 120). However, in cases where the ratios in the decision matrix used in solving the encountered problem are verbal or fuzzy, fuzzy MCDM methods have been developed due to the inadequacy of existing MCDM methods (Menteş, 2000).

METHODS

Fuzzy Sets Theory

Fuzzy set theory is an extension of classical set theory that can easily solve problems in uncertain environments. A fuzzy set $\tilde{a}$ is represented as a set of pairs (X, y). Here X represents the sample space and m: X → [0, 1] is represented in the interval. The symbol $\mu_{\tilde{a}}(x)$ expresses the membership degree of element x to the fuzzy set $\tilde{a}$. According to $\mu_{\tilde{a}}(x)$, X represents the universal set and each element x is mapped to a real number in the interval [0, 1] (Zadeh, 1965).

Definition 1: Let a ∈ F (N) be a fuzzy number, if:

(1) $x_0 \in N$; such that $\mu_{\tilde{a}}(x_0) = 1$
(2) For any $\alpha \in [0, 1]$, $\tilde{a}_\alpha = [x, \mu_{\tilde{a}_\alpha}(x) \geq \alpha]$ is a closed interval.

Here N is the set of real numbers and F(R) represents the fuzzy set.

Fuzzy Logic Membership Functions

A fuzzy set is completely characterized by its membership function. Since most fuzzy sets in use have a discourse universe X consisting of the real line X, it is impractical to list all the pairs that define a membership function. A more convenient way to define a membership function is to express it as a mathematical formula (Jang et al., 1997).

There are four main methods for establishing the fuzzy membership functions: (i) the horizontal approach (Godal and Goodman, 1980; Bharathi-Devi and Sarma, 1985), (ii) the vertical approach (Civanlar and Trussel, 1986), (iii) the pairwise comparison method (Saaty, 1980), and (iv) the membership function estimation approach with the aid of probabilistic characteristics (Dubois and Prade, 1983).

Ali et al. (2015) compared the fuzzy logic control performances using the triangular membership function, trapezoidal membership function and Gaussian membership function with the Antenna Azimuth position and analyzed the results. It was found that the triangle and trapezoidal membership functions exhibited similar responses in terms of overshoot and rise time. However, it was observed that the triangle membership function performed better in steady state behavior, especially with increasing the target position angle.

Triangular membership function

A triangular membership function is represented by three parameters {a, b, c} as follows.

Definition 2: A triangular fuzzy number $\tilde{a}$, on R is defined as the following equation 1 if the membership function $\mu_{\tilde{a}}(x)$: R → [0, 1] is defined.

$$\mu_{\tilde{a}}(x) = \begin{cases} 0, x < a \\ \frac{x-a}{b-a}, a \leq x < b \\ \frac{c-x}{c-b}, b \leq x \leq c \\ 0, x > c \end{cases} \quad (1)$$

Here a, b and c represent the lower, modal and upper values of the set $\tilde{a}_i$ respectively, all of which are crisp numbers ($-\infty < a \leq b \leq c < \infty$). A triangular fuzzy number is represented as (a, b, c). It is expressed as $\tilde{a}_i = (a_i, b_i, c_i)$.

Figure 1. Triangle membership function representation

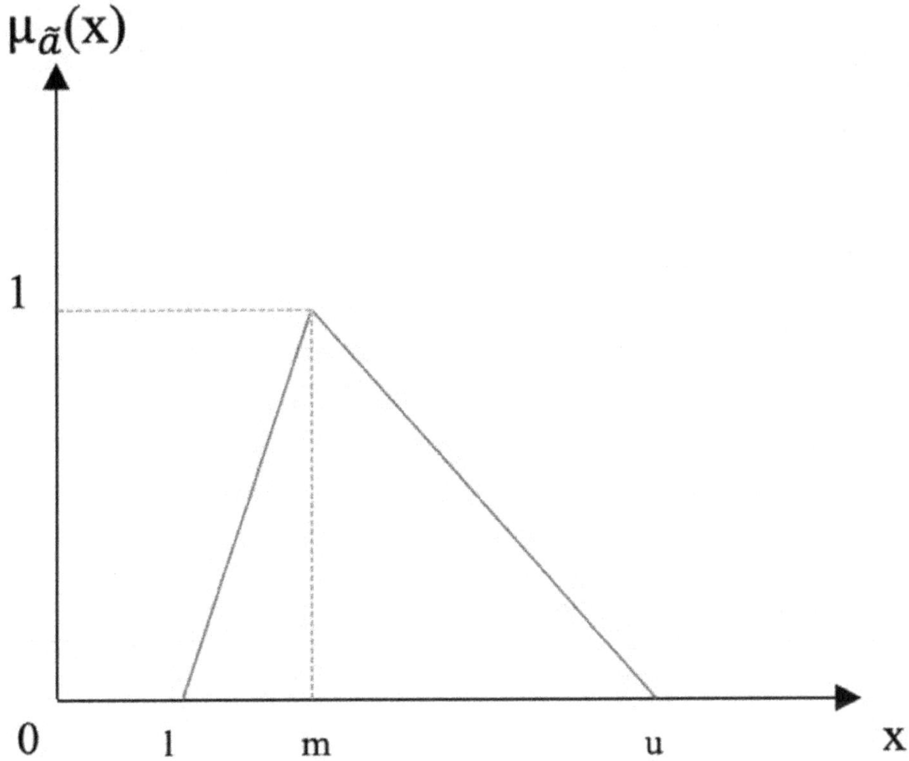

Definition 3: By the method of rank average integration representation, the rank average integration representation X $(\tilde{a}_i)$ of $\tilde{a}_i$ is as follows in equation 2 (Chen et al., 2000).

$$X(\tilde{a}_i) = \frac{a_i + 4b_i + c_i}{6} \quad (2)$$

Fuzzy CoCoSo Method

The extensions of fuzzy numbers with CoCoSo method was first proposed by Wen et al. (2019) and they implemented an application on the supplier selection problem. Fuzzy CoCoSo is used to rank alternatives according to their performance. It can easily work especially on linguistic expressions and contradictory criteria. The steps of Fuzzy CoCoSo are explained as follows (Ulutaş et al., 2021).

Step 1: The alternatives are evaluated by the decision makers (DMs) with the help of linguistic terms as shown in Table 1 and the fuzzy decision matrix $(\tilde{Z})$ is created by using equaiton 3 by taking the arithmetic average of the opinions.

Table 1. Transformation rules of linguistic variables to fuzzy numbers (Stanujkic, 2015)

Linguistic Terms	Fuzzy Numbers
Very High (VH)	(0.9, 1.0, 1.0)
High (H)	(0.7, 0.9, 1.0)
Above Average (AA)	(0.5, 0.7, 0.9)
Average (A)	(0.3, 0.5, 0.7)
Under Average (UA)	(0.1, 0.3, 0.5)
Low (L)	(0.0, 0.1, 0.3)
Very Low (VL)	(0.0, 0.0, 0.1)

$$\tilde{Z} = \left[\tilde{z}_{ij}\right]_{k\times n} = \begin{bmatrix} \tilde{z}_{11} & \cdots & \tilde{z}_{1n} \\ \vdots & \ddots & \vdots \\ \tilde{z}_{k1} & \cdots & \tilde{z}_{kn} \end{bmatrix} \# \tag{3}$$

Step 2: The decision matrix is normalized as follows using equation 4 (for cost criteria) and equation 5 (for benefit criteria). $\tilde{r}_{ij}$ represents the fuzzy normalized decision matrix in the equations.

$$\tilde{r}_{ij} = \left(r_{ij}^{l}, r_{ij}^{m}, r_{ij}^{u}\right) = \frac{\max\left(\tilde{z}_{ij}\right) - \tilde{z}_{ij}}{\max\left(\tilde{z}_{ij}\right) - \min\left(\tilde{z}_{ij}\right)} = \left(\frac{\max\left(z_{ij}^{u}\right) - z_{ij}^{u}}{\max\left(z_{ij}^{u}\right) - \min\left(z_{ij}^{l}\right)}, \frac{\max\left(z_{ij}^{u}\right) - z_{ij}^{m}}{\max\left(z_{ij}^{u}\right) - \min\left(z_{ij}^{l}\right)}, \frac{\max\left(z_{ij}^{u}\right) - z_{ij}^{l}}{\max\left(z_{ij}^{u}\right) - \min\left(z_{ij}^{l}\right)}\right) \# \tag{4}$$

$$\tilde{r}_{ij} = \left(r_{ij}^{l}, r_{ij}^{m}, r_{ij}^{u}\right) = \frac{\tilde{z}_{ij} - \min\left(\tilde{z}_{ij}\right)}{\max\left(\tilde{z}_{ij}\right) - \min\left(\tilde{z}_{ij}\right)} = \left(\frac{z_{ij}^{l} - \min\left(z_{ij}^{l}\right)}{\max\left(z_{ij}^{u}\right) - \min\left(z_{ij}^{l}\right)}, \frac{z_{ij}^{m} - \min\left(z_{ij}^{l}\right)}{\max\left(z_{ij}^{u}\right) - \min\left(z_{ij}^{l}\right)}, \frac{z_{ij}^{u} - \min\left(z_{ij}^{l}\right)}{\max\left(z_{ij}^{u}\right) - \min\left(z_{ij}^{l}\right)}\right) \# \tag{5}$$

Step 3: For each alternative, the fuzzy sum of weighted pairwise comparisons $\left(\tilde{S}_{i}\left(S_{i}^{a}, S_{i}^{b}, S_{i}^{c}\right)\right)$ and power weights $\left(\tilde{P}_{i}\left(P_{i}^{a}, P_{i}^{b}, P_{i}^{c}\right)\right)$ are calculated as shown in equations 6 and 7.

$$\tilde{S}_{i} = \left(S_{i}^{l}, S_{i}^{m}, S_{i}^{u}\right) = \sum_{j=1}^{n} \tilde{w}_{jc}\tilde{r}_{ij} = \left(\sum_{j=1}^{n} w_{jc}^{\ l} r_{ij}^{\ l}, \sum_{j=1}^{n} w_{jc}^{\ m} r_{ij}^{\ m}, \sum_{j=1}^{n} w_{jc}^{\ u} r_{ij}^{\ u}\right) \# \tag{6}$$

$$\tilde{P}_{i} = \left(P_{i}^{l}, P_{i}^{m}, P_{i}^{u}\right) =$$

$$\sum_{j=1}^{n}(\tilde{r}_{ij})^{\tilde{w}_{jc}} = \left(\sum_{j=1}^{n}(r_{ij}^{\,l})^{w_{jc}^{\,u}}, \sum_{j=1}^{n}(r_{ij}^{\,m})^{w_{jc}^{\,m}}, \sum_{j=1}^{n}(r_{ij}^{\,u})^{w_{jc}^{\,l}}\right) \# \tag{7}$$

Step 4: Three different aggregation strategies are applied to obtain the fuzzy evaluation scores $(\tilde{f}_{ia}, \tilde{f}_{ib}, \tilde{f}_{ic})$ by using equations 8, 9 and 10. For Equation 10, λ is taken as 0.5 in this application.

$$\tilde{f}_{ia} = (f_{ia}^{\,l}, f_{ia}^{\,m}, f_{ia}^{\,u}) = \frac{\tilde{P}_i + \tilde{S}_i}{\sum_{i=1}^{k}(\tilde{P}_i + \tilde{S}_i)} =$$

$$\left(\frac{P_i^{l} + S_i^{l}}{\sum_{i=1}^{k}(P_i^{u} + S_i^{u})}, \frac{P_i^{m} + S_i^{m}}{\sum_{i=1}^{k}(P_i^{m} + S_i^{m})}, \frac{P_i^{u} + S_i^{u}}{\sum_{i=1}^{k}(P_i^{l} + S_i^{l})}\right) \# \tag{8}$$

$$\tilde{f}_{ib} = (f_{ib}^{\,l}, f_{ib}^{\,m}, f_{ib}^{\,u}) = \frac{\tilde{S}_i}{\min(\tilde{S}_i)} + \frac{\tilde{P}_i}{\min(\tilde{P}_i)} =$$

$$\left(\frac{S_i^{l}}{\min(S_i^{l})} + \frac{P_i^{l}}{\min(P_i^{l})}, \frac{S_i^{m}}{\min(S_i^{l})} + \frac{P_i^{m}}{\min(P_i^{l})}, \frac{S_i^{u}}{\min(S_i^{l})} + \frac{P_i^{u}}{\min(P_i^{l})}\right) \# \tag{9}$$

$$\tilde{f}_{ic} = (f_{ic}^{\,l}, f_{ic}^{\,m}, f_{ic}^{\,u}) = \frac{\lambda(\tilde{S}_i) + (1-\lambda)(\tilde{P}_i)}{\lambda max(\tilde{S}_i) + (1-\lambda)max(\tilde{P}_i)} =$$

$$\left(\frac{\lambda(S_i^{l}) + (1-\lambda)(P_i^{l})}{\lambda\max(S_i^{u}) + (1-\lambda)\max(P_i^{u})}, \frac{\lambda(S_i^{m}) + (1-\lambda)(P_i^{m})}{\lambda\max(S_i^{u}) + (1-\lambda)\max(P_i^{u})}, \frac{\lambda(S_i^{u}) + (1-\lambda)(P_i^{u})}{\lambda\max(S_i^{u}) + (1-\lambda)\max(P_i^{u})}\right) \# \tag{10}$$

Step 5: The fuzzy evaluation scores $(\tilde{f}_{ia}, \tilde{f}_{ib}, \tilde{f}_{ic})$ are converted to crisp evaluation scores (f_{ia}, f_{ib}, f_{ic}) by using equations 11, 12 and 13 respectively.

$$f_{ia} = \frac{f_{ia}^{\,l} + f_{ia}^{\,m} + f_{ia}^{\,u}}{3} \# \tag{11}$$

$$f_{ib} = \frac{f_{ib}^{\,l} + f_{ib}^{\,m} + f_{ib}^{\,u}}{3} \# \tag{12}$$

$$f_{ic} = \frac{f_{ic}^{\,l} + f_{ic}^{\,m} + f_{ic}^{\,u}}{3} \# \tag{13}$$

Step 6: The final evaluation scores are combined to obtain the final score f_i for each alternative using equation 14. The alternative with the highest score is the best alternative.

$$f_i = (f_{ia}f_{ib}f_{ic})^{1/3} + \left(\frac{1}{3}\right)(f_{ia} + f_{ib} + f_{ic}) \tag{14}$$

APPLICATION

There are many special software and platforms for artificial intelligence applications such as voice recognition, text-to-speech, and automatic subtitling in accessibility technologies. The AI-based tools that stand out in these areas for disabled higher education students are as follows:

Voice Recognition Applications

Google Speech-to-Text: Google's voice recognition engine makes it easier for students to take notes by converting speech to text in real time. It supports many languages, including Turkish.

Otter.ai: Otter.ai is a platform that can transcribe long conversations such as meetings or lectures. It can be used to record live lectures and convert them into readable text later.

Microsoft Azure Cognitive Services - Speech-to-Text: This service from Microsoft allows students to give commands to the computer or take notes using their voices. Advanced API options allow customization according to the course content.

Text-to-Speech Applications

Kurzweil 3000: A popular educational tool especially for students with dyslexia or visual impairment, Kurzweil 3000 converts text to audio and allows students to listen to course materials.

NaturalReader: NaturalReader is an AI application that converts text to speech and offers various voice options. It can be used web-based or as an application.

Microsoft Immersive Reader: This reading tool from Microsoft offers features such as converting text to speech and increasing font size, especially for students with reading difficulties or visual impairment.

JAWS (Job Access With Speech): Developed for visually impaired users, JAWS presents texts on the computer as audio with its screen reader feature. It is especially useful for visually impaired students.

Automatic Subtitle and Translation Systems

YouTube Automatic Subtitle: YouTube has a powerful AI infrastructure that can automatically add subtitles to video content. It provides accessibility for hearing impaired students in video lessons or educational content.

Microsoft Teams and Zoom Automatic Captions: Both Microsoft Teams and Zoom offer automatic captioning in lectures. It can be used to create captions in live lectures.

Google Meet and Live Captions: Google Meet provides automatic captioning support in live lectures and meetings. Users can benefit from captioning options in many languages other than English.

DeepL and Google Translate: DeepL and Google Translate, which offer a powerful option especially for text translation, make materials in different languages accessible to students with hearing and reading disabilities.

Other Supportive Tools

Speechify: Speechify is a text-to-speech app that converts text into high-quality audio. It is a useful option for students who want to listen to lecture materials.

Transcriber for WhatsApp: This app converts WhatsApp voice messages to text, making audio content on messaging apps more accessible to students.

Within the scope of the study, according to classification which is done for AI based education technologies for disabled students, voice recognition (VOI), text-to-speech (TEX), and automatic subtitle and translation systems (AUT) and other supportive tools (OTH) were selected as alternatives for AI based accessibility technologies for higher education students with disabilities in education in the fuzzy multi-criteria decision-making model.

In this context, the relevant criteria selected to evaluate the alternatives and their explanations are given in Table 2. Cost criteria is cost oriented, and the other criteria are benefit oriented in decision making model.

For the evaluation of artificial ıntelligence-based accessibility technologies for disabled higher education students with the fuzzy CoCoSo method, the opinions of two experts in education systems were consulted in the decision-making model. The experts consist of academicians and people working on AI.

Table 2. Criteria selected for the problem

Number	Criterion	Definition
C1	Self-exploration (Hong and Kim, 2024; Ahmad and Ghapar, 2019; Han et al., 2023)	Introducing yourself through the eyes of an AI
C2	The world of work (Hong and Kim, 2024)	Explore future careers related to AI
C3	Basic work skills (Hong and Kim, 2024; Taneri, 2020)	Appling AI in various aspects of life
C4	Career decision-making (Suryani and George, 2020)	Express workplace problems using AI
C5	Career preparation (Hong and Kim, 2024; Jones et al., 2020; Dougherty et al., 2022)	AI-assisted job interviews
C6	Professional life (Hong and Kim, 2024)	Workplace greetings with AI
C7	Cost (Antunes et al., 2021)	Cost of AI tool to apply education

The steps for implementing the Fuzzy CoCoSo method are as follows.

Step 1: The alternatives were evaluated by the DMs with the help of the linguistic terms as shown in Table 1 and Table 3 and Table 4 are created. After, the fuzzy decision matrix ($\tilde{Z}$) is created in Table 5 by taking the arithmetic averages of the opinions DMs.

Table 3. CoCoSo linguistic evaluations of DMs

Criteria Alternatives	**C1**		**C2**		**C3**	
	DM1	**DM2**	**DM1**	**DM2**	**DM1**	**DM2**
VOI	UA	UA	AA	H	UA	UA
TEX	H	H	H	AA	VH	VH
AUT	H	VH	AA	A	AA	A
OTH	AA	UA	A	H	A	A
Criteria Alternatives	**C4**		**C5**			
	DM1	**DM2**	**DM1**	**DM2**		
VOI	H	AA	H	H		
TEX	H	VH	VH	VH		
AUT	AA	AA	H	AA		
OTH	H	AA	UA	L		
Criteria Alternatives	**C6**		**C7**			
	DM1	**DM2**	**DM1**	**DM2**		
VOI	VH	H	AA	AA		

continued on following page

Table 3. Continued

Criteria Alternatives	C1		C2		C3	
	DM1	**DM2**	**DM1**	**DM2**	**DM1**	**DM2**
TEX	H	AA	AA	UA		
AUT	H	H	H	H		
OTH	L	L	H	VH		

Table 4. Fuzzy evaluations of DMs according to linguistic scale

Criteria Alternatives	C1	C2	C3	C4
VOI	(0.1, 0.3, 0.5)	(0.5, 0.7, 0.9)	(0.1, 0.3, 0.5)	(0.7, 0.9, 1.0)
	(0.1, 0.3, 0.5)	(0.7, 0.9, 1.0)	(0.1, 0.3, 0.5)	(0.5, 0.7, 0.9)
TEX	(0.5, 0.7, 0.9)	(0.7, 0.9, 1.0)	(0.9, 1.0, 1.0)	(0.7, 0.9, 1.0)
	(0.7, 0.9, 1.0)	(0.5, 0.7, 0.9)	(0.9, 1.0, 1.0)	(0.9, 1.0, 1.0)
AUT	(0.7, 0.9, 1.0)	(0.3, 0.5, 0.7)	(0.5, 0.7, 0.9)	(0.5, 0.7, 0.9)
	(0.9, 1.0, 1.0)	(0.5, 0.7, 0.9)	(0.3, 0.5, 0.7)	(0.5, 0.7, 0.9)
OTH	(0.5, 0.7, 0.9)	(0.3, 0.5, 0.7)	(0.3, 0.5, 0.7)	(0.7, 0.9, 1.0)
	(0.1, 0.3, 0.5)	(0.7, 0.9, 1.0)	(0.3, 0.5, 0.7)	(0.5, 0.7, 0.9)
Criteria Alternatives	**C5**	**C6**	**C7**	
VOI	(0.7, 0.9, 1.0)	(0.9, 1.0, 1.0)	(0.5, 0.7, 0.9)	
	(0.7, 0.9, 1.0)	(0.7, 0.9, 1.0)	(0.5, 0.7, 0.9)	
TEX	(0.9, 1.0, 1.0)	(0.7, 0.9, 1.0)	(0.5, 0.7, 0.9)	
	(0.9, 1.0, 1.0)	(0.5, 0.7, 0.9)	(0.1, 0.3, 0.5)	
AUT	(0.7, 0.9, 1.0)	(0.7, 0.9, 1.0)	(0.7, 0.9, 1.0)	
	(0.5, 0.7, 0.9)	(0.7, 0.9, 1.0)	(0.7, 0.9, 1.0)	
OTH	(0.1, 0.3, 0.5)	(0, 0.1, 0.3)	(0.7, 0.9, 1.0)	
	(0, 0.1, 0.3)	(0, 0.1, 0.3)	(0.9, 1.0, 1.0)	

Table 5. Arithmetic average of DMs opinions

Criteria Alternatives	C1	C2	C3	C4
VOI	(0.1, 0.3, 0.5)	(0.6, 0.8, 0.95)	(0.1, 0.3, 0.5)	(0.6, 0.8, 0.95)
TEX	(0.6, 0.8, 0.95)	(0.6, 0.8, 0.95)	(0.9, 1.0, 1.0)	(0.8, 0.95, 1.0)
AUT	(0.8, 0.95, 1.0)	(0.4, 0.6, 0.8)	(0.4, 0.6, 0.8)	(0.5, 0.7, 0.9)
OTH	(0.3, 0.5, 0.7)	(0.5, 0.7, 0.85)	(0.3, 0.5, 0.7)	(0.6, 0.8, 0.95)
Criteria Alternatives	**C5**	**C6**	**C7**	
VOI	(0.7, 0.9, 1.0)	(0.8, 0.95, 1.0)	(0.5, 0.7, 0.9)	
TEX	(0.9, 1.0, 1.0)	(0.6, 0.8, 0.95)	(0.3, 0.5, 0.7)	
AUT	(0.6, 0.8, 0.95)	(0.7, 0.9, 1.0)	(0.7, 0.9, 1.0)	
OTH	(0.05, 0.2, 0.4)	(0, 0.1, 0.3)	(0.8, 0.95, 1.0)	

Step 2: Fuzzy decision matrix is normalized using equations 4 and 5 by considering cost oriented or benefit oriented of the selected criteria. The fuzzy normalized decision matrix is given below in Table 6.

Table 6. Fuzzy normalized decision matrix

Criteria Alternatives	C1	C2	C3	C4
VOI	(0, 0.22, 0.44)	(0.36, 0.72, 1.0)	(0, 0.22, 0.44)	(0.2, 0.6, 0.9)
TEX	(0.55, 0.77, 0.94)	(0.36, 0.72, 1.0)	(0.88, 1.0, 1.0)	(0.6, 0.9, 1.0)
AUT	(0.77, 0.94, 1.0)	(0, 0.36, 0.72)	(0.33, 0.55, 0.77)	(0, 0.4, 0.8)
OTH	(0.22, 0.44, 0.66)	(0.18, 0.54, 0.81)	(0.22, 0.44, 0.66)	(0.2, 0.6, 0.9)
Criteria Alternatives	**C5**	**C6**	**C7**	
VOI	(0.68, 0.89, 1.0)	(0.8, 0.95, 1.0)	(0.14, 0.42, 0.71)	
TEX	(0.89, 1.0, 1.0)	(0.6, 0.8, 0.95)	(0.42, 0.71, 1.0)	
AUT	(0.57, 0.78, 0.94)	(0.7, 0.9, 1.0)	(0, 0.14, 0.42)	
OTH	(0, 0.15, 0.36)	(0, 0.1, 0.3)	(0, 0.07, 0.28)	

Step 3: Fuzzy sum of weighted pairwise comparisons $\left(\tilde{S}_i\left(S_i^a, S_i^b, S_i^c\right)\right)$ and power weights $\left(\tilde{P}_i\left(P_i^a, P_i^b, P_i^c\right)\right)$ are calculated by using equations 6 and 7 for each alternative and shown in Table 7. In addition, weights of the criteria are given in Table 8.

Table 7. Fuzzy normalized decision matrix

	$\tilde{S}_i$	$\tilde{P}_i$	$\tilde{S}_i + \tilde{P}_i$
VOI	(0.11, 0.48, 1.88)	(3.74, 6.36, 6.87)	(3.86, 6.85, 8.75)
TEX	(0.23, 0.75, 2.46)	(5.87, 6.83, 6.99)	(6.11, 7.59, 9.45)
AUT	(0.14, 0.58, 2.08)	(3.25, 6.50, 6.91)	(3.40, 7.09 8.99)
OTH	(0.04, 0.27, 1.30)	(2.53, 5.84, 6.73)	(2.57, 6.11, 8.04)

Table 8. Fuzzy weights of the criteria

Criteria	**Weight**
C1	(0.07, 0.23, 0,59)
C2	(0.03, 0.06, 0.17)
C3	(0.05, 0.10, 0.27)
C4	(0.02, 0.06, 0.19)
C5	(0.06, 0.16, 0.44)
C6	(0.05, 0.12, 0.37)
C7	(0.06, 0.15, 0.44)

Step 4: The fuzzy evaluation scores $(\tilde{f}_{ia}, \tilde{f}_{ib}, \tilde{f}_{ic})$ are calculated by using equations 8, 9 and 10 and shown in Table 9.

Table 9. Fuzzy degrees of $\tilde{f}_{ia}, \tilde{f}_{ib}, \tilde{f}_{ic}$

Alternatives	$\tilde{f}_{ia}$	$\tilde{f}_{ib}$	$\tilde{f}_{ic}$
VOI	(0.11, 0.24, 0.54)	(4.30, 14.62, 49.43)	(0.40, 0.72, 0.92)
TEX	(0.17, 0.27, 0.59)	(8.16, 21.50, 63.88)	(0.64, 0.80, 1.00)
AUT	(0.09, 0.25, 0.56)	(4.99, 17.15, 54.52)	(0.36, 0.75, 0.95)
OTH	(0.07, 0.22, 0.50)	(2.00, 9.05, 35.13)	(0.27, 0.64, 0.85)

Step 5: The fuzzy evaluation scores $(\tilde{f}_{ia}, \tilde{f}_{ib}, \tilde{f}_{ic})$ are converted to crisp evaluation scores (f_{ia}, f_{ib}, f_{ic}) by using equations 11, 12 and 13 respectively and illustrated in Table 10.

Step 6: The final evaluation scores are combined to obtain the final score f_i for each alternative using equation 14. The alternative with the highest score is selected as the best alternative as seen in Table 10. When Table 10 is examined, it is seen that the best alternative is selected as the text-to-speech (TEX) alternative for the problem of prioritizing AI-based accessibility technologies for higher education students with disabilities by implementing fuzzy CoCoSo method.

Table 10. f_{ia}, f_{ib}, f_{ic} and f_i degrees

	f_{ia}	f_{ib}	f_{ic}	f_i	
VOI	0,302	22,787	0,686	9,603	3
TEX	0,347	31,183	0,817	12,849	1
AUT	0,306	25,559	0,687	10,602	2
OTH	0,266	15,396	0,590	1,99652887	4

CONCLUSION

Artificial intelligence can help ensure equality in education and support students with disabilities to realize their potential at the highest level. This technology eliminates the obstacles students face in their learning processes and enables them to progress more independently, effectively and efficiently in their education and career life.

This study provides a comprehensive evaluation of the contributions of artificial intelligence (AI) technologies to the educational processes of students withdisabilities and their role in enhancing accessibility. The primary objective of this research is to examine the impact of AI-based tools aimed at ensuring equal educational opportunities for students with disabilities and to illustrate how thesetechnologies can help overcome barriers.

According to the literature review, challenges in accessing education for individuals with disabilities include limitations of the physical environment, restrictions on social participation, and difficulties in accessing adequate support (Holloway, 2001; Liasidou, 2014). In this context, AI-supported tools and applications demonstrate significant potential in eliminating these barriers. Technologies such as speech recognition, text-to-speech, automated captioning, and chatbots that support socialinteraction notably facilitate easier access to educational materials for students with disabilities (Chen et al., 2020).

In this study, the Fuzzy CoCoSo multi-criteria decision-making method was used toevaluate various AI-based accessibility technologies. Based on expert opinions, alternatives such as speech recognition, text-to-speech, automated captioning systems, and other supportive tools were identified, and their effects on accessibility were analyzed by specific criteria. The analysis revealed that text-to-speech technology provides the highest levels of accessibility and independence for studentswith disabilities. This finding correlates with the ease of access to educational materials that text-to-speech technology provides, especially for students with visual impairments and learning disabilities such as dyslexia (Chen et al., 2020).

The findings indicate that AI-based educational technologies not only support academic success but also serve as a crucial tool in enhancing the independence, self-efficacy, and social participation of students with disabilities (Luckin et al., 2016; Ayeni et al., 2024). In this regard, universities and educational institutions areencouraged to review their accessibility policies and promote the systematic integration of AI technologies into educational programs. Additionally, institutions should ensure that their educational staff are made aware of these technologies andare equipped to use these tools effectively to support widespread adoption.

Finally, the potential of AI technologies to enhance accessibility for students with disabilities aligns with the United Nations Sustainable Development Goal of providing inclusive and equitable quality education (UN, 2020). This study, viewed from theperspective of social justice and equal opportunity, highlights a critical aspect of AI's impact in the field of disability education and serves as a guide for future, more comprehensive research in this area.

REFERENCES

Ahmad, M. F., & Ghapar, W. R. G. W. A. (2019). The era of artificial intelligence in Malaysian higher education: Impact and challenges in tangible mixed-reality learning system toward self exploration education (SEE). *Procedia Computer Science*, 163, 2–10.

Alhawiti, K. M. (2014). Natural language processing and its use in education. *International Journal of Advanced Computer Science and Applications*, 5(12).

Ali, O. A. M., Ali, A. Y., & Sumait, B. S. (2015). Comparison between the effects of different types of membership functions on fuzzy logic controller performance. *International Journal (Toronto, Ont.)*, 76, 76–83.

Alqaryouti, I. A. (2010). Inclusion the disabled students in higher education in Oman. *International Journal for cross-disciplinary subjects in education, 1*(4), 216-222.

Anderson, W. (2024). Exploring AI-Powered Assistive Technologies: Improving Accessibility for Individuals with Disabilities. *International Journal of Machine Learning for Sustainable Development*, 6(2).

Antunes, P., Karadzic, V., Santos, R., Beça, P., & Osann, A. (2011). Participatory multi-criteria analysis of irrigation management alternatives: The case of the Caia irrigation district, Portugal. *International Journal of Agricultural Sustainability*, 9(2), 334–349.

Arranz-Paraíso, S., & Arranz-Paraíso, D. (2024). Artificial Intelligence, Virtual Reality, and Augmented Reality to Enhance Visual Quality and Accessibility in Sustainable Built Environments. In *Design Strategies for Efficient and Sustainable Building Facilities* (pp. 179–199). IGI Global.

Ayeni, O. O., Al Hamad, N. M., Chisom, O. N., Osawaru, B., & Adewusi, O. E. (2024). AI in education: A review of personalized learning and educational technology. *GSC Advanced Research and Reviews*, 18(2), 261–271.

Baker, T., Smith, L., & Anissa, N. (2019). Educ-AI-tion rebooted? Exploring the future of artificial intelligence in schools and colleges.

Banes, D., & Behnke, K. (2019). The potential evolution of universal design for learning (UDL) through the lens of technology innovation. In *Universal Access through inclusive Instructional design* (pp. 323-331). Routledge.

Barua, P. D., Vicnesh, J., Gururajan, R., Oh, S. L., Palmer, E., Azizan, M. M., & Acharya, U. R. (2022). Artifcial intelligence enabled personalised assistive tools to enhance education of children with neurodevelopmental disorders-a review. *International Journal of Environmental Research and Public Health*, 19(3), 1192. DOI: 10.3390/ijerph19031192 PMID: 35162220

Bayne, S. (2015). Teacherbot: Interventions in automated teaching. *Teaching in Higher Education*, 20(4), 455–467.

Bellman, R. E., & Zadeh, L. A. (1970). Decision-making in a fuzzy environment. *Management Science*, 17(4), B-141.

Brown, M., McCormack, M., Reeves, J., Brook, D. C., Grajek, S., Alexander, B., & Weber, N. (2020). *2020 Educause Horizon Report Teaching and Learning Edition*. EDUCAUSE.

Burgstahler, S., Ladner, R. E., & Bellman, S. (2012). Strategies for increasing the participation in computing of students with disabilities. *ACM Inroads*, 3(4), 42–48.

Chan, K. S., & Zary, N. (2019). Applications and challenges of implementing artificial intelligence in medical education: Integrative review. *JMIR Medical Education*, 5(1), e13930. DOI: 10. 2196/13930 PMID: 31199295

Chen, C. Y., Hsieh, Y. T., & Liu, B. D. (2000, December). Design of pipelined mixed-signal fuzzy logic controller with linguistic hedge modifiers. In *IEEE APCCAS 2000. 2000 IEEE Asia-Pacific Conference on Circuits and Systems. Electronic Communication Systems.(Cat. No. 00EX394)* (pp. 148-151). IEEE.

Chen, X., Xie, H., Zou, D., & Hwang, G. J. (2020). Application and theory gaps during the rise of artificial intelligence in education. *Computers and Education: Artificial Intelligence*, 1, 100002.

Chen, X., Zou, D., Xie, H., & Cheng, G. (2021). Twenty years of personalized language learning. *Journal of Educational Technology & Society*, 24(1), 205–222.

Civanlar, M. R., & Trussell, H. J. (1986). Constructing membership functions using statistical data. *Fuzzy Sets and Systems*, 18(1), 1–13.

Dei, M. O. (2025). The impact of AI on the adaptation of educational materials and teaching methods to the needs of each student. *LatIA*, 3, 124–124.

Della Ventura, M. (2019). Monitoring the learning process to enhance motivation by means of learning by discovery using Facebook. In *Shaping the Future of Education, Communication and Technology: Selected Papers from the HKAECT 2019 International Conference* (pp. 117-128). Springer Singapore.

Devi, B. B., & Sarma, V. V. S. (1985). Estimation of fuzzy memberships from histograms. *Information Sciences*, 35(1), 43–59.

Dougherty, S. M., Ecton, W. G., Bonilla, S., & McGuinness, S. (2022). The effects of the COVID-19 pandemic and recession on career preparation during high school. *Peabody Journal of Education*, 97(3), 326–343.

Dubois, D., & Prade, H. (1983). Ranking fuzzy numbers in the setting of possibility theory. *Information Sciences*, 30(3), 183–224.

Geist, E. (2011). The game changer: Using iPads in college teacher education classes. *College Student Journal*, 45(4), 758769.

Godal, R. C., & Goodman, T. J. (1980). Fuzzy sets and Borel. *IEEE Transactions on Systems, Man, and Cybernetics*, 10(10), 637.

Han, B., Nawaz, S., Buchanan, G., & McKay, D. (2023, June). Ethical and pedagogical impacts of AI in education. In *International Conference on Artificial Intelligence in Education* (pp. 667-673). Cham: Springer Nature Switzerland.

Hitchings, W. E., Luzzo, D. A., Ristow, R., Horvath, M., Retish, P., & Tanners, A. (2001). The career development needs of college students with learning disabilities: In their own words. *Learning Disabilities Research & Practice*, 16, 8–17. DOI: 10.1111/0938-8982.00002

Holloway, S. (2001). The experience of higher education from the perspective of disabled students. *Disability & Society*, 16(4), 597–615.

Hong, H., & Kim, Y. (2024). Applying artificial intelligence in career education for students with intellectual disabilities: The effects on career self-efficacy and learning flow. *Education and Information Technologies*, •••, 1–20.

Hopcan, S., Polat, E., Ozturk, M. E., & Ozturk, L. (2022). Artifcial intelligence in special education: A systematic review. *Interactive Learning Environments*, 31(10), 7335–7353. DOI: 10.1080/ 10494820.2022.2067186

Hopkins, L. (2011). The path of least resistance: A voice-relational analysis of disabled students' experiences of discrimination in English universities. *International Journal of Inclusive Education*, 15(7), 711–727.

Hwang, G. J., Xie, H., Wah, B. W., & Gašević, D. (2020). Vision, challenges, roles and research issues of artificial intelligence in education. *Computers and Education: Artificial Intelligence*, 1, 100001. DOI: 10.1016/j.caeai.2020.100001

Jang, M., Cai, L., Udeani, G. O., Slowing, K. V., Thomas, C. F., Beecher, C. W., ... & Pezzuto, J. M. (1997). Cancer chemopreventive activity of resveratrol, a natural product derived from grapes. *science, 275*(5297), 218-220.

Jansen, A., & Colombo, S. (2024). Empowering AI Education by Enhancing Scalability and Accessibility of the Mix & Match Machine Learning Toolkit. *From User to Human*, 66.

Jones, A., Harkness, S., & Mondragon, N. (2020). Acts of meaning: How AI-based interviewing will transform career preparation in higher education. *EDUCAUSE Review*.

Kamber, E., Aydoğmuş, U., Aydoğmuş, H. Y., Gümüş, M., & Kahraman, C. (2024). Prioritization of drip-irrigation pump alternatives in agricultural applications: An integrated picture fuzzy BWM&CODAS methodology. *Applied Soft Computing*, 154, 111308.

Kang, C., & Cho, H. (2021). The efect of career program using group art therapy on career motivation and career decision-making self-efcacy of high school students with intellectual disabilities. *Journal of Emotional and Behavioral Disorders*, 37(1), 105–127. DOI: 10.33770/JEBD.37.1.5

Karsenti, D., Tharsis, G., Burtin, P., Venezia, F., Tordjman, G., Gillet, A., & Cavicchi, M. (2019). Adenoma and advanced neoplasia detection rates increase from 45 years of age. *World Journal of Gastroenterology*, 25(4), 447. PMID: 30700941

Kharbat, F. F., Alshawabkeh, A., & Woolsey, M. L. (2021). Identifying gaps in using artifcial intelligence to support students with intellectual disabilities from education and health perspectives. *Aslib Journal of Information Management*, 73(1), 101–128. DOI: 10.1108/AJIM-02-2020-0054

Liasidou, A. (2014). Critical disability studies and socially just change in higher education. *British Journal of Special Education*, 41(2), 120–135.

Liu, A., Ma, E., Wang, Y. C., Xu, S., & Grillo, T. (2024). AI and supportive technology experiences of customers with visual impairments in hotel, restaurant, and travel contexts. *International Journal of Contemporary Hospitality Management*, 36(1), 274–291.

Lombardi, A. R., Dougherty, S. M., & Monahan, J. (2018). Students with intellectual disabilities and career and technical education opportunities: A systematic literature review. *Journal of Disability Policy Studies*, 29(2), 82–96. DOI: 10.1177/1044207318764863

Luckin, R., Holmes, W., Griffiths, M., & Forcier, L. B. (2016). Intelligence unleashed. *An argument for AI in Education, 18.*

Madriaga, M. (2007). Enduring disablism: Students with dyslexia and their pathways into UK higher education and beyond. *Disability & Society*, 22(4), 399–412.

Martínez, I. G., Batanero, J. M. F., Cerero, J. F., & León, S. P. (2023). Analysing the impact of artifcial intelligence and computational sciences on student performance: Systematic review and meta-analysis. NAER. *Journal of New Approaches in Educational Research*, 12(1), 171–197.

Menteş, A. (2000). *Manevra ve sevk sistemi seçiminde bulanık çok kriterli karar verme* (Doctoral dissertation, Fen Bilimleri Enstitüsü).

Mills, A., Bali, M., & Eaton, L. (2023). How do we respond to generative AI in education? Open educational practices give us a framework for an ongoing process. *Journal of Applied Learning and Teaching*, 6(1), 16–30.

Mortimore, T. (2013). Dyslexia in higher education: Creating a fully inclusive institution. *Journal of Research in Special Educational Needs*, 13(1), 38–47.

Onaga, E. E., & Martoccio, T. L. (2008). Dynamic and uncertain pathways between early childhood inclusion policy and practice. *International Journal of Child Care and Education Policy*, 2, 67–75.

Prideaux, L., Patton, W., & Creed, P. (2002). Development of a theoretically derived school career program: An Australian endeavour. *International Journal for Educational and Vocational Guidance*, 2, 115–130. DOI: 10.1023/A:1016077211567

Redpath, J., Kearney, P., Nicholl, P., Mulvenna, M., Wallace, J., & Martin, S. (2013). A qualitative study of the lived experiences of disabled post-transition students in higher education institutions in Northern Ireland. *Studies in Higher Education*, 38(9), 1334–1350.

Roll, I., & Wylie, R. (2016). Evolution and revolution in artificial intelligence in education. *International Journal of Artificial Intelligence in Education*, 26, 582–599.

Romero, C., & Ventura, S. (2020). Educational data mining and learning analytics: An updated survey. *Wiley Interdisciplinary Reviews. Data Mining and Knowledge Discovery*, 10(3), e1355.

Rose, D. J. (2010). *Fallproof!: a comprehensive balance and mobility training program.* Human Kinetics.

Russell, S. J., & Norvig, P. (2016). *Artificial intelligence: a modern approach.* Pearson.

Saaty, T. L. (1980). The analytic hierarchy process (AHP). *The Journal of the Operational Research Society*, 41(11), 1073–1076.

Sibalija, J., Savundranayagam, M. Y., Orange, J. B., & Kloseck, M. (2020). Social support, social participation, & depression among caregivers and non-caregivers in Canada: A population health perspective. *Aging & Mental Health*, 24(5), 765–773. PMID: 30521370

Skinner, D., & Weisner, T. S. (2007). Sociocultural studies of families of children with intellectual disabilities. *Mental Retardation and Developmental Disabilities Research Reviews*, 13(4), 302–312. PMID: 17979204

Soner, S., & Önüt, S. (2006). Multi-criteria supplier selection: An ELECTRE-AHP application. *Sigma*, 4, 110–120.

Soresi, S., Nota, L., Ferrari, L., & Solberg, S. (2008). Career guidance for persons with disabilities. In Athanasou, J. A., & Van Esbroeck, R. (Eds.), *International Handbook of Career Guidance* (pp. 405–417). Springer.

Stanujkic, D. (2015). Extension of the ARAS method for decision-making problems with interval-valued triangular fuzzy numbers. *Informatica (Vilnius)*, 26(2), 335–355.

Subashini, P., & Krishnaveni, M. (2021). Artificial intelligence-based assistive technology. In *Artificial Intelligence Theory, Models, and Applications* (pp. 217-240). Auerbach Publications.

Suryani, A., & George, S. (2021). "Teacher education is a good choice, but I don't want to teach in schools." An analysis of university students' career decision making. *Journal of Education for Teaching*, 47(4), 590–604.

Taneri, G. U. (2020). Artificial Intelligence & Higher Education: Towards Customized Teaching and Learning, and Skills for an AI World of Work. Research & Occasional Paper Series: CSHE. 6.2020. *Center for Studies in Higher Education.*

Ulutaş, A., Popovic, G., Radanov, P., Stanujkic, D., & Karabasevic, D. (2021). A new hybrid fuzzy PSI-PIPRECIA-CoCoSo MCDM based approach to solving the transportation company selection problem. *Technological and Economic Development of Economy*, 27(5), 1227–1249.

United Nations. (2020). Sustainable development goals: Goal 4-Quality Education. Retrieved September 23, 2020, from https://www.un.org/sustainabledevelopment/education/

Vincent-Lancrin, S., & van der Vlies, R. (2020). Trustworthy Artificial Intelligence (AI) in Education: Promises and Challenges. OECD Education Working Papers, No. 218. *OECD Publishing*.

Welde, A. M., Bernes, K. B., Gunn, T. M., & Ross, S. A. (2016). Career education at the elementary school level: Student and intern teacher perspectives. *Journal of Career Development*, 43(5), 426–446. DOI: 10.1177/089484531663352

Wen, Z., Liao, H., Kazimieras Zavadskas, E., & Al-Barakati, A. (2019). Selection third-party logistics service providers in supply chain finance by a hesitant fuzzy linguistic combined compromise solution method. *Economic research-. Ekonomska Istrazivanja*, 32(1), 4033–4058.

Zadeh, L. A. (1965). Fuzzy sets. *Information and Control.*

Chapter 8
The Application of Artificial Intelligence in Educational Administration

Elisha Mupaikwa
https://orcid.org/0000-0002-0313-7139
National University of Science and Technology, Zimbabwe

ABSTRACT

To enhance the calibre of decisions, artificial intelligence technologies have been included in educational administration. The use of artificial intelligence in school administration is covered in this chapter. Out of the 130 journal articles that were downloaded from peer-reviewed journals, 50 articles were chosen for review. According to the review's findings, artificial intelligence has been applied to educational administration in several areas, including performance and assessment, faculty management, student management, course management, and student recruiting and admission. Lack of expertise and skills, ethical issues, financial difficulties, and infrastructure issues were the main obstacles to the use of AI in school administration.

INTRODUCTION

Artificial intelligence assists administrators in higher education institutions with high-volume administrative duties, such as financial management, procurement, and admissions, through a variety of technologies such as chatbots that answer students' questions, expert systems, natural language processing systems and machine learning algorithms for clustering and classification. Generally, administration is a social

DOI: 10.4018/979-8-3693-7949-3.ch008

process that deals with locating, preserving, inspiring, regulating, and combining material and human resources in an integrated system that is particularly made to accomplish predefined goals. At the heart of administration in educational contexts, Igbokwe (2023) asserts that is leadership, and that successful leadership is essential to an institution's success. In educational administration, the focus of staff support for achieving student lifetime learning should be on development programs that bolster teaching practices, offer continuous assistance and feedback, and encourage teacher cooperation. Thus an organization's ability to survive and remain relevant in its communities is made possible by this essential component. In educational administration, creating and maintaining productive teaching and learning environments requires the integration of people and resources. The relevance of educational institutions is often significantly related to the level an institution strives to address the economic developments of communities and to satisfy the general needs of the communities. The realization that education is often the primary driver of economic development in many countries, leading to the allocation of a larger portion of national budgets to educational sectors, has spurred research on educational administration. Research also confirms that competent management is necessary to achieve successful management and administration, which is necessary for educational institutions to fulfil their mandate. According to research by Galafa and Lucas (2018), educational managers in Malawi faced several difficulties, including a dearth of resources for teaching and learning, a high student-to-teacher ratio, a distance between schools and homes, a lack of infrastructure, and a lack of motivation on the part of both teachers and students. According to Galafa and Lucas (2018), these issues have a detrimental influence on Malawian schools' operations, making it more difficult for them to achieve their goals and make a meaningful contribution to the country's development. Not a single education scholar has suggested using artificial intelligence to address the issues facing educational institutions. Because of this, scholars have become interested in the role that educational administration plays in a country's economic development. These researchers have also looked into the difficulties that educational administrators confront in their workplaces. According to some experts, controlling learning environments is an issue that educational administrators encounter at all levels of educational institutions. Artificial intelligence is seen as a potential approach to address these challenges. The use of AI in education has been recognized by research as having a strong correlation with a country's economic development. This is demonstrated by a study conducted in China by Knox (2024), who states that three key concepts need to be taken into account when studying the adoption of AI in education. These are: (1) that relationships between AI and education are shaped by a broad network of actors rather than just technology designers and educators; (2) that relationships are defined by contestation rather than consensus; and (3) that AI technologies are developed within an already established education and technology context rather than emerging spontaneously. These correlations demonstrate a robust relationship between the national political economy and the intricate factors that need to be taken into account before AI is adopted and integrated into companies. The Fourth Industrial Revolution (4IR), which is defined by cutting-edge technologies like automation, the Internet of Things (IoT), AI, and other cyber-physical systems, has made the connection between AI, education, and national economic developments even more evident (Abulibdeh et al., 2024). As a result, there have been more requests for the integration of AI in educational settings; nevertheless, the literature that is currently available does not sufficiently address the uses of AI in educational management. However, according to Igbokwe (2023), artificial intelligence can be applied to a variety of educational tasks, including recruitment and admission, financial and student services, assessment and grading, student support, predictive analysis, curriculum design and development, teacher support, intelligent tutoring systems, and virtual assistants. According to studies, these are the fundamental duties of educational administration, and they have been progressively incorporating artificial intelligence. Ichim (2023) also noted the following domains in which artificial intelligence might be applied to educational management and administration:

i) Recognizing biases in university admissions;
ii) Monitoring the academic progress of students;
iii) Encouragement of Inclusive Teaching Methods;
iv) encouraging diversity in the workforce;
v) Personalized instruction;

These activities appear to represent a significant divergence from the artificial intelligence applications that are commonly associated with industry, e-commerce, and health. Thus, the first topic covered in this chapter is the fundamentals of artificial intelligence. To give a more comprehensive picture of how these various technologies are used in school administration, artificial intelligence concepts and technologies have been categorized. The chapter also looks at several educational administration jobs and how they can all be used to make use of the many types of artificial intelligence and associated technology. The review will achieve this by citing instances of artificial intelligence being used in school administration. The chapter concludes with conclusions and recommendations after delving more into the difficulties that educational institutions may encounter while implementing artificial intelligence for educational administration.

Background

Operations and strategic decision-making processes are now data-driven in all enterprises, requiring sophisticated computational skills that AI alone can provide. Knox (2024) contends that in these contexts, data-driven environments have grown more complicated than those often defined by technical explanations and marketing narratives that presuppose a clear-cut consensus regarding the goals and uses of technology in society. According to Guna, Mou, and Jiang's (2020) historical analysis of AI applications in education, companies that specialize in educational technology have created Aided Teaching systems for local language learning, classroom management, grading, and evaluation. They have also developed institute administration systems that facilitate student enrollment and inquiries. According to Meacham (2021), the development of the Bayesian inference models of decision-making dates back to 1763, marking the beginning of the use of AI in education. Later years saw the development of the Turing machine in 1950, which led to John McCarthy coining the term "Artificial Intelligence," the development of the supercomputer in 1997, IBM's Watson machine in 2011, Eugene Goostman, a first chatbot to pass the Turing test in 2014, and Charles Babbage's analytical machine in 1837, Elektro, the first robot, developed in 1939, and the neural network development by Warren S. McCulloch and Walter Pitts in 1934. The necessity to find complex solutions in organizational environments drove all of these breakthroughs. Complex problem-solving calls for multidisciplinary teamwork, dynamic problem-solving, and the possibility of many solutions. These are issues that are comparable to actual circumstances (Kunze et al., 2018). Therefore, the ability of individuals to incorporate a variety of background knowledge and experience into a dynamic collaborative process is critical to solving complex challenges (Van Den Bossche et al., 2011). Themes were created by Kamal et al. (2019) in Malaysia to examine the difficulties experienced by educational administrators. These obstacles were divided into five categories: teaching aids, classroom management, student behaviour, parent behaviour, and teacher load. The Kammal et al. (2019) study concluded that teachers needed more teaching aids in a setting where parent involvement was lacking and that administrators found it difficult to manage pupils with varying learning styles. Similar problems faced by educational administration at Nigerian educational institutions were documented by Jacob, Pajo, and Akhemedov (2002). These problems included a lack of planning data, insufficient budget, a shortage of trained teachers, inadequate facilities, and institutional corruption. This is true even with the newer data and information difficulties that administrators and school management must deal with, which have made educational decision-making more difficult. Due to the complexity and diversity of data that higher education institutions currently handle, classic decision-making models are no longer suitable for the digital technical environment and the Internet of Things. The field of educational administration has likewise been forced to confront complicated issues in a dynamic setting. There are more calls for the use of artificial intelligence in this industry due to the requirement for enhanced computing abilities and methods. One of the industries that artificial intelligence has impacted is education. As a result, researchers have been interested in the history of artificial intelligence in education, which spans more than 40 years, but their work has frequently been basic and restricted, concentrating mainly on classroom activities. As a result, research indicates that concerns regarding artificial intelligence's potential effects on education have given rise to a greater use of AI in a variety of educational contexts. However, highlighting its drawbacks, Fullan et al.,(2023) have issued a warning against the utopian adoption of AI.

The increasingly complex environment that exposes educational administrators to a wide range of information and complex circumstances that require complex non-routine decisions in situations where human computational capabilities are limited has given rise to consideration for the use of artificial intelligence in educational administrations. This has put pressure on administrators in the field of education to investigate the feasibility of using digital technologies in their decision-making procedures. Transaction processing, traditional management information, decision assistance, group decision support, and executive information systems have been the mainstays of traditional administrators' toolkits. However, these current information systems are no longer able to handle the complicated data environment of the big data environment that modern institutions today work under, thanks to the advancements of the web, the internet, and its related technologies like the Internet of Things (IoT). According to the literature, the artificial intelligence revolution has given rise to a wide range of innovations in the fields of expert systems, robotics, machine learning, natural language processing, image and speech recognition, and more. These innovations have gradually but gradually gained acceptance in the field of educational administration, and many institutions and administrators are now using these technologies to improve their services, raise the calibre of their services, and become more competitive.

Applications of artificial intelligence in education have caught the interest of many people, including researchers, educators, governments, and academics. Artificial intelligence has been employed extensively in the field of education, with a focus on research, teaching, and learning at higher education institutions. Various writers and sources have also identified and discussed their perspectives on artificial intelligence. Few studies have looked into the use of AI technology for educational administration, despite the rising interest from numerous stakeholders in the uses of AI in education. This seems to stem from the idea that, even though artificial intelligence (AI) is a valuable tool for addressing issues in education that are caused by the insufficiency of the current generation's traditional education as well as the complexity of the educational system itself, educational administrators have stuck to antiquated, frequently time-consuming, and unreliable methods of making decisions. Through e-learning, educational administrators who have embraced contemporary technologies like artificial intelligence (AI) have found that AI can tackle challenging academic issues and apply more intelligent educational technology solutions. Furthermore, teaching members and support staff are now able to perform more laborious jobs thanks to automated AI systems and ML. Guan, Mou, and Jiang (2020) conducted a historical analysis of the use of AI in educational settings and found that companies that specialize in educational technology had created Aided Teaching systems for classroom management and Institute administration systems that aided with student enrollment and inquiries. According to several studies, recent advances in AI have the potential to enable machine collaboration during group and workgroup (de Laat et al., 2020; Seeber et al., 2020; Yang et al., 2021; Siemens et al., 2022). Therefore, the application of AI in the workplace, classroom, and everyday life has changed from being limited to automation-based labour cost savings to augmenting human capabilities. This is demonstrated by generative AI tools like ChatGPT, which raise the possibility that AI can actively participate in solving complex problems. Artificial intelligence (AI) systems can analyze massive datasets—including unstructured data—in real time and find patterns or structures that can help with collaborative problem-solving and human decision-making. Artificial Intelligence (AI) has great promise for revolutionizing the way instructors and students address challenging issues in the classroom by offering individualized insights and recommendations based on data. AI partners enhance human contributions and have the ability to affect the actions taken by people as a result, thus when AI is employed in complex problem-solving, the patterns of interaction become more complex.

The relevance of social, affective, cognitive, and metacognitive components of problem-solving is increased by the influence of human AI teaming. However, regretfully, there is a significant lack of information in the literature about how these qualities manifest in collaborative human-artificial intelligence teams in challenging environments. Very few researchers have broadened this to include strategic decision-making in educational environments (Doroudi, 2022). Through the creation of adaptable learning environments and working environments that simplify the completion of routine tasks, the application of AI in educational administration and management has sparked a revolution that improves mobility and the production of knowledge capacity among administrators, lecturers, and students in academic institutions. According to a Nigerian study by Nwile and Edo (2023), the use of AI in school administration enhanced data accessibility through smart devices, which led to the simplification of administrative duties and a reduction in the amount of time needed to finish tasks. This has also made it possible for administrators to take part in international conferences, which has aided in the creation and exchange of knowledge that may be applied to wise decision-making. According to a different study by Doroudi (2022), artificial intelligence (AI) and education are related fields that mutually impact one another. As a result, many of the pioneers of AI research have attempted to make contributions to the field of education. Because of this intricate relationship, intelligent coaching, automated grading, essay scoring, and learning analytics are some common ways that individuals connect AI to education. According to the literature on the use of artificial intelligence, among other application areas, these technologies are currently being used for staff selection and recruitment, performance management, curriculum reviews and designs, financial management, student management, and educational planning in general. The literature does indicate that there is more room for artificial intelligence to be used in the fields of education and educational administration as a whole.

Artificial intelligence (AI) has been widely applied in educational practices (Artificial Intelligence in Education (AIEd)) with the advancement of computing and information processing techniques. Examples of AI applications in education include intelligent tutoring systems, teaching robots, learning analytics dashboards, adaptive learning systems, and human-computer interactions (Chen, Xieand Hwang, 2020). AI has been regarded as a potent tool to enable new paradigms for instructional design, technological development, and education research that are otherwise impossible to develop in traditional education modes since the introduction of AIEd almost at the turn of the twenty-first century (Holmes et al., 2019; Hwang et al., 2020). In particular, individualized learning, the role of the instructor, and the creation of a complex educational system are only a few of the chances, potentials, and problems that AIEd has brought forward for educational advances (Baker et al., 2019; Holmes et al., 2018; Starcic, 2019). According to Hwang et al. (2020), there are various roles that artificial intelligence (AI) can play in education. These roles include those of an intelligent instructor, tutee, learning partner, tool, or advisor for policy-making, as seen in Figure 1 below.

Figure 1. Role of AIED (Hwang et al, 2020)

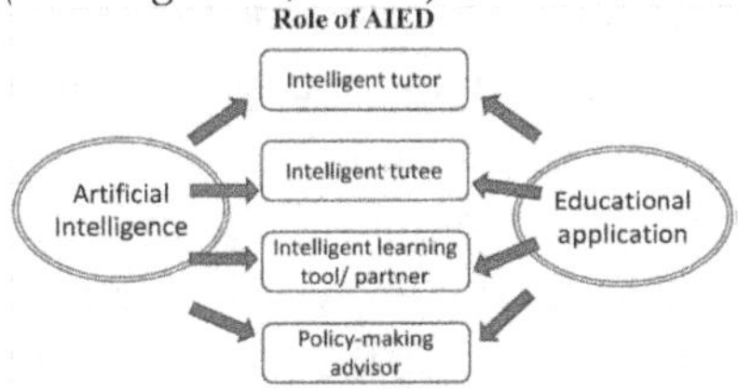

Wang, Yao, and Liu (2023) list the following as some aspects of educational management and administration that could profit from artificial intelligence applications in higher education:

Academic Registration: Enrollment, re-enrollment, suspension, withdrawal, graduation for example at George State University(Barret et al, 2019; Singh and Singh, 2021; Igbokwe, 2023).

Faculty Management: Course allocation, teaching supervision, performance management

Course Management: Scheduling, class selection, class withdrawal, course substitution

Performance Management: Grade entry, change and replacement, learning points for example, Riecken (2023).

Professional Management: Creation of majors, maintenance and updating of training programs, for example, Igbokwe(2023).

Academic Alert: Grouping warning, delayed graduation warning

Student Analysis: Learning behavior analysis, performance analysis and Prediction, for example, Igbokwe (2023).

Course Analysis: Achievement analysis, teaching quality assessment, and impact factor analysis for example in Bai (2023), Igbokwe (2023) and Somasundaram et al., (2020).

Professional Analysis: Analysis of grades and evaluation of academic style, for example, Igbokwe (2023).

Igbokwe (2023) lists intelligent tutoring systems and individualized learning as other possible uses of AI in educational management, in addition to student evaluation.

In their investigation into the application of artificial intelligence (AI) in education, Ouyang and Jiao (2021) acknowledged the significant role that these technologies may play, as well as additional potential benefits. They also developed three paradigms for using AI in educational settings: AI-directed, learner-as-recipient; AI-supported, learner-as-collaborator; and AI-empowered, learner-as-leader. These three paradigms don't seem to recognize the full range of advantages that adopting AI for educational administration might offer, and they appear to limit its application in the classroom. In their examination of AI applications, Che et al. (2020) appear to agree that, despite the growing interest in AI research, not much has been done to integrate some advanced AI technologies into educational settings, particularly when it comes to fusing these technologies with educational theories and the larger field of educational management. Among the authors who have investigated the use of artificial intelligence (AI) in educational management are Antara (2023), who looked at the opportunities and difficulties in applying AI to educational administration; Harve (2023), who looked at the various ways in which AI technologies could be applied to customize learning, automate assessments, make intelligent recommendations, and increase learner engagement; Plitnichenko (2020) on how to customize learning for different learning groups; Xia and Li (2022), where AI-enhanced teaching abilities.

METHODOLOGY

This is a review of 50 peer-reviewed journal articles downloaded from Google Scholar. The inclusion criteria were:

i) The articles were published between 2010 and 2024.
ii) Key terms used were Artificial intelligence and Educational Administration and Artificial intelligence and educational management.

A total of 130 articles were downloaded and 80 of these were found to be relevant for this book chapter.

AI in Academic Assessment and Performance Prediction

Student assessment is one of the important tasks carried out by educational administrators. AI and ML technologies are among the assessment tools that have been attributed to improving assessment. Assessment is frequently conducted at both the national and classroom levels. A variety of developing technologies have been applied in both contexts. For instance, Swieckiet al. (2022) note the value of conventional assessment techniques but also point out that AI offers potential for assessment automation through the creation of assessment tasks, the identification of peers to grade the work, and the automatic scoring of student submissions. These AI skills have then been applied to address several issues that educational institutions have had with student retention, with results from studies indicating that the quality of assessments students got frequently had an impact on the rate at which students dropped out of courses. Pradeep et al. (2015) report that there is a growing trend in the number of students quitting school every semester or year, with a lack of high-quality instruction being a contributing cause. These opinions appear to support those of Ameen et al. (2019), who assert that several elements, including the calibre of the instruction, the accessibility of instructional materials, and assessment methodologies, influence students' performance.

Chaudhury et al. (2016), Kamal and Ahuja (2017), and Usamah et al. (2013) state that in the big data-filled digital environment, determining some data includes all the features that could influence a student's performance on their internal grades, including socioeconomic conditions, demographics, learning speed, personal characteristics, school-related features, and extracurricular activities. All of these factors have a significant impact on the students' performance. Widyahastuti and Tjhin (2017) report that the integration of AI into assessment focuses on a wide range of factors that may influence students' performance. These authors posit that student performance is dependent on various attributes, including student behaviour, demographic situation and student information, psychological and socio-economic context, and so on. Student performance is one of these variables that has also been included in the predictive modelling. As a result, many researchers have realized how important it is to anticipate college performance, and there is growing interest in combining data mining and machine learning approaches to create precise predictive models. Information mining techniques were used in the study by Amin et al. (2010) to forecast college achievement for students based on academic and demographic data. Bettinger et al. (2014) investigated the use of administrative data to predict college graduation rates. The study's findings showed that a composite of parameters, including high school scores and demographic indicators, indicated a high level of predictive accuracy in determining college success. The study's conclusions showed that combining high school grades with additional variables produced a very accurate and dependable predictor of college graduation rates. They also found that financial assistance had a big impact on graduation rate forecasts. The performance of students has also been studied and predicted using AI, learning analytics, and big data analytics, especially at higher education institutions. According to Zeineddine, Braendle, and Farah (2021), big data analytics and machine learning have emerged as valuable instruments for student classification and performance prediction. Zeineddine et al. (2021) further note that these technologies have been employed in the area of educational management to identify students who may be at risk by using preliminary data collected during their years of study.

According to the literature, new technologies that combine machine learning (ML) and educational data mining (EDM) have surfaced to enhance students' learning experiences. These technologies have led to the development of several models that forecast students' grades in the courses they are enrolled in. These models offer useful insights that help students stay in such courses. By establishing a system and environment that can offer teachers remedial action suggestions and allow them to give those pupils more attention, this information can be used to identify students who are in danger early on. Additionally, by keeping a closer eye on their performance, this data can improve university student retention rates. Furthermore, Prasad and George (2022) state that pedagogical interventions that predict students' performance based on their current academic records are crucial for guaranteeing that students graduate when they are expected to and for reducing the likelihood of failure and program dropout. Therefore, Prasad and George (2022) used pre-existing variables from the literature, such as family financial assets, family spending, and personal information, to predict student performance in their investigation of machine learning approaches for tracking and predicting the performance of students in degree programs. The performance of the pupils is then accurately predicted by Pycharm, a model put forth by Prasad and George (2022), using these variables. One study by Keir et al., (2023) that looked into the use of AI in forecasting medical students' propensity to become future doctors, is among those on applications of AI in predicting student performance. The study by Keir et al., (2023) aimed to address discrepancies among screeners as a result of the volume of applications they received. They also created a machine learning model that showed how AI could be used to make reasonably accurate screening decisions for medical school admissions. Zeineddine et al. (2021) have identified several machine learning techniques that could be employed in the investigation of AI's application in student performance prediction. These tools include decision trees, neural networks, logic regressions, Naïve Bayes, K-nearest neighbour, support vector machines, and other ensemble approaches. It was feasible to increase the precision of foreseeing failing students who require prompt attention and help from specialized units in the institution using a model created by Zeineddine et al., (2021). Pallathadkaet al. (2023) is another researcher who investigated the application of AI in forecasting student performance using ML algorithms. The study used data mining and machine learning (ML) methods, such as Naïve Bayes and SVM, to predict students' total success based on past academic achievement. The results also suggested that students' interests may be related to performance. Martinez-Comesana et al. (2023) recognize the significance of data mining in artificial intelligence for forecasting student success through the extraction of behavioural patterns and information about learners and their challenges. This helps administrators identify and handle issues early by forecasting academic achievement, activity level, knowledge retention, and likelihood of dropping out. Using machine learning (ML) algorithms, Rajendran et al. (2022) contend that sociodemographic factors like age, gender, obesity, average household income, family size, and parent's marital status, as well as school-related (gender, education, and academic level) and student-related (stress and lifestyle) variables, have the potential to affect students' performance and can therefore be used by ML algorithms to predict students' performance. Neural networks, random forests, and logic regression were the main machine learning methods that were suggested for application. The study's findings demonstrated that managers utilizing AI could forecast students' performance and likelihood of graduating or dropping out by utilizing their socio-demographic traits.

AI in Student Recruitment and Admission

In both business and education, recruitment entails the identification and hiring of people with the right talent based on a predetermined set of desired traits and credentials. These days, web portals that process a lot of the data submitted by applications facilitate the enrollment and admissions processes at academic institutions. Many institutions have already included AI and ML, particularly predictive analytics, in their institutional admissions management plans for recruitment and selection. For instance, universities in many industrialized nations, including the USA, are using machine learning more and more to forecast student achievement and create new student profiles. They are also using it to increase institutional efficiency throughout the enrollment process. However, Singh and Singh (2024) claim that these schools are currently receiving thousands more applications for spots than they can accept due to the focus on massifying higher education and expanding access in many developing nations, including South Africa. Having said that, the development of machine learning and artificial intelligence (AI) coupled with their statistical ability to "read" text has made this an appealing alternative for institutions facing resource burdens and subjective limitations, especially concerning web-based services. Chatbots and machine learning technology have been employed in the recruitment process. Nawaz and Gomes (2019) conducted a study in which they found that chatbots may be effectively used in recruitment efforts and can be integrated into institutional recruitment strategies. Nawaz and Gomes (2019) observed that AI researchers are becoming more interested in education and suggested new directions for study by presenting actual data on the application of this technology in hiring.

Course Management

Course administration in academic institutions entails several responsibilities, including teacher management, curriculum development and evaluation, human resource optimization, and timetabling/course scheduling. Artificial intelligence technologies have been used in educational administration and management, and research has shown that these technologies have improved course management across university faculties. This has historically been seen as an operational task involving human labour. The task of organizing a series of lectures between instructors and students within a predetermined time frame while adhering to a variety of constraints is known as the timetabling problem. However, the application of AI has been recommended to ensure the necessity to maximize student learning amid the growing number of students and courses under resource constraints.

One of the main responsibilities in course administration that has made use of artificial intelligence technology, specifically machine learning, is time-tabling. Ahmad (2019), Huang et al., (2021), Soyemmi, Akonode, and Oloruntoba (2017), Yim and Marte (2021), and Abdennadher and Marte (2000) are a few writers who have looked into the use of AI in time-tabling. This research has led to the proposal of automated time-tabling as a solution to the problems faced by educational institutions, particularly those with huge student populations and courses given with limited resources and facilities, including lecture halls, labs, and staff. In these kinds of settings, timetabling serves the dual purposes of giving professors and instructors time to concentrate on other educational tasks and ensuring that students have adequate time for each learning activity and that courses do not overlap. According to Ahmad (2019), Universiti Tun Hussein Malaysia (UTHMM) is one of the universities that has adopted AI-driven time tabling technologies. There, an AI-driven model that made use of optimization strategies such as linear programming and Aut Colony Optimisation (ACO) was created. AI algorithms can be applied to timetabling in schools, which involves scheduling classes, preventing conflicts between lessons, and removing lecture and test overlap. According to Huang et al. (2021), the ease of use of AI-driven solutions for time-tabling and course scheduling can be helpful as the need for interdisciplinary elective courses grows and the workload associated with classroom administration gets heavier. After several time-tabulation models were put forth by researchers, a model put out by Gotlieb () in Huang et al. (2021) attempted to address the six curriculum factors: teachers, classroom, students, class, and time.

Curriculum design

The creation and design of curricula is another area in which artificial intelligence has proven beneficial to educational management and administration. In Outcome Based Education (OBE), the importance of AI in curriculum building appears to be paramount. The curriculum for OBE must particularly address the industry needs for Job Roles and the necessary knowledge, abilities, and qualities, as well as the Program Specific Outcomes (PSO) and Program Outcomes (PO). The curriculum is now set up to include a variety of courses. These courses' Course Outcomes (CO) correspond to the Program Outcome (PO). Then, it is confirmed if this satisfies the requirements of the job role. Rather than designing the curriculum in this forward-thinking manner, it would be beneficial to develop the curriculum backwards, so that it is tailored to a specific set of one or more job roles (Somasundaram et al, 2020). Several of these AI technologies are mostly in ML and NLP. AI in curriculum building allows for an entirely new process of creating learning content and developing lesson programs, evaluating program content against PSOs and COs (Ayodele et al., 2023). For instance, Somasundaram et al. (2019) suggested that in the field of engineering education, artificial intelligence (AI) might be utilized to analyze discrepancies between program outcomes and content to build interventions aimed at closing these gaps. Artificial neural networks using back-propagation, in which the assessment starts with the results and moves backwards to the program's inputs and content, are one technology that could handle this task. Somasundaram et al. (2019) cite the Indian Institute of Technology, the Indian Institute of Science, and the National Programme on Technology Enhanced Learning (NPTEL) as examples of institutions that have used artificial neural networks in curriculum building. Additionally, by creating user-centred course materials and learning resources, AI methods like machine learning (ML) may be leveraged to create inclusive curricula. Kasztelnk() goes on to list several efforts that have been put in place to assist with the creation of a curriculum powered by AI. Baker and Smith (2019) are among the researchers who have looked into the application of AI in curriculum building. They suggest that ML might be utilized to provide adaptive learning by incorporating an intelligent tutoring system into the curriculum. Additionally, learning analytics is crucial for determining learning patterns, forecasting results, and guiding curriculum development and modification (Siemens and Baker, 2012). Among the many advantages of using AI in curriculum building, according to Kasztelnk(), is the opportunity it has created for creating dynamic educational experiences that cater to the different learning demands of 21st-century learners. To meet these diverse demands and the difficulties posed by their backgrounds, individualized learning has been integrated. Furthermore, Bell et al. (2019) have employed machine learning (ML) to enhance curriculum design and adapt to the constantly evolving requirements of the school's knowledge environment. Oluyemisi() noted that ML and NLP were important in curriculum design because they allowed curriculum managers to take individual characteristics and learner requirements into account during their examination of the use of curriculum development in Nigerian tertiary institutions, thereby creating virtual assistants, intelligent tutoring systems, and adaptive learning systems.

Faculty Management

Effective faculty management involves data from a variety of university sources, including research repositories, ERPs, and student management systems. Keeping faculty data current by pulling from sources like research repositories, ERPs, HR systems, and more; creating annual faculty review reports showcasing their activities and accomplishments; setting up tenure and promotion processes across your faculty including committees and key milestones; and analyzing key metrics per campus, department, or discipline in configurable reports for strategic decision making are some of the key activities related to faculty management.

A chatbot is one of the instruments that has been utilized for faculty administration. For instance, according to Bala et al. (2017), chatbots can improve communication inside college communities by securely connecting with larger audiences, which improves the process of responding to user inquiries. Bala et al. (2017) also suggested a chatbot approach that uses sentiment analysis and natural language processing to handle complaints. According to Yang and Talha (2021), AI can be a helpful tool for managing student counselling outside of the classroom. According to Barret et al. (2019), additional advantages and uses of AI in faculty management included the development of a 24/7 universal learning access that allowed all undergraduates to study whenever and wherever they choose, utilizing a method that works for them, without having to wait for faculty members. Additionally, there is no cost for travel or lodging for students from all over the world to acquire a top-notch education. AI tools and educational software can help instructors build stronger relationships with their undergraduate students, claim Barret et al. (2019). Artificial intelligence (AI) programs can function as efficient means of communication for undergraduate students to stay in touch and confer with their teachers, addressing any questions that may come up during the course. In this approach, undergraduates might be more satisfied with their academic achievement and educational output can rise.

The strategic use of artificial intelligence (AI) in higher education is changing how teaching workload management and scheduling are done (Sanjeevi, 2024). Diverse educational contexts are giving rise to creative methods of managing the workload of faculty. AnubavamTechnologies is among the progressive technology vendors leading the charge in incorporating AI into workload distribution platforms. Institutions can obtain accurate evaluations of past data, faculty strengths, and course requirements by utilizing AI algorithms, which will result in burden assignments that are more equal and effective. Sophisticated AI algorithms are becoming essential in the quest for efficient scheduling procedures. AI is used by platforms like Creatrix Campus, created by industry pioneers like Anubavam Technologies, to smoothly integrate resource availability, class sizes, and teacher preferences. This strategy helps to maximize the utilization of the resources that are accessible in addition to removing schedule conflicts.

Challenges

Although artificial intelligence (AI) has become more popular in educational administration, research warns against the hasty adoption of these technologies in classroom settings due to numerous obstacles that educational institutions have had to overcome, especially in the areas of educational management and administration.

One obstacle that could prevent AI from being used in educational administration is the lack of expertise among educators. According to AlAli and Wardat(2024)'s study of the difficulties educational institutions experience in implementing AI, the main reasons educational administrators are reluctant to adopt AI are ethical concerns and a lack of expertise. According to Smith (2024), further difficulties in applying AI are as follows:

a) The lack of professional development and the lack of high-quality AI tools for educators
b) AI illiteracy and insufficient AI competencies among educators
c) Implicit bias in the design of AI systems. For example, an algorithm that labelled African Americans, as high-risk in Broward County
d) Barriers to equitable access to AI as a result of fewer open-source AI applications available on the market
e) Data privacy compromise that may result from the systems's unauthorised collection and processing of personal data
f) Misinformation is where AI generates false information on its own or when AI fabricates sources or reference books that do not exist, a process called hallucinating.

According to Vincent-Lancrin and van der Vlies' (2020) analysis of the benefits and drawbacks of artificial intelligence in education, policymakers face obstacles when implementing AI, one of which is building public confidence in AI systems. This is frequently connected to other issues with the responsibility, explainability, and openness of AI systems in the classroom. According to Vincent-Lancrin and van der Vlies (2020), maintaining human-centred values in AI systems' protection and security of personal data is another difficulty. When deciding whether to adopt a system, it is important to take into account a variety of factors, including the degree to which the AI system performs as intended and whether it does not perform as intended. These concerns stem from AI's potent ability to do unforeseen jobs and gather data that could have unintended and unexpected repercussions.

Recommendations

Acknowledging the existence of the above-mentioned challenges, the following recommendations are therefore suggested:

a) Investments in AI technologies in educational contexts, particularly open-source software. This will ensure equitable access to AI technologies.

b) To address ethical challenges associated with the unethical collection and processing of personal data, educational institutions need to develop acceptable use policies in the application of AI for educational management and administration. Such policies may also be developed and implemented at the national level. Additionally, the integration of AI into educational administration may improve the general acceptance of AI. Strong governance policies on the usage of AI technologies may need to be considered to minimize misinformation.
c) Training and development of users(teachers, educational managers and students) in the use of and applications of AI in education may enhance the acceptance of AI.

Recommendation for further studies

While there is abundant literature on the application of AI in education in general, the field of educational administration and AI has not been widely explored. Therefore, it is necessary to broaden research on AI in education to include the major theories of management and administration in education. Additionally, AI organisations need to invest in the development of more models of educational administration.

REFERENCES

Abulibdeh, A., Zaidan, E., & Abulibdeh, R. (2024). Navigating the confluence of Artificial intelligence and education for sustainable development in the era of industry 4.0: Challenges, opportunities, and ethical dimensions. *Journal of Cleaner Production*, 437, 140527.

AlAli, R., & Wardat, Y. (2024). Opportunities and Challenges of Integrating Generative Artificial Intelligence in Education. *International Journal of Religion*, 5(7), 784–793.

Antara, H. (2023). AI in curriculum Development: Opportunities and challenges. Hurix.com.https://www.hurix.com/wp-content/uploads/2023/06/AI-in-Curriculum-Development-Opportunities-and-Challenges.jpg

Ayanniyi, R.B. (n.d). Concepts and theories of educational administration. National Open University of Nigeria.

Ayodele, O. S., Aliu, J., Owoeye, F.O., Ajayi, E. A. and Sheidu, A.Y. (2023). The Role of Artificial Intelligence in Curriculum Development and Management. Digital Innovations and Contemporary Research in Science. *Engineering and Technology.11(2).*

Baker, R. S., & Smith, L. (2019). Using machine learning for real-time adaptation In personalized learning. *Journal of Educational Technology*, 45(2), 1–22.

Baker, T., Smith, L., & Anissa, N. (2019). *Educ-AI-tion rebooted? Exploring the Future of artificial intelligence in schools and colleges*. NESTA.

Barrett, M., Branson, L., Carter, S., DeLeon, F., Ellis, J., Gundlach, C., & Lee, D. (2019). Using Artificial Intelligence to Enhance Educational Opportunities and Student Services in Higher Education. *Inquiry. The Journal of the Virginia Community Colleges*, 22(1).

Bettinger, E. P., & Baker, R. (2014). Predicting college graduation using Administrative data: An exploratory analysis. *Center for Education Policy Analysis Working Paper*, 57.

Bossche, P. V. D., Gijselaers, W., Segers, M., Woltjer, G., & Kirschner, P. (2011). Team learning: Building shared mental models. *Instructional Science*, 39(3), 283–301.

Chaudhury, P., Mishra, S., Kumar, H., & Kishore, T. (2016). Enhancing the Capabilities of the Student Result Prediction System. Proceedings of the Second *International Conference on Information and Communication Technology for Competitive Strategies, 978-1-4503-3962.*

Chen, X., Xie, H., & Hwang, G. J. (2020). A multi-perspective study on artificial intelligence in education: Grants, conferences, journals, software tools, institutions, and researchers. *Computers & Education. Artificial Intelligence*, 1, 100005.

Chen, X., Xie, H., Zou, D., & Hwang, G. (2020). Application and theory gaps during the rise of Artificial Intelligence in Education. *Computers and Education: Artificial Intelligence*, 1, 100002.

de Laat, M., Joksimovic, S., &Ifenthaler, D. (2020). Artificial intelligence, real-time feedback and workplace learning analytics to support in situ complex problem-solving: A commentary. *The International Journal of Information and Learning Technology*. https://doi.org/.DOI: 10.1108/IJILT-03-2020-0026

Fullan, M., Azorin, C., Harris, A., & Jones, M. (2023). Artificial intelligence and school leadership: Challenges, opportunities and implications. *School Leadership & Management*, 44(4), 339–346.

Galafa, B., & Lucas, A. (2018). Challenges to educational administration and management in primary schools in Malawi. *North America Academic Research*, 1(2), 1–14.

Guan, C., Mou, J., & Jiang, Z. (2020). Artificial intelligence innovation in education: A twenty-year data-driven historical analysis. *International Journal of Innovation Studies.*, 4, 134–147.

Holmes, W., Anastopoulou, S., Schaumburg, H., & Mavrikis, M. (2018). *Technology-enhanced personalised learning: Untangling the evidence*. Robert Bosch Stiftung.

Holmes, W., Bialik, M., & Fadel, C. (2019). *Artificial intelligence in education: Promises and implications for teaching and learning*. Center for Curriculum Redesign.

Hwang, G. J., Xie, H., Wah, B. W., & Gasevc, D. (2020). Vision, challenges, roles and research issues of Artificial Intelligence in Education. *Computers & Education: Artificial Intelligence*, 1, 100001. DOI: 10.1016/j.caeai.2020.100001

Igbokwe, I. C. (2023). Application of Artificial Intelligence (AI) in Educational Management. *International Journal of Scientific and Research Publications*, 3(3). Advance online publication. DOI: 10.29322/ijsrp.13.03.2023.p13536

Kamal, P., and Ahuja, S. A. (2017). Review on Prediction of Academic Performance of Student Sat-Risk Using Data Mining Techniques. *Journal on Today's Ideas – Tomorrow's Technologies, 5(1).*

Knox, J. (2020). Artificial intelligence and education in China. *Learning, Media and Technology*. Advance online publication. DOI: 10.1080/17439884.2020.1754236

Kunze, T., Stadler, M., and Greiff, S. (2018). A look at complex problem-solving in the 21st century. *Education: Future Frontiers, 11.*

Martínez-Torresd, I. O.-P., & Kreibel, D. (2023). Impact of artificial intelligence on assessment methods in primary and secondary education: Systematic literature review. *Revista de Psicodidáctica*, 28, 93–103.

Meacham, M. (2021). A Brief History of AI and Education. *International Journal of Adult and Non-Formal Education.*, 2(4), 1–2.

Musso, M. F., Kyndt, E., Cascallar, E. C., & Dochy, F. (2013). Predicting general academic performance and identifying the differential contribution of participating variables using artificial neural networks. *Frontline Learning Research*, 1(1), 42–71. DOI: 10.14786/flr.v1i1.13

Nwaogu, G.O. (nd) Educational administration. School of human and social studies. Atlantic International University.

Ouyang, F., & Jiao, P. (2021). Artificial intelligence in education: The three paradigms. *Computers and Education: Artificial Intelligence*, 2, 100020.

Pallathadka, H., Wenda, A., Ramirez-Asís, E., Asís-López, M., Flores-Albornoz, J., & Phasinam, K. (2023). Enhancing prediction of student success: Automated machine learning approach. *Materials Today: Proceedings*, 80, 3782–3785.

Plitnichenko, L. (2020). 5 Main Roles of Artificial Intelligence in Education. ELearningIndustry. https://elearningindustry.com/5-main-roles-artificial-intelligence-in-education

Pradeep, A., Das, S., & Kizhekkethottam, J. (2015).Students' dropout factor prediction using EDM techniques. *International Conference on Soft-Computing and Networks Security (ICSNS)IEEE Xplore,* DOI: 10.1109/7292372

Prasad, A., & George, S. S. (2022). A Machine Learning Approach for Tracking and Predicting Student Performance in Degree Programs. *Proceedings of the National Conference on Emerging Computer Applications (NCECA)-2022, 4(1).*

Rajendran, S., Chamundeswari, S., & Sinha, A. A. (2022). Predicting the academic performance of middle- and high-school students using machine learning algorithms. *Social Sciences & Humanities Open*, 6, 100357.

Rodríguez-Hernandez, C. F., Musso, M., Eva Kyndt, E., & Cascallar, E. (2021). Artificial neural networks in academic performance prediction: Systematic implementation and predictor evaluation. *Computers and Education: Artificial Intelligence*, 2, 100018.

Sanjeevi, C. R. (2024). Elevating academic efficiency: The role of AI in faculty workload Management and Scheduling.

Seeber, I., Bittner, E., Briggs, R. O., Vreede, T., Vreede, G.-J., Elkins, A., Maier, R., Merz, A. B., Oeste-Reiß, S., Randrup, N., Schwabe, G., & S¨ollner, M. (2020). Machines as teammates: A research agenda on AI in team collaboration. *Information & Management*, 57(2).

Siemens, G., & Baker, R. S. (2012). Learning analytics and educational data mining: Towards communication and collaboration. *Proceedings of the 2nd International Conference on Learning Analytics and Knowledge*, 252-254

Siemens, G., Marmolejo-Ramos, F., Gabriel, F., Medeiros, K., Marrone, R., Joksimovic, S., & de Laat, M. (2022). Human and artificial cognition. *Computers & Education: Artificial Intelligence, 3*, Article 100107. https://doi.org/. caeai.2022. 100107DOI: 10.1016/j

Smith, A. T. (2024). *The impact of AI: The benefits and challenges that lie ahead for AI in education. National Parents Union.* Centre for Policy Action.

Somasundarama, M., Lathab, P., & Pandian, S. A. S. (2019). Curriculum Design Using Artificial Intelligence (AI) Back Propagation Method. 9th World Engineering Education Forum, WEEF 2019. Procedia Computer Science 172 (2020): 134–138.

Starcic, A. I. (2019). Human learning and learning analytics in the age of artificial intelligence. *British Journal of Educational Technology*, 50(6), 2974–2976.

Vincent-Lancrin, S., & van der Vlies, R. (2020). Trustworthy artificial intelligence (AI) in education: promises and challenges OECD Education Working Paper No. 218. Organisation for Economic Co-operation and Development.

Wang, B., Yao, Y., & Liu, X. (2023).Research on the Construction of Smart Educational Administration Systems in Colleges and Universities Empowered by Artificial Intelligence Technology. Proceedings of the 4th Management Science Informatization and Economic Innovation Development Conference, MSIEID 2022, December 9-11, 2022, Chongqing, China

Widyahastuti, F., & Tjhin, V. (2017). Predicting Students' Performance in Final Examination using Regression and Multilayer Perceptron. *IEEE, 978- 1-5090-4688.*

Xia, X., & Li, X. (2022). Artificial Intelligence for Higher Education Development and TeachingSkills. *Wireless Communications and Mobile Computing*, 2022, e7614337. DOI: 10.1155/2022/7614337

Yang, S. J., Ogata, H., Matsui, T., & Chen, N. S. (2021). Human-centred artificial intelligence in education: Seeing the invisible through the visible. *Computers & Education. Artificial Intelligence*, 2, 100008.

Zeineddine, H. (2021). UdoBraendle, U. and Farah, A. (2021).Classification and prediction of student performance data using various machine learning algorithms. *Computers & Electrical Engineering*, 89, 106903.

KEY TERMS AND DEFINITIONS

Artificial intelligence: The ability of machines to demonstrate reasoning and problem solving skills normally associated with humans.

Curriculum development: Conscious decisions on determining programme content and assessment strategies.

Educational administration: The process of organizing both human and non-human resources to ensure the effective delivery of instruction in an educational environment.

Faculty management: Strategies for ensuring learning units in an educational environment is productive.

Machine learning: The ability of machines to learn from data and make decisions to predict the future.

Performance management: The measurement of students' performance against expected outcomes.

Student assessment: Evaluation of student's performance in learning environment.

Student recruitment: Admission of students into a learning programme.

Chapter 9
The Role of Teachers in an AI-Enhanced Educational Landscape

Tarun Kumar Vashishth
https://orcid.org/0000-0001-9916-9575
IIMT University, India

Vikas Sharma
https://orcid.org/0000-0001-8173-4548
IIMT University, India

Mukesh Kumar Sharma
https://orcid.org/0000-0003-3071-5931
Chaudhary Charan Singh University, India

Kewal Krishan Sharma
https://orcid.org/0009-0001-2504-9607
IIMT University, India

Rajeev Sharma
https://orcid.org/0000-0002-3354-558X
IIMT Engineering College, India

ABSTRACT

The creation of artificial intelligence (AI) in training presents each possibilities and challenges, reshaping traditional coaching roles and methodologies. This paper explores the evolving position of teachers in an AI-improved instructional panorama, emphasizing the significance of human-centric abilities along with empathy, creativity, and critical wondering. While AI can automate administrative

DOI: 10.4018/979-8-3693-7949-3.ch009

tasks and offer personalized learning studies, instructors remain critical in fostering a supportive and tasty mastering surroundings. The take a look at highlights the symbiotic courting among AI equipment and educators, advocating for expert improvement and coverage reforms to maximize the benefits of AI integration. By analyzing contemporary traits and future possibilities, this paper objectives to offer a roadmap for educators navigating this transformative generation.

1. INTRODUCTION

The introduction of synthetic intelligence (AI) has catalyzed vast modifications throughout various sectors, with schooling being one of the maximum impacted fields. AI era, with its capability to revolutionize conventional teaching methodologies and administrative strategies, presents each possibilities and demanding situations for educators and inexperienced persons alike. The integration of AI in schooling promises to automate ordinary administrative obligations, including grading and attendance tracking, thereby releasing up treasured time for instructors to awareness on extra essential elements of teaching. Moreover, AI-pushed gear can offer personalized studying experiences tailor-made to man or woman pupil needs, improving the overall effectiveness of schooling. However, this technological shift additionally necessitates a re-evaluation of the traditional role of teachers. While AI can augment the academic procedure, it cannot update the important human-centric skills that instructors convey to the classroom, including empathy, creativity, and crucial wondering. These abilities are crucial for fostering a supportive and tasty studying environment that encourages scholar increase and improvement (Khazanchi & Khazanchi, 2024).

In this swiftly evolving educational panorama, instructors should adapt to new technologies at the same time as retaining the irreplaceable human elements of training. This paper explores the evolving role of teachers in an AI-more advantageous instructional placing, emphasizing the want for a balanced approach wherein generation and human abilities complement each different. It highlights the symbiotic relationship among AI tools and educators, advocating for complete expert improvement packages to equip teachers with the necessary competencies to navigate this transformative technology. Additionally, the paper discusses the importance of policy reforms to assist the effective integration of AI in schooling, ensuring that the blessings of AI are maximized at the same time as mitigating capacity drawbacks. By analyzing present day trends and destiny possibilities, this look at aims to offer a roadmap for educators and policymakers, guiding them thru the complexities of AI integration in training and ensuring that the transition complements rather than disrupts the mastering revel in (Lameras & Arnab, 2021).

1.1 Overview of AI in Education

The integration of artificial intelligence (AI) into training is reworking how educators educate and how students examine. AI technology have the capability to deal with many demanding situations inside the academic quarter, such as personalizing getting to know experiences, automating administrative duties, and supplying real-time feedback and evaluation. AI-driven adaptive getting to know systems can tailor academic content material to fulfill the individual desires of students, accommodating various learning paces and patterns. These systems analyze information on pupil overall performance to identify strengths and weaknesses, permitting personalized guidance that could decorate learning outcomes (Ayeni et al., 2024). For instance, AI can recommend specific assets or sporting events to assist college students grasp tough concepts, making sure an extra tailored academic enjoy. Administrative efficiency is every other large gain of AI in schooling. AI can deal with duties which includes grading, scheduling, and dealing with attendance, which historically consume a large amount of teachers' time. By automating these obligations, AI lets in educators to recognition extra on instructional sports and pupil engagement. For instance, automatic essay scoring systems can provide constant and objective opinions of student writing, freeing up time for instructors to concentrate on greater interactive and innovative aspects of coaching.

AI also performs a vital role in offering real-time comments and evaluation. Intelligent tutoring systems can reveal scholar development and provide instant remarks, supporting students recognize their errors and examine extra efficiently. This continuous comments loop can drastically enhance pupil overall performance and engagement, as it permits well timed intervention and assist. However, the mixing of AI in schooling is not without challenges. Concerns about facts privacy, the digital divide, and the capacity for AI to replace human instructors need to be addressed. It is essential to strike a balance in which AI complements in place of replaces the unique human components of coaching, together with emotional guide, mentorship, and the potential to inspire and inspire students (Meng et al., 2022).

In summary, AI has the potential to revolutionize schooling by way of enhancing personalization, performance, and comments mechanisms. As educators and policymakers navigate this transformative era, it is important to ensure that AI gear are implemented thoughtfully and ethically to maximize their advantages even as keeping the crucial human elements of schooling.

Figure 1. Integration of AI in education (Author)

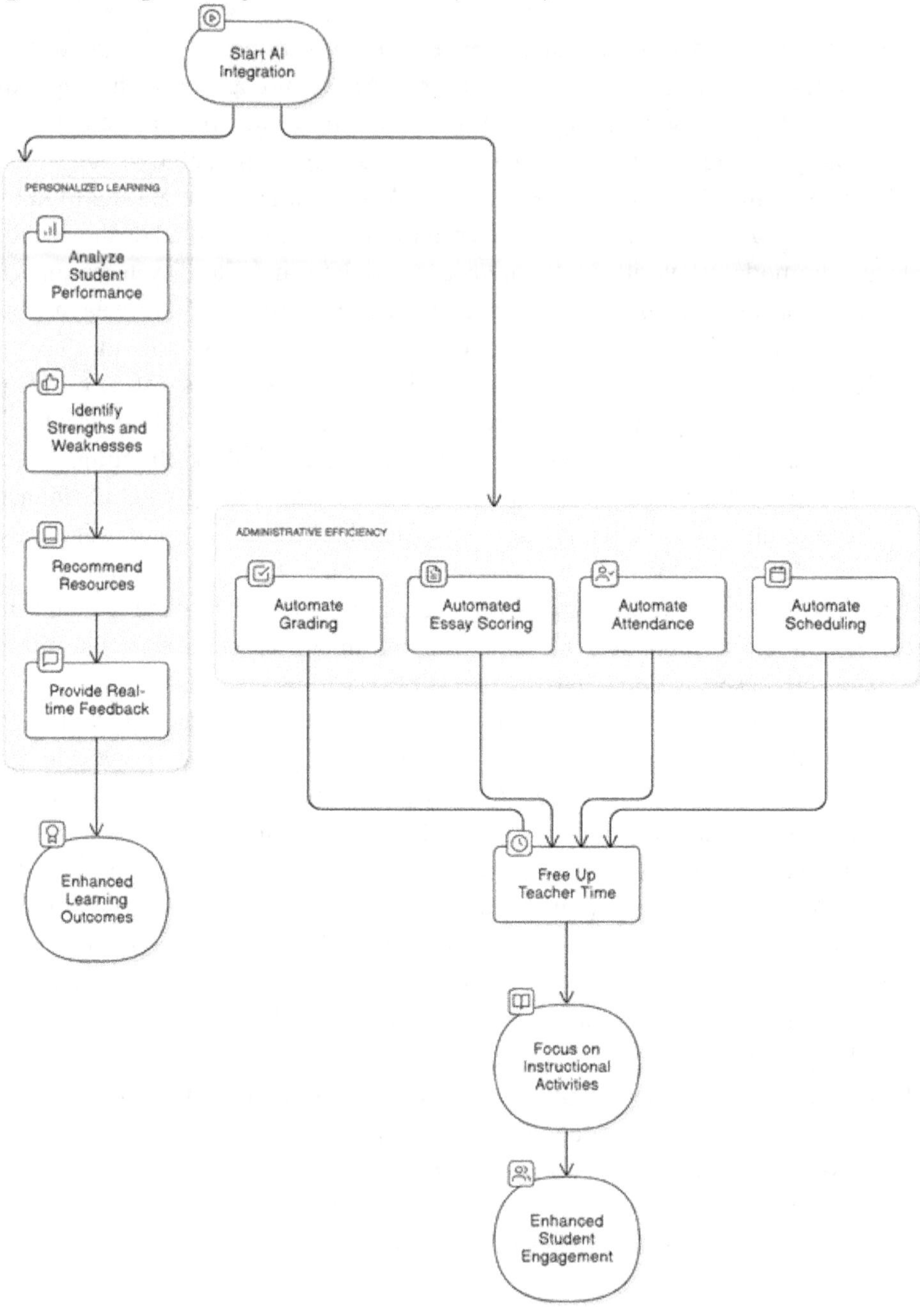

1.2 Purpose and Scope of the Paper

The purpose of this chapter is to discover the evolving position of instructors in an AI-stronger academic panorama, highlighting each the opportunities and demanding situations provided by means of the integration of synthetic intelligence into education. As AI technology end up an increasing number of well-known in classrooms, information their impact on conventional teaching roles and methodologies is essential for educators, policymakers, and stakeholders. This chapter pursuits to provide a comprehensive evaluation of the way AI can increase teaching practices, the abilities teachers want to thrive on this new surroundings, and the important policy reforms to guide this transition.

The scope of this chapter includes a detailed examination of the subsequent key areas:

AI Technologies in Education: An assessment of the numerous AI programs presently being utilized in academic settings, including adaptive studying structures, automated grading, clever tutoring systems, and administrative mission automation. This phase will discuss the abilities and barriers of these technologies.

Evolving Teaching Roles: An evaluation of how AI influences the jobs and responsibilities of instructors. This includes the shift from traditional teaching techniques to greater facilitative and mentorship roles, in which teacher's manual college students in navigating personalized studying paths and growing crucial thinking and trouble-solving capabilities (Taufikin et al., 2024).

Human-Centric Skills: Emphasis at the importance of human-centric skills such as empathy, creativity, and vital thinking inside the AI-more suitable classroom. This segment will argue that while AI can cope with many administrative and habitual obligations, the specific human qualities of teachers are irreplaceable and vital for fostering a supportive and attractive studying environment (Vashishth et al., 2024).

Professional Development: Recommendations for expert development programs to equip teachers with the talents and information had to efficiently combine AI tools into their coaching practices. This consists of schooling in virtual literacy, records interpretation, and the ethical use of AI in training (Sargiotis, 2024).

Policy Reforms: An exploration of essential coverage reforms to help the mixing of AI in education. This phase will deal with issues which includes information privacy, fairness in get right of entry to AI technologies, and the improvement of ethical recommendations for AI use in colleges.

Future Trends and Implications: A discussion of modern-day trends and destiny possibilities in AI-enhanced education. This will include predictions at the evolution of AI technology in education and their long-time period implications for coaching and learning.

By reading these areas, the chapter objectives to offer a roadmap for educators and policymakers to navigate the transformative effect of AI in schooling. It seeks to spotlight the symbiotic relationship among AI tools and educators, advocating for a balanced approach that maximizes the benefits of AI at the same time as maintaining the vital human factors of teaching (Edeni et al., 2024).

1.3 Organization of the Chapter

The rest of the chapter is organized as: Section 2 AI in Education: Opportunities and Challenges explores the potential of AI to enhance learning through personalized education, while also addressing challenges such as access inequality, ethical concerns, and data privacy issues. Section 3 The Evolving Role of Teachers within the Context of AI in Education discusses how AI reshapes teachers' roles from content deliverers to facilitators, emphasizing the need to balance traditional teaching with AI-enhanced methods. Section 4 Symbiotic Relationship between AI Tools and Educators highlights how AI tools complement teachers by supporting personalized learning and reducing administrative tasks, creating a collaborative and supportive partnership. Section 5 Professional Development for Educators focuses on the importance of continuous professional development to equip teachers with the necessary skills to effectively integrate AI into their classrooms. Section 6 Policy Reforms for AI Integration reviews necessary policy changes to ensure safe, ethical, and equitable AI implementation in education, addressing data security, privacy, and access issues. Section 7 Current Trends and Future Possibilities examines the latest AI trends in education, such as adaptive learning systems and intelligent tutoring, while considering the future possibilities of AI advancements. Section 8 Limitations and Future Research outlines the current limitations of AI in education, including bias and access issues, and identifies key areas for future research to address these challenges. Section 9 Conclusion a summary of the key points, emphasizing the ongoing need to balance AI innovation with the irreplaceable role of human educators in a rapidly evolving educational landscape.

2. AI IN EDUCATION: OPPORTUNITIES AND CHALLENGES

The integration of synthetic intelligence (AI) into the instructional sector brings a plethora of possibilities and challenges, reshaping the landscape of coaching and mastering. AI technology have the potential to revolutionize education through imparting customized mastering reports, automating administrative tasks, and presenting actual-time analytics. However, this transformation also provides good sized challenges that want to be addressed to make certain equitable and effective implementation.

Opportunities -

1. Personalized Learning:

AI can tailor educational content to meet the person desires of college students, thereby enhancing their gaining knowledge of studies. Adaptive learning systems use AI algorithms to investigate students' learning patterns, strengths, and weaknesses, presenting customized classes and sporting events. This personalized approach can help student's development at their own pace, making education more engaging and effective.

2. Automation of Administrative Tasks:

Teachers frequently spend a sizeable amount of time on administrative responsibilities along with grading, attendance monitoring, and scheduling. AI can automate these tasks, releasing up time for instructors to awareness on extra critical factors of coaching, consisting of lesson making plans and student interaction. Automated grading structures, for instance, can provide instant comments on assignments, permitting teachers to commit greater time to individualized practice.

3. Intelligent Tutoring Systems:

AI-powered tutoring structures can provide additional support to college students outside of the study room. These systems can provide motives, answer questions, and provide practice problems, supplementing traditional coaching strategies. This extra aid can be specifically useful for college kids who want greater assist or who need to explore topics in extra depth.

4. Real-Time Analytics and Insights:

AI can analyze significant amounts of data to offer actual-time insights into pupil overall performance and mastering patterns. Teachers can use those insights to pick out suffering students early, regulate coaching techniques, and provide centered interventions. This records-pushed technique can cause greater informed decision-making and stepped forward academic effects.

Challenges -

1. Equity and Access:

One of the primary demanding situations of AI in training is ensuring equitable get entry to to generation. Not all students have get entry to the essential gadgets and internet connectivity, main to a virtual divide. Schools and policymakers should cope with those disparities to make certain that everyone students can gain from AI-enhanced education.

2. Data Privacy and Security:

The use of AI in schooling involves gathering and reading vast amounts of scholar facts. Ensuring the privacy and security of this records is paramount. Schools must implement robust information protection measures and adhere to regulations to save you facts breaches and misuse of pupil data.

3. Teacher Training and Professional Development:

The success integration of AI in training calls for teachers to be correctly educated to use those technology correctly. Professional improvement programs need to be designed to equip teachers with the competencies had to integrate AI equipment into their coaching practices. This includes education in digital literacy, data interpretation, and the moral use of AI.

4. Ethical Considerations:

The use of AI in training raises several ethical troubles, consisting of the potential for bias in AI algorithms and the effect of automation on the teaching profession. Educators and policymakers must address these ethical issues to ensure that AI is used responsibly and pretty. Developing moral hints and frameworks for AI use in education is important to mitigate these dangers.

5. Dependence on Technology:

While AI gives several benefits, there's a chance of becoming overly depending on generation. It is critical to strike a stability among leveraging AI tools and keeping the human elements of teaching. Teachers play a critical function in fostering important thinking, creativity, and emotional intelligence—abilities that AI can't reflect (Kakhkharova and Tuychieva, 2024).

In conclusion, the integration of AI in education provides both substantial possibilities and challenges. By addressing the demanding situations and leveraging the possibilities, educators and policymakers can harness the ability of AI to beautify teaching and mastering reviews. A balanced and ethical technique to AI implementation is critical to ensure that each one college students benefit from those advancements at the same time as keeping the critical human factors of training.

3. THE EVOLVING ROLE OF TEACHERS WITHIN THE CONTEXT OF AI IN EDUCATION

As artificial intelligence (AI) keeps to permeate instructional environments, the role of instructors is undergoing a profound evolution. Traditionally seen as disseminators of information and facilitators of gaining knowledge of, educators now find themselves navigating a landscape wherein AI augments their skills and duties (Roberts et al., 2024). AI allows personalized learning experiences tailor-made to person pupil desires, automates administrative duties like grading and records analysis, and offers actual-time insights into pupil overall performance. Consequently, instructors are transitioning into mentors and facilitators who curate instructional stories, interpret AI-generated insights, and guide college students through crucial wondering and trouble-solving physical activities that AI can't replicate. This shift demands educators to domesticate digital literacy competencies, adaptability in integrating AI equipment into pedagogy, and an emphasis on human-centric characteristics which include empathy and creativity. Moreover, ethical concerns around statistics privacy, algorithmic bias, and equitable access to AI gear underscore the importance of educators' roles in navigating the ethical implications of AI in training whilst harnessing its potential to enhance learning outcomes (Limna et al., 2022).

3.1 Importance of Human-Centric Skills

In the realm of AI-included education, the significance of human-centric skills which include empathy, creativity, and vital wondering cannot be overstated. While AI excels in facts processing and automation, those qualities stay uniquely human and quintessential in fostering meaningful mastering studies. Empathy lets in teachers to understand college students' emotional needs, providing assist and encouragement tailor-made to man or woman instances that AI might also overlook. Creativity allows educators to design modern classes and tasks that engage students past standardized curricula, encouraging exploration and self-expression

(Petit, 2024). Critical questioning, vital for evaluating statistics and solving complex troubles, empowers college students to apply understanding in real-world contexts and navigate the ethical considerations of AI technology. Together, these talents supplement AI's analytical abilities by means of nurturing a holistic educational environment wherein students now not best collect understanding but also turn into considerate, adaptable individuals able to thriving in an AI-improved future. Thus, even as AI transforms educational methodologies, educators equipped with empathy, creativity, and important questioning continue to be pivotal in shaping students' mastering journeys and making ready them for an evolving virtual panorama (Akbar et al., 2024).

Figure 2. Importance of AI- enhanced human centric skills in education (Author)

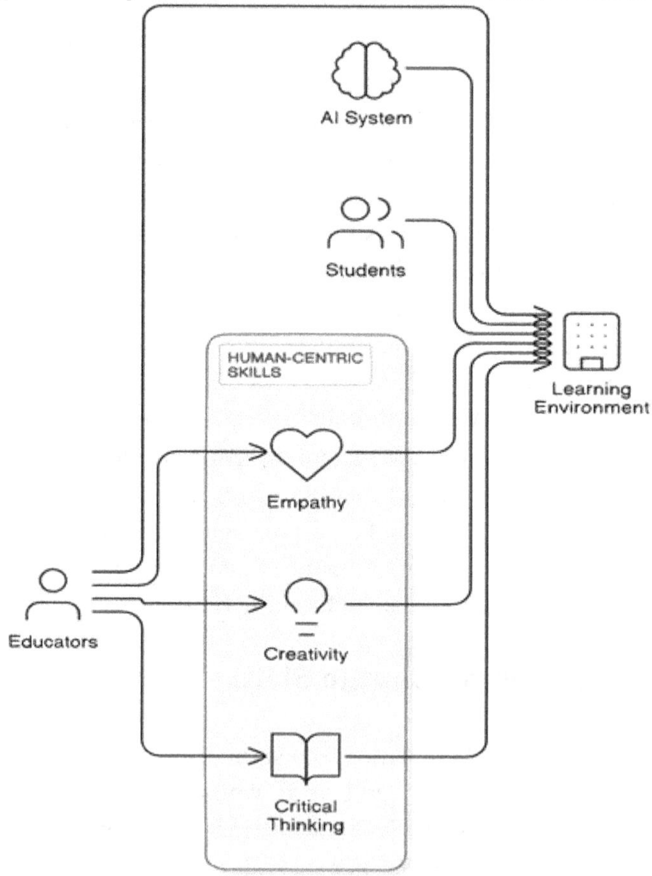

3.2 Fostering a Supportive Learning Environment

Fostering a supportive gaining knowledge of environment amidst AI integration in training calls for instructors to mixture technological improvements with interpersonal skills. AI's role in automating administrative duties and personalizing learning experiences can decorate performance and cater to man or woman pupil wishes. However, the instructor's position extends beyond mere facilitation; they serve as mentors and guides who domesticate trust, collaboration, and inclusivity within classrooms. By leveraging AI gear to music student progress and become aware of gaining knowledge of gaps, educators can tailor interventions that address each scholar's specific challenges and strengths. This personalized technique no longer simplest complements academic consequences but additionally nurtures an experience of belonging and motivation amongst beginners. Moreover, creating a supportive environment involves encouraging open conversation, positive comments, and recognize for diverse perspectives. Teachers play a crucial function in modeling nice behaviors and fostering a culture of inquiry and growth thoughts-set, wherein college student's sense empowered to explore, experiment, and study from their errors (Aghaziarati et al., 2023). Ultimately, through integrating AI technologies thoughtfully and prioritizing human-centric values, educators can create inclusive, supportive learning environments that prepare students for fulfillment in a more and more virtual and interconnected global.

Figure 3. Complementary roles of AI & teachers in instructional panorama (Author)

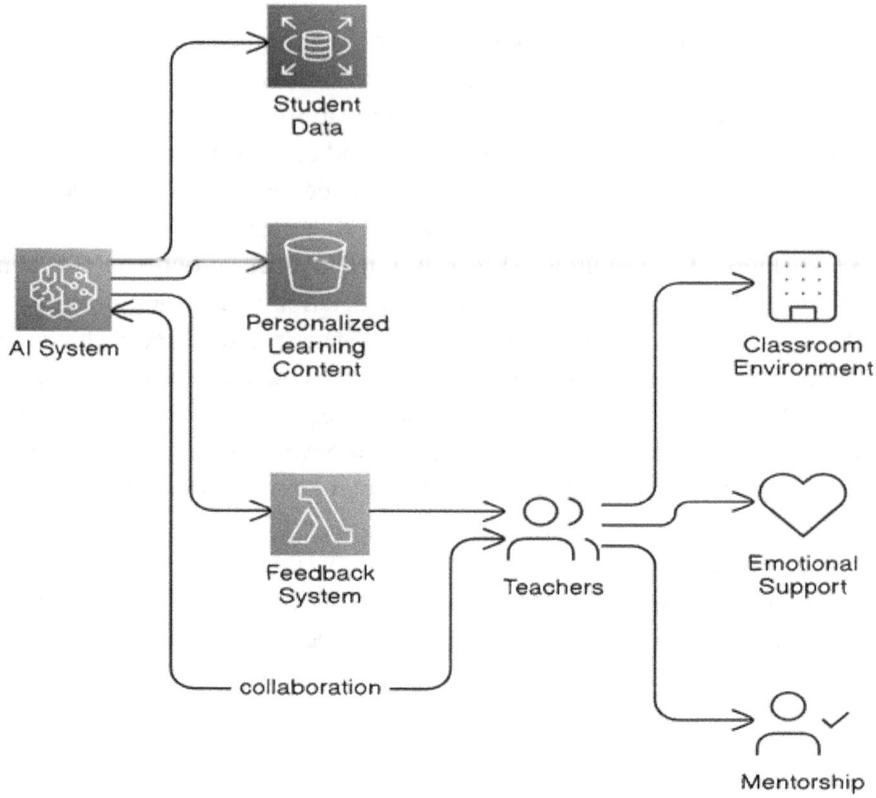

4. SYMBIOTIC RELATIONSHIP BETWEEN AI TOOLS AND EDUCATORS

The symbiotic relationship among AI tools and educators inside the realm of education underscores a dynamic collaboration aimed at enhancing coaching and gaining knowledge of results. AI technology provide educators powerful equipment to streamline administrative obligations, personalize getting to know experiences, and analyze enormous amounts of scholar facts to tell instructional strategies correctly. By automating ordinary responsibilities which includes grading checks or handling administrative workflows, AI frees up educators' time, allowing them to attention greater on individualized student help and pedagogical innovation. Furthermore, AI-driven analytics provide treasured insights into student performance tendencies and getting to know preferences, allowing teachers to tailor interventions that cater to various gaining knowledge of wishes. However, the effective integration of AI in training calls for educators to possess the expertise to interpret and observe data-pushed insights thoughtfully. Educators play a pivotal position in contextualizing AI-generated tips and adapting instructional methods primarily based on nuanced understandings of student conduct and engagement. Moreover, the human touch remains indispensable in nurturing socio-emotional talents, fostering crucial wondering, and encouraging creativity in college students—regions wherein AI assist is complementary in place of substitutive (Sperling et al., 2024).

In essence, the symbiosis between AI equipment and educators hinges on collaborative synergy, wherein AI augments instructional capacities at the same time as educators leverage their pedagogical expertise to harness the total ability of those technology. By embracing this partnership, educators can empower students with personalized gaining knowledge of experiences which might be responsive to person wishes and conducive to lifelong learning competencies vital for the destiny (Baskara, 2023).

4.1 Integration of AI in Teaching

Integrating AI in teaching represents a good sized advancement in instructional methodologies, imparting a range of revolutionary approaches to beautify learning consequences. AI equipment are more and more applied to personalize gaining knowledge of reports, adapt curriculum shipping primarily based on student performance facts, and provide real-time comments to each students and educators. Machine Learning algorithms can examine big quantities of educational facts to discover styles and tailor instructional content to character scholar desires, thereby fostering a more personalized and adaptive learning surroundings. Additionally, AI-powered digital assistants and chatbots are employed to assist administrative tasks, answer scholar inquiries, and provide tutoring assistance outdoor of traditional classroom settings. The integration of AI in teaching no longer best targets to improve educational performance however also empowers educators by means of augmenting their educational abilities and enabling them to awareness more on scholar engagement and better-order cognitive abilities. As AI keeps to conform, its role in education is expected to increase, prompting educators to evolve their coaching practices and embrace the opportunities supplied by way of these transformative technologies (Syahrizal et al., 2024).

4.2 Complementary Roles of AI and Teachers

AI and teachers play complementary roles in the instructional panorama, every bringing unique strengths to beautify studying effects. Artificial Intelligence (AI) excels in records processing, analytics, and automation, enabling personalized gaining knowledge of experiences and administrative efficiencies. AI algorithms can analyze tremendous quantities of student information to become aware of studying patterns, customize educational content, and offer centered comments, hence catering to individual learning wishes more successfully than traditional methods by myself (Zootzky and Pfeiffer, 2024).

Teachers, alternatively, deliver human-centric traits along with empathy, creativity, and critical wondering to training. These characteristics are essential in fostering a supportive and motivating learning environment where student's sense engaged and endorsed to discover their ability. Teachers interpret and contextualize AI-generated insights, presenting steerage, emotional guide, and customized mentorship that AI gear cannot reflect. Moreover, educators play a pivotal position in shaping college students' social and emotional development, nurturing their curiosity, and instilling values beyond educational success (Vashishth et al., 2023).

The symbiotic courting among AI and teachers is vital for leveraging the strengths of both approaches. While AI complements instructional efficiency and scalability, teachers provide the human contact vital for significant studying reviews. Collaboration among AI tools and educators permits a holistic method to schooling, in which era supports and amplifies teachers competencies while instructors manual and enhance the mastering journey, in the long run preparing college students for a complicated and evolving future (Gupta et al., 2024).

5. PROFESSIONAL DEVELOPMENT FOR EDUCATORS

In an AI-improved educational panorama, professional improvement for educators is important for maximizing the benefits of AI integration and ensuring that instructors are properly-organized to navigate the evolving academic environment. Effective professional improvement focuses on 3 key regions: training packages, skill enhancement, and adapting to AI technologies.

Training Programs

Training programs are essential for equipping educators with the expertise and capabilities needed to combine AI technologies efficaciously into their teaching practices. These packages need to cowl fundamental AI concepts, practical programs within the study room, and techniques for leveraging AI tools to enhance pupil learning. Training can take diverse bureaucracy, together with workshops, online courses, and arms-on sessions, ensuring that educators have get admission to continuous getting to know opportunities. By collaborating in these programs, instructors can stay updated on the modern-day advancements in AI and apprehend how to utilize these technologies to support their instructional desires.

Skill Enhancement

In addition to primary schooling, educators want to recognition on ability enhancement to maximize the benefits of AI integration. This involves growing both technical capabilities, such as records evaluation and AI device talent, and pedagogical competencies, which includes designing AI-driven personalized learning experiences. Skill enhancement also can include gaining knowledge of how to interpret AI-generated statistics to inform academic decisions and enhance student outcomes. By improving their capabilities, teachers can greater efficaciously use AI to differentiate guidance, provide well timed remarks, and create a more attractive and interactive mastering surroundings (Molefi et al., 2024).

Adapting to AI Technologies

Adapting to AI technology calls for a attitude shift and a willingness to embrace exchange. Educators have to turn out to be snug with incorporating AI into their daily workouts and be open to experimenting with new tools and strategies. This edition system consists of knowledge the moral implications of AI in training, making sure facts privacy, and maintaining a stability between era and human interplay. Teachers ought to also be organized to deal with students' questions and worries about AI, fostering a lecture room subculture that perspectives generation as a precious ally within the studying manner. By adapting to AI technology, educators can better put together their college students for a future wherein AI plays an increasingly good sized role (Kayyali, 2024).

6. POLICY REFORMS FOR AI INTEGRATION

Policy reforms are critical to aid the powerful integration of AI in education. These reforms should address numerous key regions to make certain that AI technologies are implemented in a manner that maximizes benefits for students, teachers, and academic establishments at the same time as mitigating potential risks.

6.1 Establishing Ethical Guidelines

To ensure that AI is used responsibly in training, coverage reforms ought to encompass the establishment of clean moral tips. These hints ought to cope with troubles including information privacy, scholar consent, and the prevention of bias in AI algorithms. Policies must make certain that AI packages in training are obvious and that information collected from students is used ethically and securely.

6.2 Funding and Resource Allocation

Effective AI integration requires extensive funding in technology, schooling, and infrastructure. Policies need to prioritize funding for AI equipment and sources, inclusive of hardware, software, and internet connectivity. Additionally, guidelines ought to allocate assets for ongoing professional development for educators to maintain them updated with the today's AI improvements and coaching methodologies (Rütti-Joy et al., 2024).

6.3 Curriculum Development

Curriculum reforms are vital to integrate AI literacy into education at all degrees. Policies should mandate the inclusion of AI and digital literacy within the curriculum to put together students for a future where AI is ubiquitous. This includes growing materials and sources that educators can use to educate students approximately AI principles, packages, and moral concerns (Vashishth et al., 2024).

6.4 Collaboration and Partnership

Policies have to inspire collaboration among instructional establishments, technology companies, and studies businesses to foster innovation and proportion great practices. By facilitating partnerships, policies can help faculties and educators get admission to the modern-day AI technology and insights, allowing them to put into effect AI in extra effective and innovative approaches.

6.5 Monitoring and Evaluation

To make sure the effectiveness of AI integration, guidelines have to consist of mechanisms for tracking and assessment. This entails frequently assessing the impact of AI on pupil studying results, trainer effectiveness, and general educational first-class. By continuously evaluating AI projects, policymakers can perceive regions for improvement and make statistics-driven selections to decorate AI integration (Verma et al., 2023).

6.6 Accessibility and Equity

Policy reforms need to additionally cope with problems of accessibility and fairness to make sure that each one students gain from AI technology. This includes offering support for underserved communities and ensuring that AI equipment are accessible to college students with disabilities. Policies ought to intention to bridge the virtual divide and promote inclusive schooling.

By enforcing those coverage reforms, instructional systems can create a supportive surroundings for AI integration, enhancing teaching and getting to know reviews at the same time as addressing ability challenges and ethical concerns.

6.7 Necessary Changes in Educational Policies

To efficiently combine AI into schooling, several key modifications in instructional rules are essential. These adjustments ought to awareness on creating a supportive framework that enables the ethical, equitable, and effective use of AI technologies. The following regions spotlight the critical coverage adjustments wished:

6.7.1 Ethical Standards and Data Privacy

Educational guidelines have to establish stringent moral requirements and statistics privacy guidelines. These guidelines must:

Ensure the protection of pupil facts through enforcing robust records privacy legal guidelines.

Require transparency from AI companies regarding statistics utilization and algorithmic strategies.

Mandate using impartial and truthful AI algorithms to save you discrimination and make certain equal opportunities for all college students.

6.7.2 Professional Development and Training

Policies ought to prioritize non-stop professional development for educators to assist them adapt to AI technologies. Key measures include:

Providing funding and resources for regular training programs centered on AI literacy and digital abilities (Sharma & Kumar, 2024).

Encouraging collaboration among educators and AI specialists to broaden customized education modules.

Implementing certification programs that recognize educators' talent in integrating AI into their coaching practices.

6.7.3 Curriculum and Assessment Reforms

To prepare students for a destiny driven by using AI, curriculum and assessment strategies need to be up to date. This entails:

Integrating AI and digital literacy into the core curriculum across all educational degrees.

Developing new assessment tools that leverage AI to offer personalized feedback and help differentiated studying.

Encouraging project-based and experiential learning opportunities that contain AI applications.

6.7.4 Infrastructure and Resource Allocation

Policies must make sure that faculties have the necessary infrastructure and sources to support AI integration. This consists of:

Allocating funds for upgrading technological infrastructure, such as excessive-speed internet, AI-enabled devices, and cloud computing resources.

Providing presents and monetary incentives for schools to adopt innovative AI solutions.

Ensuring equitable get entry to AI equipment and resources, mainly in under-served and rural areas.

Figure 4. Infrastructure and resource allocation for AI integration (Author)

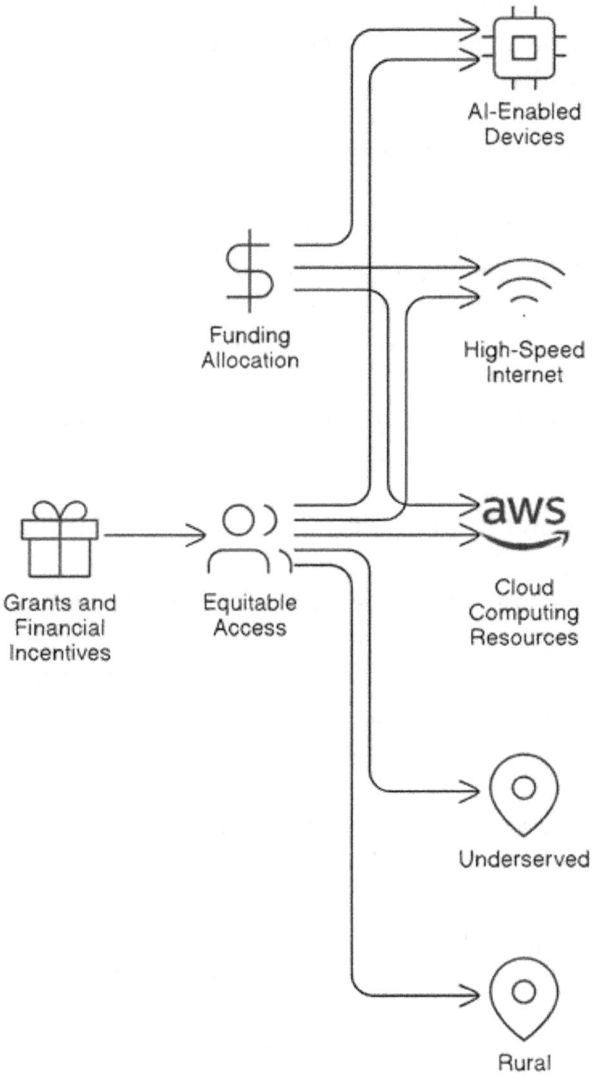

6.7.5 Inclusive Education and Accessibility

AI integration should promote inclusive training and accessibility for all students. Policies must:

Mandate the development and use of AI gear which might be accessible to college students with disabilities.

Address the digital divide with the aid of presenting aid and resources to low-profits and marginalized groups.

Promote the use of AI to create adaptive mastering environments that cater to the various needs of all college students.

6.7.6 Research and Development

To stay in advance of technological advancements, instructional rules need to support ongoing studies and improvement in AI. This involves:

Funding research tasks that explore innovative AI programs in education.

Establishing partnerships among instructional establishments, technology businesses, and research corporations.

Encouraging pilot applications and experimental studies to check new AI-driven educational methodologies and tools.

6.7.7 Monitoring and Evaluation

Continuous monitoring and assessment are essential to the fulfillment of AI integration in training. Policies ought to:

Implement frameworks for regular assessment of AI gear and their effect on teaching and getting to know effects.

Use records-pushed insights to make knowledgeable coverage selections and adjustments.

Establish responsibility mechanisms to ensure that AI implementations align with instructional dreams and moral requirements.

By making those essential modifications in instructional policies, instructional systems can create a conducive environment for the successful integration of AI, in the long run enhancing the high-quality and accessibility of training for all students.

6.8 Strategies for Effective Implementation

Effective implementation of AI in schooling calls for a multifaceted approach that involves careful making plans, collaboration, and non-stop assessment. Here are key techniques to make certain the success integration of AI technologies in instructional settings:

6.8.1 Comprehensive Planning and Vision

Define Clear Objectives: Establish clear dreams for AI integration, specializing in enhancing getting to know outcomes, personalizing education, and enhancing administrative performance.

Develop a Roadmap: Create an in depth implementation plan outlining quick-time period and lengthy-term milestones, aid allocation, and timelines.

Involve Stakeholders: Engage educators, students, parents, policymakers, and generation professionals in the making plans process to ensure various perspectives and needs are taken into consideration.

6.8.2 Building Technological Infrastructure

Invest in Infrastructure: Ensure faculties and academic establishments have access to excessive-speed net, reliable hardware, and AI-compatible software program.

Cloud Computing: Utilize cloud computing to manipulate facts storage, processing, and AI utility deployment, providing scalability and flexibility.

Pilot Projects: Start with pilot tasks to check AI equipment in managed environments before scaling up, bearing in mind adjustments and enhancements primarily based on comments.

6.8.3 Professional Development and Training

Ongoing Training Programs: Implement non-stop professional development packages focused on AI literacy, digital competencies, and the pedagogical integration of AI.

Collaborative Learning: Encourage educators to collaborate and proportion first-rate practices, fostering a community of studying and aid.

Mentorship and Support: Provide mentorship opportunities wherein experienced educators can manual their friends in efficaciously the usage of AI technologies.

8.4 Curriculum and Instructional Design

Integrate AI into Curriculum: Embed AI and virtual literacy principles into the curriculum to put together college students for an era-driven future.

Adaptive Learning: Use AI to create adaptive learning environments that provide personalized practice primarily based on person student wishes and progress.

Project-Based Learning: Encourage undertaking-based getting to know sports that contain AI applications, promoting hands-on experience and crucial thinking.

8.4.1 Policy and Ethical Considerations

Establish Ethical Guidelines: Develop and put in force ethical pointers for the usage of AI in training, making sure information privacy, transparency, and fairness.
Data Security: Implement sturdy facts security measures to defend pupil statistics and observe prison and moral requirements.
Inclusive Policies: Ensure rules aid equitable access to AI tools and assets, especially for underserved and marginalized communities.

8.4.2 Monitoring and Evaluation

Regular Assessments: Conduct normal assessments to evaluate the effectiveness of AI equipment and their impact on academic effects.
Data-Driven Decision Making: Use information analytics to tell choices, identify regions for development, and optimize AI implementations.
Feedback Mechanisms: Establish feedback loops related to educators, college students, and parents to gather insights and refine AI programs continuously (Vashishth et al., 2024).

8.4.3 Collaboration and Partnerships

Industry Partnerships: Foster partnerships with technology businesses, research establishments, and AI experts to leverage their know-how and assets.
Government Support: Advocate for authorities guide and investment for AI projects in schooling, making sure sustained investment and policy alignment.
International Collaboration: Engage in international collaborations to share information, resources, and first-class practices, enhancing global academic standards.

8.4.4 Promoting a Culture of Innovation

Encourage Innovation: Create a surroundings that encourages experimentation and innovation in teaching and studying practices.
Recognition and Incentives: Recognize and reward educators and institutions that efficaciously implement modern AI answers, promoting a lifestyle of continuous development.
Student Involvement: Involve college students within the layout and implementation of AI tools, fostering a experience of ownership and engagement inside the mastering system.

By adopting those techniques, instructional establishments can efficiently implement AI technologies, improving the fine of training and better preparing students for the future.

Figure 5. Promoting a culture of innovation in teaching with AI (Author)

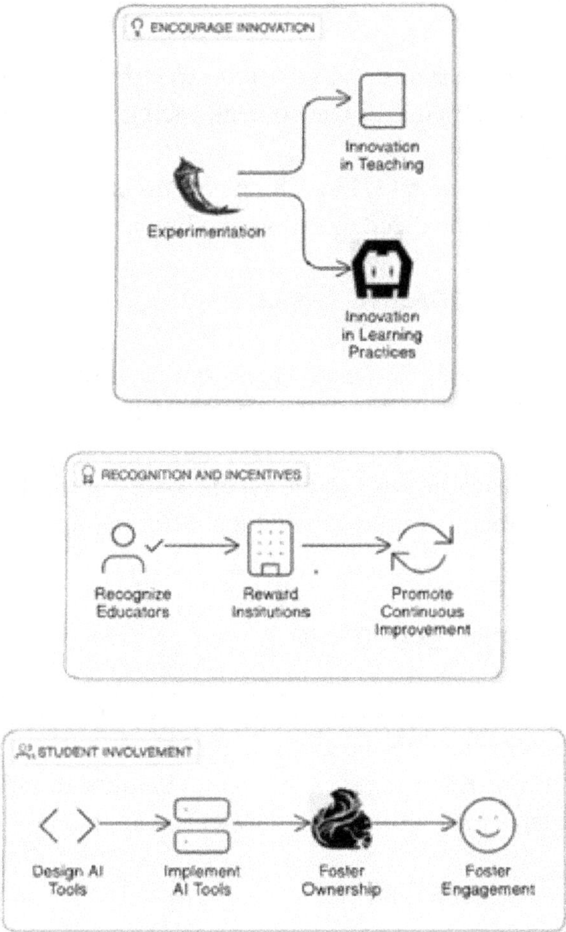

7. CURRENT TRENDS AND FUTURE POSSIBILITIES

The integration of AI in education is evolving unexpectedly, pushed by means of technological advancements and the growing recognition of AI's capability to transform mastering stories. Understanding current developments and looking ahead to future possibilities is crucial for educators, policymakers, and generation developers. Here an overview of massive trends and rising possibilities in AI-superior education:

7.1 Current Trends

Personalized Learning:

Adaptive Learning Systems: AI-powered structures examine scholar overall performance facts to tailor educational content, pacing, and sports to person getting to know styles and wishes.

Intelligent Tutoring Systems (ITS): These systems offer customized remarks and help, mimicking the personalized attention of a human coach.

Automation of Administrative Tasks:

Attendance and Grading: AI automates routine responsibilities inclusive of attendance monitoring and grading, releasing up educators to recognition on extra complex and interactive aspects of teaching.

Scheduling and Resource Allocation: AI optimizes scheduling, useful resource allocation, and different administrative functions, improving performance and reducing workload.

Enhanced Student Engagement:

Gamification: AI-pushed gamification strategies increase pupil engagement via integrating game elements into academic activities.

Interactive Learning Environments: AI creates immersive and interactive getting to know environments thru virtual reality (VR) and augmented reality (AR).

Data-Driven Decision Making:

Predictive Analytics: AI analyzes massive datasets to predict scholar consequences, discover at-chance students, and suggest interventions.

Learning Analytics: Real-time analytics provide insights into student development, assisting educators regulate practice methods directly.

AI-Powered Assessment:

Formative Assessments: AI allows continuous and formative tests, supplying immediate remarks to students and permitting ongoing improvement.

Adaptive Testing: AI adapts the problem of take a look at questions based totally on pupil responses, offering an extra accurate measure of scholar abilities.

7.2 Future Possibilities

AI and Human Collaboration:

Enhanced Teacher Roles: Teachers will increasingly more collaborate with AI, the usage of it as a device to enhance coaching, provide customized help, and recognition on developing students important thinking and creativity (Koh et al., 2023).

Professional Development: Continuous expert development will evolve to encompass AI literacy and integration capabilities, getting ready educators to correctly use AI of their teaching practices (Ding et al., 2024).

AI in Curriculum Design:

Dynamic Curricula: AI will enable the creation of dynamic and flexible curricula that can be constantly up to date based on new educational research and student performance facts.

Interdisciplinary Learning: AI will facilitate interdisciplinary mastering via connecting ideas throughout exclusive topics and providing a holistic know-how of topics (Husain, 2023).

Ethical and Inclusive AI:

Bias Reduction: Future AI systems may be designed to become aware of and mitigate biases, ensuring truthful and equitable academic possibilities for all college students (Gobara & Ahmed, 2024).

Accessibility: AI will decorate accessibility for students with disabilities, providing tailored learning experiences that cater to various desires.

Global Collaboration and Learning:

Cross-Cultural Learning: AI will permit international classrooms wherein students from distinctive parts of the sector can collaborate and research from every other in real time.

Language Translation: Advanced language translation gear will break down language barriers, making instructional sources available to a broader target market (Novawan et al., 2024).

AI-Driven Research and Innovation:

Educational Research: AI will revolutionize instructional research by using imparting new insights into getting to know methods, educational techniques, and educational results.

Innovation Hubs: Educational institutions becomes hubs of innovation, leveraging AI to experiment with new teaching methodologies and getting to know fashions.

Long-Term Impact:

Lifelong Learning: AI will assist lifelong studying by way of supplying non-stop, customized education past conventional college years.

Workforce Preparation: AI will assist put together college students for destiny careers by aligning academic stories with the abilities and understanding wished in a rapidly changing activity marketplace.

By staying abreast of these trends and watching for future tendencies, educators and institutions can proactively harness AIs capacity to decorate educational reviews and consequences.

8. LIMITATIONS AND FUTURE RESEARCH

Limitations of the Role of Teachers in an AI-Enhanced Educational Landscape -

1. Technological Access and Digital Divide: Not all schools and students have equal access to AI technologies, particularly in under-resourced areas. This digital divide can exacerbate educational inequalities, as students with limited access to AI tools may fall behind their peers who can fully engage with these innovations.

2. Teacher Training and Adaptation: Many teachers may lack sufficient training or feel overwhelmed by integrating AI into their teaching methods. As AI rapidly evolves, continuous professional development is required, which may be challenging due to resource constraints and the steep learning curve.
3. Ethical and Privacy Concerns: AI systems often collect and analyze large amounts of student data, raising concerns about privacy, consent, and data security. Teachers must balance the benefits of AI-enhanced personalization with safeguarding student information.
4. Over-reliance on AI: There is a risk of over-reliance on AI tools, which could reduce the role of teachers in making critical educational judgments. Automated systems, while powerful, may lack the human empathy, creativity, and ethical judgment needed for holistic student development.
5. Bias in AI Algorithms: AI systems may perpetuate or amplify existing biases present in their training data, leading to unfair treatment of certain student groups. Teachers may find it difficult to identify and mitigate such biases, potentially causing unintentional harm to students from marginalized backgrounds.
6. Loss of Personalized Human Interaction: While AI can enhance personalization, it cannot fully replicate the nuanced understanding and personal relationships that teachers develop with their students. The human touch, which is essential for emotional and social learning, may diminish if AI takes too central a role in classrooms.

Future Research Directions -

1. Equitable Access to AI in Education: Future research should explore strategies for providing equitable access to AI technologies across diverse schools and communities. Investigating ways to bridge the digital divide will help ensure that all students benefit from AI-enhanced education.
2. Developing Effective AI Training Programs for Teachers: Research on scalable and effective professional development programs for teachers is needed to ensure they can confidently and effectively use AI in their classrooms. This includes exploring best practices for integrating AI into pedagogical methods and ongoing support mechanisms.
3. Ethics and Policy Frameworks: Further exploration of ethical guidelines and policy frameworks is necessary to ensure that AI tools in education respect student privacy, minimize biases, and promote inclusivity. Research in this area could inform the development of transparent AI systems that align with educational goals.

4. Impact of AI on Student Learning Outcomes: More studies are needed to measure the long-term impact of AI-enhanced learning on student outcomes, including academic achievement, social-emotional development, and critical thinking skills. Research can also explore how AI complements or hinders traditional teaching methods.
5. Hybrid AI-Teacher Models: Research can explore the development of hybrid models where AI supports but does not replace the teacher's role. This includes understanding how AI can be integrated into classrooms in ways that enhance, rather than diminish, the unique contributions of teachers.
6. Addressing Algorithmic Bias in Educational AI: Future research should focus on identifying and mitigating biases within AI algorithms to ensure fairness and equity in educational outcomes. This includes studying how AI models can be refined to better serve students from diverse backgrounds.
7. Student-Teacher Dynamics in AI-Augmented Learning Environments: Research on how the integration of AI affects student-teacher interactions and classroom dynamics can provide insights into maintaining positive educational relationships in an AI-enhanced landscape.

These limitations and research directions are crucial for ensuring that AI's integration into education is both effective and equitable, while also enhancing the role of teachers in fostering a holistic learning experience.

9. CONCLUSION

The integration of synthetic intelligence in training marks a transformative generation, redefining the conventional roles of instructors while simultaneously supplying exceptional opportunities for boosting mastering studies. This paper underscores the imperative function of teachers, highlighting that in spite of the superior capabilities of AI, human-centric abilities including empathy, creativity, and crucial wondering continue to be irreplaceable. Teachers are pivotal in fostering a supportive and attractive getting to know environment, which AI tools on my own cannot acquire. The symbiotic dating between AI and educators is critical; while AI can streamline administrative obligations and provide personalized gaining knowledge of, it's miles the educators who can contextualize those equipment to meet the nuanced wishes of their college students. Professional improvement and policy reforms are critical to equip teachers with the important abilities to conform to this evolving panorama, making sure they are able to efficaciously integrate AI into their pedagogical practices. Moreover, ongoing education programs, skill enhancement initiatives, and strategies for adapting to AI technologies are essential for maximizing the advantages of AI in education. As we navigate this transformative generation, it's far essential to acknowledge and include the evolving position of instructors, ensuring they may be empowered to harness AI capability at the same time as keeping the important human factors of education. This balanced technique will pave the way for a greater enriched, equitable, and dynamic academic panorama.

REFERENCES

Aghaziarati, A., Nejatifar, S., & Abedi, A. (2023). Artificial Intelligence in Education: Investigating Teacher Attitudes. *AI and Tech in Behavioral and Social Sciences*, 1(1), 35–42.

Akbar, Y. A. A., Anuar, A., Zani, R. M., Abdullah, F. N., Sunian, E., & Sulaiman, E. (2024). Exploring the Scholarly Landscape: AI Teaching and Learning in Adult Education. *International Journal of Academic Research in Progressive Education and Development*, 13(1).

Ayeni, O. O., Al Hamad, N. M., Chisom, O. N., Osawaru, B., & Adewusi, O. E. (2024). AI in education: A review of personalized learning and educational technology. *GSC Advanced Research and Reviews*, 18(2), 261–271.

Baskara, F. R. (2023, September). Navigating pedagogical evolution: The implication of generative AI on the reinvention of teacher education. In Prosiding Seminar Nasional Universitas Jabal Ghafur (Vol. 2, pp. 409-421).

Ding, A. C. E., Shi, L., Yang, H., & Choi, I. (2024). Enhancing teacher AI literacy and integration through different types of cases in teacher professional development. *Computers and Education Open*, 6, 100178.

Edeni, C. A., Adeleye, O. O., & Adeniyi, I. S. (2024). The role of AI-enhanced tools in overcoming socioeconomic barriers in education: A conceptual analysis. *World Journal of Advanced Research and Reviews*, 21(3), 944–951.

Gobara, R. E. G. E., & Ahmed, Z. E. (2024). Preparing Students for an AI-Enhanced Future. In *AI-Enhanced Teaching Methods* (pp. 286–304). IGI Global.

Gupta, P., Sreelatha, C., Latha, A., Raj, S., & Singh, A. (2024). Navigating the Future of Education: The Impact of Artificial Intelligence on Teacher-Student Dynamics. *Educational Administration: Theory and Practice*, 30(4), 6006–6013.

Husain, N. (2023). Educational Renaissance: Unleashing the Potential of Interdisciplinary AI Integration. *Journal of Environmental Science and Technology*, 2(1), 159–166.

Kakhkharova, M., & Tuychieva, S. (2024, April). AI-Enhanced Pedagogy in Higher Education: Redefining Teaching-Learning Paradigms. In *2024 International Conference on Knowledge Engineering and Communication Systems (ICKECS)* (Vol. 1, pp. 1-6). IEEE.

Kayyali, M. (2024). Future Possibilities and Challenges of AI in Education. In Transforming Education With Generative AI: Prompt Engineering and Synthetic Content Creation (pp. 118-137). IGI Global.

Khazanchi, R., & Khazanchi, P. (2024). Generative AI to improve special education teacher preparation for inclusive classrooms. Exploring New Horizons: Generative Artificial Intelligence and Teacher Education, 159.

Koh, J., Cowling, M., Jha, M., & Sim, K. N. (2023). The Human Teacher, the AI Teacher and the AIed-Teacher Relationship. *Journal of Higher Education Theory and Practice*, 23(17).

Lameras, P., & Arnab, S. (2021). Power to the teachers: An exploratory review on artificial intelligence in education. *Information (Basel)*, 13(1), 14.

Limna, P., Jakwatanatham, S., Siripipattanakul, S., Kaewpuang, P., & Sriboonruang, P. (2022). A review of artificial intelligence (AI) in education during the digital era. *Advance Knowledge for Executives*, 1(1), 1–9.

Meng, N., Dhimolea, T. K., & Ali, Z. (2022). AI-enhanced education: Teaching and learning reimagined. In *Bridging human intelligence and artificial intelligence* (pp. 107–124). Springer International Publishing.

Molefi, R. R., Ayanwale, M. A., Kurata, L., & Chere-Masopha, J. (2024). Do in-service teachers accept artificial intelligence-driven technology? The mediating role of school support and resources. *Computers and Education Open*, •••, 100191.

Novawan, A., Walker, S. A., & Ikeda, O. (2024). The new face of technology-enhanced language learning (TELL) with artificial intelligence (AI): Teacher perspectives, practices, and challenges. *Journal of English in Academic and Professional Communication*, 10(1), 1–18.

Petit, J. (2024, March). AI-Enhanced Design Thinking in Teacher Education: A Practical Workshop. In Society for Information Technology & Teacher Education International Conference (pp. 1424-1433). Association for the Advancement of Computing in Education (AACE).

Roberts, L. N., Solomon, F. N., & Cummings, R. (2024). Navigating the AI Landscape: Student and Teacher Perceptions of AI in Assessments in High School and College Settings. In AI-Enhanced Teaching Methods (pp. 268-285). IGI Global.

Rütti-Joy, O., Winder, G., & Biedermann, H. (2024). Teacher Educator Professionalism in the Age of AI: Navigating the New Landscape of Quality Education.

Sargiotis, D. (2024). Integrating AI and Big Data in Virtual Infrastructures: Transforming Educational Landscapes for the Future. Available at *SSRN* 4789850.

Sharma, S., & Kumar, N. (2024). Navigating the Ethical Landscape of Ai-Based Resources in Education: Implications for Learning, Proper Usage, And Course Design Enhancement. *The Online Journal of Distance Education and e-Learning : TOJDEL*, 12(2), 92.

Sperling, K., Stenberg, C. J., & McGrath, C., kerfeldt, A., Heintz, F., & Stenliden, L. (2024). In search of artificial intelligence (AI) literacy in Teacher Education: A scoping review. *Computers and Education Open*, •••, 100169.

Syahrizal, S., Yasmi, F., & Mary, T. (2024). AI-Enhanced Teaching Materials for Education: A Shift towards Digitalization. *International Journal of Religion*, 5(1), 203–217.

Taufikin, M. S. I., Azifah, N., Nikmah, F., & Kuanr, J. (2024, April). The Impact of AI on Teacher Roles and Pedagogy in the 21st Century Classroom. In *2024 International Conference on Knowledge Engineering and Communication Systems (ICKECS)* (Vol. 1, pp. 1-5). IEEE.

Vashishth, T. K., Kumar, B., Panwar, R., Kumar, S., & Chaudhary, S. (2023, August). Exploring the Role of Computer Vision in Human Emotion Recognition: A Systematic Review and Meta-Analysis. In *2023 Second International Conference on Augmented Intelligence and Sustainable Systems (ICAISS)* (pp. 1071-1077). IEEE.

Vashishth, T. K., Sharma, V., Sharma, K. K., & Kumar, B. (2024). Enhancing Literacy Education in Higher Institutions with AI Opportunities and Challenges. AI-Enhanced Teaching Methods, 198-215.

Vashishth, T. K., Sharma, V., Sharma, K. K., Kumar, B., Chaudhary, S., & Panwar, R. (2024). Transforming Classroom Dynamics: The Social Impact of AI in Teaching and Learning. In AI-Enhanced Teaching Methods (pp. 322-346). IGI Global.

Vashishth, T. K., Sharma, V., Sharma, K. K., Kumar, B., Panwar, R., & Chaudhary, S. (2024). AI-Driven Learning Analytics for Personalized Feedback and Assessment in Higher Education. In Using Traditional Design Methods to Enhance AI-Driven Decision Making (pp. 206-230). IGI Global.

Verma, P. K. ., Sharma, V. ., Kumar, P. ., Sharma, S. ., Chaudhary, S. ., & Preety, P. (2023). IoT Enabled Real Time Appearance System using AI Camera and Deep Learning for Student Tracking. International Journal on Recent and Innovation Trends in Computing and Communication, 11(6s), 249□254.

Zootzky, G., & Pfeiffer, A. (2024). Educational Transformation through AI: Preparing for a New Era of Learning. In INTED2024 Proceedings (pp. 1202-1207). IATED.

KEY TERMS AND DEFINITIONS

Artificial Intelligence (AI): is the simulation of human intelligence strategies through machines, in particular laptop systems. It involves learning, reasoning, hassle-fixing, belief, and language expertise to carry out responsibilities normally requiring human intelligence.

Machine Learning (ML): is a subset of artificial intelligence that permits systems to examine and enhance from revel in without being explicitly programmed. It includes the use of algorithms and statistical fashions to investigate and draw inferences from styles in facts.

Cloud computing: is the transport of computing offerings, which includes storage, processing strength, and software program, over the internet ("the cloud"). It allows customers to get admission to and control facts and applications from far off servers, enabling scalability and flexibility in useful resource utilization.

Virtual Reality (VR): is a simulated experience created by using computer generation that immerses users in a 3-dimensional, interactive environment. Users usually interact with this environment the usage of VR headsets and controllers, which offer sensory comments and enable navigation in the virtual space.

Augmented Reality (AR): is a generation that overlays digital statistics, together with pics, films, or information, onto the real-world surroundings. This enhancement is commonly considered through gadgets like smartphones, capsules, or AR glasses, blending virtual factors with the bodily international in actual time.

Chapter 10
Edufusion:
Integrating Artificial Intelligence With Teaching Practices to Enhance Learning Experiences

Babita Chaudhary
https://orcid.org/0000-0002-7285-2830
Christ University, India

Shivani Thapliyal
Christ University, India

Aditi Arya
https://orcid.org/0009-0005-2662-3059
Christ University, India

ABSTRACT

The present research explores the influence of artificial intelligence (AI) on traditional teaching methods in the education sector. Through a comprehensive review of existing literature and empirical studies, the present research aims to elucidate the transformative potential of AI technologies in reshaping pedagogical practices and enhancing learning outcomes. The study aims to provide the integrated perspective on the ever changing dynamics influenced by the incorporation of AI in the current education system through a meticulously conducted questionnaire-based investigation involving a diverse pool of huge participants, primarily students from the region of Delhi NCR.

DOI: 10.4018/979-8-3693-7949-3.ch010

1. INTRODUCTION

Education has relied on the conventional classroom arrangement for a very long time, with the concept of a teacher teaching a group of students face-to-face collectively. While this approach served as the foundation of learning, there are certain limitations associated with it. Students have respective learning needs where traditional teaching lacks to resolve individual differences effectively. From the perspective of cognitive theories, learning is considered as the mental processing of information that involves the acquiring, constructing, coding, memorizing, storing and retrieving and non-retrieving from memory.

The education technology industry, frequently alluded to as 'EdTech', is developing, with massive interests in nations like China, the United States and India. In the present times, electronic learning or web-based learning is combined with conventional classroom learning for more effective outcomes. The first years saw how technological innovation acted when traditional classroom teaching was impacted by Coronavirus. The writing recognizes the utilization of virtual study halls, increased reality classrooms, web 2.0 advances, MOOCs, and numerous other internet learning conditions for granting training.

Earlier studies on technology-based learning found that AI based technologies were not significantly different from traditional classroom learning when it comes to effectiveness. The studies have to compare web-based instruction to face-to-face or "offline" instruction, and they have to focus specifically on objective measures of student learning. The researchers found that the students who took classes in a hybrid format (combination of online and offline) performed significantly better, on average, than did those taking courses through traditional i.e face-to-face interactions. Also, there was no significant difference found between completely online and completely face-to-face format.

In education, a learning model that depends on the consideration of contrasts in students is frequently alluded to as personalized learning. Personalized learning allows understudies to get guidance and heading when they need it. Customized learning can likewise consider a better breakdown in topic inclusion and a more flexible pathway for understudy achievement. Customized learning on a computerized platform can be acknowledged utilizing Artificial Intelligence (AI).

In addition, in today's time, when Artificial intelligence (AI) has surprised the world, it is unavoidably expected that AI based procedures be integrated into e-learning frameworks for tackling issues like programmed ID of learning styles/ mental abilities of the students really. As we all know that today's technological sophisticated world has shown a positive role of AI and Machine Learning, it is needed to adopt cost-effective and smart education globally.

Artificial intelligence in training is acquiring popularity. As clear from the discoveries of the papers, there are fewer frameworks based on the standards of artificial intelligence. The present research will study the papers in the signifying field to get better understanding on technology-based learning. In order to increase students' activity and knowledge in education, this paper will analyze the impact of developing AI-based education. This analysis generates the effectiveness of AI-based learning and if this can replace traditional based learning or not.

In a study, there were absolutely 70 articles from six SSCI diaries, top-level instructive innovation diaries in the space of instructive advances from 2007 to 2017. These diaries included PCs and Training, Instructive Innovation Society, Intuitive Learning Conditions, the English Diary of Instructive Innovation, Instructive Innovation Innovative work, and the Diary of PC Helped Learning. Overall, 6.4 articles connected with versatile/customized learning were distributed in these diaries every year. By the end of this analysis, the study will visualize how the environment is going to be impacted with the usage of AI in the educational sector and what effect this will have on the new generation students along with educators.

Studies conducted on student choices, outlook towards technology and its impact on their overall learning experience falls under this category, while considering the literature on students' classroom experiences with technology is crucial.

The aim of present research work is to investigate the preference of students and teachers towards AI driven education and their understanding of how effective it would be. We seek if today's world is in favor of the implementation of AI in education and will it actually help grow individuals' performance or not. The entire research is based on the quantitative analysis that is being conducted to emphasize on the opinion and thoughts of individuals in the education sector and from the opinion of either being a student itself, an educator or a parent. This study aims to provide valuable insights into the effectiveness and implications of AI-driven learning in the educational landscape.

Just as potential purposes of evaluation are diverse, the method used for the analysis is a questionnaire. The questionnaire is used to analyze the behavior and prospect of 3 different personalities which comprises the students and the educators. If student outcomes are the same whether the education is taken using AI or face-to-face, we should integrate AI into traditional teaching methods to strike a balance between them, thereby enhancing effectiveness. As technological capabilities grow and more customary schools embrace online training before long, schools might pick to supplant a large number of their monstrous, section level courses that are generally shown in huge auditoriums and are described by practically no singular collaboration among understudies and teachers.

The recent discovery of research adds on to the developing assortment of information on the role of artificial intelligence in training and its potential to reshape academic practices. By examining the historical development of educational technology with key milestones such as the introduction of computers in classrooms, interactive whiteboards, and the rise of online learning platforms. Investigating the theoretical foundations which support the incorporation of technology in education that may encompass learning theories, cognitive psychology, and educational philosophy.

Conceptual frameworks based on learning theories, cognitive psychology, and educational philosophy provide a conceptual platform for clarifying technology's revolutionary potential in instructional practice. Wide ranging research has been conducted to assess the influence on teaching and learning outcomes, revealing advances in student engagement, academic achievement, and critical thinking skills development. However, the literature digs into the difficulties as well, addressing the digital divide, worries about over-reliance on technology, and potential harmful impacts on social contact.

Besides, understanding the influence of artificial intelligence driven on students' performance can illuminate instructive policymakers, foundations, and teachers on the best way to harness this innovation to enhance students' achievement and encourage a more student focused way to deal with learning. In the subsequent segments of this research paper, we will dig into the literature on AI driven education, present the research methodology, analyze the outcomes, and examine the ramifications of our discoveries.

1.1 Objectives

- Comparative Effectiveness: To assess and compare the effectiveness of AI-based education in contrast to traditional teaching methods.
- Analyze technological Impact on Students: To analyze the impact of technology implementation, specifically AI, on students' learning experiences and outcomes.
- Educators' Outlook on Future Involvement: To gather insights into educators' perspectives on the potential involvement of AI-based education in the near future.
- Student Experiences with AI-driven Learning: To explore students' insights and experiences with AI-based, intelligence-driven customized learning interventions. To investigate how these encounters influence students' overall satisfaction and inspiration to learn.
- Disparities in AI Impact Across Roles: To identify and analyze any disparities in the impact of AI-driven education concerning different roles, such as students and educators.

2. LITERATURE REVIEW

The research is emphasizing the importance and implementation of AI-based education in spite of the traditional form of education. A series of studies in the past had taken place to analyze the importance of online education and if it impacts student's knowledge or not as compared to face-to-face education. In the 176 on the web learning research studies distributed somewhere in the range of 1996 and 2008 were recognized that utilized an exploratory or semi test plan and unbiasedly estimated understudy learning results. Of these 176 investigations, 99 had somewhere around one differentiation between an included on the web or mixed learning condition and up close and personal (disconnected) guidance that possibly could be utilized in the quantitative meta-examination.

In addition to the effectiveness of students, this study also focuses on the thinking of technology-based education over three individuals: be it a student, a parent or a faculty itself. Analyzing these thoughts gives a better idea of the generation of AI-based education and will it be really important to implement or is it just a myth in the tech savvy world? In order to choose how to carry out web-based learning, it is essential to comprehend the practices that exploration recommends will increase viability.

The expansion in online learning and phrasing, including the web, e-learning and distributed learning has prompted a developing interest in assessment, the majority of which has focused on assessing web-based learning designs as far as the affordances of the communication conditions (Bozik *et al.,* 2002; Chen *et al.,* 2020); clients' perceptions (Veerman *et al.,* 2000); and the kinds of abilities that clients might require (Trigwell *et al.,* 1999; Murphy, E., 2004). A notable exception is an investigation of students' fulfillment with either face-to-face or asynchronous conferencing facilities that found ladies were more fulfilled with asynchronous cooperation than men (Ocker *et al.,* 2001). A comparison of Disc Rom-based educational cost of ECG and traditional class-based educational cost found no significant distinction of either evaluation marks results or mentalities between the two groups (Jeffries *et al.,* 2003).

The expansion in online learning (and wording, including on the web, electronic learning and distributed learning) has prompted a developing interest in assessment, the vast majority of which has focused on assessing web based learning designs as far as: the affordances of the communication conditions (Bozik *et al.,* 2002; Lord, T. (2001)); clients' perceptions (Veerman *et al.,* 2000); and the sorts of abilities that clients might require (Murphy, E., 2004; Trigwell *et al.,* 1999).

Paramythis *et al., (*2003) defined that "a learning environment is considered flexible if it is capable of supervising the activities of its users; and, finally, acting upon the available knowledge on its users and the content at hand, to actively facilitate the learning process" (p. 239). This significantly emphasizes the importance and implementation of AI-based learning. The study by Muhie & Woldie, (n.d.) addresses the integration of AI into higher education to enhance teaching and learning. Based on the findings, AI allows personalised learning, automates administrative tasks, and enhances the process of immediate information about student performance. However, the road to transforming educational practices has a number of challenges with regard to gaps in skills.

Zawacki-Richter *et al.,* (2019) highlights the evolution of artificial intelligence and machine learning is getting on with many individuals, its utilization in various gadgets, applications, and administrations is becoming boundless. Sadeghi *et al.,* (2012) express that recognizable proof of student's individual learning contrasts and their impact on the growing experience is vital to successfully determining variety in execution. PCs have been used as an instructive asset (closely resembling a library or lab), as well as a method for keeping up with data sets of understudy data (Jones, C. S., 1985). At present, Artificial Intelligence is creating and spreading over all aspects of the world at a disturbing rate (Tegmark, Max, 2014). The utilization of innovation in schooling traces all the way back to the rise of first era PCs and their ensuing refreshed versions (Schindler *et al.,* 2017).

The utilization of innovation in education is far cutting edge with the development of artificial intelligence (computer-based intelligence); a framework where machines are intended to imitate people. AI is "the science and designing of making intelligent machines or a machine that acts in a manner that could be thought of as savvy if it was a person." (Mccarthy, J. (2007)). Utilization of artificial intelligence (AI) has ended up being a suitable strategy for making a significant growth opportunity for students (Conklin *et al.,* 2014). As artificial intelligence (AI) is creating and spreading over all aspects of the world at a disturbing pace (Tegmark, Max, 2014), it plays a significant job in the routine life of a human being. As the presentation of artificial intelligence (AI) is catching on with many individuals, its utilization in various applications and administrations are becoming widespread (Zawacki-Richter *et al.,* 2019). Therefore, it's time to acknowledge the important of AI in the education sector. Popenici *et al., (*2017) contended that the point of innovation in education is to build information and help instructing and advancing yet not to pack the process of content conveyance, control and appraisal in schooling.

Golonka *et al.,* (2014) completed an exhaustive study of 350 papers that contrasts the utilization of current innovations and conventional language getting the hang of instructing instruments. Slavuj *et al.,* (2017) assessed forty-two examinations from 2005-2015 which zeroed in on versatile learning frameworks. They concluded that students prefer more on technological based education rather than traditional face-to-face teaching. The utilization of Teacher-bots (processing arrangements for the regulatory piece of instructing, managing content conveyance and managerial input and supervision) and IBM Watson (Q & A PC framework that utilizes normal language to answer questions presented by a client) are some computer-based intelligence applications that are accessible to upgrade teaching and learning (Gonçalves *et al.*, 2016). Hwang *et al.*, 2018) did a precise writing survey of 90 articles somewhere in the range of 2007 and 2016 on cooperative versatile learning in different fields.

In the computerized time, complex abilities that are less simple to automate have become increasingly important. Imagination and decisive reasoning are turning out to be progressively significant in the labor market and add to a superior individual and community life (Vincent-Lancrin *et al.*, 2019). Artificial Intelligence frameworks can likewise give customized criticism and take over managerial assignments that were recently dealt with by human educators (Chen *et al.*, 2020). As computer-based intelligence innovations advance, they hold the commitment of customized and versatile learning, ongoing input, and shrewd authoritative and emotionally supportive networks (Renz *et al.*, 2020).

Evaluating studies (Malik *et al.*, 2019; Chen *et al.*, 2020) on the impact of technology on teaching and learning., we can see advances in student involvement, academic achievement and overall development of the student. Identifying successful case studies and paradigms in which technology and teaching effectively have synergies with specific tactics or approaches puts emphasis on improving learning experiences. These technologies have the potential to increase student engagement by providing personalized, interactive and immersive learning environments.

A narrative that spans historical evolution, theoretical framework and the diverse impact on educational landscapes in the dynamic domain where technology meets with teaching. As advances in natural language processing enable applications such as plagiarism detection, assessment scoring, and automated feedback provision (Goksel *et al.*, 2019; Chen *et al.*, 2020), AI has the potential to assist teachers in student assessment. The historical timeline follows the incorporation of technologies such as computers and interactive whiteboards into classrooms, highlighting the growth of educational technology.

AI integration in education, highlighting increased AI research with a focus on self-reported teacher data, essential for AI algorithm training is reviewed by Celik *et al.*, (2022). Despite this, education lags behind other industries in AI adoption, emphasising the need to compare AI usage across sectors for deeper insight. Emphasises on the role of AI competencies at school, harnesses the P21 and DigCompEdu frameworks for the advancement of learning. Individual results concern AI literacy for teachers and students, AI for personalisation and plagiarism, educator's need to keep up with emerging technologies like the Metaverse and blockchain. Ng *et al.*, (2023) underlines the need for development, not only of technical skills but also of interdisciplinary and ethical ones.

Lampropoulos, (2023) indicate that recommender systems can offer personalised learning experiences, improve learning outcomes, and foster adaptive learning. This study identified the increased academic interest in the topic and potential benefits of using the recommender systems in an educational environment. Although AI does offer solutions from a teacher's perspective, there are concerns regarding substitution of teachers. Lima *et al.*, (2024) examines the position of AI in educational institutions, with respect to optimism and concerns, raised during the research. Ethical debates related to privacy and inequality are significantly strong with insinuates looking into the implications of AI holistically rather than just enhancing educational efficiency.

Mujiono, (2023); Vistorte *et al.*, (2024) confirm that the integration of Artificial Intelligence into education increases learning outcomes and emotional assessments. AI may increase personalised learning and emotional recognition, all of which are essentials in effective learning, but to be effectively instituted, it would have to be guided by teachers through many challenges pertaining to accuracy, privacy, and ethics so that benefits could be reaped sans loss of human interaction.

Systematic review on current research indicates that AI provides the basis for emotive assessment in educational institutions, enhancing the process of emotional recognition and adaptive learning. The main challenges include problems with accuracy, privacy, and ethics. These results of research (Rane, 2024) provide further detail toward researching the refinement of AI models to address these challenges in educational contexts.

Best practices and models emerge as beacons of successful integration, demonstrating techniques that improve the learning experience. Teacher professional development emerges as a major aspect, with research emphasizing the need of training programs in ensuring appropriate technology utilization. Exploration of new technology, such as artificial intelligence and virtual reality, adds a futuristic perspective to the discussion.

The narrative weaves student perspectives into institutional support and policy ramifications in the multiple forces defining the marriage between technology and education. The review finally concludes by pointing towards future directions by suggesting more investigation of places that remain unexplored in this shifting landscape.

3. METHODOLOGY

Research Scope: The research will be certain to students' thoughts and behavior above 18 years to provide their insight and thought towards the education sector along with that it also emphasizes on the educators as it will be greatly imparting them to the tech-based education to have their opinion on the same.

Sample: The research will include a diverse pool of people for the analysis be it students or teachers of different age groups. Purposive techniques are being implemented to ensure a diverse pool of people being part of the study.

3.1. Data Collection

Quantitative Data

Surveys and Questionnaires: To evaluate the shifted viewpoints because of Artificial Intelligence (AI) on customary showing strategies, we led a questionnaire-based investigation focusing on a sample size of 200 members. Our review enveloped students, instructors, and guardians, intending to accumulate bits of knowledge into their viewpoints.

The questionnaire principally highlighted scale-based questions, permitting members to communicate nuanced views on the effect of simulated intelligence in the domain of training. By utilizing this methodology, we tried to exhaustively comprehend and dissect the different viewpoints of these three critical partners — students and educators in regard to the advancing connection between artificial intelligence and traditional educating techniques.

3.3 Research Model

Figure 1. Research model (Author's calculations)

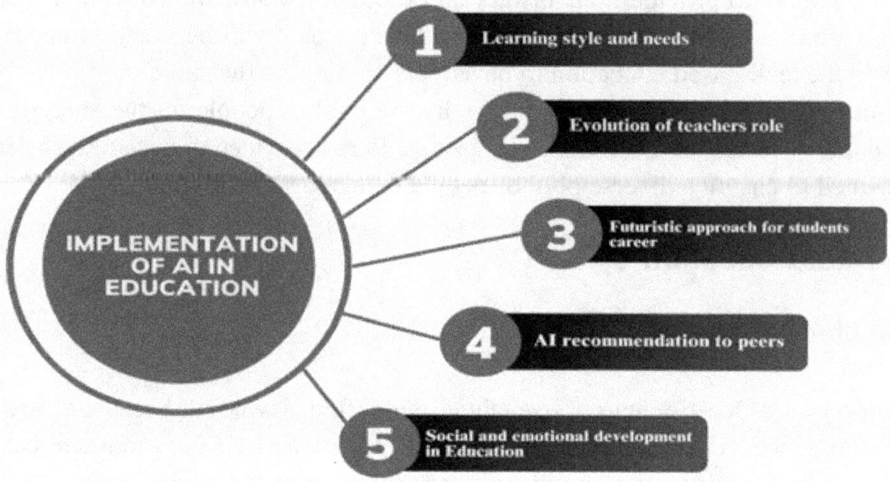

3.4 Hypothesis

1. Learning Style and Needs

H_1: There is a significant association between AI capability to adapt to different learning styles and its adaptability to understand the needs of students.

2. Evolution of Teachers Roles

H_1: AI inclusion is associated with teacher role evolution, and ongoing professional development is related to teachers' adaptability to AI-driven education.

3. Futuristic approach for Student's career

H_1: There is a significant association between the perception of AI preparing students for the digital era and the belief in AI preparing students for future employment.

4. AI Recommendation to Peers

H_1: There is a significant impact of AI providing different learning style and of suggesting AI education to peers.

5. Social and Emotional Development in Education

H_1: There is a significant relation between AI providing social and emotional development and impacting students' engagement in the learning process.

4. HYPOTHESIS TESTING

4.1. Learning Style and Needs

Table 1. Comparison of AI capability to adapt to different learning styles and to understand the needs of students

Independent Samples Test										
		Levene's Test for Equality of Variance		t-test for Equality of Means						
									95% Confidence Interval of the Difference	
		F	Sig.	t	df	Sig. (2-tailed)	Mean Difference	Std. Error Difference	Lower	Upper
Do you agree AI can adapt to the individual learning styles and needs of students	Equal variance assumed	3.196	.085	-3.670	28	.001	-2.167	.590	-3.376	-.957
	Equal variance not assumed			-5.961	22.007	.000	-2.167	.363	-2.920	-1.413

Source: Author's calculation

H_1: There is a significant association between AI capability to adapt to different learning styles and its adaptability to understand the needs of students.

By performing Levene's Test, we get **sig, level of 0.085**, assuming equal variance. The t-test applied returns a significant value of 0.085, greater than 0.05 ($p<0.05$). The negative **mean difference of (-2.167)** also suggest that **H_1 is not supported** and therefore with **95% confidence interval** (not crossing zero), further confirms statistical significance of the difference and that there is no significant association between AI capability to adapt to different learning styles and its adaptability to understand the needs of students.

4.2. Evolution of Teachers Roles

Table 2. Ongoing professional development and evolution in teacher's role

Chi-Square Tests			
	Value	df	Asymp. Sig. (2-sided)
Pearson Chi-Square	363.100[a]	15	.000
Likelihood Ratio	359.530	15	.000
No. Of Valid Cases	224		

Source: Author's calculation

H_1: AI inclusion is associated with teacher role evolution, and ongoing professional development is related to teachers' adaptability to AI-driven education.

Highly significant p-value of 0.000 which is less than 0.05 ($p<0.05$), determining association between our two categorical variables, stating the probability of the observed association between AI inclusion and teacher role evolution being extremely low. The Chi-square value of 363.100 further substantiates that H_1 is strongly supported, having a significant association to teacher role evolution, and ongoing professional development is not related to teachers' adaptability to AI-driven education.

4.3. Futuristic approach for Student's career

Table 3. AI preparing students for digital era and future employment

Chi-Square Tests			
	Value	df	Asymp. Sig. (2-sided)
Pearson Chi-Square	307.954[a]	9	.000
Likelihood Ratio	342.508	9	.000
No. Of Valid Cases	226		

Source: Author's calculation

H_1: There is a significant association between the perception of AI preparing students for the digital era and the belief in AI preparing students for future employment.

The p-value of 0.000 is highly significant, indicating that the association between the observed variables is unlikely to be due to random chances. Further, the Chi-square value test with the value of 307.954 represents the association between two variables. Since the significant value is 0.00 which is less than 0.05 ($p < 0.05$), therefore H_1 is supported with a highly significant association between the perception of AI preparing students for the digital era and the belief in AI preparing students for future employment.

4.4. AI Recommendation to Peers

Table 4. Comparison on AI providing different learning style and recommending to peers

Chi-Square Tests			
	Value	**df**	**Asymp. Sig. (2-sided)**
Pearson Chi-Square	354.826[a]	15	.000
Likelihood Ratio	359.716	15	.000
No. Of Valid Cases	226		

Source: Author's calculation

H_1: There is a significant impact of AI providing different learning style and of suggesting AI education to peers.

The significant value after the chi-square test turns out to be 0.000 less than 0.05 ($p<0.05$), which is highly significant stating statistical meaning to the observed association. Further, with the Chi-square value of 354.826, H_1 is supported. Hence, we have an association of AI providing different learning styles and of suggesting AI education to peers.

4.5. Social and Emotional Development in Education

Table 5. AI on providing social and emotional development along with engagement in learning process

		How much do you agree that AI-driven education can adequately address the social and emotional development of students in their education.	**Do you anticipate AI impacting student engagement in the learning process.**
How much do you agree that AI-driven education can adequately address the social and emotional development of students in their education.	Pearson Correlation Sig. (2-tailed) N	1 224	.856 .000 224
Do you anticipate AI impacting student engagement in the learning process.	Pearson Correlation Sig. (2-tailed) N	.856 .000 224	1 224

Source: Author's calculation

H_1: There is a significant relation between AI providing social and emotional development and impacting students' engagement in the learning process.

Significant value for both variables is 0.00 which is less than 0.05 ($p<0.05$), stating that **H_1 is supported.** The Correlation test applied to analyze the association between the variables and with the correlation coefficient value of 0.856, it implies that it has a significant relation between AI providing social and emotional development and impacting student's engagement in the learning process.

5. FINDINGS AND LIMITATIONS

Findings

The research findings indicate a significant transformation in the educational landscape. AI- driven adaptive learning systems have the potential to provide personalized learning experiences tailored to individual student needs, preferences, and learning styles. It also presents that AI can offer an advanced platform for students, enriching their learning experiences and facilitating knowledge enhancement. However, it is crucial to maintain a balanced approach when incorporating AI in education and traditional teaching methods. Thereby, surveys emphasize the essential role of human interaction in boosting the overall growth and development of students. While AI technologies provide valuable tools for innovation and personalized learning, they should enhance rather than replace traditional teaching practices to ensure comprehensive educational experiences for students.

Limitations

Our research is subject to certain drawbacks, essentially starting from its emphasis on a specific distinction for analysis. This limited degree may constrain the applicability of our findings to broader contexts, making it challenging to extrapolate interpretations universally. Furthermore, our review didn't comprehensively address the potential challenges associated with the implementation of AI in education. A notable exclusion is the lack of investigation into the obstacles that may hinder the successful integration of AI-driven teaching methods. Resistance from educators, understudies and other stakeholders can pose significant barriers, which affect the adoption and effective utilization of these technologies.

Addressing these limitations, it is essential for ensuring a thorough understanding of the ramification of artificial intelligence (AI) in education. Future research endeavors ought to strive for broader geographic representation and delve into the multifaceted challenges and complexities encompassing the execution of AI-driven teaching methods. By doing so, we can illuminate policies and practices to maximize the benefits of AI while moderating potential drawbacks and fostering a more inclusive and equitable educational landscape.

6. DISCUSSION AND CONCLUSION

Discussion

The research aims to find out how AI is affecting the way educational methodologies are carried out, with great emphasis on changes it has brought to students, teachers, and parents alike. This paper reviews a mix of different papers and their respective variables to attest to the many effects attributed to integrating AI into teaching practices in pursuit of better learning experiences. Quantitative information about the research adaptability of AI in education, analysed for 200 students, educators, and parents. We tested hypotheses about how AI can support diverse learning needs, the changing roles of teachers, its effect on career readiness, peer recommendations, and social-emotional growth.

Learning style and needs: While examining the ability of AI to adapt to different learning styles and students need, AI's ability to cater according to individualised learning style and needs was strongly indicated, backed up by study of Sadeghi *et.al.* (2012) who emphasized on the importance of recognizing individual learning differences, indicating that AI holds much promise in education. Although AI alone has not served diverse learning styles, and traditional, flexible human-centered methods remain central, which again places AI in a supporting rather than replacing role for human flexibility. AI offers possibilities for the individualisation of learning experiences, underlined by studies such as Schindler *et.al.*. (2017) & Vincent-Lancrin *et.al.* (2019), substantiating the idea of a combined approach further.

Evolution of Teachers' Roles: A clear depiction that AI is modifying the role of teachers to be moderators of personalised learning, not merely content delivery is seen as conclusion. This aligns with the findings by Popenici *et.al.* (2017), where the argument was that AI was not going to replace educators but, on the other hand, enhancing the role of educators by managing routine tasks. Further, according to Chen et al., 2020, AI can offer personalised feedback, administrative support our significant hypothesis. On the other hand, for adaptation to be successful, openness to change rather than professional development is required for better growth.

Futuristic Approach for Students' Careers: While examining the relationship between AI preparing students for digital era and its association to prepare them for future employment, the results strongly indicate strong support for the hypothesis that AI is perceived to equip students with skills needed for future career paths (Vincent-Lancrin *et.al.,* 2019). It goes without saying that with more and more digitalisation and automation happening in all sectors, AI-based education is surely standing tall in helping the youth prepare for life in a modern workforce. The reasoning behind AI-driven learning and career readiness is identical because students are increasingly expected to have experience in AI-powered tools and digital literacy within their employability supported by the argument of Gonçalves *et.al., (*2016).

AI Recommendations to peers: The findings of testings show that students who receive personalised learning with the help of AI tend to recommend AI-based education to their peers (Slavuj *et.al.,* 2017; Hwang *et.al.,* 2018). This infers a positive word-of-mouth recommendation of AI in education, based on the perception that AI will meet diverse learning styles with individualised learning experiences. As more students engage with AI-based learning platforms, their recommendations reflect increased trust in the use of AI to improve learning outcomes.

Social and emotional development in education: The strong positive correlation between the impact of AI on the social and emotional development of students and that which AI makes upon student engagement does thus show that AI-driven education has a strong, valid impact on students' engagement in fostering social and emotional development. AI's role in nurturing emotional intelligence is also substantiated by arguments of Mujiono, M. (2023) & Vistorte *et.al.,* (2024). Designing AI tools is possible for identifying and addressing the emotional states of students to offer an engaging, supportive learning environment. This indeed brings to the fore again the development of AI-driven platforms, paying special attention to emotional intelligence and nurturing the critical human aspects of education.

Overall, this research underlines that AI has the potential to make learning personal, reframe educator roles, and better align learning for the workforce; however, since AI alone cannot master diverse learning styles, it identifies a hybrid approach for learning. The paper emphasises continuous teachers' development in order for them to be able to adjust to an AI-driven educational system and calls for further qualitative and longitudinal research with a view to investigating the long-term impacts of AI on student outcomes, career readiness, and well-being. By proper integration, AI can indeed prove to be truly transformative in education.

To conclude with, the influence of Artificial Intelligence on traditional teaching and learning has been examined through various lenses, considering factors such as convenience, access, analytics, and knowledge acquisition. While online education offers evident benefits in these areas, the consensus is clear: the future of education lies in the symbiotic relationship between teachers (humans) and artificial intelligence (AI).

CONCLUSION

As featured by renowned educational researcher Prof. John Hattie, teachers stay the most influential factor in student learning success. Notwithstanding the head's ways in AI technology, human teachers possess irreplaceable characteristics that contribute to student engagement, motivation, and overall learning outcomes. (Hattie, J., 2008)

Studies supporting the reconciliation of AI in education underscore its potential to personalize learning experiences, enhance instructional effectiveness, and provide valuable insights through data analytics. For instance, a study by the International Society for Technology in Education found that 73% of educators accepted that AI could assist with tailoring instruction to meet students' unique learning styles. Additionally, a meta-analysis of over 100 studies published in the Journal of Educational Computing Research revealed that students who received guidance through AI-driven platforms consistently outflanked their peers who were taught utilizing traditional methods.

Luckin, R. (2019) research on adaptive learning systems exemplify the groundbreaking effect of AI in catering to individual student needs and preferences, further developing learning results.

However, it is essential to perceive the significance of maintaining a balanced approach to education. Over-reliance on technology can prompt the disintegration of essential human connections and interpersonal skills. Therefore, while AI advances offer valuable tools for innovation, they ought to complement rather than replace traditional teaching techniques.

In essence, the future of education lies in utilizing the qualities of both human teachers and AI technologies advancements. By effectively utilizing the unique qualities of human teachers alongside the capabilities of AI, an instructive foundation can create dynamic learning environments that encourage critical thinking, creativity, and lifelong learning skills in students. Through collaborative endeavors, educators can ensure that the educational landscape continues to evolve in ways that benefit all learners and uphold the core principles of viable educating and learning.

REFERENCES

Bozik, M., & Tracey, M. W. (2002). Content and online learning: An overview of research, theory, and practice. *Educational Media International*, 39(4), 237–246.

Celik, I., Dindar, M., Muukkonen, H., & Järvelä, S. (2022). The Promises and Challenges of Artificial Intelligence for Teachers: A Systematic Review of Research. *TechTrends*, 66(4), 616–630. DOI: 10.1007/s11528-022-00715-y

Chen, L., Chen, P., & Lin, Z. (2020). Artificial Intelligence in education: A review. *IEEE Access : Practical Innovations, Open Solutions*, 8, 75264–75278. DOI: 10.1109/ACCESS.2020.2988510

Conklin, A. L., & Hartman, J. (2014). Artificial intelligence and its effects on education. *The Journal of Effective Teaching*, 14(1), 81–86.

Gestalt psychology. (n.d.). In Encyclopedia Britannica. Retrieved 19 April 2024 from https://www.britannica.com/science/Gestalt-psychology

Goksel, N., & Bozkurt, A. (2019). Artificial Intelligence in Education: Current Insights and Future Perspectives. In Sisman-Ugur, S., & Kurubacak, G. (Eds.), *Handbook of Research on Learning in the Age of Transhumanism Hershey* (pp. 224–236). IGI Global.

Golonka, E. M., Bowles, A. R., Frank, V. M., Richardson, D. L., & Freynik, S. (2014). Technologies for foreign language learning: A review of technology types and their effectiveness. *Computer Assisted Language Learning*, 27(1), 70–105.

Gonçalves, D., Fernandes, C., Reis, A. R., Oliveira, E., & Silva, C. (2016). The use of IBM Watson in education: A review. *International Journal of Information Management*, 36(6), 787–791.

Hattie, J. (2008). *Visible Learning: A Synthesis of Over 800 Meta-Analyses Relating to Achievement* (1st ed.). Routledge., DOI: 10.4324/9780203887332

Hwang, G. J., & Fu, Q. K. (2018). Trends in the Research Design and Application of Mobile Language Learning: A Review of 2007-2016 Publications in Selected SSCI Journals. *Interactive Learning Environments*, 27, 567–581. DOI: 10.1080/10494820.2018.1486861

Jeffries, P., Gianinazzi, S., & Perotto, S. (2003). The contribution of arbuscular mycorrhizal fungi in sustainable maintenance of plant health and soil fertility. *Biology and Fertility of Soils*, 37, 1–16. DOI: 10.1007/s00374-002-0546-5

Jones, C. S. (1985). An empirical study of the evidence for contingency theories of management accounting systems in conditions of rapid change. *Accounting, Organizations and Society, Elsevier*, 10(3), 303–328.

Lampropoulos, G. (2023). Recommender systems in education: A literature review and bibliometric analysis. *Advances in Mobile Learning Educational Research*, 3(2), 829–850. DOI: 10.25082/amler.2023.02.011

Lima, G. de M., Ferreira, G. M. dos S., & Carvalho, J. de S. (2024). Automation in education: trending issues concerning Artificial Intelligence. *Educação e Pesquisa, 50*. https://doi.org/DOI: 10.1590/s1678-4634202450273857en

Lord, T. (2001). Research on the integration of technology in K-12 schools. *Journal of Educational Computing Research*, 24(1), 21–27.

Luckin, R. (2019). The learner-centered design of AI: Enabling academic innovation. *International Journal of Artificial Intelligence in Education*, 29(3), 617–622.

Malik, G., Tayal, D. K., & Vij, S. (2019). An analysis of the role of artificial intelligence in education and teaching. In *Recent Findings in Intelligent Computing Techniques* (pp. 407–417). Springer., DOI: 10.1007/978-981-10-8639-7_42

Mccarthy, J. (2007). From here to human-level AI. *Artificial Intelligence*, 171, 1174–1182.

Muhie, Y. A., & Woldie, A. B. (n.d.). Integration of Artificial Intelligence Technologies in Teaching and Learning in Higher Education. *Science and Technology*, 2020(1), 1–7. DOI: 10.5923/j.scit.202001001.01

Mujiono, M. (2023). Educational Collaboration: Teachers and Artificial Intelligence. *Jurnal Kependidikan: Jurnal Hasil Penelitian Dan Kajian Kepustakaan Di Bidang Pendidikan. Pengajaran Dan Pembelajaran*, 9(2), 618. DOI: 10.33394/jk.v9i2.7801

Murphy, E. (2004). Recognizing and promoting the role of educational technology specialists: A needs assessment. *Journal of Research on Technology in Education*, 36(2), 161–181.

Ng, D. T. K., Leung, J. K. L., Su, J., Ng, R. C. W., & Chu, S. K. W. (2023). Teachers' AI digital competencies and twenty-first century skills in the post-pandemic world. *Educational Technology Research and Development*, 71(1), 137–161. DOI: 10.1007/s11423-023-10203-6 PMID: 36844361

Ocker, R. J., & Yaverbaum, G. J. (2001). Collaborative learning environments: Exploring student attitudes and satisfaction in face-to-face and asynchronous computer conferencing settings. *Journal of Interactive Learning Research*, 12(4), 427–448.

Paramythis, A., & Reisinger, S. L. (2003). Adaptive learning environments and e-learning standards. Retrieved 4 May, 2024. https://files.eric.ed.gov/fulltext/EJ1099144.pdf

Popenici, S. A., & Kerr, S. T. (2017). Exploring the impact of artificial intelligence on teaching and learning in higher education. *Research and Practice in Technology Enhanced Learning*, 12(1), 22. PMID: 30595727

Rane, N. L. (2024). Education 4.0 and 5.0: integrating Artificial Intelligence (AI) for personalized and adaptive learning. *Journal of Artificial Intelligence and Robotics*. https://doi.org/DOI: 10.61577/jaiar.2024.100006

Renz, A., Krishnaraja, S., & Gronau, E. (2020). Demystification of artificial intelligence in education—How much AI is really in the educational technology? *International Journal of Learning Analytics and Artificial Intelligence for Education*, 2(1), 4–30.

Sadeghi, N., Kasim, Z. M., Tan, B. H., & Abdullah, F. S. (2012). Learning styles, personality types and reading comprehension performance. *English Language Teaching*, 5(4), 116–123.

Schindler, L. A., Burkholder, G. J., Morad, O. A., & Marsh, C. (2017). Computer-based technology and student engagement: A critical review of the literature. *International Journal of Educational Technology in Higher Education*, 14(1), 25.

Schunk, D. H. (2012). *Learning theories: An educational perspective* (6th ed.). Pearson Education Inc.

Slavuj, V., Meštrović, A., & Kovačić, B. (2017). Adaptivity in educational systems for language learning: A review. *Computer Assisted Language Learning*, 30(1–2), 64–90. DOI: 10.1080/09588221.2016.1242502

Tegmark, M. (2014). *Our Mathematical Universe: My Quest for the Ultimate Nature of Reality by Max Tegmark*. Alfred A. Knopf.

Trigwell, K., Prosser, M., & Waterhouse, F. (1999). Relations between teachers' approaches to teaching and students' approaches to learning. *Higher Education*, 37, 57–70. DOI: 10.1023/A:1003548313194

Veerman, A., Andriessen, J., & Kanselaar, G. (2000). Collaborative learning through computer mediated argumentation. *Learning and Instruction*, 10(4), 345–364.

Vincent-Lancrin, S., Joaquin, U., Soumyajit, K., & Gwénaël, J. (2019). *Measuring Innovation in Education 2019: What Has Changed in the Classroom?* OECD Publishing., DOI: 10.1787/9789264311671-

Vistorte, A. O. R., Deroncele-Acosta, A., Ayala, J. L. M., Barrasa, A., López-Granero, C., & Martí-González, M. (2024). Integrating artificial intelligence to assess emotions in learning environments: a systematic literature review. In *Frontiers in Psychology* (Vol. 15). Frontiers Media SA. https://doi.org/DOI: 10.3389/fpsyg.2024.1387089

Zawacki-Richter, O., Marín, V. I., Bond, M., & Gouverneur, F. (2019). Systematic review of research on artificial intelligence applications in higher education—Where are the educators? *International Journal of Educational Technology in Higher Education*, 16(1).

Chapter 11
Artificial Intelligence and the Future of Education in Bangladesh:
Impact, Challenges, and Ethical Implications of AI on Student Learning

Swapnil Tarafdar
https://orcid.org/0009-0004-9284-4178
Bangabandhu Sheikh Mujibur Rahman Digital University, Bangladesh

Sumona Afroz
https://orcid.org/0009-0003-8635-3332
Bangabandhu Sheikh Mujibur Rahman Digital University, Bangladesh

Md. Ashrafuzzaman
https://orcid.org/0000-0003-2100-9998
Bangabandhu Sheikh Mujibur Rahman Digital University, Bangladesh

ABSTRACT

This chapter highlights the transformative impact of Artificial Intelligence on the education sector in Bangladesh, reshaping the learning experience for students. It emphasizes how AI fosters personalized learning, increases access to resources, and enhances skill development, while also addressing challenges like infrastructural limitations, teacher readiness, and societal resistance. The discussion includes important ethical considerations, such as data privacy and algorithmic fairness, underscoring the need for responsible integration. By synthesizing existing literature, the paper clarifies the complex relationship between AI and education and suggests

DOI: 10.4018/979-8-3693-7949-3.ch011

avenues for further research. Collaboration among policymakers, administrators, students, and technology developers is crucial to ensure that AI benefits all learners in Bangladesh. The research highlights some key issues that are of the essence to inform the discussion on AI in education and as guidelines for developing a more inclusive and operational structure for education in Bangladesh.

1. INTRODUCTION

Artificial Intelligence (AI) has emerged as one of the most transformative forces in different verticals (Sedkaoui & Benaichouba, 2024). Artificial intelligence in education is already playing a magnificent role in digital transformation (Katsamakas et al., 2024). For the last decade, AI technologies have rapidly evolved to open up new possibilities that relate both to personalized learning and the adaptation of instructions as a means of improving student outcomes (Laak & Aru, 2024; Chen et al., 2020). From intelligent tutoring systems to automatic assessments, the use of AI stretches the limits of traditional pedagogic practices by making them much more efficient while concurrently making learning more interactive and relevant (Murdan & Halkhoree, 2024). With each passing day, educators and policymakers around the world are waking up belatedly to find that AI has a potential disruption in the classroom, moving away from one-size-fits-all models to data-driven, differentiated learning pathways comprised of immense variation in students' needs (Tan, 2023).

The integration of technology into education has been gradual in Bangladesh, especially with government reforms and digital learning initiatives that spurred the modernization of this country's educational system. However, the adoption of AI in Bangladeshi classrooms, despite the growing emphasis on digital education, remains in its infancy (Babu, 2021; K. Babu, 2021). While there are scattered examples related to the use of AI, such as those through language learning applications or exam preparation tools, challenges like infrastructure deficits, teacher training, and digital literacy stand in the way of more general diffusion among larger parts of the system. Notwithstanding the above, AI holds immense potential to address certain basic challenges facing Bangladesh, particularly overcoming inequalities created by inequitable access to quality education, especially in rural areas, and enhancing future-ready skills (Mahbub et al., 2024; K. Babu, 2021).

No doubt, AI can potentially play a significant role in the education system of Bangladesh. With its growing and young population, the pressure is huge to equip students with the competencies they need to prosper in an increasingly globalized and technology-based economy. AI uniquely befits the process of student learning and can effectively facilitate access to equal education (Sultana & Faruk, 2024). We must evaluate AI's potential considering challenges related to infrastructure, policy support, ethical data privacy issues, and algorithmic bias.

This study also discusses possibilities of the impacts of AI on student learning in Bangladesh, reviews the present state of AI adoption in education, and reveals scaling opportunities and challenges in its usage. The present research, therefore, based on a wide literature review, shall identify how AI will reshape the educational landscape in Bangladesh and hence provide practical recommendations for the benefit of policy planners, educators, and other stakeholders. It will try to answer some critical questions concerning the use of AI, inclusiveness in access to educational technologies, and how these eventually prepare students with employable skills relevant to Bangladesh.

2. LITERATURE REVIEW

2.1 Global Perspectives on AI in Education

Educators around the world welcome AI as a promise of new teaching and learning at all levels. A diverse range of educators has already harnessed the power of AI-driven technologies such as adaptive learning systems, intelligent tutoring systems, and AI-assisted assessments to construct better learning experiences (Yekollu et al., 2024). Across the globe, countries are increasing their bets with investments in AI technologies for personalized learning environments, tailoring content for the needs of a student and his learning ability (Foffano et al., 2022). For example, systems like DreamBox, Squirrel AI, and Coursera allow AI to make personalized learning experiences possible, continuous, and adaptive to students' capabilities and learning results (Yamijala et al., 2024; Sandhu et al., 2024). Platforms like Coursera are now dedicated to integrating Generative AI (GenAI) into their platforms to enhance their educational foundations, aid learners in achieving mastery, and offer personalized aid (Villasenor, 2024). Studies on AI adoption in education worldwide identify a set of critical advantages, such as the fact that many researchers analyze large volumes of student performance data in search of learning patterns, performance predictions, and suggestions for personalized learning (Ouyang et al., 2022).

The findings also highlight that AI-driven systems lead to lower dropout rates among students and improved academic performance, along with targeted support that is appropriate for the needs of students with learning disabilities. According to Patel (2024), the issue of equitably providing access to AI technologies and handling privacy issues regarding student data calls for resolution from a global perspective.

More importantly, AI has already gone deep into its work of shaping collaborative learning through the engagement of students more actively with interactive and stimulating virtual learning environments (Huang et al., 2024). Examples are AI-driven virtual learning assistants that can provide immediate feedback to students, answer student queries, and even simulate real-life scenarios for experiential learning. While the potential of AI in education is huge, actual use is highly variable throughout the world because of large variation in infrastructure, teacher preparedness, and policy support.

2.2 AI in Developing Nations: Challenges and Opportunities

Artificial Intelligence (AI) in education presents both a potential opportunity and a challenge for developing nations. This is because there are numerous factors that influence the pace at which this technology, which has the potential to revolutionize education systems in less privileged parts of the world, can facilitate access to quality education. Accessibility issues include inaccessibility to high-speed internet, lack of electricity in rural areas, and lack of technological resources (Mannan et al., 2023). Most developing countries encounter these infrastructure-related challenges. These are some of the challenges that contribute to slower integration of AI tools into most systems, especially in far-flung areas where such educational gaps have been extreme.

However, according to some developing countries, AI is a response to inequality in education. The gap that has been created can be filled by artificial intelligence-driven technologies in the case of students who stay in some regions where proper schooling or qualified teachers are not available (Nkechi et al., 2024). For instance, AI-powered learning platforms offer personalized mass education through automated learning level adaptation and local languages (Strielkowski et al., 2024). AI will also be able to support teachers in under-resourced schools by automating routine activities, including grading and providing real-time feedback, freeing educators to attend to higher-order teaching responsibilities (Kim, 2023; Bhardwaj et al., 2024).

The prospect for AI in education is encouraging in Bangladesh and most developing countries, but its implementation always turns out to be challenging due to the relatively limited resources (Horwitch, 2024). We expect that Bangladesh will adapt something from the experience of other developing countries struggling with infrastructure challenges and demonstrate how AI could realistically promote access to education and improve its quality. While this might be more receptive to governments and international organizations as well as industry associations to invest in AI technologies that can actually help to bring improvements in education in both regions, there is a dire need for multi-agency efforts to ensure effective and equitable implementation of these technologies (Hossain et al., 2024).

2.3 The Educational Landscape in Bangladesh

Access to education has rapidly improved in Bangladesh during the last decades of the twentieth century. Along with the challenges brought about by rapid population growth and some problems in building enough infrastructure within schools, initiatives such as the National Education Policy 2010 and the integration of technology in education have helped solve them. Although the revised national curriculum introduced ICT (Information and Communication Technology) in schools in 2012, thus permitting a more modern type of teaching learners' digital literacy and technological skills at both secondary and higher levels, this is greatly lacking in Bangladesh (Sultana & Haque, 2018). Despite all that, the quality of education has turned out to be severely insufficient across Bangladesh, particularly in rural and disadvantaged regions.

Even today, the gap in qualified teachers, technological resources, and infrastructural facilities is profound between urban and rural schooling (Rahaman & Akter, 2017). It is against this backdrop that AI will contribute to a significant role in solving complex problems through innovation. For instance, virtual learning platforms powered by AI can equalize the disparities in educational opportunities through customized learning content for students in the most remote villages that have no access to educational resources (Pedro et al., 2019). Schools and universities in Bangladesh, where awareness of the use of digital tools in classrooms is growing, have conducted very little research on how best to apply AI. Understanding the current environment will provide insight into those areas where applications of AI may improve student outcomes.

2.4 Existing AI Initiatives in Bangladesh's Education System

Although AI adoption in the education sector of Bangladesh is in its emergent stage, a few promising initiatives do hint at its potential to enhance learning outcomes and generally improve the educational experience. All in all, AI-based educational tools, such as interactive learning applications and online platforms, have come out to gain traction, especially in more urban areas with increased internet access and smartphone penetration. Many online learning platforms include algorithms that create personalized lessons and feedback in real time, based on the learning needs of students, to increase learning and efficiency. Other learning platforms have also started to integrate AI mechanisms within their learning modules to facilitate adaptive pathways and present insight into data.

AI-powered toolkits monitor the behavior of the student, generate the pattern of assessment to recognize gaps in learning, and send recommendations for further study material that can improve their performance in academics (Algahtani, 2024).

In fact, some universities in Bangladesh have even begun to take advantage of AI at the level of higher education. Bangladesh University of Engineering and Technology (BUET) and North South University (NSU) are among the few universities in Bangladesh that have incorporated AI into their research on computer science, engineering, and data analytics. On 11 June 2023, both these universities signed a Memorandum of Understanding (MoU) to establish collaborative academic cooperation between them. One of the important aspects of the MoU was the mutual focus on AI research and development. These two top universities plan to collaborate on researching the evolving dimensions of AI technology (The Business Post, 2023). Apart from academic research, AI also finds its place in other supporting processes, like student admission, monitoring student performance, and choosing courses (Zawacki-Richter et al., 2019). These AI-powered systems give speed and accuracy in decision-making besides easing the administrative workload to allow universities more time to concentrate on the delivery of quality education.

However, despite these advancements, the implementation of AI in primary and secondary education remains limited. This limits the use of new AI-driven learning tools that may be introduced into primary and secondary schools, especially those in rural areas. One major challenge is the absence of infrastructure in most rural schools, which shows the gap between urban and rural areas (Asadullah, 2016). This makes the disparity in access to AI-driven educational tools between these areas more critical, calling for an overall policy framework that could guarantee equitable access across all regions. Despite these challenges, the prospect that AI holds in terms of making corrections to the existing disparities in education and enhancing learning outcomes cannot be denied.

AI can help with personalized learning, automated administration, and data-driven decision-making (Singh, 2023). This, along with its potential for gap-filling in learning, timely intervention, and customized learning tracks, can bring a sea change in the Bangladesh education system. Researchers should further investigate how AI can adapt to the different educational levels in Bangladesh, not in the elite classrooms only but in each and every classroom. Both opportunities and challenges await AI in the Bangladeshi education system. With appropriate policy frameworks, investments in infrastructure, and teacher training programs, AI has the potential to shape the future of education in Bangladesh (Sikder, 2023). In this regard, inclusivity and equity are important to ensure that all students everywhere, irrespective of geographic and socio-economic backgrounds, benefit from AI-powered learning experiences.

3. IMPACT OF AI ON BANGLADESHI STUDENTS

AI in education can change the learning curve of students in Bangladesh, the access to resources, and the acquisition of the skills required in the workforce of the future (Rufai et al., 2024). The section explores how AI can provide personalized learning experiences that enhance individual academic performance by adjusting educational content to the needs of each student. We will also focus on the role AI can play in reducing educational gaps by providing equal opportunities for high-quality learning in remote areas that have poor infrastructure and teaching resources (Figure 1).

Figure 1. Impact of AI on Bangladeshi students

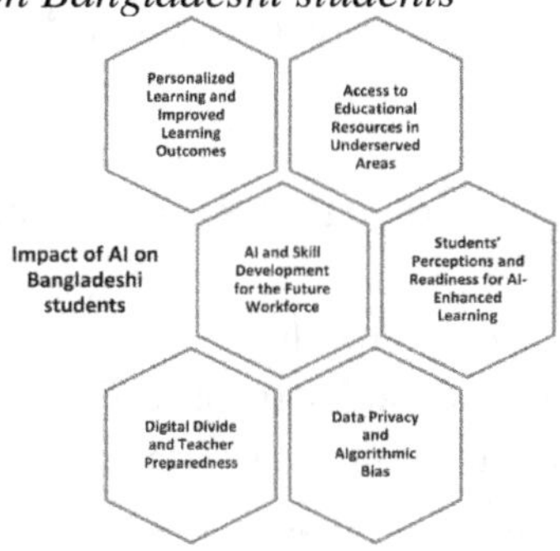

3.1 Personalized Learning and Improved Learning Outcomes

Artificial intelligence now makes it possible to shift from traditional teaching methods to more personalized modes of learning (Ivanashko et al., 2024). The AI-based learning system would adapt its teaching methodology to the relative strengths, weaknesses, and learning styles of the individuals (Ezzaim et al., 2024). Adaptive learning systems operate by continuously analyzing students' performance data and modifying the content, pace, and difficulty level to meet the unique needs of each student (Demartini et al., 2024). This may trigger a phenomenal improvement in the academic performance of Bangladeshi students, especially in highly dense classrooms where there is no scope for individual attention. In Bangladesh, in most of the classrooms, the teacher-student ratio is being seen as inappropriate. As a result, classroom size is a big concern for applying attention by the teachers towards the students (Zaman et al., 2024). Inappropriate and excessive teacher-student ratios greatly affect classroom practices (Etomes & Lyonga, 2020). That's where AI-personalized learning can bridge the learning gaps by giving remedial support to slow learners and challenging high achievers with advanced materials. Studies have shown that the capability of AI regarding instructional personalization could trigger interests, motivation, and subsequently achievement in learning (Halkiopoulos & Gkintoni, 2024).

AI systems can track student performance, providing appropriate interventions immediately when the system indicates that students are struggling in certain areas. Various platforms apply AI toward the creation of tailored lesson plans that adjust to student performance. A system on this level of personalization would be able to enable educators to identify and fix learning gaps quickly so that students do not fall behind. AI-enabled personalized learning can supplement class teachings when teacher-to-student ratios skyrocket in Bangladesh. No student will lag behind in his or her journey of education that way. All in all, AI-enabled personalized learning is going to make the educational climate more receptive to diverse student populations and hence enhance outcomes

3.2 Access to Educational Resources in Underprivileged Areas

AI can effectively democratize access to learning resources in large areas of Bangladesh, especially remote and under-resourced ones where extremely unequal educational opportunities are common (Dia et al., 2024). Generally, rural areas have to face the problem of inadequately qualified teachers and insufficient infrastructure in terms of education (Huda, 2024). AI-powered learning platforms will go a long way in helping to bridge the resource gap in such areas with quality, accessible content. This would also involve AI-enabled systems for lesson delivery, quizzes, and interactive exercises, including virtual tutors that could assist students in self-learning from any location. In this case, it further reduces dependencies on traditional classrooms, freeing the student to learn in comfort and at his own pace.

One of the greatest advantages of AI-enabled learning tools is that some systems can work fully offline or with limited network connectivity, especially critical for areas where the establishment of internet coverage is yet to be established (Wu et al., 2024). Both Shikho and Robi-10 Minute School are in the process of digitizing all the educational content to make it mobile-friendly and accessible even in areas with very low bandwidth (The Daily Star, 2022). Integrating a mix of sessions on key subjects like mathematics, science, and English, these platforms use artificial intelligence algorithms, personalizing this learning experience based on the progress the students make and what further improvements they require.

Apart from the problem of infrastructure, AI can transcend language issues in a multilingual Bangladeshi society. Supporting multiple languages, including Bangla, promotes inclusivity when delivered through AI tools for students who may struggle with the primary instructional language. This ensures that the student in the remote areas, where English proficiency might be low, would have equal opportunities for educational access as any other student in an urban setting (Murshed & Imtiaz, 2020). For example, EduHive uses AI to provide content both in Bangla and in English, hence bringing lessons closer to the local schoolchildren and thus making them more interesting. Also, AI can help bring inclusivity into education through individualized learning routes for students who have differing abilities to learn (Pedro et al., 2019). For example, students who fall behind in traditional classrooms find that adaptive learning systems, working with AI to identify strengths and weaknesses, make available selective content to catch them up at their own speed. Meanwhile, advanced learners in remote areas not privileged to have enrichment opportunities can benefit through AI by accessing more challenging material suited to their capabilities.

On the other hand, despite this enormous potential of AI to promote access and improve education in under-resourced settings, giant challenges remain. The most outstanding among these is the digital divide, overtly manifested in the lack of digital devices, electricity, and access to the internet (Horwitch, 2024). These challenges will only be surmounted through an integrated effort by the government, private sector, and international organizations in putting up the relevant infrastructural framework. The prospect of accessing devices at an affordable or subsidized price, as well as increased internet connectivity in rural areas, will open up the full potential of AI in these areas. Such gapping will allow AI to bring phenomenal transformations to schooling in backward areas of Bangladesh. It has the potential of equalizing learning opportunities and reducing dropout rates, hence generally improving learning outcomes. Greater investment and more focused interventions might enable AI to play a key role in narrowing the gap between urban and rural education, thereby enhancing equity and ensuring equal opportunities for all students, irrespective of their geographical or socio-economic background (Babu, 2021).

3.3 AI and Skill Development for the Future Workforce

Moving from a low-income to a high-income economy and emerging as a more technology-driven economy requires, among other things, a workforce with 21st-century skills that also cover critical thinking, problem-solving, and digital literacy. AI will go a long way in developing these skills among students by affording them opportunities for higher-order thinking tasks and simulations that mimic real-world problem-solving (Saeed et al., 2024). The AI technologies hold huge potential to improve project-based learning, in which the students work together on projects that are really creative, communicative, and innovative (Zhou, 2023). AI-enabled platforms can be able to create real-life scenarios where the students will be able to conduct research, analyze, and give solutions to real-life problems applicable in professional life.

Such AI-powered learning platforms could even involve the students in developing technical skills such as coding, data analysis, and machine learning that will be so crucial in today's and tomorrow's job markets (A. Alam, 2023). Consequently, AI could be used to prepare Bangladeshi students at a high level of preparedness for the challenge of the global workforce and enable them to compete in a rapidly changing world. For example, the Bangladesh ICT policy puts immense emphasis on digital skills in education; the integration of AI tools only serves to solidify this emphasis through an interactive and engaging manner in which students will learn of such competencies (Zohir, 2023).

AI can further promote continuous learning and reskilling, where students would have access to a huge volume of resources and courses that would really reflect the emergence of trends across industries (Tariq, 2024). AI will help give a culture of lifelong learning toward a more adaptable and skilled workforce, thus positioning Bangladesh for competitiveness within an increasingly globalized economy.

3.4 Challenges in AI Adoption: Digital Divide and Teacher Preparedness

Despite the promising potential of AI in education, there are two major obstacles to its implementation in Bangladesh: the digital divide and preparedness among teachers. Most AI-powered educational tools necessitate reliable internet connectivity, access to electricity, and the availability of digital devices for simple access, all of which are still scarce in most rural areas (Bulathwela et al., 2024). This widens the existing gap in education, and students in such underprivileged regions are less likely to be beneficiaries of AI-driven learning solutions, which can enhance academic experiences. According to a study of Islam et al. (2023), more than 60 percent of households in rural areas don’t have access to the internet, posing serious barriers to getting an equitable education. Urban areas receive most resources and attention, thereby widening the gap between students in urban and rural areas. In fact, if we fail to resolve this infrastructural challenge, the full potential of AI in enhancing learning outcomes may remain unrealized, thereby posing a challenge to the majority of students.

Another challenge in properly implementing AI in the classroom is preparing and training teachers for these technologies. However, most educators in Bangladesh, especially in rural areas, lack the digital literacy and technical acumen required to infuse AI tools into teaching methodologies (M. J. Alam et al., 2023). The majority of professional development programs that focus on essential skills are either incomplete or unavailable, which results in inadequate preparation of teachers for the adoption and benefits of new technologies. This skill gap diminishes educators' confidence and prohibits them from facilitating personalized learning experiences for their students.

Only widespread training programs, tailored to the specific geographical needs of the teachers, can meet this objective and actually prepare them with the knowledge and skills needed for introducing AI into their classrooms. This would involve workshops, online courses, and continuous support in collaboration with companies from the fields of education and technology. Moreover, the teachers should be involved in the development and selection processes of the AI tools so that they may go ahead and contribute much-needed insight to solving practical problems they usually face in teaching. Infrastructure improvements such as building better internet connectivity and offering affordable digital devices to students and schools complement the efforts toward addressing the problem of a digital divide. If we fail to address these challenges, they could seriously undermine the significant benefits AI brings to education and prevent certain students, especially those from disadvantaged backgrounds, from gaining the highly desired practical experience.

3.5 Ethical Concerns: Data Privacy and Algorithmic Bias

Data privacy and algorithmic bias have recently emerged as some of the hot-button ethical issues in the increased use of AI systems in education. Typical effective AI-driven educational platforms are inundated with huge amounts of data on student performance that include sensitive information such as academic performance, learning habits, and personal preferences (Kumari et al., 2024). Besides this, loose regulations related to the protection of data in Bangladesh and their non-uniform application raise the need for measures that can ensure that this data is collected, stored, and used in such a manner as to ensure student privacy. It is quite possible that information about students might fall prey to misuse or some form of ill-gotten access that might lead to problems related to privacy and security.

Moreover, training AI systems with information containing negative impacts of society will further increase biases among the population. These AI systems, for example, are bound to prove highly ineffective and even harmful if they are developed based on data from developed countries without considering the unique educational context and cultural nuances of Bangladesh. It might be an inequitable distribution of learning resources, or it might be the active marginalization of sections of students. The result would be that, in such a case, a non-diverse data set to train an AI algorithm couldn't consider the needs of students from different economic backgrounds; it may generate solutions, entirely neglecting specific challenges underprivileged sections might face.

Moreover, algorithmic bias might surface in several other forms, particularly while using biased assessment tools to evaluate the performance of students or stereotyping. This in turn brings about more critical questions concerning the development and implementation of AI algorithms in schools. It is an issue that educators and policymakers have to discuss: the ethics of the use of AI and putting in place guidelines and frameworks that protect the interests of students with intentions to prevent possible harm. This encompasses calling for transparency of AI systems and challenging the stakeholders in the use of these systems to question sources of information and methodologies employed to train the AI algorithms.

Moreover, educational institutions should lead in the training of teachers and other administrators on how to identify and address ethical issues arising from or with AI (Babu, 2021). This way, school systems will be able to help their educators think critically about the technologies they put to use and become policy advocates for equity and fairness. Equally important, a variety of new collaborations between data scientists and ethicists contribute to the creation of robust models that significantly reduce bias and enhance data privacy protection. We need to take up these ethical issues in order not only to make AI function smoothly in education but also to provide equal opportunities for success for every student. By paying attention to data privacy and striving for algorithmic equity, we have minor risks of actually leveraging the full potentials of AI while equipping a more just and equitable education setting.

3.6 Students' Perceptions and Readiness for AI-Enhanced Learning

The effectiveness of AI itself in educational settings heavily depends upon the readiness of students to perceive and receive the AI-driven learning tools (Mulaudzi & Hamilton, 2024). Coming from a traditional, teacher-centered system, adapting AI-enhanced learning faces severe cultural and psychological challenges in Bangladesh. For many students, the classroom structure is set, and the teacher regulates much outside of it. Introducing AI into this setting automatically puts the students more into autonomous, self-regulated learning models. Those students who are not very confident in AI or doubt their technology use may feel overwhelmed or resistant to such changes quite fast. Development of familiarity with AI technologies is an issue of critical importance with regard to willingness and capability to work with the AI-based learning systems in support of learning.

We need to sow the seeds for such a view about AI pretty early in an individual's educational life. AI-based school and institutional programs introduce ideas of AI in front of students in a very simple and pleasant learning way. Workshops, coding camps, or online interactive platforms where students can try out applications of AI, like a virtual tutor or adaptive learning games, would help overcome mysteries about it. We must integrate AI into the curriculum in such a way that it has relevance to the students' interests and daily lives, allowing them to build confidence and enthusiasm toward AI-enriched learning environments incrementally. The early exposure will assist in reframing their perceptions of using technology—from being just entertainment machines to realizing their potential as game-changers in educational processes.

In this regard, inclusivity plays a crucial role in preparing students from diverse backgrounds for meaningful and active engagement with AI-powered learning tools (Šumak et al., 2024). The student population from the affluent class in society may have a greater exposure to technology, whereas students from economically deprived sections may not receive enough exposure to digital learning tools, resulting in a deeper educational divide. In this context, targeted interventions would involve the provision of devices, internet connectivity, and basic training in AI literacy as a means of leveling the playing field. Schools, governments, and NGOs can all work collaboratively with one another to establish community tech centers through practical AI workshops where learners of under-resourced communities can be exposed to these technologies. In whatever case, this will enhance students' engagements and equalize the education system, where every student will gain skills and knowledge on how to use AI-powered learning systems.

4. FUTURE PROSPECTS FOR AI IN BANGLADESH'S EDUCATION

4.1 Opportunities for Deeper Integration of AI in Curriculum

The integration of AI into the curriculum brings an opportunity for modernization in Bangladeshi education, thereby gifting the students with better preparation for the digital future (Mahbub et al., 2024). AI isn't simply a matter of adoption; it is more about unlocking that opportunity for fresh curriculum design to meet evolving student and workforce needs. In this regard, the continued pervasiveness of AI tools can embed these technologies in routine teaching and learning to make the curriculum relevant, interesting, and responsive to the needs of the knowledge-based economy.

The role and function of AI in the curriculum is very evident within the STEM disciplines of science, technology, engineering, and mathematics. Integration of AI in the STEM subjects helps students to work on real-life problems, projects involving data, and developing critical thinking skills (N. Islam, 2024). Examples are AI-driven simulations, which in the future might allow students to conduct complex experiments within a virtual environment under their control and thereby enhance their understanding of complex scientific concepts beyond the constraints of physical resources. Such hands-on learning can help understand concepts in subjects like physics, biology, and chemistry—far-reaching theories coming closer through active experience-based learning.

Beyond areas in the fields of STEM, AI also tends to play an enormous role in language learning (Novawan et al., 2024). AI-powered platforms would, therefore, be able to offer customized tuition by analyzing individual learning patterns and adapting the content to suit particular students' needs. This will be quite effective, especially in Bangladesh. Therefore, it may be necessary to provide support to students who are learning local languages in addition to English. The AI-powered tools will allow students to get real-time feedback on their improvement in language proficiency and will enable them to learn at unique paces with personalized guidance that may never be possible through more conventional ways of classroom teaching. This will create a more inclusive learning environment for these students, who struggle in the traditional classrooms.

In addition, by embedding AI within cross-curricular areas of study, including subjects like ethics, social studies, and the arts, classes can provide further avenues for discussion of the impact of technologies upon society. For instance, students might consider historical trends, debate ethical issues related to the use of AI, or even create music or art with the help of AI. This helps such students understand deeper details about AI and its social implications. Such inclusion of AI in this interdisciplinary learning ensures that students experience truly multidisciplinary learning whereby they will appreciate the pervasiveness of AI in many fields. Also, such inclusion of AI within the curriculum would become imperative for lifelong learning and career readiness.

Since digital competencies are increasingly relevant in the workplace, vocational and technical education that integrates AI concepts would leave them quite prepared for the emerging sectors of their careers. Such AI-based training modules would simulate real-world, scenario-based automation, software development, and data analytics industries, thereby providing quite substantial practical experience for their future careers. It is through them that Bangladesh will have a technologically skilled workforce that can compete with the rest of the world in the artificial intelligence-driven world economy.

Another point is that incorporating AI into the curriculum can help in closing educational gaps. AI-enabled tools will provide personalized learning experiences among students in both urban and rural areas, whereby students in those deprived areas can access quality learning resources. AI lets teachers identify any lagging areas in their students and enables the teachers to take necessary actions so that no child ever falls behind. This might contribute to reducing the digital divide for equity in access to education and is another potential key benefit of AI in the Bangladeshi context. As a result, there are numerous and diverse opportunities for deeper integration of AI into the curriculum, which could help Bangladesh establish a path towards enhancing educational quality, fostering interdisciplinarity, and enhancing job preparedness. Thus, embedding AI across subjects and levels of education can make the system of education more adaptive, inclusive, and responsive to 21st-century needs. This will involve educators, policymakers, and technology providers working together in curriculum design to realize the full capacity of AI and extend its transformative power to every student.

4.2 Government and Policy Support for AI in Education

Wide-ranging government and policy support is crucial for AI to truly transform education in Bangladesh. First and foremost, policymakers have to understand the long-term gains of AI in education; they have to be proactive in creating an enabling environment for developing and implementing such technologies effectively. More concretely, this would require that financing for research and development in the field of AI-based education technologies become available; piloting of AI-powered teaching methods should be financed, and scaling up of effective programs at a national level is imperative. This means, among other things, that the government shall lead efforts to bring private technology firms, education institutions, and organizations from other countries to continuously conduct pilots and adapt new AI solutions to the unique context of Bangladesh. We can therefore identify them and accelerate the adoption of those AI tools that make the most difference to learning outcomes.

Any responsible use of AI in education should be informed by proper and sound policy frameworks. The government needs to propose guidelines on data privacy, algorithmic transparency, and ethical usage that make sure the nondiscriminatory and equitable deployment of AI tools is ensured. The government needs to ensure inclusivity in implementation, making the AI tools available to all students, regardless of their economic status (Šumak et al., 2024). This way, no students will be left behind in rural settings regarding the integration of AI. For example, the creation of national standards on AI in education ensures that states uniformly integrate AI in the curriculum, whereby the state is also able to monitor and evaluate the progress for further improvement of its integration strategy. The government is also taking other initiatives to catalyze public-private partnerships, share knowledge between the education and technology sectors, and encourage schools through grants or subsidies to use AI (Mannuru et al., 2023).

The other crucial area that necessitates significant government involvement is teacher training. The success of AI within the classroom will depend mostly on how well the educators are prepared for these tools. In this respect, the government might create countrywide professional development programs that train teachers in AI literacy and digital competency so that when full-scale AI usage arrives, they will be ready to perform. These would involve pedagogical education programs, not only on technical competencies but also on how to effectively integrate AI into the everyday current teaching methods to complement traditional pedagogies. We should also undertake public awareness campaigns to demystify AI for students and parents, building general awareness of its potential benefits. The government would accordingly streamline both technical infrastructure and human capacities to position the Bangladeshi education system for the maximum transformation potential of AI, thereby creating a foundation for skilled and tech-savvy manpower.

4.3 AI for Lifelong Learning and Continuous Skill Development

In a rapidly changing global economy, lifelong learning and continuous development of skills became the only cornerstones on which economic sustainability, let alone individual development, could survive. AI stands at the leading edge of this change, and its potential to facilitate people in the acquisition of new skills and adaptation to an ever-evolving job market is huge. AI enables learning to be more accessible and flexible and at an individual's pace for students at all career stages, fostering the lifelong learning that will be required to meet the growing need for a highly skilled workforce in Bangladesh (Rufai et al., 2024). This, in turn, necessitates the use of AI-powered tools and platforms to address these needs, thereby enhancing the competitiveness of learners in the dynamic global job market. AI-powered platforms, such as MOOCs or skill development applications, are significantly contributing to personalized learning experiences (Kaswan et al., 2024). Advanced algorithms on these platforms analyze the trend, preference, and performance of the users' learning and thereby recommend courses and study materials that precisely meet an individual's career goals and needs.

It ensures that not only will the content be fully relevant, but also the learners can move on at a pace that best fits their capabilities. Taking into consideration the wide spectrum of skills and unequal access to traditional facilities in Bangladesh, there is huge potential for personalized learning. Personalized learning AI tools keep people interested, motivated, and focused on long-term educational and professional goals (Castro et al., 2024). It should bring improved learning and a better-prepared workforce. More important is the democratization that AI enables in lifelong learning—from fresh graduates searching for work-related competencies to working adults looking to either upskill or reskill.

AI-powered platforms can introduce microcredits, for example, module-based courses that instead focus on acquiring specialized skills applicable to their respective professions (Jarvis et al., 2024). This kind of platform will allow for real-time feedback and analytics, through which learners will be able to track their progress and change their approach to learning if they need to. Developing countries like Bangladesh, where disadvantaged groups cannot access formal education or training programs, these kinds of initiatives will be very effective. Flexibility and access to AI-driven learning ensure that people in urban centers or those living in the remotest regions can keep learning for the development of skills at any stage in their life cycle, thus contributing to not only individual growth but also the economic development of the nation as a whole. Promoting an AI-supported culture of lifelong learning also nurtures a general mindset regarding the importance of adaptability and innovation.

AI also has the potential to contribute to the continuous development of skills, thereby creating a more robust and future-oriented workforce in Bangladesh. Workers can stay updated with industry trends, take up new technologies, and master all the essential skill sets that are vital in today's increasingly automated and tech-driven world. The government's support for lifelong learning with AI can only increase further on the back of partnerships between industry and educational institutions that will help facilitate training and skill development courses for Bangladesh's emerging economy (M. T. Islam et al., 2023). In this way, AI will not only build a better-informed and adaptive labor force but also place the country in a position to achieve economic growth in the long run by adequately preparing to meet the needs of the future labor market.

5. CHALLENGES IN IMPLEMENTING AI AT LARGE-SCALE

Considering the great promise of AI in education, its great impact on the educational landscape suggests several challenges for large-scale implementation in Bangladesh. The following section thus discusses infrastructural and technological limitations that make the effective deployment of AI in educational settings difficult, the need for comprehensive training and professional development on the part of teachers, and finally the socio-cultural impediments to the effective adoption of AI technologies (Figure 2). Overcoming these challenges is paramount in terms of fully gaining benefits arising from the adoption of AI in schools.

Figure 2. Challenges in implementing AI in Bangladeshi education

5.1 Infrastructure and Technological Constraints

The deplorable state of infrastructure in Bangladesh, coupled with technological limitations, has resulted in serious obstacles to the full-scale implementation of AI in education. Most schools face issues with unreliable electricity, poor internet connectivity, and minimum access to fundamental digital devices; these are especially true in rural and underprivileged areas (Al-Amin et al., 2021). Furthermore, the infrastructure regarding required digital tools is inadequate, which greatly restricts the integration of AI tools and platforms that have the highest dependence on strong structure (M. J. Alam et al., 2023). It is virtually impossible for institutions to carry out effective implementations of AI-based learning solutions with these basic building blocks of technology, thereby shrinking the chances of advanced AI-enhanced educational opportunities for students.

This indeed is the case for urban areas that enjoy better access to technology. Schools with greater resources will consistently lead the implementation of AI technologies, while those with fewer resources will inevitably regress. This, therefore, leads to a digital divide, which could establish a two-tier education system where students hailing from better backgrounds or urban areas will benefit from the integration of AI in education, while the ones from less privileged backgrounds or rural areas will lag. Such inequities, in turn, more deeply embed educational inequalities and reduce the potential of AI as a tool for democratizing education across Bangladesh.

Another critical issue is the cost associated with implementing and sustaining AI technologies. The highly inhibitive cost regarding investment in hardware, software, staff training, and continuous technical support discourages many educational institutions. Smaller schools or schools based in rural areas might face difficulties investing in such infrastructure or even maintaining these AI tools (K. E. K. Babu, 2021). Again, the insufficient funds make this task more difficult for public and private institutions. Due to budgetary constraints, schools are unable to adopt AI as an effective educational solution. Thus, the government needs to make significant investments in the development of low-cost and scalable technological solutions to fill up these gaps with collaboration with private organizations to ensure the affordability of AI implementation at all levels of education in Bangladesh.

The infrastructural and technological gaps, therefore, need to be the top priority in scaling up AI in education in Bangladesh, developing the infrastructure for internet access across the country, provision of digital devices at an affordable price, and investment in power solutions for the underserved areas. Therefore, a robust technological foundation can assist educational institutions nationwide in creating a platform that utilizes AI to enhance outcomes, equipping all students with cutting-edge learning tools.

5.2 Teacher Preparation and Continuous Professional Development

Successful integration of AI in education does not solely depend on technology; it also depends on the preparedness and capability of the teachers to integrate these tools into their teaching practices (Yue et al., 2024). Simultaneously, a significant obstacle lies in the fact that many educators in Bangladesh lack the necessary training and knowledge to effectively use AI-driven technologies (Roy et al., 2021). Since most educational systems still heavily rely on traditional approaches, it is crucial to bridge the gap between AI literacy and pedagogical skills to enable a more active role of AI in the classroom. Therefore, it's possible that teachers are either unaware of the potential benefits of AI or lack the knowledge to implement AI tools in a way that enhances, rather than disrupts, their teaching methods.

For this, extensive and easily accessible teacher training and professional development programs are highly essential. These training programs, therefore, need not be confined to AI literacy but also need to train teachers in the use of AI tools in conventional pedagogies. In fact, the practical, workshop-oriented approach may trigger the process of 'demystifying' AI by underlining its very practical applications in real-life classrooms. AI can train educators by automating big parts of educators' workloads, such as adaptive learning, personalized instructions, and administrative tasks like grading and attendance (Li & Jiang, 2024). These strategies will also integrate technology integration strategies specific to Bangladesh's unique educational contexts so that teachers can safely apply AI in meeting the needs of their students.

Continuous professional development and support must complement this initial training to help teachers adapt to the ever-evolving capabilities of AI. Continuous learning through online courses, webinars, mentorship programs, and other opportunities keeps educators updated with new AI tools and methodologies (Aithal et al., 2024). Building communities of practice—in which teachers can collaborate, share experiences, and diffuse best practices—will help create a network of peer support that enables educators to confidently experiment with AI-driven solutions in the classroom. Such collaboration will be an inspiration to innovation on the part of professionals in the way teachers develop new pedagogies together, using AI in ways that increase student engagement and positive learning outcomes.

The content of the training programs should also be based on the needs of the teachers working in different educational contexts in Bangladesh. We would tailor the training to maximize the available AI tools and resources, focusing on areas with limited access, such as rural and under-resourced areas. Training might then move to higher-order applications of AI, such as data-driven student assessments or AI-enhanced curriculum planning, at urban or more well-resourced schools. Given the varied contexts, professional development is crucial to ensure that educators throughout Bangladesh are best prepared to deploy AI technologies, taking into account the unique infrastructure and resource limitations of each school.

This is one of the major reasons why investment in teacher training and professional development is one of the most important ways to realize long-term success for AI within the education sector in Bangladesh. Confident and competent educators in the use of AI are agents of innovation, uplifting student learning experiences and driving educational transformation from below. With continuous support and learning for teachers, Bangladesh can ensure that the promise of AI-enhanced education benefits both teachers and students.

5.3 Societal and Cultural Barriers to AI Adoption

Besides technological constraints and requirements for teacher training, AI's large-scale introduction to Bangladesh's education system faces significant challenges rooted in social and cultural barriers (Hafiz & Islam, 2023). Most of such problems take root in doubt and sometimes fear toward new technologies, which include AI, in places where people have less exposure to digital tools. The concept of AI might evoke thoughts of job replacement, loss of traditional teacher roles, or even fear about losing control of learning processes. Such misunderstanding might then form the basis for resistance to the adoption of AI by parents, teachers, and students alike.

Cultural mores, especially about education, appear to cling to rote learning and teacher-centered pedagogies, which do little to help overcome this resistance (S. Islam, 2024). AI-driven, student-centered learning methods may be seen to disrupt well-worn norms and expectations of what education is and does, especially in Bangladesh, where many educators and learners are deeply accustomed to more conventional modes of instruction, such as rote memorization and standardized testing. For example, AI for adaptive learning involves the personalization of content for students. It is an unfamiliar concept and can be viewed as usurping the authority of the teacher in managing dynamics in the classroom. Similarly, the role of AI involves automating processes such as grading and lesson planning, which may raise concerns that AI could eventually replace human educators, thereby intensifying their reluctance to engage with such technologies.

These societal and cultural barriers can only be surmounted by means of focused awareness and outreach programs. In other words, policymakers, educators, and technology advocates must engage communities with regards to a fuller understanding of AI and how it can serve to improve teaching and learning without replacing them. Public awareness demystifying AI will help overcome fears and highlight the role of AI as a support tool that complements and does not replace human teaching. Success stories from local schools or communities where AI has been used effectively will also build trust and demonstrate some practical benefits of enhancements in learning outcomes.

To widely disseminate AI technology, we must consider the opinions of parents, educators, and community leaders. Workshops and seminars at public forums can present the role of AI in education, the ethics that govern its use, and how AI might serve to benefit students. This could offer a platform for students, particularly parents who have a keen interest in their children's education, to voice their concerns and receive feedback. By emphasizing how AI may extend personalized learning, enhance participation, and enable new forms of academic success, educators can offer a more supportive and positive framing of the technologies.

Other promising strategies involve embedding AI in a pilot program that effectively integrates conventional teaching techniques with AI-enhanced tools. Gradual implementation, in which AI is first introduced to support and complement, can help facilitate transition and become a driver to demonstrate value in improving student engagement and learning outcomes. These can be representative programs that show how AI and old pedagogy can coexist in order to reduce the fear in both teachers and students that some kind of revolution will sweep away familiar practices. Making greater headway in overcoming these societal and cultural obstacles necessarily involves multi-level awareness, dialogue, and gradual implementation that is inclusive. The more all parties—parents, educators, and community leaders alike—are part of the conversation regarding AI in education, the more accommodating an environment Bangladesh can build. This, in turn, would only help make the integration process smooth and foster within the mindset of the people of this country that AI is a trusted tool to help improve the quality and equity of education.

6. ETHICAL IMPLICATIONS OF AI IN EDUCATION

Artificial intelligence integration into education raises several serious ethical issues that cannot be taken lightly. The section discusses the critical issues of data privacy and security concerns, then fairness and freedom from biases within AI systems; finally, equity and access to AI technologies. By addressing these ethical considerations, stakeholders can work toward a responsible and inclusive framework for the implementation of AI in education.

6.1 Data Privacy and Security Concerns

Data used in education is very sensitive because it portrays a lot of personal information. Ignoring such data can lead to the violation of privacy, breach, and leak of personal information. Hence, the educational entity must adopt methods that ensure effective encryption of the data at rest and in transit, as well as those that control access to information, in order to prevent unauthorized persons from manipulating it. Regular security audits help in pinpointing any potential point of vulnerability and ensure that measures taken for protection are maintained and effective. We clearly need to spell out our policies on collection, usage, and sharing so that transparency in data handling is maintained. The policy would spell out what kind of data was collected, the way it would be stored, who could have access, and under what conditions third parties could access it. Good data practices will not only prevent misuse but also build confidence among students, parents, and the teaching fraternity in general that institutions value privacy and ethical standards.

What Bangladesh most needs, beyond institutional practices, is the creation of stronger and more holistic regulatory frameworks for the ethical use of AI in education (Mahbub et al., 2024). Given the variety of issues that involve responsible handling of student data, these frameworks need to consider international standards for data protection, such as the General Data Protection Regulation. These should deal with aspects concerning consent, ownership, and accountability in such a way that individuals retain control over their information and receive all necessary information for its use.

Meanwhile, policy and education stakeholders have to initiate a process that would openly discuss the ethical issues that arise from the practice of using data in AI applications, such as bias or surveillance concerns that such uses could engender and impacts on student outcomes that data-driven purposes might possibly create. Only then, under such conditions, would these stakeholders be better equipped to deal with the thorny landscape of AI and its accompanying data in education through the formulation and application of an appropriate legal and ethical framework. Therefore, data privacy and security concerns will be an integral part of deploying ethical AI within the Bangladesh education system. It is recommended that all educational institutions establish technological safeguards and regulatory frameworks for protection against sensitive information through personal engagement with policymakers. Such a structural approach to the whole issue of student data protection will form the basis of building firm ethics from which AI-driven education may grow more safely and supportively for all stakeholders concerned.

6.2 Ensuring Fairness and Avoiding Bias in AI Systems

Another critical ethical issue in AI use for education is bias in the AI systems themselves. Because of biased or non-representative datasets, algorithms within AI-powered educational tools may train and, therefore, reinforce existing biases. This kind of bias creates undervalued treatment for students from certain groups and only serves to exacerbate inequalities within an education system. For example, AI algorithms that are not trained on diverse datasets may show bias in their opinions on the type and background of learners, thus providing an unbalanced opportunity for some students at the expense of others to access educational resources.

All levels of development and deployment promote the practice of inclusion to ensure equity. In addition, making the training datasets more representative by including a wide range of demographics among the students, such as age, gender, socioeconomic background, and geographic location, helps mitigate bias in AI outputs. Regular auditing and assessment of AI systems can also eliminate biases. Audits for these aspects will not only focus on the algorithms but also extend to the data sources used for training, thereby preventing the perpetuation of stereotypes and discriminatory practices.

Educators, students, and community stakeholders can be involved in the designing and evaluation process to provide insight into the potential effects AI technologies could have on diverse student populations. This would provoke collaboration toward the creation of AI systems that keep the principle of equity and fairness at the forefront in educational settings. Focus groups, pilot programs, and feedback mechanisms empower all stakeholders to voice their concerns, provide suggestions, and ensure the AI tool truly responds to diverse student needs.

Additionally, the system should emphasize the principle of continuous training for educators regarding the ethical issues involved in AI and how to apply equity to technology use. Indeed, by equipping teachers with the knowledge to recognize and address bias, schools can foster an environment where AI serves as a tool for empowerment. Fundamentally, fairness and the absence of bias in AI systems are an issue of morality just as they are a technical challenge. As AI technologies continue to reshape education, active interest exists in the creation of systems that drive equity and inclusion, which assure equal learning opportunities for all learners. Only by making these ethical considerations paramount will the realm of education be able to balance the realization of the full potential of AI with the mitigation of its associated risks.

6.3 Addressing Equity and Access to AI Technologies

Another very serious implication of AI in education involves issues of equity and access. In Bangladesh, there exists a significant disparity in access to technology and other resources, which significantly hinders the practical implementation of AI-driven educational solutions (M. H. Rahman et al., 2024). The majority of students from rural and deprived districts either lack essential devices, effective internet connectivity, or adequate systems for receiving full benefits from AI technologies. The huge digital divide in which these students experience reduces their capacity for effective learning, hence keeping the wheel of systemic inequalities spinning and deprivations heavier than that of their urban counterparts.

A policy framework that would guarantee the learning of all students with or without socio-economic disadvantages in the use of AI technologies should be devised by the stakeholders in the light of these equity issues. Government intervention is hence imperative to this end. This would involve devices at subsidized costs, development and expansion of the internet, and investment in infrastructure that allows easy access to AI resources. Furthermore, this may provide an avenue toward government and private partnerships in creating community technology hubs. These hubs will further encourage learning and engagement by offering AI tools, training, and support for the students and educators through collaboration.

We must implement awareness and training programs that promote AI literacy in addition to expanding technological access. Regardless of one's early exposure to technology, training in how to effectively use AI tools is relevant for students and educators alike. Every educational institution may, therefore, set up training programs that embed AI literacy within the curriculum to enable students to have important skills needed for life in a technologically intensive environment. The programs will equally create awareness among people on how AI works, the accruable benefits from it, and its limitations, hence ensuring that students become not only consumers of technology but informed users who can actively engage with AI systems.

Besides that, partnerships with local communities, NGOs, and international agencies will go a long way in enhancing equity in access to AI. These could be some form of collaborative projects that aim to bridge the resource, training, and support gap required for the underserved communities. The projects that involve the community allow them to get to know the needs of the community they serve and work toward a solution to meet those needs. It thus means that in the inclusive use of AI stakeholders, equal opportunities for bridging digital divides are possible, providing all students with equal experiences of AI-enhanced learning. Equity and access to AI technologies are more than just provision; it is about cultivating a culture that supports inclusiveness and empowerment. Equity and access to AI technologies are areas that the Bangladesh government needs to focus on so that the coming educational landscape provides equity in a manner that every child is prepared to face the challenges in the world with a constantly growing envelope of AI.

7. CONCLUSION

The integration of AI into the education system in Bangladesh would fundamentally alter our understanding of learning and our preparation for a dynamic job market. The chapter has discussed the various impacts AI is having among Bangladeshi students, including personalized learning, increased access to resources, and the development of a more skilled workforce. Infrastructure will not support large-scale implementation; there is a dire need for large-scale teacher capacity building, and people may resist the adoption of technologies. Several ethical considerations, ranging from data protection issues to questions relating to equity and access in the use of AI technology, exist. Key findings both highlight potential benefits of AI in education and address critical challenges to meaningful integration. Bangladesh has yet to conduct research on the long-term implications for educational equity, innovative models for teacher training, and the effectiveness assessment of AI tools in diverse educational settings. AI in education will have a brighter future with collaboration among government entities, institutions of learning, developers of technology, and society. In attaining all this, Bangladesh can ensure improvement in its educational landscape and the introduction of its students to a more technologically driven world by fostering an inclusive and ethical approach in the integration of AI. We can harness this huge promise to improve education for all learners in Bangladesh with strategic planning and commitment.

REFERENCES

Aithal, P. S., Prabhu, S., & Aithal, S. (2024). Future of Higher Education through Technology Prediction and Forecasting. SSRN *Electronic Journal*. https://doi.org/DOI: 10.2139/ssrn.4901474

Al-Amin, M., Al Zubayer, A., Deb, B., & Hasan, M. (2021). Status of tertiary level online class in Bangladesh: Students' response on preparedness, participation and classroom activities. *Heliyon*, 7(1). PMID: 33506126

Alam, A. (2023). Intelligence unleashed : An argument for AI-enabled learning ecologies with real world examples of today and a peek into the future. *AIP Conference Proceedings*. Advance online publication. DOI: 10.1063/5.0129803

Alam, M. J., Pervez, A. K. M. K., Kabir, M. S., Amin, M. R., & Bhuiya, R. A. (2023). The Challenges and Prospects of e-learning in Higher Education in Bangladesh- A review. *Asian Journal of Education and Social Studies*, 43(1), 10–19. DOI: 10.9734/ajess/2023/v43i1931

ALGAHTANI, A. (2024). A Comparative Study of AI-Based Educational Tools: Evaluating User Interface Experience and Educational Impact. *Journal of Theoretical and Applied Information Technology*, 102(5).

Asadullah, M. N. (2016). Do Pro-Poor Schools reach out to the poor? Location choice of BRAC and ROSC schools in Bangladesh. *The Australian Economic Review*, 49(4), 432–452. DOI: 10.1111/1467-8462.12180

Babu, K. (2021). Artificial intelligence, its applications in different sectors and challenges: Bangladesh context. In *Advanced sciences and technologies for security applications* (pp. 103–119). https://doi.org/DOI: 10.1007/978-3-030-88040-8_4

Babu, K. E. K. (2021). Artificial intelligence in Bangladesh, its applications in different sectors and relevant challenges for the government: An analysis. *International Journal of Public Law and Policy*, 7(4), 319. DOI: 10.1504/ijplap.2021.118891

Bhardwaj, K., Garima, N., & Sudan, S. (2024). Artificial intelligence's role and future implementation in education. In *Advances in educational technologies and instructional design book series* (pp. 160–175). https://doi.org/DOI: 10.4018/979-8-3693-2728-9.ch007

Bulathwela, S., Pérez-Ortiz, M., Holloway, C., Cukurova, M., & Shawe-Taylor, J. (2024). Artificial intelligence alone will not democratise education: On Educational Inequality, Techno-Solutionism and Inclusive Tools. *Sustainability*, 16(2), 781. DOI: 10.3390/su16020781

Castro, G. P. B., Chiappe, A., Rodriguez, D. F. B., & Sepulveda, F. G. (2024). Harnessing AI for Education 4.0: Drivers of Personalized Learning. *The Electronic Journal of e-Learning, 22*(5), 01–14. https://doi.org/DOI: 10.34190/ejel.22.5.3467

Chen, L., Chen, P., & Lin, Z. (2020). Artificial Intelligence in Education: A review. *IEEE Access : Practical Innovations, Open Solutions*, 8, 75264–75278. DOI: 10.1109/access.2020.2988510

Demartini, C. G., Sciascia, L., Bosso, A., & Manuri, F. (2024). Artificial Intelligence Bringing Improvements to Adaptive Learning in Education: A case study. *Sustainability*, 16(3), 1347. DOI: 10.3390/su16031347

Desk, T. (2023, June 15). NSU teams up with BUET for research, AI development. *The Business Post*. https://businesspostbd.com/corporate/2023-06-16/nsu-teams-up-with-buet-for-research-ai-development-2023-06-16

Dia, R. R., Akif, A., Islam, Q. T., & Hossain, M. A. (2024). Interactive Cares Bangladesh: Empowering Bangladesh's Future Through Education and the SDGs. SAGE Publications: SAGE Business Cases Originals.

Etomes, S. E., & Lyonga, F. I. N. (2020). STUDENT-TEACHER RATIO AND STUDENTS'ACADEMIC PERFORMANCE IN PUBLIC UNIVERSITIES: THE CASE OF THE UNIVERSITY OF BUEA, CAMEROON. *European Journal of Education Studies*, 7(6).

Ezzaim, A., Dahbi, A., Aqqal, A., & Haidine, A. (2024). AI-based learning style detection in adaptive learning systems: a systematic literature review. *Journal of Computers in Education*. https://doi.org/DOI: 10.1007/s40692-024-00328-9

Foffano, F., Scantamburlo, T., & Cortés, A. (2022). Investing in AI for social good: An analysis of European national strategies. *AI & Society*, 38(2), 479–500. DOI: 10.1007/s00146-022-01445-8 PMID: 35528248

Hafiz, N., & Islam, A. (2023, October 1). *Impact of artificial intelligence in closing the gender gap among women-led industries: a developing country perspective*. https://dspace.bracu.ac.bd/xmlui/handle/10361/22802

Halkiopoulos, C., & Gkintoni, E. (2024). Leveraging AI in E-Learning: Personalized Learning and Adaptive Assessment through Cognitive Neuropsychology—A Systematic Analysis. *Electronics (Basel)*, 13(18), 3762. DOI: 10.3390/electronics13183762

Horwitch, M. (2024, August). The AI Challenge for National Technology Strategy. In *2024 Portland International Conference on Management of Engineering and Technology (PICMET)* (pp. 1-11). IEEE.

Horwitch, M. "The AI Challenge for National Technology Strategy," *2024 Portland International Conference on Management of Engineering and Technology (PICMET)*, Portland, OR, USA, 2024, pp. 1-11, https://doi.org/DOI: 10.23919/picmet64035.2024.10653430

Hossain, M. K., Srivastava, A., Oliver, G. C., Islam, M. E., Jahan, N. A., Karim, R., Kanij, T., & Mahdi, T. H. (2024). Adoption of artificial intelligence and big data analytics: An organizational readiness perspective of the textile and garment industry in Bangladesh. *Business Process Management Journal.* Advance online publication. DOI: 10.1108/bpmj-11-2023-0914

Huang, F., Wang, Y., & Zhang, H. (2024). Modelling generative AI acceptance, Perceived Teachers' enthusiasm and Self-Efficacy to English as a Foreign Language learners' Well-Being in the Digital era. *European Journal of Education.* Advance online publication. DOI: 10.1111/ejed.12770

Huda, S. (2024). Challenges of Using Multimedia Tools in the Teaching and Learning Process: Instance from a college of Bangladesh. *Journal of Management and Business Education*, 7(3), 435–451. DOI: 10.35564/jmbe.2024.0024

Islam, M. M., Shaheen, S. M., Roy, R. K., Islam, A., & Hossain, M. D. (2023). Pandemic-Led Challenges for Rural Students in Bangladesh. *IAFOR Journal of Education*, 11(3), 113–136.

Islam, M. T., Hasan, M. M., Redwanuzzaman, M., & Hossain, M. K. (2023). Practices of artificial intelligence to improve the business in Bangladesh. *Social Sciences & Humanities Open*, 9, 100766. DOI: 10.1016/j.ssaho.2023.100766

Islam, N. (2024). Synthesizing sociological dimensions into engineering programs: Challenges for the sociology teachers in Bangladesh. *Social Sciences & Humanities Open*, 10, 101079. DOI: 10.1016/j.ssaho.2024.101079

Islam, S. (2024). British Columbian and Bangladeshi secondary science teachers' views on the role of professional learning communities in the growth of their knowledge for teaching. *UBC Library Open Collections.* https://doi.org/DOI: 10.14288/1.0444124

Ivanashko, O., Kozak, A., Knysh, T., & Honchar, K. (2024). The role of artificial intelligence in shaping the future of education: opportunities and challenges. *Futurity Education*, 126–146. https://doi.org/DOI: 10.57125/fed.2024.03.25.08

Jarvis, A., Ho, A., & Lim, G. (2024). Impressing Artificial Intelligence: Automated Job Interview training in Professional English subjects. *RELC Journal.* Advance online publication. DOI: 10.1177/00336882241245449

Kaswan, K. S., Dhatterwal, J. S., & Ojha, R. P. (2024). AI in personalized learning. In *CRC Press eBooks* (pp. 103–117). https://doi.org/DOI: 10.1201/9781003376699-9

Katsamakas, E., Pavlov, O. V., & Saklad, R. (2024). Artificial intelligence and the transformation of higher education institutions. *arXiv (Cornell University)*. https://doi.org//arxiv.2402.08143DOI: 10.48550

Kim, J. (2023). Leading teachers' perspective on teacher-AI collaboration in education. *Education and Information Technologies*. Advance online publication. DOI: 10.1007/s10639-023-12109-5

Kumari, G. V., Chapa, B. P., Chaitanya, N. K., Mahajan, R. G., & Shahakar, M. (2024). Introduction to data-driven intelligent systems. In *CRC Press eBooks* (pp. 1–18). https://doi.org/DOI: 10.1201/9781003388449-1

Laak, K., & Aru, J. (2024). AI and personalized learning: bridging the gap with modern educational goals. *arXiv (Cornell University)*. https://doi.org//arxiv.2404.02798DOI: 10.48550

Li, X., & Jiang, Y. (2024). Artificial intelligence in education: Opportunities, current status, and prospects. *Geographical Research Bulletin*, 3, 146–174.

Mahbub, S., Wafik, H. A., Arif, Z., Rahman, M., Uddin, A., & Azim, I. B. (2024). AI Consciousness and Technological Advancement in Bangladesh's Higher Education: AI Awareness among the Learners.

Mannan, M., Mustafa, Z. B., Aziz, S. F. B. A., & Maruf, T. I. (2023). Technology adoption for higher education in Bangladesh–development and validation. *Journal of Education and Social Sciences*, 24(1), 1–9.

Mannuru, N. R., Shahriar, S., Teel, Z. A., Wang, T., Lund, B. D., Tijani, S., Pohboon, C. O., Agbaji, D., Alhassan, J., Galley, J., Kousari, R., Ogbadu-Oladapo, L., Saurav, S. K., Srivastava, A., Tummuru, S. P., Uppala, S., & Vaidya, P. (2023). Artificial intelligence in developing countries: The impact of generative artificial intelligence (AI) technologies for development. *Information Development*. Advance online publication. DOI: 10.1177/02666669231200628

Mulaudzi, L., & Hamilton, J. (2024). Student perspectives on optimising AI tools to enhance personalised learning in higher education. *Interdisciplinary Journal of Education Research*, 6(s1), 1–15. DOI: 10.38140/ijer-2024.vol6.s1.03

Murdan, A. P., & Halkhoree, R. (2024, June). Integration of Artificial Intelligence for educational excellence and innovation in higher education institutions. In 2024 1st International Conference on Smart Energy Systems and Artificial Intelligence (SESAI) (pp. 1-6). IEEE.

Murshed, S. M., & Imtiaz, M. (2020). Inclusive practices in Bangladesh. In *BRILL eBooks* (pp. 159–174). https://doi.org/DOI: 10.1163/9789004432789_011

Nkechi, A. A., Ojo, A. O., & Eneh, O. A. (2024). Impact of artificial intelligence in achieving quality education. In *Artificial intelligence*. https://doi.org/DOI: 10.5772/intechopen.1004871

Novawan, A., Walker, S. A., & Ikeda, O. (2024). The new face of technology-enhanced language learning (TELL) with artificial intelligence (AI): Teacher perspectives, practices, and challenges. *Journal of English in Academic and Professional Communication*, 10(1), 1–18.

Ouyang, F., Zheng, L., & Jiao, P. (2022). Artificial intelligence in online higher education: A systematic review of empirical research from 2011 to 2020. *Education and Information Technologies*, 27(6), 7893–7925. DOI: 10.1007/s10639-022-10925-9

Patel, S. (2024, September 9). *AI-DRIVEN EDUCATIONAL INTERVENTIONS: AN EMPIRICAL STUDY ON THEIR EFFICACY IN IMPROVING ACADEMIC PERFORMANCE*. https://iaeme-library.com/index.php/IJETR/article/view/IJETR_09_02_013

Pedro, F., Subosa, M., Rivas, A., & Valverde, P. (2019). *Artificial intelligence in education : challenges and opportunities for sustainable development*. https://hdl.handle.net/20.500.12799/6533

Rahaman, M. M., & Akter, N. (2017). ICT used in education sector considering primary and secondary level schools in rural areas: A study of Sylhet division in Bangladesh. *IOSR Journal of Business and Management*, 19(4), 1–6.

Rahman, M. H., Ahmad, A. B., & Sawal, M. Z. H. B. M. (2024). The influence of personal factors on resistance to technology adoption in university libraries in Bangladesh. *Information Development*. Advance online publication. DOI: 10.1177/02666669241257196

Report, T. (2023, June 12). NSU, BUET join hands for collaborative research and AI development. *The Business Standard*. https://www.tbsnews.net/economy/corporates/nsu-buet-join-hands-collaborative-research-and-ai-development-648266

Roy, G., Babu, R., Kalam, M. A., Yasmin, N., Zafar, T., & Nath, S. R. (2021). Response, readiness and challenges of online teaching amid COVID-19 pandemic: The case of higher education in Bangladesh. *The Educational and Developmental Psychologist*, 40(1), 40–50. DOI: 10.1080/20590776.2021.1997066

Rufai, A. A., Khan, M. S. H., & Hasan, M. (2024). An exploration of pedagogical approaches in teaching artificial intelligence courses: Experience from undergraduates students of Bangladesh. *Social Sciences & Humanities Open*, 10, 101075. DOI: 10.1016/j.ssaho.2024.101075

Saeed, M. M. A., Saeed, R. A., Ahmed, Z. E., Gaid, A. S. A., & Mokhtar, R. A. (2024). AI technologies in engineering education. In *Advances in educational technologies and instructional design book series* (pp. 61–87). https://doi.org/DOI: 10.4018/979-8-3693-2728-9.ch003

Sandhu, R., Channi, H. K., Ghai, D., Cheema, G. S., & Kaur, M. (2024). An Introduction to Generative AI Tools for Education 2030. In *Advances in educational technologies and instructional design book series* (pp. 1–28). https://doi.org/DOI: 10.4018/979-8-3693-2440-0.ch001

Sedkaoui, S., & Benaichouba, R. (2024). Generative AI as a transformative force for innovation: A review of opportunities, applications and challenges. *European Journal of Innovation Management*. Advance online publication. DOI: 10.1108/ejim-02-2024-0129

Sikder, A. S. (2023). Artificial Intelligence-Enabled Transformation in Bangladesh: Overcoming Challenges for Socio-Economic Empowerment.: AI-Driven Transformation in Bangladesh. *International Journal of Imminent Science & Technology*, 1(1), 77–96.

Singh, R. J. (2023). Transforming higher education: The power of artificial intelligence. International Journal of Multidisciplinary Research in Arts. *Science and Technology*, 1(3), 13–18.

Strielkowski, W., Grebennikova, V., Lisovskiy, A., Rakhimova, G., & Vasileva, T. (2024). AI-driven adaptive learning for sustainable educational transformation. *Sustainable Development*. Advance online publication. DOI: 10.1002/sd.3221

Sultana, M., & Haque, M. S. (2018). The cause of low implementation of ICT in education sector considering higher education: A study on Bangladesh. *Canadian Social Science*, 14(12), 67–73.

Sultana, R., & Faruk, M. (2024). Does artificial intelligence increase learners' sustainability in higher education: Insights from Bangladesh. *Journal of Data Information and Management*, 6(2), 161–172. DOI: 10.1007/s42488-024-00121-4

Šumak, B., López-de-Ipiña, D., Dziabenko, O., Correia, S. D., de Carvalho, L. M. S., Lopes, S., . . . Pušnik, M. (2024, May). AI-Based Education Tools for Enabling Inclusive Education: Challenges and Benefits. In 2024 47th MIPRO ICT and Electronics Convention (MIPRO) (pp. 472-477). IEEE.

Tan, S. (2023). Exploiting Disruptive Innovation in Learning and Teaching. In *Learning Intelligence* (pp. 149–176). Innovative and Digital Transformative Learning Strategies., DOI: 10.1007/978-981-19-9201-8_4

Tariq, M. U. (2024). The role of AI in skilling, upskilling, and reskilling the workforce. In *Advances in educational technologies and instructional design book series* (pp. 408–420). https://doi.org/DOI: 10.4018/979-8-3693-2440-0.ch023

The Daily Star. (2022, March 29). Shikho aspires to make learning more accessible. *The Daily Star*. https://www.thedailystar.net/supplements/get-set-study-abroad/news/shikho-aspires-make-learning-more-accessible-2993831

Villasenor, A. (2024, September 4). *AI Grading in Peer Reviews: Enhancing Coursera's Learning Experience with Faster, High-Quality Feedback*. Coursera Blog. https://blog.coursera.org/ai-grading-in-peer-reviews-enhancing-courseras-learning-experience-with-faster-high-quality-feedback/

Wu, S., Chen, N., Xiao, A., Zhang, P., Jiang, C., & Zhang, W. (2024). AI-Empowered Virtual Network Embedding: A Comprehensive survey. *IEEE Communications Surveys and Tutorials*, 1. Advance online publication. DOI: 10.1109/comst.2024.3424533

Yamijala, S. M. S., Chodisetty, R. S. C. M., Chakravorty, C., & Sai, K. P. (2024). AI-Powered Learning revolutionizing smart education with personalized learning styles. In *Advances in educational technologies and instructional design book series* (pp. 191–212). https://doi.org/DOI: 10.4018/979-8-3693-8151-9.ch007

Yekollu, R. K., Ghuge, T. B., Biradar, S. S., Haldikar, S. V., & Kader, O. F. M. A. (2024). AI-Driven Personalized Learning Paths: Enhancing education through Adaptive Systems. In *Algorithms for intelligent systems* (pp. 507–517). https://doi.org/DOI: 10.1007/978-981-97-3191-6_38

Yue, M., Jong, M. S., & Ng, D. T. K. (2024). Understanding K–12 teachers' technological pedagogical content knowledge readiness and attitudes toward artificial intelligence education. *Education and Information Technologies*. Advance online publication. DOI: 10.1007/s10639-024-12621-2

Zaman, M. P. A., Hasan, N., Islam, M. H., & Amin, M. R. (2024). Evaluating the impact of primary education in Bangladesh: An In-Depth Investigation of Bagha Upazila in the Rajshahi District. *Indonesian Research Journal on Education*, 4(1). Advance online publication. DOI: 10.31004/irje.v4i1.420

Zawacki-Richter, O., Marín, V. I., Bond, M., & Gouverneur, F. (2019). Systematic review of research on artificial intelligence applications in higher education – where are the educators? *International Journal of Educational Technology in Higher Education*, 16(1). Advance online publication. DOI: 10.1186/s41239-019-0171-0

Zhou, Z. (2023). Project-Based Learning for Quality Art Teacher Development in the age of AI. www.clausiuspress.com. https://doi.org/DOI: 10.23977/curtm.2023.060607

Zohir, S. (2023). A Framework to Assess Digital Transformation in a Technologically Less-Developed Country: Challenges and Opportunities in Bangladesh. https://ergonline.org/digitalization-in-a-technologically-less-developed-country/

Chapter 12
The Utilization of Artificial Intelligence in Higher Education Institutions in Germany:
Opportunities and Challenges of AI in HEIs

Christopher Bohlens
https://orcid.org/0009-0001-9653-2743
Leuphana University of Lüneburg, Germany

ABSTRACT

This part analyzes the integration of Artificial Intelligence (AI) in German Higher Education Institutions (HEIs), highlighting its transformative potential and associated challenges. AI technologies are increasingly employed to enhance teaching, streamline administration, and accelerate research. Despite their benefits, concerns regarding transparency, equity, data privacy, and accountability are raised. Anticipated European regulations, such as the proposed Artificial Intelligence Act, are expected to further shape AI application in academia. Using empirical case studies from German universities, this manuscript illustrates successful AI integration while addressing the challenges of balancing innovation with ethical and legal considerations. The manuscript concludes with strategic recommendations for policymakers, educators, and technology developers to promote responsible AI adoption, emphasizing the importance of ethical frameworks, human oversight, and interdisciplinary collaboration. This study provides valuable insights into the current and future landscape of AI in HEIs.

DOI: 10.4018/979-8-3693-7949-3.ch012

INTRODUCTION AND BACKGROUND

The incorporation of Artificial Intelligence (AI) into the realm of higher education is fundamentally transforming the operational paradigms of academic institutions, encompassing pedagogical methodologies, administrative functionalities, and research endeavors. AI presents unparalleled opportunities to augment operational efficiency, customize educational experiences, streamline administrative processes, and stimulate innovative research initiatives. As universities across the globe confront the disruptive potential of AI, German Higher Education Institutions (HEIs) are positioned at the vanguard of this evolution, actively investigating the prospects of AI while addressing the associated legal, ethical, and operational complexities.

Within German HEIs, AI is being utilized in diverse applications—ranging from adaptive learning systems that customize instructional content for individual learners, to AI-enhanced administrative frameworks that refine admissions processes and scheduling logistics, as well as research instruments that analyze extensive datasets with unmatched speed and precision. Nevertheless, in conjunction with these technological advancements, apprehensions regarding transparency, equity, privacy, and the necessity for human oversight have emerged, particularly in critical domains such as student evaluations, admissions procedures, and the preservation of academic integrity.

Regulatory structures, including the European General Data Protection Regulation (GDPR) and forthcoming AI-centric legislation, play an instrumental role in influencing the implementation of AI within educational contexts. German universities are required to comply with stringent data protection regulations while ensuring that AI systems operate with transparency and accountability. Furthermore, there exists an increasing imperative for interdisciplinary cooperation among educators, technologists, and policymakers to guarantee that AI frameworks are conceived and employed in manners that resonate with the principles of academic freedom, equity, and justice.

This investigation into the role of AI in German higher education aspires to furnish a thorough examination of the prevailing landscape, elucidating both the prospects and obstacles that lie ahead. By analyzing the practical utilizations of AI, pertinent legal frameworks, ethical implications, and prospective trajectories, this discourse provides significant insights for educators, administrators, and policymakers as they navigate the evolving integration of AI within academic settings. As the utilization of AI in higher education continues to proliferate, it is imperative to ensure that these technologies are employed judiciously to enhance educational outcomes while preserving the integrity of academic institutions.

INTRODUCTION TO UTILIZATION OF AI

Introduction and Background

The emergence of Artificial Intelligence (AI) has instigated a revolutionary shift across a myriad of sectors, fundamentally transforming the operational dynamics and service delivery mechanisms of organizations. The realm of higher education is not immune to this transformation. The extensive potential of AI to augment educational methodologies and outcomes is profound, impacting domains such as individualized learning experiences, administrative optimization, and the advancement of research initiatives (Luckin & Holmes, 2016; Williamson et al., 2023). As academic institutions globally endeavor to assimilate AI into their operational frameworks, the imperative of executing such integration in an effective and ethically responsible manner becomes of utmost importance.

In Germany, recognized for its esteemed higher education framework and unwavering dedication to research prowess, the incorporation of AI within academic establishments presents both formidable challenges and promising opportunities. German Higher Education Institutions (HEIs) are progressively embracing AI technologies to facilitate diverse functions, encompassing admissions protocols, student support services, and the enhancement of research capacities. Nevertheless, this technological adoption is fraught with critical ethical and legal considerations, particularly in relation to data privacy, academic integrity, and the risk of bias in AI-informed decision-making processes (Akgun & Greenhow, 2022; Cantner et al., 2022; Perset et al., 2024; Rammer et al., 2024; Slimi & Carballido, 2023).

This chapter establishes a foundation for an in-depth investigation of AI's role in German HEIs by delineating the current landscape of AI integration, the obstacles encountered, and the regulatory frameworks that oversee AI deployment within educational contexts. It aspires to furnish a foundational comprehension of the subject matter, which will be expounded upon in the ensuing chapters.

The Role of AI in Higher Education

Artificial Intelligence possesses significant transformative capacity within higher education institutions on a global scale. Its applications extend from augmenting pedagogical and learning experiences to refining administrative operations and propelling academic research forward. AI technologies, including machine learning, natural language processing, and predictive analytics, provide avant-garde solutions to intricate educational dilemmas (Zawacki-Richter et al., 2019). For instance, AI-driven adaptive learning platforms are capable of customizing educational material to cater to the unique requirements of individual students, thereby facilitating more effective and engaging learning experiences (Garcia & Adams, 2023; Holmes et al., 2021; Luckin & Holmes, 2016; Stobierski, 2019).

In administrative frameworks, AI can optimize processes such as student admissions, assessment grading, and resource allocation, liberating essential time for educators and administrators to concentrate on more strategic endeavors (Mcafee & Brynjolfsson, 2017). Moreover, the capacity of AI to analyze extensive datasets can bolster decision-making in critical areas such as curriculum design, strategies for student retention, and institutional planning (Arqawi et al., 2022; Daniel, 2014).

Nonetheless, the assimilation of AI within educational environments is accompanied by a myriad of challenges. Issues pertaining to data privacy, the transparency of AI algorithms, and the potential for technology to perpetuate existing biases are central to the ongoing discourse (Eubanks, 2018). These concerns are particularly salient within the higher education context, where the principles of academic freedom, equity, and integrity hold paramount significance.

The Context of German Higher Education

The higher education system in is distinguished by its pronounced focus on research and its dedication to delivering superior educational experiences to a heterogeneous student demographic. The nation's universities are globally acknowledged for their academic excellence and research contributions, particularly in disciplines such as engineering, natural sciences, and social sciences (DAAD, 2023; Deutscher Akademischer Austauschdienst, 2023). Consequently, the incorporation of artificial intelligence (AI) into German higher education institutions (HEIs) constitutes a pivotal domain of advancement, carrying profound implications for the prospective trajectory of the nation's educational framework (Cantner et al., 2022).

Several German universities have commenced experiments with AI technologies across various functions. These endeavors underscore the capacity of AI to enhance the efficiency and efficacy of higher education institutions (Biederbeck et al., 2023; Pisica et al., 2023; Tobor, 2024; Universität Bielefeld, 2024; Universität zu Köln, 2024).

Notwithstanding these progressions, the application of AI within German HEIs is accompanied by considerable debate. The nation's stringent data protection legislation, epitomized by the General Data Protection Regulation (Regulation - 2016/679 - EN - GDPR - EUR-Lex, 2016), imposes notable limitations on the acquisition, retention, and utilization of personal data. Such regulations necessitate meticulous contemplation regarding the implementation of AI technologies, especially in connection with student data and academic records.

Furthermore, ongoing discussions persist regarding the ethical ramifications of AI in educational contexts. Scholars and policymakers have expressed apprehensions regarding the potential of AI to exacerbate existing disparities, both within the academic environment and in the wider labor market (Madan & Ashok, 2023; Memarian & Doleck, 2023; Wang et al., 2023). In light of these concerns, certain German universities have instituted ethical frameworks for the application of AI, striving to ensure that the utilization of these technologies adheres to the principles of equity, transparency, and accountability.

Key Takeaways

The incorporation of AI into German higher education represents a complex and multifaceted challenge, encompassing both considerable opportunities and significant hurdles. As elucidated in this chapter, AI possesses the capacity to transform pedagogical practices, learning methodologies, and administrative functions within HEIs; however, it concurrently engenders critical ethical and legal inquiries that necessitate careful navigation. The subsequent chapters will provide a more in-depth examination of these matters, investigating the specific implementations of AI in German universities, the regulatory structures that govern its application, and the broader ramifications for the future of higher education in Germany.

REGULATORY AND ETHICAL CHALLENGES OF AI IN GERMAN HIGHER EDUCATION

Opening Remarks

As Artificial Intelligence (AI) continues to gain traction within the realm of higher education, it presents a multitude of regulatory and ethical dilemmas. For German Higher Education Institutions (HEIs), effectively addressing these intricacies necessitates a comprehensive understanding of both national and European legal paradigms. This chapter delves into the principal regulatory and ethical considerations pertinent to the deployment of AI within German universities, encompassing issues such as data privacy, transparency, and equity, while offering a comparative examination with analogous challenges encountered by other European nations.

Legal Frameworks Governing AI in German HEIs

Germany's methodology for regulating AI within higher education is fundamentally anchored in its overarching legal framework, particularly the General Data Protection Regulation (GDPR), recognized as one of the most stringent data protection statutes globally. The rigorous stipulations outlined in the GDPR regarding data processing and the necessity for consent present considerable obstacles for universities aspiring to leverage AI technologies for objectives such as predictive analytics and tailored educational experiences.

A predominant legal issue within this framework pertains to the collection and processing of student information. AI systems employed for student assistance, including learning analytics platforms, necessitate access to extensive volumes of personal data, encompassing academic performance and behavioral trends. In accordance with the GDPR, universities are mandated to ensure that such data is processed in a manner that is lawful, transparent, and confined to specific purposes, requiring the explicit consent of the students concerned (Mahieu et al., 2019; Wecks et al., 2024).

Complementing the GDPR, the German Federal Data Protection Act (BDSG - Bundesdatenschutzgesetz, 1978) imposes supplementary responsibilities on HEIs. For instance, it necessitates that universities designate a Data Protection Officer (DPO) tasked with supervising adherence to data protection regulations. Furthermore, the BDSG prescribes that institutions must implement both technical and organizational measures to protect personal data, a requirement that is particularly pertinent in the context of AI systems that manage sensitive information.

Ethical Considerations in AI Implementation

The integration of artificial intelligence within educational frameworks engenders a multitude of ethical dilemmas that transcend mere legal adherence. Among the most significant concerns is the likelihood that artificial intelligence may intensify pre-existing disparities within higher education. For example, algorithmic biases have the potential to yield discriminatory results in critical areas such as admissions and grading, thereby disproportionately impacting students hailing from marginalized communities (Bodemer, 2023; Nassar & Kamal, 2021; Noble, 2018).

Another paramount ethical consideration is the issue of transparency. AI systems frequently function as "black boxes," rendering it challenging for stakeholders to comprehend the mechanisms by which decisions are rendered (Burrell, 2016). Such opacity threatens to erode trust in AI technologies, particularly in high-stakes contexts like student evaluation. To mitigate this concern, several German universities have embraced the principles of explainability and accountability, thereby ensuring that

AI systems operate transparently and that their outputs can be rigorously examined and contested by both students and faculty (Hagendorff, 2020).

The ethical application of artificial intelligence in research also constitutes a significant concern. Academic institutions must guarantee that AI-driven research adheres to the principles of academic integrity and does not infringe upon the rights of research participants. This encompasses considerations regarding informed consent, the employment of AI for surveillance or monitoring purposes, and the potential misuse of AI tools for objectives such as data fabrication or plagi(Gison, 2024)arism (Floridi & Cowls, 2019; Gison, 2024; von Garrel & Mayer, 2023).

Comparative Analysis: Germany and Other European Contexts

While Germany has made notable advancements in the regulation of artificial intelligence in higher education, it is not solitary in confronting these challenges. Other European nations, including the United Kingdom and France, have likewise struggled with the intricacies involved in the integration of AI into their educational systems (Perset et al., 2024).

In the United Kingdom, the regulatory framework governing AI in education is similarly influenced by the GDPR, while also being shaped by national policies pertaining to technology and innovation. The Office for Students, which serves as the regulatory body for higher education in the UK, has issued guidelines regarding the ethical utilization of data analytics, underscoring the necessity for transparency, accountability, and fairness in AI applications (Students, 2018, 2021). This approach contrasts with the German model, which places a stronger emphasis on data protection and privacy.

Conversely, France has adopted a more centralized methodology for regulating artificial intelligence in education, with the government assuming a pivotal role in establishing standards and guidelines. The French Digital Council has delineated a national strategy for AI that encompasses specific provisions for education, such as the formulation of AI ethics charters for universities and research institutions (Villani et al., 2018). This stands in contrast to Germany's more decentralized framework, wherein individual universities possess greater autonomy in formulating their AI policies.

Despite these variances, there exist commonalities across European contexts. All three nations acknowledge the imperative for robust ethical frameworks to steer the application of AI in education and have undertaken initiatives to engage stakeholders in the formulation of these frameworks. There is also a collective apprehension regarding the potential of AI to reinforce existing social inequalities, along with a recognition of the necessity for transparency and accountability in AI systems (EU Commission, 2020).

Future Directions and Policy Recommendations

In anticipation of future developments, there exist multiple domains in which German higher education institutions (HEIs) can enhance their regulatory and ethical frameworks pertaining to artificial intelligence (AI). Primarily, there is an exigent requirement for more explicit guidelines regulating the ethical deployment of AI within educational contexts, particularly with respect to matters such as algorithmic bias and the entitlements of students to contest decisions generated by AI systems. The establishment of a national code of conduct for AI in education, akin to those suggested in the United Kingdom and France, could serve as a significant benchmark for universities.

Furthermore, German universities ought to emphasize transparency in their application of AI technologies, ensuring that both students and faculty are comprehensively apprised of the methodologies employed by AI systems and the potential implications they may harbor for educational outcomes. This initiative could encompass the creation of AI literacy programs designed for students and academic personnel, with the objective of elucidating AI technologies and cultivating an environment characterized by trust and collaboration (Hornberger et al., 2023).

Lastly, there exists a pressing need for enhanced collaboration among universities, policymakers, and industry stakeholders to cultivate AI systems that are not only efficacious but also ethical and equitable. This approach could entail the formation of multi-stakeholder advisory boards tasked with supervising AI initiatives, as well as forging partnerships with technology firms to develop AI instruments that resonate with the values and priorities of the higher education sector.

Overall Assessment

The assimilation of AI into the landscape of German higher education introduces both considerable prospects and formidable challenges. Although the nation possesses a comprehensive legal framework governing the utilization of AI, there remain critical ethical dilemmas that warrant attention. By drawing insights from the experiences of other European nations and engaging in a proactive discourse regarding the role of AI in education, German HEIs can formulate policies and practices that capitalize on the advantages of AI while concurrently safeguarding the rights and interests of their students and staff.

PRACTICAL EXAMPLES AND CASE STUDIES OF AI IN GERMAN HIGHER EDUCATION

Contextual Overview

The integration of artificial intelligence (AI) within German higher education institutions (HEIs) is becoming increasingly prevalent, motivated by an escalating demand for innovative methodologies to optimize academic procedures, research endeavors, and administrative operations. Although AI presents substantial potential to enhance operational efficiency, elevate educational outcomes, and stimulate research activities, its deployment across various institutions has yielded heterogeneous results. This chapter investigates concrete instances from prominent German universities, elucidating successful AI assimilation while concurrently addressing the challenges and constraints encountered in particular scenarios.

AI in Academic Applications

A particularly promising domain for AI application within German HEIs is the sphere of personalized learning and academic assistance. Adaptive learning technologies underpinned by AI are revolutionizing student interaction with course materials, providing bespoke educational experiences that adapt to individual needs and learning modalities (Hüsch et al., 2024; Zawacki-Richter et al., 2019).

For instance, the Technical University of Munich (TUM) has introduced AI-enhanced instruments that customize student learning experiences in extensive online courses. Through AI-based algorithms, students are presented with personalized study recommendations, thereby enhancing engagement and retention metrics (Haase, 2024b; Mikalef et al., 2019; Pyper, 2024; Technische Universität München, 2023). These AI frameworks analyze student data in real time, including quiz performances and participation statistics, to suggest targeted learning resources, assisting students in comprehending challenging concepts more effectively.

Nevertheless, despite the utility of these AI instruments in fostering personalized learning experiences, their deployment engenders concerns regarding student data privacy and transparency. Institutions are obligated to meticulously regulate the introduction of these technologies, ensuring adherence to the European General Data Protection Regulation (GDPR) to protect students' personal information. It is also imperative to maintain transparency in the decision-making processes of AI systems, as students must have confidence that the recommendations generated by these systems are equitable and impartial (Holmes et al., 2021).

AI in Administrative Functions

In addition to its applications within academic settings, artificial intelligence (AI) is progressively being employed to enhance administrative functions within German higher education institutions (HEIs), thus facilitating the optimization of decision-making processes, admissions procedures, and student service operations. The deployment of AI technologies allows for the comprehensive analysis of substantial data sets, thereby promoting more efficient operational frameworks within university departments (Jo, 2024; Mcafee & Brynjolfsson, 2017).

Furthermore, AI applications are actively utilized in student support services. For example, AI-enabled chatbots are increasingly being harnessed to address prevalent student inquiries, offering continuous assistance across areas such as course registration, examination schedules, and campus-related services. Technical University of Munich (TUM) has effectively implemented AI chatbots to manage over 80% of routine inquiries, thus liberating human personnel to concentrate on more intricate tasks (Haase, 2024a, 2024b; Rasul et al., 2023). These AI-oriented solutions not only enhance response times but also enrich the overall student experience, particularly within larger universities encountering substantial volumes of inquiries.

Nevertheless, the integration of AI into administrative functions presents a distinct array of challenges. A significant concern pertains to the propensity for AI systems to replicate biases embedded within historical data, which may culminate in discriminatory implications in processes such as admissions. It is imperative for universities to conduct meticulous audits of AI systems to ensure the non-reinforcement of existing inequities; additionally, they must devise and implement strategies aimed at mitigating bias and ensuring equitable outcomes (Landers & Behrend, 2022; Veale et al., 2018).

Challenges in Scaling AI in German HEIs

While the aforementioned examples underscore the successful integration of artificial intelligence within various contexts, substantial challenges persist in the effort to scale AI across all German higher education institutions (HEIs). A significant barrier is the inadequacy of funding and infrastructural support necessary for the expansive integration of AI technologies. Smaller universities, in particular, frequently lack the financial resources required to invest in the essential technology and expertise (Williamson et al., 2023).

Moreover, there exists resistance from both faculty members and students concerning the perceived "automation" of the educational process. Numerous educators express apprehension that the introduction of AI may jeopardize the humanistic aspects of teaching and learning, especially in domains necessitating nuanced judgment and emotional intelligence, such as mentorship and feedback provided to students (Williamson et al., 2023).

To address these challenges, German universities must prioritize the training and upskilling of faculty members in artificial intelligence literacy, ensuring that they are adequately prepared to collaborate with AI tools and seamlessly integrate them into both their pedagogical and administrative functions. Furthermore, institutions are compelled to formulate comprehensive AI policies that engage with both the prospective benefits and ethical dilemmas associated with the employment of AI within higher education (Floridi & Cowls, 2019).

Navigating Uncertainty, Fostering Competencies, and Redefining Assessment

The increasing integration of artificial intelligence (AI) within academic practice has engendered a considerable degree of uncertainty. Numerous educators and educational institutions encounter a lack of definitive guidance or consensus regarding the adaptation of pedagogical strategies and learning methodologies in light of this technological advancement. This absence of orientation has resulted in unresolved inquiries concerning optimal practices for the incorporation of AI, thereby perpetuating an ongoing atmosphere of disquietude within scholarly communities.

Conversely, universities have initiated efforts to build upon insights garnered from prior digitalization strategies. These institutions are now taking proactive measures to integrate AI into their educational frameworks. This transition is approached with a focus on promoting a culture of empowerment, wherein essential processes are being instituted to facilitate the assimilation of AI tools and systems within the academic milieu.

Notwithstanding the prevailing uncertainties, both educators and learners are increasingly employing AI tools in their routine academic endeavors. This escalating dependence on AI underscores the imperative for secure and equitable access to such technologies. It is essential to ensure that all constituents of the academic community can engage with AI tools devoid of impediments, thereby preserving equity and fostering opportunities for all.

Furthermore, the cultivation of AI competencies is becoming imperative across all strata of academia. The ability to comprehend, interpret, and proficiently utilize AI systems and their outputs has emerged as a fundamental skill set for students, educators, and administrative personnel alike. As AI continues to advance, it is essential that the capabilities of those who engage with it also evolve, ensuring that they can critically interact with AI-generated outputs and utilize these tools to enhance both learning and teaching.

The emergence of AI likewise presents challenges to conventional academic practices and self-conceptions. It compels educators and institutions to reevaluate entrenched methodologies, particularly concerning assessment. The escalating impact of AI has accentuated the necessity for a paradigm shift towards a novel evaluative culture, one that accurately reflects the capabilities and ramifications of these nascent technologies. This transformation, which has long been overdue, has become increasingly urgent as AI propels the metamorphosis of academic environments (Budde et al., 2024; Hense et al., 2023).

Summing Up

Artificial Intelligence has commenced the transformation of the framework of higher education in Germany, presenting pioneering solutions to both scholarly and administrative obstacles. Although certain institutions, have adeptly incorporated AI within their operational structures, there persist considerable challenges that must be addressed, particularly regarding the assurance of equity, transparency, and the safeguarding of personal information. In progressing towards the successful implementation of AI within German Higher Education Institutions, it will be critical to achieve an equilibrium between technological advancement and the ethical responsibilities inherent in higher education, ensuring that AI functions as an instrument for the enhancement, rather than the substitution, of the human dimensions of pedagogy, learning, and administration.

LABELING AND TRANSPARENCY

Beginning

As Artificial Intelligence (AI) increasingly infiltrates higher education, the imperative of ensuring transparency in its implementation has emerged as a vital concern for both educational institutions and regulatory bodies. Transparency is essential for sustaining trust in AI systems, particularly within academic environments where fairness, accountability, and clarity are of utmost importance. In the domain of German higher education institutions (HEIs), the imposition of labeling requirements for AI systems guarantees that students, faculty, and administrators possess comprehensive awareness of the AI technologies being utilized and their repercussions on academic and administrative operations. This chapter investigates the frameworks pertaining to transparency and labeling that govern the utilization of AI within German HEIs, scrutinizing the manner in which these institutions adhere to national and European regulations, including the General Data Protection

Regulation (GDPR), as well as the ethical considerations inherent in transparency concerning AI applications.

The Importance of Transparency in AI

Transparency constitutes a fundamental aspect of the ethical utilization of AI technologies. It guarantees that AI systems function in manners that are comprehensible to users, thus enabling them to trust and interact with the technology in a meaningful way. Within the educational framework, transparency pertains to the elucidation of the operational mechanisms of AI tools to students, faculty, and administrators, ensuring that they are cognizant of how decisions are formulated and what data is being processed.

For example, AI-driven systems employed in grading, admissions, or course recommendations must exhibit transparency in their processes to avert any perceived or actual biases. Recent research has indicated that when students lack awareness regarding the operational functionality of AI systems, there exists a potential risk of eroded trust, which may result in resistance or disengagement (Pasquale, 2015). Consequently, German HEIs are compelled to ensure that transparency is integrally woven into the deployment of AI from both legal and ethical standpoints.

Labeling Requirements in AI Applications

German academic institutions, akin to numerous entities throughout Europe, are governed by the stipulations outlined in the General Data Protection Regulation (GDPR), which underscores the necessity of maintaining transparency in the collection and processing of data. Correspondingly, the imposition of labeling requirements is necessitated to guarantee that artificial intelligence systems explicitly convey their operational status, particularly when they engage in the processing of personal data or execute automated decision-making. The GDPR stipulates that individuals must be apprised if decisions that affect them are derived from automated processing, which constitutes a vital component of upholding transparency (Voigt & Von Dem Bussche, 2017).

In practical application, this stipulates that AI-enhanced instruments utilized in student evaluations, admissions, and administrative functions must incorporate labeling that apprises users of the AI's involvement in the decision-making process. One hyperechogenic example will be, students interacting with AI-facilitated academic advising platforms receive notifications at each juncture regarding the manner in which the system formulates recommendations predicated on their academic history and performance metrics (Beutel et al., 2019). Such labels not only augment trust in the system but also empower students to interrogate or seek further elucidation regarding decisions rendered by AI.

The labeling of AI systems transcends mere compliance and also engages with the broader ethical dilemmas associated with fairness and accountability. Labeling serves to inform users when their interactions are mediated by AI, thereby enabling them to comprehend and contest automated decisions when deemed necessary. At RWTH Aachen University, for example, the institution has instituted an AI transparency protocol that guarantees all AI-generated decisions in domains such as grading or resource distribution are appropriately labeled and elucidated to both students and staff (Barthel & Ciesielski, 2023; Brauner et al., 2023; Kaulbach, 2024; RWTH Aachen, 2024b, 2024c, 2024a; Solis, 2023).

The Role of Explainability and Accountability

Explainability is intrinsically linked to transparency and labeling. Explainability pertains to the capacity to articulate the decision-making processes of AI systems in a manner comprehensible to humans. This aspect is of particular significance within higher education, where AI-informed decisions—such as grading, admissions, or plagiarism detection—can wield considerable repercussions for students (Deck et al., 2024).

Accountability in the realm of AI necessitates that universities uphold oversight mechanisms to assure that AI systems are not only explicable but also subject to audit. This entails the regular examination of AI decisions, particularly in sensitive contexts such as grading or admissions, to ensure that biases do not manifest and that the systems consistently adhere to ethical and legal standards (Gunning et al., 2019; Landers & Behrend, 2022; Lepri et al., 2018)

Ethical and Legal Challenges in Transparency

While transparency constitutes a fundamental requisite, it simultaneously engenders numerous challenges. A principal impediment to achieving transparency in artificial intelligence (AI) lies in the intrinsic complexity of numerous AI algorithms, particularly those pertaining to deep learning models, which are frequently characterized as "black boxes" owing to their limited interpretability (Burrell, 2016). Even when underscored by altruistic intentions, elucidating the methodologies through which specific AI systems arrive at their conclusions can prove to be technically arduous, thereby complicating the ability of higher education institutions (HEIs) to satisfy their obligations regarding transparency (Liaison, 2024).

An additional challenge manifests in the necessity to reconcile transparency with the imperative of privacy. While the General Data Protection Regulation (GDPR) mandates transparency, it concurrently enforces stringent regulations concerning data privacy, compelling universities to adeptly navigate this intricate balance. An excessive disclosure of the operational intricacies of AI systems may inadvertently unveil sensitive information, thereby engendering privacy-related apprehensions. Consequently, German HEIs are compelled to formulate strategies that permit the dissemination of sufficient information to guarantee transparency while simultaneously safeguarding individual privacy.

Furthermore, the imperative of upholding fairness within automated systems presents a significant concern. The pursuit of transparency transcends mere user notification; it also encompasses the critical prevention of biases that may adversely affect vulnerable student demographics. AI systems that are trained on historical datasets may inadvertently sustain pre-existing inequalities, thus necessitating that universities establish transparency mechanisms that concurrently address concerns related to fairness (Binns, 2021). In Germany, multiple universities have proactively integrated fairness auditing tools into their AI systems, ensuring that outcomes are meticulously evaluated for potential biases prior to their application in authentic educational contexts (Chen et al., 2024; von Garrel & Mayer, 2023; Zimmermann, 2024).

Case Studies on Transparency and Labeling in German HEIs

Numerous German universities have undertaken proactive initiatives to guarantee transparency and comply with labeling requirements within their AI systems. Another hypo theoretical example would, the AI technologies employed in student admissions are supplemented by comprehensive transparency reports, elucidating the processes involved in data handling and decision-making. The university has also instituted a coherent labeling system that apprises applicants of the utilization of AI in decision-making procedures, thereby fostering trust in the system (Solis, 2023; Stahl & Wright, 2018).

At several universities, the AI-driven plagiarism detection system offers comprehensive explanations to both students and faculty regarding the methodologies employed in document analysis and flagging. The labeling system informs students in advance that their submissions will be subjected to AI processing, while faculty members benefit from transparency reports that delineate the rationale behind the algorithm's decisions (Hutson, 2024; Joamets, 2022; Mittelstadt et al., 2016). These initiatives have augmented the credibility of the system and have contributed to alleviating concerns related to fairness and potential algorithmic biases.

Synthesis of Findings

The requirements for transparency and labeling constitute indispensable elements of ethically and legally compliant AI systems within German higher education. As AI increasingly integrates into academic and administrative frameworks, the assurance that these systems are transparent, explicable, and accountable is vital for preserving trust, fairness, and ethical standards. German HEIs are at the vanguard of implementing transparency measures; however, challenges persist in reconciling transparency with privacy, ensuring fairness, and rendering complex AI systems interpretable. Looking ahead, the establishment of a robust framework for transparency and labeling will be imperative as universities continue to adopt AI technologies within their educational ecosystems.

LEGAL FRAMEWORKS AND CASE LAW PERTAINING TO AI

As Artificial Intelligence (AI) becomes increasingly embedded within the framework of higher education, the imperative to ensure legal compliance and to navigate the legal ramifications of its implementation is of utmost significance for universities. In Germany, the legal architecture governing the application of AI in educational contexts is influenced by both national statutes and European legislation, including but not limited to the General Data Protection Regulation (GDPR), the German Federal Data Protection Act (BDSG), and various emergent regulations specifically crafted to address concerns pertinent to AI. This chapter delves into the legal frameworks that oversee the deployment of AI within German higher education institutions (HEIs), alongside noteworthy case law that has significantly influenced AI policy within the educational domain. By scrutinizing these frameworks and legal precedents, this chapter aims to furnish a comprehensive understanding of how AI must be administered in alignment with regulatory stipulations, as well as how the legal landscape is adapting in response to the burgeoning presence of AI in academic settings.

The General Data Protection Regulation (GDPR) and AI

The GDPR represents the most extensive regulatory framework governing the utilization of personal data within the European Union (EU), and it directly pertains to the application of AI technologies in the sphere of higher education. AI systems frequently engage in the processing of substantial volumes of personal data, encompassing student records, academic performance metrics, and behavioral information, thereby rendering GDPR compliance a paramount concern for universities. In accordance with the GDPR, data controllers—such as universities—are obligated to guarantee that AI systems process data in a manner that is lawful, equitable, and transparent (Voigt & Von Dem Bussche, 2017).

A principal element of the GDPR is the stipulation for informed consent, which necessitates that universities must adequately inform students, staff, and other relevant stakeholders when their data is subjected to processing by AI systems. This requirement bears specific implications for the application of AI in domains such as admissions, grading, and personalized learning platforms. For example, it is imperative that students are informed when AI methodologies are employed to assess their academic performance, and they must possess the right to contest automated determinations should they perceive these outcomes as unjust or erroneous (DPA, 2024; Holmes et al., 2021; Kieslich et al., 2022; Lim et al., 2023; Mittelstadt et al., 2016).

Another significant consideration under the GDPR is the right to explanation, which grants individuals the entitlement to seek clarification regarding the rationale behind an AI system's specific decision-making process. This provision is particularly pertinent in the context of higher education, where students' academic trajectories may be impacted by AI-generated decisions concerning grades, course placements, and various academic outcomes (Mittelstadt et al., 2016).

The German Federal Data Protection Act (BDSG) and AI

In conjunction with the General Data Protection Regulation (GDPR), Germany has enacted its own Federal Data Protection Act (BDSG), which delineates supplementary guidelines for the utilization of artificial intelligence (AI) within educational institutions. The BDSG augments the GDPR by establishing explicit stipulations for the processing of data, particularly concerning public entities such as universities. A salient characteristic of the BDSG is the mandatory designation of a Data Protection Officer (DPO) across all higher education institutions that engage in extensive processing of personal data (Mahieu et al., 2019; Mergel et al., 2023; Neumann et al., 2024; Rochel, 2021; Voigt & Von Dem Bussche, 2017).

The DPO is tasked with the obligation of ensuring that AI systems adhere to the stipulations set forth by both the GDPR and the BDSG. This responsibility encompasses the execution of routine audits of AI systems to ascertain compliance with privacy regulations and to guarantee that data subjects are adequately informed regarding the utilization of their personal information. Furthermore, the DPO supervises the application of the principle of privacy by design, which necessitates the foundational incorporation of privacy considerations in the design of AI systems, thereby limiting the collection and utilization of personal data to the greatest extent feasible (J. P. Albrecht, 2016).

An illustrative instance of the BDSG's influence on AI within German higher education institutions (HEIs), which uncovered that its AI-driven student evaluation system was acquiring an excess of data beyond what was requisite for its intended objectives. Consequently, the university's DPO mandated the reconfiguration of the system to ensure that it would gather solely the data essential for the generation of academic evaluations, thereby securing compliance with both the GDPR and the BDSG (Khosravi et al., 2023).

Emerging AI-Specific Regulations and Initiatives

In recent years, the European Union has initiated efforts to formulate regulations specifically pertaining to artificial intelligence, including the proposed Artificial Intelligence Act (AIA), which aspires to establish a legal framework for the development, deployment, and utilization of AI systems within the EU. Upon its enactment, this act will engender substantial ramifications for the application of AI in higher education, as it seeks to categorize AI systems according to risk levels and impose varying regulatory obligations contingent upon the degree of risk involved (Nikolinakos, 2023; Proposal for a Regulation of the European Parliament and of the Council Laying down Harmonised Rules on Artificial Intelligence (Artificial Intelligence Act) and Amending Certain Union Legislative Acts, 2021).

For instance, AI systems employed in critical areas such as admissions or grading may be designated as high-risk, necessitating that universities implement stringent measures for transparency, accountability, and data governance. The AIA further accentuates the necessity for human oversight, which is imperative within the educational sphere to guarantee that AI-generated decisions are subject to challenge and review by human educators or administrators (Bullock et al., 2024; Veale & Borgesius, 2021).

In anticipation of these impending regulations, several German higher education institutions have proactively commenced the implementation of compliance strategies.

Notable Case Law and Legal Precedents

As artificial intelligence becomes increasingly integrated into the higher education sector, the incidence of legal disputes pertaining to AI systems is on the rise. In Germany, several pivotal legal cases have emerged that elucidate the manner in which

AI-related legal dilemmas are being navigated within the realm of higher education (P.-G. Albrecht et al., 2024; Boobier, 2022; Karras et al., 2024; Zimmermann, 2024).

One prominent case pertained to the deployment of an AI-driven plagiarism detection system at a German university, wherein a student contested the verdict rendered by the system, asserting that the algorithm unjustly identified his work as plagiarized due to deficiencies in its pattern recognition capabilities. The judicial ruling articulated that although AI instruments possess substantial utility in identifying instances of plagiarism, academic institutions must ascertain that the utilization of such technologies does not supplant human evaluative judgment. This decision emphasized the critical necessity of human oversight in AI applications and the imperative for transparency regarding the operational mechanisms of these tools (Berrezueta Guzman et al., 2023; Gasparyan et al., 2017; Niehues et al., 2022; Schwartmann, 2024).

Another significant legal case revolved around the application of AI within admissions processes at a German university. The institution had instituted an AI system for the assessment of applications; however, a collective of applicants initiated litigation, contending that the algorithm exhibited bias against certain socio-economic demographics. The court determined that while AI could serve as an adjunct in admissions processes, universities are mandated to conduct bias assessments to guarantee that their systems do not disproportionately disadvantage particular groups (Androniceanu, 2023; Bahr, 2024; Haderecker & Binder, 2024; Jack, 2023; Reckling, 2024; Van Busum & Fang, 2023; *VG München, 08.05.2024—M 3 E 24.1136*, 2024; *VG München, 28.11.2023—M 3 E 23.4371*, 2023). This case underscores the paramount significance of fairness and equity in the deployment of AI systems for academic decision-making.

Future Directions for AI Regulation in Higher Education

As artificial intelligence continues to advance, the legal frameworks overseeing its application within higher education will likewise evolve. In the forthcoming years, one can anticipate heightened regulatory scrutiny of AI systems, particularly concerning issues of fairness, accountability, and transparency. Academic institutions must remain vigilant in ensuring that their AI systems adhere to both established legal standards such as the GDPR and BDSG, as well as emergent AI-specific regulations like the Artificial Intelligence Act.

Moreover, legal scholars and policymakers are advocating for the establishment of more comprehensive ethical guidelines to augment existing legal frameworks. These guidelines will prioritize the design and implementation of AI systems that honor the principles of academic freedom, equity, and fairness (Binns, 2021). In pursuit of this objective, German higher education institutions are likely to formulate more extensive AI governance structures that encompass routine audits, mechanisms for bias detection, and enhanced human oversight.

Wrap-Up

The legal frameworks regulating the use of artificial intelligence within German higher education institutions are both robust and continue to adapt in response to the rapid advancements in AI technologies. The GDPR and BDSG lay a solid foundation for the regulation of data protection and privacy, while emerging regulations such as the Artificial Intelligence Act aim to address broader ethical and accountability concerns related to AI utilization in educational contexts. Case law has also contributed significantly to the shaping of AI policy, accentuating the necessity for human oversight, fairness, and transparency. In the future, German higher education institutions will need to persist in their adaptation to these legal challenges, ensuring that AI technologies are employed in a manner that is both legally compliant and ethically sound.

FUTURE DIRECTIONS AND RECOMMENDATIONS

Starting point

Artificial Intelligence (AI) is positioned to revolutionize the landscape of higher education globally, with Germany being no exception to this transformative trend. As Higher Education Institutions (HEIs) in Germany progressively incorporate and assimilate AI technologies, the forthcoming era is anticipated to present both substantial opportunities and considerable challenges. This chapter critically examines the prospective future trajectories of AI within German HEIs, concentrating on the domains of pedagogy, research, and administrative functions. Additionally, it proffers a set of recommendations for policymakers, educators, and technologists aimed at ensuring the implementation of AI occurs in a manner that fosters educational equity, academic excellence, and technological innovation, while remaining compliant with legal and ethical standards.

AI in Pedagogy: Enhancing Teaching and Learning

One of the most compelling applications of AI in the realm of higher education resides in its capacity to augment teaching and learning processes. AI-driven personalized learning systems present the potential to customize educational content according to the distinct needs, learning styles, and progress of individual students, which could markedly enhance learning outcomes (Zawacki-Richter et al., 2019). Adaptive learning platforms that modify the pace and intricacy of lessons in real-time based on student performance metrics are currently undergoing trials in German HEIs. In the foreseeable future, these systems may achieve broader implementation, thereby transforming conventional classrooms into dynamic, AI-enhanced learning environments (Al-Zahrani & Alasmari, 2024; Bećirović & Mattoš, 2024; Wecks et al., 2024).

Furthermore, AI could facilitate more effective feedback mechanisms, delivering immediate and comprehensive responses to students regarding assignments, quizzes, and examinations. AI-based tutoring systems, empowered by natural language processing (NLP) technologies, could provide tailored assistance in disciplines where students encounter the most difficulty (Akiba & Fraboni, 2023; Luckin & Holmes, 2016). For example, institutions such as RWTH Aachen and the Technical University of Munich (TUM) are piloting AI tools designed to offer on-demand tutoring for STEM disciplines, thereby significantly enhancing student retention and engagement levels.

Nevertheless, as AI becomes increasingly embedded within pedagogical frameworks, concerns arise regarding the potential depersonalization of the educational experience. Consequently, it is imperative for educators and institutions to ensure that AI serves as a supportive tool rather than a replacement for human instructors. Future developments in AI-enhanced pedagogy should prioritize hybrid models wherein AI complements faculty instruction, thereby allowing educators to devote more time to creative, critical, and interpersonal teaching endeavors (Holmes et al., 2021; Luckin & Holmes, 2016).

AI in Research: Accelerating Discovery and Innovation

The significance of artificial intelligence (AI) in the realm of research constitutes a domain with substantial potential for advancement. Renowned for their research capabilities, German universities possess the opportunity to harness AI technologies to expedite discoveries across various domains, encompassing both the natural sciences and the humanities. The capacity of AI to process extensive datasets with greater speed and efficiency than conventional methodologies empowers researchers to discern patterns, anticipate trends, and derive insights in manners that were previously unattainable (Akiba & Fraboni, 2023; Carobene et al., 2024; Mcafee & Brynjolfsson, 2017).

Leading the charge in AI-enhanced research in Germany is the Max Planck Society, which has incorporated AI systems within its laboratories to automate data analysis and augment research productivity (Broekhuizen et al., 2023; Majeed & Hwang, 2024; Max Planck Society, 2024). The application of AI systems has facilitated the examination of substantial datasets in genetics, physics, and environmental science, thereby assisting in the revelation of novel discoveries that would have necessitated years to realize through traditional methodologies.

In the domains of social sciences and humanities, AI is fostering innovative research techniques such as text mining and sentiment analysis, which are capable of processing and analyzing extensive corpora of literature, historical documents, and data from social media platforms (Broekhuizen et al., 2023; Daniel, 2014; Khosravi et al., 2023). For example, AI systems are currently employed to investigate trends in political discourse, scrutinize historical texts for linguistic patterns, and examine the progression of cultural trends over time.

In anticipation of future developments, German higher education institutions (HEIs) ought to prioritize interdisciplinary collaborations wherein AI technologies are both developed and implemented in close collaboration between computer scientists and subject matter experts across various fields. This approach will guarantee that AI tools are specifically designed to cater to the unique requirements of diverse research disciplines and to augment, rather than supplant, human insight (Bardakci et al., 2024; Elken, 2024; Kezar, 2005).

AI in Administration: Efficiency and Ethical Considerations

The integration of AI technologies into administrative functions within German HEIs is already underway, yet there exists potential for even greater integration in forthcoming years. AI possesses the capability to optimize administrative processes such as admissions, course scheduling, and resource management (Charalabidis et al., 2024).

Looking ahead, AI-driven administrative tools have the potential to further refine decision-making processes by providing instantaneous insights regarding student enrollment trends, financial performance, and faculty workload distribution. Predictive analytics could serve to identify students who are at risk of discontinuing their studies, thereby enabling institutions to intervene proactively with targeted support strategies (Arqawi et al., 2022; Wecks et al., 2024).

Nevertheless, the growing dependence on AI within administrative contexts also gives rise to ethical dilemmas. It is imperative that AI systems are architected to be transparent, equitable, and accountable. In the absence of stringent oversight, there exists a risk that AI could perpetuate or intensify existing biases, particularly in critical areas such as admissions and recruitment. To mitigate these concerns, universities should establish explicit ethical frameworks governing the utilization of AI in administrative decision-making processes, thereby ensuring that human oversight remains an integral aspect of all AI systems (Binns, 2021; Veale et al., 2018).

Recommendations for Policymakers, Educators, and Technologists

As artificial intelligence (AI) continues to advance, it is imperative for German higher education institutions (HEIs) to formulate comprehensive strategies to effectively navigate the myriad opportunities and challenges that it presents. The subsequent recommendations are designed to ensure the responsible and efficacious implementation of AI within the realm of higher education:

Develop AI Literacy Programs: It is crucial that both students and faculty acquire a foundational comprehension of AI technologies. AI literacy programs ought to be incorporated into curricula across various disciplines to guarantee that all constituents of the academic community possess an understanding of AI's operational mechanisms and its broader implications. This approach will empower students and staff to engage critically with AI systems and cultivate a culture of informed AI utilization.

Implement Clear Ethical Guidelines: It is essential for universities to formulate and enforce ethical guidelines that govern the application of AI in both academic and administrative spheres. These guidelines should comprehensively address matters such as bias, transparency, privacy, and accountability, thereby ensuring that AI systems are congruent with the foundational values of education).

Foster Interdisciplinary Collaboration: To fully harness the potential of AI, it is vital to facilitate interdisciplinary collaboration among computer scientists and subject matter experts. Institutions should endeavor to establish environments wherein experts from diverse fields can collaborate to design AI systems that specifically cater to distinct academic and research requirements.

Ensure Human Oversight: AI systems ought to serve as complements to, rather than substitutes for, human decision-making. In contexts such as pedagogy, research, or administration, human oversight is indispensable to ensuring that AI systems are employed ethically and effectively. Institutions should implement frameworks that permit regular evaluations of AI systems, ensuring that they operate as intended and continue to align with institutional values.

Prepare for Regulatory Changes: As European regulations surrounding AI continue to evolve, it is critical for German universities to proactively anticipate legal requirements to ensure compliance. This preparation entails readiness for forthcoming regulations such as the EU Artificial Intelligence Act, which will impose more stringent requirements on high-risk AI systems utilized in educational settings. Institutions should consistently review and revise their AI policies to maintain compliance with both national and EU regulatory standards.

Recommendations for University Leaders

To begin with, it is imperative that all students cultivate or enhance their foundational proficiencies in the utilization of artificial intelligence (AI). In order to accomplish this objective, it is critical that AI-related competencies are systematically integrated across all academic curricula. Program directors must receive an unequivocal directive to formulate curricula that encompass the development of AI competencies, thereby equipping students to engage with AI in substantively impactful manners.

Furthermore, this directive encompasses the deliberation surrounding the permissibility or prohibition of AI utilization during examinations. The dilemma is not merely a binary choice between the presence or absence of AI, but rather an inquiry into how academic programs can present a thoughtfully curated array of assessment modalities that are congruent with their educational objectives. These modalities should reflect the multifaceted influences of AI on both learning and evaluation processes, affording flexibility while upholding the principles of academic integrity.

Moreover, faculty members exhibit a pronounced enthusiasm for augmenting their understanding of AI, necessitating that universities facilitate avenues for such professional enrichment. To this end, institutions of higher learning must establish dedicated spaces and resources aimed at AI-centric training and broaden continuing education initiatives specifically designed to enhance AI competencies among instructional personnel.

Additionally, when integrating AI tools into pedagogical practices, the principles of equitable access and data privacy must be prioritized. This necessitates the provision of university-wide licenses for AI tools that incur costs, ensuring that all students have the opportunity to utilize these technologies irrespective of their financial circumstances. Through this approach, universities can cultivate an inclusive educational environment wherein all students can engage with AI on an equitable basis.

Finally, universities will be more adept at confronting the challenges introduced by AI tools through collaborative efforts. This necessitates the establishment of an open and critical dialogue among institutions, underpinned by the development of appropriate platforms and formats to facilitate such discussions. The exchange of experiences, best practices, and obstacles will empower universities to navigate the intricate challenges associated with AI integration with greater efficacy (Budde et al., 2024; Hense et al., 2023).

In the End

The prospective landscape of AI in German higher education is replete with promise, presenting the potential to transform pedagogy, research, and administration. Nevertheless, the realization of this potential necessitates meticulous planning, ethical considerations, and adherence to regulatory frameworks. German HEIs must prioritize the conscientious integration of AI technologies, ensuring that such integration enhances educational outcomes while safeguarding the rights and interests of students, faculty, and staff. By promoting interdisciplinary collaboration, instituting ethical guidelines, and guaranteeing human oversight, German universities can assume a leadership role in shaping the future of AI within higher education.

CONCLUSION AND IMPLICATIONS FOR THE FUTURE

Summary of Key Findings

In the course of this investigation into the role of Artificial Intelligence (AI) within German Higher Education Institutions (HEIs), we have observed the transformative impact of AI on diverse facets of academia, encompassing pedagogy, research, administration, and regulatory adherence. The incorporation of AI holds substantial promise for the enhancement of educational quality by facilitating tailored learning experiences, optimizing administrative efficiencies, and expediting the process of research discovery. Concurrently, the advent of AI engenders significant ethical, legal, and social dilemmas, notably concerning issues of transparency, equity, and accountability.

In prior sections, we scrutinized the regulatory frameworks that govern the application of AI in higher education, including the General Data Protection Regulation (GDPR) and the nascent AI-specific regulations emerging within the European Union. These regulatory structures are pivotal in ensuring the responsible utilization of AI technologies, safeguarding the privacy and rights of students, staff, and faculty members. Moreover, we explored practical instances and case studies from German universities that have adeptly integrated AI tools across various domains, alongside the obstacles encountered during their implementation.

The ethical dilemmas associated with AI, such as bias, data privacy, and the imperative for human oversight, were underscored as critical challenges that necessitate attention to preserve trust in these systems. The instances of AI-mediated admissions and grading mechanisms illustrate that, despite the potential for AI to enhance operational efficiency, it is crucial for human educators to remain integral to the decision-making processes to uphold standards of fairness and transparency.

Implications for Policymakers and Educators

The ascendance of artificial intelligence within the realm of higher education engenders both prospects and obstacles for policymakers. On one hand, the integration of AI has the potential to enhance educational outcomes and facilitate more efficient operational practices within universities. Conversely, it demands the formulation of comprehensive legal and ethical frameworks to oversee its deployment. Policymakers are compelled to devise explicit guidelines that advocate for the responsible utilization of AI, ensuring that these technologies do not inadvertently jeopardize the well-being of students or personnel. Their focus should be directed toward establishing regulations that promote transparency, equity, and accountability within AI systems, while simultaneously nurturing innovation and enabling institutions to reap the benefits of technological progress.

Educators also possess a crucial responsibility in shaping the trajectory of AI in higher education. Although AI can offer significant assistance in domains such as personalized learning and administrative functions, it must not supplant the human aspect of education. Faculty members must remain integral to the educational experience, providing the emotional intelligence, critical analysis, and mentorship that artificial intelligence is incapable of replicating. It is imperative for educators to receive training on the effective utilization of AI tools, comprehending their limitations and exploring ways in which they can be assimilated into pedagogical practices in manners that augment, rather than detract from, the educational experience.

Future Directions for AI in Higher Education

Looking ahead, the trajectory of artificial intelligence within the realm of German higher education will hinge upon the meticulous equilibrium between innovation and regulatory frameworks. As AI technologies perpetually advance, it is imperative for universities to exhibit adaptability, continuously evolving in response to emerging tools while ensuring that their application is congruent with the institution's foundational principles of academic freedom, equity, and integrity. Institutions of higher learning must allocate resources towards the development of AI literacy initiatives to guarantee that both students and staff possess the requisite knowledge and competencies to critically and ethically engage with AI technologies.

Furthermore, interdisciplinary collaboration will prove essential for fully realizing the potential of AI within the academic landscape. It is crucial that computer scientists, educators, and policymakers collaborate to construct AI systems tailored to the distinctive requirements of higher education, thereby ensuring that these technologies are employed in manners that are advantageous to the academic community in its entirety. In addition, as AI becomes increasingly entrenched in research practices, one can anticipate significant advancements across various disciplines, spanning from the humanities to the sciences, as AI tools facilitate novel methods for researchers to process and analyze data.

Final words

Artificial intelligence embodies a formidable instrument for the future trajectory of higher education, possessing the capacity to transform the operational frameworks of universities and the modalities through which students engage in learning. Nevertheless, the successful assimilation of AI will necessitate strategic planning, ethical deliberation, and continuous dialogue among educators, technologists, and policymakers. By confronting the challenges associated with transparency, fairness, and accountability, German higher education institutions can leverage the advantages of AI to augment their academic missions while concurrently safeguarding the rights and interests of all constituents within the university community.

As we transition into this new epoch of AI-enhanced education, the pivotal objective will be to ensure that these technologies function as instruments for human empowerment, fostering profound learning experiences, promoting innovation, and bolstering educators in their quest to inspire the forthcoming generation of critical thinkers, creators, and leaders.

REFERENCES

Aachen, R. W. T. H. (2024a). *Funktionen RWTHgpt (RWTHgpt)—IT Center Help*. https://help.itc.rwth-aachen.de/service/1808737e10424937b76e564ed15d8028/article/a7be8edd80274621aae6bebfddd3f459/

Aachen, R. W. T. H. (2024b). *RWTH setzt auf eigenes KI-Tool—RWTH AACHEN UNIVERSITY - Deutsch*. https://www.rwth-aachen.de/cms/root/die-rwth/aktuell/pressemitteilungen/juli-2024/~bipvlz/rwth-setzt-auf-eigenes-ki-tool/

Aachen, R. W. T. H. (2024c). *RWTHgpt—IT Center Help*. https://help.itc.rwth-aachen.de/service/1808737e10424937b76e564ed15d8028/

Akgun, S., & Greenhow, C. (2022). Artificial intelligence in education: Addressing ethical challenges in K-12 settings. *AI and Ethics*, 2(3), 431–440. DOI: 10.1007/s43681-021-00096-7 PMID: 34790956

Akiba, D., & Fraboni, M. C. (2023). AI-Supported Academic Advising: Exploring ChatGPT's Current State and Future Potential toward Student Empowerment. *Education Sciences*, 13(9), 9. Advance online publication. DOI: 10.3390/educsci13090885

Al-Zahrani, A. M., & Alasmari, T. M. (2024). Exploring the impact of artificial intelligence on higher education: The dynamics of ethical, social, and educational implications. *Humanities & Social Sciences Communications*, 11(1), 1–12. DOI: 10.1057/s41599-024-03432-4

Albrecht, J. P. (2016). How the GDPR Will Change the World. *European Data Protection Law Review*, 2(3), 287–289. DOI: 10.21552/EDPL/2016/3/4

Albrecht, P.-G., Borkowski, S., & König, L. (2024, July 23). *Deutsche Hochschulen wagen erste Regulationsschritte*. Forschung und Lehre. https://www.forschung-und-lehre.de/management/deutsche-hochschulen-wagen-erste-regulationsschritte-6550

Androniceanu, A. (2023). The new trends of digital transformation and artificial intelligence in public administration. *Administratie Si Management Public*, 40, 147–155.

Arqawi, S., Zitawi, E., Rabaya, A., Abunasser, B., & Abu-Naser, S. (2022). Predicting University Student Retention using Artificial Intelligence. *International Journal of Advanced Computer Science and Applications*, 13. Advance online publication. DOI: 10.14569/IJACSA.2022.0130937

Bahr, M. (2024, June 12). *VG München: Und noch einmal: Kein Zugang zum Masterstudium, da Täuschung durch KI-erzeugtes Essay.* https://www.dr-bahr.com/news/und-noch-einmal-kein-zugang-zum-masterstudium-da-taeuschung-durch-ki-erzeugtes-essay.html

Bardakci, S., Yelbay Yilmaz, Y., & Dilek Avsaroglu, M. (2024). Global diffusion of quality assurance research in higher education: A study on collaboration and concepts. *Higher Education Research & Development*, 43(3), 657–672. DOI: 10.1080/07294360.2023.2253157

Barthel, J., & Ciesielski, R. (2023, May 15). *Universitäten: Regeln zu ChatGPT oft unklar.* tagesschau.de. https://www.tagesschau.de/wissen/technologie/ki-chatgpt-uni-wissenschaft-101.html

BDSG - Bundesdatenschutzgesetz. (1978). https://www.gesetze-im-internet.de/bdsg_2018/index.html

Bećirović, S., & Mattoš, B. (2024). *Artificial Intelligence in the Transformation of Higher Education: Threats.* Promises and Implementation Strategies., DOI: 10.1108/978-1-83549-480-620241002

Berrezueta Guzman, S., Paulsen, M., & Krusche, S. (2023). *Plagiarism Detection and its Effect on the Learning Outcomes.* 99–108. https://doi.org/DOI: 10.1109/CSEET58097.2023.00021

Biederbeck, A., Giesbert, A., Karolyi, H., Kempka, A., Opel, S., Sperl, A., & de Witt, C. (2023). *KI-Leitfaden der FernUniversität in Hagen: Grundsätze und Orientierungshilfen für die Nutzung von Künstlicher Intelligenz in Lehre und Studium.* https://www.fernuni-hagen.de/zli/docs/6716_ki-leitfaden_-_din_a4_-_web.pdf

Binns, R. (2021). *Fairness in Machine Learning: Lessons from Political Philosophy* (arXiv:1712.03586). arXiv. https://doi.org//arXiv.1712.03586DOI: 10.48550

Bodemer, O. (2023, November 27). Artificial Intelligence in Governance: A Comprehensive Analysis of AI Integration and Policy. *Medium.* https://oliverbodemer.medium.com/artificial-intelligence-in-governance-a-comprehensive-analysis-of-ai-integration-and-policy-8fc1a4a342c5

Boobier, T. (2022). *AI and the Future of the Public Sector: The Creation of Public Sector 4.0.* John Wiley & Sons.

Brauner, P., Hick, A., Philipsen, R., & Ziefle, M. (2023). What does the public think about artificial intelligence?—A criticality map to understand bias in the public perception of AI. *Frontiers of Computer Science*, 5. Advance online publication. DOI: 10.3389/fcomp.2023.1113903

Broekhuizen, T., Dekker, H., de Faria, P., Firk, S., Nguyen, D. K., & Sofka, W. (2023). AI for managing open innovation: Opportunities, challenges, and a research agenda. *Journal of Business Research*, 167, 114196. DOI: 10.1016/j.jbusres.2023.114196

Budde, J., Tobor, J., & Friedrich, J. (2024). *Blickpunkt – Künstliche Intelligenz: Wo stehen die deutschen Hochschulen?* (Hochschulforum Digitalisierung, Ed.). Hochschulforum Digitalisierung. https://www.che.de/download/blickpunkt-kuenstliche-intelligenz-wo-stehen-die-deutschen-hochschulen/

Bullock, J. B., Chen, Y.-C., Himmelreich, J., Hudson, V. M., Korinek, A., Young, M. M., & Zhang, B. (2024). *The Oxford Handbook of AI Governance*. Oxford University Press.

Burrell, J. (2016). How the machine 'thinks': Understanding opacity in machine learning algorithms. *Big Data & Society*, 3(1), 2053951715622512. DOI: 10.1177/2053951715622512

Cantner, U., Dauchert, H., Hölzle, K., & Stolz, C. (2022). Challenges on the Digitalisation of the Universities in the European Higher Education Area: The Case of Germany. In *Transformation Fast and Slow* (pp. 78–102). Brill. https://doi.org/ DOI: 10.1163/9789004520912_005

Carobene, A., Padoan, A., Cabitza, F., Banfi, G., & Plebani, M. (2024). Rising adoption of artificial intelligence in scientific publishing: Evaluating the role, risks, and ethical implications in paper drafting and review process. [CCLM]. *Clinical Chemistry and Laboratory Medicine*, 62(5), 835–843. DOI: 10.1515/cclm-2023-1136 PMID: 38019961

Charalabidis, Y., Medaglia, R., & van Noordt, C. (2024). *Research Handbook on Public Management and Artificial Intelligence*. Edward Elgar Publishing.

Chen, Z., Chen, C., Yang, G., He, X., Chi, X., Zeng, Z., & Chen, X. (2024). Research integrity in the era of artificial intelligence: Challenges and responses. *Medicine*, 103(27), e38811. DOI: 10.1097/MD.0000000000038811 PMID: 38968491

Commission, E. U. (2020, February 19). *White Paper on Artificial Intelligence: A European approach to excellence and trust - European Commission*. https://commission.europa.eu/publications/white-paper-artificial-intelligence-european-approach-excellence-and-trust_en

DAAD. (2023, July 1). *Get to know the higher education system*. Www.Study-in-Germany.De. https://www.study-in-germany.de/en/plan-your-studies/study-options/higher-education-system/

Daniel, B. (2014). Big Data and analytics in higher education: Opportunities and challenges. *British Journal of Educational Technology*, 46. Advance online publication. DOI: 10.1111/bjet.12230

Deck, L., Schoeffer, J., De-Arteaga, M., & Kühl, N. (2024). A Critical Survey on Fairness Benefits of Explainable AI. *The 2024 ACM Conference on Fairness, Accountability, and Transparency*, 1579–1595. https://doi.org/DOI: 10.1145/3630106.3658990

Deutscher Akademischer Austauschdienst, D. (Ed.). (2023, June). *Studieren und Forschen in Deutschland kommentierte WWW-Links*. DAAD. https://static.daad.de/media/daad_de/pdfs_nicht_barrierefrei/in-deutschland-studieren-forschen-lehren/ifa_weblinks_de.pdf

DPA. (2024, March 15). *KI-Nutzung an der Uni beschäftigt Justiz*. https://www.forschung-und-lehre.de/recht/ki-nutzung-an-der-uni-beschaeftigt-justiz-6309

Elken, M. (2024). Collaborative design of governance instruments in higher education. *Studies in Higher Education*, 49(6), 1095–1106. DOI: 10.1080/03075079.2023.2258905

Eubanks, V. (2018). *Automating Inequality: How High-tech Tools Profile, Police, and Punish the Poor* (Illustrated Edition). St Martin's Press.

Floridi, L., & Cowls, J. (2019). A Unified Framework of Five Principles for AI in Society. *Harvard Data Science Review*. Advance online publication. DOI: 10.1162/99608f92.8cd550d1

Garcia, P. A., & Adams, D. J. (2023). Data-Driven Decision Making: Leveraging Analytics and AI for Strategic Advantage. *Research Studies of Business, 1*(02), Article 02.

Gasparyan, A. Y., Nurmashev, B., Seksenbayev, B., Trukhachev, V. I., Kostyukova, E. I., & Kitas, G. D. (2017). Plagiarism in the Context of Education and Evolving Detection Strategies. *Journal of Korean Medical Science*, 32(8), 1220–1227. DOI: 10.3346/jkms.2017.32.8.1220 PMID: 28665055

Gison, C. (2024, April 8). The Role of AI in Preventing Plagiarism and Ensuring Content Originality. *Medium*. https://medium.com/@chasegison/the-role-of-ai-in-preventing-plagiarism-and-ensuring-content-originality-4b53d07949ea

Gunning, D., Stefik, M., Choi, J., Miller, T., Stumpf, S., & Yang, G.-Z. (2019). XAI-Explainable artificial intelligence. *Science Robotics*, 4(37), eaay7120. Advance online publication. DOI: 10.1126/scirobotics.aay7120 PMID: 33137719

Haase, K. (2024a, February 11). *LMU und TU suchen noch nach dem richtigen Umgang mit Künstlicher Intelligenz.* Süddeutsche.de. https://www.sueddeutsche.de/muenchen/kuenstliche-intelligenz-lmu-tu-unsicherheit-studierende-1.6350153

Haase, K. (2024b, July 29). *Lern-Chatbot der TU München: Hilfe ja - Lösung nein.* Süddeutsche.de. https://www.sueddeutsche.de/muenchen/ki-chatbot-chat-gpt-muenchen-tum-studium-lux.9NsArTJGvyeeHESKeNJias

Haderecker, J., & Binder, J. (2024, March 15). *Mit KI-Hilfe an die Uni: Zwei weitere Bewerber abgelehnt.* BR24. https://www.br.de/nachrichten/bayern/mit-ki-hilfe-an-die-uni-zwei-weitere-bewerber-abgelehnt,U76Xlxf

Hagendorff, T. (2020). The Ethics of AI Ethics: An Evaluation of Guidelines. *Minds and Machines*, 30(1), 99–120. DOI: 10.1007/s11023-020-09517-8

Hense, J., Goertz, L., Budde, J., & Friedrich, J. (2023). Monitor Digitalisierung 360°—Wo stehen die deutschen Hochschulen. *Hochschulforum Digitalisierung. Arbeitspapier*, (68), 85.

Holmes, W., Porayska-Pomsta, K., Holstein, K., Sutherland, E., Baker, T., Shum, S., Santos, O. C., Rodrigo, M., Cukurova, M., Bittencourt, I., & Koedinger, K. (2021). Ethics of AI in Education: Towards a Community-Wide Framework. *International Journal of Artificial Intelligence in Education*, 32. Advance online publication. DOI: 10.1007/s40593-021-00239-1

Hornberger, M., Bewersdorff, A., & Nerdel, C. (2023). What do university students know about Artificial Intelligence? Development and validation of an AI literacy test. *Computers and Education: Artificial Intelligence*, 5, 100165. DOI: 10.1016/j.caeai.2023.100165

Hüsch, M., Horstmann, N., & Breiter, A. (2024). *CHECK - Künstliche Intelligenz in Studium und Lehre.* https://www.che.de/download/check-ki-2024/

Hutson, J. (2024). Rethinking Plagiarism in the Era of Generative AI. *Journal of International Communication*, 4. Advance online publication. DOI: 10.54963/jic.v4i1.220

Jack, P. (2023, November 28). *AI 'could reinforce bias' in university admissions.* Times Higher Education (THE). https://www.timeshighereducation.com/news/ai-could-reinforce-bias-university-admissions

Jo, H. (2024). From concerns to benefits: A comprehensive study of ChatGPT usage in education. *International Journal of Educational Technology in Higher Education*, 21(1), 35. DOI: 10.1186/s41239-024-00471-4

Joamets, K. (2022). Plagiarism as a Legal Phenomenon and Algorithm-Based Decision Making. *TalTech Journal of European Studies*, 12, 146–164. DOI: 10.2478/bjes-2022-0015

Karras, O., Lorenz, A.-L., & Auer, S. (2024, September 26). *Chancen einer KI-gestützten Wissenschaft*. Forschung und Lehre. https://www.forschung-und-lehre.de/forschung/chancen-einer-ki-gestuetzten-wissenschaft-6667

Kaulbach, L.-L. (2024, August 9). *Neuer Meilenstein erreicht – RWTHgpt • IT Center Blog*. https://blog.rwth-aachen.de/itc/2024/08/09/neuer-meilenstein-erreicht-rwthgpt/

Kezar, A. J. (2005). Redesigning for Collaboration within Higher Education Institutions: An Exploration into the Developmental Process. *Research in Higher Education*, 46, 831–860. DOI: 10.1007/s11162-004-6227-5

Khosravi, H., Sadiq, S., & Amer-Yahia, S. (2023). Data management of AI-powered education technologies: Challenges and opportunities. *Journal of Learning Letters*. https://doi.org/DOI: 10.59453//XLUD7002

Kieslich, K., Keller, B., & Starke, C. (2022). Artificial intelligence ethics by design. Evaluating public perception on the importance of ethical design principles of artificial intelligence. *Big Data & Society*, 9(1), 20539517221092956. DOI: 10.1177/20539517221092956

Landers, R., & Behrend, T. (2022). Auditing the AI Auditors: A Framework for Evaluating Fairness and Bias in High Stakes AI Predictive Models. *The American Psychologist*, 78. Advance online publication. DOI: 10.1037/amp0000972 PMID: 35157476

Lepri, B., Oliver, N., Letouzé, E., Pentland, A., & Vinck, P. (2018). Fair, Transparent, and Accountable Algorithmic Decision-making Processes. *Philosophy & Technology*, 31(4), 611–627. DOI: 10.1007/s13347-017-0279-x

Liaison. (2024, February 14). *Ethical Considerations for AI in Higher Education: Ensuring Fairness and Transparency*. Liaison. https://www.liaisonedu.com/ethical-considerations-for-ai-in-higher-education-ensuring-fairness-and-transparency/

Lim, T., Gottipati, S., & Cheong, M. (2023). *Ethical Considerations for Artificial Intelligence in Educational Assessments*., DOI: 10.4018/979-8-3693-0205-7.ch003

Luckin, R., & Holmes, W. (2016). *Intelligence Unleashed: An argument for AI in Education*.

Madan, R., & Ashok, M. (2023). AI adoption and diffusion in public administration: A systematic literature review and future research agenda. *Government Information Quarterly*, 40(1), 101774. DOI: 10.1016/j.giq.2022.101774

Mahieu, R., van Hoboken, J., & Asghari, H. (2019). *Responsibility for Data Protection in a Networked World – On the Question of the Controller, 'Effective and Complete Protection' and Its Application to Data Access Rights in Europe* (SSRN Scholarly Paper 3256743). https://doi.org/DOI: 10.2139/ssrn.3256743

Majeed, A., & Hwang, S. O. (2024). Towards Unlocking the Hidden Potentials of the Data-Centric AI Paradigm in the Modern Era. *Applied System Innovation*, 7(4), 4. Advance online publication. DOI: 10.3390/asi7040054

Max Planck Society. (2024). *Research on Artificial Intelligence (AI) at the Max Planck Society*. https://www.mpg.de/19142520/artifical-intelligence

Mcafee, A., & Brynjolfsson, E. (2017). *Machine, Platform, Crowd*. WW Norton.

Memarian, B., & Doleck, T. (2023). Fairness, Accountability, Transparency, and Ethics (FATE) in Artificial Intelligence (AI) and higher education: A systematic review. *Computers and Education: Artificial Intelligence*, 5, 100152. DOI: 10.1016/j.caeai.2023.100152

Mergel, I., Dickinson, H., Stenvall, J., & Gasco, M. (2023). Implementing AI in the public sector. *Public Management Review*, 0(0), 1–14. DOI: 10.1080/14719037.2023.2231950

Mikalef, P., Boura, M., Lekakos, G., & Krogstie, J. (2019). Big data analytics and firm performance: Findings from a mixed-method approach. *Journal of Business Research*, 98, 261–276. DOI: 10.1016/j.jbusres.2019.01.044

Mittelstadt, B. D., Allo, P., Taddeo, M., Wachter, S., & Floridi, L. (2016). The ethics of algorithms: Mapping the debate. *Big Data & Society*, 3(2), 2053951716679679. DOI: 10.1177/2053951716679679

Nassar, A., & Kamal, M. (2021). Ethical Dilemmas in AI-Powered Decision-Making: A Deep Dive into Big Data-Driven Ethical Considerations. *International Journal of Responsible Artificial Intelligence*, 11(8), 8.

Neumann, O., Guirguis, K., & Steiner, R. (2024). Exploring artificial intelligence adoption in public organizations: A comparative case study. *Public Management Review*, 26(1), 114–141. DOI: 10.1080/14719037.2022.2048685

Niehues, N., Fischer, E., Jeremias, C., & Dieterich, P. (2022). *Prüfungsrecht* (8., vollständig neubearbeitete Edition). C.H.Beck.

Nikolinakos, N. T. (2023). *EU Policy and Legal Framework for Artificial Intelligence, Robotics and Related Technologies—The AI Act*. Springer Nature.

Noble, S. U. (2018). *Algorithms of Oppression: How Search Engines Reinforce Racism* (Illustrated Edition). Combined Academic Publ.

Pasquale, F. (2015). *The Black Box Society: The Secret Algorithms That Control Money and Information*. Harvard University Press. https://www.jstor.org/stable/j.ctt13x0hch

Perset, K., Russo, L., & Oder, N. (2024, June 11). *OECD AI Review of Germany: A new phase for Germany's AI strategy*. OECD.AI Policy Observatory. https://oecd.ai/en/wonk/review-germany-2024

Pisica, A. I., Edu, T., Zaharia, R. M., & Zaharia, R. (2023). Implementing Artificial Intelligence in Higher Education: Pros and Cons from the Perspectives of Academics. *Societies (Basel, Switzerland)*, 13(5), 5. Advance online publication. DOI: 10.3390/soc13050118

Pyper, J. (2024, July 1). *Heilbronner Studenten entwickeln KI für einen leichteren Studienalltag*. swr.online. https://www.swr.de/swraktuell/baden-wuerttemberg/heilbronn/heilbronner-studenten-entwickeln-kuenstliche-intelligenz-100.html

Rammer, C., Doherr, T., Kinne, J., & Lenz, D. (2024). *KI-Einsatz in Unternehmen in Deutschland*.

Rasul, T., Nair, S., Kalendra, D., Robin, M., Santini, F., Ladeira, W., Sun, M., Day, I., Rather, A., & Heathcote, L. (2023)... *The Role of ChatGPT in Higher Education: Benefits, Challenges, and Future Research Directions.*, 6. Advance online publication. DOI: 10.37074/jalt.2023.6.1.29

Reckling, C. (2024, August 13). *VG München: KI-Einsatz im Prüfungsrecht*. https://www.anwalt.de/rechtstipps/vg-muenchen-ki-einsatz-im-pruefungsrecht-230279.html

Regulation - 2016/679 - EN - GDPR - EUR-Lex (2016). https://eur-lex.europa.eu/eli/reg/2016/679/oj

Rochel, J. (2021). Ethics in the GDPR: A Blueprint for Applied Legal Theory. *International Data Privacy Law*, 11(2), 209–223. DOI: 10.1093/idpl/ipab007

Schwartmann, R. (2024, May 14). *Was es beim Einsatz von KI rechtlich zu beachten gibt*. Forschung und Lehre. https://www.forschung-und-lehre.de/lehre/autonom-wie-ein-tier-6415

Slimi, Z., & Carballido, B. (2023). Navigating the Ethical Challenges of Artificial Intelligence in Higher Education: An Analysis of Seven Global AI Ethics Policies. *TEM Journal*, 590–602. https://doi.org/DOI: 10.18421/TEM122-02

Solis, T. (2023, May 6). *Die ChatGPT-Richtlinien der 100 größten deutschen Universitäten*. Scribbr. https://www.scribbr.de/ki-tools-nutzen/chatgpt-universitaere-richtlinien/

Stahl, B., & Wright, D. (2018). Ethics and Privacy in AI and Big Data: Implementing Responsible Research and Innovation. *IEEE Security and Privacy*, 16, 26–33. DOI: 10.1109/MSP.2018.2701164

Stobierski, T. (2019, August 26). *The Advantages of Data-Driven Decision-Making | HBS Online*. Business Insights Blog. https://online.hbs.edu/blog/post/data-driven-decision-making

Students, O. for. (2018, March 26). *OfS privacy—Office for Students* (Worldwide). Office for Students. https://www.officeforstudents.org.uk/

Students, O. for. (2021, January 26). *Notifications—Office for Students* (Worldwide). Office for Students. https://www.officeforstudents.org.uk/

Technische Universität München. (2023, July 25). *Regeln für den Umgang mit KI in der Wissenschaft*. https://www.tum.de/aktuelles/alle-meldungen/pressemitteilungen/details/regeln-fuer-den-umgang-mit-ki-in-der-wissenschaft

Tobor, J. (2024, February 7). Blickpunkt: Leitlinien zum Umgang mit generativer KI. *Hochschulforum Digitalisierung*. https://hochschulforumdigitalisierung.de/news/blickpunkt-ki-leitlinien/

Universität Bielefeld. (2024). *ChatGPT - Universität Bielefeld*. https://www.uni-bielefeld.de/themen/pruefungsrecht/chatgpt/

Universität zu Köln. (2024). *ChatGPT*. https://verwaltung.uni-koeln.de/stabsstelle02.1/content/faq/data/chatgpt/index_ger.html

Van Busum, K., & Fang, S. (2023). Analysis of AI Models for Student Admissions: A Case Study. *Proceedings of the 38th ACM/SIGAPP Symposium on Applied Computing*, 17–22. https://doi.org/DOI: 10.1145/3555776.3577743

Veale, M., & Borgesius, F. Z. (2021). Demystifying the Draft EU Artificial Intelligence Act—Analysing the good, the bad, and the unclear elements of the proposed approach. *Computer Law Review International*, 22(4), 97–112. DOI: 10.9785/cri-2021-220402

Veale, M., Van Kleek, M., & Binns, R. (2018). Fairness and Accountability Design Needs for Algorithmic Support in High-Stakes Public Sector Decision-Making. *Proceedings of the 2018 CHI Conference on Human Factors in Computing Systems*, 1–14. https://doi.org/DOI: 10.1145/3173574.3174014

Villani, C., Bonnet, Y., Schoenauer, M., Berthet, C., Levin, F., Cornut, A. C., & Rondepierre, B. (2018). *For a meaningful artificial intelligence: Towards a french and european strategy*. Conseil national du numérique.

Voigt, P., & Von Dem Bussche, A. (2017). *The EU General Data Protection Regulation (GDPR)*. Springer International Publishing., DOI: 10.1007/978-3-319-57959-7

von Garrel, J., & Mayer, J. (2023). Artificial Intelligence in studies—Use of ChatGPT and AI-based tools among students in Germany. *Humanities & Social Sciences Communications*, 10(1), 1–9. DOI: 10.1057/s41599-023-02304-7

Wang, T., Lund, B. D., Marengo, A., Pagano, A., Mannuru, N. R., Teel, Z. A., & Pange, J. (2023). Exploring the Potential Impact of Artificial Intelligence (AI) on International Students in Higher Education: Generative AI, Chatbots, Analytics, and International Student Success. *Applied Sciences (Basel, Switzerland)*, 13(11), 11. Advance online publication. DOI: 10.3390/app13116716

Wecks, J. O., Voshaar, J., Plate, B. J., & Zimmermann, J. (2024). *Generative AI Usage and Academic Performance* (arXiv:2404.19699). arXiv. https://doi.org//arXiv.2404.19699DOI: 10.48550

Williamson, B., Eynon, R., Knox, J., & Davies, H. (2023). *Critical perspectives on AI in education: Political economy, discrimination, commercialization, governance and ethics* (pp. 553–570). https://doi.org/DOI: 10.4337/9781800375413.00037

Zawacki-Richter, O., Marín, V. I., Bond, M., & Gouverneur, F. (2019). Systematic review of research on artificial intelligence applications in higher education – where are the educators? *International Journal of Educational Technology in Higher Education*, 16(1), 39. DOI: 10.1186/s41239-019-0171-0

Zimmermann, V. (2024, June 21). *Artificial intelligence in Germany: Status quo, opportunities and options for economic policy measures*. KfW Research. https://www.kfw.de/PDF/Download-Center/Konzernthemen/Research/PDF-Dokumente-Fokus-Volkswirtschaft/Fokus-englische-Dateien/Fokus-2024-EN/Focus-No.-463-June-2024-AI.pdf

Chapter 13
Exploring Knowledge, Will, Skills, Technological Support, and Use of ChatGPT in Higher Education:
A Cross-Sectional Survey

Sadia Muzaffar Bhutta
https://orcid.org/0000-0003-0343-8932
Aga Khan University, Pakistan

Sohail Ahmad
https://orcid.org/0000-0001-7344-0566
Aga Khan University, Pakistan

Aisha Naz Ansari
https://orcid.org/0000-0003-0938-8980
Aga Khan University, Pakistan

Afaq Ahmed
School of Education and Human Development, Texas A&M University, College Station, USA

Kiran Qasim Ali
Aga Khan University, Pakistan

DOI: 10.4018/979-8-3693-7949-3.ch013

ABSTRACT

The rise of Generative AI chatbots like ChatGPT has sparked debate about their role in higher education. This cross-sectional survey examined students' perceived knowledge, willingness, skills, technological support, and usage of ChatGPT. Using the KWSTU questionnaire, data from 1,218 university students in Sindh, Pakistan, revealed high knowledge and willingness but moderate skill and usage levels. The ChatGPT was reported to have been used for different purposes including reading, writing, and classroom participation. Technological support remained at the lowest end suggesting that the universities were not providing enough support for creating awareness about and necessary orientation to use ChatGPT. Further analysis showed that willingness, skills, and technological support positively predict ChatGPT usage, with willingness being the strongest predictor. Public university students showed a greater inclination to use ChatGPT, while gender had no impact. These findings suggest implications for policy, practice, and research in higher education as AI continues to advance rapidly.

INTRODUCTION

The rapid advancement of technology has penetrated every realm of life including education. A plethora of evidence reveals that the use of technology can enhance the effectiveness of teaching-learning processes in several ways (Sofany & Haggar, 2020; Viberg et al, 2023). For instance, technology can increase access to knowledge and education, promote transparency in assessment, and encourage interactive and personalised learning. In recent times, exponential growth has been observed in technology integration in education, particularly during the COVID-19 pandemic. This growth was further boosted by the integration of Artificial Intelligence (AI) in various aspects of education. Such as personalised learning, intelligent tutoring, automatic grading, and feedback (Vincent-Lancrin & Vlies, 2020; Woll & Wylie, 2016).

Among various AI developments in education, the launch of AI Chatbots (e.g., Chat Generative Pre-Trained Transformer - ChatGPT) has stimulated a heated discussion among educationists regarding its benefits and consequences for teaching learning, particularly in higher education (Atlas, 2023; Farrokhnia et al., 2023). The ChatGPT by Open AI was launched for public use on November 22, 2022, and gained considerable attention as evidenced by its success to surplus million users within a few days (Arif et al., 2023). This tool has been designed using a language model that is pre-trained with a large amount of data, and it is still evolving (Atlas, 2023; Zhia, 2023). It aimed to generate human-like text on a given prompt or conversation potentially engaging the user in natural, open-ended conversation on numerous topics (Atlas, 2023).

The growing literature suggests that ChatGPT can be used in numerous fields including public health (Sinha et al., 2023), agriculture (Gaddikeri et al., 2023), and data science (Hassani & Silva, 2023). Concurrently, it is equally relevant for teachers and students in higher education as it can serve as an assistance tool (Ansari et al., 2023). The literature as well as the general narrative around ChatGPT usage in higher education claims that it improves writing as it generates texts on request around any topic, summarises lengthy manuscripts, and assists in improving quality (Halaweh, 2023). Moreover, it enhances research abilities by delivering data, resources, ideas for uncharted territory, a variety of readings, and support for formulating hypotheses and writing papers (Ansari et al., 2023; Atlas, 2023; Kasneci et al., 2023). It also provides an individualised learning environment along with instant feedback (Ansari et al., 2023; Sok & Heng, 2023). On the flip side, there are also several potential risks including cheating in online exams, plagiarism in graded assignments, and theses writing (Iqbal et al., 2022; Susnjak, 2022) which can negatively affect students' higher-order thinking (i.e., critical thinking, problem-solving, creativity), and reading and writing skills (Farrokhnia et al., 2023).

The application of ChatGPT in academia has become a prominent and widely discussed topic in recent times and has attracted attention from the world as evidenced by our recent systematic review (Ansari et al., 2023). Its potential to revolutionise education means that students and teachers in higher education may increasingly adopt it for various purposes, potentially transforming the way learning takes place. However, this adoption for teaching and learning is not straightforward, as it depends on various key factors including access to the tool, awareness about it, willingness to adopt it, and proficiency in using it.

The literature from international as well as national contexts depicts that the concept is still in its infancy and requires attention to carry out empirical studies to understand baseline knowledge, attitudes, skills, and perceptions among higher education graduate students towards using ChatGPT for academic purposes. Therefore, this study aimed to explore the perceived knowledge, will, skills, technological support, and uses of ChatGPT by students in higher education. The study is guided by two major research questions.

1. What is the perceived level of students' knowledge, will, skills, technological support, and use of ChatGPT across public and private universities in the province of Sindh, Pakistan?
2. Do students' knowledge, will, skill, and technological support predict the use of ChatGPT controlling for their gender and the type of university they are enrolled in?

LITERATURE REVIEW

This section provides an overview of existing literature, beginning with a historical perspective on AI and tracing its evolution to the emergence and uses of ChatGPT. It also examines evidence-based factors contributing to the use of ChatGPT and explores the implications of students using ChatGPT for academic purposes.

AI from Historical Perspective

The history of technology integration in education goes back a few decades when computer-based training (CBT) and computer-aided instruction (CAI) were initially used in education (Beck et al, 1984). Early on, technology was frequently considered a supplementary tool rather than a crucial component of the curriculum. The introduction of the Internet in the 1990s further revolutionised the use of technology in education by providing instructors and students with a wealth of information and channels for communication (Kozma, 2008). As hardware, software, and communication continue to evolve, technology integration today grows and changes. Over time the progression of various educational technologies gained popularity in education and COVID-19 played a significant role since major technological adaptation has been observed (Shenoy et al., 2020). Educational institutions quickly shifted to online and mixed learning methods as schools closed and social distance became necessary (Carrillo & Flores, 2020). The usage of digital tools, communication platforms, and online resources to assist remote instruction significantly increased because of this abrupt change. The process of adaptation and upgradation of technology continued in the post-pandemic era.

In recent times, technology integration has gained significant escalation since technologies started using artificial intelligence (Arif et al., 2023). The utilisation of AI is not only limited to education, but it has also been extended to other fields including medicine, agriculture, and engineering (Kung et al, 2023; Ali & Aysan, 2023). AI is a clever machine, especially intelligent computer programmes, that is a combination of science and engineering (Mccarthy, 2023). Besides, AI refers to computer software that has been trained to interact with the world in ways that would typically require human intelligence (Lukin et al., 2016).

AIEd offers various opportunities for learning including providing personal intelligent tutors, support for collaborative learning, and an authentic virtual environment (Woll & Wylie, 2016; Lukin et al., 2016). In addition, AI in education assists in personalising learning, supporting children with special needs, and aids in assessing novel skills (Vincent-Lancrin & Vlies, 2020). This can be concluded that AI technology in education has the power to unleash the potential of the users.

Keeping in view the current trends it can be anticipated that the integration of AI in education will gain more popularity as it has already achieved milestones.

ChatGPT in Teaching and Learning

With advancements in technology, the possibilities for more authentic learning processes have increased. AI, for example, is used to provide more accurate and personalised feedback based on students' proficiency levels (Wulff et al., 2023). AI has also been employed for various other purposes to enhance students' learning experiences. Studies on AI and chatbots show that students frequently utilise them for completing assignments, academic writing, and language learning, albeit sometimes with low quality (Chen et al., 2023; Huang et al., 2022; Wang et al., 2023).

Additionally, students generally have a positive perception of ChatGPT in education, appreciating its potential applications in providing immediate feedback, answering questions, and supporting personalised and adaptive learning (Limna et al., 2023; Lozano & Blanco Fontao, 2023). However, concerns about the accuracy of information, the potential loss of personal interaction with teachers, and the need for privacy and data security persist (Adams et al., 2023; Kiryakova & Angelova, 2023). ChatGPT is seen as a tool that can support teaching activities, reduce educators' workload, and stimulate critical thinking and creativity in learners (Ansari et al., 2023; Klimova et al., 2024). Students have the proficiency, willingness, and requisite technological infrastructure to use ChatGPT, with a large majority attesting to its ability to augment their learning experience and facilitate task and assignment completions (Adams et al., 2023). However, concerns about unethical use and the danger of learners completely trusting ChatGPT without verifying the authenticity of generated texts emphasise the need for careful monitoring and a balance between the use of ChatGPT and human interaction for effective adoption in language learning and teaching (Vo & Nguyen, 2024).

In teaching, AI is widely used to support instruction and reduce the workload of teachers (Ahmad et al., 2024). It has been used in diverse classrooms and makes it possible to cater to the individual needs of students (Grissom et al., 2013). Teachers are also increasingly using chatbots for clerical tasks like outlining, planning ideas, and creating resources (Ansari et al., 2023). Recent systematic reviews have identified that AI in education (AIEd) improves assessment through adaptive feedback and grading systems (Celik et al., 2022; Zawacki-Richter et al., 2019).

Factors Predicting the Use of ChatGPT

The current literature presents mixed findings regarding the factors that predict students' use of ChatGPT. Studies employing the unified theory of acceptance and use of technology (UTAUT) model have identified significant predictors of higher education students' behavioural intentions and actual usage of ChatGPT. According to Arthur et al. (2024), factors such as hedonic motivation, performance expectancy, effort expectancy, and social influence significantly predict students' behavioural intentions. Additionally, behavioural intention and facilitating conditions were found to influence the actual use of ChatGPT. The study also revealed that habit, age, and gender moderate the relationship between these factors and ChatGPT usage.

An exploratory analysis among Peruvian university students by Diaz-Leon & Iraola-Real (2024) indicated that women have a greater intention to use ChatGPT and use it more frequently than men. The analysis also highlighted that socio-demographic variables, including gender and study mode, influence the intention to use and actual use of ChatGPT. Furthermore, Alshammari & Alshammari (2024) found that performance expectancy and facilitating conditions significantly influence students' intentions to use ChatGPT.

In summary, the use of ChatGPT among students is influenced by various factors such as hedonic motivation, performance expectancy, effort expectancy, and social influence. Gender plays a significant role, with women showing a greater intention and more frequent use of ChatGPT compared to men. Technological support, including performance expectancy and facilitating conditions, also significantly influences students' intentions.

Potential Benefits and Risks of ChatGPT

The development of advanced AI technologies, particularly the recent launch of ChatGPT (generative pre-trained transformer) by OpenAI in late 2022, has led to significant growth in the augmentation of AI. ChatGPT's impressive ability to produce well-structured, logical, and informative responses has attracted a considerable number of subscribers, exceeding one million within its first week of launch. As the leading natural language processing model, ChatGPT utilises an extensive dataset of human conversations for practical application using the OpenAI language model, and demonstrates human-like response generation capabilities, with a focus on personalised and interactive assistance (Caldarini et al., 2022; Atlas, 2023; Naumova, 2023; Plebani, 2023; Susnjak, 2022; Farhi et al., 2023; Jeljeli et al., 2022). The widespread popularity of technology often hinges on its user-friendly interface and utility (Davis, 1989). In the academic realm, ChatGPT has gained prominence for its capacity to enhance writing processes by generating on-demand texts on diverse subjects, condensing lengthy articles for time efficiency, and improving overall readability (Halaweh, 2023). Literature supports the idea that ChatGPT excels in providing solutions, answering complex questions, crafting essays, and expediting the learning process for its users. Moreover, its utility extends to research development, as it displays an ability to analyse and organise substantial data with minimal input (Atlas, 2023; Kasneci et al., 2023). An array of international studies has explored the potential of ChatGPT in the realm of academic writing and scholarly publications (Zhia, 2023; Chaudhry et al., 2023; Hosseini et al., 2023; Cotton et al., 2023). A study by Zhu et al. (2023) suggests that the implementation of ChatGPT can augment educational experiences through the provision of individualised support, facilitation of knowledge retrieval, and cultivation of critical thinking abilities. According to the authors, with sensible usage, ChatGPT has the potential to function as a practical resource that may assist students in enhancing their writing, research, and problem-solving proficiencies. Nevertheless, some voice apprehensions over the possibility of excessive dependence on AI, noting issues such as the suppression of originality, innovation, and independent thought because ChatGPT can produce well-structured texts from any input. That may lead to discrimination against those students who have not used it (Farrokhnia et al., 2023). Additionally, the existing body of literature indicates several potential risks, including instances of cheating in online assessments and plagiarism in graded work (Iqbal et al., 2022; Susnjak, 2022; Cotton et al., 2023). Also, human higher-order thinking abilities may be adversely affected by the use of ChatGPT, given its capability to execute any specified job and the potential for enhancing dependency (Farrokhnia et al., 2023; Rahman & Watanobe, 2023; Raman et al., 2023). The potential for bias in AI systems has been a subject of significant concern across academia. Examples include, first, the susceptibility of AI systems to inherit biases from historical or cultural practices reflected in the training data, which could be adopted by the algorithm (Larsen, 2021). Second, high-stake patterns of AI failures, including biased predictions, emphasising the need for trustworthy AI principles and practices to address such issues (Li et al., 2021). Third, machine learning and AI systems have the computational capacity to make a significantly higher number of decisions and interactions, potentially amplifying the harm caused by biased decisions (Saluja et al., 2022).

METHODOLOGY

The current chapter is extracted from a mixed-methods research aiming to investigate students' and faculty's perceptions and experiences of using ChatGPT in higher education. The study was approved by the Ethical Review Committee of the Aga Khan University. This paper focuses on quantitative data which was collected from students enrolled in selected public and private universities of the province of Sindh using a cross-sectional survey. The cross-sectional survey was guided by two research questions focusing on students' data through i) examining the variation in students' perceptions of knowledge, will, skill, technological support, and use of ChatGPT in higher education, and ii) exploring predictors for students' use of ChatGPT.

Sample

This study involved 1,218 university students from six universities (public=3; private=3) in Sindh – a province of Pakistan. A multi-stage sampling technique was used to recruit a representative sample. Of the seven divisions, five were excluded either because of: i) the absence of universities; or ii) the unavailability of multi-disciplinary universities with education departments. Consequently, two divisions were selected for the sample. In the second stage, universities from these two divisions, which offered both undergraduate and graduate-level degree programmes in various disciplines including education, were selected for data collection. Of the two selected divisions, only one has a representation of the public and private sectors while the other division only has representation of the former. Given the population in the two selected divisions, four universities (public =1; private = 3) were selected from the first division while the two public sector universities were recruited from the second[1] division. This strategic selection helped to recruit the equal representation of public and private sector universities in the final sample. Interestingly, the distribution of students across public and private universities was representative of high enrolment[2] in the public universities of Sindh (HEDR Statistics, 2023).

Survey Questionnaire

The conceptual model of Knezek and Christensen (2000) served as a guiding source to develop a suitable framework for the study. The Knezek and colleagues' model comprised of three factors: will (attitudes, beliefs, openness to change); skill (ability, experience, and acceptance of technology); and technological tools encompassing specific tools. A plethora of empirical studies have supported the Will-Skill-Tool (WST) model's validity and its role in explaining technology integration in education (e.g., Agyei & Voogt, 2011; Grant, 2019; Knezek et al., 2003; Petko, 2012; Scully et al., 2021; Velazquez, 2007).

Previous studies on the integration of technology in higher education revealed that positive attitude and confidence (will), competency to use technology (skills), and access to technology (technological support) are important for the effective use of any technology (e.g., Christensen & Knezek, 2008; Knezek & Christenson,

2016; Tondeur et al., 2012). This is because, positive attitudes, competence, and technological resources are considered essential for effective technology integration (Agyei & Voogt, 2011; Buabeng-Andoh, 2012). However, we added to the framework two other factors: 'knowledge' and 'use' as the former is fundamentally important in providing foundational information and the latter is the logical output of the model. The output – *use* - was also an outcome variable in determining the prediction power of the rest of the four factors (i.e., knowledge, will, skill, and technological support) controlling for relevant demographic characteristics. This resulted in the emergence of KWSTU framework as presented in Figure 1, which was used for developing a questionnaire.

Figure 1. Adapted model for ChatGPT Questionnaire (KWSTU)

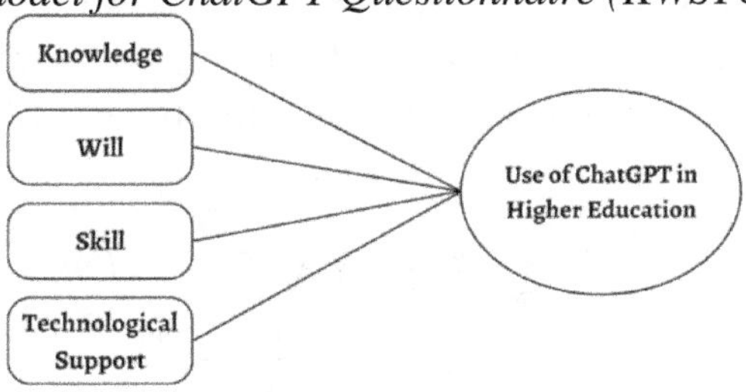

The KWSTU questionnaire encompassed five constructs: knowledge, will, skill, technological support, and the use of ChatGPT. The development of this questionnaire was based solely on a thorough literature review, authors' experiences, and experts' opinions. The first draft of the questionnaire comprised 34 items organised in five constructs, each assessed on a 4-point Likert scale, indicating extent ("Not at all" to "to a greater extent").

The content validity was established using Lawshe's (1975) approach to the Content Validity Index (CVI). The questionnaire underwent review by both national and international experts (n=9), who used a three-point scale to make their judgments on its relevance (1= not relevant; 2= moderately relevant; 3= relevant) and clarity (1= ambiguous; 2= moderately clear; 3= clear). These experts have diverse experience including research, teaching in higher education, and technology integration in the teaching and learning process. Based on experts' qualitative feedback, the authors made minor amendments in the language of items for better readability. The CVR was computed, and its value was determined to be excellent, as indicated in Table 1.

Table 1. Content validation of KWSTU - ChatGPT questionnaire

CVI	Value	Remarks
Relevance	1	Excellent
Clarity	0.963	Excellent

In order to validate the five-factor structure of the questionnaire, confirmatory factor analysis was employed (Field, 2013; Kang, 2013). After conducting CFA with three iterations, the final model was generated which revealed good model indices with no factor loading less than 0.50, as a result four statements were excluded. The final version of KWSTU questionnaire included thirty statements with five distinct factors, revealing a good model fit with acceptable values of CFI (0.973), TLI (0.970), NFI (0.968), RMSEA (0.077), SRMR (0.069). Values of internal consistency as presented in Table 2 fell in acceptable range for all constructs as well as overall KWSTU providing evidence for the questionnaire's reliability.

Table 2. Cronbach's Alpha of KWSTU - ChatGPT questionnaire

Construct	Cronbach's Alpha	No. of items
Knowledge	0.829	8
Will	0.815	5
Skill	0.811	5
Technological Support	0.753	3
Use	0.893	9
Overall	0.911	30

Data Collection

The data collection commenced following approval from the Ethics Review Committee (ERC) and permission from the selected universities. Quantitative data were gathered through a hybrid approach involving both direct and online administration. Survey Monkey was used for online administration of the questionnaire where the link was sent via email and WhatsApp to the participants. However, in some instances, where there was low/no response to online link, a blended approach was used. For instance, a printed version of the QR code was given to the data collectors to visit the universities in person and ask the respondents to scan and complete the questionnaire. This helped in increasing the response rate. On average, respondents spent 10-15 minutes completing the questionnaire.

Data Analysis

The quantitative data were analysed using SPSS version 25. For the first research question, descriptive statistics were employed to ascertain measures of central tendency and standard deviation for overall and construct scores as well as item-level analysis. For the second research question, inferential statistics using multiple linear regression where the use of ChatGPT was added into the equation as an outcome variable while knowledge, will, skill, and technological support were regressed as predictors after controlling for student gender and university type. This allows us to account for the potential influence of the predictors on the use of ChatGPT. All the assumptions of multiple linear regression were fulfilled at various stages to ensure appropriate prediction of the model (Allison, 1999; Tabachnick & Fidel, 2019). First, bivariate correlations were examined to explore the correlation between the outcome variable and predictors. Of the six predictors, one did not correlate (knowledge) with the use of ChatGPT, therefore, it was excluded from the model. Second, a multicollinearity diagnostic was run to investigate possible multicollinearity. The average Variance Inflation Factor (VIF) was 1.20 (closer to 1) with no VIF above 1.5, and the tolerance values were closer to 1, with no value below 0.4 (Allison, 1999), therefore, both the conditions confirmed no collinearity among the predictors (Field, 2013). Furthermore, the model also met the assumptions of normality, linearity, and homoscedasticity for residuals in the model (Tabachnick & Fidel, 2019).

RESULTS

The participants included relatively more females (55%) than males (45%), with the majority falling in the age bracket of 20 to 25 years. Students from public universities participated more (70%) than their counterparts enrolled in the private sector (30%), reflecting the higher enrolment rates in public universities, which are three times higher than the private universities (HEDR Statistics, 2023). Most of the participants were full-time students, with only a fraction being part-time (7%). Similarly, most of the participants were solely studying, with only a fraction (15%) performing a professional job while studying. Regarding assessment types, the majority (71%) reported being assessed through examinations. Meanwhile, a quarter (24%) experienced a combination of examinations and open-book assignments, and a small fraction (5%) were assessed exclusively through open-book assignments.

Students' views about ChatGPT: An overall pattern of KWSTU constructs

Table 3 encapsulates the overall perceptions of students regarding ChatGPT in higher education focused on the KWSTU questionnaire. The findings indicate that students possess a reasonable level of both technical and functional knowledge about ChatGPT (M=2.99; SD=0.66), even though it was introduced a few months before the launch of the study. Additionally, the scores related to the 'Will' construct suggest that students exhibit positive attitude towards ChatGPT (M=2.78; SD=0.75). Furthermore, students possess a variety of technical skills (M=2.54; SD=0.73) to effectively use and engage with ChatGPT. However, they perceive limited support from their universities in terms of access and capacity enhancement to utilise ChatGPT efficiently (M=2.00; SD=0.85). Notably, the data also revealed a diverse range of ChatGPT usage among students for various academic purposes, spanning from individual to classroom levels (M=2.48; SD=0.77).

Table 3. Descriptives of perceived levels of KWSTU

Construct	Mean (SD)
Knowledge	2.99 (0.66)
Will	2.78 (0.75)
Skill	2.54 (0.73)
Technological Support	2.00 (0.85)
Use	2.48 (0.77)

Perceived Knowledge of ChatGPT

Table 4 summarises the students' perceived knowledge including technical and functional aspects of ChatGPT where the score ranged from 3.2 to 2.7.

Table 4. Item-wise analysis of perceived knowledge of ChatGPT

Items	Mean (SD)
ChatGPT is an AI tool.	3.2 (1.0)
ChatGPT performs various tasks.	3.2 (0.9)
ChatGPT is a pre-trained language model.	3.1 (1.0)
How to use ChatGPT.	3.0 (0.9)

continued on following page

Table 4. Continued

Items	Mean (SD)
ChatGPT can promote a copy-paste culture.	3.0 (1.0)
ChatGPT uses users' data.	2.9 (1.0)
Limitation of ChatGPT.	2.8 (0.9)
Ethical considerations of ChatGPT.	2.7 (1.0)

The results indicate that students have demonstrated a clear understanding of both technical and functional aspects of ChatGPT. For instance, students reported their awareness of ChatGPT as an AI tool operating on a pre-trained language model along with acknowledging its limitations. Respondents also displayed familiarity with ChatGPT's utility and its capacity to undertake diverse tasks. Moreover, scoring pattern also revealed an optimal level of understanding of the ethical considerations surrounding ChatGPT's usage, particularly its utilisation of user data to enhance the model. However, it is noteworthy that there is considerable variability in responses, indicating a high degree of dispersion among students' knowledge levels. This suggests that while some students possess a robust understanding, others may still have limited knowledge about ChatGPT's workings.

Perceived Will to Use ChatGPT

Table 5 presents students' willingness to use ChatGPT where the score ranged from 2.9 to 2.5 clearly illustrating a higher degree of confidence and enthusiasm regarding the use of ChatGPT by them.

Table 5. Item-wise analysis of perceived will to use ChatGPT

Items	Mean (SD)
Comfortable interacting with ChatGPT.	2.9 (1.0)
Enthusiastic to explore ChatGPT.	2.9 (1.0)
Optimistic to adapt learning with ChatGPT.	2.8 (1.0)
ChatGPT allows self-paced learning.	2.8 (1.0)
ChatGPT improves high order thinking skills.	2.5 (1.0)

Students reported feeling comfortable interacting with ChatGPT indicating that they might be familiar with giving appropriate prompts to get the desired output. A relatively higher score on enthusiasm to explore ChatGPT signifies that they were eager to stay abreast with continuous advancement in this newly launched AI tool. Furthermore, students not only illustrated their optimism to adapt learning habits with ChatGPT, but they also acknowledged its positive role in allowing them to use it as a personalised learning tool that facilitates self-paced learning. Interestingly, a relatively lower score on ChatGPT's role in improving higher-order thinking reflects their ability to consider the consequences of using this new tool which they are willing to adopt for academic purposes. However, it is important to note that there is a significant degree of variability in their responses, indicating a wide range of perspectives among students. Largely, the analysis of this construct at the item level suggests that students generally exhibit a positive attitude, particularly in their willingness to use ChatGPT in higher education.

Perceived Skill to Use ChatGPT

Table 6 demonstrates students' perceived skills to use ChatGPT where the score ranged from 2.7 to 2.3 illuminating a moderate degree of overall competence to utilise the tool.

Table 6. Item-wise analysis of perceived skill to use ChatGPT

Items	Mean (SD)
Utilise features of ChatGPT.	2.7 (1.0)
Modify ChatGPT-generated information for my tasks.	2.7 (1.0)
Critically evaluate ChatGPT-generated information.	2.6 (1.0)
Technical skills to interact with ChatGPT.	2.5 (0.9)
Troubleshooting skills while using ChatGPT.	2.3 (1.0)

Students reported that they possess adequate skills to utilise features of ChatGPT, which may include customising the tool for personal assistance. Moreover, students rated their skills in modifying ChatGPT-generated information for their task in hand relatively high. While students have rated their skills of utilising features of ChatGPT to generate information and customising this information for their tasks relatively higher, interestingly, they rated their skills relatively lower on critically evaluating that information and technical skills to interact with ChatGPT to generate the information (i.e., giving appropriate prompt). As mentioned earlier, the lowest scoring aspect of compendium of skills is troubleshooting which is an important competence to learn and maintain momentum of using any AI tool including ChatGPT. Notably, there is a significant degree of variability in their responses, indicating a wide range of perspectives among students. Mostly, the analysis of this construct suggests that students generally exhibit a certain level of competence in using ChatGPT for their tasks.

Perceived Provision of Technological Support to Use ChatGPT

Table 7 presents students' perceived views on technological support they received at the institutional level to use ChatGPT. As it was the lowest scoring construct the mean score at the item level ranges 2.1 to 1.9 unveiling a lower degree of overall technological support.

Table 7. Item-wise analysis of provision of technological support to use ChatGPT

Items	Mean (SD)
University updates about ChatGPT.	2.1 (1.0)
University provides training to use ChatGPT.	2.1 (1.0)
University purchased ChatGPT-4.	1.9 (1.0)

Students reported limited updates and training concerning the awareness and use of ChatGPT. Similarly, universities are less inclined to provide students with access to subscribed ChatGPT features, typically requiring a paid version. The perceptions of students suggest that universities are generally less proactive in responding to ChatGPT by providing access to additional features, keeping students informed about such tools, and offering training on their usage. Notably, there is a significant degree of variability in their responses, indicating a wide range of perspectives among students. This suggests that technological support varies across different groups when it comes to using ChatGPT.

Perceived Use of ChatGPT

Table 8 illustrates students' use of ChatGPT for several academic tasks. The mean score at the item level ranges from 2.8 to 2.3 revealing that students utilise ChatGPT for diverse academic tasks.

Table 8. Item-wise analysis of students' use of ChatGPT

Items	Mean (SD)
Idea generation for assignment.	2.8 (1.0)
Proofread and refined assignments.	2.5 (1.0)
Research purpose.	2.5 (1.0)
Written communication practice.	2.5 (1.0)
Classroom participation.	2.4 (1.0)

continued on following page

Table 8. Continued

Items	Mean (SD)
Paraphrase and rewrite copied text for assignment.	2.4 (1.0)
Read summaries of books.	2.4 (1.0)
Scan and skim academic readings.	2.4 (1.0)
Write complete assignment.	2.3 (1.0)

Students claimed to use ChatGPT for generating ideas related to their assigned tasks, as well as for proofreading their written drafts to enhance the quality of their assignments. Students also reported utilising ChatGPT for research-related purposes, including brainstorming research questions, conducting literature reviews, formulating methodologies, and analysing collected data. Encouragingly, students are harnessing ChatGPT to enhance their language skills, including written communication and reading skills. However, students have shown less inclination to use ChatGPT for writing complete assignments. This suggests that students view their use of ChatGPT for basic level such as generating ideas and refining drafts rather than solely relying on it for entire assignment writing. Notably, there is a significant degree of variability in their responses, reflecting a diverse range of ChatGPT uses among students.

Multiple regression model

Table 9 explains the prediction powers of five factors (i.e., will, skill, technological support, student gender, and university type) on students' use of ChatGPT.

Table 9. Predictors of the use of ChatGPT

Predictors	Standardised Coefficient (Beta)
Will	0.315***
Skill	0.283***
Technological Support	0.219***
Student Gender *(Male = 1; Female = 2)*	0.005 (ns)
University Type *(Public = 1; Private = 2)*	-0.179***
$R^2 = 0.419$	
[F (5, 1139) = 165.762, p<0.001]	
*p<0.05; **p<0.01; ***p<0.001	

The analysis of multiple linear regression determined the factors predicting students' use of ChatGPT in higher education. The model presents four predictors which explained 41.9% of the variance (R^2= 0.419). The F-test indicates that all three components of WST (i.e., will, skill, and technological support) and the type of university, along with the outcome variable (i.e., the use of ChatGPT), in the model had a significant linear relationship [$F(5, 1139) = 165.762, p<0.001$]. Notably, among these, the key predictors for the use of ChatGPT are students perceived will, skill, and technological support related to ChatGPT, significantly contributing to the use of ChatGPT with strong variances explained of 31%, 28%, and 21.9%, respectively. This indicates that students who perceive themselves as confident, competent, and well-supported are more likely to use ChatGPT for their academic tasks compared to those who lack confidence, competence, and resource provisions.

Furthermore, the type of university explained 17.9% of the variance in the use of ChatGPT for academic tasks. This underscores that students enrolled in public universities tend to use ChatGPT more frequently than their counterparts in private universities. However, gender did not significantly contribute to the use of ChatGPT, suggesting that students of both genders utilise ChatGPT for their academic tasks.

DISCUSSION

The results reveal university students' collective perceived knowledge, will, skill, and technological support in using ChatGPT in higher education. Despite ChatGPT's recent introduction in November 2022, the findings indicate that students have quickly adapted to and gained a reasonable level of both technical and functional knowledge about the tool. This suggests that ChatGPT's design and ease of use have facilitated its rapid adoption. Interestingly, the data also revealed diverse ChatGPT usage among students for various academic purposes, ranging from individual study assistance to collaborative learning tasks within classrooms.

The statistics revealed that students reported to have positive attitudes towards ChatGPT, reflecting their openness and willingness to embrace it as a valuable academic tool. This positive disposition has led to increased adoption and integration of ChatGPT into their learning practices. Furthermore, many students reported having the necessary skills to effectively use and engage with ChatGPT. This underscores the importance of students feeling confident in their ability to interact with ChatGPT, indicating that they perceive themselves as competent users capable of leveraging technology to support their learning and academic tasks. However, students perceive limited support from their universities in terms of access and capacity enhancement for using ChatGPT efficiently. This indicates that students' knowledge of ChatGPT has stimulated both their positive attitudes towards and competence in using it for their academic tasks. Meanwhile, the support provided by the university to access ChatGPT has also affected their use of it.

The results revealed a consistent pattern with the findings of systematic reviews (i.e., Ansari et al., 2023; Imran & Almusharraf, 2023; Faisa, 2024; Montenegro-Rueda et al., 2023) indicating that students in higher education frequently use ChatGPT for academic tasks ranging from receiving to producing new knowledge. The available evidence suggests that students use ChatGPT in higher education for several reasons. First, ChatGPT serves as a helpful tool for teaching and understanding fundamental concepts, accelerating access to material, and completing assignments (Arista et al., 2023; Domenech, 2023). Students also use ChatGPT to search for information and generate initial ideas for tackling academic topics, appreciating its easy search capabilities, quick responses, and summarized information (Costa et al., 2024). It is important to note that more than one-third of university students use ChatGPT for writing assessments, and it has the potential to boost student engagement by providing immersive, dynamic, and customized learning environments (Arista et al., 2023; Ahmad et al., 2024).

However, there are concerns about the accuracy of the information provided by ChatGPT, interestingly students are reluctant to rely solely on it and acknowledge its advantages as well as limitations (Costa et al., 2024). Ethical considerations are also a concern, with potentially negative consequences leading to recommendations for responsible use and clear guidelines in educational institutions (Hasanein & Sobaih, 2023). Having said that, other factors such as effort expectancy, performance expectancy, and knowledge sharing significantly influence students' adoption and use of ChatGPT in higher education (Duong et al., 2023). Therefore, it is reasonable to state that students are using ChatGPT in higher education for academic assistance to enhance their academic productivity. However, this usage raises concerns about accuracy, limitations, and ethical considerations that need to be addressed by higher education institutions.

The possible impacts of ChatGPT on students range from acquiring knowledge to developing skill sets and attitudes towards using ChatGPT for their academic tasks. When students begin using ChatGPT, they recognise its potential to help them understand complex concepts, enhance the quality of learning, and facilitate faster learning among university students (Awal, 2024; Schonberger, 2023). This generally favors students to develop positive attitude towards using ChatGPT as a learning resource because they perceive it as a tool that facilitates and improves their educational experience (Ajlouni et al., 2023; Estrada-Araoz et al., 2024). In the same vein, the use of ChatGPT has the potential to enhance students' critical thinking skills and stimulate their creativity, but it also presents a challenge for educators to modify existing teaching approaches and assessments to boost these skills (Klimova et al., 2024). Additionally, the integration of ChatGPT offers novel avenues for interactive learning and individualised assistance, fostering students' understanding and exploration of complex concepts (Klimova et al., 2024). The other possible factors influencing university students' attitudes and usage of ChatGPT include ease of use, positive attitude towards technology, social influence, perceived usefulness, behavioral and cognitive influences, low perceived risks, and low anxiety (Abdaljaleel et al., 2024). This also includes effort expectancy, performance expectancy, intentions to use ChatGPT, and knowledge sharing have been identified as significant factors influencing higher education students' actual usage of ChatGPT (Duong et al., 2023). However, concerns have been raised about the potential for ChatGPT to diminish students' creativity and critical thinking skills, potentially leading to ethical misconduct (Awal, 2024; Schonberger, 2023). There are also concerns about ChatGPT generating inaccurate results, which can lead to apprehensions and anxiety among some students (Ajlouni et al., 2023; Estrada-Araoz et al., 2024). To sum up, the positive attitudes and skills of students have stimulated their use of ChatGPT, which has impacted their learning. While ChatGPT can enhance learning experiences and skills development, there are concerns about its potential to diminish critical thinking skills and ethical implications.

This study considered KWSTU as an adapted theoretical framework, which assumes that being knowledgeable, enthusiastic, competent, and resourceful leads to the use of a technological tool - in this case, ChatGPT. The findings are consistent with this theoretical framework, indicating that students have acquired a reasonable level of both technical and functional knowledge about ChatGPT. They exhibit positive attitudes towards ChatGPT, and their willingness to embrace it as a valuable academic tool has led to increased adoption and integration into their learning practices. They reported possessing the necessary skills to effectively use and engage with ChatGPT and feel confident in their ability to interact with the tool is crucial for successful integration. Therefore, their positive attitudes and openness towards ChatGPT (will), perceived competence in using and engaging with ChatGPT (skill), and the technological support ChatGPT provides for their learning (tool) direct them to use ChatGPT for their academic tasks. In conclusion, the integration of technological tools, including AI tools, by students requires a combination of knowledge, will, skill, and technological support.

CONCLUSION

This study provides valuable insights into the early adoption and usage of ChatGPT among higher education students in Sindh, Pakistan. Despite the recent introduction of ChatGPT, the findings demonstrate that students have quickly adapted to and embraced this AI tool, showing a strong willingness to integrate it into their academic routines. The positive attitudes and foundational knowledge students possess about ChatGPT have facilitated its adoption, although the study also highlights gaps in the technological support provided by universities.

Students' perceived competence in using ChatGPT, coupled with their willingness, significantly predicts their actual use of the tool. However, the moderate levels of skill and usage suggest that while students are open to leveraging ChatGPT, they may lack the full capability to use it effectively across all academic tasks. This underscores the importance of not only fostering positive attitudes but also providing adequate training and support to enhance students' technical skills and confidence in using AI tools like ChatGPT.

The study also reveals a disparity in support between public and private universities, indicating a need for institutions to play a more active role in promoting and facilitating the use of emerging technologies. Universities should develop policies that address potential biases inherent in AI systems, ensuring these tools do not perpetuate or exacerbate existing inequities within the student population. Moreover, the findings emphasise the benefits and challenges of integrating AI into education. While ChatGPT offers significant potential for enhancing learning experiences, there are valid concerns regarding accuracy, critical thinking, and ethical considerations that must be addressed by higher education institutions. The integration of AI tools in assessment practices, for example, requires careful policy considerations. AI-powered plagiarism detection and proctoring systems can enhance the integrity of exams and assignments, but their use must be balanced with concerns about student privacy, academic freedom, and the potential for false positives.

In conclusion, the successful integration of AI tools like ChatGPT in higher education hinges on a combination of knowledge, will, skill, and technological support. As AI continues to evolve, universities must ensure that students are not only equipped with the necessary technical skills but are also guided in the ethical and effective use of these tools to enrich their academic pursuits. Additionally, at a broader institutional level, the adoption of AI tools can have far-reaching implications for the higher education landscape. Policymakers should consider the potential impact of AI on the job market, as automation may displace certain roles within universities, and ensure that policies are in place to support the reskilling and redeployment of affected staff.

REFERENCES

Abdaljaleel, M., Barakat, M., Alsanafi, M., Salim, N. A., Abazid, H., Malaeb, D., Mohammed, A. H., Hassan, B. A. R., Wayyes, A. M., Farhan, S. S., El-Khatib, S., Rahal, M., Sahban, A., Abdelaziz, D. H., Mansour, N. O., AlZayer, R., Khalil, R., Fekih-Romdhane, F., Hallit, R., & Sallam, M. (2024). A multinational study on the factors influencing university students' attitudes and usage of ChatGPT. *Scientific Reports*, 14(1), 1983. DOI: 10.1038/s41598-024-52549-8 PMID: 38263214

Adams, D., Chuah, K. M., Devadason, E., & Azzis, M. S. A. (2023). From novice to navigator: Students' academic help-seeking behaviour, readiness, and perceived usefulness of ChatGPT in learning. *Education and Information Technologies*, 1–18.

Ahmad, S., Ahmed, A., Bhutta, S. M., & Ansari, A. N. (2024). Transforming Teaching Learning With Chatbots in Higher Education: Quest, Opportunities and Challenges for Quality Enhancement. The Evolution of Artificial Intelligence in Higher Education, 111-127.

Ajlouni, A. O., Wahba, F. A. A., & Almahaireh, A. S. (2023). Students' Attitudes Towards Using ChatGPT as a Learning Tool: The Case of the University of Jordan. *International Journal of Interactive Mobile Technologies*, 17(18). Advance online publication. DOI: 10.3991/ijim.v17i18.41753

Allison, P. D. (1999). *Multiple regression: A primer*. Pine Forge Press.

Alshammari, S. H., & Alshammari, M. H. (2024). Factors Affecting the Adoption and Use of ChatGPT in Higher Education. [IJICTE]. *International Journal of Information and Communication Technology Education*, 20(1), 1–16. DOI: 10.4018/IJICTE.339557

Ansari, A. N., Ahmad, S., & Bhutta, S. M. (2023). Mapping the global evidence around the use of ChatGPT in higher education: A systematic scoping review. *Education and Information Technologies*, 1–41.

Arista, A., Shuib, L., & Ismail, M. A. (2023, November). A Glimpse of chatGPT: An Introduction of Features, Challenges, and Threads in Higher Education. In *2023 International Conference on Informatics, Multimedia, Cyber and Informations System (ICIMCIS)* (pp. 694-698). IEEE. DOI: 10.1109/ICIMCIS60089.2023.10349057

Arthur, F., Salifu, I., & Abam Nortey, S. (2024). Predictors of higher education students' behavioural intention and usage of ChatGPT: The moderating roles of age, gender and experience. *Interactive Learning Environments*, 1–27. DOI: 10.1080/10494820.2024.2362805

Awal, M. R. (2024). *Curse or blessing? Students' experience from ChatGPT with an application of Colaizzi's phenomenological descriptive method of enquiry and content analysis*. Higher Education, Skills and Work-Based Learning.

Chen, Y., Jensen, S., Albert, L. J., Gupta, S., & Lee, T. (2023). Artificial intelligence (AI) student assistants in the classroom: Designing chatbots to support student success. *Information Systems Frontiers*, 25(1), 161–182. DOI: 10.1007/s10796-022-10291-4

Costa, R., Costa, A. L., & Carvalho, A. A. (2024). Use of ChatGPT in Higher Education: A Study with Graduate Students. In *Digital Transformation in Higher Education Institutions* (pp. 121–137). Springer Nature Switzerland. DOI: 10.1007/978-3-031-52296-3_7

Diaz-Leon, I., & Iraola-Real, I. (2024). The Use of ChatGPT by Peruvian University Students: An Exploration of Actual Use and Intention to Use. *RISTI - Revista Iberica de Sistemas e Tecnologias de Informacao, 69*, 89-101.

Domenech, J. (2023, June). ChatGPT in the classroom: friend or foe? In *9th International Conference on Higher Education Advances (HEAd'23)* (pp. 339-347). Editorial Universitat Politècnica de València. DOI: 10.4995/HEAd23.2023.16179

Duong, C. D., Vu, T. N., & Ngo, T. V. N. (2023). Applying a modified technology acceptance model to explain higher education students' usage of ChatGPT: A serial multiple mediation model with knowledge sharing as a moderator. *International Journal of Management Education*, 21(3), 100883. DOI: 10.1016/j.ijme.2023.100883

Estrada-Araoz, E. G., Paredes-Valverde, Y., Quispe-Herrera, R., Gallegos-Ramos, N. A., Rivera-Mamani, F. A., & Romaní-Claros, A. (2024). Investigando la actitud de los estudiantes universitarios hacia el uso del ChatGPT como recurso de aprendizaje. *Data and Metadata*, 3, 268–268. DOI: 10.56294/dm2024268

Faisal, E. (2024, April). Unlock the potential for Saudi Arabian higher education: A systematic review of the benefits of ChatGPT. [). Frontiers Media SA.]. *Frontiers in Education*, 9, 1325601. DOI: 10.3389/feduc.2024.1325601

Field, A. (2013). *Discovering statistics using IBM SPSS statistics* (4th ed.). SAGE.

Hasanein, A. M., & Sobaih, A. E. E. (2023). Drivers and Consequences of ChatGPT Use in Higher Education: Key Stakeholder Perspectives. *European Journal of Investigation in Health, Psychology and Education*, 13(11), 2599–2614. DOI: 10.3390/ejihpe13110181 PMID: 37998071

Huang, W., Hew, K. F., & Fryer, L. K. (2022). Chatbots for language learning—Are they really useful? A systematic review of chatbot-supported language learning. *Journal of Computer Assisted Learning*, 38(1), 237–257. DOI: 10.1111/jcal.12610

Imran, M., & Almusharraf, N. (2023). Analyzing the role of ChatGPT as a writing assistant at higher education level: A systematic review of the literature. *Contemporary Educational Technology*, 15(4), ep464. DOI: 10.30935/cedtech/13605

Kang, H. (2013). A guide on the use of factor analysis in the assessment of construct validity. *Journal of Korean Academy of Nursing*, 43(5), 587–594. DOI: 10.4040/jkan.2013.43.5.587 PMID: 24351990

Kiryakova, G., & Angelova, N. (2023). ChatGPT—A challenging tool for the university professors in their teaching practice. *Education Sciences*, 13(10), 1056. DOI: 10.3390/educsci13101056

Klimova, B., Pikhart, M., & Al-Obaydi, L. H. (2024). Exploring the potential of ChatGPT for foreign language education at the university level. *Frontiers in Psychology*, 15, 1269319. DOI: 10.3389/fpsyg.2024.1269319 PMID: 38655215

Klimova, B., Pikhart, M., & Al-Obaydi, L. H. (2024). Exploring the potential of ChatGPT for foreign language education at the university level. *Frontiers in Psychology*, 15, 1269319. DOI: 10.3389/fpsyg.2024.1269319 PMID: 38655215

Limna, P., Kraiwanit, T., Jangjarat, K., Klayklung, P., & Chocksathaporn, P. (2023). The use of ChatGPT in the digital era: Perspectives on chatbot implementation. *Journal of Applied Learning and Teaching*, 6(1), 64–74.

Lozano, A., & Blanco Fontao, C. (2023). Is the education system prepared for the irruption of artificial intelligence? A study on the perceptions of students of primary education degree from a dual perspective: Current pupils and future teachers. *Education Sciences*, 13(7), 733. DOI: 10.3390/educsci13070733

Montenegro-Rueda, M., Fernández-Cerero, J., Fernández-Batanero, J. M., & López-Meneses, E. (2023). Impact of the implementation of ChatGPT in education: A systematic review. *Computers*, 12(8), 153. DOI: 10.3390/computers12080153

Schönberger, M. (2023). ChatGPT in higher education: the good, the bad, and the University. *Universitat Politecnica de Valencia, 10.*

Tabachnick, B. G., & Fidell, L. S. (2019). *Using multivariate statistics* (7th ed.). Pearson.

Vo, T. K. A., & Nguyen, H. (2024). Generative Artificial Intelligence and ChatGPT in Language Learning: EFL Students' Perceptions of Technology Acceptance. *Journal of University Teaching & Learning Practice*, 21(06). Advance online publication. DOI: 10.53761/fr1rkj58

Wang, T., Lund, B. D., Marengo, A., Pagano, A., Mannuru, N. R., Teel, Z. A., & Pange, J. (2023). Exploring the potential impact of artificial intelligence (AI) on international students in higher education: Generative AI, chatbots, analytics, and international student success. *Applied Sciences (Basel, Switzerland)*, 13(11), 6716. DOI: 10.3390/app13116716

ENDNOTES

1 There were only two public sector universities which fulfil the inclusion criteria and both were selected.

2 The current statistics of the higher education commission reveal 75% enrolment in public and 25% enrolment in private universities in the province of Sindh (HEDR Statistics, 2023).

Compilation of References

Aachen, R. W. T. H. (2024a). *Funktionen RWTHgpt (RWTHgpt)—IT Center Help.* https://help.itc.rwth-aachen.de/service/1808737e10424937b76e564ed15d8028/article/a7be8edd80274621aae6bebfddd3f459/

Aachen, R. W. T. H. (2024b). *RWTH setzt auf eigenes KI-Tool—RWTH AACHEN UNIVERSITY - Deutsch.* https://www.rwth-aachen.de/cms/root/die-rwth/aktuell/pressemitteilungen/juli-2024/~bipvlz/rwth-setzt-auf-eigenes-ki-tool/

Aachen, R. W. T. H. (2024c). *RWTHgpt—IT Center Help.* https://help.itc.rwth-aachen.de/service/1808737e10424937b76e564ed15d8028/

Abbas, N., Imran, A., Manzoor, R., Hussain, T., & Hussain, M H A I. (2023, August 16). Role of Artificial Intelligence Tools in Enhancing Students' Educational Performance at Higher Levels., 36-49. https://doi.org/DOI: 10.55529/jaimlnn.35.36.49

Abdaljaleel, M., Barakat, M., Alsanafi, M., Salim, N. A., Abazid, H., Malaeb, D., Mohammed, A. H., Hassan, B. A. R., Wayyes, A. M., Farhan, S. S., El-Khatib, S., Rahal, M., Sahban, A., Abdelaziz, D. H., Mansour, N. O., AlZayer, R., Khalil, R., Fekih-Romdhane, F., Hallit, R., & Sallam, M. (2024). A multinational study on the factors influencing university students' attitudes and usage of ChatGPT. *Scientific Reports*, 14(1), 1983. DOI: 10.1038/s41598-024-52549-8 PMID: 38263214

Abdamia, N., Puteh, F., & Jah, N J A. (2023, April 10). Investigating Learning Modalities among Diploma Students., 12(2). https://doi.org/DOI: 10.6007/ijarped/v12-i2/16552

Abu-Ghuwaleh, M., & Saffaf, R. (2023). Integrating AI and NLP with project-based learning in STREAM education.

Abuhassna, H., Awae, F., Adnan, M. A., Daud, M., & Almheiri, A. S. (2024). The information age for education via artificial intelligence and machine learning: A bibliometric and systematic literature analysis. *International Journal of Information and Education Technology (IJIET)*, 14(5).

Abulibdeh, A., Zaidan, E., & Abulibdeh, R. (2024). Navigating the confluence of Artificial intelligence and education for sustainable development in the era of industry 4.0: Challenges, opportunities, and ethical dimensions. *Journal of Cleaner Production*, 437, 140527.

Adams, D., Chuah, K. M., Devadason, E., & Azzis, M. S. A. (2023). From novice to navigator: Students' academic help-seeking behaviour, readiness, and perceived usefulness of ChatGPT in learning. *Education and Information Technologies*, •••, 1–18.

Afzal, S., Dempsey, B., D'Helon, C., Mukhi, N., Pribic, M., Sickler, A., & Wilde, L. (2019). The personality of AI systems in education: Experiences with the Watson tutor, a one-on-one virtual tutoring system. *Childhood Education*, 95(1), 44–52. DOI: 10.1080/00094056.2019.1565809

Aghaziarati, A., Nejatifar, S., & Abedi, A. (2023). Artificial Intelligence in Education: Investigating Teacher Attitudes. *AI and Tech in Behavioral and Social Sciences*, 1(1), 35–42.

Ahmad, S., Umirzakova, S., Mujtaba, G., Amin, M., & Whangbo, T. K. (2023, January 1). Education 5.0: Requirements, Enabling Technologies, and Future Directions. Cornell University. https://doi.org//arxiv.2307.15846DOI: 10.48550

Ahmad, A. Y. A. B. (2024). Ethical implications of artificial intelligence in accounting: A framework for responsible ai adoption in multinational corporations in Jordan. *International Journal of Data and Network Science*, 8(1), 401–414.

Ahmad, M. F., & Ghapar, W. R. G. W. A. (2019). The era of artificial intelligence in Malaysian higher education: Impact and challenges in tangible mixed-reality learning system toward self exploration education (SEE). *Procedia Computer Science*, 163, 2–10.

Ahmad, S. F., Alam, M. M., Rahmat, M. K., Mubarik, M. S., & Hyder, S. I. (2022). Academic and administrative role of artificial intelligence in education. *Sustainability*, 14(3), 1101.

Ahmad, S. F., Han, H., Alam, M. M., Rehmat, M. K., Irshad, M., Arraño-Muñoz, M., & Ariza-Montes, A. (2023, June 9). Impact of artificial intelligence on human loss in decision making, laziness and safety in education. *Palgrave Macmillan*, 10(1). Advance online publication. DOI: 10.1057/s41599-023-01787-8 PMID: 37325188

Ahmad, S. F., Rahmat, M. K., Mubarik, M. S., Alam, M. M., & Hyder, S. I. (2021). Artificial intelligence and its role in education. *Sustainability*, 13(22), 12902.

Aithal, P. S., Prabhu, S., & Aithal, S. (2024). Future of Higher Education through Technology Prediction and Forecasting. SSRN *Electronic Journal*. https://doi.org/ DOI: 10.2139/ssrn.4901474

Aizenberg, E., & Van Den Hoven, J. (2020). Designing for human rights in AI. *Big Data & Society*, 7(2), 2053951720949566.

Ajlouni, A. O., Wahba, F. A. A., & Almahaireh, A. S. (2023). Students' Attitudes Towards Using ChatGPT as a Learning Tool: The Case of the University of Jordan. *International Journal of Interactive Mobile Technologies*, 17(18). Advance online publication. DOI: 10.3991/ijim.v17i18.41753

Akbar, Y. A. A., Anuar, A., Zani, R. M., Abdullah, F. N., Sunian, E., & Sulaiman, E. (2024). Exploring the Scholarly Landscape: AI Teaching and Learning in Adult Education. *International Journal of Academic Research in Progressive Education and Development*, 13(1).

Akgun, S., & Greenhow, C. (2022). Artificial intelligence in education: Addressing ethical challenges in K-12 settings. *AI and Ethics*, 2(3), 431–440. PMID: 34790956

Akiba, D., & Fraboni, M. C. (2023). AI-Supported Academic Advising: Exploring ChatGPT's Current State and Future Potential toward Student Empowerment. *Education Sciences*, 13(9), 9. Advance online publication. DOI: 10.3390/educsci13090885

Akter, S., McCarthy, G., Sajib, S., Michael, K., Dwivedi, Y. K., D'Ambra, J., & Shen, K. N. (2021). Algorithmic bias in data-driven innovation in the age of AI. *International Journal of Information Management*, 60, 102387.

Al Darayseh, A. (2023). Acceptance of artificial intelligence in teaching science: Science teachers' perspective. *Computers and Education: Artificial Intelligence*, 4, 100132.

AlAli, R., & Wardat, Y. (2024). Opportunities and Challenges of Integrating Generative Artificial Intelligence in Education. *International Journal of Religion*, 5(7), 784–793.

Alam, A. (2023). Harnessing the Power of AI to Create Intelligent Tutoring Systems for Enhanced Classroom Experience and Improved Learning Outcomes. In *Intelligent Communication Technologies and Virtual Mobile Networks* (pp. 571–591). Springer Nature Singapore.

Alam, A. (2023). Intelligence unleashed : An argument for AI-enabled learning ecologies with real world examples of today and a peek into the future. *AIP Conference Proceedings*. Advance online publication. DOI: 10.1063/5.0129803

Al-Amin, M., Al Zubayer, A., Deb, B., & Hasan, M. (2021). Status of tertiary level online class in Bangladesh: Students' response on preparedness, participation and classroom activities. *Heliyon*, 7(1). PMID: 33506126

Alam, M. J., Pervez, A. K. M. K., Kabir, M. S., Amin, M. R., & Bhuiya, R. A. (2023). The Challenges and Prospects of e-learning in Higher Education in Bangladesh- A review. *Asian Journal of Education and Social Studies*, 43(1), 10–19. DOI: 10.9734/ajess/2023/v43i1931

Alasadi, E. A., & Baiz, C. R. (2023). Generative AI in education and research: Opportunities, concerns, and solutions. *Journal of Chemical Education*, 100(8), 2965–2971.

Albrecht, P.-G., Borkowski, S., & König, L. (2024, July 23). *Deutsche Hochschulen wagen erste Regulationsschritte*. Forschung und Lehre. https://www.forschung-und-lehre.de/management/deutsche-hochschulen-wagen-erste-regulationsschritte-6550

Albrecht, J. P. (2016). How the GDPR Will Change the World. *European Data Protection Law Review*, 2(3), 287–289. DOI: 10.21552/EDPL/2016/3/4

Alekseeva, L., Azar, J., Giné, M., Samila, S., & Taska, B. (2021). The demand for AI skills in the labor market. *Labour Economics*, 71, 102002.

Alexander, B. (2020). *Academia next: The futures of higher education*. Johns Hopkins University Press.

ALGAHTANI, A. (2024). A Comparative Study of AI-Based Educational Tools: Evaluating User Interface Experience and Educational Impact. *Journal of Theoretical and Applied Information Technology*, 102(5).

AlGhamdi, R., Buhari, S M., & Alassafi, M O. (2020, November 1). FROM TEACHING TO COACHING: A CASE STUDY OF A TECHNICAL COMMUNICATION COURSE. International Academy of Technology, Education and Development. https://doi.org/DOI: 10.21125/iceri.2020.0285

Alhawiti, K. M. (2014). Natural language processing and its use in education. *International Journal of Advanced Computer Science and Applications*, 5(12).

Alinezhad, A., & Khalili, J. (2019). *New methods and applications in multiple attribute decision making (MADM)* (Vol. 277). Springer.

Ali, O. A. M., Ali, A. Y., & Sumait, B. S. (2015). Comparison between the effects of different types of membership functions on fuzzy logic controller performance. *International Journal (Toronto, Ont.)*, 76, 76–83.

Alkan, N., & Kahraman, C. (2021). Circular intuitionistic fuzzy TOPSIS method: Pandemic hospital location selection. *Journal of Intelligent & Fuzzy Systems*, 42(1), 1–22.

Allison, P. D. (1999). *Multiple regression: A primer*. Pine Forge Press.

Almansour, M., & Alfhaid, F. M. (2024). Generative artificial intelligence and the personalization of health professional education: A narrative review. *Medicine*, 103(31), e38955. PMID: 39093806

Alowais, S. A., Alghamdi, S. S., Alsuhebany, N., Alqahtani, T., Alshaya, A., Almohareb, S. N., Aldairem, A., Alrashed, M., Saleh, K. B., Badreldin, H. A., Yami, M. S. A., Harbi, S. A., & Albekairy, A. (2023, September 22). Revolutionizing healthcare: The role of artificial intelligence in clinical practice. *BioMed Central*, 23(1). Advance online publication. DOI: 10.1186/s12909-023-04698-z PMID: 37740191

Alqaryouti, I. A. (2010). Inclusion the disabled students in higher education in Oman. *International Journal for cross-disciplinary subjects in education, 1*(4), 216-222.

Alshammari, S. H., & Alshammari, M. H. (2024). Factors Affecting the Adoption and Use of ChatGPT in Higher Education. [IJICTE]. *International Journal of Information and Communication Technology Education*, 20(1), 1–16. DOI: 10.4018/IJICTE.339557

Al-Zahrani, A. M., & Alasmari, T. M. (2024). Exploring the impact of artificial intelligence on higher education: The dynamics of ethical, social, and educational implications. *Humanities & Social Sciences Communications*, 11(1), 1–12. DOI: 10.1057/s41599-024-03432-4

Anderson, W. (2024). Exploring AI-Powered Assistive Technologies: Improving Accessibility for Individuals with Disabilities. *International Journal of Machine Learning for Sustainable Development*, 6(2).

Androniceanu, A. (2023). The new trends of digital transformation and artificial intelligence in public administration. *Administratie Si Management Public*, 40, 147–155.

Annuš, N. (2023, May 25). Chatbots in Education: The impact of Artificial Intelligence based ChatGPT on Teachers and Students., 7(4), 366-370. https://doi.org/DOI: 10.59287/ijanser.739

Ansari, A. N., Ahmad, S., & Bhutta, S. M. (2023). Mapping the global evidence around the use of ChatGPT in higher education: A systematic scoping review. *Education and Information Technologies*, •••, 1–41.

Antara, H. (2023). AI in curriculum Development: Opportunities and challenges. Hurix.com.https://www.hurix.com/wp-content/uploads/2023/06/AI-in-Curriculum-Development-Opportunities-and-Challenges.jpg

Antunes, P., Karadzic, V., Santos, R., Beça, P., & Osann, A. (2011). Participatory multi-criteria analysis of irrigation management alternatives: The case of the Caia irrigation district, Portugal. *International Journal of Agricultural Sustainability*, 9(2), 334–349.

Arista, A., Shuib, L., & Ismail, M. A. (2023, November). A Glimpse of chatGPT: An Introduction of Features, Challenges, and Threads in Higher Education. In *2023 International Conference on Informatics, Multimedia, Cyber and Informations System (ICIMCIS)* (pp. 694-698). IEEE. DOI: 10.1109/ICIMCIS60089.2023.10349057

Arqawi, S., Zitawi, E., Rabaya, A., Abunasser, B., & Abu-Naser, S. (2022). Predicting University Student Retention using Artificial Intelligence. *International Journal of Advanced Computer Science and Applications*, 13. Advance online publication. DOI: 10.14569/IJACSA.2022.0130937

Arranz-Paraíso, S., & Arranz-Paraíso, D. (2024). Artificial Intelligence, Virtual Reality, and Augmented Reality to Enhance Visual Quality and Accessibility in Sustainable Built Environments. In *Design Strategies for Efficient and Sustainable Building Facilities* (pp. 179–199). IGI Global.

Arthur, F., Salifu, I., & Abam Nortey, S. (2024). Predictors of higher education students' behavioural intention and usage of ChatGPT: The moderating roles of age, gender and experience. *Interactive Learning Environments*, •••, 1–27. DOI: 10.1080/10494820.2024.2362805

Artificial intelligence for science: The easy and hard problems. (2024, September 3). https://www.aimodels.fyi/papers/arxiv/artificial-intelligence-science-easy-hard-problems

Asadullah, M. N. (2016). Do Pro-Poor Schools reach out to the poor? Location choice of BRAC and ROSC schools in Bangladesh. *The Australian Economic Review*, 49(4), 432–452. DOI: 10.1111/1467-8462.12180

Ashrafi, A., Zareravasan, A., Rabiee Savoji, S., & Amani, M. (2022). Exploring factors influencing students' continuance intention to use the learning management system (LMS): A multi-perspective framework. *Interactive Learning Environments*, 30(8), 1475–1497.

Atanassov, K. (1986). Intuitionistic fuzzy sets. *Fuzzy Sets and Systems*, 20(1), 87–96.

Atanassov, K. (2020). Circular intuitionistic fuzzy sets. *Journal of Intelligent & Fuzzy Systems*, 39(5), 5981–5986.

Attaran, M., Stark, J., & Stotler, D. (2018). Opportunities and challenges for big data analytics in US higher education: A conceptual model for implementation. *Industry and Higher Education*, 32(3), 169–182.

Awal, M. R. (2024). *Curse or blessing? Students' experience from ChatGPT with an application of Colaizzi's phenomenological descriptive method of enquiry and content analysis*. Higher Education, Skills and Work-Based Learning.

Ayala-Pazmiño, M. (2023, May 2). Artificial Intelligence in Education. *Exploring the Potential Benefits and Risks.*, 8(3), 892–899. DOI: 10.33386/593dp.2023.3.1827

Ayanniyi, R.B. (n.d). Concepts and theories of educational administration. National Open University of Nigeria.

Aydogmus, H. Y., Turkan, Y. S., & Aydogmus, U. (2023). A Bibliometric Analysis of Higher Education and the Sustainable Development Goals. In Advances in educational marketing, administration, and leadership book series (pp. 1–25). https://doi.org/DOI: 10.4018/978-1-6684-8356-5.ch001

Ayeni, O. O., Al Hamad, N. M., Chisom, O. N., Osawaru, B., & Adewusi, O. E. (2024). AI in education: A review of personalized learning and educational technology. *GSC Advanced Research and Reviews*, 18(2), 261–271.

Ayodele, O. S., Aliu, J., Owoeye, F.O., Ajayi, E. A. and Sheidu, A.Y. (2023). The Role of Artificial Intelligence in Curriculum Development and Management. Digital Innovations and Contemporary Research in Science. *Engineering and Technology.11(2).*

Azcona, D. (2019). Artificial Intelligence in computer science and mathematics education (Doctoral dissertation, Dublin City University).

Babu, K. (2021). Artificial intelligence, its applications in different sectors and challenges: Bangladesh context. In *Advanced sciences and technologies for security applications* (pp. 103–119). https://doi.org/DOI: 10.1007/978-3-030-88040-8_4

Babu, K. E. K. (2021). Artificial intelligence in Bangladesh, its applications in different sectors and relevant challenges for the government: An analysis. *International Journal of Public Law and Policy*, 7(4), 319. DOI: 10.1504/ijplap.2021.118891

Bahr, M. (2024, June 12). *VG München: Und noch einmal: Kein Zugang zum Masterstudium, da Täuschung durch KI-erzeugtes Essay.* https://www.dr-bahr.com/news/und-noch-einmal-kein-zugang-zum-masterstudium-da-taeuschung-durch-ki-erzeugtes-essay.html

Bahroun, Z., Anane, C., Ahmed, V., & Zacca, A. (2023). Transforming education: A comprehensive review of generative artificial intelligence in educational settings through bibliometric and content analysis. *Sustainability*, 15(17), 12983.

Baillifard, A., Gabella, M., Lavenex, P. B., & Martarelli, C. S. (2023, January 1). Implementing Learning Principles with a Personal AI Tutor: A Case Study. Cornell University. https://doi.org/DOI: 10.48550/arXiv.2309

Baker, T., Smith, L., & Anissa, N. (2019). Educ-AI-tion rebooted? Exploring the future of artificial intelligence in schools and colleges.

Baker, R. S., & Smith, L. (2019). Using machine learning for real-time adaptation In personalized learning. *Journal of Educational Technology*, 45(2), 1–22.

Baker, T., Smith, L., & Anissa, N. (2019). *Educ-AI-tion rebooted? Exploring the Future of artificial intelligence in schools and colleges.* NESTA.

Balta, N. (2023, June 15).. . *Embracing the Future: AI's Transformative Potential in Educational Research*, 6(2), 1–2. DOI: 10.31757/euer.624

Baneres, D., Rodríguez-Gonzalez, M. E., & Serra, M. (2019). An early feedback prediction system for learners at-risk within a first-year higher education course. *IEEE Transactions on Learning Technologies*, 12, 249–263.

Banes, D., & Behnke, K. (2019). The potential evolution of universal design for learning (UDL) through the lens of technology innovation. In *Universal Access through inclusive Instructional design* (pp. 323-331). Routledge.

Baradwaj, B. K., & Pal, S. (2011). Mining educational data to analyze students' performance. *International Journal of Advanced Computer Science and Applications*, 2, 63–69.

Bardakci, S., Yelbay Yilmaz, Y., & Dilek Avsaroglu, M. (2024). Global diffusion of quality assurance research in higher education: A study on collaboration and concepts. *Higher Education Research & Development*, 43(3), 657–672. DOI: 10.1080/07294360.2023.2253157

Barrett, M., Branson, L., Carter, S., DeLeon, F., Ellis, J., Gundlach, C., & Lee, D. (2019). Using Artificial Intelligence to Enhance Educational Opportunities and Student Services in Higher Education. *Inquiry. The Journal of the Virginia Community Colleges*, 22(1).

Barthel, J., & Ciesielski, R. (2023, May 15). *Universitäten: Regeln zu ChatGPT oft unklar*. tagesschau.de. https://www.tagesschau.de/wissen/technologie/ki-chatgpt-uni-wissenschaft-101.html

Barua, P. D., Vicnesh, J., Gururajan, R., Oh, S. L., Palmer, E., Azizan, M. M., & Acharya, U. R. (2022). Artifcial intelligence enabled personalised assistive tools to enhance education of children with neurodevelopmental disorders-a review. *International Journal of Environmental Research and Public Health*, 19(3), 1192. DOI: 10.3390/ijerph19031192 PMID: 35162220

Baskara, F. R. (2023, September). Navigating pedagogical evolution: The implication of generative AI on the reinvention of teacher education. In Prosiding Seminar Nasional Universitas Jabal Ghafur (Vol. 2, pp. 409-421).

Bates, T., Cobo, C., Mariño, O., & Wheeler, S. (2020). Can artificial intelligence transform higher education? *International Journal of Educational Technology in Higher Education*, 17, 1–12.

Bayne, S. (2015). Teacherbot: Interventions in automated teaching. *Teaching in Higher Education*, 20(4), 455–467.

BDSG - Bundesdatenschutzgesetz. (1978). https://www.gesetze-im-internet.de/bdsg_2018/index.html

Bećirović, S., & Mattoš, B. (2024). *Artificial Intelligence in the Transformation of Higher Education: Threats*. Promises and Implementation Strategies., DOI: 10.1108/978-1-83549-480-620241002

Belenguer, L. (2022). AI bias: Exploring discriminatory algorithmic decision-making models and the application of possible machine-centric solutions adapted from the pharmaceutical industry. *AI and Ethics*, 2(4), 771–787. PMID: 35194591

Bellman, R. E., & Zadeh, L. A. (1970). Decision-making in a fuzzy environment. *Management Science*, 17(4), B-141.

Benbya, H., Davenport, T. H., & Pachidi, S. (2020). Artificial intelligence in organizations: Current state and future opportunities. *MIS Quarterly Executive*, 19(4).

Bengio, Y., Hinton, G. E., Yao, A. C., Song, D., Abbeel, P., Darrell, T., Harari, Y. N., Zhang, Y., Lan, X., Shalev-Shwartz, S., Hadfield, G. K., Mouret, J., Maharaj, T., Hutter, F., Baydin, A. G., McIlraith, S. A., Gao, Q., Acharya, A., Krueger, D., & Mindermann, S. (2024, May 24). Managing extreme AI risks amid rapid progress. *American Association for the Advancement of Science*, 384(6698), 842–845. DOI: 10.1126/science.adn0117 PMID: 38768279

Bentley, C., Aicardi, C., Poveda, S., Magela Cunha, L., Kohan Marzagao, D., Glover, R., & Acar, O. A. (2023). A framework for responsible AI education. Available at *SSRN* 4544010.

Bernacki, M. L., Greene, M. J., & Lobczowski, N. G. (2021). A systematic review of research on personalized learning: Personalized by whom, to what, how, and for what purpose(s*)?Educational Psychology Review*, 33(4), 1675–1715. DOI: 10.1007/s10648-021-09615-8

Berrezueta Guzman, S., Paulsen, M., & Krusche, S. (2023). *Plagiarism Detection and its Effect on the Learning Outcomes*. 99–108. https://doi.org/DOI: 10.1109/CSEET58097.2023.00021

Bettinger, E. P., & Baker, R. (2014). Predicting college graduation using Administrative data: An exploratory analysis. *Center for Education Policy Analysis Working Paper*, 57.

Bhardwaj, K., Garima, N., & Sudan, S. (2024). Artificial intelligence's role and future implementation in education. In *Advances in educational technologies and instructional design book series* (pp. 160–175). https://doi.org/DOI: 10.4018/979-8-3693-2728-9.ch007

Bhutoria, A. (2022). Personalized education and artificial intelligence in the United States, China, and India: A systematic review using a human-in-the-loop model. *Computers and Education: Artificial Intelligence*, 3, 100068.

Biederbeck, A., Giesbert, A., Karolyi, H., Kempka, A., Opel, S., Sperl, A., & de Witt, C. (2023). *KI-Leitfaden der FernUniversität in Hagen: Grundsätze und Orientierungshilfen für die Nutzung von Künstlicher Intelligenz in Lehre und Studium*. https://www.fernuni-hagen.de/zli/docs/6716_ki-leitfaden_-_din_a4_-_web.pdf

Bodemer, O. (2023, November 27). Artificial Intelligence in Governance: A Comprehensive Analysis of AI Integration and Policy. *Medium*. https://oliverbodemer.medium.com/artificial-intelligence-in-governance-a-comprehensive-analysis-of-ai-integration-and-policy-8fc1a4a342c5

Boobier, T. (2022). *AI and the Future of the Public Sector: The Creation of Public Sector 4.0*. John Wiley & Sons.

Boran, F. E., Genç, S., Kurt, M., & Akay, D. (2009). A multi-criteria intuitionistic fuzzy group decision making for supplier selection with TOPSIS method. *Expert Systems with Applications*, 36(8), 11363–11368.

Bossche, P. V. D., Gijselaers, W., Segers, M., Woltjer, G., & Kirschner, P. (2011). Team learning: Building shared mental models. *Instructional Science*, 39(3), 283–301.

Bota-Avram, C. (2023). Bibliometric analysis of sustainable business performance: Where are we going? A science map of the field. *Economic research-. Ekonomska Istrazivanja*, 36(1), 2137–2176.

Bozik, M., & Tracey, M. W. (2002). Content and online learning: An overview of research, theory, and practice. *Educational Media International*, 39(4), 237–246.

Bradford, S. C. (1934). Sources of information on specific subjects. *Engineering (London)*, 137, 85–86.

Brauner, P., Hick, A., Philipsen, R., & Ziefle, M. (2023). What does the public think about artificial intelligence?—A criticality map to understand bias in the public perception of AI. *Frontiers of Computer Science*, 5. Advance online publication. DOI: 10.3389/fcomp.2023.1113903

Brendel, A. B., Mirbabaie, M., Lembcke, T. B., & Hofeditz, L. (2021). Ethical management of artificial intelligence. *Sustainability*, 13(4), 1974.

Broekhuizen, T., Dekker, H., de Faria, P., Firk, S., Nguyen, D. K., & Sofka, W. (2023). AI for managing open innovation: Opportunities, challenges, and a research agenda. *Journal of Business Research*, 167, 114196. DOI: 10.1016/j.jbusres.2023.114196

Brown, M., McCormack, M., Reeves, J., Brook, D. C., Grajek, S., Alexander, B., & Weber, N. (2020). *2020 Educause Horizon Report Teaching and Learning Edition*. EDUCAUSE.

Budde, J., Tobor, J., & Friedrich, J. (2024). *Blickpunkt – Künstliche Intelligenz: Wo stehen die deutschen Hochschulen?* (Hochschulforum Digitalisierung, Ed.). Hochschulforum Digitalisierung. https://www.che.de/download/blickpunkt-kuenstliche-intelligenz-wo-stehen-die-deutschen-hochschulen/

Bulathwela, S., Pérez-Ortiz, M., Holloway, C., Cukurova, M., & Shawe-Taylor, J. (2024). Artificial intelligence alone will not democratise education: On educational inequality, techno-solutionism and inclusive tools. *Sustainability*, 16(2), 781.

Bulathwela, S., Pérez-Ortiz, M., Holloway, C., Cukurova, M., & Shawe-Taylor, J. (2024). Artificial intelligence alone will not democratise education: On Educational Inequality, Techno-Solutionism and Inclusive Tools. *Sustainability*, 16(2), 781. DOI: 10.3390/su16020781

Bullock, J. B., Chen, Y.-C., Himmelreich, J., Hudson, V. M., Korinek, A., Young, M. M., & Zhang, B. (2024). *The Oxford Handbook of AI Governance*. Oxford University Press.

Bulut, O., Beiting-Parrish, M., Casabianca, J. M., Slater, S., Jiao, H., Song, D., Ormerod, C. M., Fabiyi, D. G., Ivan, R., Walsh, C., Rios, O., Wilson, J. M., Yildirim-Erbasli, S. N., Wongvorachan, T., Liu, J. X., Tan, B., & Morilova, P. (2024, June 27). The Rise of Artificial Intelligence in Educational Measurement: Opportunities and Ethical Challenges. Cornell University. https://doi.org/DOI: 10.48550/arXiv.2406

Bureau, U. C. (2024, April 19). Starting Up AI. https://www.census.gov/library/working-papers/2024/adrm/CES-WP-24-09.html

Burgstahler, S., Ladner, R. E., & Bellman, S. (2012). Strategies for increasing the participation in computing of students with disabilities. *ACM Inroads*, 3(4), 42–48.

Burrell, J. (2016). How the machine 'thinks': Understanding opacity in machine learning algorithms. *Big Data & Society*, 3(1), 2053951715622512. DOI: 10.1177/2053951715622512

Cantner, U., Dauchert, H., Hölzle, K., & Stolz, C. (2022). Challenges on the Digitalisation of the Universities in the European Higher Education Area: The Case of Germany. In *Transformation Fast and Slow* (pp. 78–102). Brill. https://doi.org/DOI: 10.1163/9789004520912_005

Carbonell, J. R. (1970). AI in CAI: An artificial-intelligence approach to computer-assisted instruction. *IEEE Transactions on Man-Machine Systems*, 11(4), 190–202. DOI: 10.1109/TMMS.1970.299942

Carobene, A., Padoan, A., Cabitza, F., Banfi, G., & Plebani, M. (2023, November 30). Rising adoption of artificial intelligence in scientific publishing: Evaluating the role, risks, and ethical implications in paper drafting and review process. *De Gruyter*, 62(5), 835–843. DOI: 10.1515/cclm-2023-1136 PMID: 38019961

Carvalho, L., Martinez-Maldonado, R., Tsai, Y. S., Markauskaite, L., & De Laat, M. (2022). How can we design for learning in an AI world? *Computers and Education: Artificial Intelligence*, 3, 100053.

Castro, G. P. B., Chiappe, A., Rodriguez, D. F. B., & Sepulveda, F. G. (2024). Harnessing AI for Education 4.0: Drivers of Personalized Learning. *The Electronic Journal of e-Learning, 22*(5), 01–14. https://doi.org/DOI: 10.34190/ejel.22.5.3467

Celik, I., Dindar, M., Muukkonen, H., & Järvelä, S. (2022). The Promises and Challenges of Artificial Intelligence for Teachers: A Systematic Review of Research. *TechTrends*, 66(4), 616–630. DOI: 10.1007/s11528-022-00715-y

Chamorro-Atalaya, O., Huarcaya-Godoy, M., Durán-Herrera, V., Nieves-Barreto, C., Suarez-Bazalar, R., Cruz-Telada, Y., Alarcón-Anco, R., Huayhua-Mamani, H., Vargas-Díaz, A., & Balarezo-Mares, D. (2023, September 30). Application of the Chatbot in University Education: A Systematic Review on the Acceptance and Impact on Learning. *Tresorix Ltd*, 22(9), 156–178. DOI: 10.26803/ijlter.22.9.9

Chan, K. S., & Zary, N. (2019). Applications and challenges of implementing artificial intelligence in medical education: Integrative review. *JMIR Medical Education*, 5(1), e13930. DOI: 10. 2196/13930 PMID: 31199295

Charalabidis, Y., Medaglia, R., & van Noordt, C. (2024). *Research Handbook on Public Management and Artificial Intelligence*. Edward Elgar Publishing.

Chassignol, M., Khoroshavin, A., Klimova, A., & Bilyatdinova, A. (2018). Artificial Intelligence trends in education: A narrative overview. *Procedia Computer Science*, 136, 16–24. DOI: 10.1016/j.procs.2018.08.233

Chaudhry, M. A., & Kazim, E. (2022). Artificial Intelligence in Education (AIEd): A high-level academic and industry note 2021. *AI and Ethics*, 2(1), 157–165. PMID: 34790953

Chaudhury, P., Mishra, S., Kumar, H., & Kishore, T. (2016). Enhancing the Capabilities of the Student Result Prediction System. Proceedings of the Second *International Conference on Information and Communication Technology for Competitive Strategies, 978-1-4503-3962.*

Chen, C. Y., Hsieh, Y. T., & Liu, B. D. (2000, December). Design of pipelined mixed-signal fuzzy logic controller with linguistic hedge modifiers. In *IEEE APCCAS 2000. 2000 IEEE Asia-Pacific Conference on Circuits and Systems. Electronic Communication Systems.(Cat. No. 00EX394)* (pp. 148-151). IEEE.

Chen, C. (2017). Science mapping: A systematic review of the literature. *Journal of Data and Information Science*, 2(2), 1–40.

Chen, L., Chen, P., & Lin, Z. (2020). Artificial intelligence in education: A review. *IEEE Access : Practical Innovations, Open Solutions*, 8, 75264–75278.

Chen, L., Chen, P., & Lin, Z. (2020). Artificial Intelligence in Education: A review. *IEEE Access : Practical Innovations, Open Solutions*, 8, 75264–75278. DOI: 10.1109/access.2020.2988510

Chen, L., Chen, P., & Lin, Z. (2020). Artificial Intelligence in education: A review. *IEEE Access : Practical Innovations, Open Solutions*, 8, 75264–75278. DOI: 10.1109/ACCESS.2020.2988510

Chen, X., Xie, H., & Hwang, G. J. (2020). A multi-perspective study on artificial intelligence in education: Grants, conferences, journals, software tools, institutions, and researchers. *Computers & Education. Artificial Intelligence*, 1, 100005.

Chen, X., Xie, H., Zou, D., & Hwang, G. (2020). Application and theory gaps during the rise of Artificial Intelligence in Education. *Computers and Education: Artificial Intelligence*, 1, 100002.

Chen, X., Xie, H., Zou, D., & Hwang, G. J. (2020). Application and theory gaps during the rise of artificial intelligence in education. *Computers and Education: Artificial Intelligence*, 1, 100002.

Chen, X., Zou, D., Xie, H., & Cheng, G. (2021). Twenty years of personalized language learning. *Journal of Educational Technology & Society*, 24(1), 205–222.

Chen, Y., Jensen, S., Albert, L. J., Gupta, S., & Lee, T. (2023). Artificial intelligence (AI) student assistants in the classroom: Designing chatbots to support student success. *Information Systems Frontiers*, 25(1), 161–182. DOI: 10.1007/s10796-022-10291-4

Chen, Z. (2023, September 13). Ethics and discrimination in artificial intelligence-enabled recruitment practices. *Palgrave Macmillan*, 10(1). Advance online publication. DOI: 10.1057/s41599-023-02079-x

Chen, Z., Chen, C., Yang, G., He, X., Chi, X., Zeng, Z., & Chen, X. (2024). Research integrity in the era of artificial intelligence: Challenges and responses. *Medicine*, 103(27), e38811. DOI: 10.1097/MD.0000000000038811 PMID: 38968491

Chine, D. R., Brentley, C., Thomas-Browne, C., Richey, J. E., Gul, A., Carvalho, P. F., & Koedinger, K. R. (2022, July). Educational equity through combined human-AI personalization: A propensity matching evaluation. In *International Conference on Artificial Intelligence in Education* (pp. 366-377). Cham: Springer International Publishing.

Chiu, T. K. (2023). The impact of Generative AI (GenAI) on practices, policies and research direction in education: A case of ChatGPT and Midjourney. *Interactive Learning Environments*, •••, 1–17.

Chiu, T. K., Moorhouse, B. L., Chai, C. S., & Ismailov, M. (2023). Teacher support and student motivation to learn with Artificial Intelligence (AI) based chatbot. *Interactive Learning Environments*, •••, 1–17.

Choung, H., David, P., & Ling, T. W. (2024). Acceptance of AI-Powered Facial Recognition Technology in Surveillance Scenarios: Role of Trust, Security, and Privacy Perceptions. *Technology in Society*, •••, 102721.

Chui, M., Manyika, J., & Miremadi, M. (2016). Where machines could replace humans-and where they can't (yet). *The McKinsey Quarterly*, •••, 1–12.

Çil, İ., Tokat, M. A., Türkan, Y. S., & Doğan, N. (2014). "E-guidance and counseling decision support system in elementary and high schools", H. U. Journal of Education, 29, (29-2),34-56.

Çil, İ., Tokat, M. A., Türkan, Y. S., & Doğan, N. (2014). E-guidance and counseling decision support system in elementary and high schools. *H. U. Journal of Education*, 29, (29-2),34-56.

Civanlar, M. R., & Trussell, H. J. (1986). Constructing membership functions using statistical data. *Fuzzy Sets and Systems*, 18(1), 1–13.

Cointe, N., Bonnet, G., & Boissier, O. (2016, May). Ethical Judgment of Agents' Behaviors in Multi-Agent Systems. In AAMAS,1106-1114.

Colchester, K., Hagras, H., Alghazzawi, D., & Aldabbagh, G. (2017). A survey of artificial intelligence techniques employed for adaptive educational systems within e-learning platforms. *Journal of Artificial Intelligence and Soft Computing Research*, 7(1), 47–64. DOI: 10.1515/jaiscr-2017-0004

Collins, G. S., Dhiman, P., Navarro, C. L. A., Ma, J., Hooft, L., Reitsma, J. B., & Moons, K. G. (2021). Protocol for development of a reporting guideline (TRIPOD-AI) and risk of bias tool (PROBAST-AI) for diagnostic and prognostic prediction model studies based on artificial intelligence. *BMJ Open*, 11(7), e048008. PMID: 34244270

Commission, E. U. (2020, February 19). *White Paper on Artificial Intelligence: A European approach to excellence and trust - European Commission.* https://commission.europa.eu/publications/white-paper-artificial-intelligence-european-approach-excellence-and-trust_en

Conklin, A. L., & Hartman, J. (2014). Artificial intelligence and its effects on education. *The Journal of Effective Teaching*, 14(1), 81–86.

Copeland, J. (1993). *Artificial intelligence: A philosophical introduction.* John Wiley & Sons.

Córdova, P. R., & Vicari, R. M. (2022, August). Practical ethical issues for artificial intelligence in education. In International Conference on Technology and Innovation in Learning, Teaching and Education (pp. 437-445). Cham: Springer Nature Switzerland.

Costa, R., Costa, A. L., & Carvalho, A. A. (2024). Use of ChatGPT in Higher Education: A Study with Graduate Students. In *Digital Transformation in Higher Education Institutions* (pp. 121–137). Springer Nature Switzerland. DOI: 10.1007/978-3-031-52296-3_7

DAAD. (2023, July 1). *Get to know the higher education system.* Www.Study-in-Germany.De. https://www.study-in-germany.de/en/plan-your-studies/study-options/higher-education-system/

Daniel, B. (2014). Big Data and analytics in higher education: Opportunities and challenges. *British Journal of Educational Technology*, 46. Advance online publication. DOI: 10.1111/bjet.12230

Dave, M., & Patel, N. (2023, May 26). Artificial intelligence in healthcare and education. *Springer Nature*, 234(10), 761–764. DOI: 10.1038/s41415-023-5845-2 PMID: 37237212

Davenport, T H., & Glaser, J. (2022, October 31). Factors governing the adoption of artificial intelligence in healthcare providers. Springer Science+Business Media, 1(1). https://doi.org/DOI: 10.1007/s44250-022-00004-8

Davis, C. (2024). Artificial Intelligence in Education: Enhancing Learning Experiences through Personalized Adaptation. *International Journal of Cyber and IT Service Management*, 4(1), 26–32.

de Laat, M., Joksimovic, S., &Ifenthaler, D. (2020). Artificial intelligence, real-time feedback and workplace learning analytics to support in situ complex problem-solving: A commentary. *The International Journal of Information and Learning Technology*. https://doi.org/.DOI: 10.1108/IJILT-03-2020-0026

Deacon, T., & Plumbley, M. D. (2024, June). Working with AI Sound: Exploring the Future of Workplace AI Sound Technologies. In *Proceedings of the 3rd Annual Meeting of the Symposium on Human-Computer Interaction for Work* (pp. 1-21).

Deck, L., Schoeffer, J., De-Arteaga, M., & Kühl, N. (2024). A Critical Survey on Fairness Benefits of Explainable AI. *The 2024 ACM Conference on Fairness, Accountability, and Transparency*, 1579–1595. https://doi.org/DOI: 10.1145/3630106.3658990

Dei, M. O. (2025). The impact of AI on the adaptation of educational materials and teaching methods to the needs of each student. *LatIA*, 3, 124–124.

Delen, I., Sen, N., Ozudogru, F., & Biasutti, M. (2024). Understanding the growth of artificial intelligence in educational research through bibliometric analysis. *Sustainability*, 16(16), 6724.

Della Ventura, M. (2019). Monitoring the learning process to enhance motivation by means of learning by discovery using Facebook. In *Shaping the Future of Education, Communication and Technology: Selected Papers from the HKAECT 2019 International Conference* (pp. 117-128). Springer Singapore.

Demartini, C. G., Sciascia, L., Bosso, A., & Manuri, F. (2024). Artificial Intelligence Bringing Improvements to Adaptive Learning in Education: A case study. *Sustainability*, 16(3), 1347. DOI: 10.3390/su16031347

Dermeval, D., Paiva, R., Bittencourt, I. I., Vassileva, J., & Borges, D. (2018). Authoring tools for designing intelligent tutoring systems: A systematic review of the literature. *International Journal of Artificial Intelligence in Education*, 28, 336–384.

Desk, T. (2023, June 15). NSU teams up with BUET for research, AI development. *The Business Post*. https://businesspostbd.com/corporate/2023-06-16/nsu-teams-up-with-buet-for-research-ai-development-2023-06-16

Deutscher Akademischer Austauschdienst, D. (Ed.). (2023, June). *Studieren und Forschen in Deutschland kommentierte WWW-Links*. DAAD. https://static.daad.de/media/daad_de/pdfs_nicht_barrierefrei/in-deutschland-studieren-forschen-lehren/ifa_weblinks_de.pdf

Devi, B. B., & Sarma, V. V. S. (1985). Estimation of fuzzy memberships from histograms. *Information Sciences*, 35(1), 43–59.

Dia, R. R., Akif, A., Islam, Q. T., & Hossain, M. A. (2024). Interactive Cares Bangladesh: Empowering Bangladesh's Future Through Education and the SDGs. SAGE Publications: SAGE Business Cases Originals.

Diaz-Leon, I., & Iraola-Real, I. (2024). The Use of ChatGPT by Peruvian University Students: An Exploration of Actual Use and Intention to Use. *RISTI - Revista Iberica de Sistemas e Tecnologias de Informacao, 69*, 89-101.

Dilmaghani, S., Brust, M. R., Danoy, G., Cassagnes, N., Pecero, J., & Bouvry, P. (2019). Privacy and security of big data in AI systems: A research and standards perspective, in *Proc. IEEE Int. Conf. Big Data*, 5737–5743.

Ding, A. C. E., Shi, L., Yang, H., & Choi, I. (2024). Enhancing teacher AI literacy and integration through different types of cases in teacher professional development. *Computers and Education Open*, 6, 100178.

Domenech, J. (2023, June). ChatGPT in the classroom: friend or foe? In *9th International Conference on Higher Education Advances (HEAd'23)* (pp. 339-347). Editorial Universitat Politècnica de València. DOI: 10.4995/HEAd23.2023.16179

Dönmez, E. (2024). The Future of Education: AI-Supported Reforms in the USA and China. In *Global Agendas and Education Reforms: A Comparative Study* (pp. 135–150). Springer Nature Singapore.

Dougherty, S. M., Ecton, W. G., Bonilla, S., & McGuinness, S. (2022). The effects of the COVID-19 pandemic and recession on career preparation during high school. *Peabody Journal of Education*, 97(3), 326–343.

DPA. (2024, March 15). *KI-Nutzung an der Uni beschäftigt Justiz.* https://www.forschung-und-lehre.de/recht/ki-nutzung-an-der-uni-beschaeftigt-justiz-6309

Dubois, D., & Prade, H. (1983). Ranking fuzzy numbers in the setting of possibility theory. *Information Sciences*, 30(3), 183–224.

Duong, C. D., Vu, T. N., & Ngo, T. V. N. (2023). Applying a modified technology acceptance model to explain higher education students' usage of ChatGPT: A serial multiple mediation model with knowledge sharing as a moderator. *International Journal of Management Education*, 21(3), 100883. DOI: 10.1016/j.ijme.2023.100883

Durak, G., Çankaya, S., Özdemir, D., & Can, S. (2024). Artificial intelligence in education: A bibliometric study on its role in transforming teaching and learning. *International Review of Research in Open and Distributed Learning*, 25(3), 219–244.

Du, Y. (2024). The Digital Divide: Mapping the Ethics of Artificial Intelligence. *Journal of Student Research*, 13(2).

Dwivedi, Y. K., Hughes, L., Ismagilova, E., Aarts, G., Coombs, C., Crick, T., & Williams, M. D. (2021). Artificial Intelligence (AI): Multidisciplinary perspectives on emerging challenges, opportunities, and agenda for research, practice and policy. *International Journal of Information Management*, 57, 101994.

Dwivedi, Y. K., Kshetri, N., Hughes, L., Slade, E. L., Jeyaraj, A., & Kar, A. K.. (2023). "So what if ChatGPT wrote it?" multidisciplinary perspectives on opportunities, challenges, and implications of generative conversational AI for research, practice, and policy. *International Journal of Information Management*, 71, 102642. DOI: 10.1016/j.ijinfomgt.2023.102642

Dwivedi, Y. K., Kshetri, N., Hughes, L., Slade, E. L., Jeyaraj, A., Kar, A. K., & Wright, R. (2023). Opinion Paper:"So what if ChatGPT wrote it?" Multidisciplinary perspectives on opportunities, challenges and implications of generative conversational AI for research, practice and policy. *International Journal of Information Management*, 71, 102642.

Eden, C. A., Chisom, O. N., & Adeniyi, I. S. (2024). Integrating AI in education: Opportunities, challenges, and ethical considerations. Magna Scientia Advanced Research and Reviews, 10(2), 006-013.

Edeni, C. A., Adeleye, O. O., & Adeniyi, I. S. (2024). The role of AI-enhanced tools in overcoming socioeconomic barriers in education: A conceptual analysis. *World Journal of Advanced Research and Reviews*, 21(3), 944–951.

Elken, M. (2024). Collaborative design of governance instruments in higher education. *Studies in Higher Education*, 49(6), 1095–1106. DOI: 10.1080/03075079.2023.2258905

Estrada-Araoz, E. G., Paredes-Valverde, Y., Quispe-Herrera, R., Gallegos-Ramos, N. A., Rivera-Mamani, F. A., & Romaní-Claros, A. (2024). Investigando la actitud de los estudiantes universitarios hacia el uso del ChatGPT como recurso de aprendizaje. *Data and Metadata*, 3, 268–268. DOI: 10.56294/dm2024268

Etomes, S. E., & Lyonga, F. I. N. (2020). STUDENT-TEACHER RATIO AND STUDENTS'ACADEMIC PERFORMANCE IN PUBLIC UNIVERSITIES: THE CASE OF THE UNIVERSITY OF BUEA, CAMEROON. *European Journal of Education Studies*, 7(6).

Etzioni, A., & Etzioni, O. (2017). Incorporating ethics into artificial intelligence. *The Journal of Ethics*, 21, 403–418.

Eubanks, V. (2018). *Automating Inequality: How High-tech Tools Profile, Police, and Punish the Poor* (Illustrated Edition). St Martin's Press.

Ezzaim, A., Dahbi, A., Aqqal, A., & Haidine, A. (2024). AI-based learning style detection in adaptive learning systems: a systematic literature review. *Journal of Computers in Education*. https://doi.org/DOI: 10.1007/s40692-024-00328-9

Faisal, E. (2024, April). Unlock the potential for Saudi Arabian higher education: A systematic review of the benefits of ChatGPT. [). Frontiers Media SA.]. *Frontiers in Education*, 9, 1325601. DOI: 10.3389/feduc.2024.1325601

Ferrara, E. (2023). Fairness and bias in artificial intelligence: A brief survey of sources, impacts, and mitigation strategies. *Sci*, 6(1), 3.

Field, A. (2013). *Discovering statistics using IBM SPSS statistics* (4th ed.). SAGE.

Fiero, A. W., & Beier, E. (2022). New global developments in data protection and privacy regulations: Comparative analysis of European Union, United States, and Russian legislation. *Stan. J. Int'l L.*, 58, 151.

Florea, A. M., & Radu, S. (2019, May). Artificial intelligence and education. In 2019 22nd International Conference on Control Systems and Computer Science (CSCS) (pp. 381-382). IEEE.

Floridi, L., & Cowls, J. (2019). A Unified Framework of Five Principles for AI in Society. *Harvard Data Science Review*. Advance online publication. DOI: 10.1162/99608f92.8cd550d1

Foffano, F., Scantamburlo, T., & Cortés, A. (2022). Investing in AI for social good: An analysis of European national strategies. *AI & Society*, 38(2), 479–500. DOI: 10.1007/s00146-022-01445-8 PMID: 35528248

Fontenelle-Tereshchuk, D. (2024, January 10). Academic writing and ChatGPT: Students transitioning into college in the shadow of the COVID-19 pandemic. Springer Science+Business Media, 3(1). https://doi.org/DOI: 10.1007/s44217-023-00076-5

Fullan, M., Azorin, C., Harris, A., & Jones, M. (2023). Artificial intelligence and school leadership: Challenges, opportunities and implications. *School Leadership & Management*, 44(4), 339–346.

Galafa, B., & Lucas, A. (2018). Challenges to educational administration and management in primary schools in Malawi. *North America Academic Research*, 1(2), 1–14.

Garcia, P. A., & Adams, D. J. (2023). Data-Driven Decision Making: Leveraging Analytics and AI for Strategic Advantage. *Research Studies of Business, 1*(02), Article 02.

García-Peñalvo, F. J., & Corell, A. (2020). The COVID-19: The enzyme of the digital transformation of teaching or the reflection of a methodological and competence crisis in higher education. *Campus Virtuales*, 9(2), 83–98.

Garfield, E. (1980). Citation indexing. *Journal of Information Science*, 2(1), 47–47.

Gasparyan, A. Y., Nurmashev, B., Seksenbayev, B., Trukhachev, V. I., Kostyukova, E. I., & Kitas, G. D. (2017). Plagiarism in the Context of Education and Evolving Detection Strategies. *Journal of Korean Medical Science*, 32(8), 1220–1227. DOI: 10.3346/jkms.2017.32.8.1220 PMID: 28665055

Gayan Nayanajith, D.A. (2020). Customers' Perceptions of E-Security and Ease of Use on Artificial Intelligence Enabled E-Banking Adoption.

Geist, E. (2011). The game changer: Using iPads in college teacher education classes. *College Student Journal*, 45(4), 758769.

George, B., & Wooden, O. (2023). Managing the strategic transformation of higher education through artificial intelligence. *Administrative Sciences*, 13(9), 196.

Gerlich, M. (2023). Perceptions and acceptance of artificial intelligence: A multi-dimensional study. *Social Sciences*, 12(9), 502.

Gestalt psychology. (n.d.). In Encyclopedia Britannica. Retrieved 19 April 2024 from https://www.britannica.com/science/Gestalt-psychology

Ge, Z., & Hu, Y. (2020, April 1). Innovative Application of Artificial Intelligence (AI) in the Management of Higher Education and Teaching. *IOP Publishing*, 1533(3), 032089–032089. DOI: 10.1088/1742-6596/1533/3/032089

Gison, C. (2024, April 8). The Role of AI in Preventing Plagiarism and Ensuring Content Originality. *Medium*. https://medium.com/@chasegison/the-role-of-ai-in-preventing-plagiarism-and-ensuring-content-originality-4b53d07949ea

Gobara, R. E. G. E., & Ahmed, Z. E. (2024). Preparing Students for an AI-Enhanced Future. In *AI-Enhanced Teaching Methods* (pp. 286–304). IGI Global.

Godal, R. C., & Goodman, T. J. (1980). Fuzzy sets and Borel. *IEEE Transactions on Systems, Man, and Cybernetics*, 10(10), 637.

Godin, B. (2006). On the origins of bibliometrics. *Scientometrics*, 68(1), 109–133. DOI: 10.1007/s11192-006-0086-0

Goksel, N., & Bozkurt, A. (2019). Artificial Intelligence in Education: Current Insights and Future Perspectives. In Sisman-Ugur, S., & Kurubacak, G. (Eds.), *Handbook of Research on Learning in the Age of Transhumanism Hershey* (pp. 224–236). IGI Global.

Golonka, E. M., Bowles, A. R., Frank, V. M., Richardson, D. L., & Freynik, S. (2014). Technologies for foreign language learning: A review of technology types and their effectiveness. *Computer Assisted Language Learning*, 27(1), 70–105.

Gonçalves, D., Fernandes, C., Reis, A. R., Oliveira, E., & Silva, C. (2016). The use of IBM Watson in education: A review. *International Journal of Information Management*, 36(6), 787–791.

González-Calatayud, V., Prendes-Espinosa, P., & Roig-Vila, R. (2021). Artificial intelligence for student assessment: A Systematic Review. *Applied Sciences (Basel, Switzerland)*, 11(12), 5467. DOI: 10.3390/app11125467

González, R. A. G., & Bonilla, M. H. S. (2022). Education and artificial intelligence: Immersive theme nodes. *Electronic Journal of Educational Technology*, 82, 59–77. DOI: 10.21556/edutec.2022.82.2633

Graesser, A. C. (2009). Inaugural editorial for Journal of Educational Psychology. *Journal of Educational Psychology*, 101(2), 259–261. DOI: 10.1037/a0014883

Graesser, A. C., Chipman, P., Haynes, B. C., & Olney, A. (2005). AutoTutor: An intelligent tutoring system with mixed-initiative dialogue. *IEEE Transactions on Education*, 48(4), 612–618. DOI: 10.1109/TE.2005.856149

Graesser, A. C., Conley, M. W., & Olney, A. M. (2012a). Intelligent tutoring systems. In Graham, S., & Harris, K. (Eds.), APA Educational Psychology Handbook: Vol. 3. *Applications to Learning and Teaching* (pp. 451–473). American Psychological Association.

Graesser, A. C., D'Mello, S. K., Hu, X., Cai, Z., Olney, A., & Morgan, B. (2012b). AutoTutor. In McCarthy, P., & Boonthum-Denecke, C. (Eds.), *Applied natural language processing: Identification, investigation, and resolution (ss* (pp. 169–187). IGI Global. DOI: 10.4018/978-1-60960-741-8.ch010

Graesser, A. C., Person, N. K., & Magliano, J. P. (1995). Collaborative dialogue patterns in naturalistic one-toone tutoring. *Applied Cognitive Psychology*, 9(6), 1–28. DOI: 10.1002/acp.2350090604

Graesser, A. C., Wiemer-Hastings, K., Wiemer-Hastings, P., & Kreuz, R.Tutoring Research Group. (1999). AutoTutor:A simulation of a human tutor. *Cognitive Systems Research*, 1(1), 35–51. DOI: 10.1016/S1389-0417(99)00005-4

Guan, C., Mou, J., & Jiang, Z. (2020). Artificial intelligence innovation in education: A twenty-year data-driven historical analysis. *International Journal of Innovation Studies.*, 4, 134–147.

Guan, H. (2023). Advantages and Challenges of Using Artificial Intelligence in Primary and Secondary School Education. *Journal of Education. Humanities and Social Sciences*, 22, 377–383.

Guechair, S. (2024). Artificial intelligence in education: A comprehensive bibliometric study on scopus (2010-2024). *Atras Journal*, 5(3), 445–463.

Gunning, D., Stefik, M., Choi, J., Miller, T., Stumpf, S., & Yang, G.-Z. (2019). XAI-Explainable artificial intelligence. *Science Robotics*, 4(37), eaay7120. Advance online publication. DOI: 10.1126/scirobotics.aay7120 PMID: 33137719

Gupta, P., Sreelatha, C., Latha, A., Raj, S., & Singh, A. (2024). Navigating the Future of Education: The Impact of Artificial Intelligence on Teacher-Student Dynamics. *Educational Administration: Theory and Practice*, 30(4), 6006–6013.

Gutiérrez-Salcedo, M., Martínez, M. Á., Moral-Munoz, J. A., Herrera-Viedma, E., & Cobo, M. J. (2018). Some bibliometric procedures for analyzing and evaluating research fields. *Applied Intelligence*, 48, 1275–1287. DOI: 10.1007/s10489-017-1105-y

Haase, K. (2024a, February 11). *LMU und TU suchen noch nach dem richtigen Umgang mit Künstlicher Intelligenz.* Süddeutsche.de. https://www.sueddeutsche.de/muenchen/kuenstliche-intelligenz-lmu-tu-unsicherheit-studierende-1.6350153

Haase, K. (2024b, July 29). *Lern-Chatbot der TU München: Hilfe ja - Lösung nein.* Süddeutsche.de. https://www.sueddeutsche.de/muenchen/ki-chatbot-chat-gpt-muenchen-tum-studium-lux.9NsArTJGvyeeHESKeNJias

Haddow, G. (2013). Bibliometric research. In *Research methods: Information, systems and contexts* (pp. 219–244). Tilde University Press.

Haderecker, J., & Binder, J. (2024, March 15). *Mit KI-Hilfe an die Uni: Zwei weitere Bewerber abgelehnt.* BR24. https://www.br.de/nachrichten/bayern/mit-ki-hilfe-an-die-uni-zwei-weitere-bewerber-abgelehnt,U76Xlxf

Hafiz, N., & Islam, A. (2023, October 1). *Impact of artificial intelligence in closing the gender gap among women-led industries: a developing country perspective.* https://dspace.bracu.ac.bd/xmlui/handle/10361/22802

Hagendorff, T. (2020). The Ethics of AI Ethics: An Evaluation of Guidelines. *Minds and Machines*, 30(1), 99–120. DOI: 10.1007/s11023-020-09517-8

Halkiopoulos, C., & Gkintoni, E. (2024). Leveraging AI in E-Learning: Personalized Learning and Adaptive Assessment through Cognitive Neuropsychology—A Systematic Analysis. *Electronics (Basel)*, 13(18), 3762. DOI: 10.3390/electronics13183762

Han, B., Nawaz, S., Buchanan, G., & McKay, D. (2023, June). Ethical and pedagogical impacts of AI in education. In *International Conference on Artificial Intelligence in Education* (pp. 667-673). Cham: Springer Nature Switzerland.

Hannan, E., & Liu, S. (2023). AI: New source of competitiveness in higher education. *Competitiveness Review*, 33(2), 265–279.

Hasanein, A. M., & Sobaih, A. E. E. (2023). Drivers and Consequences of ChatGPT Use in Higher Education: Key Stakeholder Perspectives. *European Journal of Investigation in Health, Psychology and Education*, 13(11), 2599–2614. DOI: 10.3390/ejihpe13110181 PMID: 37998071

Hashim, S., Omar, M. K., Ab Jalil, H., & Sharef, N. M. (2022). Trends on technologies and artificial intelligence in education for personalized learning: Systematic literature. *Journal of Academic Research in Progressive Education and Development*, 12(1), 884–903.

Hasselgren, C., & Oprea, T. I. (2024, January 23). Artificial Intelligence for Drug Discovery: Are We There Yet? *Annual Reviews*, 64(1), 527–550. DOI: 10.1146/annurev-pharmtox-040323-040828 PMID: 37738505

Hattie, J. (2008). *Visible Learning: A Synthesis of Over 800 Meta-Analyses Relating to Achievement* (1st ed.). Routledge., DOI: 10.4324/9780203887332

Hense, J., Goertz, L., Budde, J., & Friedrich, J. (2023). Monitor Digitalisierung 360°—Wo stehen die deutschen Hochschulen. *Hochschulforum Digitalisierung. Arbeitspapier*, (68), 85.

Hernández-Blanco, A., Herrera-Flores, B., Tomás, D., & Navarro-Colorado, B. (2019). A systematic review of deep learning approaches to educational data mining. *Complexity*, 2019(2019), 1306039.

Hinton, G. E. (2007). Learning multiple layers of representation. *Trends in Cognitive Sciences*, 11, 428–434. PMID: 17921042

Hitchings, W. E., Luzzo, D. A., Ristow, R., Horvath, M., Retish, P., & Tanners, A. (2001). The career development needs of college students with learning disabilities: In their own words. *Learning Disabilities Research & Practice*, 16, 8–17. DOI: 10.1111/0938-8982.00002

Hmoud, M., Swaity, H., Hamad, N., Karram, O., & Daher, W. (2024). Higher education students' task motivation in the generative artificial intelligence context: The case of chatgpt. *Information (Basel)*, 15(1), 33.

Holloway, S. (2001). The experience of higher education from the perspective of disabled students. *Disability & Society*, 16(4), 597–615.

Holmes, W., Anastopoulou, S., Schaumburg, H., & Mavrikis, M. (2018). *Technology-enhanced personalised learning: Untangling the evidence*. Robert Bosch Stiftung.

Holmes, W., Bialik, M., & Fadel, C. (2019). *Artificial intelligence in education: Promises and implications for teaching and learning*. Center for Curriculum Redesign.

Holmes, W., Bialik, M., & Fadel, C. (2019). *Artificial intelligence in education:promises and implications for teaching and learning*. Center for Curriculum Redesign.

Holmes, W., Porayska-Pomsta, K., Holstein, K., Sutherland, E., Baker, T., Shum, S. B., & Koedinger, K. R. (2022). Ethics of AI in education: Towards a community-wide framework. *International Journal of Artificial Intelligence in Education*, •••, 1–23.

Holmes, W., Porayska-Pomsta, K., Holstein, K., Sutherland, E., Baker, T., Shum, S., Santos, O. C., Rodrigo, M., Cukurova, M., Bittencourt, I., & Koedinger, K. (2021). Ethics of AI in Education: Towards a Community-Wide Framework. *International Journal of Artificial Intelligence in Education*, 32. Advance online publication. DOI: 10.1007/s40593-021-00239-1

Hong, H., & Kim, Y. (2024). Applying artificial intelligence in career education for students with intellectual disabilities: The effects on career self-efficacy and learning flow. *Education and Information Technologies*, •••, 1–20.

Hopcan, S., Polat, E., Ozturk, M. E., & Ozturk, L. (2022). Artifcial intelligence in special education: A systematic review. *Interactive Learning Environments*, 31(10), 7335–7353. DOI: 10.1080/ 10494820.2022.2067186

Hopkins, L. (2011). The path of least resistance: A voice-relational analysis of disabled students' experiences of discrimination in English universities. *International Journal of Inclusive Education*, 15(7), 711–727.

Hornberger, M., Bewersdorff, A., & Nerdel, C. (2023). What do university students know about Artificial Intelligence? Development and validation of an AI literacy test. *Computers and Education: Artificial Intelligence*, 5, 100165. DOI: 10.1016/j.caeai.2023.100165

Horwitch, M. (2024, August). The AI Challenge for National Technology Strategy. In *2024 Portland International Conference on Management of Engineering and Technology (PICMET)* (pp. 1-11). IEEE.

Horwitch, M. "The AI Challenge for National Technology Strategy," *2024 Portland International Conference on Management of Engineering and Technology (PICMET)*, Portland, OR, USA, 2024, pp. 1-11, https://doi.org/DOI: 10.23919/picmet64035.2024.10653430

Hossain, M. K., Srivastava, A., Oliver, G. C., Islam, M. E., Jahan, N. A., Karim, R., Kanij, T., & Mahdi, T. H. (2024). Adoption of artificial intelligence and big data analytics: An organizational readiness perspective of the textile and garment industry in Bangladesh. *Business Process Management Journal*. Advance online publication. DOI: 10.1108/bpmj-11-2023-0914

Houwen, B. B., Nass, K. J., Vleugels, J. L., Fockens, P., Hazewinkel, Y., & Dekker, E. (2023). Comprehensive review of publicly available colonoscopic imaging databases for artificial intelligence research: Availability, accessibility, and usability. *Gastrointestinal Endoscopy*, 97(2), 184–199. PMID: 36084720

Huang, C., Zhang, Z., Mao, B., & Yao, X. (2022). An overview of artificial intelligence ethics. *IEEE Transactions on Artificial Intelligence*, 4(4), 799–819.

Huang, F., Wang, Y., & Zhang, H. (2024). Modelling generative AI acceptance, Perceived Teachers' enthusiasm and Self-Efficacy to English as a Foreign Language learners' Well-Being in the Digital era. *European Journal of Education*. Advance online publication. DOI: 10.1111/ejed.12770

Huang, J., Saleh, S., & Liu, Y. (2021). A review on artificial intelligence in education. *Academic Journal of Interdisciplinary Studies*, 10(3), 206–217. DOI: 10.36941/ajis-2021-0077

Huang, W., Hew, K. F., & Fryer, L. K. (2022). Chatbots for language learning—Are they really useful? A systematic review of chatbot-supported language learning. *Journal of Computer Assisted Learning*, 38(1), 237–257. DOI: 10.1111/jcal.12610

Huda, S. (2024). Challenges of Using Multimedia Tools in the Teaching and Learning Process: Instance from a college of Bangladesh. *Journal of Management and Business Education*, 7(3), 435–451. DOI: 10.35564/jmbe.2024.0024

Hurley, R. (2019). *Data Science: A Comprehensive Guide to Data Science, Data Analytics, Data Mining, Artificial Intelligence, Machine Learning, and Big Data*. Independently Published.

Husain, N. (2023). Educational Renaissance: Unleashing the Potential of Interdisciplinary AI Integration. *Journal of Environmental Science and Technology*, 2(1), 159–166.

Hüsch, M., Horstmann, N., & Breiter, A. (2024). *CHECK - Künstliche Intelligenz in Studium und Lehre*. https://www.che.de/download/check-ki-2024/

Hutson, J. (2024). Rethinking Plagiarism in the Era of Generative AI. *Journal of International Communication*, 4. Advance online publication. DOI: 10.54963/jic.v4i1.220

Hwang, G. J., & Fu, Q. K. (2018). Trends in the Research Design and Application of Mobile Language Learning: A Review of 2007-2016 Publications in Selected SSCI Journals. *Interactive Learning Environments*, 27, 567–581. DOI: 10.1080/10494820.2018.1486861

Hwang, G. J., Xie, H., Wah, B. W., & Gašević, D. (2020). Vision, challenges, roles and research issues of artificial intelligence in education. *Computers and Education: Artificial Intelligence*, 1, 100001. DOI: 10.1016/j.caeai.2020.100001

Ifenthaler, D., & Gibson, D. (Eds.). (2020). *Adoption of data analytics in higher education learning and teaching*. Springer.

Igbokwe, I. C. (2023). Application of Artificial Intelligence (AI) in Educational Management. *International Journal of Scientific and Research Publications*, 3(3). Advance online publication. DOI: 10.29322/ijsrp.13.03.2023.p13536

Ilham, R., Giatman, M., & Maksun, H. (2024). artificial intelligence research in education: A bibliometric analysis. *Journal of Education*, 6(2), 13467–13479.

Imran, M., & Almusharraf, N. (2023). Analyzing the role of ChatGPT as a writing assistant at higher education level: A systematic review of the literature. *Contemporary Educational Technology*, 15(4), ep464. DOI: 10.30935/cedtech/13605

Islam, M. M., Shaheen, S. M., Roy, R. K., Islam, A., & Hossain, M. D. (2023). Pandemic-Led Challenges for Rural Students in Bangladesh. *IAFOR Journal of Education*, 11(3), 113–136.

Islam, M. T., Hasan, M. M., Redwanuzzaman, M., & Hossain, M. K. (2023). Practices of artificial intelligence to improve the business in Bangladesh. *Social Sciences & Humanities Open*, 9, 100766. DOI: 10.1016/j.ssaho.2023.100766

Islam, N. (2024). Synthesizing sociological dimensions into engineering programs: Challenges for the sociology teachers in Bangladesh. *Social Sciences & Humanities Open*, 10, 101079. DOI: 10.1016/j.ssaho.2024.101079

Islam, S. (2024). British Columbian and Bangladeshi secondary science teachers' views on the role of professional learning communities in the growth of their knowledge for teaching. *UBC Library Open Collections*. https://doi.org/DOI: 10.14288/1.0444124

Ivanashko, O., Kozak, A., Knysh, T., & Honchar, K. (2024). The role of artificial intelligence in shaping the future of education: opportunities and challenges. *Futurity Education*, 126–146. https://doi.org/DOI: 10.57125/fed.2024.03.25.08

Ivanova, M., Grosseck, G., & Holotescu, C. (2024, February). Unveiling insights: a bibliometric analysis of artificial intelligence in teaching. In Informatics (Vol. 11, No. 1, p. 10). MDPI.

Jack, P. (2023, November 28). *AI 'could reinforce bias' in university admissions.* Times Higher Education (THE). https://www.timeshighereducation.com/news/ai-could-reinforce-bias-university-admissions

Jang, M., Cai, L., Udeani, G. O., Slowing, K. V., Thomas, C. F., Beecher, C. W., ... & Pezzuto, J. M. (1997). Cancer chemopreventive activity of resveratrol, a natural product derived from grapes. *science, 275*(5297), 218-220.

Jansen, A., & Colombo, S. (2024). Empowering AI Education by Enhancing Scalability and Accessibility of the Mix & Match Machine Learning Toolkit. *From User to Human*, 66.

Jarvis, A., Ho, A., & Lim, G. (2024). Impressing Artificial Intelligence: Automated Job Interview training in Professional English subjects. *RELC Journal.* Advance online publication. DOI: 10.1177/00336882241245449

Jeffries, P., Gianinazzi, S., & Perotto, S. (2003). The contribution of arbuscular mycorrhizal fungi in sustainable maintenance of plant health and soil fertility. *Biology and Fertility of Soils*, 37, 1–16. DOI: 10.1007/s00374-002-0546-5

Joamets, K. (2022). Plagiarism as a Legal Phenomenon and Algorithm-Based Decision Making. *TalTech Journal of European Studies*, 12, 146–164. DOI: 10.2478/bjes-2022-0015

Jo, H. (2024). From concerns to benefits: A comprehensive study of ChatGPT usage in education. *International Journal of Educational Technology in Higher Education*, 21(1), 35. DOI: 10.1186/s41239-024-00471-4

Jones, A., Harkness, S., & Mondragon, N. (2020). Acts of meaning: How AI-based interviewing will transform career preparation in higher education. *EDUCAUSE Review.*

Jones, C. S. (1985). An empirical study of the evidence for contingency theories of management accounting systems in conditions of rapid change. *Accounting, Organizations and Society, Elsevier*, 10(3), 303–328.

Kadaruddin, K. (2023, August 2). Empowering Education through Generative AI. *Innovative Instructional Strategies for Tomorrow's Learners.*, 4(2), 618–625. DOI: 10.56442/ijble.v4i2.215

Kakhkharova, M., & Tuychieva, S. (2024, April). AI-Enhanced Pedagogy in Higher Education: Redefining Teaching-Learning Paradigms. In *2024 International Conference on Knowledge Engineering and Communication Systems (ICKECS)* (Vol. 1, pp. 1-6). IEEE.

Kallio, T. J., Kallio, K. M., & Blomberg, A. (2020). From professional bureaucracy to competitive bureaucracy–redefining universities' organization principles, performance measurement criteria, and reason for being. *Qualitative Research in Accounting & Management*, 17(1), 82–108.

Kamal, P., and Ahuja, S. A. (2017). Review on Prediction of Academic Performance of Student Sat-Risk Using Data Mining Techniques. *Journal on Today's Ideas – Tomorrow's Technologies, 5(1).*

Kamalov, F., Calonge, D. S., & Gurrib, I. (2023, August 16). New Era of Artificial Intelligence in Education: Towards a Sustainable Multifaceted Revolution. *Multidisciplinary Digital Publishing Institute*, 15(16), 12451–12451. DOI: 10.3390/su151612451

Kamalov, F., & Gurrib, I. (2023, January 1). New Era of Artificial Intelligence in Education: Towards a Sustainable Multifaceted Revolution. Cornell University. https://doi.org/DOI: 10.48550/arXiv.2305

Kamber, E., Aydoğmuş, U., Aydoğmuş, H. Y., Gümüş, M., & Kahraman, C. (2024). Prioritization of drip-irrigation pump alternatives in agricultural applications: An integrated picture fuzzy BWM&CODAS methodology. *Applied Soft Computing*, 154, 111308.

Kang, C., & Cho, H. (2021). The efect of career program using group art therapy on career motivation and career decision-making self-efcacy of high school students with intellectual disabilities. *Journal of Emotional and Behavioral Disorders*, 37(1), 105–127. DOI: 10.33770/JEBD.37.1.5

Kang, H. (2013). A guide on the use of factor analysis in the assessment of construct validity. *Journal of Korean Academy of Nursing*, 43(5), 587–594. DOI: 10.4040/jkan.2013.43.5.587 PMID: 24351990

Karras, O., Lorenz, A.-L., & Auer, S. (2024, September 26). *Chancen einer KI-gestützten Wissenschaft*. Forschung und Lehre. https://www.forschung-und-lehre.de/forschung/chancen-einer-ki-gestuetzten-wissenschaft-6667

Karsenti, D., Tharsis, G., Burtin, P., Venezia, F., Tordjman, G., Gillet, A., & Cavicchi, M. (2019). Adenoma and advanced neoplasia detection rates increase from 45 years of age. *World Journal of Gastroenterology*, 25(4), 447. PMID: 30700941

Kaswan, K. S., Dhatterwal, J. S., & Ojha, R. P. (2024). AI in personalized learning. In *CRC Press eBooks* (pp. 103–117). https://doi.org/DOI: 10.1201/9781003376699-9

Kaulbach, L.-L. (2024, August 9). *Neuer Meilenstein erreicht – RWTHgpt • IT Center Blog*. https://blog.rwth-aachen.de/itc/2024/08/09/neuer-meilenstein-erreicht-rwthgpt/

Kavitha, P., Moorthy, B. K., Sudharshan, P. S., & Aarthi, T. (2018). Mapping artificial intelligence and education. In 2018 International Conference on Communication, Computing and Internet of Things (IC3IoT); IEEE: Piscataway, NJ, USA, pp. 165–168.

Kayyali, M. (2021). Positive Impact of High Technology on Higher Education.

Kayyali, M. (2024). Future Possibilities and Challenges of AI in Education. In Transforming Education With Generative AI: Prompt Engineering and Synthetic Content Creation (pp. 118-137). IGI Global.

Kayyali, M. (2024b). Immersive Technologies: Virtual and Augmented Reality in Higher Education. In Reshaping Learning with Next Generation Educational Technologies (pp. 99-114). IGI Global.

Kayyali, M. (2024a). Future possibilities and challenges of AI in education. In *Transforming education with generative AI: Prompt engineering and synthetic content creation* (pp. 118–137). IGI Global.

Kayyali, M. (2024c). The Future of Higher Education in an Uncertain World. In *Building Resilient Education Models Post Crisis* (pp. 42–55). IGI Global.

Keller, F. S. (1968). Good-bye, teacher.... *Journal of Applied Behavior Analysis*, 1(1), 79–89. DOI: 10.1901/jaba.1968.1-79 PMID: 16795164

Kelly, S., Kaye, S. A., & Oviedo-Trespalacios, O. (2023). What factors contribute to the acceptance of artificial intelligence? A systematic review. *Telematics and Informatics*, 77, 101925.

Keskin, D., & Sevli, O. 2024, Eğitimde Yapay Zekâ Ve Etik. International Topkapı Congress III.

Kezar, A. J. (2005). Redesigning for Collaboration within Higher Education Institutions: An Exploration into the Developmental Process. *Research in Higher Education*, 46, 831–860. DOI: 10.1007/s11162-004-6227-5

Khaldi, H., & Prado-Gascó, V. (2021). Bibliometric maps and co-word analysis of the literature on international cooperation on migration. *Quality & Quantity*, 55, 1845–1869. DOI: 10.1007/s11135-020-01085-4

Kharbat, F. F., Alshawabkeh, A., & Woolsey, M. L. (2021). Identifying gaps in using artifcial intelligence to support students with intellectual disabilities from education and health perspectives. *Aslib Journal of Information Management*, 73(1), 101–128. DOI: 10.1108/AJIM-02-2020-0054

Khare, K., Stewart, B., & Khare, A. (2018). Artificial intelligence and the student experience: An institutional perspective. The International Academic Forum (IAFOR).

Khare, K., & Stewart, B. (2018). Artificial Intelligence and the Student Experience: An Institutional Perspective. *IAFOR Journal of Education*, 6(3), 63–78.

Khazanchi, R., & Khazanchi, P. (2024). Generative AI to improve special education teacher preparation for inclusive classrooms. Exploring New Horizons: Generative Artificial Intelligence and Teacher Education, 159.

Khosravi, H., Sadiq, S., & Amer-Yahia, S. (2023). Data management of AI-powered education technologies: Challenges and opportunities. *Journal of Learning Letters*. https://doi.org/DOI: 10.59453//XLUD7002

Khosravi, H., Shum, S B., Chen, G., Conati, C., Tsai, Y., Kay, J., Knight, S., Martínez-Maldonado, R., Sadiq, S., & Gašević, D. (2022, January 1). Explainable Artificial Intelligence in education. Elsevier BV, 3, 100074-100074. https://doi.org/DOI: 10.1016/j.caeai.2022.100074

Kieslich, K., Keller, B., & Starke, C. (2022). Artificial intelligence ethics by design. Evaluating public perception on the importance of ethical design principles of artificial intelligence. *Big Data & Society*, 9(1), 20539517221092956. DOI: 10.1177/20539517221092956

Kim, J. (2020). The influence of perceived costs and perceived benefits on AI-driven interactive recommendation agent value. *Journal of Global Scholars of Marketing Science*, 30(3), 319–333.

Kim, J. (2023). Leading teachers' perspective on teacher-AI collaboration in education. *Education and Information Technologies*. Advance online publication. DOI: 10.1007/s10639-023-12109-5

Kim, N. (2023, February 28)... *Strengthening the Self-feedback on College Writing Classes.*, 17(1), 47–62. DOI: 10.46392/kjge.2023.17.1.47

Kirkpatrick, K. (2015). The moral challenges of driverless cars. *Communications of the ACM*, 58(8), 19–20.

Kiryakova, G., & Angelova, N. (2023). ChatGPT—A challenging tool for the university professors in their teaching practice. *Education Sciences*, 13(10), 1056. DOI: 10.3390/educsci13101056

Klimova, B., Pikhart, M., & Al-Obaydi, L. H. (2024). Exploring the potential of ChatGPT for foreign language education at the university level. *Frontiers in Psychology*, 15, 1269319. DOI: 10.3389/fpsyg.2024.1269319 PMID: 38655215

Knox, J. (2020). Artificial intelligence and education in China. *Learning, Media and Technology*. Advance online publication. DOI: 10.1080/17439884.2020.1754236

Koçoğlu, F. Ö., Emre, ˙. I. E., & Erol, Ç. S. (2017). Observation of Success Status of Employees in E-Learning Courses in Organizations with Data Mining. *International Journal of E-Adoption*, 9, 38–49.

Koh, J., Cowling, M., Jha, M., & Sim, K. N. (2023). The Human Teacher, the AI Teacher and the AIed-Teacher Relationship. *Journal of Higher Education Theory and Practice*, 23(17).

Kohnke, L. (2024). Exploring EAP students' perceptions of GenAI and traditional grammar-checking tools for language learning. *Computers and Education: Artificial Intelligence*, 7, 100279.

Kooli, C. (2023). Chatbots in education and research: A critical examination of ethical implications and solutions. *Sustainability*, 15(7), 5614.

Kosmas, P., Nisiforou, E., & Vrasidas, C. (2024). Transforming higher education teaching through the integration of virtual and augmented reality. In *INTED2024 Proceedings* (pp. 2604-2612). IATED.

Kumari, G. V., Chapa, B. P., Chaitanya, N. K., Mahajan, R. G., & Shahakar, M. (2024). Introduction to data-driven intelligent systems. In *CRC Press eBooks* (pp. 1–18). https://doi.org/DOI: 10.1201/9781003388449-1

Kunze, T., Stadler, M., and Greiff, S. (2018). A look at complex problem-solving in the 21st century. *Education: Future Frontiers, 11.*

Lameras, P., & Arnab, S. (2021). Power to the teachers: An exploratory review on artificial intelligence in education. *Information (Basel)*, 13(1), 14.

Lampropoulos, G. (2023). Recommender systems in education: A literature review and bibliometric analysis. *Advances in Mobile Learning Educational Research*, 3(2), 829–850. DOI: 10.25082/amler.2023.02.011

Landers, R., & Behrend, T. (2022). Auditing the AI Auditors: A Framework for Evaluating Fairness and Bias in High Stakes AI Predictive Models. *The American Psychologist*, 78. Advance online publication. DOI: 10.1037/amp0000972 PMID: 35157476

Larsson, S., & Heintz, F. (2020). Transparency in artificial intelligence. *Internet Policy Review*, 9(2).

LeCun, Y., Bengio, Y., & Hinton, G. (2015). Deep learning. *Nature*, 521(7553), 436–444. PMID: 26017442

LeCun, Y., Bottou, L., Bengio, Y., & Haffner, P. (1998). Gradient-based learning applied to document recognition. *Proceedings of the IEEE*, 86(11), 2278–2324. DOI: 10.1109/5.726791

Lepri, B., Oliver, N., Letouzé, E., Pentland, A., & Vinck, P. (2018). Fair, Transparent, and Accountable Algorithmic Decision-making Processes. *Philosophy & Technology*, 31(4), 611–627. DOI: 10.1007/s13347-017-0279-x

Leslie, D., Burr, C., Aitken, M., Cowls, J., Katell, M., & Briggs, M. (2021). Artificial intelligence, human rights, democracy, and the rule of law: a primer. arXiv preprint arXiv:2104.04147.

Liaison. (2024, February 14). *Ethical Considerations for AI in Higher Education: Ensuring Fairness and Transparency*. Liaison. https://www.liaisonedu.com/ethical-considerations-for-ai-in-higher-education-ensuring-fairness-and-transparency/

Liao, S. M. (Ed.). (2020). *Ethics of artificial intelligence*. Oxford University Press.

Liasidou, A. (2014). Critical disability studies and socially just change in higher education. *British Journal of Special Education*, 41(2), 120–135.

Li, J. (2023, July). Big data and artificial intelligence in education: A bibliometrics study from 2010 to 2023. In *2023 IEEE World Conference on Applied Intelligence and Computing (AIC)* (pp. 400-406). IEEE.

Lima, G. de M., Ferreira, G. M. dos S., & Carvalho, J. de S. (2024). Automation in education: trending issues concerning Artificial Intelligence. *Educação e Pesquisa, 50*. https://doi.org/DOI: 10.1590/s1678-4634202450273857en

Limna, P., Jakwatanatham, S., Siripipattanakul, S., Kaewpuang, P., & Sriboonruang, P. (2022). A review of artificial intelligence (AI) in education during the digital era. *Advance Knowledge for Executives*, 1(1), 1–9.

Limna, P., Kraiwanit, T., Jangjarat, K., Klayklung, P., & Chocksathaporn, P. (2023). The use of ChatGPT in the digital era: Perspectives on chatbot implementation. *Journal of Applied Learning and Teaching*, 6(1), 64–74.

Lim, T., Gottipati, S., & Cheong, M. (2023). *Ethical Considerations for Artificial Intelligence in Educational Assessments*., DOI: 10.4018/979-8-3693-0205-7.ch003

Lin, Y., & Yu, Z. (2024). A bibliometric analysis of artificial intelligence chatbots in educational contexts. *Interactive Technology and Smart Education*, 21(2), 189–213.

Liu, A., Ma, E., Wang, Y. C., Xu, S., & Grillo, T. (2024). AI and supportive technology experiences of customers with visual impairments in hotel, restaurant, and travel contexts. *International Journal of Contemporary Hospitality Management*, 36(1), 274–291.

Liu, G., & Ma, C. (2024). Measuring EFL learners' use of ChatGPT in informal digital learning of English based on the technology acceptance model. *Innovation in Language Learning and Teaching*, 18(2), 125–138.

Liu, J., Kong, X., Xia, F., Bai, X., Wang, L., Qing, Q., & Lee, I. (2018). Artificial intelligence in the 21st century. *IEEE Access : Practical Innovations, Open Solutions*, 6, 34403–34421. DOI: 10.1109/ACCESS.2018.2819688

Li, X., & Jiang, Y. (2024). Artificial intelligence in education: Opportunities, current status, and prospects. *Geographical Research Bulletin*, 3, 146–174.

Lombardi, A. R., Dougherty, S. M., & Monahan, J. (2018). Students with intellectual disabilities and career and technical education opportunities: A systematic literature review. *Journal of Disability Policy Studies*, 29(2), 82–96. DOI: 10.1177/1044207318764863

Lopes, J. M., Silva, L. F., & Massano-Cardoso, I. (2024). AI Meets the Shopper: Psychosocial Factors in Ease of Use and Their Effect on E-Commerce Purchase Intention. *Behavioral Sciences (Basel, Switzerland)*, 14(7), 616. PMID: 39062439

Lord, T. (2001). Research on the integration of technology in K-12 schools. *Journal of Educational Computing Research*, 24(1), 21–27.

Lozano, A., & Blanco Fontao, C. (2023). Is the education system prepared for the irruption of artificial intelligence? A study on the perceptions of students of primary education degree from a dual perspective: Current pupils and future teachers. *Education Sciences*, 13(7), 733. DOI: 10.3390/educsci13070733

Luckin, R., & Holmes, W. (2016). *Intelligence Unleashed: An argument for AI in Education*.

Luckin, R., Holmes, W., Griffiths, M., & Forcier, L. B. (2016). Intelligence unleashed. *An argument for AI in Education, 18.*

Luckin, R. (2019). The learner-centered design of AI: Enabling academic innovation. *International Journal of Artificial Intelligence in Education*, 29(3), 617–622.

Luckin, R., Holmes, W., Griffiths, M., & Forcier, L. B. (2016). *Intelligence unleashed: An argument for AI in Education*. Pearson.

M U D., & Thombre, D. (2023, June 24). Admission BOT: Unleashing the Potential of Neural Networks in Streamlining the Admission Process., 5(3). https://doi.org/ DOI: 10.36948/ijfmr.2023.v05i03.3989

Madan, R., & Ashok, M. (2023). AI adoption and diffusion in public administration: A systematic literature review and future research agenda. *Government Information Quarterly*, 40(1), 101774. DOI: 10.1016/j.giq.2022.101774

Madriaga, M. (2007). Enduring disablism: Students with dyslexia and their pathways into UK higher education and beyond. *Disability & Society*, 22(4), 399–412.

Maghsudi, S., Lan, A., Xu, J., & van Der Schaar, M. (2021). Personalized education in the artificial intelligence era: What to expect next. *IEEE Signal Processing Magazine*, 38(3), 37–50.

Mahbub, S., Wafik, H. A., Arif, Z., Rahman, M., Uddin, A., & Azim, I. B. (2024). AI Consciousness and Technological Advancement in Bangladesh's Higher Education: AI Awareness among the Learners.

Mahieu, R., van Hoboken, J., & Asghari, H. (2019). *Responsibility for Data Protection in a Networked World – On the Question of the Controller, 'Effective and Complete Protection' and Its Application to Data Access Rights in Europe* (SSRN Scholarly Paper 3256743). https://doi.org/DOI: 10.2139/ssrn.3256743

Majeed, A., & Hwang, S. O. (2024). Towards Unlocking the Hidden Potentials of the Data-Centric AI Paradigm in the Modern Era. *Applied System Innovation*, 7(4), 4. Advance online publication. DOI: 10.3390/asi7040054

Majjate, H., Bellarhmouch, Y., Jeghal, A., Yahyaouy, A., Tairi, H., & Zidani, K. A. (2023). AI-powered academic guidance and counseling system based on student profile and interests. *Applied System Innovation*, 7(1), 6.

Malik, G., Tayal, D. K., & Vij, S. (2019). An analysis of the role of artificial intelligence in education and teaching. In *Recent Findings in Intelligent Computing Techniques* (pp. 407–417). Springer., DOI: 10.1007/978-981-10-8639-7_42

Mannan, M., Mustafa, Z. B., Aziz, S. F. B. A., & Maruf, T. I. (2023). Technology adoption for higher education in Bangladesh–development and validation. *Journal of Education and Social Sciences*, 24(1), 1–9.

Mannuru, N. R., Shahriar, S., Teel, Z. A., Wang, T., Lund, B. D., Tijani, S., Pohboon, C. O., Agbaji, D., Alhassan, J., Galley, J., Kousari, R., Ogbadu-Oladapo, L., Saurav, S. K., Srivastava, A., Tummuru, S. P., Uppala, S., & Vaidya, P. (2023). Artificial intelligence in developing countries: The impact of generative artificial intelligence (AI) technologies for development. *Information Development*. Advance online publication. DOI: 10.1177/02666669231200628

Maphosa, V., & Maphosa, M. (2023). Artificial intelligence in higher education: A bibliometric analysis and topic modeling approach. *Applied Artificial Intelligence*, 37(1), 2261730.

Marjanovikj-Apostolovski, M. (2024). ChatGPT as a learning tool in an undergraduate advanced academic english course at south east european university. Journal of Teaching English for Specific and Academic Purposes, 243-254.

Markauskaite, L., Marrone, R., Poquet, O., Knight, S., Martinez-Maldonado, R., Howard, S., & Siemens, G. (2022). Rethinking the entwinement between artificial intelligence and human learning: What capabilities do learners need for a world with AI? *Computers and Education: Artificial Intelligence*, 3, 100056.

Marshall, S. J. (2018). Shaping the University of the Future. Springer, 10, 978-981.

Martínez, I. G., Batanero, J. M. F., Cerero, J. F., & León, S. P. (2023). Analysing the impact of artifcial intelligence and computational sciences on student performance: Systematic review and meta-analysis. NAER. *Journal of New Approaches in Educational Research*, 12(1), 171–197.

Martínez-Torresd, I. O.-P., & Kreibel, D. (2023). Impact of artificial intelligence on assessment methods in primary and secondary education: Systematic literature review. *Revista de Psicodidáctica*, 28, 93–103.

Max Planck Society. (2024). *Research on Artificial Intelligence (AI) at the Max Planck Society*. https://www.mpg.de/19142520/artifical-intelligence

Mayeke, N. R., Arigbabu, A. T., Olaniyi, O. O., Okunleye, O. J., & Adigwe, C. S. (2024). Evolving Access Control Paradigms: A Comprehensive Multi-Dimensional Analysis of Security Risks and System Assurance in Cyber Engineering. *Asian Journal of Research in Computer Science*, 17(5), 108–124.

Mcafee, A., & Brynjolfsson, E. (2017). *Machine, Platform, Crowd*. WW Norton.

Mccarthy, J. (2007). From here to human-level AI. *Artificial Intelligence*, 171, 1174–1182.

McGrath, C., Pargman, T. C., Juth, N., & Palmgren, P. J. (2023). University teachers' perceptions of responsibility and artificial intelligence in higher education-An experimental philosophical study. *Computers and Education: Artificial Intelligence*, 4, 100139.

Meacham, M. (2021). A Brief History of AI and Education. *International Journal of Adult and Non-Formal Education.*, 2(4), 1–2.

Meckler, L., & Verma, P. (2022) Teachers are on alert for inevitable cheating after the release of ChatGPT. The Washington Post. Available at: https://www.washingtonpost.com/education/2022/12/28/chatbot-cheating-ai-chatbotgpt-teachers/ (Accessed August 15, 2024).

Mehendale, P. (2023). Personalization in Education through AI. *European Journal of Advances in Engineering and Technology*, 10(3), 60–65.

Mellul, C. (2018). Emerging technologies in higher education and the workplace: An assessment. *Future*, •••, 223.

Memarian, B., & Doleck, T. (2023). Fairness, Accountability, Transparency, and Ethics (FATE) in Artificial Intelligence (AI) and higher education: A systematic review. *Computers and Education: Artificial Intelligence*, 5, 100152. DOI: 10.1016/j.caeai.2023.100152

Meng, N., Dhimolea, T. K., & Ali, Z. (2022). AI-enhanced education: Teaching and learning reimagined. In *Bridging human intelligence and artificial intelligence* (pp. 107–124). Springer International Publishing.

Menteş, A. (2000). *Manevra ve sevk sistemi seçiminde bulanık çok kriterli karar verme* (Doctoral dissertation, Fen Bilimleri Enstitüsü).

Mer, A. (2023). Artificial intelligence in human resource management: Recent trends and research agenda. Digital Transformation, Strategic Resilience. *Cyber Security and Risk Management*, 111, 31–56.

Mergel, I., Dickinson, H., Stenvall, J., & Gasco, M. (2023). Implementing AI in the public sector. *Public Management Review*, 0(0), 1–14. DOI: 10.1080/14719037.2023.2231950

Metli, A. (2023). Articles on education and artificial intelligence: A bibliometric analysis. Journal of Social Sciences and Education, 6(Education Special Issue), 279-312.

Mikalef, P., Boura, M., Lekakos, G., & Krogstie, J. (2019). Big data analytics and firm performance: Findings from a mixed-method approach. *Journal of Business Research*, 98, 261–276. DOI: 10.1016/j.jbusres.2019.01.044

Mills, A., Bali, M., & Eaton, L. (2023). How do we respond to generative AI in education? Open educational practices give us a framework for an ongoing process. *Journal of Applied Learning and Teaching*, 6(1), 16–30.

Minaei-Bidgoli, B., Kashy, D. A., Kortemeyer, G., & Punch, W. F. (2003, November). Predicting student performance: an application of data mining methods with an educational web-based system. In 33rd Annual Frontiers in Education, 2003. FIE 2003. (Vol. 1, pp. T2A-13). IEEE.

Mingers, J., & Leydesdorff, L. (2015). A review of theory and practice in scientometrics. *European Journal of Operational Research*, 246(1), 1–19.

Mittelstadt, B. D., Allo, P., Taddeo, M., Wachter, S., & Floridi, L. (2016). The ethics of algorithms: Mapping the debate. *Big Data & Society*, 3(2), 2053951716679679. DOI: 10.1177/2053951716679679

Mohd Rahim, N. I., & Iahad, A., N., Yusof, A. F., & A. Al-Sharafi, M. (2022). AI-based chatbots adoption model for higher-education institutions: A hybrid PLS-SEM-neural network modelling approach. *Sustainability*, 14(19), 12726.

Molefi, R. R., Ayanwale, M. A., Kurata, L., & Chere-Masopha, J. (2024). Do in-service teachers accept artificial intelligence-driven technology? The mediating role of school support and resources. *Computers and Education Open*, •••, 100191.

Mon, B. F., Wasfi, A., Hayajneh, M., Slim, A., & Ali, N. A. (2023). Reinforcement Learning in Education: A Literature Review. *Informatics (MDPI)*, 10(3), 74. DOI: 10.3390/informatics10030074

Montenegro-Rueda, M., Fernández-Cerero, J., Fernández-Batanero, J. M., & López-Meneses, E. (2023). Impact of the implementation of ChatGPT in education: A systematic review. *Computers*, 12(8), 153. DOI: 10.3390/computers12080153

Mortimore, T. (2013). Dyslexia in higher education: Creating a fully inclusive institution. *Journal of Research in Special Educational Needs*, 13(1), 38–47.

Muhie, Y. A., & Woldie, A. B. (2020, January 1). Integration of Artificial Intelligence Technologies in Teaching and Learning in Higher Education., 10(1), 1-7. http://www.sapub.org/global/showpaperpdf.aspx?doi=10.5923/j.scit.20201001.01

Muhie, Y. A., & Woldie, A. B. (n.d.). Integration of Artificial Intelligence Technologies in Teaching and Learning in Higher Education. *Science and Technology*, 2020(1), 1–7. DOI: 10.5923/j.scit.202001001.01

Mujiono, M. (2023). Educational Collaboration: Teachers and Artificial Intelligence. *Jurnal Kependidikan: Jurnal Hasil Penelitian Dan Kajian Kepustakaan Di Bidang Pendidikan. Pengajaran Dan Pembelajaran*, 9(2), 618. DOI: 10.33394/jk.v9i2.7801

Mulaudzi, L., & Hamilton, J. (2024). Student perspectives on optimising AI tools to enhance personalised learning in higher education. *Interdisciplinary Journal of Education Research*, 6(s1), 1–15. DOI: 10.38140/ijer-2024.vol6.s1.03

Mullangi, K., Dhameliya, N., Anumandla, S. K. R., Yarlagadda, V. K., Sachani, D. K., Vennapusa, S. C. R., & Patel, B. (2023). AI-Augmented Decision-Making in Management Using Quantum Networks. *Asian Business Review*, 13(2), 73–86.

Mullowney, M. W., Duncan, K., Elsayed, S. S., Garg, N., Hooft, J. J. J. V. D., Martin, N. I., Meijer, D., Terlouw, B. R., Biermann, F., Blin, K., Durairaj, J., González, M. G., Helfrich, E. J. N., Huber, F., Leopold-Messer, S., Rajan, K., Rond, T. D., Santen, J. V., Sorokina, M., & Medema, M. H. (2023, September 11). Artificial intelligence for natural product drug discovery. *Nature Portfolio*, 22(11), 895–916. DOI: 10.1038/s41573-023-00774-7 PMID: 37697042

Muniasamy, A., & Alasiry, A. (2020). Deep Learning: The Impact on Future eLearning. *International Journal of Emerging Technologies in Learning*, 15(1), 188–199. DOI: 10.3991/ijet.v15i01.11435

Murdan, A. P., & Halkhoree, R. (2024, June). Integration of Artificial Intelligence for educational excellence and innovation in higher education institutions. In 2024 1st International Conference on Smart Energy Systems and Artificial Intelligence (SESAI) (pp. 1-6). IEEE.

Murphy, R. F. (2019). Artificial intelligence applications to support k-12 teachers and teaching: A review of promising applications, opportunities, and challenges. Perspective. *RAND Corporation* (1-20).

Murphy, E. (2004). Recognizing and promoting the role of educational technology specialists: A needs assessment. *Journal of Research on Technology in Education*, 36(2), 161–181.

Murshed, S. M., & Imtiaz, M. (2020). Inclusive practices in Bangladesh. In *BRILL eBooks* (pp. 159–174). https://doi.org/DOI: 10.1163/9789004432789_011

Musso, M. F., Kyndt, E., Cascallar, E. C., & Dochy, F. (2013). Predicting general academic performance and identifying the differential contribution of participating variables using artificial neural networks. *Frontline Learning Research*, 1(1), 42–71. DOI: 10.14786/flr.v1i1.13

Nassar, A., & Kamal, M. (2021). Ethical dilemmas in AI-powered decision-making: A deep dive into big data-driven ethical considerations. *International Journal of Responsible Artificial Intelligence*, 11(8), 1–11.

Nassar, A., & Kamal, M. (2021). Ethical Dilemmas in AI-Powered Decision-Making: A Deep Dive into Big Data-Driven Ethical Considerations. *International Journal of Responsible Artificial Intelligence*, 11(8), 8.

Neumann, O., Guirguis, K., & Steiner, R. (2024). Exploring artificial intelligence adoption in public organizations: A comparative case study. *Public Management Review*, 26(1), 114–141. DOI: 10.1080/14719037.2022.2048685

Ng, D. T. K., Leung, J. K. L., Su, J., Ng, R. C. W., & Chu, S. K. W. (2023). Teachers' AI digital competencies and twenty-first century skills in the post-pandemic world. *Educational Technology Research and Development*, 71(1), 137–161. DOI: 10.1007/s11423-023-10203-6 PMID: 36844361

Nguyen, A., Ngo, H. N., Hong, Y., Dang, B., & Nguyen, B. P. T. (2023). Ethical principles for artificial intelligence in education. *Education and Information Technologies*, 28(4), 4221–4241. PMID: 36254344

Niehues, N., Fischer, E., Jeremias, C., & Dieterich, P. (2022). *Prüfungsrecht* (8., vollständig neubearbeitete Edition). C.H.Beck.

Nieto-Morote, A., & Ruz-Vila, F. (2012). A fuzzy multi-criteria decision-making model for construction contractor prequalification. *Automation in Construction*, 25, 8–19.

Nikolic, S., Daniel, S., Haque, R., Belkina, M., Hassan, G. M., Grundy, S., & Sandison, C. (2023). ChatGPT versus engineering education assessment: A multidisciplinary and multi-institutional benchmarking and analysis of this generative artificial intelligence tool to investigate assessment integrity. *European Journal of Engineering Education*, 48(4), 559–614.

Nikolinakos, N. T. (2023). *EU Policy and Legal Framework for Artificial Intelligence, Robotics and Related Technologies—The AI Act*. Springer Nature.

Nilsson, N. J. (1991). Logic and artificial intelligence. *Artificial Intelligence*, 47(1-3), 31–56.

Nilsson, N. J. (1998). *Artificial intelligence: a new synthesis*. Morgan Kaufmann.

Nkechi, A. A., Ojo, A. O., & Eneh, O. A. (2024). Impact of artificial intelligence in achieving quality education. In *Artificial intelligence*. https://doi.org/DOI: 10.5772/intechopen.1004871

Noble, S. U. (2018). *Algorithms of Oppression: How Search Engines Reinforce Racism* (Illustrated Edition). Combined Academic Publ.

Nong, L., Liu, G., Tang, C., & Chen, Y. (2023). The Design and Implementation of Campus informatization in Chinese Universities: A Conceptual Framework. *Sustainability*, 15(6), 4732.

Novawan, A., Walker, S. A., & Ikeda, O. (2024). The new face of technology-enhanced language learning (TELL) with artificial intelligence (AI): Teacher perspectives, practices, and challenges. *Journal of English in Academic and Professional Communication*, 10(1), 1–18.

Núñez, J L M., Harris, P., Fernández, R P., Abbas, A., & Radovanović, D. (2023, January 1). Does intrinsic motivation mediate perceived artificial intelligence (AI) learning and computational thinking of students during the COVID-19 pandemic? Elsevier BV, 4, 100128-100128. https://doi.org/DOI: 10.1016/j.caeai.2023.100128

Nwaogu, G.O. (nd) Educational administration. School of human and social studies. Atlantic International University.

Nye, B. D. (2015). Intelligent tutoring systems by and for the developing world: A review of trends and approaches for educational technology in a global context. *International Journal of Artificial Intelligence in Education*, 25(2), 177–203. DOI: 10.1007/s40593-014-0028-6

O'Neil, C. (2016). *Weapons of Math Destruction: How Big Data Increases Inequality and Threatens Democracy*. Crown Publishing Group.

Ober, T M., Lehman, B., Gooch, R., Oluwalana, O., Solyst, J., Phelps, G., & Hamilton, L S. (2023, August 7). Culturally Responsive Personalized Learning: Recommendations for a Working Definition and Framework. Wiley, 2023(1), 1-14. https://doi.org/DOI: 10.1002/ets2.12372

Ocker, R. J., & Yaverbaum, G. J. (2001). Collaborative learning environments: Exploring student attitudes and satisfaction in face-to-face and asynchronous computer conferencing settings. *Journal of Interactive Learning Research*, 12(4), 427–448.

Okulich-Kazarin, V., Artyukhov, A., Skowron, Ł., Artyukhova, N., & Wołowiec, T. (2024). When Artificial Intelligence Tools Meet" Non-Violent" Learning Environments (SDG 4.3): Crossroads with Smart Education. Sustainability (2071-1050), 16(17).

Olabanji, S. O., Oladoyinbo, O. B., Asonze, C. U., Oladoyinbo, T. O., Ajayi, S. A., & Olaniyi, O. O. (2024). Effect of adopting AI to explore big data on personally identifiable information (PII) for financial and economic data transformation. Available at *SSRN* 4739227.

Omrani, N., Rivieccio, G., Fiore, U., Schiavone, F., & Agreda, S. G. (2022). To trust or not to trust? An assessment of trust in AI-based systems: Concerns, ethics and contexts. *Technological Forecasting and Social Change*, 181, 121763.

Onaga, E. E., & Martoccio, T. L. (2008). Dynamic and uncertain pathways between early childhood inclusion policy and practice. *International Journal of Child Care and Education Policy*, 2, 67–75.

Onesi-Ozigagun, O., Ololade, Y. J., Eyo-Udo, N. L., & Ogundipe, D. O. (2024, April 10). REVOLUTIONIZING EDUCATION THROUGH AI: A COMPREHENSIVE REVIEW OF ENHANCING LEARNING EXPERIENCES. *Fair East Publishers*, 6(4), 589–607. DOI: 10.51594/ijarss.v6i4.1011

Orozco, M. P., Pytel, P., & Pollo-Cattaneo, M. F. (2020). Implementation methodology of a chatbot as a virtual tutor in the educational field for universities in Latin America. In Serna, E.M. (Ed.), Formative Research in Engineering(pp. 218–226). Antioquia Research Institute (IAI).

Ouyang, F., & Jiao, P. (2021). Artificial intelligence in education: The three paradigms. *Computers and Education: Artificial Intelligence*, 2, 100020.

Ouyang, F., Zheng, L., & Jiao, P. (2022). Artificial intelligence in online higher education: A systematic review of empirical research from 2011 to 2020. *Education and Information Technologies*, 27(6), 7893–7925.

Owoc, M. L., Sawicka, A., & Weichbroth, P. (2019, August). Artificial intelligence technologies in education: benefits, challenges and strategies of implementation. In *IFIP International Workshop on Artificial Intelligence for Knowledge Management* (pp. 37-58). Cham: Springer International Publishing.

Pallathadka, H., Wenda, A., Ramirez-Asís, E., Asís-López, M., Flores-Albornoz, J., & Phasinam, K. (2023). Enhancing prediction of student success: Automated machine learning approach. *Materials Today: Proceedings*, 80, 3782–3785.

Pannu, A. (2015). Artificial intelligence and its application in different areas. *Artificial Intelligence*, 4(10), 79–84.

Paramythis, A., & Reisinger, S. L. (2003). Adaptive learning environments and e-learning standards. Retrieved 4 May, 2024. https://files.eric.ed.gov/fulltext/EJ1099144.pdf

Park, D. Y., & Kim, H. (2023). Determinants of intentions to use digital mental healthcare content among university students, faculty, and staff: Motivation, perceived usefulness, perceived ease of use, and parasocial interaction with AI Chatbot. *Sustainability*, 15(1), 872.

Pasquale, F. (2015). *The Black Box Society: The Secret Algorithms That Control Money and Information*. Harvard University Press. https://www.jstor.org/stable/j.ctt13x0hch

Patel, S. (2024, September 9). *AI-DRIVEN EDUCATIONAL INTERVENTIONS: AN EMPIRICAL STUDY ON THEIR EFFICACY IN IMPROVING ACADEMIC PERFORMANCE*. https://iaeme-library.com/index.php/IJETR/article/view/IJETR_09_02_013

Pedro, F., Subosa, M., Rivas, A., & Valverde, P. (2019). *Artificial intelligence in education : challenges and opportunities for sustainable development*. https://hdl.handle.net/20.500.12799/6533

Pedro, F., Subosa, M., Rivas, A., & Valverde, P. (2019). Artificial intelligence in education: Challenges and opportunities for sustainable development.

Perkins, M. (2023, February 22). Academic integrity considerations of AI Large Language Models in the post-pandemic era: ChatGPT and beyond. *University of Wollongong*, 20(2). Advance online publication. DOI: 10.53761/1.20.02.07

Perset, K., Russo, L., & Oder, N. (2024, June 11). *OECD AI Review of Germany: A new phase for Germany's AI strategy*. OECD.AI Policy Observatory. https://oecd.ai/en/wonk/review-germany-2024

Petit, J. (2024, March). AI-Enhanced Design Thinking in Teacher Education: A Practical Workshop. In Society for Information Technology & Teacher Education International Conference (pp. 1424-1433). Association for the Advancement of Computing in Education (AACE).

Pisica, A. I., Edu, T., Zaharia, R. M., & Zaharia, R. (2023). Implementing Artificial Intelligence in Higher Education: Pros and Cons from the Perspectives of Academics. *Societies (Basel, Switzerland)*, 13(5), 5. Advance online publication. DOI: 10.3390/soc13050118

Plitnichenko, L. (2020). 5 Main Roles of Artificial Intelligence in Education. ELearningIndustry. https://elearningindustry.com/5-main-roles-artificial-intelligence-in-education

Pokrivcakova, S. (2019). Preparing teachers for the application of AI-powered technologies in foreign language education. *Journal of Language and Cultural Education*, 7(3), 135–153. DOI: 10.2478/jolace-2019-0025

Polat, H., Topuz, A. C., Yildiz, M., Taslibeyaz, E., & Kursun, E. (2024). A bibliometric analysis of research on chatgpt in education. *International Journal of Technology in Education*, 7(1), 59–85.

Popenici, S. A., & Kerr, S. T. (2017). Exploring the impact of artificial intelligence on teaching and learning in higher education. *Research and Practice in Technology Enhanced Learning*, 12(1), 22. PMID: 30595727

Pradeep, A., Das, S., & Kizhekkethottam, J. (2015).Students' dropout factor prediction using EDM techniques. *International Conference on Soft-Computing and Networks Security (ICSNS)IEEE Xplore,* DOI: 10.1109/7292372

Prahani, B., Rizki, I., Jatmiko, B., Suprapto, N., & Tan, A. (2022). Artificial intelligence in education research during the last ten years: A review and bibliometric study. [iJET]. *International Journal of Emerging Technologies in Learning*, 17(8), 169–188.

Prasad, A., & George, S. S. (2022). A Machine Learning Approach for Tracking and Predicting Student Performance in Degree Programs. *Proceedings of the National Conference on Emerging Computer Applications (NCECA)*-2022, *4(1).*

Preston, J., & Bishop, M. (2006). Essays on Searle and Artificial Intelligence, Oxford: Clarendon Press, 2002, pp. xvi+ 410.

Prideaux, L., Patton, W., & Creed, P. (2002). Development of a theoretically derived school career program: An Australian endeavour. *International Journal for Educational and Vocational Guidance*, 2, 115–130. DOI: 10.1023/A:1016077211567

Pua, S., Ahmad, N. A., & Khambari, M. N. M. (2021). Identification and analysis of core topics in educational artificial intelligence research: A bibliometric analysis. *Cypriot Journal of Educational Sciences*, 16(3), 995–1009.

Pyper, J. (2024, July 1). *Heilbronner Studenten entwickeln KI für einen leichteren Studienalltag*. swr.online. https://www.swr.de/swraktuell/baden-wuerttemberg/heilbronn/heilbronner-studenten-entwickeln-kuenstliche-intelligenz-100.html

Radu, C., Ciocoiu, C. N., Veith, C., & Cătălin, R. (2024). Artificial intelligence and competency-based education: A bibliometric analysis. *Amfiteatru Economic*, 26(65), 220–240.

Rahaman, M. M., & Akter, N. (2017). ICT used in education sector considering primary and secondary level schools in rural areas: A study of Sylhet division in Bangladesh. *IOSR Journal of Business and Management*, 19(4), 1–6.

Rahman, M. H., Ahmad, A. B., & Sawal, M. Z. H. B. M. (2024). The influence of personal factors on resistance to technology adoption in university libraries in Bangladesh. *Information Development*. Advance online publication. DOI: 10.1177/02666669241257196

Rajendran, S., Chamundeswari, S., & Sinha, A. A. (2022). Predicting the academic performance of middle- and high-school students using machine learning algorithms. *Social Sciences & Humanities Open*, 6, 100357.

Rammer, C., Doherr, T., Kinne, J., & Lenz, D. (2024). *KI-Einsatz in Unternehmen in Deutschland.*

Rane, M V., Apte, V M., Nerkar, V N., Roja, M M., & Rajput, K. (2021, March 5). Automated Timetabling System for University Course. https://doi.org/DOI: 10.1109/esci50559.2021.9396906

Rane, N. L. (2024). Education 4.0 and 5.0: integrating Artificial Intelligence (AI) for personalized and adaptive learning. *Journal of Artificial Intelligence and Robotics*. https://doi.org/DOI: 10.61577/jaiar.2024.100006

Rani, M., Bala, J., & Varjani, S. (2023, June 19).. . *Scope and Challenges of Multimedia in Education Sector.*, 5(3). Advance online publication. DOI: 10.36948/ijfmr.2023.v05i03.3868

Rao, P. K., & Shukla, A. (2023). Sustainable strategic management: A bibliometric analysis. *Business Strategy and the Environment*, 32(6), 3902–3914.

Rasheed, Z., Ghwanmeh, S., & Abualkishik, A. Z. (2023). Harnessing Artificial Intelligence for Personalized Learning: A Systematic Review. *Data and Metadata*, 2, 146–146.

Rasul, T., Nair, S., Kalendra, D., Robin, M., Santini, F., Ladeira, W., Sun, M., Day, I., Rather, A., & Heathcote, L. (2023).. . *The Role of ChatGPT in Higher Education: Benefits, Challenges, and Future Research Directions.*, 6. Advance online publication. DOI: 10.37074/jalt.2023.6.1.29

Rathnayake, C., & Gunawardana, A. (2023). The role of generative ai in enhancing human resource management recruitment, training, and performance evaluation perspectives. *International Journal of Stochastic Analysis*, 8(11), 13–22.

Reckling, C. (2024, August 13). *VG München: KI-Einsatz im Prüfungsrecht*. https://www.anwalt.de/rechtstipps/vg-muenchen-ki-einsatz-im-pruefungsrecht-230279.html

Redding, S. (2016). Competencies and personalized learning. *Handbook On Personalized Learning For States, Districts, And Schools*, 3-18.

Redpath, J., Kearney, P., Nicholl, P., Mulvenna, M., Wallace, J., & Martin, S. (2013). A qualitative study of the lived experiences of disabled post-transition students in higher education institutions in Northern Ireland. *Studies in Higher Education*, 38(9), 1334–1350.

Regulation - 2016/679 - EN - GDPR - EUR-Lex (2016). https://eur-lex.europa.eu/eli/reg/2016/679/oj

Renz, A., Krishnaraja, S., & Gronau, E. (2020). Demystification of artificial intelligence in education—How much AI is really in the educational technology? *International Journal of Learning Analytics and Artificial Intelligence for Education*, 2(1), 4–30.

Report, T. (2023, June 12). NSU, BUET join hands for collaborative research and AI development. *The Business Standard*. https://www.tbsnews.net/economy/corporates/nsu-buet-join-hands-collaborative-research-and-ai-development-648266

Resnick, M. (2024, March 27). Generative AI and Creative Learning: Concerns, Opportunities, and Choices. https://doi.org/DOI: 10.21428/e4baedd9.cf3e35e5

Rieckmann, M. (2018). Learning to transform the world: Key competencies in Education for Sustainable Development. Issues and trends in education for sustainable development, 39(1), 39-59.

Riedl, M. O. (2019). Human-centered artificial intelligence and machine learning. *Human Behavior and Emerging Technologies*, 1, 33–36.

Roberts, L. N., Solomon, F. N., & Cummings, R. (2024). Navigating the AI Landscape: Student and Teacher Perceptions of AI in Assessments in High School and College Settings. In AI-Enhanced Teaching Methods (pp. 268-285). IGI Global.

Rochel, J. (2021). Ethics in the GDPR: A Blueprint for Applied Legal Theory. *International Data Privacy Law*, 11(2), 209–223. DOI: 10.1093/idpl/ipab007

Rodgers, W., Murray, J. M., Stefanidis, A., Degbey, W. Y., & Tarba, S. Y. (2023). An artificial intelligence algorithmic approach to ethical decision-making in human resource management processes. *Human Resource Management Review*, 33(1), 100925.

Rodrigues, M., Silva, R., Borges, A. P., Franco, M., & Oliveira, C. (2024). Artificial intelligence: Threat or asset to academic integrity? A bibliometric analysis. *Kybernetes*.

Rodríguez-Hernandez, C. F., Musso, M., Eva Kyndt, E., & Cascallar, E. (2021). Artificial neural networks in academic performance prediction: Systematic implementation and predictor evaluation. *Computers and Education: Artificial Intelligence*, 2, 100018.

Rodway, P., & Schepman, A. (2023, January 1). The impact of adopting AI educational technologies on projected course satisfaction in university students. Elsevier BV, 5, 100150-100150. https://doi.org/DOI: 10.1016/j.caeai.2023.100150

Roll, I., & Wylie, R. (2016). Evolution and revolution in artificial intelligence in education. *International Journal of Artificial Intelligence in Education*, 26(2), 582–599. DOI: 10.1007/s40593-016-0110-3

Romero, C., & Ventura, S. (2020). Educational data mining and learning analytics: An updated survey. *Wiley Interdisciplinary Reviews. Data Mining and Knowledge Discovery*, 10(3), e1355.

Rose, D. J. (2010). *Fallproof!: a comprehensive balance and mobility training program*. Human Kinetics.

Roy, G., Babu, R., Kalam, M. A., Yasmin, N., Zafar, T., & Nath, S. R. (2021). Response, readiness and challenges of online teaching amid COVID-19 pandemic: The case of higher education in Bangladesh. *The Educational and Developmental Psychologist*, 40(1), 40–50. DOI: 10.1080/20590776.2021.1997066

Rufai, A. A., Khan, M. S. H., & Hasan, M. (2024). An exploration of pedagogical approaches in teaching artificial intelligence courses: Experience from undergraduates students of Bangladesh. *Social Sciences & Humanities Open*, 10, 101075. DOI: 10.1016/j.ssaho.2024.101075

Ruiz-Rojas, L. I., Acosta-Vargas, P., De-Moreta-Llovet, J., & González, M. (2023, July 25). Empowering Education with Generative Artificial Intelligence Tools: Approach with an Instructional Design Matrix. *Multidisciplinary Digital Publishing Institute*, 15(15), 11524–11524. DOI: 10.3390/su151511524

Ruiz-Rojas, L. I., Acosta-Vargas, P., De-Moreta-Llovet, J., & Gonzalez-Rodriguez, M. (2023). Empowering education with generative artificial intelligence tools: Approach with an instructional design matrix. *Sustainability*, 15(15), 11524.

Russell, S. J., & Norvig, P. (2016). *Artificial intelligence: a modern approach*. Pearson.

Rütti-Joy, O., Winder, G., & Biedermann, H. (2024). Teacher Educator Professionalism in the Age of AI: Navigating the New Landscape of Quality Education.

Ryan, M. (2020). In AI we trust: Ethics, artificial intelligence, and reliability. *Science and Engineering Ethics*, 26(5), 2749–2767. PMID: 32524425

Saaida, M. B. (2023). AI-Driven transformations in higher education: Opportunities and challenges. *International Journal of Educational Research and Studies*, 5(1), 29–36.

Saaty, T. L. (1980). The analytic hierarchy process (AHP). *The Journal of the Operational Research Society*, 41(11), 1073–1076.

Sadeghi, N., Kasim, Z. M., Tan, B. H., & Abdullah, F. S. (2012). Learning styles, personality types and reading comprehension performance. *English Language Teaching*, 5(4), 116–123.

Saeed, M. M. A., Saeed, R. A., Ahmed, Z. E., Gaid, A. S. A., & Mokhtar, R. A. (2024). AI technologies in engineering education. In *Advances in educational technologies and instructional design book series* (pp. 61–87). https://doi.org/DOI: 10.4018/979-8-3693-2728-9.ch003

Sandhu, R., Channi, H. K., Ghai, D., Cheema, G. S., & Kaur, M. (2024). An Introduction to Generative AI Tools for Education 2030. In *Advances in educational technologies and instructional design book series* (pp. 1–28). https://doi.org/DOI: 10.4018/979-8-3693-2440-0.ch001

Sanjeevi, C. R. (2024). Elevating academic efficiency: The role of AI in faculty workload Management and Scheduling.

Santos, S. M. A. V., da Silva, C. G., de Carvalho, I. E., & de Castilho, L. P., das Neves Meroto, M. B., Tavares, P. R., dos Reis Pires, R., de Oliveira Rodrogues Moniz, S. S. (2024). The art of personalization of education: Artificial Intelligence on the stages of special education. *Contrıbuciones. Ciencia y Sociedad*, 17(2), e4971–e4971.

Sargiotis, D. (2024). Integrating AI and Big Data in Virtual Infrastructures: Transforming Educational Landscapes for the Future. Available at *SSRN* 4789850.

Schiff, D. (2022). Education for AI, not AI for education: The role of education and ethics in national AI policy strategies. *International Journal of Artificial Intelligence in Education*, 32(3), 527–563.

Schindler, L. A., Burkholder, G. J., Morad, O. A., & Marsh, C. (2017). Computer-based technology and student engagement: A critical review of the literature. *International Journal of Educational Technology in Higher Education*, 14(1), 25.

Schmidt, P., Biessmann, F., & Teubner, T. (2020). Transparency and trust in artificial intelligence systems. *Journal of Decision Systems*, 29(4), 260–278.

Schönberger, M. (2023). ChatGPT in higher education: the good, the bad, and the University. *Universitat Politecnica de Valencia, 10.*

Schunk, D. H. (2012). *Learning theories: An educational perspective* (6th ed.). Pearson Education Inc.

Schwartmann, R. (2024, May 14). *Was es beim Einsatz von KI rechtlich zu beachten gibt.* Forschung und Lehre. https://www.forschung-und-lehre.de/lehre/autonom-wie-ein-tier-6415

Schwartz, R., Schwartz, R., Vassilev, A., Greene, K., Perine, L., Burt, A., & Hall, P. (2022). Towards a standard for identifying and managing bias in artificial intelligence (Vol. 3, p. 00). US Department of Commerce, National Institute of Standards and Technology.

Sedkaoui, S., & Benaichouba, R. (2024). Generative AI as a transformative force for innovation: A review of opportunities, applications and challenges. *European Journal of Innovation Management.* Advance online publication. DOI: 10.1108/ejim-02-2024-0129

Seeber, I., Bittner, E., Briggs, R. O., Vreede, T., Vreede, G.-J., Elkins, A., Maier, R., Merz, A. B., Oeste-Reiß, S., Randrup, N., Schwabe, G., & S¨ollner, M. (2020). Machines as teammates: A research agenda on AI in team collaboration. *Information & Management*, 57(2).

Seo, K., Tang, J., Roll, I., Fels, S., & Yoon, D. (2021). The impact of artificial intelligence on learner–instructor interaction in online learning. *International Journal of Educational Technology in Higher Education*, 18, 1–23. PMID: 34778540

Shahzad, M. F., Xu, S., & Javed, I. (2024). ChatGPT awareness, acceptance, and adoption in higher education: The role of trust as a cornerstone. *International Journal of Educational Technology in Higher Education*, 21(1), 46.

Sharma, R. C., Kawachi, P., & Bozkurt, A. (2019). The landscape of artificial intelligence in open, online and distance education: Promises and concerns. *Asian Journal of Distance Education*, 14(2), 1–2.

Sharma, R., Kumar, P., Singh, D. K., Suri, D., Rajput, P., & Kumar, S. (2024, April). The intersection of ai, ethics, and education: a bibliometric analysis. In *2024 International Conference on Computing and Data Science (ICCDS)* (pp. 1-6). IEEE.

Sharma, S., & Kumar, N. (2024). Navigating the Ethical Landscape of Ai-Based Resources in Education: Implications for Learning, Proper Usage, And Course Design Enhancement. *The Online Journal of Distance Education and e-Learning : TOJDEL*, 12(2), 92.

Shmueli, G., & Ray, S. (2024). Reimagining the Journal Editorial Process: An AI-Augmented Versus an AI-Driven Future. *Journal of the Association for Information Systems*, 25(1), 10.

Shneiderman, B. (2020). Human-centered artificial intelligence: Three fresh ideas. *AIS Transactions on Human-Computer Interaction*, 12(3), 109–124.

Shrivastava, R. (2022). Teachers fear ChatGPT will make cheating easier than ever. Forbes. Available at: https://www.forbes.com/sites/rashishrivastava/2022/12/12/teachers-fear-chatgpt-will-make-cheating-easier-than-ever/?sh=5b0ab2ac1eef (Accessed on July 5, 2024).

Shukla, A. K., Janmaijaya, M., Abraham, A., & Muhuri, P. K. (2019). Engineering applications of artificial intelligence: A bibliometric analysis of 30 years (1988–2018). *Engineering Applications of Artificial Intelligence*, 85, 517–532. DOI: 10.1016/j.engappai.2019.06.010

Siau, K., & Wang, W. (2020). Artificial intelligence (AI) ethics. *Journal of Database Management*, 31(2), 74–87.

Sibalija, J., Savundranayagam, M. Y., Orange, J. B., & Kloseck, M. (2020). Social support, social participation, & depression among caregivers and non-caregivers in Canada: A population health perspective. *Aging & Mental Health*, 24(5), 765–773. PMID: 30521370

Siemens, G., Marmolejo-Ramos, F., Gabriel, F., Medeiros, K., Marrone, R., Joksimovic, S., & de Laat, M. (2022). Human and artificial cognition. *Computers & Education: Artificial Intelligence, 3*, Article 100107. https://doi.org/. caeai.2022.100107DOI: 10.1016/j

Siemens, G., & Baker, R. S. (2012). Learning analytics and educational data mining: Towards communication and collaboration. *Proceedings of the 2nd International Conference on Learning Analytics and Knowledge*, 252-254

Sijing, L., & Lan, W. (2018, August). Artificial intelligence education ethical problems and solutions. In 2018 13th International Conference on Computer Science & Education (ICCSE) (pp. 1-5). IEEE.

Sikder, A. S. (2023). Artificial Intelligence-Enabled Transformation in Bangladesh: Overcoming Challenges for Socio-Economic Empowerment.: AI-Driven Transformation in Bangladesh. *International Journal of Imminent Science & Technology*, 1(1), 77–96.

Sil, P., Chaudhuri, P., & Raman, B. (2024, January 1). Can AI Assistance Aid in the Grading of Handwritten Answer Sheets? Springer Science+Business Media, 291-298. https://doi.org/DOI: 10.1007/978-3-031-64312-5_35

Sing, C. C., Teo, T., Huang, F., Chiu, T. K., & Xing Wei, W. (2022). Secondary school students' intentions to learn AI: Testing moderation effects of readiness, social good and optimism. *Educational Technology Research and Development*, 70(3), 765–782.

Singh, B., & Kaunert, C. (2024). Future of Digital Marketing: Hyper-Personalized Customer Dynamic Experience with AI-Based Predictive Models. In Revolutionizing the AI-Digital Landscape (pp. 189-203). Productivity Press.

Singh, R. J. (2023). Transforming higher education: The power of artificial intelligence. International Journal of Multidisciplinary Research in Arts. *Science and Technology*, 1(3), 13–18.

Skinner, D., & Weisner, T. S. (2007). Sociocultural studies of families of children with intellectual disabilities. *Mental Retardation and Developmental Disabilities Research Reviews*, 13(4), 302–312. PMID: 17979204

Slavuj, V., Meštrović, A., & Kovačić, B. (2017). Adaptivity in educational systems for language learning: A review. *Computer Assisted Language Learning*, 30(1–2), 64–90. DOI: 10.1080/09588221.2016.1242502

Sleeter, C., & Carmona, J. F. (2017). *Un-standardizing curriculum: Multicultural teaching in the standards-based classroom*. Teachers College Press.

Slimi, Z., & Carballido, B. (2023). Navigating the Ethical Challenges of Artificial Intelligence in Higher Education: An Analysis of Seven Global AI Ethics Policies. *TEM Journal*, 590–602. https://doi.org/DOI: 10.18421/TEM122-02

Smerdon, D. (2024). AI in essay-based assessment: Student adoption, usage, and performance. *Computers and Education: Artificial Intelligence*, 7, 100288.

Smith, A. T. (2024). *The impact of AI: The benefits and challenges that lie ahead for AI in education. National Parents Union*. Centre for Policy Action.

Sohn, K., & Kwon, O. (2020). Technology acceptance theories and factors influencing artificial Intelligence-based intelligent products. *Telematics and Informatics*, 47, 101324.

Solis, T. (2023, May 6). *Die ChatGPT-Richtlinien der 100 größten deutschen Universitäten*. Scribbr. https://www.scribbr.de/ki-tools-nutzen/chatgpt-universitaere-richtlinien/

Somasundarama, M., Lathab, P., & Pandian, S. A. S. (2019). Curriculum Design Using Artificial Intelligence (AI) Back Propagation Method. 9th World Engineering Education Forum, WEEF 2019. Procedia Computer Science 172 (2020): 134–138.

Soner, S., & Önüt, S. (2006). Multi-criteria supplier selection: An ELECTRE-AHP application. *Sigma*, 4, 110–120.

Song, P., & Wang, X. (2020). A bibliometric analysis of worldwide educational artificial intelligence research development in recent twenty years. *Asia Pacific Education Review*, 21(3), 473–486.

Soresi, S., Nota, L., Ferrari, L., & Solberg, S. (2008). Career guidance for persons with disabilities. In Athanasou, J. A., & Van Esbroeck, R. (Eds.), *International Handbook of Career Guidance* (pp. 405–417). Springer.

Southgate, E. (2020, July 27). Artificial intelligence, ethics, equity and higher education: a 'beginning-of-the-discussion' paper. https://apo.org.au/node/307359

Sperling, K., Stenberg, C. J., & McGrath, C., kerfeldt, A., Heintz, F., & Stenliden, L. (2024). In search of artificial intelligence (AI) literacy in Teacher Education: A scoping review. *Computers and Education Open*, •••, 100169.

Spring, M., Faulconbridge, J., & Sarwar, A. (2022). How information technology automates and augments processes: Insights from Artificial-Intelligence-based systems in professional service operations. *Journal of Operations Management*, 68(6-7), 592–618.

Stahl, B., & Wright, D. (2018). Ethics and Privacy in AI and Big Data: Implementing Responsible Research and Innovation. *IEEE Security and Privacy*, 16, 26–33. DOI: 10.1109/MSP.2018.2701164

Stanujkic, D. (2015). Extension of the ARAS method for decision-making problems with interval-valued triangular fuzzy numbers. *Informatica (Vilnius)*, 26(2), 335–355.

Starcic, A. I. (2019). Human learning and learning analytics in the age of artificial intelligence. *British Journal of Educational Technology*, 50(6), 2974–2976.

Stobierski, T. (2019, August 26). *The Advantages of Data-Driven Decision-Making | HBS Online*. Business Insights Blog. https://online.hbs.edu/blog/post/data-driven-decision-making

Strielkowski, W., Grebennikova, V., Lisovskiy, A., Rakhimova, G., & Vasileva, T. (2024). AI-driven adaptive learning for sustainable educational transformation. *Sustainable Development*. Advance online publication. DOI: 10.1002/sd.3221

Strzalkowski, P., Strzalkowska, A., Chhablani, J., Pfau, K., Errera, M. H., Roth, M., & Guthoff, R. (2024). Evaluation of the accuracy and readability of ChatGPT-4 and Google Gemini in providing information on retinal detachment: A multicenter expert comparative study. *International Journal of Retina and Vitreous*, 10(1), 61. PMID: 39223678

Strzelecki, A. (2023). To use or not to use ChatGPT in higher education? A study of students' acceptance and use of technology. *Interactive Learning Environments*, •••, 1–14. DOI: 10.1080/ 10494820.2023.2209881

Students, O. for. (2018, March 26). *OfS privacy—Office for Students* (Worldwide). Office for Students. https://www.officeforstudents.org.uk/

Students, O. for. (2021, January 26). *Notifications—Office for Students* (Worldwide). Office for Students. https://www.officeforstudents.org.uk/

Stupp, C. (2019). Fraudsters used AI to mimic CEO's voice in unusual cybercrime case: Scams using artificial intelligence are a new challenge for companies, Accessed: Feb. 10, 2022. [Online]. Available: https://www.wsj.com/articles/fraudsters-use-ai-tomimic-ceos-voice-in-unusual-cybercrime-case-11567157402

Subashini, P., & Krishnaveni, M. (2021). Artificial intelligence-based assistive technology. In *Artificial Intelligence Theory, Models, and Applications* (pp. 217-240). Auerbach Publications.

Sudaryanto, M. R., Hendrawan, M. A., & Andrian, T. (2023). The Effect of Technology Readiness, Digital Competence, Perceived Usefulness, and Ease of Use on Accounting Students Artificial Intelligence Technology Adoption. In *E3S Web of Conferences* (Vol. 388, p. 04055). EDP Sciences.

Sullins, J. P. (2011). When is a robot a moral agent? In Anderson, M., & Anderson, S. L. (Eds.), *Machine Ethics* (pp. 151–161). Cambridge Univ. Press.

Sultana, M., & Haque, M. S. (2018). The cause of low implementation of ICT in education sector considering higher education: A study on Bangladesh. *Canadian Social Science*, 14(12), 67–73.

Sultana, R., & Faruk, M. (2024). Does artificial intelligence increase learners' sustainability in higher education: Insights from Bangladesh. *Journal of Data Information and Management*, 6(2), 161–172. DOI: 10.1007/s42488-024-00121-4

Šumak, B., López-de-Ipiña, D., Dziabenko, O., Correia, S. D., de Carvalho, L. M. S., Lopes, S., . . . Pušnik, M. (2024, May). AI-Based Education Tools for Enabling Inclusive Education: Challenges and Benefits. In 2024 47th MIPRO ICT and Electronics Convention (MIPRO) (pp. 472-477). IEEE.

Suryani, A., & George, S. (2021). "Teacher education is a good choice, but I don't want to teach in schools." An analysis of university students' career decision making. *Journal of Education for Teaching*, 47(4), 590–604.

Sutton, R. S., & Barto, A. G. (2018). *Reinforcement Learning: An Introduction*. MIT Press.

Syahrizal, S., Yasmi, F., & Mary, T. (2024). AI-Enhanced Teaching Materials for Education: A Shift towards Digitalization. *International Journal of Religion*, 5(1), 203–217.

Szmidt, E., & Kacprzyk, J. (2004). A similarity measure for intuitionistic fuzzy sets and its application in supporting medical diagnostic reasoning, In International conference on artificial intelligence and soft computing (pp. 388-393). Berlin, Heidelberg: Springer Berlin Heidelberg.

Tabachnick, B. G., & Fidell, L. S. (2019). *Using multivariate statistics* (7th ed.). Pearson.

Talan, T. (2021). Artificial intelligence in education: A bibliometric study. *International Journal of Research in Education and Science*, 7(3), 822–837.

Taneja, K., Maiti, P., Kakar, S., Guruprasad, P., Rao, S., & Goel, A K. (2024, January 1). Jill Watson: A Virtual Teaching Assistant Powered by ChatGPT. Springer Science+Business Media, 324-337. https://doi.org/DOI: 10.1007/978-3-031-64302-6_23

Taneri, G. U. (2020). Artificial Intelligence & Higher Education: Towards Customized Teaching and Learning, and Skills for an AI World of Work. Research & Occasional Paper Series: CSHE. 6.2020. Center for Studies in Higher Education.

Tan, S. (2023). Exploiting Disruptive Innovation in Learning and Teaching. In *Learning Intelligence* (pp. 149–176). Innovative and Digital Transformative Learning Strategies., DOI: 10.1007/978-981-19-9201-8_4

Tapalova, O., & Zhiyenbayeva, N. (2022). Artificial intelligence in education: AIEd for personalised learning pathways. *Electronic Journal of e-Learning*, 20(5), 639–653.

Tariq, M. U. (2024). The role of AI in skilling, upskilling, and reskilling the workforce. In *Advances in educational technologies and instructional design book series* (pp. 408–420). https://doi.org/DOI: 10.4018/979-8-3693-2440-0.ch023

Taufikin, M. S. I., Azifah, N., Nikmah, F., & Kuanr, J. (2024, April). The Impact of AI on Teacher Roles and Pedagogy in the 21st Century Classroom. In *2024 International Conference on Knowledge Engineering and Communication Systems (ICKECS)* (Vol. 1, pp. 1-5). IEEE.

Technische Universität München. (2023, July 25). *Regeln für den Umgang mit KI in der Wissenschaft*. https://www.tum.de/aktuelles/alle-meldungen/pressemitteilungen/details/regeln-fuer-den-umgang-mit-ki-in-der-wissenschaft

Tegmark, M. (2014). *Our Mathematical Universe: My Quest for the Ultimate Nature of Reality by Max Tegmark*. Alfred A. Knopf.

Teng, Y., Zhang, J., & Sun, T. (2023). Data-driven decision-making model based on artificial intelligence in higher education system of colleges and universities. *Expert Systems: International Journal of Knowledge Engineering and Neural Networks*, 40(4), e12820.

The Daily Star. (2022, March 29). Shikho aspires to make learning more accessible. *The Daily Star*. https://www.thedailystar.net/supplements/get-set-study-abroad/news/shikho-aspires-make-learning-more-accessible-2993831

Timmermans, J., Stahl, B. C., Ikonen, V., & Bozdag, E. (2010). The ethics of cloud computing: A conceptual review, in Proc. IEEE 2nd Int. Conf. Cloud Comput. Technol. Sci., 614–620.

Tlili, A., Sun, T., Denden, M., Kinshuk, K., Graf, S., Fei, C., & Wang, H. (2023, May 23). Impact of personality traits on learners' navigational behavior patterns in an online course: A lag sequential analysis approach. *Frontiers of Medicine*, 14. Advance online publication. DOI: 10.3389/fpsyg.2023.1071985 PMID: 37292512

Tobor, J. (2024, February 7). Blickpunkt: Leitlinien zum Umgang mit generativer KI. *Hochschulforum Digitalisierung*. https://hochschulforumdigitalisierung.de/news/blickpunkt-ki-leitlinien/

Torres, M. T. M., Álvarez, L. M. S., & Osorio, A. S. O. (2022). Initialstudy of a chatbot for virtual modality students from the inter-American school of librarianship. *Library Research*, 36(90), 13–30. DOI: 10.22201/iibi.24488321xe.2022.90.58452

Trigwell, K., Prosser, M., & Waterhouse, F. (1999). Relations between teachers' approaches to teaching and students' approaches to learning. *Higher Education*, 37, 57–70. DOI: 10.1023/A:1003548313194

Turan, T., Turan, G., & Küçüksille, E. (2022). Yapay zekâ etiği: Toplum üzerine etkisi. *Mehmet Akif Ersoy Üniversitesi Fen Bilimleri Enstitüsü Dergisi*, 13(2), 292–299.

Turing, A. M. (1950). Computing machinery and intelligence-AM Turing. *Mind*, 59(236), 433–450.

Tybroski, M. (2023). Developing Career Readiness Among Collegiate Student Staff Members (Doctoral dissertation, Arizona State University).

U.S. Department of Education. Artificial Intelligence and Future of Teaching and Learning: Insights and Recommendations., Washington, DC, (2023)

Ulu, M., & Türkan, Y. S. (2024). *Bibliometric Analysis of Traffic Accident Prediction Studies from 2003 to 2023: Trends, Patterns, and Future Directions*. Traffic Transportation.

Ulutaş, A., Popovic, G., Radanov, P., Stanujkic, D., & Karabasevic, D. (2021). A new hybrid fuzzy PSI-PIPRECIA-CoCoSo MCDM based approach to solving the transportation company selection problem. *Technological and Economic Development of Economy*, 27(5), 1227–1249.

United Nations. (2020). Sustainable development goals: Goal 4-Quality Education. Retrieved September 23, 2020, from https://www.un.org/sustainabledevelopment/education/

Universität Bielefeld. (2024). *ChatGPT - Universität Bielefeld*. https://www.uni-bielefeld.de/themen/pruefungsrecht/chatgpt/

Universität zu Köln. (2024). *ChatGPT*. https://verwaltung.uni-koeln.de/stabsstelle02.1/content/faq/data/chatgpt/index_ger.html

Ünlü, R. (2019). An assessment of imbalanced control chart pattern recognition by artificial neural networks. In *Artificial Intelligence and Machine Learning Applications in Civil* (pp. 240–258). Mechanical, and Industrial Engineering., DOI: 10.4018/978-1-7998-0301-0.ch013

Vacalares, S. T., Clarin, E., Lapid, R., Malaki, M., Plaza, V., & Barcena, M. (2023, May 30). Factors affecting the writing skills of the education students: A descriptive study. *GSC Online Press*, 18(2), 1192–1201. DOI: 10.30574/wjarr.2023.18.2.0931

Valerio, A. (2024). Anticipating the impact of artificial intelligence in higher education: Student awareness and ethical concerns in Zamboanga City, Philippines. *Cognizance Journal of Multidisciplinary Studies*, 4(6), 10–47760.

Van Busum, K., & Fang, S. (2023). Analysis of AI Models for Student Admissions: A Case Study. *Proceedings of the 38th ACM/SIGAPP Symposium on Applied Computing*, 17–22. https://doi.org/DOI: 10.1145/3555776.3577743

Van der Vorst, T., & Jelicic, N. (2019). Artificial Intelligence in Education: Can AI bring the full potential of personalized learning to education? 30th European Conference of the International Telecommunications Society (ITS): "Towards a Connected and Automated Society", Helsinki, Finland, 16th-19th June, 2019, International Telecommunications Society (ITS), Calgary

Varnosfaderani, S. M., & Forouzanfar, M. (2024, March 29). The Role of AI in Hospitals and Clinics: Transforming Healthcare in the 21st Century. *Multidisciplinary Digital Publishing Institute*, 11(4), 337–337. DOI: 10.3390/bioengineering11040337 PMID: 38671759

Vashishth, T. K., Sharma, V., Sharma, K. K., & Kumar, B. (2024). Enhancing Literacy Education in Higher Institutions with AI Opportunities and Challenges. AI-Enhanced Teaching Methods, 198-215.

Vashishth, T. K., Sharma, V., Sharma, K. K., Kumar, B., Chaudhary, S., & Panwar, R. (2024). Transforming Classroom Dynamics: The Social Impact of AI in Teaching and Learning. In AI-Enhanced Teaching Methods (pp. 322-346). IGI Global.

Vashishth, T. K., Sharma, V., Sharma, K. K., Kumar, B., Panwar, R., & Chaudhary, S. (2024). AI-Driven Learning Analytics for Personalized Feedback and Assessment in Higher Education. In Using Traditional Design Methods to Enhance AI-Driven Decision Making (pp. 206-230). IGI Global.

Vashishth, T. K., Kumar, B., Panwar, R., Kumar, S., & Chaudhary, S. (2023, August). Exploring the Role of Computer Vision in Human Emotion Recognition: A Systematic Review and Meta-Analysis. In *2023 Second International Conference on Augmented Intelligence and Sustainable Systems (ICAISS)* (pp. 1071-1077). IEEE.

Veale, M., & Borgesius, F. Z. (2021). Demystifying the Draft EU Artificial Intelligence Act—Analysing the good, the bad, and the unclear elements of the proposed approach. *Computer Law Review International*, 22(4), 97–112. DOI: 10.9785/cri-2021-220402

Veale, M., Van Kleek, M., & Binns, R. (2018). Fairness and Accountability Design Needs for Algorithmic Support in High-Stakes Public Sector Decision-Making. *Proceedings of the 2018 CHI Conference on Human Factors in Computing Systems*, 1–14. https://doi.org/DOI: 10.1145/3173574.3174014

Veerman, A., Andriessen, J., & Kanselaar, G. (2000). Collaborative learning through computer mediated argumentation. *Learning and Instruction*, 10(4), 345–364.

Verma, P. K. ., Sharma, V. ., Kumar, P. ., Sharma, S. ., Chaudhary, S. ., & Preety, P. (2023). IoT Enabled Real Time Appearance System using AI Camera and Deep Learning for Student Tracking. International Journal on Recent and Innovation Trends in Computing and Communication, 11(6s), 249□254.

Villani, C., Bonnet, Y., Schoenauer, M., Berthet, C., Levin, F., Cornut, A. C., & Rondepierre, B. (2018). *For a meaningful artificial intelligence: Towards a french and european strategy*. Conseil national du numérique.

Villasenor, A. (2024, September 4). *AI Grading in Peer Reviews: Enhancing Coursera's Learning Experience with Faster, High-Quality Feedback*. Coursera Blog. https://blog.coursera.org/ai-grading-in-peer-reviews-enhancing-courseras-learning-experience-with-faster-high-quality-feedback/

Vincent-Lancrin, S., & van der Vlies, R. (2020). Trustworthy artificial intelligence (AI) in education: promises and challenges OECD Education Working Paper No. 218. Organisation for Economic Co-operation and Development.

Vincent-Lancrin, S., & van der Vlies, R. (2020). Trustworthy Artificial Intelligence (AI) in Education: Promises and Challenges. OECD Education Working Papers, No. 218. *OECD Publishing*.

Vincent-Lancrin, S., Joaquin, U., Soumyajit, K., & Gwénaël, J. (2019). *Measuring Innovation in Education 2019: What Has Changed in the Classroom?* OECD Publishing., DOI: 10.1787/9789264311671-

Vistorte, A. O. R., Deroncele-Acosta, A., Ayala, J. L. M., Barrasa, A., López-Granero, C., & Martí-González, M. (2024). Integrating artificial intelligence to assess emotions in learning environments: a systematic literature review. In *Frontiers in Psychology* (Vol. 15). Frontiers Media SA. https://doi.org/DOI: 10.3389/fpsyg.2024.1387089

Vittorini, P., Menini, S., & Tonelli, S. (2021). An AI-based system for formative and summative assessment in data science courses. *International Journal of Artificial Intelligence in Education*, 31(2), 159–185. DOI: 10.1007/s40593-020-00230-2

Vivar, J. M. F., & Peñalvo, F. J. G. (2023). Reflexiones sobre la ética, potencialidades y retos de la Inteligencia Artificial en el marco de la Educación de Calidad (ODS4). *Comunicar: Revista Cientifica De Comunicacion y Educacion*, (74), 37–47.

Voigt, P., & Von Dem Bussche, A. (2017). *The EU General Data Protection Regulation (GDPR)*. Springer International Publishing., DOI: 10.1007/978-3-319-57959-7

von Garrel, J., & Mayer, J. (2023). Artificial Intelligence in studies—Use of ChatGPT and AI-based tools among students in Germany. *Humanities & Social Sciences Communications*, 10(1), 1–9. DOI: 10.1057/s41599-023-02304-7

Vo, T. K. A., & Nguyen, H. (2024). Generative Artificial Intelligence and ChatGPT in Language Learning: EFL Students' Perceptions of Technology Acceptance. *Journal of University Teaching & Learning Practice*, 21(06). Advance online publication. DOI: 10.53761/fr1rkj58

Wang, B., Yao, Y., & Liu, X. (2023).Research on the Construction of Smart Educational Administration Systems in Colleges and Universities Empowered by Artificial Intelligence Technology. Proceedings of the 4th Management Science Informatization and Economic Innovation Development Conference, MSIEID 2022, December 9-11, 2022, Chongqing, China

Wang, L., Fu, T., Du, Y., Gao, W., Huang, K., Liu, Z., Chandak, P., Liu, S., Katwyk, P. V., Deac, A., Anandkumar, A., Bergen, K. J., Gomes, C. P., Ho, S., Kohli, P., Lasenby, J., Leskovec, J., Liu, T., Manrai, A. K., & Žitnik, M. (2023, August 2). Scientific discovery in the age of artificial intelligence. *Nature Portfolio*, 620(7972), 47–60. DOI: 10.1038/s41586-023-06221-2 PMID: 37532811

Wang, T., Lund, B., Marengo, A., Pagano, A., Mannuru, N. R., Teel, Z. A., & Pange, J. (2023, May 31). Exploring the Potential Impact of Artificial Intelligence (AI) on International Students in Higher Education: Generative AI, Chatbots, Analytics, and International Student Success. *Multidisciplinary Digital Publishing Institute*, 13(11), 6716–6716. DOI: 10.3390/app13116716

Wang, W., & Siau, K. (2019). Artificial intelligence, machine learning, automation, robotics, future of work and future of humanity: A review and research agenda. *Journal of Database Management*, 30(1), 61–79.

Wartman, S. A., & Combs, C. D. (2018). Medical education must move from the information age to the age of artificial intelligence. *Academic Medicine*, 93(8), 1107–1109. DOI: 10.1097/ACM.0000000000002044 PMID: 29095704

Welde, A. M., Bernes, K. B., Gunn, T. M., & Ross, S. A. (2016). Career education at the elementary school level: Student and intern teacher perspectives. *Journal of Career Development*, 43(5), 426–446. DOI: 10.1177/089484531663352

Wen, Z., Liao, H., Kazimieras Zavadskas, E., & Al-Barakati, A. (2019). Selection third-party logistics service providers in supply chain finance by a hesitant fuzzy linguistic combined compromise solution method. *Economic research-. Ekonomska Istrazivanja*, 32(1), 4033–4058.

Westgarth, T., Chen, W., Hay, G., & Heath, R. (2022). Understanding UK Artificial Intelligence R&D commercialisation and the role of standards. Tech. rep. For the Department of Digital, Culture, Media and Sport, and the Office for Artificial Intelligence. Oxford Insights. URL: https://assets. publishing. service. gov. uk/ government/uploads/system/uploads/attachment_data.

Widyahastuti, F., & Tjhin, V. (2017). Predicting Students' Performance in Final Examination using Regression and Multilayer Perceptron. *IEEE, 978- 1-5090-4688.*

Wiering, M. A., & Van Otterlo, M. (2012). Reinforcement learning. *Adaptation, Learning, And Optimization*, 12(3), 729.

Williamson, B., Eynon, R., Knox, J., & Davies, H. (2023). *Critical perspectives on AI in education: Political economy, discrimination, commercialization, governance and ethics* (pp. 553–570). https://doi.org/DOI: 10.4337/9781800375413.00037

Wollny, S., Schneider, J., Di Mitri, D., Weidlich, J., Rittberger, M., & Drachsler, H. (2021). Are we there yet?-a systematic literature review on chatbots in education. *Frontiers in Artificial Intelligence*, 4, 654924. DOI: 10.3389/frai.2021.654924 PMID: 34337392

Wu, S., Chen, N., Xiao, A., Zhang, P., Jiang, C., & Zhang, W. (2024). AI-Empowered Virtual Network Embedding:A Comprehensive survey. *IEEE Communications Surveys and Tutorials*, 1. Advance online publication. DOI: 10.1109/comst.2024.3424533

Xia, Q., Chiu, T. K., & Chai, C. S. (2023). The moderating effects of gender and need satisfaction on self-regulated learning through Artificial Intelligence (AI). *Education and Information Technologies*, 28(7), 8691–8713.

Xia, X., & Li, X. (2022). Artificial Intelligence for Higher Education Development and TeachingSkills. *Wireless Communications and Mobile Computing*, 2022, e7614337. DOI: 10.1155/2022/7614337

Xu, Z. (2007). Intuitionistic fuzzy aggregation operators. *IEEE Transactions on Fuzzy Systems*, 15(6), 1179–1187.

Xu, Z. (2024). AI in education: Enhancing learning experiences and student outcomes. *Appl. Comput. Eng*, 51, 104–111.

Yadav, K. (2019). Disruptive innovative technologies in higher education. *International Journal of Advanced Education and Research*, 4(1), 49–54.

Yamijala, S. M. S., Chodisetty, R. S. C. M., Chakravorty, C., & Sai, K. P. (2024). AI-Powered Learning revolutionizing smart education with personalized learning styles. In *Advances in educational technologies and instructional design book series* (pp. 191–212). https://doi.org/DOI: 10.4018/979-8-3693-8151-9.ch007

Yanamala, A. K. Y., Suryadevara, S., & Kalli, V. D. R. (2024). Balancing Innovation and Privacy: The Intersection of Data Protection and Artificial Intelligence. *International Journal of Machine Learning Research in Cybersecurity and Artificial Intelligence*, 15(1), 1–43.

Yang, S. J., Ogata, H., Matsui, T., & Chen, N. S. (2021). Human-centred artificial intelligence in education: Seeing the invisible through the visible. *Computers & Education. Artificial Intelligence*, 2, 100008.

Yang, S., & Bai, H. (2020). The integration design of artificial intelligence and normal students' education. [). IOP Publishing.]. *Journal of Physics: Conference Series*, 1453(1), 012090. DOI: 10.1088/1742-6596/1453/1/012090

Yekollu, R. K., Bhimraj Ghuge, T., Sunil Biradar, S., Haldikar, S. V., & Farook Mohideen Abdul Kader, O. (2024, February). AI-Driven Personalized Learning Paths: Enhancing Education Through Adaptive Systems. In International Conference on Smart Data Intelligence (pp. 507-517). Singapore: Springer Nature Singapore.

Yekollu, R. K., Ghuge, T. B., Biradar, S. S., Haldikar, S. V., & Kader, O. F. M. A. (2024). AI-Driven Personalized Learning Paths: Enhancing education through Adaptive Systems. In *Algorithms for intelligent systems* (pp. 507–517). https://doi.org/DOI: 10.1007/978-981-97-3191-6_38

Yilmaz, G. (2017). Restoranlarda Bahşiş İle İlgili Yayınlanan Makalelerin Bibliyometrik Analizi. Seyahat ve Otel İşletmeciliği Dergisi, 65–79. https://doi.org/DOI: 10.24010/soid.335082

Yue, M., Jong, M. S., & Ng, D. T. K. (2024). Understanding K–12 teachers' technological pedagogical content knowledge readiness and attitudes toward artificial intelligence education. *Education and Information Technologies*. Advance online publication. DOI: 10.1007/s10639-024-12621-2

Yu, L., & Yu, Z. (2023). Qualitative and quantitative analyses of artificial intelligence ethics in education using VOSviewer and CitNetExplorer. *Frontiers in Psychology*, 14, 1061778. PMID: 36968737

Yu, P. K. (2020). Legal Studies Research Paper Series The Algorithmic Divide and Equality in the Age of Artificial Intelligence. *Florida Law Review*, 72(19), 331–389.

Yuskovych-Zhukovska, V., Poplavska, T., Diachenko, O., Mishenina, T., Topolnyk, Y., & Gurevych, R. (2022). Application of artificial intelligence in education. Problems and opportunities for sustainable development. *BRAIN. Broad Research in Artificial Intelligence and Neuroscience*, 13(1Sup1), 339-356.

Zadeh, L. A. (1965). Fuzzy sets. *Information and Control.*

Zafari, M., Bazargani, J. S., Sadeghi-Niaraki, A., & Choi, S. M. (2022). Artificial intelligence applications in K-12 education: A systematic literature review. *IEEE Access : Practical Innovations, Open Solutions*, 10, 61905–61921. DOI: 10.1109/ACCESS.2022.3179356

Zaman, M. P. A., Hasan, N., Islam, M. H., & Amin, M. R. (2024). Evaluating the impact of primary education in Bangladesh: An In-Depth Investigation of Bagha Upazila in the Rajshahi District. *Indonesian Research Journal on Education*, 4(1). Advance online publication. DOI: 10.31004/irje.v4i1.420

Zawacki-Richter, O., Marín, V. I., Bond, M., & Gouverneur, F. (2019). Systematic review of research on artificial intelligence applications in higher education – where are the educators? *International Journal of Educational Technology in Higher Education*, 16(1). Advance online publication. DOI: 10.1186/s41239-019-0171-0

Zawacki-Richter, O., Marín, V. I., Bond, M., & Gouverneur, F. (2019). Systematic review of research on artificial intelligence applications in higher education–where are the educators? *International Journal of Educational Technology in Higher Education*, 16(1), 1–27.

Zawacki-Richter, O., Marín, V. I., Bond, M., & Gouverneur, F. (2019). Systematic review of research on artificial intelligence applications in higher education—Where are the educators? *International Journal of Educational Technology in Higher Education*, 16(1).

Zeineddine, H. (2021). UdoBraendle, U. and Farah, A. (2021).Classification and prediction of student performance data using various machine learning algorithms. *Computers & Electrical Engineering*, 89, 106903.

Zhang, Y., Yang, X., & Tong, W. (2024). University students' attitudes toward ChatGPT profiles and their relation to ChatGPT intentions. *International Journal of Human-Computer Interaction*, •••, 1–14.

Zheltukhina, M. R., Sergeeva, O. V., Masalimova, A. R., Budkevich, R. L., Kosarenko, N. N., & Nesterov, G. V. (2024). A bibliometric analysis of publications on ChatGPT in education: Research patterns and topics. *Online Journal of Communication and Media Technologies*, 14, e202405.

Zhou, Y., Freedman, R., Glass, M., Michael, J. A., Rovick, A. A., & Evens, M. W. (1999, July). Delivering hints in a dialogue-based intelligent tutoring system. In *AAAI/IAAI* (pp. 128-134).

Zhou, Z. (2023). Project-Based Learning for Quality Art Teacher Development in the age of AI. www.clausiuspress.com. https://doi.org/DOI: 10.23977/curtm.2023.060607

Zimmerle, J C. (2021, January 2). Safe, Sound, and Private: Promoting Data Protection for Students. Taylor & Francis, 38(1), 1-18. https://doi.org/DOI: 10.1080/07380569.2021.1882203

Zimmermann, V. (2024, June 21). *Artificial intelligence in Germany: Status quo, opportunities and options for economic policy measures*. KfW Research. https://www.kfw.de/PDF/Download-Center/Konzernthemen/Research/PDF-Dokumente-Fokus-Volkswirtschaft/Fokus-englische-Dateien/Fokus-2024-EN/Focus-No.-463-June-2024-AI.pdf

Zohir, S. (2023). A Framework to Assess Digital Transformation in a Technologically Less-Developed Country: Challenges and Opportunities in Bangladesh. https://ergonline.org/digitalization-in-a-technologically-less-developed-country/

Zootzky, G., & Pfeiffer, A. (2024). Educational Transformation through AI: Preparing for a New Era of Learning. In INTED2024 Proceedings (pp. 1202-1207). IATED.

Zou, Y., Zhong, N., Chen, Z., & Zhao, W. (2024). Bridging digitalization and sustainability in universities: A Chinese green university initiative in the digital era. *Journal of Cleaner Production*, 469, 143181.

About the Contributors

Gamze Sart completed her undergraduate education at Bogazici University in the Department of Political Science and International Relations. She completed her first master's degree in the Institute of Social Sciences, Department of Psychology in Harvard and Istanbul Commerce University. She completed her second master's degree in the Social Sciences Institute, Department of Educational Sciences in Bogazici University. She received her doctorate from Stanford and Bogazici University, Faculty of Social Sciences, Department of Educational Sciences. Associate Professor Gamze Sart is a faculty member of the Hasan Ali Yucel Education Faculty (HAYEF) and is currently carrying on academic studies at Istanbul University Cerrahpasa (IUC) on the "Innovation and Technology-Oriented Future of Higher Education".

Funda Hatice Sezgin completed her undergraduate education in Faculty of economics in University of Istanbul. She did master of business administration degree (MBA) in Econometrics of University of Istanbul, and doctor of econometrics in Marmara University. Her research interests are time series analysis, panel data analysis and statistical methods. She works in the department of industrial engineering at Istanbul University-Cerrahpasa.

***

Sumona Afroz is a final-year undergraduate student in the Department of Educational Technology and Engineering (EdTE) at Bangabandhu Sheikh Mujibur Rahman Digital University, Bangladesh (BDU). Actively engaged in research, she has contributed to multiple papers focusing on innovative teaching methods, ICT integration in education, and blended learning. She authored the book *Technology in Education and Smart Bangladesh*, showcased at the Amar Ekushey Book Fair 2024. Sumona also achieved notable success as the 2nd Runner-up at the Hult Prize competition held at BDU. With a strong academic background and a commitment to advancing educational practices, she aims to make significant contributions to the field of Educational Technology.

Sohail Ahmad is a doctoral candidate (Education) at the University of Cambridge and the Aga Khan University Institute for Educational Development, Pakistan. Currently, he is working as Research Specialist at AKU-IED. He has experience in large-scale research through working on various nation-wide studie s on science and mathematics education in Pakistan. Most of his academic work revolves around the quality of education, mainly pedagogical quality and its impact on students' learning outcomes, from school to higher education. He has published on pedagogical quality, student learning, higher education, quality assurance, and use of technology in higher education.

Afaq Ahmed is currently a PhD candidate in the Department of Teaching, Learning and Culture at the Texas A&M University, College Station, Tx. He has earlier served as a Lecturer at the Government Elementary College of Education, Hussainabad, and a Research Associate at the Aga Khan University Institute for Educational Development, Karachi. He has also and worked on teaching license policy in Sindh province. His research area includes education policy, teacher education, technologies and quality of teaching.

Aisha Naz Ansari is a research specialist at Aga Khan University Institute for Educational Development (AKU-IED), Pakistan. She completed an MPhil Education from the AKU-IED and holds a B.Ed (Hons.) degree from Sukkur IBA University. She has published more than twenty (20) research articles and research blogs in international and national journals and forums. Her research areas include systematic reviews, educational technology, educational psychology, holistic student development, teacher education, public-private partnerships, and classroom teaching and learning. ORCID: https://orcid.org/0000 -0003 -0938 -8980.

Md. Ashrafuzzaman is an Assistant Professor in the Department of Educational Technology and Engineering (EdTE) at Bangabandhu Sheikh Mujibur Rahman Digital University, Bangladesh. Previously, he worked as a Research Coordinator in the EIA-DU-OU (UK) Research Collaboration Programme at the Institute of Education and Research (IER), University of Dhaka (DU). He has completed his BEd (Hons), MEd, and MPhil from IER, DU. He has fourteen years of experience in teaching and educational research, focusing on teachers' training programs, underprivileged children's education, English language education, classroom practice, teaching methods and techniques, assessment and feedback practice, ICT in education, blended learning, and Educational Technology.

Ufuk Aydogmus received his Bachelor of Science from the department of Industrial Engineering at Selcuk University and a Master of Science degree from Osmangazi University. He is PhD student in the department of Industrial Engineering. His research interest include supply chain management, MCDM and Industry 4.0. He has been working as a lecturer at Alanya Alaaddin Keykubat University since 2013.

Christopher Bohlens is a junior researcher at Leuphana University of Lüneburg and serves as the head of the Science Working Group at Transparency International Germany. With a strong background in student advocacy, Christopher has represented student interests on a national scale during his years in student self-administration. He is a dedicated expert in promoting student participation and ensuring their voices are heard in university quality assurance processes. He is also active in the field of quality assurance and quality management of Higher Education Institutions (HEIs), where he is involved in many functions and areas. Additionally, he is an active advocate for Freedom of Information, open data, transparency legislation, and the application of Administrative Law. Christopher's academic journey includes studies in business administration, economics, political science, and law at Hamburg University of Applied Sciences, Leuphana University, and FernUni Hagen.

Miftachul Huda is a researcher at Faculty of Human Sciences, Universiti Pendidikan Sultan Idris Malaysia. His research interest includes the field of educational studies: moral, Islamic and multicultural education, learning theory, adaptive teaching and learning technology. He has been experienced in working on research for more than five years. Contributing several works, he is currently the member of the advisory editorial board in some international journals. Traveling in some countries with scholarly intent makes him extensive experience on his research expertise in international trend and issues. Thus, he commits to contributing his knowledge to the benefit of society through professional and social activities.

Rituraj Jain is currently working in the Department of Information Technology, Marwadi University, Rajkot, GUjarat, India. He has published many papers in International Journals and Conferences. He has published 4 books. He is an Oracle Database SQL Certified Expert. He is also associated with professional bodies like the Indian Society of Technical Education (ISTE), Computer Science Teachers Association (CSTA), Academy & Industry Research Collaboration Center (AIRCC), International Association of Computer Science and Information Technology (IACSIT), International Association of Engineers (IAENG). His research interests include Cloud Computing, Machine Learning, Deep Learning, Fuzzy Logic, IoT, Genetic Algorithms, Big Data and Software Engineering.

Eren Kamber is a Assistant Professor specializing in industrial engineering. He earned his bachelor's degree from Istanbul Technical University in 2009 and his master's degree in engineering management from Alanya Alaaddin Keykubat University in 2019. In 2023, he completed his Ph.D. in industrial engineering at Istanbul Technical University, focusing his dissertation on "Green Logistics Location Selection with Circular Intuitionistic Fuzzy CODAS (CIFS-CODAS) Method." Kamber continues his academic career in the Department of Industrial Engineering at the Rafet Kayış Faculty of Engineering at Alanya Alaaddin Keykubat University, where he has been working since 2018. He teaches courses such as statistical quality control, project management, and organizational behavior. Kamber's academic research focuses on multi-criteria decision-making methods and fuzzy logic techniques. He has published numerous articles in national and international journals and presented at international conferences. His work covers topics such as pump selection in agricultural irrigation systems, green logistics, and Industry 4.0 awareness. Additionally, he has contributed book chapters on sustainability from an industrial engineering perspective and has served as an editor for several academic books. Eren Kamber's academic expertise and specialization in multi-criteria decision-making provide significant contributions to industrial applications.

Mustafa Kayyali I am an ardent advocate for excellence in higher education, driven by a relentless pursuit of quality, recognition, and innovation. My journey in academia started with a Master's in Quality Management and Evaluation in Higher Education from Universitat Oberta de Catalunya, followed by a Ph.D. in Quality Management from Azteca University. These academic pursuits have laid a strong foundation for my expertise in Accreditation, Quality Assurance, and Higher Education Rankings. As an entrepreneur, researcher, translator, and publisher, I am deeply involved in various facets of the academic world. My diverse interests encompass Management, Translation, Interpretation, and Academic consulting, contributing to a well-rounded understanding of the industry. Throughout my career, I have made significant contributions to academic literature, with more than 20 published papers and 7 book chapters to my name. Additionally, I take pride in having translated 5 books, bridging language gaps, and promoting knowledge exchange on a global scale. I am committed to fostering positive change in higher education and contributing to its continuous improvement.

Damodharan Palaniappan works as an Associate Professor & Head in the Department of Information Technology, Marwadi University, Rajkot, Gujarat. He completed his Ph.D. at Anna University, Chennai, M.E. in Computer Science and Engineering at C.I.E.T, Coimbatore and B.E. in Computer Science and Engineering at CSI College of Engineering, Ketty, Nilgiri. He has 19 years' experience of teaching and research. Currently, he guides 6 Ph.D. research scholars. He has authored 8 book chapters, and he has published research papers in reputed journals. His interested areas of research are Data Mining, Image Processing, Software, Machine Learning and Deep Learning.

Kumar Parmar I am an Assistant Professor with a strong foundation in Computer Science and Engineering, currently pursuing my PhD at Marwadi University. With a Master's in Computer Engineering and extensive teaching experience across various institutions, I am dedicated to fostering a dynamic and innovative learning environment. My expertise spans Operating Systems, Linux Administration, Cybersecurity, IoT, and Software Engineering, Machine Learning, Deep learning. In addition to teaching, I have contributed to research with multiple publications and patents, and I am actively involved in guiding projects, mentoring students, and coordinating academic clubs. My professional journey is driven by a passion for continuous learning and collaboration

Kewal Krishan Sharma is a professor in computer sc. in IIMT University, Meerut, U.P, India. He did his Ph.D. in computer network with this he has MCA, MBA and Law degree also. He did variously certification courses also. He has an overall experience of around 33 year in academic, business and industry. He wrote a number of research papers and books.

Mukesh Krishan Sharma is a Professor and Head in Department of Mathematics, Chaudhary Charan Singh University, Meerut, U.P, India. He is an active academician and researcher in the field of computer science and mathematics.

Rajeev Sharma is the Assistant professor in IIMT Engineering College, Meerut. He has more than 15 years of teaching as well as administrative experience. He has a conference Proceeding on Modified CPU Scheduling Process to his Credit published by Springer Nature. He has published five research papers and reputed journals. He has attended many conferences, workshops, FDP's and symposium and presented research papers. His research area is fuzzy logic, Neural Networks and CPU scheduling.

Vikas Sharma completed his Graduation and Post Graduation from Chaudhary Charan Singh University, Meerut, U.P. Currently Pursuing his Ph.D. in Computer Science and Engineering from Govt. Recognized University. Presently, he is working as an Assistant Professor in the Department of Computer Science and Applications, IIMT University, Meerut, U.P. He has been awarded as Excellence in teaching award 2019. He is the reviewer member of some reputed journals. He has published several book chapters and research papers of national and international reputed journals.

Premavathi T, working as Assistant Professor in the Department of Computer Engineering – Artificial Intelligence, Marwadi University, Rajkot, Gujarat. I did B.E in Computer Science and Engineering at Dhanalakshmi Srinivasan Engineering College, Perambalur, TamilNadu and I did her M.E in Software Engineering with Distinction in Anna University. I am currently pursuing Ph.D. at the Marwadi University. I am having 14+ years of experiences in teaching. My area of interests are Machine Learning, Deep Learning, Big data analystics, etc.

Swapnil Tarafdar is a final-year undergraduate student in the Department of Educational Technology and Engineering (EdTE) at Bangabandhu Sheikh Mujibur Rahman Digital University, Bangladesh. With a strong academic background, he leads various projects and research, bringing significant success. Engaged in research on Educational Technology, ICT in Education, Machine Learning projects, and Data Analysis, he has also worked as a junior journalist at bdnews24.com. Notably, he was the 2nd Runner-up at the Hult Prize competition held at BDU and awarded as a Galactic Problem Solver at the NASA International Space Apps Challenge 2022. Swapnil authored the book, *Technology in Education and Smart Bangladesh*, showcased at the Amar Ekushey Book Fair 2024.

Yusuf Sait Turkan is working as Associate Professor in the Department of Industrial Engineering of Istanbul University - Cerrahpasa, Turkey. He is a also the coordinator of Distance Industrial Engineering Program at Istanbul University Open and Distance Faculty. He has completed his PhD and Master of Science in Industrial Engineering at the Istanbul University. His research interest include system simulation, metaheuristic algorithms and machine learning applications.

Tarun Kumar Vashishth is an active academician and researcher in the field of computer science with 22 years of experience. He earned Ph.D. Mathematics degree specialized in Operations Research; served several academic positions such as HoD, Dy. Director, Academic Coordinator, Member Secretary of Department Research Committee, Assistant Center superintendent and Head Examiner in university examinations. He is involved in academic development and scholarly activities. He is member of International Association of Engineers, The Society of Digital Information and Wireless Communications, Global Professors Welfare Association, International Association of Academic plus Corporate (IAAC), Computer Science Teachers Association and Internet Society. His research interest includes Cloud Computing, Artificial Intelligence, Machine Learning and Operations Research; published more than 35 research articles with 2 books and 40 book chapters in edited books. He is contributing as member of editorial and reviewers boards in conferences and various computer journals published by CRC Press, Taylor and Francis, Springer, IGI global and other universities.

Hacer Yumurtaci Aydogmus received her Bachelor of Science in 2001 from Industrial Engineering Department. After undergraduate work, she began working as a research assistant at Istanbul University until 2013. She has Master of Science degree from Yıldız Technic University Business Management and doctor degree from Istanbul University Industrial Engineering Department. She is working at Faculty of Engineering -which was founded in 2010 as a part of Akdeniz University and has become a part of Alanya Alaaddin Keykubat University (ALKU) in 2015- as an associate Professor.

Index

A

B

C

D

E

M

P

R

S

T

U

W

www.ingramcontent.com/pod-product-compliance
Lightning Source LLC
LaVergne TN
LVHW080611300926
849162LV00005B/1115